"Wooden Horses" by Reginald Marsh

THE ANNALS
OF
AMERICA

THE ANNALS OF AMERICA

Volume 15

1929 - 1939

The Great Depression

William Benton, *Publisher*

ENCYCLOPÆDIA BRITANNICA, INC.

Chicago London Toronto Geneva Sydney Tokyo Manila

The editors wish to express their gratitude for permission to reprint
material from the following sources:

Stane Adamic for Selection 62, from *Harper's Monthly Magazine*, November 1934, Copyright © 1945 by Harper's Magazine, Inc.

American Academy of Political and Social Science for Selection 80, from *The Annals* of the American Academy of Political and Social Science, 1936.

The American Mercury Magazine of Torrence, California, for Selection 3, from *The American Mercury*, Vol. XVI, no. 64, April 1929. Also for Selection 4, from *The American Mercury*, Vol. XVI, no. 63, March 1929. Also for Selection 5, from *The American Mercury*, Vol. XVI, no. 61, January 1929.

The Atlantic Monthly and W. L. White for Selection 104, from *The Atlantic Monthly*, Copyright © 1937 by The Atlantic Monthly Company, Boston, Mass. The Atlantic Monthly and James Stewart for Selection 114, from *The Atlantic Monthly*, Copyright © 1938 by The Atlantic Monthly Company, Boston, Mass.

Basic Books, Inc. for Selection 128, from *The Atomic Age*, ed. by Morton Grodzins and Eugene Rabinowitch, © 1963 by Basic Books, Inc., Publishers, New York.

William Beard and Miriam B. Vagts for Selection 20, from *The Myth of Rugged American Individualism*, University Microfilms, Inc., O.P. Title 17, 409, Copyright 1931 by Harper & Brothers, Copyright 1932 by Charles A. Beard, copyright renewed 1959 by William Beard and Mrs. Miriam B. Vagts.

Brandt & Brandt for Selection 117, from *A Southerner Discovers the South*, Copyright 1938 by Jonathan Daniels.

Dorothy Chamberlain for Selection 84, from *The New Republic*, 1936.

Violet Hemming Clark for Selection 74, from *Harper's Monthly Magazine*, December 1935. Copyright © 1935 by Harper's Magazine, Inc.

Malcolm Cowley for Selection 34, from *Think Back on Us: A Contemporary Chronicle of the 1930's*, University of Southern Illinois Press, 1967. Originally printed in *The New Republic*, August 17, 1932.

Harcourt, Brace & World, Inc. for Selection 2, from *Middletown*, by Robert S. and Helen M. Lynd, Copyright 1929 by Harcourt, Brace & World, Inc., Copy-

CODED SOURCES IN THIS VOLUME

FDR — *The Public Papers and Addresses of Franklin D. Roosevelt.* Compiled by Samuel P. Rosenman. In 13 vols. New York, 1938-1950.

5 F. Supp. 182 — *Federal Supplement.* Cases Argued and Determined in the District Courts of the United States Court of Claims. St. Paul, Minn., 1934. Vol. 5, pp. 182ff.

PRFA — [United States Department of State] *Papers Relating to Foreign Affairs.* Compiled annually since 1861 except for 1869 with supplements issued periodically. Title changed to *Papers Relating to Foreign Relations of the United States* in 1870 and to *Foreign Relations of the United States* in 1947. Washington, 1862 *et seq.*

Record — *Congressional Record.* A record of the proceedings of Congress from March 3, 1873, to date, arranged by number of Congress and by session. Washington, 1874 *et seq.*

Record, App. — *Congressional Record Appendix.* A supplement to the *Congressional Record* (see above), paged separately and also arranged by Congress and session.

Statutes — *The Public Statutes at Large of the United States of America from the Organization of the Government in 1789, etc., etc.* In 79 vols. as of August 1966. 1845 *et seq.* Vol. 48, Washington, 1934.

TWA — *This Was America.* Edited by Oscar Handlin. Cambridge, 1949.

United States Reports [Supreme Court].

285 U.S. 262 — Vol. 285, pp. 262ff.;

295 U.S. 495 — Vol. 295, pp. 495ff.;

297 U.S. 288 — Vol. 297, pp. 288ff.

VSD — *Vital Speeches of the Day.* Published twice a month. New York, 1934 *et seq.*

Contents

Introduction, xvii
Chronology, 1929-1939, xxiii
Maps, xliv

THE GREAT DEPRESSION
In Pictures

The nation's trust in Republican prosperity passed to Herbert
Hoover in 1928; in the autumn of 1929 chaos was loosed upon the
American economy. The spiral of speculation and inflated prices
that had drawn nothing but encouragement from government
and only an occasional half-hearted warning from financial
circles ended suddenly and forever. Within months millions were
jobless, and, in the absence of effective remedial action, violence
and revolt became serious possibilities.

If the farmers were no less surprised than the rest of the
country at the Crash of 1929, they had generally less to lose.
Agriculture had been seriously depressed since 1921, as the great
expansion of production during the war had turned quickly
to overproduction and falling prices. Congress had resisted
helpful legislation and considerable time passed even after
the Crash before any relief was attempted.

Like Wilson, Roosevelt was primarily concerned in domestic
problems but found himself drawn more and more into foreign
affairs. The spirit of isolationism was even stronger in Congress
and across the nation than it had been before World War I,
and this, combined with America's non-support of the League
of Nations, held in check a great potential obstacle to the
bald aggression in Europe and Asia.

Asides on Depression 321-332

Fortunately there was a great deal more to occupy the nation's
attention during the Depression than its problems; the tenacity
of the people's grasp on normality was strikingly demonstrated
with the aid of sports, some sensational journalism, and the ever-
growing entertainment industry. But for the thoroughly
dispossessed, the nation determined to continue with no more
disruption than was absolutely necessary.

Art and Society 421-430

The Depression served at least one useful purpose, that of
bringing artists alienated in varying degrees from American life
into deeper and broader contact with America and the American
environment. The Federal Arts Projects encouraged a good
deal of work in this direction, and from the photographers of
the Farm Security Administration came some classic studies of
rural America. In literature the intensely personal concerns of the
Lost Generation gave way quickly to a new social awareness.

The Dispossessed 531-540

Before any of the farm relief programs of the New Deal
could begin to function, the disaster of Depression was
compounded in the Middle West by drought and the Dust
Bowl it created. Thrown off buried farms, thousands of homeless
and jobless families headed West. Their cheap labor was
welcome everywhere, their problems nowhere. Together with
the urban unemployed, they represented a generation of
wasted human resources and growing human tragedy.

Introduction

The birthdate of the Great Bull Market of 1929 may for convenience be given as March 26. In the preceding two or three weeks there had been a good deal of anxiety about the attitude of the Federal Reserve Board and of newly inaugurated President Herbert Hoover toward the speculative activities in the stock market that had been going on for several years. On that day — March 26 — there was a break, following a series of secret meetings of the Board in Washington. Rumors flew this way and that, and at one time the averages were 15 points under those of the previous day. But before the market closed that afternoon an announcement by the president of the First National City Bank of New York gave heart to shareholders large and small, and the market was off on the wildest binge it has ever known. Between the end of March and the beginning of June there were a few more nervous days, but after the latter date all stops were removed and the market almost literally sailed off into the blue and out of sight.

There were some ominous signs. The construction industry had suffered a recession in 1928; expenditures for capital improvements were sharply down; the farmers continued to lag behind the rest of the economy, as they had since about 1922; and the European financial picture was not encouraging. But a patient flushed with fever does not notice such things. A few old hands did notice, and sold out in August and September. But most people thought they were crazy. Wasn't everybody buying stocks, and selling stocks, and making money? Wouldn't the boom go on forever? Paper fortunes grew before men's very eyes, and many mortgaged their futures, sometimes secretly, to purchase stocks on margins that were often as low as the legal 10 percent. It was mainly these small shareholders, owning most of the value of their shares on credit, who were caught when the Crash came.

And what a crash it was! Frederick Lewis Allen described some of those hectic, unforgettable days of late October 1929 in his bestseller *Only Yesterday* (see Selection 7). "Five thousand shares, ten thousand shares appeared at a time on the laboring ticker at fearful recessions in price. Not only were innumerable small traders being sold out, but big ones, too, protagonists of the new economic era who a few weeks before had counted themselves millionaires. Again and again the specialist in a stock would find himself surrounded by brokers fighting to sell — and nobody at all even thinking of buying. To give one single example: during the bull market, the common stock of the White

Sewing Machine Company had gone as high as 48; on Monday, October 28, it had closed at 11⅛. On that black Tuesday [October 29], somebody — a clever messenger boy for the exchange, it was rumored — had the bright idea of putting in an order to buy at 1; and in the temporarily complete absence of other bids he actually got his stock for a dollar a share!"

By the end of the day, the blackest of all black days in the market's history, nearly sixteen and a half million shares had been traded — a record that stood for nearly forty years — and the average price of fifty leading stocks had fallen nearly forty points. (It should be noted that if 16,500,000 shares were sold, the same number were bought — so somebody still had money.) The panic took almost no time to reach other exchanges, including those in Europe, and it started a downward slide that did not reach bottom for two years. By that time two-thirds of the value of all listed securities had been wiped away.

The Crash was perhaps a natural enough result of the world-wide speculation that had preceded it; but it was not only a result, it was also a cause of even more dire effects. Despite the insistence of President Hoover and Secretary of the Treasury Mellon that conditions were "fundamentally sound" and that prosperity was "just around the corner," a deflationary trend set in that endured, to all intents and purposes, for a decade — or until the prosperity brought on by World War II put an end to it. Businessmen had lost their confidence in the economy and ceased to invest in new productive capacity, bankers and mortgage holders called loans and were chary of making new ones, unemployment soared — a fourth of the labor force was out of work by 1932 — and the buying power of the nation was paralyzed.

President Hoover did what he could, but he was hampered by the traditions of his party, by his own inability to accept the necessity of really far-reaching measures, and, after the election in 1930, by anti-administration majorities in both houses of Congress. The financial collapse of Western Europe in the spring of 1931 was the last straw, and Hoover, a good man who had been dealt a low blow by history, waged a desultory campaign in 1932 and knew as well as anyone that he could not possibly win against a new face in American politics, Franklin Delano Roosevelt, who was supported not only by Democrats but by most progressive Republicans as well. (See Selections 36 and 38-39.)

The keynote of the Roosevelt approach and indeed of the whole early New Deal was sounded in a speech that FDR made in May 1932, before he was even a candidate. "It is common sense," he said, "to take a method and try it. If it fails, admit it frankly and try another. But above all, try something." This was good advice for a country that, as Roosevelt understood better than anyone, had to fear above everything else fear itself (see Selection 43). "Nameless, unreasoning, unjustified terror," he called it, which "paralyzes needed efforts to convert retreat into advance."

There were reasons enough to be frightened. Beginning with Michigan in mid-February 1933, state after state closed its banks. In the eight days preceding March 4, Inauguration Day, more than $1.5 billion was withdrawn from the banks that were still open throughout the nation. Unemployment was more severe than ever, and the breadlines for men and women on relief seemed to be the only places where people congregated during that dark winter. Prices fell steadily, yet there was still no one to buy. (For descriptions of the misery and distress throughout the country at the time, see Selections 21, 28-29, 31, 37, and 41-42.)

Responses to the Depression took various forms. Roosevelt himself identified three of them in a speech in 1934, in the course of which he distinguished between relief, recovery, and reform (see Selection 58). The Hoover Administration had concentrated on relief, making few efforts for recovery and none at all for reform. Some of the legislation passed during the whirlwind "Hundred Days" — the first three months of the New Deal — fell into the same category; for example, measures for unemployment relief, for federal supervision of investment securities, and for prevention of mortgage foreclosures on homes. But these were temporary stopgaps; of more importance were the measures for recovery (see Selection 45), among them the Agricultural Adjustment Act (see Selections 49, 61, and 71), the act establishing the Tennessee Valley Authority (see Selections 18 and 98), and, most important and controversial of all, the National Industrial Recovery Act (NIRA), which established the National Recovery Administration (NRA).

The Blue Eagle program, as it was called after the emblem that participating businesses were allowed to display, was representative of both the successes and failures of the early New Deal. A prime example of taking a method and trying it, it brought about a temporary improvement in conditions that was extremely heartening. But the act generated a tangle of rules and regulations, was essentially unenforceable, and furthermore was of doubtful constitutionality — a point that was confirmed when the law was struck down by a unanimous Supreme Court in the famous Schechter Poultry decision of May 1935. (For an excerpt from that decision and for other views of the NRA and of the impulse that gave birth to it, see Selections 44, 59-60, and 64-66.)

By that time the emphasis was on reform rather than relief or recovery. Roosevelt's advisers — the "Brain Trust," as they were called, because so many of them came from the universities — were saying that far-reaching changes were required in the country's social and economic structure, and that no amount of temporary or ad hoc legislation could end the Depression, much less put the country on a progressive footing and avoid future disasters. "We have not weeded out the overprivileged," Roosevelt declared in his annual message to Congress in 1935, proposing the Second New Deal, "and we have not effectively lifted up the underprivileged." (See Selection 67.)

The pressure from the country was for doing just those things, and during that year two tremendously important items of legislation were passed by an overwhelmingly Democratic Congress. One was the Social Security Act (see Selections 68 and 101). This first law was limited, but the coverage of the government insurance system that it created would be progressively extended during the next thirty years. The other was the National Labor Relations, or Wagner, Act, which outlawed a large number of "unfair practices" on the part of employers and established a strong National Labor Relations Board (NLRB) to enforce the law. Labor had its troubles during the '30s. Violence marked many strikes; labor racketeering became a serious problem; and the effort to organize the major U.S. industries — for example, steel, coal, automobiles — resulted in widespread attacks on labor's monopolistic tendencies. But the

Wagner Act was one of labor's greatest triumphs. (See Selections 78, 80, 102-103, and 109-110.)

There was no question about Roosevelt's running again in 1936, and the Republicans had little if any hope of beating him. They nominated Alfred M. Landon of Kansas, a moderate, who promised to continue most of the New Deal programs — but in a more businesslike fashion. Roosevelt took every state but two, Maine and Vermont, for the greatest electoral college victory in history, and Jim Farley, FDR's campaign manager, produced a notable political quip. Maine had traditionally gone Republican or Democratic as the nation as a whole did, occasioning the old saw: "As Maine goes, so goes the nation." Farley saw his opportunity and remarked: "As Maine goes, so goes Vermont." (For Selections dealing with the election and with its aftermath, see numbers 86-90.)

The Supreme Court had not only struck down the NRA; it had also, in unanimous or near-unanimous decisions, invalidated several other New Deal measures considered important by the Administration. Landon had warned during the campaign that Roosevelt, if elected, would tamper with the Court. Roosevelt had refused to answer the charge, but in February 1937, without informing congressional leaders in advance, he sent Congress a message proposing a reform of the court system including the right to replace up to six Supreme Court justices if they were over 70 years old. The uproar over this alleged "court-packing plan" may have surprised even the President, who suffered a stinging political defeat when the Senate defeated the proposal in July by a vote of 70 to 22. But though he lost the battle, he won the war, for beginning in the spring of 1937 the same Court that had overturned much important New Deal legislation began to put its imprimatur on even more important measures, including a minimum wage law for women, and the Wagner and Social Security Acts. (See Selection 95.)

Others besides the Justices (at least until 1937) disapproved of the New Deal. The Administration and the President were widely attacked — from both the right and the left. Fascism seemed to some to be the wave of the future, and various American versions of its noxious doctrine were voiced from about 1935 on. Governor Huey P. Long of Louisiana and Father Charles E. Coughlin of Detroit were not exactly Fascists, but they were not wholly non-Fascist, either. Long wanted to "soak the rich" and "share the wealth" among all U.S. citizens, or at least all Louisiana citizens; Father Coughlin wanted to reinstitute traditional morality, "drive the money changers from the temple," and go back to the gold standard. It was probably fortunate for the country that neither got very far.

All of the criticism from the right was not so violent. Californian Francis E. Townsend had a simple idea: the federal government should give every American over 60 the sum of $200 a month, which they would have to spend before the beginning of the next month, and all of the nation's problems would be solved. Throughout the country, 5,000,000 old people joined Townsend Clubs, and for a while it looked as if they just might be able to elect a Republican in 1936. But Roosevelt, with his ear for the political *mot juste,* referred to them as the "lunatic fringe," and the threat vanished. He was to use language with similar effect in subsequent elections; as he himself conceded — or boasted —

in 1940, "I am an old campaigner, and I love a good fight." (See, for some statements by and about conservatives during the '30s, Selections 63, 69-70, 79, 87-88, 104, 106, 108, 119, and 122.)

If the right felt that the Roosevelt Administration was doing too much, leftists characteristically felt that it was not doing enough. To FDR's three Rs — relief, recovery, and reform — they added a fourth: revolution. There had been much talk in the early part of the decade about whether the country would experience a social and economic revolution, perhaps similar to Russia's fifteen years before. George Soule (see Selection 35) didn't think so; Norman Thomas agreed, but, unlike Soule, regretted the fact (see Selection 81). Disaffected veterans marched on Washington in July 1932 but dispersed, their ardor cooled, when they were met by troops with drawn bayonets. (General Douglas MacArthur, in charge of the troops, called them "a bad-looking mob animated by the spirit of revolution," but Will Rogers said they were "the best behaved of any fifteen thousand hungry men assembled anywhere in the world" and added: "Just think what fifteen thousand clubwomen would have done to Washington even if they weren't hungry." See Selection 34 for still another viewpoint.) And a certain number of Americans joined the Communist Party or became fellow travelers (see Selection 120). The number was never very large, a fact that was surprising, considering the circumstances, to European leftwingers.

The radical impulse in the United States during the '30s was more likely to express itself in a kind of non-philosophical anarchism or nihilism that was much different from its European counterpart, although a proletarian movement agitated all the arts, especially the popular arts of journalism, cartooning, and musical comedy. Thus Woody Guthrie spoke for a multitude, by no means all of them "Okies," when he twanged his guitar and sang in his nasal voice: "So Long (It's Been Good to Know Yuh)" (Selection 97). Their desire was simply to "git," as they say in the Southwest; to escape the misery and despair that weighed them down, not by overturning the government, but by traveling — as Americans have always done when things were bad. (See Selections 126-127 for various views of the problem of "the nation's dust bowl." Selection 127 is an extract from John Steinbeck's *The Grapes of Wrath*, perhaps the finest American novel to come out of the decade.)

The radical impulse also found a kind of muted expression in the effect of the WPA — the Works Progress Administration — in the cultural sphere. The various programs that this New Deal agency set up were the first governmental recognition in the country's history that artists existed and had problems of their own. The funded theaters, guide-books, art and architecture projects, state historical research projects, folklore retrieval programs, and the like were new and important. They made artists think of themselves as citizens. (See, for example, Selection 123.)

The most popular arts of all were hardly touched by radicalism or proletarianism. These were the movies and especially radio, which reached its zenith during the decade. In retrospect, radio and television have probably affected our history far more than the NRA, although of course we didn't know it then. (See, among others, Selections 3, 10, 54, 63, and 84-85.)

Some modern historians, indeed, think it was Roosevelt himself — called

"That Man in Washington" by conservatives who hated him as no President since Lincoln had been hated — who really defused the bomb of revolution. The quickness with which he acted in the early days of 1933, the fortitude and strength that he seemed to exude, not least his jaunty cheerfulness and his wit, may have given enough people the feeling that the country would survive without an eruption so that a revolution became unnecessary. In any event, it did not happen.

The tendency at the time was to think of America's problems as being almost wholly domestic. Of course this wasn't true, as everyone knows now and as a few knew then. The United States did not cease because of the Depression to be involved in foreign relations, or even to think of itself at last as a world power (see Selection 12). And a small number of farsighted men tried to sound a warning of what was coming.

Nathaniel Peffer was one of these, reacting in 1933 to the Japanese invasion of Manchuria (see Selection 46). Roosevelt called for a "quarantine" of the "aggressors" in 1937 (see Selection 107); Ambassador Joseph C. Grew protested against Japan's "New Order" in 1938 (see Selection 118). The war clouds gathered and grew blacker. The poets saw what was coming, perhaps better than anyone; Kenneth Fearing's "Dirge" and Robinson Jeffers' "Rearmament" were both published in the same year, 1935 (see Selections 72 and 75), and other poets had similar things to say (see, for example, Selections 13, 94, and 124).

The most ominous note of all was struck by Albert Einstein. He had fled the Nazis in 1933 and come to the United States, where he was able to continue his work in peace. But peace, he knew, was neither inevitable nor permanent; and in 1939 he became deeply concerned over some experiments that were being performed in Germany. He wrote President Roosevelt in August 1939 (see Selection 128): "In the course of the last four months it has been made probable . . . that it may be possible to set up a nuclear chain reaction in a large mass of uranium. . . . This new phenomenon would also lead to the construction of bombs. . . . A single bomb of this type, carried by boat and exploded in a port, might very well destroy the whole port together with some of the surrounding territory."

It is unclear how receptive President Roosevelt and his advisers were to the scientific facts described by Einstein in this famous letter. But they could not help being struck by the last paragraph, which mentioned what no one could mistake for a mere coincidence. "I understand that Germany has actually stopped the sale of uranium from the Czechoslovakian mines which she has taken over," Einstein said. "That she should have taken such early action might perhaps be understood on the ground that the son of the German Under-Secretary of State . . . is attached to the Kaiser-Wilhelm-Institut in Berlin where some of the American work on uranium is now being repeated."

However it happened, the world learned six years later that the American government had taken the hint. The people of Hiroshima were the first to know.

Chronology: 1929 - 1939

1929

Feb. 11. Owen D. Young and J. P. Morgan as U.S. representatives meet in Paris with Committee on German Reparations to revise Dawes Plan of 1924. Young Plan lowers amount due from Germany and extends time for payment. It also lowers debts among Allies and sets up Bank for International Settlements.

May 27. Supreme Court confirms right of the President to prevent passage of legislation by the pocket veto (holding of a bill presented for signature for 10 days when Congress adjourns within the period limit so that the bill cannot become law).

June 15. In Agricultural Marketing Act, Congress seeks to stabilize farm prices by means of a Federal Farm Board that aids financing of agricultural markets. Act does not contain price-fixing measures that had resulted in President Coolidge's veto of McNary-Haugen Bill of 1927.

July 1. National origins immigration quota law goes into effect. In same year, consuls are authorized to refuse admission to any applicant who might become a "public charge."

Sept. 24. In first instrument flight, Lieu-tenant James Doolittle flies entirely by radio signals received in his airplane.

Oct. 24. Several weeks' decline in stock prices becomes panic, and 13 million shares are sold. House of Morgan tries to halt drop by buying but, except for a momentary lull, is unsuccessful. **Oct. 29.** Selling begins again, and more than 16 million shares change hands. By mid-November, loss in stock paper values is about $26 billion. End of unprecedented speculation is not directly related to decline in earning power of industry or expansion of consumer debt, but it marks the beginning of 10 years of depression.

In this year, manufacture of nearly 3 million cars for the first time puts the automobile industry ahead of all others in value produced.

Robert S. and Helen Lynd of Columbia University publish *Middletown*, classic sociological study of Muncie, Indiana.

Thomas Wolfe publishes *Look Homeward, Angel,* his first novel; *Of Time and the River* is published in 1935 and *The Web and the Rock* in 1939. All are to some extent autobiographical. William Faulkner publishes *Sartoris*, first novel in cycle on the fate of the South; others are *The Sound and the*

Fury in the same year, *As I Lay Dying* in 1930, *Sanctuary* in 1931, and *Absalom, Absalom!* in 1936. Ernest Hemingway publishes *A Farewell to Arms.*

Museum of Modern Art is founded in New York City; collection consists of international art of late nineteenth and twentieth centuries.

1930

Jan. 21-April 22. At London Naval Conference, five major naval powers continue principles of 1921 agreements without major changes; they do not discuss limitation of air or land armaments. The U.S., Britain, and Japan agree to limit cruiser construction; France and Italy do not. The U.S. Senate ratifies treaty in July.

Feb. 10. Almost 190 corporations and persons are arrested in Chicago on charges of violating the Prohibition amendment. They have done $50 million national business in liquor, selling more than 7 million gallons of whisky.

March 30. Captain Frank M. Hawks succeeds in first transcontinental glider flight. Departing San Diego, California, he reaches New York City in one week.

May 26. The Supreme Court holds unanimously that buying liquor is not a violation of the Prohibition amendment.

June 17. President Hoover signs Smoot-Hawley Tariff, although in May a petition signed by more than 1,000 economists has protested it and urged him to veto it if passed. Tariff raises duties so drastically on almost 900 articles that it results in sharp decline in international trade, and a deepening depression.

July 3. Congress creates Veterans Administration, which combines all federal agencies for aid to former servicemen under one department.

Sept. 9. U.S. State Department, fearing further unemployment, orders restrictions on immigration that prohibit almost any laborer from entering the country.

Nov. 4. In first defeat since 1916, Republicans lose majority in the House of Representatives and eight seats in the Senate.

Dec. 2. Unsuccessful in his attempts to establish self-help relief for unemployment through states and local organizations, President Hoover finally asks Congress for $100 to $150 million for public works, announcing that unemployment has reached about 4,500,000. Message also blames Depression on world conditions beyond control of the U.S.

Dec. 11. New York City's Bank of the United States closes as result of stock market crash. Bank has 60 branches and almost half a million depositors. During this year, more than 1,300 banks in the U.S. are forced to close.

State Department publishes 1928 J. Reuben Clark interpretation of Monroe Doctrine as relating only to European powers vis-à-vis Western Hemisphere states and not primarily to U.S. relations with Hemisphere nations. Memorandum repudiates Roosevelt Corollary of 1904 and improves hemispheric relations.

Lowell Observatory, Arizona, photographically identifies planet Pluto; discovery confirms mathematical prediction of Percival Lowell 16 years earlier and is significant advance in mathematical astronomy.

1930 census shows population of 122,775,000, which includes 4,107,000 immigrants arrived since 1920. Illiteracy is lower than ever before, at 4.3 percent. Average life expectancy at birth is 61 years, an increase of 11 years since 1900. In a survey made this year, it is found that one of every five Americans owns an automobile.

Federal Bureau of Narcotics is formed as a unit of the Treasury Department to handle licensing of narcotics handlers, import permits, and law enforcement in cooperation with states.

Dr. Karl Landsteiner receives Nobel Prize for Medicine for his work on human blood groups. Born in Austria, Landsteiner has become an American citizen.

Louis Bamberger and his sister, Mrs. Felix Fuld, found the Institute for Advanced Study at Princeton University; Albert Einstein joins Institute in 1933.

I'll Take My Stand, cooperative book by 12 Southern writers, defends concrete, regional forms of writing.

Sinclair Lewis is first American to be awarded the Nobel Prize for Literature.

Hart Crane publishes *The Bridge,* a series of poems based on the Brooklyn Bridge as a symbol of American art and engineering.

Marc Connelly receives the Pulitzer Prize for *Green Pastures,* a play about Negro religion based on Roark Bradford's novel *Ol' Man Adam an' His Chillun.*

Grant Wood exhibits "American Gothic" in Chicago; painting is one of his first after change from pseudo-Impressionist style to technique influenced by Flemish primitives.

1930 - 1935

Ernest O. Lawrence builds first cyclotron, making possible atomic fission, in 1930. Harold C. Urey discovers isotope of hydrogen with atomic weight of 2 (deuterium, or heavy hydrogen) in 1931. In 1935 Arthur J. Dempster discovers uranium-235, sole natural element that is fissionable and plentiful.

1931

Jan. 19. Wickersham Commission, appointed by President Hoover to recommend means of enforcing Prohibition amendment, reports that enforcement is almost impossible because profits from illegal sale of liquor are great and the public, in general, does not favor the law. Commission recommends changes in the amendment and federal enforcement only instead of state-federal measures.

January. Unemployment is estimated at between 4 and 5 million. **Sept.-Oct.** In spreading bank panic, more than 800 U.S. banks close. Americans start hoarding gold for fear the U.S. will go off the gold standard.

Feb. 26. President Hoover vetoes Veterans Compensation Act, which authorizes loans equal to half the value of 1924 bonus allowances; Act is passed over his veto on following day.

March 3. "Star-Spangled Banner," words of which have been written by Francis Scott Key in 1814, is officially made U.S. national anthem.

May 1. The 102-story Empire State Building, tallest in the world, is dedicated and opened in New York City.

Oct. 5. Clyde Pangborn and Hugh Herndon complete first nonstop transpacific flight; trip from Japan to Washington State takes about 41 hours.

Dec. 26. Musical political satire *Of Thee I Sing,* by George S. Kaufman, Ira and George Gershwin, and Morrie Ryskind, opens in New York City. Enormously popular, it becomes first musical comedy to win the Pulitzer Prize.

Alphonse ("Scarface Al") Capone, Chicago gangster who has an annual income of at least $20 million, is imprisoned for income tax evasion.

J. G. Lansky first detects radio wave interference from the Milky Way after noticing a steady hissing sound when his radio aerial is turned in that direction.

Lincoln Steffens, foremost muckraker at turn of the century, publishes his *Autobiography,* in which he favors a more revolutionary approach to reform than his earlier efforts.

Pearl Buck publishes *The Good Earth,* which tops best seller lists for two years; in 1938 she wins the Nobel Prize for Literature.

International Bible Students Association becomes Jehovah's Witnesses; in 1939 organization is incorporated under the name Watch Tower Bible and Tract Society of Pennsylvania.

1931 - 1933

June 20, 1931. President Hoover proposes an international moratorium on war debts and reparations because of worldwide depression. Moratorium is initially set at one year; token payments are made in 1933, after which all nations except Finland suspend payments entirely.

1932

Jan. 22. Reconstruction Finance Corporation (RFC) is established with Charles G. Dawes as head, and U.S. government becomes major source of business capital.

Measure provides that credit of federal government be used to support railroads and financial institutions and to revive the economy by aiding business corporations. New government corporation is capitalized at $500 million, with $2 billion borrowing power. By end of year, RFC has loaned about $1,500,000,000 to U.S. financial institutions.

Feb. 2. The U.S. attends disarmament conference at Geneva, Switzerland, called by League of Nations. President Hoover's proposals for scrapping of all offensive weapons and reduction of land armaments by one-third are rejected. Meeting produces no important results.

Feb. 27. In effort to bolster U.S. foreign credit and counteract gold hoarding, Congress passes Glass-Steagall Act, which releases about $750 million of U.S. gold to industry and business. Gold has been part of that used to support U.S. currency.

March 3. Twentieth ("Lame Duck") Amendment is submitted to the states for ratification. It provides that Congress shall convene on January 3 after fall elections, that terms of President and Vice-President shall start on January 20 rather than March 4, and that in the event of the death of the President-elect before inauguration, the Vice-President-elect shall succeed to the office. Amendment is declared ratified on February 6, 1933.

March 23. Passage of Norris-LaGuardia Anti-Injunction Act is a distinct gain for labor, since it prohibits injunctions in most labor disputes. Use of injunctions has been challenged since Sherman Antitrust Act of 1890.

April 30. Convention of Socialist Labor Party meets and nominates Verne L. Reynolds of New York for President. **May 21.** Socialist Party nominates Norman Thomas of New York. **May 28.** Communist Party nominates William Z. Foster of New York; his running mate is a Negro, James W. Ford of Alabama. **June 14.** Republicans meet at Chicago and renominate President Hoover and Vice-President Curtis. **June 27.** Democrats meet at Chicago and nominate Governor Franklin Delano Roosevelt of New York for President on the fourth ballot, with John Nance Garner of Texas as his running mate. **July 5.** Prohibition Party meets and nominates William D. Upshaw of Georgia. **July 10.** Farmer-Labor Party nominates Jacob S. Coxey of Ohio. Republican platform calls for government economy; a protective tariff; participation in international monetary conference; further limits on immigration; the gold standard; veterans' pensions; and revision of the Prohibition amendment. Democratic platform calls for government economy; tariff for revenue; state unemployment and old-age insurance; participation in international monetary conference; banking and financial reform, largely to be achieved by federal regulation; every possible aid to farmers; veterans' pensions for men with service-connected disabilities; and repeal of Prohibition.

May 21. Amelia Earhart lands in Ireland after 13½-hour, 2,026-mile flight from Newfoundland, becoming first woman to fly alone across the Atlantic. Four years earlier she has been first woman passenger to fly the Atlantic.

May 29. One thousand veterans of World War I arrive in Washington, D.C., to urge full cash payment of veterans' bonuses. During June they are joined by about 14,000 more. **June 15.** House of Representatives passes bill to provide full payment of bonuses, but Senate defeats it two days later. Most veterans then leave for home with funds provided by the government, but many stay in Washington despite efforts of Washington police to evict them. **July 28-29.** After two deaths have occurred, President Hoover sends federal troops and tanks, commanded by General Douglas MacArthur, to disperse the veterans.

July 21. Faced with rapidly increasing unemployment, President Hoover approves Emergency Relief Act, which broadens scope of RFC, including help to agriculture; raises amount of authorized financing of business and industry; and provides for financing of state and local public works.

July 22. Congress passes Federal Home Loan Bank Act, recommended by President Hoover in 1931. Act authorizes 12 federal regional banks to protect homeowners by granting loans and to encourage new construction for relief of unemployment. Land banks to aid farmers, authorized by Congress in 1916, are also strengthened.

July. Depression reaches low point. Farm purchasing power is almost one-half that of 1929; monthly wages are 60 percent of 1929; dividends are about 57 percent; industry operates at half 1929 volume; more than 5,000 banks, especially rural ones, have closed since 1930; average monthly unemployment is 12 million. President Hoover and Vice-President Curtis, as well as Cabinet members, cut their own salaries and plan federal public works to ease unemployment.

July-October. During election campaign, Roosevelt promises program of social reconstruction and federal support of the economy aimed at the "forgotten man." He stresses distribution of the wealth with least possible federal interference. Hoover stresses private enterprise, calling Roosevelt's program socialistic; he warns that if the "new deal" (a phrase used by Roosevelt in his acceptance speech) is adopted, "the grass will grow in the streets . . . the weeds will overrun the fields."

Nov. 8. Roosevelt is elected by popular vote of 22,810,000 to Hoover's 15,759,000. Electoral vote is Roosevelt, 472; Hoover, 59. Roosevelt wins in all states except Delaware, Pennsylvania, Connecticut, New Hampshire, Vermont, and Maine. Democrats win control in Congress amounting to almost two-thirds of the Senate and almost three-quarters of the House.

November. Government-appointed Committee on the Costs of Medical Care recommends state-sponsored medical care supported by taxes or insurance for the medically indigent. American Medical Association calls idea idealistic, cumbersome, impersonal, and bureaucratic.

December. Enthusiasm for technocracy reaches height; idea of Howard Scott of New York City, scheme involves regulation of national affairs by experts in place of elected officials, and price controls based on units of energy.

Wisconsin enacts first unemployment insurance law in the U.S.

American Federation of Labor adopts new constitution, confirming traditional "craft union" structure; membership by this year is about 2,500,000.

James T. Farrell publishes first volume of his Studs Lonigan trilogy, *Young Lonigan;* trilogy deals with life in deteriorating middle-class section of Chicago. Remaining volumes are *The Young Manhood of Studs Lonigan* in 1934 and *Judgment Day* in 1935. Erskine Caldwell publishes *Tobacco Road,* a realistic examination of Southern poor whites.

Ferde Grofé completes his *Grand Canyon Suite,* which becomes one of the best-known American musical compositions throughout the world. One of most popular songs of this year is "Brother, Can You Spare a Dime?"

Nebraska capitol at Lincoln is completed. Designed by Bertram Goodhue, it is first important public building that attempts use of modern or original style in architecture and sculpture.

1932 - 1933

Jan. 7, 1932. The U.S. protests Japanese occupation of Manchuria, which has started in 1931. Secretary of State Henry Stimson announces that the U.S. will not recognize any arrangement violating the Open Door in China or imposed on China by force in violation of treaties. **March 3.** Japan expels Chinese forces from Shanghai. **March 11.** League of Nations adopts Stimson nonrecognition policy, and Japan withdraws from China but not from Manchuria. **Oct.** Special commission appointed by League to investigate Japanese activity in Manchuria decries Japan's actions and recommends making Manchuria an autonomous state of China with safeguards for Japanese interests. **March 1933.** Japan withdraws from the League of Nations.

1933

Feb. 25. First U.S. aircraft carrier is christened *Ranger,* after John Paul Jones's ship, by Mrs. Herbert Hoover.

March 4. Franklin D. Roosevelt is inaugurated as President; inaugural address inspires public confidence, attacks Hoover administration measures for failure of economic recovery, and sets the stage for the vigorous economic and social experiments of the New Deal. Inaugural also proclaims U.S. "good neighbor" policy, at first toward the world, and later applied especially to the Western Hemisphere.

March 5. On Sunday after inauguration, President Roosevelt proclaims a national bank holiday from March 6 through March 9. By this time, about one-half of all U.S. banks have failed or suspended payments, especially in small cities and rural areas, and almost all states have closed or placed restrictions on banks. National holiday suspends activity of the Federal Reserve System and all financial institutions and bans transactions in bullion or currency. **March 13.** Banks begin to reopen, and by end of the month about three-quarters of banks are operating, confidence in banks and currency is restored, large-scale runs and failures cease, stocks go up, and hoarded gold begins to return to the Treasury. Roosevelt has acted under authority of a 1917 wartime measure, but Congress has approved action by passing the Emergency Banking Relief Act on March 9.

March 9. Congress meets in special session called by President Roosevelt to deal with financial crisis, but Roosevelt continues session until June 16 to handle farm relief and unemployment; session is later called the "Hundred Days" of the New Deal. By June 16 Congress has enacted a wide program of social and economic experiments that goes far beyond economic recovery goals. Many laws passed are later changed or extended by supplementary laws and by interpretation by the courts.

March 12. President Roosevelt begins new policy of speaking directly to the people by means of radio in fireside chats; in first talk, he explains the emergency measures he has taken to stem the financial panic.

March 20. President Roosevelt signs Economy Act. It aims at saving about $500 million by cutting government salaries, de-

partmental budgets, and veterans' pensions, especially those paid to ex-servicemen without service-connected disabilities. Act actually saves about half of amount desired.

March 22. President Roosevelt signs act that legalizes sale of beers and wines of 3.2 percent or less alcohol volume and places revenues on sales.

March 31. Civilian Conservation Corps (CCC) is formed to employ young men of 18 to 25 years of age in such projects as reforestation, flood control, soil erosion control, and road construction. Program is run by War, Interior, Labor, and Agriculture departments, with army officers directing work and camps. At point of maximum enrollment, CCC has 500,000 members, and by 1942 it has employed about 3 million men.

April 19. The U.S. goes off the gold standard, and prices in the U.S. go up. Emergency Banking Relief Act of March 9 has authorized withdrawal by the Treasury of all gold and gold certificates and prohibited exporting and hoarding of gold.

May 12. Congress creates Federal Emergency Relief Administration (FERA) under Harry L. Hopkins to contribute $500 million of federal funds to state relief agencies. Contributions are outright grants, not loans as in Hoover administration relief measures.

May 12. Creation of Agricultural Adjustment Administration (AAA) provides financial aid to farmers, attempts to reduce crop surpluses by making direct payments to farmers who cut down acreage planted in surplus commodities, and raises farm income by controlling prices of basic crops. Some of these features are held unconstitutional by the Supreme Court in 1936.

May 18. Tennessee Valley Authority (TVA) is established as a government corporation set up to coordinate and develop all aspects of resources of the Tennessee River Valley, which covers parts of seven states. Plan includes social and economic improvement of people, as well as conservation, flood control, and rural electrification. These principles of regional planning have long been urged by conservationists and by Senator George Norris of Nebraska, who has sponsored similar measures that have been vetoed in 1928 and 1931 by Presidents Coolidge and Hoover as government interference with private enterprise.

May 27. Federal Securities "Truth in Securities" Act requires that reliable information on all new securities offered for sale be given to investors by means of public sworn statements to the Federal Trade Commission (FTC).

May 27. A Century of Progress International Exposition opens in Chicago; it celebrates Chicago's centennial and marks public acceptance of modern architectural technique and design.

June 6. Congress establishes the U.S. Employment Service, which, jointly with states, establishes and maintains employment agencies.

June 12-July 27. At London conference on tariffs and currency stabilization, the U.S. declines to cooperate in international currency stabilization program with gold standard nations; proposal for bilateral tariff agreements without such stabilization is rejected by European nations. Conference fails.

June 13. Home Owners' Loan Corporation (HOLC) is created to give financial help to nonfarm homeowners by refinancing mortgages and providing advances for taxes, repairs, and maintenance. Eventually, Corporation makes loans involving more than 1 million mortgages.

June 13. Congress passes National Industrial Recovery Act (NIRA), which embodies three programs. First, to be handled by National Recovery Administration (NRA), attempts to reduce unemployment and stimulate business by setting up system of self-regulation in industry, with agreed-on fair trade codes, under government supervision; cooperating industries are to be exempt from antitrust laws, and courts may issue injunctions against code violators; the President may approve proposed codes and prescribe them; General Hugh S. Johnson is appointed head of the NRA. Second, National Labor Board (later National Labor Relations Board, NLRB), headed by Senator Robert F. Wagner of New York, is created to guarantee the right of labor to bargain collectively through its own representatives; Act also sets up enforcement machinery. Third, Public Works Administration (PWA), under leadership of Secretary of the Interior Harold L. Ickes, is established to provide employment and stimulate business by providing purchasing power; PWA is to provide funds of $3,300,000,000 for construction of public projects. NIRA is invalidated by the Supreme Court in 1935 on the grounds that it gives the Executive excessive power, that the Constitution does not provide for such legislation, and that the Act regulates businesses not engaged in interstate commerce.

June 15. National Guard (state forces partially supported by the federal government) is made part of the Army of the United States in wartime and in national emergencies declared by Congress.

June 16. Farm Credit Act is passed to help in refinancing farm mortgages and financing crops. These functions and other farm credit operations of the federal government are combined in a single agency, the Farm Credit Administration (FCA).

June 16. Banking (Glass-Steagall) Act establishes Federal Deposit Insurance Corporation (FDIC), guaranteeing individual bank deposits up to $5,000 against bank failures.

June. Emergency Housing Division, a branch of the PWA, is organized to finance slum clearance and private housing projects.

October. Commodity Credit Corporation is organized to keep farm prices up by lending money to farmers so that they can hold their produce instead of selling on a low market.

Nov. 8. Civil Works Administration is set up under the leadership of Harry L. Hopkins; a further unemployment relief program, it aims to make jobs for 4 million people on new federal, state, and local projects. Eventually about $1 billion is spent on nearly 400,000 work projects.

Nov. 16. President Roosevelt, hoping for increased foreign trade, establishes diplomatic relations with the Soviet Union, which has not been recognized by the U.S. since 1917. Soviet Union promises to discontinue propaganda against U.S. government and to recognize rights of U.S. citizens in Russia.

Dec. 5. Twenty-first Amendment to the Constitution, which repeals the Prohibition amendment, is declared ratified.

Dec. 26. At Montevideo Conference of U.S. and Latin-American nations, Secretary of State Cordell Hull for the U.S. and representatives of all other nations declare that no state has the right to intervene in the internal or external affairs of another. President Roosevelt echoes this for the U.S. two days later in saying that the U.S. is "from now on . . . opposed to armed intervention."

Fiorello La Guardia is elected mayor of New York City on liberal fusion ticket, ending 16-year rule of Tammany Hall, characterized by corruption; La Guardia is reelected in 1937 and 1941.

Affected seriously by the Depression, 2,000 rural schools do not open for the fall semester; 200,000 teachers are out of work; and about 2,300,000 eligible children are not in school; in addition, a number of colleges and universities are forced to close.

Thomas Hunt Morgan of California Institute of Technology receives the Nobel Prize for Medicine for his investigations and discoveries concerning the chromosome in the transmission of heredity. Morgan has written *The Theory of the Gene.*

U.S. District Court voids ban on James Joyce's novel *Ulysses,* which has repeatedly been burned and confiscated as obscene by U.S. Post Office. Judge John M. Woolsey, in his decision, calls it "a sincere and honest book" and says, "I do not detect anywhere the leer of a sensualist." Ruling helps establish new legal criteria of obscenity in literature and art. Erskine Caldwell's *God's Little Acre* is similarly cleared in case brought by New York Society for the Prevention of Vice.

Gertrude Stein's *Autobiography of Alice B. Toklas,* actually her own rather than her secretary's, sells widely, although her other books have had small audiences.

The Great Lakes are linked with the Gulf of Mexico when the Illinois Waterway is opened.

1934

Jan. 1. Dr. Francis E. Townsend of Long Beach, California, proposes his old-age pension plan, providing that all U.S. citizens more than 60 years old receive $200 per month; funds are to be raised by taxes on business transactions. Townsend feels that plan will stabilize the U.S. economy, since pensioners must spend each month's pension within one month.

Jan. 30. Gold Reserve Act of this year gives the President flexible, but limited powers to regulate the value of the dollar in order to give government control of dollar devaluation and to increase prices of goods. On the following day, the President proclaims value of the dollar is 59.06 cents in relation to its gold content.

Jan. 31. Congress creates Federal Farm Mortgage Corporation to provide further aid for debt-ridden farmers through easier credit terms.

Feb. 2. President Roosevelt establishes Export-Import Bank of Washington to provide financial help through various credit devices in an attempt to encourage foreign trade.

Feb. 23. Crop Loan Act sets up a fund of $40 million to extend crop financing measure of previous year.

February. Civil Works Administration (CWA) is dismantled. Federal Emergency Relief Administration (FERA) takes over relief burdens and continues operation until 1935.

February. U.S. postmaster general cancels all domestic airmail contracts on ground of collusion among airlines in fixing prices. Army Air Corps takes over delivery of airmail until May, when private lines resume service under supervision of Interstate Commerce Commission.

March 24. After rejection by the Philippines of an independence act passed in 1933, Tydings-McDuffie Act establishes the Commonwealth of the Philippines and provides for complete independence in 1946.

Under the Commonwealth, U.S. supervision is decreased and includes only controls over such matters as defense and foreign affairs. Manuel Quezon is elected first president in 1935 after ratification of new constitution.

March 27. Vinson Naval Parity Act authorizes construction of airplanes and ships up to limits of naval treaties of 1922 and 1930, providing for building of 100 ships and 1,000 planes over five years. Construction is held up until 1938, however, since Congress does not appropriate enough money for program.

March 28. For the first time, President Roosevelt is defied by Congress when his veto of bill increasing government salaries and veterans' pensions is overridden.

April 7-June 28. Jones-Connally Farm Relief Act, Bankhead Cotton Control Act, Jones-Costigan Sugar Act, and Kerr-Smith Tobacco Control Act are passed in effort to cut production of surplus agricultural commodities. In some cases, reduction of acreage is voluntary as specified by the AAA; but in others it is compulsory, and violators are subject to taxes on excess production. Tax aspect of acts is invalidated by the Supreme Court in 1936.

April 13. Congress passes Johnson Debt Default Act, which prohibits U.S. loans to any nation that is in default on war debt payments.

April 23. Senator Gerald P. Nye of North Dakota is appointed to head committee investigating role of munitions manufacturers and financiers in involving the U.S. in World War I for profit to be gained from sale of arms and from loans. Although evidence gathered is not conclusive, publicity increases isolationist feeling in the U.S.

April 27. Home Owners' Loan Act extends funds of act of 1933 to encourage home building and maintenance.

May 18. In effort to control widespread crime, Congress enacts several laws that authorize use of federal powers against crimes involving more than one state and against federal agents; in addition, the death penalty is established for kidnapping across state lines, a result of kidnap-murder of son of Charles A. Lindbergh.

May 23. Du Pont laboratories researcher Dr. Wallace H. Carothers produces an immensely strong synthetic fiber that he calls polymer 66. It is patented later under the name nylon, and first use is bristles for toothbrushes.

May 29. New treaty with Cuba abrogates Platt Amendment of 1901, which has made Cuba virtually a U.S. protectorate. Ambassador to Cuba Sumner Welles has negotiated treaty with conservative Cuban government and dictator Fulgencio Batista.

June 6. Securities and Exchange Commission (SEC) is formed to license stock exchanges, control trading in securities, and correct dishonest practices in the markets.

June 7. Corporate Bankruptcy Act provides for reorganization of bankrupt corporations on formal request or consent of two-thirds of their creditors.

June 12. Reciprocal Trade Agreements Act gives the President power to raise or lower tariffs 50 percent by agreement with other governments. By 1938, agreements have been reached with 18 nations, with which trade is increased about 40 percent but with little effect on total foreign trade. However, gesture of reciprocal adjustment eases foreign resentment of generally high U.S. tariffs.

June 18. Wheeler-Howard Indian Reorganization Act reverses trend toward decline of tribal societies by returning lands open to sale to tribal ownership; Dawes Severalty (General Allotment) Act of 1887 has divided tribal lands for sale to individuals and has been a conspicuous failure.

June 28. Federal Housing Administration is established to insure housing loans made by private financial organizations. In 1937 establishment of the U.S. Housing Authority extends loans to local governments for public housing.

Aug. 6. U.S. troops and administrators are withdrawn from Haiti after 19 years; U.S. financial aid has stabilized Haitian economy, and political order has been restored. U.S. financial control continues until 1947.

Nov. 6. In fall elections Democrats gain nine seats in the Senate and nine in the House of Representatives.

Nov. 6. Nebraska adopts constitutional amendment written by Senator George Norris and becomes the first state in the U.S. with a unicameral legislature.

November. Author Upton Sinclair is Democratic candidate for governor of California on EPIC ("end poverty in California") program; he is defeated by a massive coalition of regular parties and business interests.

Censorship of moving pictures is begun by the Catholic Legion of Decency; program meets little resistance.

Federal Communications Commission (FCC) replaces Federal Radio Commission; it is authorized to control all foreign and interstate radio, telegraph, and cable communications.

1934 - 1935

Roosevelt administration measures, while creating employment, raising incomes, improving labor conditions, stemming tide of bank and business failures, and inspiring a sense of hopefulness, are violently opposed by a number of factions. The American Liberty League, formed by conservatives, opposes prolabor legislation and increase of tax rate on high incomes. Old-age pension plans and Share-the-Wealth plans advocated by Francis E. Townsend, Senator Huey P. Long of Louisiana, and Reverend Gerald L. K. Smith call for direct payments to U.S. citizens. Father Charles E. Coughlin (the "Radio Priest") of Michigan organizes the National Union for Social Justice, favoring inflation and isolationism, and speaks to a wide audience, condemning labor, Communists, international financiers, Jews, and President Roosevelt. The New Deal is called Communist, Socialist, Bolshevik, and un-American, and work projects are called boondoggling, but most Americans are heartened by obvious lifting of the Depression.

1934 - 1936

F. Scott Fitzgerald publishes his novel of character disintegration *Tender Is the Night;* his last volume of short stories, *Taps at Reveille,* appears in 1935 and a series of essays, "The Crack-Up," in 1936.

1935

Jan. 4. President Roosevelt in his message to Congress sets goal of economic security for the ordinary man through social reform, rather than emphasizing revival of the national economy and business; he also recommends further solutions to unemployment.

Jan. 29. Senate fails to ratify agreement providing for U.S. participation in the Permanent Court of International Justice, although it has been authorized by President Hoover in 1929 and is approved by President Roosevelt. Vote is barely short of necessary two-thirds majority.

April 8. Passage of Emergency Relief Appropriation Act establishes the Works Progress Administration (WPA), which continues until 1943. Act ends direct federal relief payments but continues to provide relief by employing workers on public projects. By 1943, nearly 15 million people have been employed at various times. Important specialized projects are National Youth Administration, which employs needy students and other youths; Federal Arts Project, in which artists decorate public buildings, index works of art, and teach in first federal project involving the fine arts; Federal Theater Project, which helps experimental theater and brings live theater to many towns for the first time since the advent of radio and movies; Federal Writers' Project, which compiles many local histories and publishes historic archives.

April 27. Soil Conservation Service is established to try to halt soil erosion in the Great Plains, where the most destructive drought ever known in the Middle West has turned the land into a dust bowl. Many have left their farms and become "Okies," moving to other areas in hope of finding work.

May 1. Resettlement Administration (RA) is established to help or resettle farm families living on marginal or submarginal land. Under the program, unproductive farmland is shifted to soil conservation and reforestation programs, model towns are built, and family ownership of small farms is supported.

May 11. Rural Electrification Administration (REA) is established by President Roosevelt to build power lines and provide electricity to areas not served by private companies; measure encourages rural power cooperatives and municipally owned power systems. By 1940, number of farms receiving electricity has almost tripled from 1935 figure (12.6 percent).

June 7. National Resources Committee is formed to collect information, make estimates, and plan development of such natural resources as water, land, and mining areas, as well as human resources.

July 5. Because of Supreme Court invalidation of the NRA, a new National Labor Relations Board is established by the Wagner Act. Board is to supervise labor negotiations, guaranteeing collective bargaining rights of employees and controlling unfair labor practices of employers. Many states also enact similar legislation. Board is upheld by the Supreme Court in 1937.

Aug. 14. Social Security Act establishes federal payroll tax to finance a cooperative federal-state system of unemployment insurance, as well as grants to states to support and encourage state systems of relief to the blind, to dependent children, and for maternity and infant care. Old-age and, later, survivors' pensions are to be paid directly by the federal government.

Aug. 24. Banking Act of 1935 refines and strengthens operation of the Federal Reserve System.

Aug. 28. Public Utility Holding Company Act places various aspects of public utility industry under authority of the Federal Trade Commission, the Federal Power Commission, and the Securities and Exchange Commission and counteracts monopolies by forbidding financial consolidation of public utility systems that is not necessary for efficient operation.

Aug. 28. After the Supreme Court invalidates an earlier measure designed to allow farmers to hold bankrupt farms, Congress passes Frazier-Lemke Amendment to Federal Bankruptcy Act, which provides a three-year grace period for farmers whose mortgages are foreclosed; during period they may retain their properties by payment of a reasonable rent to be determined by the courts.

Aug. 30. Revenue Act of 1935 (Wealth Tax Act) increases income tax rates in high income brackets, individual as well as corporate, and raises gift and estate taxes. Act affects individuals with incomes of more than $50,000 and taxes incomes of more than $1 million up to 75 percent.

Aug. 31. Neutrality Act of 1935 is passed; it gives the President power to declare an embargo on arms, but not raw materials, to belligerents in case of European war and to allow U.S. citizens to travel on belligerent vessels only at their own risk. Desire to separate U.S. financial interests from foreign wars, as well as Italy's apparent designs on Ethiopia, is responsible for proposal.

Sept. 8. Dr. Carl A. Weiss shoots Senator Huey P. Long in the capitol of Louisiana. Long has become virtually a dictator of Louisiana and has become powerful in national politics. Before his death (two days later), he has been planning to form a third political party.

Sept. 25. Maxwell Anderson's verse drama *Winterset* opens; it is inspired by the Sacco-Vanzetti case. **Oct. 10.** *Porgy and Bess* opens in New York City; folk opera by George Gershwin based on *Porgy*, a play by Dorothy and DuBose Heyward, it runs for only four months but eventually is revived many times and is shown in U.S. road shows, as well as in Europe, Latin America, and the Soviet Union. Clifford Odets' *Awake and Sing,* play about life in the Bronx, is immediately popular; in the same year three other plays by Odets, *Till the Day I Die, Paradise Lost,* and *Waiting for Lefty,* are shown in New York City.

Nov. 9. Committee for Industrial Organization is founded by the heads of eight unions within the American Federation of Labor to develop industry-wide unions that include clerical and unskilled workers, as well as skilled workers who are eligible for the A.F.L.

President Roosevelt places all remaining public lands in the U.S. under conservation program.

Fear of radicals results in pressure by the American Legion and Daughters of the American Revolution on state governments to require loyalty oaths of teachers; eventually they are successful in 19 states.

Pan American Airways begins transpacific air service from San Francisco to Manila.

1936

Jan. 15. Japan, which has denounced the Washington Naval Treaty of 1922 dealing with reduction of navies and maintenance of the Open Door in China, withdraws from the London Naval Conference. **March 25.** Britain, France, and the U.S. agree to minor and fairly ineffectual limitations on naval armaments.

Jan. 24. Congress passes Adjusted Compensation Act over President Roosevelt's veto; Act provides for immediate payment, if requested, of veterans' bonus certificates. More than $1,500,000,000 in benefits is paid out to about 3 million veterans by the middle of the year.

Feb. 29. Neutrality Act of 1936 extends 1935 act to May 1937 and adds prohibition of credit or loans to belligerent nations.

Feb. 29. Since Agricultural Adjustment Act of 1933 has been invalidated by the Supreme Court in January, Congress passes Soil Conservation and Domestic Allotment Act; law aims to continue policies of restriction of surplus crops, as well as to conserve soil by compensation for cutting acreage of soil-depleting crops and planting soil-improving and -conserving crops.

April 26. Socialist Labor Party nominates John W. Aiken of Massachusetts for President. **May 5.** Prohibition Party meets and nominates Dr. D. Leigh Colvin of New York. **May 22.** Socialist Party meets and nominates Norman Thomas of New York. **June 11.** Republicans at Cleveland nominate Governor Alfred M. Landon of Kansas for President and Colonel Frank Knox of Illinois for Vice-President. **June 19.** Representative William Lemke of North Dakota announces that he is the presidential candidate on the Union Party ticket; Union Party is backed by Father Coughlin's National Union for Social Justice. **June 23.** Democrats meet at Philadelphia and renominate President Roosevelt and Vice-President Garner. Roosevelt is endorsed by several progressive and labor organizations. **June 24.** Communists meet and nominate Earl Browder of Kansas. Republican platform criticizes "unconstitutionality" of the New Deal and usurping of congressional power by the executive but proposes no alternatives to major New Deal measures. Democratic platform stands on New Deal record. Roosevelt criticizes despotism of "economic royalists."

June 19. Robinson-Patman Act is passed; it prohibits prices so low that competition is destroyed and pricing that encourages monopolies or reduces competition. Its greatest effect is on chain stores involved in interstate commerce.

June 22. Revenue Act of 1936 provides, among other things, for taxation of undistributed profits of corporations, in addition to already existing corporation income tax. Act is widely attacked by industry as hampering the practice of setting aside funds for expansion and as a cushion of support for slow periods.

June 26. Merchant Marine Act attempts to strengthen U.S. merchant fleet by direct subsidy instead of by existing ocean mail contracts; Act also creates U.S. Maritime Commission.

June 30. Congress passes Walsh-Healey Public Contracts Act, specifying labor conditions for employees of firms having government contracts; established minimum wages are to be paid, 8-hour day and 40-hour week are to be maintained, and child labor is prohibited.

Nov. 3. After bitterly fought campaign, in which about 80 percent of U.S. newspapers support Governor Landon, President Roosevelt wins election by a popular vote of 27,753,000 to Landon's 16,675,000. Electoral vote is Roosevelt, 523; Landon, 8; Roosevelt carries every state but Maine and Vermont; this is greatest electoral majority in any election involving two or more candidates. Election results in about 80 percent Democratic membership in both House and Senate.

Dec. 1. President Roosevelt opens Inter-American Conference for Maintenance of Peace at Buenos Aires, Argentina; Conference adopts agreement pledging consultation among Western Hemisphere nations whenever any of them is threatened by foreign aggression.

Dec. 11. King Edward VIII of England abdicates his throne after British government refuses to accept as queen American divorcée Wallis Warfield Simpson. Succeeded by his brother George VI, Edward is given the title duke of Windsor.

By this year, the gross national debt has risen to about $34 billion, as opposed to more than $22 billion at beginning of Roosevelt administration. Income of government has risen, but its expenditures have gone up at a greater rate, largely because of relief measures.

Boulder (Hoover) Dam on the Colorado River is completed; reservoir (Lake Mead) back of dam has total capacity of more than 10 trillion gallons of water, the largest man-made lake in the world. Dam is the highest in the world to this time.

Robert M. Hutchins, president of the University of Chicago, publishes *The Higher Learning in America,* a manifesto of the movement against progressive education and the elective system in colleges.

Margaret Mitchell publishes her Pulitzer Prize novel, *Gone with the Wind;* before her death in 1949, the Civil War and Reconstruction novel sells about 8 million copies in 40 countries, almost certainly the greatest sale of any novel published in the U.S. Movie made from book wins Academy award for 1939.

Dramatist Eugene O'Neill receives the Nobel Prize for Literature.

Henry R. Luce begins publication of *Life,* weekly photographic news and feature magazine, inaugurating an era of photojournalism; he has bought title of satire magazine discontinued in this year.

1936 - 1939

Although the U.S. remains officially neutral in the Spanish Civil War, American opinion favors the Loyalists. Hundreds go to Spain to fight the Fascist insurgents, just as men from many European countries join in a conflict that becomes a World War II proving ground.

1937

Jan. 6. Because of Spanish Civil War, started in previous year, Congress passes joint resolution forbidding export of munitions to either side in Spain; resolution is necessary because previous neutrality acts apply only to wars between nations; it hampers mainly Loyalists, however, since Insurgents are supplied by Germany and Italy. **May 1.** Neutrality Act of 1937 is passed in effort to remedy shortcomings of previous ones. In addition to prohibiting shipment of arms on U.S. vessels, travel on belligerent vessels is made unlawful, and belligerents who purchase nonmilitary goods in the U.S. are required to pay for them immediately and transport them in their own ships. The latter is called the "cash and carry" clause. **Sept. 14.** Executive order restrains U.S. munitions trade arising from Japanese attack on China; because of Japan's large merchant fleet, this is largely to China's disadvantage.

Jan. 20. President Roosevelt is inaugurated at first January 20 inauguration, as provided by the Twentieth Amendment; he promises further measures against continuing economic depression that leaves "one-third of a nation ill-housed, ill-clad, ill-nourished."

January. Auto workers at General Motors' Fisher body plants in Flint, Michigan, stage first major sit-down strike in the U.S.; strikers entrench themselves in factories and, despite Michigan court ruling that they are in violation of property rights, are highly successful. Strikes and sit-downs continue, especially in the automobile and steel industries. General Motors recognizes the United Auto Workers in February, and U.S. Steel signs contract in the spring rather than risk a strike.

Feb. 5. In an effort to win Supreme Court approval of New Deal legislation, President Roosevelt proposes reorganization of the federal judiciary. Plan to increase the number of Supreme Court justices from 9 to 15 is resisted by Congress and the press as an attempt to "pack" the Court and leads to first serious political defeat for Roosevelt, but practical success is gained when the Court, in a series of decisions between March and May, upholds the Social Security Act, the Wagner Labor Relations Act, and other important New Deal measures. In addition, Roosevelt is able to appoint seven new justices within the next four years because of death or retirement of elderly incumbents.

March 1. Important gains by organized labor are achieved when United States Steel Corporation accepts first union contract with United Steel Workers-CIO; contract raises wages, lowers hours, and provides for overtime pay. **April 26.** A further gain is the Guffey-Vinson Bituminous Coal Act, which reenacts valid parts of earlier New Deal laws that seek to regulate production and labor conditions in the soft coal industry; the Supreme Court has held parts of original law unconstitutional.

May 30. "Little Steel" companies, led by Republic Steel, refuse to recognize steel union; union demonstrators outside of Republic plant in South Chicago are fired on by police, who kill 4 and injure 84; incident is known as "Memorial Day Massacre." Recognition by independent steel companies is not achieved until 1941.

July 22. Congress passes Bankhead-Jones Farm Tenant Act, which seeks to promote family farm ownership, discourage tenant farming and sharecropping, and improve labor conditions of migrant workers. Act establishes the Farm Security Administration (FSA), which takes over work of the Resettlement Administration.

Aug. 26. Judicial Procedure Reform Act is signed; it allows federal judges, including those of the Supreme Court, to retire at 70 with full pensions after 10 or more years of service.

Sept. 1. U.S. Housing Authority is established by the U.S. Housing Act to provide loans to local authorities for low-cost housing and rent subsidies.

Oct. 5. President Roosevelt, convinced that international measures are necessary to preserve world peace, urges a quarantine of aggressors by all peace-loving nations; U.S. opinion, however, is still predominantly isolationist, and move is not popular among some groups.

Nov. 10. Brazil adopts new constitution, which gives President Getúlio Vargas far-reaching powers to stem disturbances by radicals. Although Vargas government is considered Fascist by many, the U.S. does not acknowledge this and acts immediately to diminish German influence in Brazil. By March 1939 the U.S. and Brazil have signed several agreements guaranteeing to Brazil funds for improving its economy.

Nov. 15-Dec. 21. Congress meets in special session called by President Roosevelt, who recommends legislation involving farmers, labor, conservation, and government reorganization. Congress fails to act largely because Southern Democrats have by now joined Republicans in opposing most administration policies.

Dec. 12. U.S. gunboat *Panay* is attacked by Japanese planes in Chinese waters and sunk; 2 of crew are killed and 30 injured. **Dec. 14.** The U.S. demands that Japan apologize, pay reparations, and guarantee that such incidents will not recur. Japan sends formal apologies and guarantees on the same day.

December. Senator Robert M. La Follette's committee reports, after investigation of means of suppressing labor unions, that various companies use espionage, strikebreakers, vigilantes against organizers, blacklisting of union members, and even private armies supplied from private arsenals.

Musical comedy *I'd Rather Be Right*, by George S. Kaufman and Moss Hart, with songs by Richard Rodgers and Lorenz Hart, is a satire on President Roosevelt. International Ladies' Garment Workers' Union produces *Pins and Needles*, a musical comedy that becomes enormously successful; one of its most popular songs is "Sing Me a Song with Social Significance."

1937 - 1940

Supreme Court invalidates Oregon conviction of labor organizer on the ground that a speech given at an orderly meeting is not a public danger. In the same year, Georgia conviction of a Communist organizer is reversed. In following years, Supreme Court rules that the states may not infringe on liberties specified in the Fourteenth Amendment, upholding, in 1938, the right to distribute religious tracts without a license; in 1939, the right of peaceful assemblage; in 1940, the right to collect funds for religious organizations and the right of peaceful picketing.

1938

Jan. 3. President Roosevelt in his annual message points out that world unrest makes it vital for the U.S. to keep itself defensively strong. Later in January, he proposes to Congress increased appropriations for defense tools and naval construction.

Jan. 6. President Roosevelt sends message to House of Representatives warning against passage of Ludlow Resolution, which would make a national referendum necessary for a declaration of war except in a case of invasion. Roosevelt asserts that such a measure would encourage violation of American rights by foreign nations and leave the President helpless to deal with foreign affairs. Resolution is returned to committee and shelved in the House.

Feb. 16. Second Agricultural Adjustment Act (AAA) extends acreage and crop quotas financed from government revenue, authorizes wheat crop insurance, and attempts to establish an "ever normal granary" by crop carry-over in government storage to stabilize supplies and prices.

March 18. Mexican government expropriates foreign oil concessions; the U.S. accepts negotiated cash compensation in 1941.

May 17. Naval Expansion (Vinson Naval) Act authorizes building of a "two-ocean navy" over the next 10 years. Earlier treaties on naval limitation lapse during this year.

May 26. House Committee on Un-American Activities is established by Congress; Committee is to investigate organizations of Communist, Fascist, Nazi, and other "un-American" character. Martin Dies of Texas is made chairman.

May 27. Congress passes Revenue Act of 1938 without President Roosevelt's approval. Act nominally reduces corporation taxes; its effect, however, is to reduce taxes of large corporations while increasing those of small firms.

June 16. Temporary National Economic Committee (TNEC) is established after President Roosevelt has proposed measures to counteract monopolies and increasing centralization of economic power in industry. Committee is to investigate monopolies, price-fixing, and restraint of competition and trade. Committee makes its recommendations in 1941 after one and a half years of public hearings.

June 21. Emergency Relief Appropriation is signed; President Roosevelt has addressed the Congress and the nation in April asking for expansion of relief and business aid programs to combat new business recession that has begun in the previous summer.

June 23. Civil Aeronautics Authority is formed as an independent agency of the federal government to supervise most aspects of nonmilitary flying.

June 24. Federal Food, Drug, and Cosmetic Act controls misbranding and false advertising claims by manufacturers; misbranding is to be handled by Food and Drug Administration and advertising by Federal Trade Commission.

June 25. Fair Labor Standards Act (Wages and Hours Law), enacted by Congress using interstate commerce power, is signed. It sets an increasing scale of minimum wages and descending scale of maximum hours, as well as prohibiting child labor in industries engaged in, or affected by, interstate commerce. In 1941 Supreme Court holds Act constitutional, overruling 1918 and 1922 decisions against such legislation.

July 5. President Roosevelt calls the lagging economic conditions in the South the "nation's number one economic problem" in message to conference meeting to investigate Southern conditions. Report, issued publicly in August, confirms that low living standards in Southern states hamper development.

Sept. 27. President Roosevelt appeals personally to Chancellor Adolf Hitler of Germany and Premier Benito Mussolini of Italy for cooperation in the peaceful solution of unsettled European problems. By this time Germany has reoccupied the Rhineland, signed Anti-Comintern Pact with Italy and Japan, annexed Austria, and is ready to take over the Sudetenland of Czechoslovakia either by agreement or force.

Oct. 6. U.S. Ambassador Joseph C. Grew protests to Japan its violations of the Open Door in China. Japan replies that present and future world conditions make the Open Door obsolete. U.S. State Department refuses to recognize Japan's "new order."

Oct. 30. "Invasion from Mars," radio play produced by Orson Welles based on H. G. Wells's *War of the Worlds,* causes widespread panic when listeners (in spite of frequent disclaimers during play) think vivid account of attack from Mars is a bona fide news broadcast.

October. Gallup Poll shows that most Americans approve Munich Agreement, signed by Germany, Italy, Britain, and France on September 30, which gives all Sudetenland and Czech military fortifications to Germany in order to keep peace in Europe.

Nov. 8. Although President Roosevelt has intervened in primaries in effort to help liberal Democrats, Republicans gain 81 House seats and 8 Senate seats in fall elections. Democrats retain majorities, but this is first gain for Republicans since 1928.

November. Committee for Industrial Organization, expelled from the American Federation of Labor, which refuses to recognize industrial unions, holds convention and creates independent body with name changed to Congress of Industrial Organizations (CIO); leading unions are steel, auto, garment, and mine workers. John L. Lewis is elected first president.

December. At International Conference of American States in Lima, Roosevelt Corollary of the Monroe Doctrine becomes one of joint responsibility in Western Hemisphere affairs; American nations proclaim mutual solidarity in case of any threat to the peace, security, or territorial integrity of an American state.

December. In first case challenging inequality of education in the South, the Supreme Court holds that a Negro must be admitted to University of Missouri Law School, since no other facilities for legal education exist in the area.

1939

Jan. 4. President Roosevelt devotes most of his annual message to warning of danger to international peace and democracy by aggressors in Europe. **Jan. 5.** Roosevelt's 1940 budget, submitted to Congress, includes about $1,320,000,000 for national defense. **Jan. 12.** The President asks further defense appropriations of $525 million, including air defense program.

Feb. 27. Supreme Court finds sit-down strikes illegal; in past few years, sit-down strikes have involved about 500,000 workers in textile, steel, rubber, oil, and shipbuilding industries and have proved one of labor's most effective weapons.

March 4-April 29. President Roosevelt asks Congress for still further defense appropriations.

March 15. Germany invades Czechoslovakia. **March 22.** Germany annexes Lithuanian Baltic port of Memel and, two days later, demands from Poland passage through the Polish Corridor to Danzig. **March 31.** England and France promise help to Poles if they are threatened. **April 7.** Italy invades Albania. **April 13.** England and France offer help to Greece and Rumania in case of aggression. The U.S., maintaining a policy of strict neutrality in spite of strong anti-German and anti-Italian feeling, observes events in Europe while Germany and Italy continue aggression.

April 3. Administrative Reorganization Act of 1939 is signed; Act consolidates and coordinates many specialized agencies formed since turn of the century, many of them by the New Deal. President Roosevelt has for two years recommended simplifying government setup, but measures have been defeated by Republicans and conservative Democrats who feel that passage will give President dictatorial powers.

April 15. President Roosevelt asks Hitler and Mussolini to guarantee that they will not attack 31 European and Near Eastern nations. Hitler replies that Germany is only righting the wrongs of Versailles.

May 10. Three branches of the Methodist Church, with about 7,500,000 members, are reunited after splits of main body in 1830 and 1844.

May 22. Germany and Italy sign a military alliance.

June 28. Pan American World Airways institutes regular transatlantic passenger flights with *Dixie Clipper,* a "flying boat" carrying 22 passengers from New York to Lisbon, Portugal; flight takes about 24 hours.

June. WPA rolls are reduced when Congress refuses to appropriate amounts asked for by President Roosevelt to handle further unemployment following 1937 business recession. Emergency Relief Appropriations Act of 1939 limits time of employment on government projects, reduces wages, and abolishes Federal Theater Project. As a re-

sult, WPA workers hold nationwide strike, and many lose their jobs.

July 13. Congress passes amendments to Social Security Act that broaden it as to age, payments, and categories of persons covered.

July 25. U.S. Senate ratifies U.S.-Panama treaty worked out in 1936 by President Roosevelt and President Harmodio Arias of Panama; treaty gives Panama most commercial rights of an independent state and puts it on more equal basis with the U.S. in management of Panamanian affairs. Delay in ratification has been caused by opposition of U.S. naval and military authorities.

Aug. 2. Albert Einstein writes to President Roosevelt to tell him that atomic fission can be used to make bombs and that two German physicists have achieved fission of uranium. Einstein has been asked by a number of prominent physicists to inform Roosevelt of the danger if Germany succeeds in using atomic fission explosives. Einstein has come to the U.S. in 1933 after the Nazi ascendancy in Germany.

Aug. 23. Germany and the Soviet Union sign agreement that neither will attack the other, nor remain neutral in case of attack by another nation.

Aug. 24. President Roosevelt appeals to Poland, Germany, and Italy, urging arbitration, conciliation, or negotiation of German-Polish conflict to avoid war. Poland accepts offer, choosing conciliation.

Sept. 1. Germany invades Poland without declaration of war. **Sept. 3.** Britain and France declare war on Germany, and Belgium declares itself neutral.

Sept. 4. After sinking the day before of

British passenger ship *Athenia* by a submarine, killing 30 American passengers, Secretary of State Cordell Hull advises Americans to travel to Europe only under most extreme necessity.

Sept. 5. The U.S. declares neutrality; on September 3, President Roosevelt has said in radio talk that, although he is aware the nation is not neutral in thought, it must remain neutral in policy. **Sept. 8.** In order to facilitate action, Roosevelt declares a limited emergency.

Sept. 17. German forces demand Polish surrender after reaching Warsaw. On the same day, the Soviet Union invades Poland, and most resistance stops. **Sept. 28.** Germany and Soviet Union divide Poland into German and Soviet areas, and a week later the last Polish forces surrender.

Oct. 2. Declaration of Panama specifies certain Western Hemisphere ocean safety zones south of Canada, in which naval action by belligerents is forbidden.

Nov. 2. Congress, meeting in special session called by President Roosevelt, repeals arms embargo clauses of Neutrality Act of 1937 and authorizes trade with belligerents on a cash-and-carry basis.

Nov. 30. Soviet Union invades Finland. Four months later, after a winter campaign in which Soviet armor is often at a disadvantage, Finno-Russian peace treaty is signed.

John Steinbeck publishes *The Grapes of Wrath,* Pulitzer Prize novel of displaced Oklahoma farm family migrating to California. In previous years, he has published *Tortilla Flat, In Dubious Battle,* and *Of Mice and Men.*

1939 - 1940

Aug. 2, 1939. President Roosevelt signs Hatch Act limiting political activity of government personnel; Act prohibits most federal employees from taking part in campaigns, accepting money from persons on relief, and using offices to influence federal elections. **July 20, 1940.** Amendment to Hatch Act limits annual national political expenses of parties to $3 million and individual campaign contributions to $5,000.

A PORTFOLIO OF MAPS

Reclamation of Resources

In 1934 President Roosevelt remarked: "Unlike most of the leading nations of the world, we have so far failed to create a national policy for the development of our land and water resources." The national domain had always been the responsibility of the federal government, but this had not prevented exploitation of the land and its resources. Early in the 19th century national leadership had abdicated responsibility for internal improvements, and there had never been any concerted agricultural policies to reclaim the soil wasted by erosion and irresponsible farming.

It was President Theodore Roosevelt who first took both an active interest and effective action in the problems of conservation and rural life, but it was not until the New Deal that broad national policies were formulated in the matters of land, water, and forest reclamation. The seriousness of the problem was dramatized by the drought and subsequent "dust bowl" of the early 1930s. The administration met the situation with such programs as the Tennessee Valley Authority, created in 1933; the Soil Conservation Act of 1935; and the Civilian Conservation Corps. The CCC was devised to cope with unemployment and conservation at the same time. This vast public works project was one of the most successful devices of the New Deal, for it aided the more than 2½ million men who participated in it as well as benefiting the nation by preserving its natural resources.

The most notable — and controversial — plan for area redevelopment undertaken by the New Deal was the Tennessee Valley Authority. This large program of federal enterprise involved flood control, electric power transmission, fertilizer production, regional planning, and general agricultural renewal. Since the TVA, a number of other regional and local development projects involving flood control and the production of cheap electric power have been built.

Maps prepared by Uni-Map Inc., Palatine, Ill.
for Encyclopaedia Britannica, Inc.

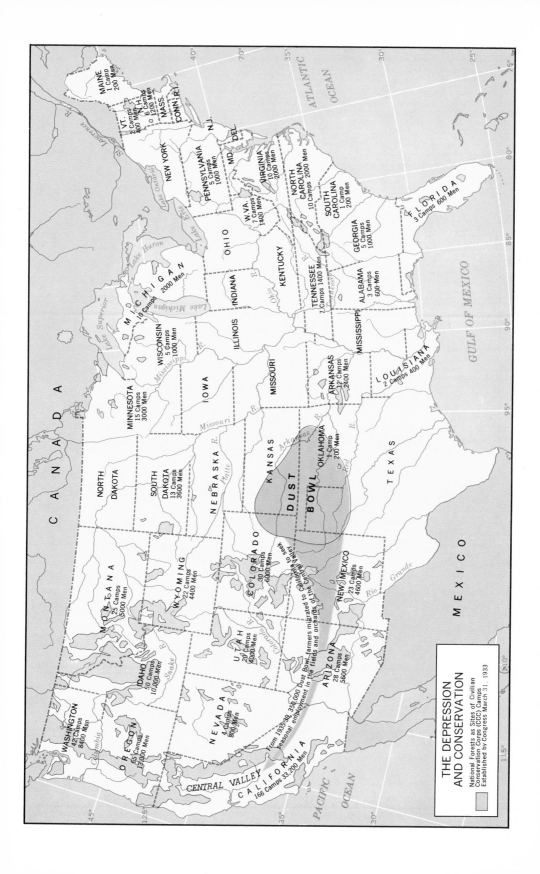

THE DEPRESSION
AND CONSERVATION

☐ National Forests as Sites of Civilian
Conservation Corps (CCC) Camps
Established by Congress March 31, 1933

CANADA

MEXICO

MEXICO

ATLANTIC OCEAN

GULF OF MEXICO

PACIFIC OCEAN

DUST BOWL

CENTRAL VALLEY

MAINE
1 Camp
200 Men

VT.
2 Camps
400 Men

N.H.
6 Camps
1200 Men

MASS.
CONN. R.I.

NEW YORK

PENNSYLVANIA
5 Camps
1000 Men

N.J.

MD. DEL.

VIRGINIA
10 Camps
2000 Men

W.VA.
7 Camps
1400 Men

NORTH CAROLINA
10 Camps 2000 Men

SOUTH CAROLINA
1 Camp
200 Men

GEORGIA
5 Camps
1000 Men

FLORIDA
3 Camps 600 Men

OHIO

INDIANA

KENTUCKY

TENNESSEE
7 Camps 1400 Men

ALABAMA
3 Camps
600 Men

MISSISSIPPI

MICHIGAN
2000 Men
10 Camps

WISCONSIN
5 Camps
1000 Men

ILLINOIS

IOWA

MISSOURI

ARKANSAS
12 Camps
2400 Men

LOUISIANA
2 Camps 400 Men

MINNESOTA
15 Camps
3000 Men

NORTH DAKOTA

SOUTH DAKOTA
13 Camps
3600 Men

NEBRASKA

KANSAS

OKLAHOMA
1 Camp
200 Men

TEXAS

MONTANA
25 Camps
5000 Men

WYOMING
22 Camps
4400 Men

COLORADO
30 Camps
6000 Men

NEW MEXICO
23 Camps
4600 Men

IDAHO
50 Camps
10,000 Men

UTAH
20 Camps
4000 Men

ARIZONA
28 Camps
5600 Men

WASHINGTON
42 Camps
8400 Men

OREGON
55 Camps
13,000 Men

NEVADA
4 Camps
800 Men

CALIFORNIA
166 Camps 33,200 Men

From 1935-39, 350,000 Dust Bowl farmers migrated to California to seek seasonal employment in the fields and orchards of the Central Valley

Lake Superior
Lake Michigan
Lake Huron
Lake Erie
Lake Ontario

St. Lawrence R.

Mississippi R.
Missouri R.
Ohio R.
Tennessee R.
Arkansas R.
Red R.
Platte R.
Columbia R.
Snake R.
Rio Grande

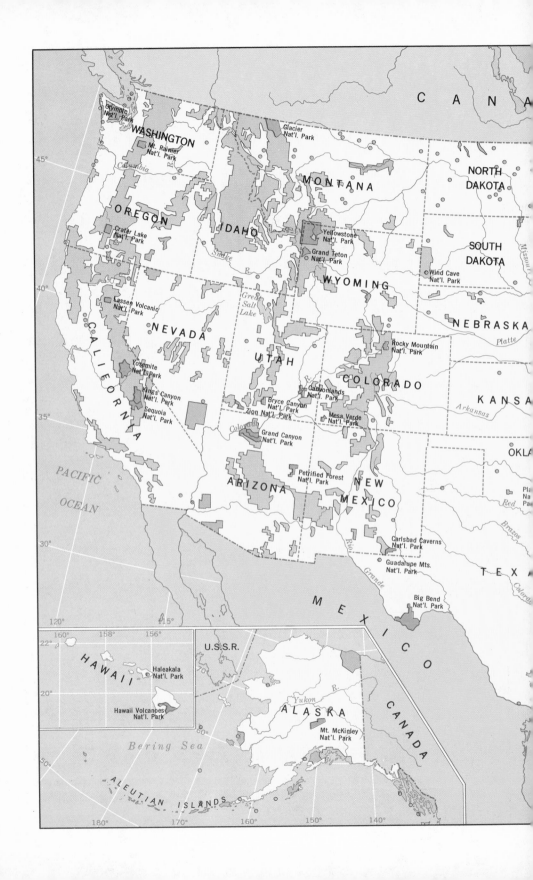

NATIONAL PARKS, FORESTS
AND WILDLIFE REFUGES

National Park

National Forest

National Wildlife Refuge

CANADA

Isle Royale Nat'l. Park

Lake Superior

MAINE

Acadia Nat'l. Park

MINNESOTA

MICHIGAN

Lake Huron

VT.

N.H.

WISCONSIN

Lake Michigan

NEW YORK

MASS.

CONN. R.I.

IOWA

Lake Ontario

Lake Erie

PENNSYLVANIA

NEW JERSEY

40°

Mississippi R.

ILLINOIS

INDIANA

OHIO

MARYLAND DEL.

Shenandoah Nat'l. Park

MISSOURI

Ohio R.

KENTUCKY

WEST VIRGINIA

VIRGINIA

35°

Mammoth Cave Nat'l. Park

TENNESSEE

Tennessee R.

Great Smoky Mts. Nat'l. Park

NORTH CAROLINA

ARKANSAS

SOUTH CAROLINA

ATLANTIC

Hot Springs Nat'l. Park

MISS.

ALABAMA

GEORGIA

OCEAN

LOUISIANA

Mississippi R.

30°

BAHAMA ISLANDS

GULF OF MEXICO

FLORIDA

25°

Everglades Nat'l. Park

CUBA

95°

90°

85°

80°

St. Lawrence R.

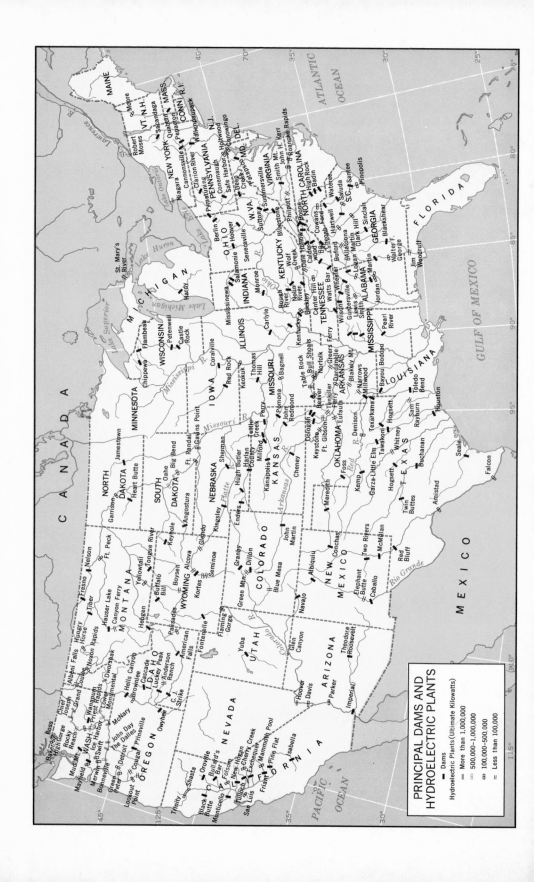

PRINCIPAL DAMS AND
HYDROELECTRIC PLANTS

Hydroelectric Plants (Ultimate Kilowatts)
■ More than 1,000,000
▤ 500,000–1,000,000
▨ 100,000–500,000
Ⅱ Less than 100,000

⧦ Dams

1929

1.

Richard Müller-Freienfels: The Mechanization of American Life

Richard Müller-Freienfels, professor of aesthetics and psychology at the Berlin Academy of Music, published in Germany a work whose English translation later appeared as the Mysteries of the Soul. *His purpose was to present a discussion, not of the characteristics of contemporary civilization but of the underlying, often unconscious, motivations and attitudes that were manifested as an external image. The translation, which appeared in 1929, included a chapter (reprinted here in part) on "The Americanization of the Soul."*

Source: *Mysteries of the Soul,* translated by Bernard Miall, New York, 1929, pp. 252-262.

The second chief characteristic of Americanism is the technicalization or mechanization of life. Not that we Western Europeans are deficient in technique, but nowhere is it so obtrusive as in America. In Europe it is a servant — at least, in theory — but in America it is the almost undisputed despot of life. The decisive point is not the existence but the different valuation of technical methods and knowledge. In Europe at least, in intellectual circles, such terms as "mechanical" or "machine-made" are employed as terms of censure, which are opposed to "organic" or "artistic." In the same way the word "technique" seems often to savor of the superficial, unintellectual, and inartistic. The average American sets an absolute and positive value on technique.

In the American cities it is not only the finished wares that are displayed in the stores; if possible they are actually manufac-tured before the eyes of the passing crowd. You will see the pressing machine at work in the shop windows, stretching, folding, and pressing a suit of clothes in the course of a few minutes; cigarmakers will show anyone who cares to linger before their windows how cigars are made by hand and machine; or you may see — and this is quite an appetizing sight — how sweets and pastry are made and cooked by neat and pretty young women.

Technique is not, as it should be in theory, a means to an end, but is becoming an end in itself. The clatter of machinery, which we find disturbing, is music to the true American ear. Only by the fact that he does not inwardly rebel against it can we explain the fact that the American's nerves do not suffer from noise like those of the European, who is distressed by these things because he inwardly protests against them.

In a purely external sense, the mechanization of life is conditioned by the size of the country. To be sure, we Europeans too have need of our railways, telegraphs, and telephones; but in America these are far more essential if the different parts of the continent are to be connected. A vast network of railways covers the land; the telegraph and the telephone, both largely American inventions, have reached a high degree of development. The airmail is a necessity, not a kind of sport, as with us. Above all, the motorcar is not a luxury but an article of everyday utility, which is obvious from the shabby condition of most of the cars one sees. The majority of the railways, whether above or below ground, are single lines for one-way traffic, and there are separate tracks for the express trains. In the dwelling houses, people ascend to their apartments, not by the stairs but by elevators; in the larger buildings there are frequently a dozen or more elevators at the inmates' disposal, and they may even be divided into express and local elevators.

In the eyes of the American all these things have a positive value. The average European takes his guest to the ancient churches of his city; he shows you streets and localities that have a sentimental interest; it will seldom occur to him to invite you to visit the slaughterhouse or a car factory. In Chicago the slaughterhouses are regarded as the thing best worth seeing, and after them the factories, docks, etc. It is not that we Europeans never inspect a dock or a factory, but we do so out of curiosity, or as a matter of unemotional interest, and not in a spirit of almost religious respect as does the genuine American.

In the country I was repeatedly taken to see wireless apparatus, which reproduced the greatest variety of messages with a considerable amount of noise. *What* was heard, whether Beethoven or jazz music, did not interest my hosts in the least; all that they considered was the technique of transmission and reception — technique as an end in itself.

This general mechanization of life is, of course, due to the cooperation of a number of factors. The lack of domestic servants . . . has of necessity resulted in the mechanization, even in the home, of many tasks which in Europe are performed by human labor. While visiting American acquaintances who lived in the country, I was repeatedly led into the kitchen by my hostess, where she showed me her laboratory. Mechanical contrivances did the work of washing and drying plates and dishes; electrical machines prepared the inevitable ice cream; and there were cooking appliances and vacuum cleaners with refinements quite unknown to us. All these things are devised for "comfort," but American comfort is not what we call comfort in Europe. To us the word conveys a sense of ease and coziness.

The American railway cars, with their spaciousness and their convenient corridors which enable one to pass through the whole train more readily than is possible on most European expresses, are entirely comfortable, but they are not "cozy." The elevated railroads and their stations answer their purpose efficiently, but they are hideous, naked iron scaffoldings, in comparison with which the Berlin elevated railway has a positively artistic appearance. The underground railways are rapid, but excruciatingly noisy, and their atmosphere is intolerable. The asphalt or concrete motor roads are practical, but they are terribly prosaic in a charming landscape; and now they run even through such a park as the Central Park of New York, compared with which the greater part of the Berlin Tiergarten is a poem.

It is pleasant to be invited for a run into the country, perhaps on a Sunday afternoon; but the motorist has no intention of stopping in some picturesque little country town, to enjoy the hospitality of a comfortable inn. In the States, an excursion by road is a technical enterprise. The American driver will tell you proudly how many miles an hour he is traveling, and how many he intends to travel. And what does one see? Hundreds of cars ahead of one, hundreds behind, and one meets thousands! We go in search of nature in order to escape from the technical and mechanical side of life; without machinery and technique the American cannot enjoy nature at all.

Everyone who has visited the United States will be able to recall similar characteristics, all of which go to prove the same thing, namely, that the whole of life has been mechanized in a far greater degree than with us. Psychologically speaking, all these traits may be referred to an intellectual attitude on the part of the American, which is not indeed unknown in Europe, but is found in a purer form in America, and this attitude may be described as the rationalization of the soul. By rationalization I mean the prevalence of practical thinking, of the concentration of the intellect on the practical, useful, and efficient, and the obverse of this attitude is the repression and suppression of all that is merely agreeable, emotional, and irrational in the personality. This rationality, as a form of thinking and willing, expresses itself in constructions and instruments and machines which impress the purposeful will of humanity, with the aid of the inorganic forces of nature, on the outer world. The machine is above all the typical creation and manifestation of the utilitarian and practical reason. It is pure practicality, embodied rationality.

Even organic and intellectual life are mechanized in accordance with the ideal of the rationally operating machine. A cow or a pig, which the German peasant will regard as a personality, and for which he often feels affection, is in America a machine for producing meat and leather. How should any personal relation to the animal be possible when animals are "produced" by the thousand? Even man himself is be-

coming mechanized, is considered solely with regard to his performance.

What are the holders of the great athletic records but machines for boxing, playing baseball, or running? And the workers in the factories? They too are machines, which indefatigably exercise the same function, a function rationally acquired, without any personal relation to the thing which they are making. How should the individual worker have any personal relation to his work when he is only one of thousands, who are all cooperating in a task which he cannot survey as a whole? Strictly speaking, the factory worker is not even a complete machine, but only a portion of a machine, with no more independence than a cogwheel or driving belt. Taylorism and Fordism are the systematic accomplishment of this mechanization of the human being.

If we now take a rapid survey of Europe and the rest of the world, we shall find everywhere the same tendency to mechanization and technicalization, even though it is less pronounced. Even in Europe the machine is thrusting itself between the worker and his work; even here it is not only the work that is being mechanized but the man as well. It is true that the opposing forces are greater, but they are gradually losing their strength. In respect of the tyranny of technique, we are becoming more and more Americanized.

THE STANDARDIZATION OF LIFE

THE MATHEMATIZATION and technicalization of life is connected inextricably with a further trait of Americanism — with the *typicalization*, or, to use the American expression, the *standardization* of life. Nowadays, one may also call this *Fordization*, since Mr. Ford is regarded as peculiarly representative of his country. Standardization is a consequence of mass production, mathematization, and mechanization, for it implies the unlimited mass production — for the most part by mechanical means — of a definite type of product. The most importunate result of this process is the Ford car that rattles along every street.

This standardization will be obvious even to anyone crossing the continent. There are, of course, great differences in different parts of the States, yet they are trifling compared with the uniformity which exists by their side. Compared with the special characteristics of German or Italian landscapes, in which every village almost, and at all events every town of any size, has an individuality of its own, the differences between American cities are trifling. At all events, an observant eye will note the conspicuous appearance of the same features everywhere, in spite of obvious differences. This typification will be seen in the most prominent features as well as in the least conspicuous. If you go shopping, you will everywhere find the same standard wares in the window. All the men seem to be clothed by the same tailor, and all the women seem to have bought their hats at the same shop. As a matter of fact, they buy the same things in different shops. Everything reaches a most respectable standard, but everywhere this standard has the effect of a leveling, a standardization.

The most remarkable thing is that even the people impress one as having been standardized. All these clean-shaven men, all these girls, with their doll-like faces, which are generally painted, seem to have been produced somewhere in a Ford factory, not by the dozen but by the thousand. In no other country are the individuals reduced to such a dead-level as in the United States, and this appears all the more remarkable when we reflect that nowhere is there such a disorderly mixture of races and peoples as in this El Dorado of the needy and adventurous of all countries.

And yet, surprisingly enough, after a few years as a rule, and certainly after a few generations, the immigrant, whether he was English, German, Russian, Syrian, or Greek, has become "an American." And this transformation affects even his features! We can understand that as regards his clothing and other externals he will do his best not to look a "greenhorn"; but it is not so easy to understand that even the member of such a race as the Jewish, which has preserved its type for thousands of years, will after a little while impress one as being not a Jew but an American. And if this transformation affects the features, which would seem to be independent of the will, it is naturally far more perceptible in the bearing and behavior, in speech and accent, and in social manners.

As in the case of "quantification" and mechanization, so in that of typification we are confronted by a different valuation. In Europe, time out of mind, people have preferred to maintain a distance, and therefore a difference, between races and classes and other social groups, and even between individuals. Distance, uniqueness, and originality are European values which are foreign to the American. His values are the very reverse of these: adherence to type, agreement, similarity. In the Middle Ages the classes were divided by dress, custom, and many other characteristics; there was no intercourse between them.

Even in Europe time has brought many changes; even in Europe the bourgeois is victorious, and noblemen and peasants alike wear bourgeois clothes. Nevertheless, these differences persist, even though they may not be visible; the spirit of caste still survives; classes and professional groups still regard one another with disfavor; the educated man looks down on the man of the people, and the man of the people is resentful of education; the officer has a special standing, and so forth.

In America these differences do not exist. There the only difference that counts is a man's quantitative achievement and success, which in the last resort is expressed in dollars. Here is a marshal's baton which everyone carries in his knapsack. It does not matter how he makes his way; whether he succeeds as a professor, or a merchant, or an artisan, there is only the one method of valuation. There are no insuperable barriers, such as that of noble birth. If a man fails in one calling, he adopts another. No one looks down on a man who fails as a professor and then becomes a hotel-keeper, provided he is successful.

This lack of social discrimination impresses the newcomer. People treat one another with a peculiarly equalitarian politeness, which to us often seems an obtrusive cordiality, but which is an attribute of the type, not of the individual. The American sees in his neighbor not a certain Mr. M ——— or Mrs. N ———, but simply an impersonal being, with whom he can exchange opinions, or rather the usual phrases, concerning the weather or the last glove-fight. This reduction of all to a dead-level has of course its advantages, but it deprives life of much that is desirable, and, above all, of a perception of personal quality.

Just as the American does not discriminate between the professions, so he has no perception of all those factors that in Europe separate, differentiate, and discriminate. What of the political parties, for example? In Europe they are divided by their social and political ideals. There are, of course, political differences in America, but, in the first place, they are very few, and, in the second, they are very slight. The European is surprised to find how little difference there is between the tendencies of the two principal parties, the Republicans and the Democrats. Men change their party without conscientious scruples, and they are not therefore accused of moral weakness.

Even religion does not create such radical divisions as in Europe, although the number of sects and confusions is far greater than with us. But there is no "Centre" party, as in Germany; no anti-Semitism as we understand it, no instinctive feeling of enmity against another ethnological species. Even

such associations as the Ku Klux Klan do not attack any particular group of opponents, but simply wage war on all that is un-American — that is, on all that is not typical. If a thing is untypical it is worthless.

Further, the difference between the sexes is not so great as it is — or used to be — with us. Women do not constitute a downtrodden caste; they are so dominant that some Europeans have spoken of gynocracy. Even the young girl behaves with an independence which is startling to the European, and seems to him "unfeminine"; and conversely, he often detects feminine traits in the American man. In both cases he is mistaken; the sexes have not interchanged their roles; it is only that the differences are not so extreme. Even age does not constitute a social difference in the States. While with us the relation of adults to children (like that of the husband to the wife) is from the sociological point of view very like that of master and servant, in America youth enjoys much more extensive rights. The result may often be regarded by the European as lack of respect, disobedience, and libertinism, but it is not so regarded in America, since the adult does not ask for respect and subordination.

Human typification finds an aesthetic expression in an "ideal beauty," which is propagated daily in a thousand magazines, cinemas, and theaters, and in which all the characteristic differences of race, sex, age, and class have completely disappeared.

This lack of differentiation between individuals, and the resulting exclusiveness of type, naturally manifests itself externally by a sharp discrimination against all that does not belong to this type. And this explains the American attitude to *color*, which some Europeans find so difficult to understand. This, apparently, is a flat contradiction of the general tolerance and equalitarianism of the American. The colored person (and the category includes those whose ascendants include a Negro even at a distance of three or four generations) is simply and absolutely debarred from absorption into the type, so that in most of the states of the Union, marriage between the races is forbidden by law.

In theory this harshness is justified on eugenic grounds, since it is assumed that hybrids must naturally inherit the worst qualities of both races. But in actual fact there are other motives at work. Despite the ostensible attitude of the American, the decisive point is the fact that the very visible somatic differences of the two races cannot be overlooked and are incompatible with unity of type. Unity of type can only be achieved if all that would destroy it is excluded.

Is this standardization American in the ethnographical sense, or is it "Americanistic"; in other words, is it a universal feature? Once again we are compelled to admit that while it is most accentuated in America, it is making its appearance everywhere in Europe. Not only things and industrial products are being standardized but, in an ever increasing degree, human beings also, even in Europe. The beardless face of the man, the doll-like face of the woman whose features are made "stylistic" and inorganic by means of rouge and powder and lip salve — even in Europe these are becoming more and more prevalent. In our great cities, in particular, we have in Europe also a reduction to a dead-level which hardly differs from that to be observed in America.

2.

Robert S. and Helen Merrell Lynd: The Automobile and Family Life

In 1925 a team of sociologists headed by Robert and Helen Lynd took up residence in Muncie, Indiana, to study the effects of modern inventions and the resulting increase of leisure on contemporary life. They remained in Muncie for about a year, interviewing the residents and collecting statistical data. Their findings were published in 1929 in a book entitled Middletown, *as Muncie was fictitiously renamed. The portion of the book that deals with the impact of the automobile on family life is reprinted below in part. In the 1930s the Lynds returned to Muncie, this time to study the effect of the Depression on that city.* Middletown *and* Middletown in Transition, *as the second study was called, were received with much acclaim and are frequently referred to by social historians.*

Source: *Middletown: A Study in Contemporary American Culture,* New York, 1929: "Inventions Remaking Leisure."

The first real automobile appeared in Middletown in 1900. About 1906 it was estimated that "there are probably 200 in the city and county." At the close of 1923 there were 6,221 passenger cars in the city, one for every 6.1 persons, or roughly two for every three families. Of these 6,221 cars, 41 percent were Fords; 54 percent of the total were cars of models of 1920 or later, and 17 percent models earlier than 1917.

These cars average a bit over 5,000 miles a year.

For some of the workers and some of the business class, use of the automobile is a seasonal matter, but the increase in surfaced roads and in closed cars is rapidly making the car a year-round tool for leisure time as well as getting-a-living activities. As, at the turn of the century, business-class people began to feel apologetic if they did not have a telephone, so ownership of an automobile has' now reached the point of being an accepted essential of normal living.

Into the equilibrium of habits, which constitutes for each individual some integration in living, has come this new habit, upsetting old adjustments and blasting its way through such accustomed and unquestioned dicta as "Rain or shine, I never miss a Sunday morning at church"; "A high-school boy does not need much spending money"; "I don't need exercise, walking to the office keeps me fit"; "I wouldn't think of moving out-of-town and being so far from my friends"; "Parents ought always to know where their children are." The newcomer is most quickly and amicably incorporated into those regions of behavior in which men are engaged in doing impersonal, matter-of-fact things; much more contested is its advent where emotionally charged sanctions and taboos are concerned.

No one questions the use of the auto for transporting groceries, getting to one's place of work or to the golf course, or in place of the porch for "cooling off after supper" on a hot summer evening; however much the activities concerned with getting a living may be altered by the fact that a factory can draw from workmen within a radius of forty-five miles, or however much old labor union men resent the intrusion of this new alternate way of spending an evening, these things are hardly major issues. But when auto riding tends to replace the traditional call in the family parlor as a way of approach between the unmarried, "the home

is endangered," and all-day Sunday motor trips are a "threat against the church"; it is in the activities concerned with the home and religion that the automobile occasions the greatest emotional conflicts.

Group-sanctioned values are disturbed by the inroads of the automobile upon the family budget. A case in point is the not uncommon practice of mortgaging a home to buy an automobile. Data on automobile ownership were secured from 123 working-class families. Of these, 60 have cars. Forty-one of the 60 own their homes. Twenty-six of these 41 families have mortgages on their homes. Forty of the 63 families who do not own a car own their homes. Twenty-nine of these have mortgages on their homes. Obviously, other factors are involved in many of Middletown's mortgages.

That the automobile does represent a real choice in the minds of some at least is suggested by the acid retort of one citizen to the question about car ownership: "No, sir, we've *not* got a car. *That's* why we've got a home." According to an officer of a Middletown automobile financing company, 75 to 90 percent of the cars purchased locally are bought on time payment, and a workingman earning $35 a week frequently plans to use one week's pay each month as payment for his car.

The automobile has apparently unsettled the habit of careful saving for some families. "Part of the money we spend on the car would go to the bank, I suppose," said more than one working-class wife. A businessman explained his recent inviting of social oblivion by selling his car by saying: "My car, counting depreciation and everything, was costing mighty nearly $100 a month, and my wife and I sat down together the other night and just figured that we're getting along, and if we're to have anything later on, we've just got to begin to save." The "moral" aspect of the competition between the automobile and certain accepted expenditures appears in the remark of another businessman, "An automobile is a luxury, and no one has a right to one if he can't afford it. I haven't the slightest sympathy for anyone who is out of work if he owns a car."

Men in the clothing industry are convinced that automobiles are bought at the expense of clothing, and the statements of a number of the working-class wives bear this out:

"We'd rather do without clothes than give up the car," said one mother of nine children. "We used to go to his sister's to visit, but by the time we'd get the children shoed and dressed there wasn't any money left for carfare. Now no matter how they look, we just poke 'em in the car and take 'em along."

"We don't have no fancy clothes when we have the car to pay for," said another. "The car is the only pleasure we have."

Even food may suffer: "I'll go without food before I'll see us give up the car," said one woman emphatically; and several who were out of work were apparently making precisely this adjustment.

Twenty-one of the twenty-six families owning a car for whom data on bathroom facilities happened to be secured live in homes without bathtubs. Here we obviously have a new habit cutting in ahead of an older one and slowing down the diffusion of the latter.

Meanwhile, advertisements pound away at Middletown people with the tempting advice to spend money for automobiles for the sake of their homes and families: "Hit the trail to better times!" says one such advertisement.

Another depicts a gray-haired banker lending a young couple the money to buy a car and proffering the friendly advice: "Before you can save money, you first must make money. And to make it you must have health, contentment, and full command of all your resources. . . . I have of-

ten advised customers of mine to buy cars, as I felt that the increased stimulation and opportunity of observation would enable them to earn amounts equal to the cost of their cars."

Many families feel that an automobile is justified as an agency holding the family group together. "I never feel as close to my family as when we are all together in the car," said one business-class mother; and one or two spoke of giving up Country Club membership or other recreations to get a car for this reason. "We don't spend anything on recreation except for the car. We save every place we can and put the money into the car. It keeps the family together," was an opinion voiced more than once. Sixty-one percent of 337 boys and 60 percent of 423 girls in the three upper years of the high school say that they motor more often with their parents than without them.

But this centralizing tendency of the automobile may be only a passing phase; sets in the other direction are almost equally prominent. "Our daughters [eighteen and fifteen] don't use our car much because they are always with somebody else in their car when we go out motoring," lamented one business-class mother. And another said, "The two older children [eighteen and sixteen] never go out when the family motors. They always have something else on."

"In the '90s we were all much more together," said another wife. "People brought chairs and cushions out of the house and sat on the lawn evenings. We rolled out a strip of carpet and put cushions on the porch step to take care of the unlimited overflow of neighbors that dropped by. We'd sit out so all evening. The younger couples perhaps would wander off for half an hour to get a soda but come back to join in the informal singing or listen while somebody strummed a mandolin or guitar." "What on earth *do* you want me to do? Just sit around home all evening!" retorted a popular high-school girl of today when her father discouraged her going out motoring for the evening with a young blade in a rakish car waiting at the curb.

The fact that 348 boys and 382 girls in the three upper years of the high school placed "use of the automobile" fifth and fourth respectively in a list of twelve possible sources of disagreement between them and their parents suggests that this may be an increasing decentralizing agent.

An earnest teacher in a Sunday-school class of working-class boys and girls in their late teens was winding up the lesson on the temptations of Jesus: "These three temptations summarize all the temptations we encounter today: physical comfort, fame, and wealth. Can you think of any temptation we have today that Jesus didn't have?" "Speed!" rejoined one boy. The unwanted interruption was quickly passed over. But the boy had mentioned a tendency underlying one of the four chief infringements of group laws in Middletown today, and the manifestations of Speed are not confined to "speeding."

"Auto Polo next Sunday!!" shouts the display advertisement of an amusement park near the city. "It's motor insanity — too fast for the movies!" The boys who have cars "step on the gas," and those who haven't cars sometimes steal them: "The desire of youth to step on the gas when it has no machine of its own," said the local press, "is considered responsible for the theft of the greater part of the [154] automobiles stolen from [Middletown] during the past year."

The threat which the automobile presents to some anxious parents is suggested by the fact that of thirty girls brought before the Juvenile Court in the twelve months preceding September 1, 1924, charged with "sex crimes," for whom the place where the offense occurred was given in the records,

Library of Congress

Billboard along the highway near Los Angeles, Calif., 1936; photo by Dorothea Lange

nineteen were listed as having committed the offense in an automobile. Here again the automobile appears to some as an "enemy" of the home and society.

Sharp, also, is the resentment aroused by this elbowing new device when it interferes with old-established religious habits. The minister trying to change people's behavior in desired directions through the spoken word must compete against the strong pull of the open road strengthened by endless printed "copy" inciting to travel. Preaching to 200 people on a hot, sunny Sunday in midsummer on "The Supreme Need of To-day," a leading Middletown minister denounced "automobilitis — the thing those people have who go off motoring on Sunday instead of going to church. If you want to use your car on Sunday, take it out Sunday morning and bring some shut-ins to church and Sunday school; then in the afternoon, if you choose, go out and worship God in the beauty of nature — but don't neglect to worship Him indoors too."

This same month there appeared in the *Saturday Evening Post*, reaching approximately one family in six in Middletown, a two-page spread on the automobile as an "enricher of life," quoting "a bank president in a Midwestern city" as saying, "A man who works six days a week and spends the seventh on his own doorstep certainly will not pick up the extra dimes in the great thoroughfares of life." "Some sunny Sunday very soon," said another two-page spread in the *Post,* "just drive an Overland up to your door — tell the family to hurry the packing and get aboard — and be off with smiles down the nearest road — free, loose, and happy — bound for green wonderlands." Another such advertisement urged Middletown to "Increase Your Weekend Touring Radius."

If we except the concentrated group pressure of wartime, never perhaps since the days of the camp meeting have the citizens of this community been subjected to such a powerfully focused stream of habit diffusion. To get the full force of this appeal, one must remember that the nearest lakes or hills are one hundred miles from Middletown in either direction and that an afternoon's motoring brings only mile upon mile of level stretches like Middletown itself.

3.

Robert E. Sherwood: Renaissance in Hollywood

The first sound motion picture, or "talkie," was The Jazz Singer; *starring Al Jolson, it was released in 1927. It was evident from its phenomenal success that the motion picture industry, which had since World War I transformed American taste in entertainment, was itself about to be transformed. The effect of that transformation was eagerly anticipated by Robert E. Sherwood in an article entitled "Renaissance in Hollywood." Sherwood was a dramatist, an occasional screenwriter, and a drama and movie critic. His article, a portion of which is reprinted here, appeared in H. L. Mencken's* American Mercury *in 1929.*

Source: *American Mercury,* April 1929.

As one who has written about the movies and talked about them at great length, and actually gone to see them, regularly, for many years, I am now enjoying myself heartily at the prospect of sensitive souls rushing forth to defend the ebbing silent drama against the swelling talkies; for these same souls, a year ago, noticed the screen only as one would notice a roadside signboard, which shut off part of the landscape and added nothing of beauty to the rest. They who once spoke of the movie as the backhouse of the drama are now protesting loudly because the Vitaphone, the Movietone, and the Photophone are degrading a noble art!

Formerly, they either ignored the activities on the screen entirely, or else they observed them, as from a great height, with a faintly nauseous contempt. Now, if one may judge from their impassioned outcries, they seem to regard the cinema as a virginal muse who has been assaulted on Parnassus by an unprincipled satyr from the laboratories of the Radio Corporation of America.

Here is a specimen of their complaints against the talkies; it is picked from a letter to the movie editor of a New York newspaper and printed by him in his department:

> To try to resonate a film is to protest that the film is not a complete and self-fulfilled art medium, and nobody of sense would say that about the cinema today. . . . In any perfect art medium there are brief strokes which achieve the utmost in imaginative suggestiveness, and piling on extraneous sense-ticklers is then only to distract and annoy, in short, to vitiate the fine effect.

I don't know just how that word "resonate" crept in, but I suppose it is intended to mean, in this new application, to add sound. Its user evidently feels that those who practise resonation are in a class with the novelty manufacturers who insert ornamental clocks into the abdomen of the Venus of Milo. He believes that the lily does not need a new coat of gilt — that well enough might well be let alone.

Since when did the movies, in the minds of such people, become inviolate? Since when did the industry presided over by Adolph Zukor, William Fox, Sam Goldwyn, Carl Laemmle, Joe Schenck, and the brothers Warner come to be known as a "complete and self-fulfilled art medium"? I gather that all this has happened since the Vitaphone first caused Conrad Nagel to lisp.

It is not my purpose to defend the talkies as they have appeared up to the present time; such a defense would be beyond the limits of my capabilities, or of Clarence Darrow's, for that matter. No one is in a position to deny that the machines themselves are still this side of perfection — they groan, squawk, and shriek — or that they have been used thus far with lamentable ineptitude. Most of the talkies that I have seen have combined the worst features of a bad movie and a bad play, and if anyone can conceive anything more awful than that, may he refrain from telling me about it.

Nevertheless, and in the face of all the obvious arguments that may be offered to refute me, I contend that the talkies have come as a veritable blessing, that they are exercising a profoundly salutary influence upon the movie industry, and that the revolution which they caused will come to be known, in time, as a memorable Renaissance. They have shaken the insecure and essentially phony foundations of Hollywood, and beneath the resultant heaps of wreckage lies much of the fatheaded incompetence and stupid conceit that has dominated the movie during the protracted period of its infancy.

When people consider the present upheaval in Hollywood, they think only of its effect on stars who happen to be deficient in elocution. They are either delighted or stunned by contemplation of the possibility that Miss Clara Bow may be lost to the public because her voice doesn't screen well. That, of course, is largely nonsense. What matters infinitely more than the tonal quality of the star's voice, or the perfection of his or her articulation, is the nature of the star's cerebral functions. For every one representative of the Beverly Hills nobility who will be sent to the guillotine in the near future because of faulty diction, there will be a dozen who are decapitated because they lack the capacity to memorize three or four sentences at a time and to retain them for as long as ten minutes.

Nor are the stars the only ex-aristocrats who are now being compelled to exchange their Hispano-Suizas for tumbrils. You will observe among them large numbers of lordly directors, golf-playing scenario and subtitle writers, and even (and herein lies the greatest cause for rejoicing) manicured executives. Their voices don't count, but other qualifications, or the want of them, are becoming of increasing importance.

Consider the director: he is an impressive fellow who gained his experience in stock companies of the lower order or in medicine shows, and then was conducted, by a friendly fate, to the old Vitagraph plant in

Brooklyn or the Triangle plant in Hollywood. He has risen to his present eminence largely because he could outtalk and outbluff his betters. He is, in effect, a high-pressure salesman who has been able to sell himself to the illiterate gentlemen by whom he is employed. Although he is not intelligent, he is clever enough to recognize the merit of ideas originated by a Chaplin, a von Stroheim, a Lubitsch or a Murnau, and to appropriate these ideas and use them as his own. Such frauds can and do exist outside the movie industry; but it is in this industry, ignorantly conducted and sloppily disorganized as it has been, that they have reached their highest state of glorification.

The director now confronts the talkies. He has pooh-poohed them resolutely — has dismissed them as "a mere toy" — and has alluded frequently to the good taste of the public and to the deathless art of pantomime; but he now realizes that he must either demonstrate his ability to make talking pictures or return to the medicine shows. He selects the former course, feeling that he will have no difficulty in applying what he is pleased to term the technique of the speaking stage. He learned that technique in his stock-company and medicine-show days and is unaware that the speaking stage has undergone any changes since then.

The actual production of talkies cramps the director to an uncomfortable extent. He has to prepare his scenes in advance, which means that he must exercise a certain amount of intelligent forethought. He must work with actors who know their business and are therefore apt to be smarter than he is. Worst of all, he may not talk himself while the scenes are being photographed and recorded; he must sit, mute and impotent, and long for the old times when he could shout through the megaphone, "Now pull the skirt a little higher, sweetheart! Give us just a *little* more of the thigh. . . . No! No! NO! *Cut!*"

It should be apparent that this type of film director (and he is *the* type of film director) is soon to pass on to other fields. With him will go his by-products, the scenario and subtitle writers, or yes-men. The departure of these fawning fellows from their fat jobs will be mourned by no one but their dependents. Of all the classes of laborers in the Southern California vineyards, these have been the lowliest and most ignoble. While the movies have developed several great directors, many fine actors, two or three first-rate financiers, and a number of meritorious scenic artists, technicians, and even press agents, they have not, in the thirty years of their existence, developed more than one writer who is worthy of mention; that lone exception is the gifted Miss Anita Loos, and she quit this chambermaid's employment as soon as she could afford to do so. The writer will now be boosted into a position of importance that is equal, at least, to that of the director. He will assume the same privilege of responsibility that is enjoyed (or regretted, as the case may be) by the playwright. He will have a great deal to say about the preparation and production of a picture, and his remarks won't all be variations of the affirmative yes.

As to the executives, they are either going out entirely or are being humbled to positions more nearly commensurate with their talents, because the movie industry is no longer its old, easygoing self. It is now rapidly coming under the domination of those august corporations which control the patents on the Vitaphone, Movietone, and Photophone; namely, the General Electric, Western Electric, American Telephone and Telegraph, and the Radio Corporation of America. Whatever else may be said of these bodies, they unquestionably possess the virtue of competence. If they hire a man to design a new electric toaster or to distribute condensers, they do so because they believe him to be the best toaster designer or condenser distributor obtainable, not because he happens to be someone's nephew from the old hometown in Latvia.

That is why we hear statements from the usually astute Joe Schenck to the effect that the "talkies are no more than a passing phase" and that the public is too smart to be permanently deluded by sound. Mr. Schenck is merely venting his rage at the invasion of his own territory by interests that are shrewder and more powerful than he is; having planned to get control of the movies himself, he is embittered by the thought that his disrupted industry is about to become a minor item in the vast scheme of Big Business. Efficiency and economy are entering the movies with the new regime, and waste and extravagance are going out. The very preeminence of Hollywood as a world production center is seriously threatened, and the Golden Calf that Hollywood has worshiped these many years is now being replaced by the gods of Wall Street and Schenectady, N.Y.

One would be inclined to shed tears of sympathy for the old order were this what it might appear to be: another triumph of the machine age, another victory of stuffy babbittry over charming, devil-may-care bohemianism. But it happens to be nothing of the sort. It is no more than the expected victory of a superior form of industrialism over an inferior one.

II

THUS, WE HAVE BEFORE US the immensely agreeable spectacle provided by a group of morons who, accustomed to fabulous affluence, are now confronted with unemployment, and who are giving out interviews to representatives of the fan magazines, condemning the talkies as hopelessly inartistic. They have seen the end of that which has been, if I understand correctly the meaning of a somewhat esoteric term, a racket.

Who will take their places? Will every dumbbell who loses his or her job in Hollywood be replaced at once by a mental giant? That, of course, is extremely improbable. There aren't that many mental giants in all creation.

Most of the new directors, actors, and writers have been recruited from the Broadway theater — experience in dealing with the spoken word being now of paramount, universal, and first national importance. The movie merchants are in a state of panicky indecision as a result of the unexpected dawn of the Noise Era on the screen, and they are shrieking for help from those who have composed dialogue and recited it out loud. Members of the Dramatists' Guild and of the Actors' Equity Association, saddened by the present epidemic of starvation on Broadway, are now rushing gleefully to Hollywood, engaging in chop-licking exercises as they go. One notices the titles of recent or forthcoming super-features — *Interference, Coquette, Show Boat, The Trial of Mary Dugan, Broadway, The Barker,* and *The Front Page* — and realizes that the big celluloid merchants have been buying up all the recent theatrical smash hits, whether they have any legitimate place on the screen or not.

Some of the newcomers in Hollywood are being encouraged to write original stories for the talkies; but most of them are being put to the wearisome work of adaptation. How the movie people love that word "adapt!" Anything that has been adapted must be good! As an instance of the present tendency: the keen-visioned executives of that mammoth corporation Paramount-Famous-Lasky hired George Abbott in the hope that he would bring to the talkies some of the considerable talent that he has displayed as writer and director of rough and rowdy plays of the "Broadway" type; but instead of assigning him to a story that had been written by himself, or by Ring Lardner, or some other native, they set him to work directing a venerable bit of French hokum called *The Bishop's Candlesticks,* which was derived originally from an episode in *Les Misérables* and which has seen service as a vaudeville dramalet ever since! And that ruthlessly wise poetess Dorothy Parker was lured to the Metro-Goldwyn-Mayer studio in Hollywood for the purpose of writing dialogue for *Madame X!* If they could get him, they would doubtless turn Eugene O'Neill loose on *Rebecca of Sunnybrook Farm.*

All these raids on Broadway are inspired by the belief, prevalent in and out of the movie business, that a talking picture is necessarily no more than a photographic and phonographic recording of a stage play. That, too, is nonsense. The movie is still as independent of the play as it is of the fugue. It has established for itself an identity of its own, through the medium of such pictures as *The Last Laugh,* the Chaplin comedies, and even the newsreels, and the fact of added talk (instead of printed subtitles) fails to alter this identity in any essential respect.

I saw a talkie the other day in which one of the characters, opening a letter that had been handed to him, read every word of it to the audience, though there was no occasion for him to do so. On the stage, he would have to read it aloud; otherwise, the audience would have no way of knowing its contents. On the screen, a close-up of the letter could easily be inserted into the film, and the literate members of the audience could explain it to their companions. But the director of this picture had forgotten about the obvious advantages which the movies enjoy; he was thinking of the "technique of the speaking stage," as he dimly remembered it, and he consequently obeyed the ancient laws of the theater and observed its limitations. No one had told him that the ancient laws of the theater are no longer enforced, not even in the theater.

However, these early bonehead plays won't continue at the present rate forever. The movie moguls have found themselves in a horribly embarrassing position and are not entirely responsible for their immediate actions. That which a man will do when caught with his pants down is not to be accepted as evidence of what he will do when those garments have been restored to their rightful position and duly buttoned.

The movie people — whether they be the Goldwyns and Laemmles of the old order, or the Sarnoffs and Owen D. Youngs of the new — will learn a great deal in the years to come. Some of it will be new knowledge, but the bulk of it will be a relearning of old lessons. It will be discovered (and soon) that if the former white hopes of Hollywood don't understand how to write, direct, or deliver spoken dialogue, neither do the bright boys of Broadway understand the art of expression in terms of pictures that move.

The latter are obsessed with the idea that a talking picture must be all talk — an idea which they have brought with them from the theater. On the stage, of course, it is essential that the dialogue be kept going, continuously, it being always difficult and usually impossible for a playwright, actor, or director to invent business which will hold the audience's interest for more than a few seconds. On the screen, business has been developed to such an extent that it is far more eloquent, far more telling than the printed or spoken word could ever be. . . .

Custom and usage have done a lot for the movie, which has arisen from a nickel novelty to a "complete and self-fulfilled art medium," because people have demonstrated their ability to accept and believe anything in which they are sufficiently interested. The mechanical whirr of the projection machine is ignored; the distant shadows of reality are acquiescently accepted as reality itself. The audience sees walruses fighting for their lives in *Nanook of the North* — cracker orphans fighting for their lives in *Stark Love* — leopards fighting for their lives in *Chang* — and is moved and stirred, and terrified by them, just as it is moved, stirred, and terrified by the sight of Jack Gilbert, clad in a doughboy suit, charging bolt upright into the teeth of a German machine-gun nest.

If custom and usage have enabled us to accept one mechanical process with so much implicit faith, I don't see why we should be forbidden, for artistic reasons, to accept another. The invention of the talkie apparatus, which tends to make the camera more nearly complete as a reproductive organ, has always seemed to me to be an inevitable development in the progress of the moving picture, just as color photography and stereopticon photography are inevitable developments of the future. If an art medium is to be ground out through a machine, then there is no earthly reason why that machine should not be as proficient as the Hoovers can make it.

In them can be entrusted the confidence of the great fun-loving public. If the problems that they confront were artistic ones, there might be some question of their ability to solve them; but these are purely mechanical problems, and they are now engaging the attention of the most resourceful engineers in the employ of the General Electric, the R.C.A. and the other formidable corporations.

We may well have faith in engineers. They can accomplish anything. They produced a machine that rolled across the country last fall and gathered some 21 million votes. They can be counted on to remove the squawks, the shrieks, and the lisps from the talking movies.

III

AND THEN WHAT? When the lisp has been cured, and when Mr. Zukor and his brethren are producing talkies that are as meritorious, in their way, as *The Last Laugh, The Big Parade, The Thief of Bagdad,* and *The Gold Rush* were in theirs, what will become of the tottering theater? Well-nigh ruined already by competition offered by the film

parlors, the dance halls, lonely suburban roads (suitable for evening parking), the radio, and countless other alibi-providing menaces, how will the theater survive against this new invention, which assails the eyes, ears, nose, and throat at one and the same time?

Already, the movie industry has gained, from the talkies, an advantage which enables it to fight the theater on its own grounds. It now possesses, for the first time in its history, the power to discriminate between one type of audience and another.

In the old days, every picture that was sent forth from Hollywood was rated a failure unless it was designed to appeal to everyone, everywhere. The moviemakers had to please countless millions of people, in all parts of the world, if they wanted to keep out of the red ink. They had to tickle the sex-hungry flappers in Chicago, and at the same time appease the censors in Kansas; they had to respect the sensibilities of Mexican patriots, British patriots, German patriots, and Abyssinian patriots; they had to avoid unhappy endings and intimations of expectant motherhood.

The theatrical business, on the other hand, could be organized on a series of different levels, as the magazine business, the automobile business, and every other business is organized. The casual visitor to New York could be reasonably sure of finding one type of play at the Guild Theatre, another at the New Amsterdam, another at the Empire, and another at the Minskys' palace of elegant burlesque in Second Avenue. The Theatre Guild could prosper by producing plays for its large group of supporters, and the Minskys could expect a reasonable profit from theirs.

The same situation is now possible of realization in the movies. The Messrs. Warner, who were the first hardy pioneers to use the Vitaphone, have proved that they could make talking pictures at an extraordinarily cheap rate (about one-tenth the cost of the usual silent film), and that they could make substantial sums of money even though their products might not be shown in the smaller towns where the theaters have not as yet been equipped with the talkie apparatus, or in foreign countries where the language is unknown. They produced the Al Jolson picture, *The Singing Fool*, at less than the cost of an ordinary musical revue, and from the presentation of that picture in only one theater in one city, they have already retrieved their original investment. The Warners don't have to worry whether or not the squareheads in Kokomo or the peons in Chihuahua consider *The Singing Fool* good entertainment. They, and all the other film producers, are at last in a position to thumb their noses at the rabble.

This means that pictures can and will be made solely for those smaller but more appreciative groups whom the movie moguls have previously ignored. And for every member of such groups who finds that the screen is beginning to be worthy of his attention, there will be one less customer for the despondent theatrical managers to mulct.

The future of the theater depends on one consideration — its ability to give its audience something which they can't obtain, more cheaply and more conveniently, in the neighboring cinema palaces. If the Warner brothers can put on a better show than the Shubert brothers can, then the loyal supporters of art will forget that the Shuberts are representatives of that illustrious institution which has harbored the genius of a Shakespeare, a Garrick, a Sheridan, a Booth, and a Mae West, and will go to the upstart Warners for their entertainment.

In which event, the Shuberts will do well to abandon their passing shows and welcome into their theaters the Warners' product; which is exactly what, with characteristic sagacity, they are now doing.

4.

WILLIAM HENRY NUGENT: The Sports Section

The newspapers reflected and at the same time nourished the mania for sports in the Twenties. In even the most dignified papers, principles of accurate reporting were ignored, promotion and sports news became confused, and the amount of newspaper space devoted to sports increased. William Nugent traced the evolution of the sports column and its specialized jargon in an article published in March 1929, from which the following selection is taken.

Source: *American Mercury*, March 1929.

THE UNITED STATES LEARNED its first lessons in sports journalism and sports slang from the British Isles, where flowered the first public prints dedicated to horse racing, the hunt, the chase, cockfighting, prizefighting, and other such pursuits and spectacles. The writers for these periodicals invented a special style and vocabulary that are still used by our modern sports-page literati. . . .

It will not seem strange that we inherited sports journalism from the British Isles if it is further recalled that we also imported the organization of sport, the solemnities, the ceremonies, the rules, the first prizefight manager, the promoter, and the feudal distinction between amateur and professional. Again, despite those who applaud the English sporting spirit and blame everything wicked on Americans, the British initiated us into the mysteries of commercialism, faking, and publicity. But they gave us the good with the bad. The English, Irish, and Scotch immigrants in the last century helped to break down the wall of puritanical prejudice against organized play. They acted as teachers. Think of all the English and the Irish pugilists, the Scotch golf professionals! In time, the pupils learned to play as well as their instructors, and even better, and competed against them in international contests.

Anyone, then, who would trace the evolution of the present-day American sports section and its slang should examine certain early periodicals in England and their imitators in the United States. . . .

The first important sporting weekly in the United States appeared in New York on Dec. 10, 1831. It was the *Spirit of the Times: the American Gentlemen's Newspaper.* This pioneer lived until 1901, when it merged with the *Horseman* of Chicago. Horace Greeley, as a young printer, set type on it in 1832. Its editor and owner, William Trotter Porter, who came of horse-loving Vermont stock, attended Dartmouth, learned the printer's trade at a Bible House at Andover, Mass., and at twenty-one descended upon New York City with the notion that a national sporting paper devoted principally to horseracing would be a profitable venture. . . .

He advocated and ballyhooed the same sports played up in the papers across the Atlantic. It pleased him when his overseas contemporaries called the *Spirit* the *Bell's Life* of the Western world. He sprinkled his columns with hunting stories about the buffalo, the wildcat, the turkey, the panther, and the 'possum. He had articles on old sledge, the brag steamboats on the Missis-

sippi, an Answers to Queries column, a few woodcuts, dramatic reviews, jokes, and an occasional serial novel. He popularized poker and "peaknuckle" by printing their rules and answering questions on their problems. . . .

The *Spirit,* as masculine as *Godey's Ladies' Book* was feminine, was read by horsemen, breeders, farmers, college students, Army officers, congressmen, gamblers, pugilists, ball players, bartenders, all the knowing ones. Daniel Webster, a friend of Porter's, took it at Washington while the Senate was in session and at Boston when he returned home. The success of the *Spirit* gave birth to seven other papers bearing the same title. At the outbreak of the Civil War it had, according to sworn testimony in a libel suit, a circulation of 100,000. Only one weekly in America, aside from the religious press, had more, *Bonner's New York Ledger.* Thousands of subscribers seceded with the South in 1861 and never came back.

By encouraging cricket in the '40s and '50s, just as he had sponsored other hyphenated pastimes here, Porter nearly made it the national game and indirectly helped to establish baseball. Up to a few years before the Civil War, indeed, cricket had more advocates in the nation than baseball. Elevens sprang up, not only in New York and in Philadelphia but even in Detroit and Naugatuck, Conn. The All-United States beat All-Canada in an international match and the victors considered challenging the parent Marylebone Club of London, which is to cricket what St. Andrew's is to golf.

The St. George Cricket Club, instituted by British residents in New York, built a clubhouse on Bloomingdale Road, and its members bowled and batted and drank tea just as they had done in the Old Country. They ignored the jibes directed at them by ribald passersby. How unlike the attitude of the sensitive Philadelphians in 1828, who abandoned their wickets in a field at Camden, N.J., when onlookers and newspapers laughed at them for wasting time at a boy's pastime!

In 1844 the activities of the English gentlemen encouraged a group of young men who had offices in Wall Street to consider exercising after office hours, but instead of playing cricket they voted for the town-ball of their boyhood. They rented a field near Madison Square, but later moved to the Elysian Fields, Hoboken. They gathered twice a week and imitated the St. Georgians by building a clubhouse, keeping a scorebook, and fixing a system of fines for nonattendance. This Knickerbocker Ball Club wrote out regulations in 1845 for a new game that it called baseball. It caught on. Just as the small-town Babbitts of today in plus fours play golf because it is the recreation of the Rockefellers, so did the young men of Brooklyn and in New York in the '50s organize baseball clubs in imitation of high-toned Wall Street. The game took because Porter gave it publicity.

He printed the first rules, the first scores, the first picture of a match in progress, the first box score, the first allusion to it as the national game, and the first dope stories, and gave wide space to the first convention in 1858, when the players voted to make nine innings a game instead of calling it when the first side had tallied twenty-one aces. Cricketers, native and foreign-born, switched to baseball and carried over many terms to the newer game, among them, *lucky breaks, fielding average, batting average, batter* (instead of the old fashioned *striker*), *fly(ing) ball, innings* (instead of *hands in*).

Henry Chadwick, an Englishman who wrote on cricket for the *Spirit of the Times*, first edited Spalding's *Baseball Guide* and won a press agent's title of the Father of Baseball. Harry Wright, another Englishman who played cricket with the St. George Club and baseball with the Knickerbocker Club, organized the first salaried nine, the Cincinnati Red Stockings, in 1868, and later managed teams in the National League of Professional Baseball Clubs which he helped to launch.

The *Spirit* also boomed prizefighting in America, introducing the London prizering code and the Marquis of Queensberry rules. For a considerable period the American ring, long a bootleg institution, was really only a branch of the English ring. It was under the control of Englishmen and Irishmen; they did the fighting, the managing, the training, the faking, the promoting, and the collecting. . . .

The *Spirit of the Times,* in the '70s, imitated its two transatlantic contemporaries and introduced amateur boxing, football, rowing, and track and field competitions into America. Curtis, whom Wilkes had engaged as his editor in the '70s, was the Chambers of the United States, forming the New York Athletic Club, defining an amateur athlete (a rewrite of the English definition), and aiding in establishing the present Amateur Athletic Union. For good and for evil, the old *Spirit* for half a century was the chief propagandist of British professional and amateur sports, their slang and their journalism, in the republic.

The second important sports weekly was born in New York in 1845 and still lives. It is the *National Police Gazette*. It circulated early among police officers, criminals, the Fancy, barbers, and saloonkeepers. It picked up stories of British criminals until the American underworld had developed its own heroes. Each week is summarized the nation's rapes, burglaries, murders, and hangings. But it remained for a rival, the *Illustrated Police News* of Boston, to set a different alliterative headline each week over the countrywide harvest of executions, *e.g.,* "Spine Stretching," "Legally Lassoed" and "Justly Jerked."

The *Police Gazette* later added news about boxing, cockfighting, and other pastimes. Wilkes, before going to the *Spirit of the Times,* had edited it, but it never had the *Spirit's* literary tone or class of readers. . . .

The New York *Clipper* cruised the journalistic seas from 1853 to 1924, carrying boxing, baseball, and theatrical news, and, from 1897 onward, stage news only. It docked for the last time four years ago in the office of Sime Silverman's *Variety*. The *Clipper* not only helped to spread underworld and sporting argot from abroad but also contributed idioms from the English-speaking stage and circus lot. Other weeklies containing sports news blossomed between 1830 and 1890. To note a few, there were the *Whip,* the *Rake,* the *Flash,* the *Sunday Times,* the *Sunday Mercury,* and the New York *Sportsman. Leslie's Weekly* and *Harper's Weekly* pictured important athletic events. Thomas Nast drew sketches of the Heenan and Sayers fight for the New York *Illustrated News.* But the *Spirit of the Times,* the *Police Gazette,* and the *Clipper* were the big three in sports journalism in the last century.

Even before the Civil War some newspaper editors, though they looked on athletics as the province of the weeklies, printed news of any event that aroused public interest. The New York *Herald,* from its establishment in 1835 until 1885, assigned Uncle Joe Elliott, superintendent of its delivery room, to double as a reporter of prizefights and horse races. Seated at the ringside, he dictated a story to a stenographer, who later transcribed the notes for a copyreader to cut down and polish. *Herald* pony-express riders, in May 1847, carrying Elliott's story of how Yankee Sullivan vanquished Caunt the Englishman early in the morning on a dew-covered battleground at Harper's Ferry, galloped from the ringside to New York in time for the *Herald* to print the yarn only two days after the mill.

Less than two years later, Elliott, in relating how Tom Hyer had won the championship of America by flaxing out Yankee Sullivan in eighteen minutes at Rock Creek, Md., dispatched from Baltimore to New York the first prize-fight message ever sent

over Morse's five-year-old magnetic telegraph. This epochal dispatch, plus other pugilistic intelligence, filled the entire front page next day. In April 1860, the *Herald's* presses rumbled day and night for four days to provide an eager public with accounts of the "great international match" between the Benecia Boy, an American blacksmith's helper, and Tom Sayers, an English bricklayer's laborer, a landmark in ring history. Bennett did not send a representative from the home office but economically clipped his report from English and American exchanges. The *Herald* also reported horse races, especially the matches between Northern and Southern thoroughbreds, yacht races, and the early baseball games.

James Gordon Bennett, the younger, himself a long-distance pedestrian and polo player, offered cups in the '70s to winners in college rowing races and track and field events. Out of this developed the present Poughkeepsie Regatta and the annual intercollegiate meets. In the '80s he introduced polo to Newport and found space in his paper for news about it, as well as about golf and tennis, old pastimes still indifferent to newspaper publicity. His *Evening Telegram,* established in 1867, had a clientele among boxing and baseball zealots. When Elliott was superannuated in the late '80s, the *Herald* engaged Billy Edwards, champion emeritus of the lightweights and bouncer at the Hoffman House, to dictate a blow-by-blow account of boxing bouts to a shorthand reporter. Thus he was the founder of a long hokum dynasty of prizefighters who "expert" for the newspapers at higher salaries than are paid to city editors.

Toppy Maguire, a contemporary of Elliott, served the New York *Sun* as a boxing and racing authority for thirty years. Sometimes Charles A. Dana accompanied him to a fight. Arthur Brisbane, while London correspondent of the New York *Sun,* cabled stories about Sullivan's visit to the Prince of Wales, and at other times wrote about the bare-knuckle fights between Smith and Kilrain, Mitchell and Sullivan. The puritanical New York *Tribune* preached against prizefights and horse races, but its reporters were assigned to them and turned in excellent yarns.

These early American sports writers, through oral and printed tradition, inherited a ready-made vocabulary. For a while the editors of conservative newspapers with traditions of good writing toned down their excessive slang, but today all editors allow their sports writers greater liberties than those granted to reporters in the other departments of the paper. Many terms and wisecracks borrowed from the past still survive, some without change and some with slight changes due to the wear and tear of colloquial speech. American sports writers yet use a lot of this standing-metal slang, but they likewise create their share of new phrases, idioms, and nicknames. Baseball experts, adapting boxing diction to baseball, introduced *initial sack, hot corner,* and so on.

William Randolph Hearst bought the New York *Journal* in 1895. Before turning his talents three years later to his war with Spain, he had worked out the modern newspaper sports section. Finding his rivals running from three to seven columns of sport news daily, he doubled, trebled, and quadrupled the space, and on occasional Sundays issued a bicycle or a horse supplement of twelve pages. . . .

Hearst not only invented the present-day sports page make-up; he whooped things up all along the line, putting the final crusher on the weekly as an authority in athletics. Before he breezed in with his open purse, other papers had appended the names of the writers at the ends of sports stories. The New York *World,* for instance, had baseball chatter signed by De Wolfe Hopper, the actor, who had already discovered the poem "Casey At the Bat," and Dominick McCaffery, the heavyweight contender of 1889, explained over his own name that John L. Sullivan beat down Jake Kilrain, not by face hits but by blows to the heart.

The New York *Illustrated News,* in 1889, appointed John L. Sullivan sports editor, with the understanding that he would sit two hours a day at his desk. John L. collected his salary for eight months, but did no work. He blustered in once, bought the staff a drink, and then refused to come again. The publishers, after frequent telegrams to Boston, ultimately cut him off the payroll.

Hearst placed the new by-line rig on a better basis. He signed his champions to a contract and, instead of giving them an impecunious $50 a week, paid out real money. He paid James J. Corbett and Bob Fitzsimmons, successors to Sullivan, $5,000 a year each for the right to put their signatures in facsimile over articles. Furthermore, he did not ask them to associate with the staff, but gave them a ghost writer, Robert H. Davis, to do the work of composition. He hired other champions, Hobart on tennis, Bald on bicycling, Batchelder on wheeling, and Heffelfinger, the Yale hero, on football. Amos Rusie, the Giant's pitcher, told how he threw puzzling curves; Arthur Irwin, manager of the Giants, charted the science of the hit-and-run; and under the shaky facsimile signatures of two dinge jockeys, A. Hamilton and Willie Sims, appeared the story, "How A Horse Race Is Ridden." Hearst, in 1896 and 1897, had signed up nearly every sports champion. Of late the price of by-lines has gone up. Dempsey was paid $45,000 a year for his name, and Tunney is said to have received a still higher sum.

Hearst built up a staff of experts, including Ralph Paine of Yale on rowing, Charles Dryden on baseball, and Paul Armstrong on boxing. The *World,* in 1889, had boasted that Nellie Bly, in interviewing John L. Sullivan and his trainer, William Muldoon, to the extent of three columns both before and after the Kilrain fight, had been the first woman to achieve such a feat. The

Journal assigned Winifred Black to visit New Haven, and in the fall of 1895 appeared a five-and-a-half column story and three sketches headed: "At Old Yale. The Journal's Woman Reporter Trains With the Little Boys in Blue. Once Around the Clock With the Lads Who Will Uphold Yale's Prestige. The First Time a Woman Was Invited to Dinner by a College Football Team."

The *Sun*, the *Herald*, and the *World* spread out on college football reports, running seven and more columns with sketches. Hearst ran wild in covering the Yale-Princeton game in 1895. He printed two-and-a-half pages, with five sketches, one seven columns wide, and two diagrams showing "How the Ball Moved." Richard Harding Davis filled a whole page, aside from pictures, plus a breakover. Heffelfinger presented a technical description, and Jim Corbett in a signed story approved of football by saying: "It has a tendency to make a man a strong, healthy animal and it is all right. I consider football as played today rough sport, but not brutal." Both the team captains signed statements. On Monday Captain Thorne of Yale told his own story of how he made that great run. Not only did Hearst splurge on football but he gave space to other pastimes and a big prizefight called for five pages. All this before 1898.

Other publishers in 1896, and for a long time thereafter, shrilled that he was prostituting journalism by his yellow methods. Today the innovations of 1896 have become commonplace. All publishers have adopted those identical methods, with the eight- and the ten-page sports section, the banner headlines, the cartoons, the pictures. Even the New York *Times* and the Associated Press, within the last few years, have allowed their sports writers to sign their names to stories. Others have gone into the market and bid away champions from

Hearst. As a result of adopting his devices and newer ones, such as the double-measure sports column popularized by Grantland Rice of the Nashville *Banner*, the New York *Mail* and the New York *Herald Tribune*, a feature that has a thousand imitators, other papers have overhauled and passed him.

Since the World War the sporting section has grown tremendously. The *Editor and Publisher* has computed that the New York *World* devotes 40 percent of its local news on weekdays to sports and that the *Herald Tribune* gives over no less than 60 percent. All large city newspapers now surrender four or five pages to sports news on weekdays and eight and even ten pages on Sunday. . . .

To supply this demand, the Associated Press has lately organized a segregated sports department with twelve men on its staff. The International News, out of a total of 45,000 words in a full thirteen-hour report, carried 5,000 words on sports. The United Press is sending out three times the amount it transmitted a year ago. Publishers agree that circulation, prestige, and reader interest are created by sports news. . . .

Today, America leads the universe in sports journalism. Our syndicated specialists sell baseball stories and box scores to Japan and Mexico, prizefight and polo yarns to the press of the world. Readers in the British Isles know the cartoons of Bud Fisher, Tad, and Edgren. Slang from our sports sections has found its way to England, often in movie captions, until nervous Bloomsbury critics write letters to the London *Times* that we are corrupting, that is, americanizing, the mother tongue. Few seem to know that many of these words are making a return trip to their place of origin. For it was the British who taught them to us when they gave us our first lessons in sporting journalism.

5.

E. Boyd Barrett: The Catholic Church Faces America

Catholic Americans were criticized in the 1920s by their non-Catholic compatriots for putting loyalty to church and Rome before loyalty to country and by European Catholics for not being properly subservient to Rome. The distrust of Protestant Americans was brought emphatically to the fore during "Al" Smith's campaign for the presidency, while the strained relationship between European and American Catholics was manifested in the fact that there were only four American cardinals, despite the large number of Catholics in the United States. The dilemma of the Catholic Church in America is analyzed in the following selection, taken from an article by E. Boyd Barrett that was published in 1929.

Source: *American Mercury*, January 1929.

FREE USE IS BEING MADE of late of the expression "American Catholic Church," and the suggestion of its otherness, its distinctiveness from the Roman Catholic Church is working in the public mind. . . . Alarmists have gone so far as to affirm that there is a widening breach between the Catholic Church in the United States and the Catholic Church as it exists in Europe. A leading Protestant journal, the *Congregationalist*, has voiced the opinion that "here in America, Roman Catholic authority, theory, and practice are being profoundly modified — so much so that it becomes apparent that there is developing in this country a Catholicism that, except in its historic associations and its formal connections, is more American than Roman." . . .

Has it, then, come to pass that the dark foreboding of Leo XIII is realized? Has the fear which he expressed as far back as 1899, in a letter to the American bishops, come true — the fear that among American Catholics there exists a desire for a church different from the Church as it exists throughout the world? Is Americanism, the bugaboo of every Italian professor of theology from Milan to Reggio, a *fait accompli*?

It is too often overlooked that European Catholics have always regarded the Catholic Church of this country with a considerable amount of suspicion, not unmixed with disdain. . . . Their misgivings are founded on the recollection of Pius X's rebuke of that Americanism which regards "the *active* virtues as more important than the passive, and as more deserving of encouragement in practice" (*Pascendi Gregis*). They believe that Paul Sabatier was correct in ascribing to American Catholics "a Liberal Catholicism which takes its color from its surroundings," and they think of all American Catholics as more or less tainted with this liberalism.

Since the day when Montalembert congratulated American Catholics on "adopting the inevitable conditions of modern society" Rome has grown more and more uneasy about the state of the Church in this country. Although economically dependent upon it, and compliant in conferring minor dignities on American ecclesiastics and laymen, she has been cautious and conservative in her attitude, as though anticipating trouble. . . .

It is only a trifling matter, but it is not without its effect in creating in Europe a mildly lurid idea of American ecclesiasticism, that in such places as Louvain and Rome, where American seminarists are to be found, they soon become conspicuous for their disregard of the decorous deportment required of European students of theology. Boys from Boston, Chicago, and Philadelphia, finding themselves buckled to the ankles in long woolen cassocks, indoors and out, delight in shocking their pious brethren by performing acrobatic feats, little in harmony with the Latin idea of modesty. The strange *Americani* go even further. They demand the right to swim in the lakes, to play football, and even, to the undisguised horror of their fellow students, to appraise the muscular development of *nude* gladiators and disc throwers!

When the present writer was at Louvain he was witness to a veritable panic of disedification among Continental seminarists occasioned by the fact that three young American religious (one of them the present editor of *America*) had traveled from the States to Louvain via Madrid instead of coming, as befitted holy men, as the crow flies. In such trivialities one finds a tolerable index of the reaction of conservative ecclesiastical Europe to the antitraditionalism of American Catholics.

II

ONE CANNOT SEE IN ITS TRUE PERSPECTIVE that quality inherent in the Catholic Church of this country that has been called Americanism unless one take at least a summary view of the development of the Church in our midst.

Until the third decade of the 19th century, Catholics comprised little above 2 percent of the population, and were a negligible factor in the communal life, but from 1830 onward their numbers increased rapidly, thanks to immigration. For a long period the Church was disorganized and incapable of coping with the situation created by the arrival of innumerable poor, uneducated, European Catholics, who spoke strange languages and brought with them their native customs, and not a few superstitious practices. In the middle of the century, Catholicism was little in favor and suffered from the hostility of the American Party and the Know Nothing movement.

But with incredible speed a vast, highly organized church emerged, consisting of 100 bishops, 25,000 priests, and 20 million adherents, controlling several thousand churches, schools, halls, hospitals, and orphan asylums, and a few hundred journals. From a sense of inferiority, Catholics have passed to a reaction resembling a sense of superiority. They have set afoot multimembered clubs and associations that boast of gigantic material resources and very considerable political power. Having emerged, they sense their freedom. They are naturally grateful to the Constitution which made it possible for them to find themselves and which protects their interests. Though as a body deeply devoted to their church, they have no considerable acquaintance with her history, nor with those Catholic politico-theological principles which occupy largely the minds of educated European Catholics. They see in the American Constitution a good and a just law, and they glory in it. They have never experienced any conflict between the practice of their religion and the Constitution, and they are reluctant to believe that any such conflict is in the region of possibility.

Having this background in view, one can readily understand why the first salient feature of American Catholicism (the Catholicism of Gibbons, Ireland, Keane, O'Connell, O'Gorman, Kain, and Alfred E. Smith) should be what amounts to a veritable religious faith in the American ideal of democracy. This faith found its most striking illustration in the chorus of Catholic applause which greeted the publication in the *Atlantic Monthly* of Governor Smith's politico-religious Credo. Catholics, lay and clerical, accepted his exposition of Catholicism as the expression of their own cherished convictions.

No Catholic ventured to protest or to question its orthodoxy; no bishop uttered a syllable of criticism. Catholic theologians vied with each other in defending it, and it was registered in Catholic minds as ecclesiastically approved. Nevertheless, in that Credo there were many very daring statements; there were declarations concerning equality of religions, freedom of conscience, noninterference of the Church, freedom of education, and so forth, which, while thoroughly in consonance with American ideals of democracy, were much less clearly in consonance with the Vatican Decrees and certain teachings of Pius IX's Syllabus. . . .

In contrast to this first salient feature of American Catholicism, namely, its faith in democracy, we have a second no less characteristic feature which seems strangely out of harmony with the spirit of democracy. I refer to the tendency of the American Catholic Church to display its power, together with its belief in the wisdom and righteousness of so doing. One need only recall to mind the nationwide Catholic effort (which was, indeed, in its way a triumphant success) to stage a stupendous, public, religious ceremony in Chicago, the Eucharistic Congress, in order to realize that American Catholics believe in showing their strength. . . .

No doubt the effect of so much emphasis on power — especially Catholic American power — is to enhance the American Catholic's sense of pride and independence in all directions, not only *vis-à-vis* of other churches, but even of Rome!

III

It may not be out of place at this point to inquire into the reason of this self-assertiveness, amounting sometimes to a form of combativeness — this pronounced affirmation of power which we have been considering. I have said above that "from a sense of inferiority, American Catholics have passed to a reaction resembling a sense of superiority." But the superiority does not ring true. There is, as any psychoanalyst can detect, an ambivalent inferiority that is still stronger. The truth of the matter is that Catholics are acutely conscious of being, in some degree, unpopular. They feel that many are ill-disposed toward them — that in many there is an unjustifiable hostility against them. This feeling found ample confirmation in the recent presidential campaign.

How do Catholics explain this fact? Most of them, taking their cue from Cardinal Gibbons, assert that the Church is "the victim of the foulest slanders," that "upon her fair and heavenly brow her enemies have put a hideous mask," that there exists a hatred of Catholicism based upon the misrepresentations of centuries of inherited dislike. Other Catholics there are, more supernatural in outlook, who hold that dislike of Catholicism originates in the fact that "the truth of the Church" stands as a reproach to unbelievers — that the Church is hated and rejected through "obstinacy." This opinion, however, rests upon the assumption that "the truth of the Church is self-evident," a theory which is not widely admitted in this country.

The reasons given by non-Catholics for their dislike of Catholicism are very different. Non-Catholics are naturally unwilling to admit the existence in their minds of either "inherited hatred" or "obstinacy." They confess, however, to finding it irritating to see papal flags and papal titles flaunted in America. They resent such incidents as the halting of the Lindbergh procession before St. Patrick's Cathedral in New York, and the highly official reception given to Cardinal Bonzano in the Municipal Building on June 17, 1926. They found it objectionable that, as the Free-thinkers' Protest expressed it, "the alderman's chamber should have been converted into a Catholic Cathedral." All such matters are perhaps trifling in themselves, but they are none the less pregnant of provocation.

A more serious reason for the unpopularity of Catholicism in this country is the fact that there is no give and take with the Catholic Church. It will not meet the other churches halfway, and above all, will not tolerate criticism. "The Church bears criticism very badly," said one friendly Protestant critic. The Church hits back when criticized, said Mr. Heywood Broun, or to put it in his precise words, "There is not a single New York editor who does not live in terror of this group" (The *Nation*, May 9, 1928). . . .

Catholic popularity suffers further wreckage in a certain lack of tactfulness among her apologists. In order to glorify Catholicism, fictions that are annoying to non-Catholic Americans, such as that which makes of Jefferson a plagiarist of the Jesuit Bellarmine, are trotted out. Thus, at Detroit, in October 1927, Cardinal Hayes, no doubt with perfect sincerity, but nonetheless hurtingly, amplified the exploded theory. "The Virginia Bill of Rights," declared His Eminence, "was taken almost verbatim from the writings of the Venerable Robert Bellarmine. . . . The principles, almost the very language of the Declaration of Independence were written by the Venerable Bellarmine." The line of thought behind propaganda of this kind is provoking to non-Catholics; it amounts, in a word, to the principle that all good emanates from Rome. . . .

From such isolated instances one may not of course conclude that all Catholic propaganda is ill-conceived. Neither may one conclude from isolated cases of Catholic resentment at criticism that all literary Catholics are bears. It would be absurd to do so. But in seeking for the causes of the unquestioned animosity of great numbers of Americans toward Catholicism, one feels justified in indicating, as a likely factor, a wrong method of approach on the part of responsible Catholics to the American people. Catholics themselves feel that, as Catholics, they do not hit it off with the bulk of the people. And it may well be that the reason is a corporate lack of tact in propaganda.

IV

ALTHOUGH THE AVERAGE AMERICAN SEES in the Catholic Church of this country a pretty accurate and complete replica of that complexus of beliefs and practices which he classifies as Romanism, European Catholics visiting America sense a distinctiveness, an otherness about American Catholicism. No doubt all the essentials of Catholicism are the same: mass, confession, communion, and so forth. But there is a difference of spirit, a novel attitude toward the world, a strangeness in methods of propaganda and church administration — above all, a marked lack of traditionalism. Things are done and said here in the name of the Church which are neither done nor said in the name of the Church in Europe.

Recently, at Omaha, Bishop Rummel, addressing himself to Catholic women teachers, spoke as follows: "As citizens of the United States, you have a right to vote whether you wear religious garb or not. It is a wise thing to exercise that right, not only this year but every year." By these words he publicly authorized the nuns of his diocese to register and vote. This advice naturally implied the advice to keep *au courant* with political events, "not only this year but every year." In other words, he told them that it was *wiser* for them to adapt themselves to the political exigencies of the times than to persevere in their traditional holy seclusion. Elsewhere in America other bishops gave similar advice to nuns, thus repudiating all the stored-up religious traditions and canonical enactments of a thousand years. Nuns who before had feared to glance through a window lest they should violate "holy rule" by taking an interest in the world, must now study political platforms!

Now for another example of American Catholic distinctiveness. In January last, a prominent New York priest, Father Francis P. Duffy, made an address in public that attracted the notice of the press. He said: "If the pope were a civil ruler and waged war on the United States, I would take up arms against him, and the Sixty-ninth Regiment [of which Father Duffy is the chaplain] would be the first to combat him." . . .

On the question of the temporal power of the pope — the eternal Roman question — if we are to believe Mr. Michael Williams, "the overwhelming [Catholic] American doctrine" is "firmly against the resumption of the pope's acknowledged place as head of a state." However creditable to the political wisdom of American Catholics this view may be, it is in distinct disaccord with Roman feeling and Roman teaching. No less so is the common attitude of American Catholics, lay and clerical, toward the binding force of papal encyclicals. Except insofar as they are nullifiable (hypothetically), encyclicals, for Roman Catholics, have the same binding force on mind and will as infallible decrees. But for the average American Catholic they are, to use Mr. Williams' phrase, merely "considered opinions of an individual pope, . . . not always or of necessity laying down binding laws of the Church." . . .

Perhaps the most fundamental difference, however, which exists between the American Catholic and his European brother lies in the comparative indifference which the former displays toward dogma. Apparently he is satisfied to practice his religion and derive spiritual comfort therefrom. He is little concerned with theological notions or with the metaphysical background thereof. This indifference to dogma leaves him wholly unaware of the fact that in espousing democracy with such ardor, and in interpreting Catholicism in terms of democracy as he does, he has come perilously near aligning himself with the Modernists. . . .

In regions proximate to the practice of Catholicism in this country, we find again an American Catholic way which would surprise, if not shock, a European. We find the most delicate and exotic forms of Catholic piety paraded before the public — given the utmost publicity — and managed in a "big business" spirit, which seems strangely out of place. . . .

What is characteristically American Catholic in all this is a certain readiness to appeal to a very composite religious citizenship for interest in pious enterprises, which the majority of citizens clearly differentiate from high spirituality. Whether these enterprises indicate a tendency toward materializing religion, one cannot tell. Color, however, is lent to such a view by remarks made by Bishop McNicholas of Cincinnati (*The Catholic News*, Aug. 11, 1928). Speaking of the decay of preaching he said: "We are engrossed in too many material affairs. We are not weighed down with the responsibility of teaching through the spoken Word of God." He added that "priests were too busy about many things" — referring no doubt to their building and organizing schemes, and their planning of spectacular devotions.

Among the lower ranks of the American clergy there is avowed dislike of all things tending toward the italianizing of the Church in this country. There are signs of jealousy of Roman interference, an inclination perhaps to attach something short of their due importance to mandates and *motu proprios* from Rome. Nationalism, while not being openly avowed, is latent in the attitude of these priests. At Scranton it took its extremest form when Polish Catholics set up an independent American Catholic Church and severed their connection with Rome. It would be too much to say that the Scranton spirit is shared by a considerable portion of the clergy, for among them in general there is at least a sentimental attachment to Rome and to the pope, but, on the other hand, there is a strong and widespread desire for a thoroughly americanized Church. Whether this ideal will ever be realized in a canonically established American Church similar to the Gallican Church of the 17th century, or whether Rome would prefer to let America go rather than submit to the indignity of a Gallican compromise remains to be seen. . . .

It is not possible to doubt that the Holy See disapproves of the stand taken up by Governor Smith and the Catholics, lay and clerical, of this country on the question of the relationship between the Church and the State. Already last January the pope issued his reply to Governor Smith's Credo by emphatically reaffirming the Vatican Decrees. But in spite of this diplomatic hint, the American bishops have not receded one inch from the position they took in support of Governor Smith, nor have they issued any repudiation of his doctrines. Implicitly they, like he, "relegate to the limbo of defunct controversy" the decrees that Pius XI insists upon. . . .

VI

THE DEFEAT THAT GOVERNOR SMITH suffered last November in no way mitigates the seriousness of the crisis which faces the Catholic Church; if anything, it intensifies it. He carried with him, as far as one can judge, 95 percent of the Catholic vote; and in every Catholic vote cast for him there was an implicit endorsement of his Credo, and to no little extent a challenge to Rome. For the first time in history a great Catholic popular vote has been freely, conscientiously, and independently taken by the bishops, priests, religious, and lay Catholics of a nation on an issue which clearly involved papal claims. And the result was, as I say, 95 to 1 in favor of "the American doctrine of absolute separation of Church and State."

Though, from the standpoint of the electoral college, Governor Smith's defeat was overwhelming, his popular vote was so large and his personal popularity was so unequivocally demonstrated that Rome will foresee the likelihood of another Smith-Hoover contest in some years to come. And she will have fears lest the next Catholic candidate for the presidency will yield even more ground, will wander even farther in to the morass of heresy than Governor Smith.

To check this Catholic landslide from the conservatism of the Vatican Decrees, Pius XI will have to act quickly and firmly. He has no choice but to administer a sharp rebuke to his recalcitrant American children and to assert his authority. No doubt he will wait a little while until the election heat has cooled down. . . .

Will the American Catholics, lay and clerical, submit to a papal rebuke? Will they repudiate the popular, liberal Credo of Governor Smith that they hailed with so much fervor a short while back? They will *perhaps* profess their readiness to submit, but the step they have already taken is irrevocable: they can never again *think* in harmony with the doctrines of Pius IX and Leo XIII.

Thus there will be no choice before His Holiness but to yield to the "Americanism" of St. Patrick's, as he yielded to the "Americanism" of the Gesu, or else stir up a crisis more momentous than any that has tortured the Church since the Council of Nicaea.

6.

William E. Borah: Western Farming and the Tariff

The Farm Bloc in Congress fought the Smoot-Hawley Tariff Bill, partly because it perpetuated the so-called "flexible provision" of the Fordney-McCumber Tariff of 1922, according to which a Tariff Commission was empowered to make ongoing adjustments in the tariff rate. The Commission, by failing to lower the tariff on industrial goods, had proved unresponsive to Western farm interests. The speech by the Farm Bloc leader, Senator Borah of Idaho, reprinted in part below, was addressed to that point. It was delivered on September 26, 1929, during a special session of Congress convened the previous April for the explicit purpose of aiding the farmer and revising the tariff. Despite the Farm Bloc's opposition, the Commission's power remained intact in the Smoot-Hawley Act.

Source: *Record*, 71 Cong., 1 Sess., pp. 3969-3975.

I DESIRE TO SUBMIT some observations on the question which is now before the Senate, involving what are known as the flexible provisions of the tariff bill.

We have had flexible provisions in the law for about seven years. The first question which we naturally ask ourselves is: What has been accomplished in the way of eliminating or reducing the inequalities between industry and agriculture? That is, and has been for some time in this country, the most important matter connected with the question of the tariff. It has for some time been a serious national problem.

The second proposition which presents itself to our minds is: What has been achieved in the way of reducing the cost of living or, as it were, protecting the consumers under the present system or under the Tariff Law as it was enacted in 1922?

Let us first, Mr. President, recall the circumstances and conditions under which the law of 1922 was enacted. It was here for consideration and became a law shortly after the war, at a time when economic conditions were unsettled and when it was most difficult to determine the facts upon which we assumed to base our duties, the cost of production at home and abroad. I think it is fair to say, at least it was my understanding, that the Tariff Law of 1922 was enacted with the design of holding the prices of industrial articles or manufactured goods as nearly to the war level as was possible or practicable under the law; the duties upon commodities were placed so high that it would seem practically to preclude the importation of goods from foreign countries.

It was believed, owing to conditions in Europe and the necessity of Europe to manufacture and to sell, that unless the wall was practically prohibitive the goods would inevitably come over. I think it was clearly understood at the time among those who were responsible for the bill that the duties were based upon that condition of affairs, and for its purpose that objective.

Since that time the most remarkable economic changes which have ever occurred in the same period of time in the world's history have taken place. It was assumed, even by the leader of the tariff discussion upon this side, the much-abused but sincere senator from Utah [Mr. Smoot], that the first and primary and greatest task of the Tariff Commission under the flexible-tariff provision would be to trim down and reduce tariff duties. He so stated, and I have no doubt it was stated with entire sincerity, because, as I say, it was understood at the time that the conditions under which we were levying the duties were such that all doubts were resolved in favor of high duties and upon the assumption that economic changes would ensue, it was presumed that reductions would inevitably follow under the provisions of the flexible tariff.

As an illustration of the view I desire to present to the Senate, let us review the workings of the Tariff Commission with reference to this particular question of reduction. What have they accomplished in these seven years? What reductions have been made? What relief has been given to the consumers of the country under a law enacted at a time when there was practically a condition of war?

To my mind the record is one which condemns the Tariff Commission if we are to regard its operations as having anything whatever to do with the question of reducing tariff rates. In that respect it has been as inflexible as one could well conceive any law to be. I take the position that not a single reduction of any moment whatever has been brought about or been recommended by the Tariff Commission; that not 1 cent of the tremendous burden laid upon the consumers of this country by reason of conditions under which the tariff was enacted has been lifted by the action of the Tariff Commission during these seven years. . . .

Mr. President, seven years have passed,

United Press International

Sen. William Borah; photograph taken in 1928 when he was a candidate for President

seven years which were calculated to give play to this Commission in accomplishing, or at least in directing, a course indicating a purpose to relieve the consumers of the nation from what I conceive to be unjust rates in many particulars, and also to bring about more nearly equality between the industrialists and the agriculturists of the United States in the matter of tariff duties.

The best evidence of the fact that the Tariff Commission has been without effect, that it has accomplished little or nothing along the lines which it was supposed to work, is the fact that the last presidential campaign in part was fought out on the proposition of adjusting the inequalities of the Tariff Law now upon the statute books. Although seven years had passed, so egregious, so pronounced were the conditions with reference to the tariff that the last campaign turned, in a large measure, upon an adjustment of tariff duties.

The Commission had accomplished, as we felt in the campaign, practically nothing. I submit to my Republican friends: Suppose we had said in the campaign, "These inequalities exist: this readjustment is necessary; but we are going to leave it to the Tariff Commission instead of doing it as a Congress": what do you think would have been the effect upon the voters of the United States? Suppose we had said then that we proposed to shirk our responsibility, to abandon our sovereign obligation imposed upon us by the Constitution, and leave it to six or seven men sitting behind closed doors to adjust tariff rates, what the effect would have been in the campaign no man would have dared to say. Who would have ventured to say to the voters, "We, the Congress, will not seek to adjust the rates; we are going to shirk that duty; we are going to leave you to the tender mercies of a Tariff Commission." Had any Republican orator made such a statement, I suspect the candidate for the presidency would have repudiated it. . . .

If our friends upon this side who believe in the flexible-tariff provision, and believe that it is capable of ironing out inequalities or adjusting rates where it is necessary to adjust them, have the confidence in it which they express, will they not permit the industrial duties in the law to remain as they are and wait until the Tariff Commission can iron them out? In other words, in view of the fact that we are importing less than 4 percent of the manufactured stuff that is consumed in this country, will they not be willing to show their faith in the flexible-tariff provision by permitting duties of that kind to remain upon the statute books until the Tariff Commission, through this flexible-tariff law, may iron them out? Will not the President say to this chamber, "Lay off on your industrial duties. Primarily, this is a session for agricultural relief. Lay off of your industrial duties until our Tariff Commission can adjust them satisfactorily."

Mr. President, the time to do justice to the agricultural interests is right now, in this session. That was the fight in the campaign.

That was the object of calling the session. If we permit this bill to pass as it is written, how long will it take the Tariff Commission to iron out the inequalities? I asked an expert last night, and he said 135 years at the rate at which they had been going recently.

We went into the campaign pledging ourselves to rectify the agricultural situation, and one of the methods was said to be through tariff legislation. Now is the time to do it; and I say that it not only devolves upon you and upon me but it devolves upon the President to see that these schedules are right, and to pass our O.K. upon them at this session, and not transfer them to the remote consideration of a tariff commission. So I say, Mr. President, in all fairness and in all justice, the President having conceived that it is his duty to shape the terms of this bill, we ought to have his judgment as to the measure as it now stands.

Senators of the West, this is the only body left in the government where we have anything like an equality. This is the only body left where there is anything like an equality in shaping the economic policies of the country as between the industrial interests and agriculture. We cannot conceal the fact that there is an economic conflict in that situation. The industrial interests are naturally indisposed toward duties upon farm products, or upon raw materials, as was so well illustrated in this bill with reference to manganese. They are naturally desirous — it is human nature to desire — that their raw materials be free, and that their food products be free.

It has not been so very long since we were fighting in this chamber against absolute free trade for agriculture and highly protective duties for industry. There is an inevitable and natural conflict there.

This is the only body left where there is anything like an equality in that tremendously important fight. In this body the vote of California is equal to the vote of Pennsylvania. In this body the vote of Oregon is equal to the vote of Massachusetts. In this body the vote of Washington is equal to the vote of New York or of any other great Eastern state. This is the only place where there can be anything like an equality of position and of prestige and of power in working out and shaping the policies which relate to the whole nation.

Understand me, my friends. I again say that I am not speaking as a tariff-for-revenue advocate. I am not speaking against the protective system; but I do say in all sincerity that the protective system with reference to industrial schedules has grown and expanded until it has reached the point where it is practically an embargo, and by reason of that fact there is an inequality between the agricultural and the industrial interests, and it never can be otherwise so long as that continues.

Where is that matter to be fought out? Are we Western senators to be asked to transfer our power in that contest to a Tariff Commission, where the West will have one vote at most? Without challenging the integrity of the men who may sit upon that Commission, Tom Reed once said that no man rises above his environment, and my experience with the Tariff Commission is that Tom Reed was absolutely right.

The able senator from Pennsylvania [Mr. Reed] the other day spoke movingly of his interest in agriculture, of his sympathy for the farmer, and of the fact that he had more farmers in his state than several of us Western senators had in all of our states combined. I do not challenge the senator's sincerity of expression or sincerity of attitude; but your farmer, Senator, is as different from our farmer economically as night from day. Your farmer lives in the midst of a great industrial region. He can diversify his crops to meet the demand. His market is next door. He can dump his products into the hopper even from his farm. We are 1,000, 2,000, 3,000 miles from the market; and our economic situation is as different from that of your farmer as if we were in two different countries.

I do not challenge what the senator stated was his feeling in regard to the matter; but I say that he, like the Tariff Commission, has no more conception of the agricultural question, as we see it, than we have of many of his economics.

This is a vast country, a tremendous country, of vastly varied interests. We in the West are now a developing country, a growing country. We are like this country was when Clay was speaking and when the men of his time were making the fight. Protection is more applicable to us than to any other part of the country, and more necessary in order that we may develop; and it is because of that fact that we must necessarily guard the power that we have and the rights we have upon this floor.

Therefore, aside from all other questions, I am unwilling to leave the West and the great agricultural interests to the control or direction or decision or judgment of a Tariff Commission; that is to say, a Tariff Commission whose judgment finally crystallizes into rates, which is the design of this bill.

Wall Street Lays An Egg.

Headline, *Variety*, October 1929

1929-1931

7.

The Stock Market Crash

October 1929 made a shambles of the American myths of the "self-regulating economy" and "rugged individualism." The stock market had shown signs of weakness as early as September; and on October 24, "Black Thursday," it suffered unprecedented losses. A rally on Friday and a gain on Monday, stimulated by a group of New York bankers, promised hope for a moment but ended in complete collapse on Tuesday the 29th. The Treasury Department, to stave off panic, announced that "the recession . . . is purely a technical reaction and is not due to any general decline in business conditions." But business conditions went into a downward spiral that wrecked the entire economy. Seldom if ever had the confidence of the whole nation been so completely shattered by a single event in war or peace. By mid-November the value of the New York Stock Exchange listings had dropped over 40 percent — a loss of $26 billion. The following selection contains two accounts of the crash: an afternoon newspaper story of the October 24 decline, and a chapter from Frederick Lewis Allen's Only Yesterday *giving a résumé of the end of prosperity.*

Source: *Minneapolis Star*, October 24, 1929.
    Only Yesterday, New York, 1931, Ch. 13.

BILLIONS AGAIN CLIPPED FROM VALUES AS STOCKS GO INTO NEW TAILSPIN

LEADERS CRASH IN ONE OF WORST BREAKS IN HISTORY

TRADES AT RATE OF 14 MILLION SHARES

TRADERS SURGE ABOUT BROKERAGE HOUSES — SEE HOLDINGS WIPED OUT

Wave after wave of selling again moved down prices on the Stock Exchange today and billions of dollars were clipped from values.

Traders surged about the brokerage offices watching their holdings wiped out, and scenes on the floor of the Exchange were of the kind never before witnessed. It was one of the worst breaks in history, with all leaders crashing down through resistance barriers.

United Press International

Crowd on Wall Street after the stock market collapsed, Oct. 29, 1929; New York Stock Exchange is the building on the right

Reaction is Sudden

The reaction came with the same abruptness as the one yesterday in which billions of dollars in value were lost.

For a time, in the morning, the market was showing signs of rallying power. Banking support was given the leaders, and U.S. Steel staged a substantial recovery that was carried over to the other pivotal shares.

Then new waves of selling out of poorly margined accounts started another reaction.

Tickers at 12:20 were 68 minutes behind. All records for volume were being broken.

Sales to noon amounted to 5,711,200 shares. This was at the rate of 14,000,000 shares for a full day.

Big Drops Recorded

At 12:20, U.S. Steel was down to 195, off 9; Consolidated Gas, 111, off 11½; Montgomery Ward, 60, off 23¼; Johns Manville, 145, off 35; General Electric, 289, off 25; Westinghouse, 165, off 25; Sears Roebuck, 117, off 17¾; American Can, 138, off 16½; American Telephone, 250, off 21½; American & Foreign Power,

93, off 21; Radio, 49¾, off 18¼; Columbia Gas, 83, off 14¾; National Cash Register, 83, off 17; General Motors, 50, off 7⅞; Standard of New Jersey, 67, off 6½; Missouri-Kansas-Texas, 44⅛, off 7⅞; Atlantic Refining, 40, off 9; and Chrysler, 45, off 6.

Curb prices also broke precipitately, especially the utilities, where tremendous unloading took place in Cities Service. Bonds were unsettled and, shortly after the opening, values began to melt away.

At the outset, prices were highly irregular, the majority lower with losses ranging to 8 points. Gains where they occurred ranged from fractions to 11 points.

Nervousness was still apparent in many quarters. An evidence of this was the trading in American Water Works, which declined 17¼ points to 103.

Sell Orders Pile Up

Vast numbers of orders to sell flowed into brokerage offices overnight, necessitating execution in big blocks. Many represented forced liquidation of weakly margined accounts. The dealings continued to mount up to record proportions.

Oil issues were slightly firmer, featured by Sinclair Consolidated Oil, which opened 15,000 shares at 27½, up ½. Utilities were showing a better tone in the early dealings, although several were depressed to new low ground earlier.

Street Near Panic

Wall Street yesterday was thrown into the nearest approximation of a stock market panic experience in years.

A new and wholly unexpected avalanche of selling swept over the market, carrying scores of stocks down from $10 to $96 a share, and wiping out more than $3,000,000,000 in paper values in the brief interval of about an hour, an average of about $50,000,000 a minute.

Small Traders Wiped Out

While brokers acknowledged that thousands of small traders undoubtedly had been completely wiped out, the senior partner of one of the largest commission houses stated that a tremendous amount of stock, having been held over a period of months, was sold at a profit. It was pointed out also that, while such a precipitous decline would have had disastrous results a few years ago, when margins of only about 10 percent were required, what with present margins of from 33 to 50 percent, both brokerage houses and banks were more than amply protected.

Sales Reach 6,368,300

Total sales of 6,368,300 shares were piled up, of which about 2,600,000 shares changed hands between 2 and 3 o'clock. This turnover exceeded the 6,091,800 shares of Monday, and was the largest since March 26, when more than 8,000,000 shares were traded. The ticker did not print the final quotation until an hour and three-quarters after the close.

FREDERICK LEWIS ALLEN:
Fear, Panic, and Forced Selling

EARLY IN SEPTEMBER the stock market broke. It quickly recovered, however; indeed, on September 19 the averages as compiled by the *New York Times* reached an even higher level than that of September 3. Once more it slipped, farther and faster, until by October 4 the prices of a good many stocks had coasted to what seemed first-class bargain levels. Steel, for example, after having touched 261¾ a few weeks earlier, had dropped as low as 204; American Can, at the closing on October 4, was nearly twenty points below its high for the year; General Electric was over fifty points below its high; Radio had gone down from 114¾ to 82½.

A bad break, to be sure, but there had been other bad breaks, and the speculators who escaped unscathed proceeded to take advantage of the lesson they had learned in June and December of 1928 and March and May of 1929: when there was a break it was a good time to buy. In the face of all this tremendous liquidation, brokers' loans as compiled by the Federal Reserve Bank of New York mounted to a new high record on October 2, reaching $6,804,000,000 — a sure sign that margin buyers were not deserting the market but coming into it in numbers at least undiminished. (Part of the increase in the loan figure was probably due to the piling up of unsold securities in dealers' hands, as the spawning of investment trusts and the issue of new common stock by every manner of business concern continued unabated.)

History, it seemed, was about to repeat itself, and those who picked up Anaconda at 109¾ or American Telephone at 281 would count themselves wise investors. And sure enough, prices once more began to climb. They had already turned upward before that Sunday in early October when Ramsay MacDonald sat on a log with Herbert Hoover at the Rapidan Camp and talked over the prospects for naval limitation and peace.

Something was wrong, however. The decline began once more. The wiseacres of Wall Street, looking about for causes, fixed upon the collapse of the Hatry financial group in England (which had led to much forced selling among foreign investors and speculators), and upon the bold refusal of the Massachusetts Department of Public Utilities to allow the Edison Company of Boston to split up its stock. They pointed, too, to the fact that the steel industry was undoubtedly slipping, and to the accumulation of "undigested" securities. But there was little real alarm until the week of October 21. The consensus of opinion, in the meantime, was merely that the equinoctial storm of September had not quite blown over. The market was readjusting itself into a "more secure technical position." . . .

The expected recovery in the stock market did not come. It seemed to be beginning on Tuesday, October 22, but the gains made during the day were largely lost during the last hour. And on Wednesday, the 23rd, there was a perfect Niagara of liquidation. The volume of trading was over 6 million shares, the tape was 104 minutes late when the 3 o'clock gong ended trading for the day, and the *New York Times* averages for fifty leading railroad and industrial stocks lost 18.24 points — a loss which made the most abrupt declines in previous breaks look small. Everybody realized that an unprecedented number of margin calls must be on their way to insecurely margined traders, and that the situation at last was getting serious. But perhaps the turn would come tomorrow. Already the break had carried prices down a good deal farther than the previous breaks of the past two years. Surely it could not go on much longer.

The next day was Thursday, October 24.

On that momentous day stocks opened moderately steady in price, but in enormous volume. Kennecott appeared on the tape in a block of 20,000 shares, General Motors in another of the same amount. Almost at once the ticker tape began to lag behind the trading on the floor. The pressure of selling orders was disconcertingly heavy. Prices were going down. . . . Presently they were going down with some rapidity. . . . Before the first hour of trading was over, it was already apparent that they were going down with an altogether unprecedented and amazing violence. In brokers' offices all over the country, tape-watchers looked at one another in astonishment and perplexity. Where on earth was this torrent of selling orders coming from?

The exact answer to this question will probably never be known. But it seems probable that the principal cause of the break in prices during that first hour on October 24 was not fear. Nor was it short selling. It was forced selling. It was the dumping on the market of hundreds of thousands of shares of stock held in the name of miserable traders whose margins were exhausted or about to be exhausted. The gigantic edifice of prices was honeycombed with speculative credit and was now breaking under its own weight.

Fear, however, did not long delay its coming. As the price structure crumbled, there was a sudden stampede to get out from under. By 11 o'clock traders on the floor of the Stock Exchange were in a wild scramble to "sell at the market." Long before the lagging ticker could tell what was happening, word had gone out by telephone and telegraph that the bottom was dropping out of things, and the selling orders redoubled in volume. The leading stocks were going down two, three, and even five points between sales. Down, down, down. . . . Where were the bargain hunters who were supposed to come to the rescue at times like this? Where were the investment trusts, which were expected to provide a cushion for the market by making new purchases at low prices? Where were the big operators who had declared that they were still bullish? Where were the powerful bankers who were supposed to be able at any moment to support prices? There seemed to be no support whatever. Down, down, down. The roar of voices which rose from the floor of the Exchange had become a roar of panic.

United States Steel had opened at 205½. It crashed through 200 and presently was at 193½. General Electric, which only a few weeks before had been selling above 400, had opened this morning at 315 — now it had slid to 283. Things were even worse with Radio: opening at 68¾, it had gone dismally down through the sixties and the fifties and forties to the abysmal price of 44½. And as for Montgomery Ward, vehicle of the hopes of thousands who saw the chain store as the harbinger of the new economic era, it had dropped headlong from 83 to 50. In the space of two short hours, dozens of stocks lost ground which it had required many months of the bull market to gain.

Even this sudden decline in values might not have been utterly terrifying if people could have known precisely what was happening at any moment. It is the unknown which causes real panic. . . .

At 7 o'clock that night the tickers in a thousand brokers' offices were still chattering; not till after 7:08 did they finally record the last sale made on the floor at 3 o'clock. The volume of trading had set a new record — 12,894,650 shares. ("The time may come when we shall see a 5 million-share day," the wise men of the Street had been saying twenty months before!) Incredible rumors had spread wildly during the early afternoon — that eleven speculators had committed suicide, that the Buffalo and Chicago exchanges had been closed, that troops were guarding the New York Stock Exchange against an angry mob. The country had known the bitter taste of panic. And although the bankers' pool had prevented for the moment an utter collapse, there was no gainsaying the fact that the

economic structure had cracked wide open.

Things looked somewhat better on Friday and Saturday. Trading was still on an enormous scale, but prices for the most part held. At the very moment when the bankers' pool was cautiously disposing of as much as possible of the stock which it had accumulated on Thursday and was thus preparing for future emergencies, traders who had sold out higher up were coming back into the market again with new purchases, in the hope that the bottom had been reached. (Hadn't they often been told that "the time to buy is when things look blackest"?) The newspapers carried a very pretty series of reassuring statements from the occupants of the seats of the mighty; Herbert Hoover himself, in a White House statement, pointed out that "the fundamental business of the country, that is, production and distribution of commodities, is on a sound and prosperous basis." But toward the close of Saturday's session, prices began to slip again. And on Monday the rout was under way once more.

The losses registered on Monday were terrific — 17½ points for Steel, 47½ for General Electric, 36 for Allied Chemical, 34½ for Westinghouse, and so on down a long and dismal list. All Saturday afternoon and Saturday night and Sunday the brokers had been struggling to post their records and go over their customers' accounts and sent out calls for further margin, and another avalanche of forced selling resulted. The prices at which Mr. Whitney's purchases had steadied the leading stocks on Thursday were so readily broken through that it was immediately clear that the bankers' pool had made a strategic retreat. As a matter of fact, the brokers who represented the pool were having their hands full plugging up the "air-holes" in the list — in other words, buying stocks which were offered for sale without any bids at all in sight. Nothing more than this could have been accomplished, even if it could have been wisely attempted. Even six great banks could hardly stem the flow of liquidation from the entire United States. They could only guide it a little, check it momentarily here and there.

Once more the ticker dropped ridiculously far behind, the lights in the brokers' offices and the banks burned till dawn, and the telegraph companies distributed thousands of margin calls and requests for more collateral to back up loans at the banks. Bankers, brokers, clerks, messengers, were almost at the end of their strength; for days and nights they had been driving themselves to keep pace with the most terrific volume of business that had ever descended upon them. It did not seem as if they could stand it much longer.

But the worst was still ahead. It came the next day, Tuesday, October 29.

The big gong had hardly sounded in the great hall of the Exchange at 10 o'clock Tuesday morning before the storm broke in full force. Huge blocks of stock were thrown upon the market for what they would bring. Five thousand shares, 10,000 shares appeared at a time on the laboring ticker at fearful recessions in price. Not only were innumerable small traders being sold out, but big ones, too, protagonists of the new economic era who a few weeks before had counted themselves millionaires. Again and again the specialist in a stock would find himself surrounded by brokers fighting to sell — and nobody at all even thinking of buying.

To give one single example: during the bull market, the common stock of the White Sewing Machine Company had gone as high as 48; on Monday, October 28, it had closed at 11⅛. On that black Tuesday, somebody — a clever messenger boy for the Exchange, it was rumored — had the bright idea of putting in an order to buy at 1 — and in the temporarily complete absence of other bids he actually got his stock for a dollar a share!

The scene on the floor was chaotic. Despite the jamming of the communication system, orders to buy and sell — mostly to sell — came in faster than human beings could possibly handle them; it was on that day that an exhausted broker, at the close of the session, found a large wastebasket which he had stuffed with orders to be executed and had carefully set aside for safekeeping — and then had completely forgotten. Within half an hour of the opening the volume of trading had passed 3 million shares, by 12 o'clock it had passed 8 million, by half-past one it had passed 12 million, and when the closing gong brought the day's madness to an end the gigantic record of 16,410,030 shares had been set. Toward the close there was a rally, but by that time the average prices of fifty leading stocks, as compiled by the *New York Times,* had fallen nearly forty points. Meanwhile there was a near-panic in other markets — the foreign stock exchanges, the lesser American exchanges, the grain market.

So complete was the demoralization of the stock market and so exhausted were the brokers and their staffs and the Stock Exchange employees, that at noon that day, when the panic was at its worst, the Governing Committee met quietly to decide whether or not to close the Exchange. To quote from an address made some months later by Richard Whitney:

> In order not to give occasion for alarming rumors, this meeting was not held in the Governing Committee Room but in the office of the president of the Stock Clearing Corporation directly beneath the Stock Exchange floor. . . . The forty governors came to the meeting in groups of two and three as unobtrusively as possible. The office they met in was never designed for large meetings of this sort, with the result that most of the governors were compelled to stand, or to sit on tables. As the meeting progressed, panic was raging overhead on the floor. . . . The feeling of those present was revealed by their habit of continually lighting cigarettes, taking a puff or two, putting them out and lighting new ones — a practice which soon made the narrow room blue with smoke. . . .

Two of the Morgan partners were invited to the meeting and, attempting to slip into the building unnoticed so as not to start a new flock of rumors, were refused admittance by one of the guards and had to remain outside until rescued by a member of the Governing Committee. After some deliberation, the governors finally decided not to close the Exchange.

It was a critical day for the banks, that Tuesday, the 29th. Many of the corporations which had so cheerfully loaned money to brokers through the banks in order to obtain interest at 8 or 9 percent were now clamoring to have these loans called — and the banks were faced with a choice between taking over the loans themselves and running the risk of precipitating further ruin. It was no laughing matter to assume the responsibility of millions of dollars' worth of loans secured by collateral which by the end of the day might prove to have dropped to a fraction of its former value. That the call money rate never rose above 6 percent that day, that a money panic was not added to the stock panic, and that several Wall Street institutions did not go down into immediate bankruptcy was due largely to the nerve shown by a few bankers in stepping into the breach. The story is told of one banker who went grimly on authorizing the taking over of loan after loan until one of his subordinate officers came in with a white face and told him that the bank was insolvent. "I dare say," said the banker, and went ahead unmoved. He knew that if he did not, more than one concern would face insolvency.

The next day — Wednesday, October 30 — the outlook suddenly and providentially brightened. The directors of the Steel Corporation had declared an extra dividend; the directors of the American Can Company had not only declared an extra dividend but had raised the regular dividend. There was another flood of reassuring statements — though by this time a cheerful statement

from a financier fell upon somewhat skeptical ears. Julius Klein, Mr. Hoover's assistant secretary of commerce, composed a rhapsody on continued prosperity. John J. Raskob declared that stocks were at bargain prices and that he and his friends were buying. John D. Rockefeller poured Standard Oil upon the waters: "Believing that fundamental conditions of the country are sound and that there is nothing in the business situation to warrant the destruction of values that has taken place on the exchanges during the past week, my son and I have for some days been purchasing sound common stocks."

Better still, prices rose — steadily and buoyantly. Now at last the time had come when the strain on the Exchange could be relieved without causing undue alarm. At 1:40 o'clock Vice-President Whitney announced from the rostrum that the Exchange would not open until noon the following day and would remain closed all day Friday and Saturday — and to his immense relief the announcement was greeted, not with renewed panic but with a cheer.

Throughout Thursday's short session the recovery continued. Prices gyrated wildly — for who could arrive at a reasonable idea of what a given stock was worth, now that all settled standards of value had been upset? — but the worst of the storm seemed to have blown over. The financial community breathed more easily; now they could have a chance to set their houses in order.

It was true that the worst of the panic was past. But not the worst prices. There was too much forced liquidation still to come as brokers' accounts were gradually straightened out, as banks called for more collateral, and terror was renewed. The next week, in a series of short sessions, the tide of prices receded once more — until at last on November 13 the bottom prices for the year 1929 were reached. Beside the figures hung up in the sunny days of September they made a tragic showing:

	High price Sept. 3, 1929	Low price Nov. 13, 1929
American Can	181⅞	86
American Telephone & Telegraph	304	197¼
Anaconda Copper	131½	70
General Electric	396¼	168⅛
General Motors	72¾	36
Montgomery Ward	137⅞	49¼
New York Central	256⅜	160
Radio	101	28
Union Carbide & Carbon	137⅞	59
United States Steel	261¾	150
Westinghouse E. & M.	289⅞	102⅝
Woolworth	100⅜	52¼
Electric Bond & Share	186¾	50¼

The *New York Times* averages for fifty leading stocks had been almost cut in half, falling from a high of 311.90 in September to a low of 164.43 on November 13; and the *Times* averages for twenty-five leading industrials had fared still worse, diving from 469.49 to 220.95.

The Big Bull Market was dead. Billions of dollars' worth of profits — and paper profits — had disappeared. The grocer, the window cleaner, and the seamstress had lost their capital. In every town there were families which had suddenly dropped from showy affluence into debt. . . .

Coolidge-Hoover Prosperity was not yet dead, but it was dying. Under the impact of the shock of panic, a multitude of ills which hitherto had passed unnoticed or had been offset by stock-market optimism began to beset the body economic, as poisons seep through the human system when a vital organ has ceased to function normally. Although the liquidation of nearly $3 billion of brokers' loans contracted credit, and the Reserve Banks lowered the rediscount rate, and the way in which the larger banks and corporations of the country had survived the emergency without a single failure of large proportions offered real encouragement, nevertheless the poisons were there: over-production of capital; overambitious expansion of business concerns; over-pro-

duction of commodities under the stimulus of installment buying and buying with stock-market profits; the maintenance of an artificial price level for many commodities; the depressed condition of European trade. No matter how many soothsayers of high finance proclaimed that all was well, no matter how earnestly the President set to work to repair the damage with soft words, and White House conferences, a major depression was inevitably under way.

Nor was that all. Prosperity is more than an economic condition; it is a state of mind. The Big Bull Market had been more than the climax of a business cycle; it had been the climax of a cycle in American mass thinking and mass emotion. There was hardly a man or woman in the country whose attitude toward life had not been affected by it in some degree and was not now affected by the sudden and brutal shattering of hope. With the Big Bull Market gone and prosperity going, Americans were soon to find themselves living in an altered world which called for new adjustments, new ideas, new habits of thought, and a new order of values. The psychological climate was changing; the ever-shifting currents of American life were turning into new channels.

The Post-war Decade had come to its close. An era had ended.

1930

8.

SHERWOOD ANDERSON: Lift Up Thine Eyes

In 1913 it took fourteen hours to assemble a Ford car. In 1914, using the endless chain conveyor, the same job took ninety-three minutes. By 1925 a completed Ford rolled off the assembly line every ten seconds. Ford and other manufacturers were proud of their technological achievements, proud of the conditions they provided for their workers, and proud of the services their products could perform. But to the writer Sherwood Anderson, the industrial culture and commercialism of America created an unchallenging, valueless void. In the following article the near-poetic staccato prose, conforming to his subject matter, brought out the tensions underlying the mechanized life of the worker.

Source: *Nation*, May 28, 1930.

IT IS A BIG ASSEMBLING PLANT in a city of the Northwest. They assemble there the Bogel car. It is a car that sells in large numbers and at a low price. The parts are made in one great central plant and shipped to the places where they are to be assembled. There is little or no manufacturing done in the assembling plant itself. The parts come in. These great companies have learned to use the railroad cars for storage.

At the central plant everything is done on schedule. As soon as the parts are made they go into railroad cars. They are on their way to the assembling plants scattered all over the United States and they arrive on schedule.

The assembling plant assembles cars for a certain territory. A careful survey has been made. This territory can afford to buy so and so many cars per day.

"But suppose the people do not want the cars?"

"What has that to do with it?"

People, American people, no longer buy cars. They do not buy newspapers, books, foods, pictures, clothes. Things are sold to people now. If a territory can take so and so many Bogel cars, find men who can make them take the cars. That is the way things are done now.

In the assembling plant everyone works "on the belt." This is a big steel conveyor, a kind of moving sidewalk, waist-high. It is a great river running down through the plant. Various tributary streams come into the main stream, the main belt. They bring tires, they bring headlights, horns, bumpers for cars. They flow into the main stream. The main stream has its source at the freight cars, where the parts are unloaded, and it flows out to the other end of the factory and into other freight cars.

The finished automobiles go into the freight cars at the delivery end of the belt. The assembly plant is a place of peculiar tension. You feel it when you go in. It never lets up. Men here work always on tension. There is no let-up to the tension. If you can't stand it get out.

It is the belt. The belt is boss. It moves always forward. Now the chassis goes on the belt. A hoist lifts it up and places it just so. There is a man at each corner. The chassis is deposited on the belt and it begins to move. Not too rapidly. There are things to be done.

How nicely everything is calculated. Scientific men have done this. They have watched men work. They have stood looking, watch in hand. There is care taken about everything. Look up. Lift up thine eyes. Hoists are bringing engines, bodies, wheels, fenders. These come out of side streams flowing into the main stream. They move at a pace very nicely calculated. They will arrive at the main stream at just a certain place at just a certain time.

In this shop there is no question of wages to be wrangled about. The men work but eight hours a day and are well paid. They are, almost without exception, young, strong men. It is, however, possible that eight hours a day in this place may be much longer than twelve or even sixteen hours in the old carelessly run plants.

They can get better pay here than at any other shop in town. Although I am a man wanting a good many minor comforts in life, I could live well enough on the wages made by the workers in this place. Sixty cents an hour to begin and then, after a probation period of sixty days, if I can stand the pace, seventy cents or more.

To stand the pace is the real test. Special skill is not required. It is all perfectly timed, perfectly calculated. If you are a body upholsterer, so many tacks driven per second. Not too many. If a man hurries too much too many tacks drop on the floor. If a man gets too hurried he is not efficient. Let an expert take a month, two months, to find out just how many tacks the average good man can drive per second.

There must be a certain standard maintained in the finished product. Remember that. It must pass inspection after inspection.

Do not crowd too hard.

Crowd all you can.

Keep crowding.

There are fifteen, twenty, thirty, perhaps fifty such assembling plants, all over the country, each serving its own section. Wires pass back and forth daily. The central office — from which all the parts come — at Jointville is the nerve center. Wires come in and go out of Jointville. In so and so many hours Williamsburg, with so and so many men, produced so and so many cars.

Now Burkesville is ahead. It stays ahead. What is up at Burkesville? An expert flies there.

The man at Burkesville was a major in the army. He is the manager there. He is a cold, rather severe, rather formal man. He has found out something. He is a real Bogel man, an ideal Bogel man. There is no foolishness about him. He watches the belt. He does not say foolishly to himself, "I am the boss here." He knows the belt is boss.

He says there is a lot of foolishness talked about the belt. The experts are too expert, he says. He has found out that the belt can be made to move just a little faster than the experts say. He has tried it. He knows. Go and look for yourself. There are the men out there on the belt, swarming along the belt, each in his place. They are all right, aren't they?

Can you see anything wrong?

Just a trifle more speed in every man. Shove the pace up just a little, not much. With the same number of men, in the same number of hours, six more cars a day.

That's the way a major gets to be a colonel, a colonel a general. Watch that fellow at Burkesville, the man with the military stride, the cold steady voice. He'll go far.

Everything is nicely, perfectly calculated in all the Bogel assembling plants. There are white marks on the floor everywhere. Everything is immaculately clean. No one smokes, no one chews tobacco, no one spits. There are white bands on the cement floor along which the men walk. As they work, sweepers follow them. Tacks dropped on the floor are at once swept up. You can tell by the sweepings in a plant where there is too much waste, too much carelessness. Sweep everything carefully and frequently. Weigh the sweepings. Have an expert examine the sweepings. Report to Jointville.

Jointville says: "Too many upholsterers' tacks wasted in the plant at Port Smith. Belleville produced one hundred and eleven cars a day, with seven hundred and forty-nine men, wasting only nine hundred and six tacks."

It is a good thing to go through the plant now and then, select one man from all the others, give him a new and bigger job, just like that, offhand. If he doesn't make good, fire him.   .

It is a good thing to go through the plant occasionally, pick out some man, working apparently just as the others are, fire him.

If he asks why, just say to him, "You know."

He'll know why all right. He'll imagine why.

The thing is to build up Jointville. This country needs a religion. You have got to build up the sense of a mysterious central thing, a thing working outside your knowledge.

Let the notion grow and grow that there is something superhuman at the core of all this.

Lift up thine eyes, lift up thine eyes.

The central office reaches down into your secret thoughts. It knows, it knows.

Jointville knows.

Do not ask questions of Jointville. Keep up the pace.

Get the cars out.

Get the cars out.

Get the cars out.

The pace can be accelerated a little this year. The men have all got tuned into the old pace now.

Step it up a little, just a little.

They have got a special policeman in all the Bogel assembling plants. They have got a special doctor there. A man hurts his finger a little. It bleeds a little, a mere scratch. The doctor reaches down for him. The finger is fixed. Jointville wants no blood poisonings, no infections.

The doctor puts men who want jobs through a physical examination, as in the army. Try his nerve reactions. We want only the best men here, the youngest, the fastest.

Why not?

We pay the best wages, don't we?

The policeman in the plant has a special job. That's queer. It is like this. Now and then the big boss passes through. He selects a man off the belt.

"You're fired."

"Why?"

"You know."

Now and then a man goes off his nut. He goes fan-toed. He howls and shouts. He grabs up a hammer.

A stream of crazy profanity comes from his lips.

There is Jointville. That is the central thing. That controls the belt.

The belt controls me.

It moves.

It moves.

It moves.

I've tried to keep up.

I tell you I have been keeping up.

Jointville is God.

Jointville controls the belt.

The belt is God.

God has rejected me.

You're fired.

Sometimes a man, fired like that, goes nutty. He gets dangerous. A strong policeman on hand knocks him down, takes him out.

You walk within certain definite white lines.

It is calculated that a man, rubbing automobile bodies with pumice, makes thirty thousand and twenty-one arm strokes per day. The difference between thirty thousand and twenty-one and twenty-eight thousand and four will tell a vital story of profits or loss at Jointville.

Do you think things are settled at Jointville, or at the assembling plants of the Bogel car scattered all over America? Do you think men know how fast the belt can be made to move, what the ultimate, the final pace will be, can be?

Certainly not.

There are experts studying the nerves of men, the movements of men. They are watching, watching. Calculations are always going on. The thing is to produce goods and more goods at less cost. Keep the standard up. Increase the pace a little.

Stop waste.

Calculate everything.

A man walking to and from his work between white lines saves steps. There is a tremendous science of lost motion not perfectly calculated yet.

More goods at less cost.

Increase the pace.

Keep up standards.

It is so you advance civilization.

In the Bogel assembling plants, as at Jointville itself, there isn't any laughter. No one stops work to play. No one fools around or throws things, as they used to do in the old factories. That is why Bogel is able to put the old-fashioned factories, one by one, out of business.

It is all a matter of calculation. You feel it when you go in. You feel rigid lines. You feel movement. You feel a strange tension in the air. There is a quiet terrible intensity.

The belt moves. It keeps moving. The day I was there a number of young boys had come in. They had been sent by a Bogel car dealer, away back somewhere in the country. They had driven in during the night and were to drive Bogel cars back over country roads to some dealer. A good many Bogel cars go out to dealers from the assembling plants, driven out by boys like that.

Such boys, driving all night, fooling along the road, getting no sleep.

They have a place for them to wait for the cars in the Bogel assembling plants. You have been at dog shows and have seen how prize dogs are exhibited, each in his nice clean cage. They have nice clean cages like that for country boys who drive in to Bogel assembling plants to get cars.

The boys come in. There is a place to lie down in there. It is clean. After the boy goes into his cage a gate is closed. He is fastened in.

If a country boy, sleepy like that, waiting for his car, wandered about in a plant he might get hurt.

There might be damage suits, all sorts of things.

Better to calculate everything. Be careful. Be exact.

Jointville thought of that. Jointville thinks of everything. It is the center of power, the new mystery.

Every year in America Jointville comes nearer and nearer being the new center. Men nowadays do not look to Washington. They look to Jointville.

Lift up thine eyes, lift up thine eyes.

9.

"The Death of Mother Jones"

The life of Mary "Mother" Jones came to an end in 1930, one hundred years after it had begun. This song, which mourns her death, also celebrates her vigorous and effective dedication to the cause of American labor. Especially renowned were her fearlessness and talent for plotting strike strategy. She shared her talents with many groups but was especially close to the miners. Her predilection for calling the workers her children earned her the affectionate title of "Mother." The song appeared shortly after she died.

Source: *Songs of Work and Freedom*, Edith Fowke and Joe Glazer, eds., New York, 1960.

☙ THE DEATH OF MOTHER JONES

The world today is mourning the death of Mother Jones;
Grief and sorrow hover around the miners' homes.
This grand old champion of labor has gone to a better land,
But the hard-working miners, they miss her guiding hand.

Through the hills and over the valleys in every mining town,
Mother Jones was ready to help them; she never let them down.
In front with the striking miners she always could be found;
She fought for right and justice; she took a noble stand.

With a spirit strong and fearless, she hated that which was wrong;
She never gave up fighting until her breath was gone.
May the workers all get together to carry out her plan,
And bring back better conditions for every laboring man.

10.

ERNST TOLLER: Aimee Semple McPherson and the Movies

*After World War I the German dramatist Ernst Toller traveled in both the
United States and the Soviet Union hopefully seeking the basis for a better world.
The book that emerged from his travels,* Quer Durch Reisebilder und Reden
*("Travel Sketches and Discourses," 1930), compared the two nations and found
neither to be satisfactory. An English translation retitled* Which World: Which Way?
*appeared in 1931. Aimee Semple McPherson and the "talkies" were two features
of post-World War I America that engaged Toller's interest as a dramatist.
Aimee McPherson became nationally prominent in about 1923 (her disappearance,
to which Toller alludes, occurred in 1926), and the "talkies" emerged in 1927.*

Source: TWA, pp. 506-514.

How WOULD YOU PICTURE the founder of a church? Lean, the ascetic face framed by a quivering beard, wearing a hair shirt, the loins engirdled with a cord? You must revise your picture.

In Los Angeles lives Aimee Semple McPherson, who would certainly carry off the prize in any ordinary beauty competition. Her blonde hair has the gleam which so delights the hairdressers; dark lashes shade her large blue eyes; her nose is strong but noble; her lips are finely set, her hands narrow, the fingers long. She wears a white cape, the folds of which are very decorative. On her bosom gleams a large white cross worked with silver thread; on her left shoulder a bunch of orchids. Her hair is carefully waved; well-applied make-up gives her face the sweetness necessary in America: her hands are well cared for and manicured.

She is the founder and prophetess of a large church which numbers thousands of adherents, and which is called the Church of the Smiling Light. How could a church be otherwise named in a country where the dead are made up? "Keep smiling," even in death, is the motto here.

Aimee is the daughter of a farmer. Brought up in the solitude of the Canadian prairie, at the age of sixteen she made the acquaintance of a Baptist, fell in love at first sight, married him, and went with him to China to win the heathen to the eternal bliss of the evangelical heaven. Her husband died, she returned to America, met McPherson, lived with him for a year, unhappily; separated from him and, supported by her mother, began to preach, in halls, theaters, and churches. Ultimately she gained a parish. Rich adherents gave her money to build the Angels' Church in Los Angeles, which can accommodate a congregation of some 5,000.

Behind the pulpit is the platform, fitted up with all the latest technical contrivances. Right and left rise tiers for the choir of male and female angels, hundreds strong.

Aimee heals by prayer. Aimee heals by the laying on of hands. The farmers of the West revere her as a saint. For eight years she behaves like a saint. But Aimee is too young and too beautiful to remain always a saint. One day she vanishes. She is seen one morning on the beach of Santa Monica with her lady secretary, bathing in a fashionable costume — and is never seen again. The secretary is questioned, but can give no information — Aimee has vanished.

Believers go in their thousands to the seashore, kneel down and pray for Aimee's soul. Divers seek her at the bottom of the sea; two men lose their lives in an effort to save her. Airplanes circle about the spot where she vanished; the aviators throw Aimee's favorite flowers into the sea. Aimee is reckoned as dead. The one who mourns her most is her mother. But in the end the old lady is an American — she goes to the life-insurance company and draws the not inconsiderable consolation.

Some weeks later great jubilation breaks out in the Church of the Smiling Light. Joyful messages are hurried to Aimee's mother. Aimee writes to say that she is alive; Mexican bandits had robbed her and held her prisoner in the California desert, but with the help of God she had broken free; like the children of Israel she has wandered many miles through the dusty wilderness and is now lying in a hospital in Arizona. The police try to catch the bandits. Accompanied by the district attorney, by photographers with movie cameras, Aimee travels back through the desert to the house in which she had languished. But the house is nowhere to be found. Aimee goes back to Los Angeles by a special train, and in a wonderful triumphal procession is conveyed to the church, where she joins with the true believers in thanks to God for her deliverance.

Some reporters, disbelieving heathens, cast doubts on her story, make investigations on their own, let out that her car had been seen in Carmel, that she had passed sweet days of love with her handsome young radio mechanic in a country house in that town. Only tangible evidence is lacking. Then a document in her handwriting, ordering fresh vegetables for dinner in profane words, is found in front of the house in which she had lived. This document is photographed and published.

The authorities take action. Aimee comes to judgment. She denies all. The document is a work of the devil. Smiling scornfully, the district attorney hands it over to the jury, whereupon God has mercy upon the saint; the document disappears before it has been seen by the last juryman, and Aimee is acquitted. The halo round Aimee's head grows. It is not even dimmed when her adversaries discover that she possesses a private account, with a nice fat balance. This money, so her enemies say, she appropriated from the subscriptions given by the faithful for social work. Even this charge misses fire. A dozen adherents declare that they have given her the money against a rainy day. Aimee remains unconquerable. Every day she preaches in the church.

I went twice to her services; once I heard her speak on the radio. Theatrical producers make a pilgrimage to Aimee and learn the art of production from her. I have never witnessed more impressive spectacles. One Sunday evening she presented, with her choir, an oratorio entitled "Christ the Bridge." The words were written by herself; the settings were designed by her; gestures and movements were arranged by her — but the music was borrowed from *The Merry Widow*. For her chorales she always turns to the melodies of popular songs; no operetta is safe.

In this oratorio Jesus appears — as Carpenter, as Shepherd, as Teacher, as Fisherman, as Sailor, as Doctor, as Everyman, as Servant, as the King of Kings. Across a bridge, which rises behind the altar, He steps slowly forward, always in the costume demanded by the verse, while the chorus, adorned with ever-fresh symbols and instruments, accompany Him. For example, to

United Press International

Aimee Semple McPherson with some of the 2,000 persons who participated in a religious pageant in her Angelus Temple, 1936

the tune of "Vilja, Vilja, my woodmaiden," Aimee and the chorus sing:

> *Sailor, sailor, sailor,*
> *Sailor from Galilee!*
> *Oh, oh, oh!*
> *Darkness is falling,*
> *Tempests are rising,*
> *Oh, oh, oh!*

All singers, male and female, wear sailor caps on their heads and carry oars in their hands, so that they can control the waves with vigorous movements. Aimee also wears a cap, but hers is made of silk and is richly embroidered. She wears hers at a more coquettish angle than the others; her oar is bigger and costlier and glitters with paste diamonds. Aimee's adornments are always more splendid than the adornments of the chorus girls. If they wear paper crowns, Aimee, as a sign of her chosen mission, wears a gilded crown agleam with gems.

Aimee not only sings, she conducts the choir; she "produces" the actor who plays the role of Jesus; she keeps her eye on the microphone which carries her words to

hundreds of thousands; for Aimee is a modern woman who understands advertising and has an hour on the radio.

Once a week she exhibits the sick whom she has healed. Indeed, Upton Sinclair told me that she engages lots of the healed at a good daily fee; but then, as you know, Upton Sinclair is a heathen. Women, men, children appear on the stage. Each testifies that he has been cured of a great illness by Aimee's hand alone. "Consumption of the spine," breaks in Aimee, "and now quite healthy. *Isn't that lovely?* Tumor, and cured. *Isn't it beautiful?*"

Every Thursday evening Aimee baptizes, for, says she, the baptism of children is valueless. She sprinkles grownups with water. We must step into the water; in the water one is buried with the Lord, and like Him is resurrected. Every year she baptizes 3,000 persons. The floor of the stage sinks, a large swimming pool is rolled in; Aimee changes her clothes and, supported by a young man, stands in the water. The convert appears, clothed in a white garment; Aimee and the young man seize him, bend him down, duck him in the water, and lift him out again. The resurrected one flings his arms delightedly on high and cries out in an ecstatic voice: "Hallelujah! Hallelujah!" Sometimes father, mother, and child come; Aimee baptizes all at the same time, and she claps her hands with approval when the converts fall into an ecstasy. But she does not forget to remove the microphone from the pulpit and put it near the swimming pool.

The facial expressions and the gestures of this woman must be seen! She has just raised her hearers and herself to the highest pitch of ecstasy — she sees that the microphone is not fixed in the right position, and with a calculated movement she changes its position; and as she leans toward it she utters a biblical phrase in a more emphatic voice: "Ye who hear me over the radio, soon will ye see me. Shortly a talkie will be made showing our church, and I will see to it that this film is shown in your local theater."

Suddenly the telephone bells ring, for there is also a telephone near the pulpit. Aimee takes up the receiver and announces that 360 veterans of the Civil War are listening in. Hurriedly she turns on a wild patriotic song of prayer for the old graybeards.

Aimee takes care to provide constant entertainment. Solo singers appear, the band plays symphonies composed by Aimee herself and jazz dances. On the stage, living pictures are shown amid changing scenery. These living pictures accompany her preaching. What would happen, she preached on one occasion, if Eve had not eaten the apple? The red curtain of the stage opens. In front of a flowery landscape stand Adam and Eve. Adam in a brown leather farmer's kit; Eve in a dress of gold and with a wreath on her head. Aimee turns to the picture, claps her hands. "You look delightful, quite charming!" She turns back to the congregation. "Eve gave Adam the apple."

On the stage Adam takes the apple and swallows it greedily! "And naturally Eve said: 'Leave me some of it,' but Adam had devoured it, stalk and core." And even this sin had its meaning. If Eve had not sinned we should not have had the Bible and should not have got on familiar terms with God.

What would have happened if Jesus had never been born? We should not have Christmas celebrations in America! We are the grandest, cleanest, most God-beloved of nations; nobody else knows as we do how to give Christmas presents.

What would have happened if God had not come to Sister Aimee McPherson? What indeed! She tells her life story; she praises herself; she begins to sing, and she closes with the cry: "Who will pray with Sister Aimee McPherson?"

She turns to the first balcony, to the second, to the orchestra.

"Every man who is happy, say 'Amen.' "

"Amen!" rings out.

"Every man who loves Jesus, say 'Hallelujah!' "

"Hallelujah!" rings out.

"Raise your hands high, you in the second balcony."

"Now those in the first."

The hands of the faithful go quickly up.

In the spring Aimee is going to Palestine. She has chartered a ship, and intends to go with her archangels through the sacred places, singing and glorifying. Cook's, who have given her preferential terms, will conduct the tour.

DOUGLAS FAIRBANKS AND MARY PICKFORD have had the courage to make a talkie out of the *Taming of the Shrew*. The attempt is a complete failure. In spite of a good deal of Shakespeare's verse, nothing of Shakespeare's spirit remains. This example demonstrates better than any theory where the limits of the talking film are fixed. A work written for the stage cannot simply be transferred to the screen. The stage has laws formed and developed over thousands of years; the talking film, which has burst through the boundaries of time and space, has yet to find its laws.

On the whole, the talkies are artistically and technically a backward step. They repeat the mistakes and stupidities which the silent film made in the first years of its development. Dozens of new talkies are produced every month in America. The worst trash, the sickliest romanticism, the stupidest make-believe tumble over one another. If only they were amusing! But they are boring and soporific. The inevitable naked chorus-girls' legs; always the same stupid love chatter, always the same happy ending. In answer to my inquiry as to why the happy ending had been raised to an absolute law, a producer in one of the largest studios in Hollywood said: "The American public demands it. They want to find in the movies the justification of their lives. They want to be assured that their hard struggle for existence has some idealistic purpose behind it."

The answer did not convince me. It is part of American "Cant." The producers father their own wishes on the public. True, America is a young nation, and young nations, like young men, like to foster the illusion of eternal life, in their dreams to soften the hard lines of reality. They lie about social disharmonies and spiritual conflicts; they shut themselves off from the inexorableness of cosmic destiny and of death. Is it not noteworthy that every corpse in America is embalmed, that when a man is lying in his coffin wadding is stuck into his mouth to puff out the sunken cheeks, and that he is then made up?

Of the dozens of American talkies which I saw, one stands out as definitely a great performance — the Negro film, *Hallelujah*. The producer is King Vidor, whom we in Germany know as the creator of *The Great Parade*, and who is undoubtedly the most

distinguished American producer. Every one of these magnificent Negro actors is an amateur discovered by King Vidor. What faces! What gestures! What songs! What dances! What choral singing! They are splendid in their wildness, their naturalness, their creative grief. *Hallelujah* shows the greatest possibilities of the talking film. If producers, actors, and authors master film technique and "the word," they will turn out talkies to take a place as works of art beside those of the theater. I lay stress on "the word," for the spoken word must find its own peculiar power, its own style.

The talking film has two great possibilities: imaginative and documentary. For some weeks there has existed on Broadway a film-theater called the Newsreel. It exhibits nothing but news from all over the world. The newspaper has become alive. If one reads, over one's breakfast coffee, that, in the words of Goethe, far away in Turkey, people are fighting one another, one is not particularly disturbed. But when the news comes in the form of pictures, sounds, and words, the visions compel one to share the destiny of men who work and suffer in the furthermost corners of the earth. In other words, this living newspaper, like all newspapers, has an important political function. What is shown and what is not shown, what is photographed and how it is photographed, are matters of importance. I foresee a time when these talking-screen newspapers will be on the Left or on the Right in politics. These are true documents, which might bring nations closer together, but which in unscrupulous hands might just as easily serve to alienate peoples!

Even in elections the talkies are pressed into service. In the New York mayoralty election, tens of thousands of people blocked Broadway of an evening. Across a traffic island gleamed a white screen. On the screen pictures flickered; the pictures began to speak. Favorite singers sang couplets; bands played shrill jazz tunes; then the candidate, Mr. Jimmy Walker, appeared on the screen, smiled, bowed, and made his great election speech, in which — with a comical mixture of ingratiating, bigoted, philistine, boorish, and jingoistic phrases — the populace was exhorted to elect him, the faithful son of a poor Irishman, to be the mayor of this city, chosen of God, the most beautiful and richest ever built. Pictures followed which showed with blatant bombast how many subways, skyscrapers, museums, Mr. Walker had personally built up to now. Finally, the American comedian, Eddie Cantor, appeared, and, in a crude but very witty song, jibed at the people who reproached "our Jimmy" with always wearing elegantly creased trousers. The effect was stupendous.

The American talkie is making rapid strides. Money in plenty is there, in such plenty as we in Germany scarcely even dream of. From the venturesomeness and the energy of the Americans we can take example, but the American talkie will not develop beyond the limits imposed by a public opinion dominated by finance. It will become brilliant on the technical side, but as a document, or as an expression of artistic truth, it will accomplish something only in exceptional cases.

A few words about the American theater. I went to New York with great expectations, but found little there. Commercialism is even stronger there than in Berlin. Every production implies the investment of capital. For, apart from a few societies which possess their own buildings and have their own companies, a theater has to be rented and actors engaged for every new play. Therefore, managers are shy of experiments. Only the New York Theater Guild and a few amateur groups dare to put on plays which differ from the common run, either in form or matter. The theater is overrun with detective stories, drawing-room comedies, revues, and musical comedies.

Ibsen, Strindberg, Wedekind, so far as the American public is concerned, never existed. Therefore, things are regarded as audacious which we in Europe consider practically innocuous. If one attempts to treat sexual conflicts with a tenth of the frankness of Strindberg or Wedekind, that is taken as evidence of boundless courage. This estimate is not surprising in a country where actors are arrested for daring to produce a play the scene of which is a brothel. In God's own country, which calls itself the land of freedom, there are few signs of spiritual freedom. You may have read that O'Neill's *Strange Interlude* was banned in Boston. When Bourdet's *La Prisonnière* was produced in New York, certain members of the public took offense. Whereupon the actors, the producer, and the audience were conveyed in trucks to the police station.

As in the movies, so in the theater; people here want to be sheltered from the conflicts of social life. Both the German and the Russian theaters are much more alive and much more aware of the times in which we live than is the New York theater. The American drama is an outlet for the pleasure-loving, possessing classes. Woe to the authors who show the reverse side of American prosperity. They will not be performed; this is the case with Upton Sinclair. Only small studio theaters will sponsor them.

The theater is always dependent upon the social atmosphere of a country. The unrest which throbs today through the continent of America will ere long be detected in the American theater. Pessimists, whom public opinion in America will not tolerate (a characteristic it shares with Wilhelm II!), have bitter, much-needed truths to tell their country.

——————◆——————

Everybody is ignorant, only on different subjects.

WILL ROGERS

11.

Southern Agrarians Take Their Stand

I'll Take My Stand: The South and the Agrarian Tradition was an anthology of essays by twelve Southerners that appeared in 1930. Contributors included the poets John Crowe Ransom, Allen Tate, and Robert Penn Warren, who, in the Twenties, belonged to a group that called itself the Fugitives. It evolved as one of the most influential American literary movements of the twentieth century, forming the core of Southern literary renaissance. The "Statement of Principles" that introduced I'll Take My Stand is reprinted below. It reflected the group's desire to forestall the formless confusion of the present by seeking identity in the Southern past.

Source: *I'll Take My Stand,* New York, 1930: "Introduction: A Statement of Principles."

THE AUTHORS CONTRIBUTING TO THIS BOOK are Southerners, well acquainted with one another and of similar tastes, though not necessarily living in the same physical community, and perhaps only at this moment aware of themselves as a single group of men. By conversation and exchange of letters over a number of years it had developed that they entertained many convictions in common, and it was decided to make a volume in which each one should furnish his views upon a chosen topic. This was the general background. But background and consultation as to the various topics were enough; there was to be no further collaboration. And so no single author is responsible for any view outside his own article.

It was through the good fortune of some deeper agreement that the book was expected to achieve its unity. All the articles bear in the same sense upon the book's title subject: all tend to support a Southern way of life against what may be called the American or prevailing way; and all as much as agree that the best terms in which to represent the distinction are contained in the phrase, "Agrarian *versus* Industrial."

But after the book was under way it seemed a pity if the contributors, limited as they were within their special subjects, should stop short of showing how close their agreements really were. On the contrary, it seemed that they ought to go on and make themselves known as a group already consolidated by a set of principles which could be stated with a good deal of particularity. This might prove useful for the sake of future reference, if they should undertake any further joint publication. It was then decided to prepare a general introduction for the book which would state briefly the common convictions of the group. This is the statement. To it every one of the contributors in this book has subscribed.

Nobody now proposes for the South, or for any other community in this country, an independent political destiny. That idea is thought to have been finished in 1865. But how far shall the South surrender its moral, social, and economic autonomy to the victorious principle of Union? That question remains open. The South is a minority section that has hitherto been jealous of its minority right to live its own kind of life. The South scarcely hopes to determine the other sections, but it does propose to determine itself, within the utmost limits of legal action. Of late, however, there is the melancholy fact that the South itself has wavered a little and shown signs of wanting to join up behind the common or American industrial ideal. It is against that tendency that this book is written. The younger Southerners, who are being converted frequently to the industrial gospel, must come back to the support of the Southern tradition. They must be persuaded to look very critically at the advantages of becoming a "new South" which will be only an undistinguished replica of the usual industrial community.

But there are many other minority communities opposed to industrialism and wanting a much simpler economy to live by. The communities and private persons sharing the agrarian tastes are to be found widely within the Union. Proper living is a matter of the intelligence and the will, does not depend on the local climate or geography, and is capable of a definition which is general and not Southern at all. Southerners have a filial duty to discharge to their own section. But their cause is precarious and they must seek alliances with sympathetic communities everywhere. The members of the present group would be happy to be counted as members of a national agrarian movement.

Industrialism is the economic organization of the collective American society. It means the decision of society to invest its economic resources in the applied sciences. But the word "science" has acquired a certain sanctitude. It is out of order to quarrel with science in the abstract, or even with the applied sciences when their applications are made subject to criticism and intelligence. The capitalization of the applied sciences has now become extravagant and uncritical; it has enslaved our human energies to a degree now clearly felt to be burdensome.

The apologists of industrialism do not like to meet this charge directly; so they often take refuge in saying that they are devoted simply to science! They are really devoted to the applied sciences and to practical production. Therefore it is necessary to employ a certain skepticism even at the expense of the Cult of Science, and to say, It is an Americanism, which looks innocent and disinterested, but really is not either.

The contribution that science can make to a labor is to render it easier by the help of a tool or a process, and to assure the laborer of his perfect economic security while he is engaged upon it. Then it can be performed with leisure and enjoyment. But the modern laborer has not exactly received this benefit under the industrial regime. His labor is hard, its tempo is fierce, and his employment is insecure. The first principle of a good labor is that it must be effective, but the second principle is that it must be enjoyed. Labor is one of the largest items in the human career; it is a modest demand to ask that it may partake of happiness.

The regular act of applied science is to introduce into labor a laborsaving device or a machine. Whether this is a benefit depends on how far it is advisable to save the labor. The philosophy of applied science is generally quite sure that the saving of labor is a pure gain, and that the more of it the better. This is to assume that labor is an evil, that only the end of labor or the material product is good. On this assumption labor becomes mercenary and servile, and it is no wonder if many forms of modern labor are accepted without resentment though they are evidently brutalizing. The act of labor as one of the happy functions of human life has been in effect abandoned, and is practised solely for its rewards.

Even the apologists of industrialism have been obliged to admit that some economic evils follow in the wake of the machines. These are such as overproduction, unemployment, and a growing inequality in the distribution of wealth. But the remedies proposed by the apologists are always homeopathic. They expect the evils to disappear when we have bigger and better machines, and more of them. Their remedial programs, therefore, look forward to more industrialism. Sometimes they see the system righting itself spontaneously and without direction: they are Optimists. Sometimes they rely on the benevolence of capital, or the militancy of labor, to bring about a fairer division of the spoils: they are Cooperationists or Socialists. And sometimes they expect to find super-engineers, in the shape of Boards of Control, who will adapt production to consumption and regulate prices and guarantee business against fluctuations: they are Sovietists.

With respect to these last it must be insisted that the true Sovietists or Communists — if the term may be used here in the European sense — are the Industrialists themselves. They would have the government set up an economic super-organization, which in turn would become the government. We therefore look upon the Communist menace as a menace indeed, but not as a Red one; because it is simply according to the blind drift of our industrial development to expect in America at last much the same economic system as that imposed by violence upon Russia in 1917.

Turning to consumption, as the grand end which justifies the evil of modern labor, we find that we have been deceived. We have more time in which to consume and many more products to be consumed. But the tempo of our labors communicates itself to our satisfactions, and these also become brutal and hurried. The constitution of the natural man probably does not permit him to shorten his labor-time and enlarge his consuming-time indefinitely. He has to pay the penalty in satiety and aimlessness. The modern man has lost his sense of vocation.

Religion can hardly expect to flourish in an industrial society. Religion is our submission to the general intention of a nature that is fairly inscrutable; it is the sense of our rôle as creatures within it. But nature industrialized, transformed into cities and artificial habitations, manufactured into commodities, is no longer nature but a highly simplified picture of nature. We receive the illusion of having power over nature, and lose the sense of nature as something mysterious and contingent. The God of nature under these conditions is merely an amiable expression, a superfluity, and the philosophical understanding ordinarily carried in the religious experience is not there for us to have.

Nor do the arts have a proper life under industrialism, with the general decay of sensibility which attends it. Art depends, in general, like religion, on a right attitude to nature; and in particular on a free and disinterested observation of nature that occurs only in leisure. Neither the creation nor the understanding of works of art is possible in an industrial age except by some local and unlikely suspension of the industrial drive.

The amenities of life also suffer under the curse of a strictly business or industrial civilization. They consist in such practices as manners, conversation, hospitality, sympathy, family life, romantic love — in the social exchanges which reveal and develop sensibility in human affairs. If religion and the arts are founded on right relations of man-to-nature, these are founded on right relations of man-to-man.

Apologists of industrialism are even inclined to admit that its actual processes may have upon its victims the spiritual effects just described. But they think that all can be made right by extraordinary educational efforts, by all sorts of cultural institutions and endowments. They would cure the poverty of the contemporary spirit by hiring experts to instruct it in spite of itself in the historic culture. But salvation is hardly to be encountered on that road. The trouble with the life-pattern is to be located at its economic base, and we cannot rebuild it by pouring in soft materials from the top. The young men and women in colleges, for example, if they are already placed in a false way of life, cannot make more than an inconsequential acquaintance with the arts and humanities transmitted to them. Or else the understanding of these arts and humanities will but make them the more wretched in their own destitution.

The "Humanists" are too abstract. Humanism, properly speaking, is not an abstract system but a culture, the whole way in which we live, act, think, and feel. It is a kind of imaginatively balanced life lived out in a definite social tradition. And, in the concrete, we believe that this, the genuine humanism, was rooted in the agrarian life of the older South and of other parts of the country that shared in such a tradition. It was not an abstract moral "check" derived from the classics — it was not soft material poured in from the top. It was deeply founded in the way of life itself — in its tables, chairs, portraits, festivals, laws, marriage customs. We cannot recover our native humanism by adopting some standard of taste that is critical enough to question the contemporary arts but not critical enough to question the social and economic life which is their ground.

The tempo of the industrial life is fast, but that is not the worst of it; it is accelerating. The ideal is not merely some set form of industrialism, with so many stable industries, but industrial progress, or an incessant extension of industrialization. It never proposes a specific goal; it initiates the infinite series. We have not merely capitalized certain industries; we have capitalized the laboratories and inventors, and undertaken to employ all the laborsaving devices that come out of them. But a fresh laborsaving device introduced into an industry does not emancipate the laborers in that industry so much as it evicts them. Applied at the expense of agriculture, for example, the

new processes have reduced the part of the population supporting itself upon the soil to a smaller and smaller fraction.

Of course no single laborsaving process is fatal; it brings on a period of unemployed labor and unemployed capital, but soon a new industry is devised which will put them both to work again, and a new commodity is thrown upon the market. The laborers were sufficiently embarrassed in the meantime, but, according to the theory, they will eventually be taken care of. It is now the public which is embarrassed; it feels obligated to purchase a commodity for which it had expressed no desire, but it is invited to make its budget equal to the strain. All might yet be well, and stability and comfort might again obtain, but for this: partly because of industrial ambitions and partly because the repressed creative impulse must break out somewhere, there will be a stream of further laborsaving devices in all industries, and the cycle will have to be repeated over and over. The result is an increasing disadjustment and instability.

It is an inevitable consequence of industrial progress that production greatly outruns the rate of natural consumption. To overcome the disparity, the producers, disguised as the pure idealists of progress, must coerce and wheedle the public into being loyal and steady consumers, in order to keep the machines running. So the rise of modern advertising — along with its twin, personal salesmanship — is the most significant development of our industrialism. Advertising means to persuade the consumers to want exactly what the applied sciences are able to furnish them. It consults the happiness of the consumer no more than it consulted the happiness of the laborer. It is the great effort of a false economy of life to approve itself. But its task grows more difficult every day.

It is strange, of course, that a majority of men anywhere could ever as with one mind become enamored of industrialism: a system that has so little regard for individual wants. There is evidently a kind of thinking that rejoices in setting up a social objective which has no relation to the individual. Men are prepared to sacrifice their private dignity and happiness to an abstract social ideal, and without asking whether the social ideal produces the welfare of any individual man whatsoever. But this is absurd. The responsibility of men is for their own welfare and that of their neighbors; not for the hypothetical welfare of some fabulous creature called society.

Opposed to the industrial society is the agrarian, which does not stand in particular need of definition. An agrarian society is hardly one that has no use at all for industries, for professional vocations, for scholars and artists, and for the life of cities. Technically, perhaps, an agrarian society is one in which agriculture is the leading vocation, whether for wealth, for pleasure, or for prestige — a form of labor that is pursued with intelligence and leisure, and that becomes the model to which the other forms approach as well as they may. But an agrarian regime will be secured readily enough where the superfluous industries are not allowed to rise against it. The theory of agrarianism is that the culture of the soil is the best and most sensitive of vocations, and that therefore it should have the economic preference and enlist the maximum number of workers.

These principles do not intend to be very specific in proposing any practical measures.

How may the little agrarian community resist the Chamber of Commerce of its county seat, which is always trying to import some foreign industry that cannot be assimilated to the life-pattern of the community? Just what must the Southern leaders do to defend the traditional Southern life? How may the Southern and the Western agrarians unite for effective action? Should the agrarian forces try to capture the Democratic Party, which historically is so closely affiliated with the defense of individualism, the small community, the state, the South? Or must the agrarians — even the Southern ones — abandon the Democratic Party to its fate and try a new one?

What legislation could most profitably be championed by the powerful agrarians in the Senate of the United States? What anti-industrial measures might promise to stop the advances of industrialism, or even undo some of them, with the least harm to those concerned? What policy should be pursued by the educators who have a tradition at heart? These and many other questions are of the greatest importance, but they cannot be answered here.

For, in conclusion, this much is clear: If a community, or a section, or a race, or an age, is groaning under industrialism, and well aware that it is an evil dispensation, it must find the way to throw it off. To think that this cannot be done is pusillanimous. And if the whole community, section, race, or age thinks it cannot be done, then it has simply lost its political genius and doomed itself to impotence.

In profound appreciation/Of the Boll Weevil and what he has done/
As the herald of prosperity/This monument was erected/
By the citizens of/ Enterprise, Coffee County, Alabama.

Inscription, 1930s. The South was being ruined by the one-crop system; the weevil forced the growing of other crops

12.

Edwin L. James: America as a World Power

Despite the attempt to isolate the nation from international obligations that began with the repudiation of the commitments made by President Wilson at Versailles, the United States in reality could not totally ignore the rest of the world after World War I. Economic interests, if no other, dictated that there be sufficient international cooperation to assure a permanent peace. In 1921 and 1922 the United States took part in the Washington Conference on disarmament and further cooperation came in 1928 with the signing of the Pact of Paris that outlawed aggressive war. Nevertheless, isolationism, reinforced by the belief that another European war was impossible, was the dominant mood of U.S. foreign policy. "Men of goodwill throughout the world are working earnestly . . . to perfect the equipment . . . for peace," President Hoover assured his audience on Armistice Day 1929, "but there is something . . . infinitely more powerful than the work of all ambassadors and ministers. . . . That is to . . . create respect and confidence, to stimulate esteem between peoples — this is the far greatest guaranty of peace." Some observers of American policy felt that leadership based on goodwill and moral earnestness was insufficient. One such critic was the journalist and foreign correspondent Edwin L. James.

Source: *International Digest*, October 1930: "Our World Power and Moral Influence."

THE MATERIAL SITUATION of the United States of America is such that the resulting political influence is enormous, so enormous that a failure to place its true value on it may be explained by the circumstance that it has not yet made its real force felt to a degree that will surely materialize.

There is no country where the power of the dollar has not reached. There is no capital which does not take the United States into consideration at almost every turn. Conversely, there is no zone where our interests are not involved. Isolation is a myth. We are not isolated and cannot be isolated. The United States is ever present.

Officially, our government stays out of world organizations. We scorn the League of Nations; we continue to shy at the World Court. But such things count for less and less. We must deal with the world and the world must deal with us. Let there be an international conference, and the imponderable influences bring the United States there. A conference on reparations, we are there. The International Bank is set up, an American is made president. The World Court meets, an American is put on the bench. A naval conference gathers, and the whole business hangs largely on the American position. And so on, ad infinitum.

It is always the case that the American position is among the most important. Such is one of the prices of our power. Few world problems arise in which the influence of the United States will not swing the decision if we take a real interest. Opposition to the United States is a serious undertaking. Our dollars are powerful; there are so many of them.

Take the tariff. Such is the breadth of the trade of the United States that no nation ignores our markets. A higher duty voted in

Washington affects work in countless cities abroad. Conversely, higher duties voted in foreign capitals may affect work in our cities from one seaboard to the other.

It is always a question of what the United States does or is going to do. No European nation plans peace without taking America into account. Nor will any European nation plan war without seeking to find out what is the attitude of Washington on the issues at stake. Supplies of credit, food, and munitions from the United States mean one situation, especially if our Navy guarantees our shipments crossing the Atlantic successfully, and the lack of those supplies means quite another thing. Geneva can make no blockade which we do not recognize because there are no League members who will take a serious chance of antagonizing the United States.

Indeed, the position and power of this country is rapidly reaching the point when it will be said that we have gained the relative position which Great Britain held from the Battle of Waterloo up to 1914, which France held for approximately a century preceding, and which through history belonged for varying periods to various nations. For all the indications point to this being our century.

To a large degree world greatness has been thrust upon us. It has come to us through the force of circumstances not all of our own making. That, by chance, may explain why nationally we have not come fully to realize where we are.

But there are signs in every direction that the situation which has been so mobile, with everything moving in our direction, is becoming stabilized. The current toward the United States is slackening. Things should tend to stabilize. In other words, in the next decade our progress will not be so great because it cannot bring the same increase in power as we enjoyed in the last ten years.

Furthermore, what we win in the next ten years we shall have to strive for to a much greater degree than since the war.

The game of keeping our own markets for ourselves by shutting out foreign goods and at the same time enjoying the markets of other countries is going to be more and more difficult. Europe is back on its feet again and able to compete with us in the world markets.

But if the shake-up is largely over, it was surely to our advantage. The aftermath of the war has left the United States sitting on the top of the world. The predominance of our economic and financial position extends in every direction and is an example being used by the exponents of the movement for a federated Europe and an economically united British Commonwealth of Nations.

It is generally realized in the United States how great the nation is economically. But there is not yet a realization of the great political power our material position has brought us. And whether we will use that power when we feel it as other nations have or whether we will use it in a new and different manner — there is the greatest question of world politics.

Just as an American observer who has been living in Europe gets the idea, on returning to the United States, that popularly there is an underestimation of the political power which America's material position has given us, he also finds what, looked upon from the other side, seems to be an exaggeration of the moral world influence of the United States.

America's great world political position is not due primarily to our moral leadership but primarily to our wealth and economic position. That is true because it is not to our moral teachings that the rest of the world responds, but to our material power. If we were a poor and weak nation the world would today care no more about what we thought than did the world before the Great War.

It is not difficult to understand why the Old World does not take our exhortations to heart any more. There is the old story of the League of Nations. There is the World

Court. There are other things, like the International Bank — all of which seem to represent our advice to others as to how to do their business, while we do ours some other way.

Now those who still believe that "the moral sense" of America is a real factor in international affairs will surely cite the Kellogg Pact as an example of how we do good and do it altruistically. But no one who has lived in Europe in recent years can believe in the dominant moral effect of the Kellogg Pact as an active factor in world affairs. Almost the only attraction Europe ever saw in it was the line the United States signed on. No European nation promised anything in the antiwar pact that it had not already agreed to in the covenant of the League of Nations. But there was the signature of the United States, which seemed to promise the cooperation of our great material power in curbing the aggressor in another war. And that made a powerful appeal. But this appeal lay not in any new religion the Kellogg Pact brought to a soul-hungry world. It was based on the great political power of America because of our enormous wealth and potential military and naval power.

Does anyone believe seriously that the deference and respect Britain has shown for us in the past decade represent a belief in our moral superiority, a realization of a superior civilization on this side of the Atlantic or a better system of government and social order? Not at all. Britain is extremely practical in foreign affairs. There is no new approval of America and Americans, but there is a realization of our material power as something to be reckoned with seriously, and Britain does just that.

It is no exaggeration to say that Europe sees us as nationally selfish in our refusal to commit ourselves in any way as to measures to be taken to maintain peace or to restore peace if it is broken. While we say it is to preserve our precious liberty, other nations say we seek to preserve our right to trade with warring nations or to do whatever else may be to our advantage, as we see it at any given time.

Perhaps it is not becoming in some of our European critics to draw from our position the conclusion that we are worse than other nations. We follow the line of foreign policy they followed, generally speaking, when they were in our relative position. There would be better support for our contention that we are no worse than they were and would be if they could. But the situation does make it difficult for us to contend successfully that we are better than other nations. They do not believe it.

Of course, there have been, in the past, indications pointing to a real influence of our moral advice. In the first five years after the World War the nations of Europe, on their backs and seeking American aid, took all pains to avoid offending us and therefore appeared to give careful and weighty consideration to our altruistic advice. The succeeding five years changed that. Today, Europe, to a rapidly increasing degree, feels itself getting back to where it may treat with us on a plane of equality. And that puts Europe in a position to do what the Old World likes about our advice. More and more we shall hear that words unaccompanied by acts will not be taken as seriously as in the past.

But Europeans do know the importance of America in the world. Because they are more used to studying and judging world affairs than we are, they realize, perhaps better than we do, just how important is the United States. Their eyes are on us all the time. They must reckon with us; they must do business with us. And so they must know what we are doing and what we may be going to do. That gives us our great importance and out of that grows our influence. Although not exercised as actively as it will be later on, American world political power is interestingly important not only because of its might, but because of its present underdevelopment.

13.

Archibald MacLeish: "American Letter"

Archibald MacLeish was one of the many American artists and writers who migrated to Europe after the war, and, like most of them, he projected a sense of decay and despair into his art. In 1928 he returned to America and in 1930, the same year that he became the first editor of Fortune *magazine, he published a collection of poems,* New Found Land, *many of which attested to his homesickness for the old world of Europe and his difficulty in readjusting to and defining the new world of America. "American Letter (for Gerald Murphy)" is one of the best known of the poems that MacLeish wrote during this period, and it reflects the divided feelings of a large number of intellectuals at the time. But such feelings were of course not confined to the early 1930s. Americans from Franklin and Jefferson to Peace Corps volunteers in the 1960s have shared a yearning to be citizens not only of America but also of other lands — and at the same time have recognized MacLeish's warning question: "How can a wise man have two countries?"*

Source: *New Found Land,* Boston and New York, 1930.

AMERICAN LETTER
for Gerald Murphy

The wind is east but the hot weather continues,
Blue and no clouds, the sound of the leaves thin,
Dry like the rustling of paper, scored across
With the slate-shrill screech of the locusts.
                    The tossing of
Pines is the low sound. In the wind's running
The wild carrots smell of the burning sun.
Why should I think of the dolphins at Capo di Mele?
Why should I see in my mind the taut sail
And the hill over St.-Tropez and your hand on the tiller?
Why should my heart be troubled with palms still?
I am neither a sold boy nor a Chinese official
Sent to sicken in Pa for some Lo-Yang dish.
This is my own land, my sky, my mountain:
This — not the humming pines and the surf and the sand
At the Ferme Blanche, nor Port Cros in the dusk and the harbor
Floating the motionless ship and the sea-drowned star.
I am neither Po Chü-i nor another after
Far from home, in a strange land, daft
For the talk of his own sort and the taste of his lettuces.

This land is my native land. And yet
I am sick for home for the red roofs and the olives,
And the foreign words and the smell of the sea fall.
How can a wise man have two countries?
How can a man have the earth and the wind and want
A land far off, alien, smelling of palm trees
And the yellow gorse at noon in the long calms?

It is a strange thing — to be an American.
Neither an old house it is with the air
Tasting of hung herbs and the sun returning
Year after year to the same door and the churn
Making the same sound in the cool of the kitchen
Mother to son's wife, and the place to sit
Marked in the dusk by the worn stone at the wellhead —
That — nor the eyes like each other's eyes and the skull
Shaped to the same fault and the hands' sameness.
Neither a place it is nor a blood name.
America is West and the wind blowing.
America is a great word and the snow,
A way, a white bird, the rain falling,
A shining thing in the mind and the gulls' call.
America is neither a land nor a people,
A word's shape it is, a wind's sweep —
America is alone: many together,
Many of one mouth, of one breath,
Dressed as one — and none brothers among them:
Only the taught speech and the aped tongue.
America is alone and the gulls calling.

It is a strange thing to be an American.
It is strange to live on the high world in the stare
Of the naked sun and the stars as our bones live.
Men in the old lands housed by their rivers.
They built their towns in the vales in the earth's shelter.
We first inhabit the world. We dwell
On the half earth, on the open curve of a continent.
Sea is divided from sea by the day-fall. The dawn
Rides the low east with us many hours;
First are the capes, then are the shorelands, now
The blue Appalachians faint at the day rise;
The willows shudder with light on the long Ohio:
The Lakes scatter the low sun: the prairies
Slide out of dark: in the eddy of clean air
The smoke goes up from the high plains of Wyoming:
The steep Sierras arise: the struck foam

Flames at the wind's heel on the far Pacific.
Already the noon leans to the eastern cliff:
The elms darken the door and the dust-heavy lilacs.

It is strange to sleep in the bare stars and to die
On an open land where few bury before us:
(From the new earth the dead return no more.)
It is strange to be born of no race and no people.
In the old lands they are many together. They keep
The wise past and the words spoken in common.
They remember the dead with their hands, their mouths dumb.
They answer each other with two words in their meeting.
They live together in small things. They eat
The same dish, their drink is the same and their proverbs.
Their youth is like. They are like in their ways of love.
They are many men. There are always others beside them.
Here it is one man and another and wide
On the darkening hills the faint smoke of the houses.
Here it is one man and the wind in the boughs.

Therefore our hearts are sick for the south water.
The smell of the gorse comes back to our night thought.
We are sick at heart for the red roofs and the olives;
We are sick at heart for the voice and the foot fall.
Therefore we will not go though the sea call us. . . .

This, this is our land, this is our people,
This that is neither a land nor a race. We must reap
The wind here in the grass for our soul's harvest:
Here we must eat our salt or our bones starve.
Here we must live or live only as shadows.
This is our race, we that have none, that have had
Neither the old walls nor the voices around us,
This is our land, this is our ancient ground —
The raw earth, the mixed bloods and the strangers,
The different eyes, the wind, and the heart's change.
These we will not leave though the old call us.
This our country-earth, our blood, our kind.
Here we will live our years till the earth blind us —

The wind blows from the east. The leaves fall.
Far off in the pines a jay rises.
The wind smells of haze and the wild ripe apples.

I think of the masts at Cette and the sweet rain.

14.

Sinclair Lewis: The American Fear of Literature

*In 1930 Sinclair Lewis became the first American to receive the Nobel Prize for Literature. In his novels — * Main Street, Babbitt, Dodsworth, *and* Elmer Gantry *are the best known — Lewis had satirically exposed the hypocrisy of American middle-class life, and many outraged Americans felt that by offering the prize to Lewis the Nobel Committee was criticizing American culture rather than honoring American literature. Lewis' acceptance speech berated the American sensitivity to criticism. The speech, a revised version of which is reprinted here, was delivered on December 12, 1930, in Stockholm's Stock Exchange Hall.*

Source: *Address by Sinclair Lewis Before the Swedish Academy, December 12, 1930,* New York, n.d., pp. 9-23.

Members of the Swedish Academy; Ladies and Gentlemen:

Were I to express my feeling of honor and pleasure in having been awarded the Nobel Prize in Literature, I should be fulsome and perhaps tedious, and I present my gratitude with a plain "Thank you."

I wish, in this address, to consider certain trends, certain dangers, and certain high and exciting promises in present-day American literature. To discuss this with complete and unguarded frankness — and I should not insult you by being otherwise than completely honest, however indiscreet — it will be necessary for me to be a little impolite regarding certain institutions and persons of my own greatly beloved land.

But I beg of you to believe that I am in no case gratifying a grudge. Fortune has dealt with me rather too well. I have known little struggle, not much poverty, many generosities. Now and then I have, for my books or myself, been somewhat warmly denounced — there was one good pastor in California who, upon reading my

Elmer Gantry, desired to lead a mob and lynch me; while another holy man in the state of Maine wondered if there was no respectable and righteous way of putting me in jail. And, much harder to endure than any raging condemnation, a certain number of old acquaintances among journalists, what in the galloping American slang we call the "I Knew Him When Club," have scribbled that since they know me personally, therefore I must be a rather low sort of fellow and certainly no writer. But if I have now and then received such cheering brickbats, still I, who have heaved a good many bricks myself, would be fatuous not to expect a fair number in return.

No, I have for myself no conceivable complaint to make, and yet for American literature in general, and its standing in a country where industrialism and finance and science flourish and the only arts that are vital and respected are architecture and the film, I have a considerable complaint.

I can illustrate by an incident which chances to concern the Swedish Academy and myself and which happened a few days ago, just before I took ship at New York for Sweden. There is in America a learned and most amiable old gentleman who has been a pastor, a university professor, and a diplomat. He is a member of the American Academy of Arts and Letters and no few universities have honored him with degrees. As a writer he is chiefly known for his pleasant little essays on the joy of fishing. I do not suppose that professional fishermen, whose lives depend on the run of cod or herring, find it altogether an amusing occupation, but from these essays I learned, as a boy, that there is something very important and spiritual about catching fish, if you have no need of doing so.

This scholar stated, and publicly, that in awarding the Nobel Prize to a person who has scoffed at American institutions as much as I have, the Nobel Committee and the Swedish Academy had insulted America. I don't know whether, as an ex-diplomat, he intends to have an international incident made of it, and perhaps demand of the American government that they land marines in Stockholm to protect American literary rights, but I hope not.

I should have supposed that to a man so learned as to have been made a Doctor of Divinity, a Doctor of Letters, and I do not know how many other imposing magnificences, the matter would have seemed different; I should have supposed that he would have reasoned, "Although personally I dislike this man's books, nevertheless the Swedish Academy has in choosing him honored America by assuming that the Americans are no longer a puerile backwoods clan, so inferior that they are afraid of criticism, but instead a nation come of age and able to consider calmly and maturely any dissection of their land, however scoffing."

I should even have supposed that so international a scholar would have believed that Scandinavia, accustomed to the works of Strindberg, Ibsen, and Pontoppidan, would not have been peculiarly shocked by a writer whose most anarchistic assertion has been that America, with all her wealth and power, has not yet produced a civilization good enough to satisfy the deepest wants of human creatures.

I believe that Strindberg rarely sang the "Star-spangled Banner" or addressed Rotary Clubs, yet Sweden seems to have survived him.

I have at such length discussed this criticism of the learned fisherman not because it has any conceivable importance in itself but because it does illustrate the fact that in America most of us — not readers alone but even writers — are still afraid of any literature which is not a glorification of everything American, a glorification of our faults as well as our virtues. To be not only a best-seller in America but to be really beloved, a novelist must assert that all American men are tall, handsome, rich, honest, and powerful at golf; that all country towns are filled with neighbors who do nothing from day to day save go about being kind to one another; that although American girls may be wild, they change always into perfect wives and mothers; and that, geographically, America is composed solely of New York, which is inhabited entirely by millionaires; of the West, which keeps unchanged all the boisterous heroism of 1870; and of the South, where everyone lives on a plantation perpetually glossy with moonlight and scented with magnolias.

It is not today vastly more true than it was twenty years ago that such novelists of ours as you have read in Sweden, novelists like Dreiser and Willa Cather, are authentically popular and influential in America. As it was revealed by the venerable fishing Academician whom I have quoted, we still most revere the writers for the popular magazines who in a hearty and edifying chorus chant that the America of 120 million population is still as simple, as pastoral,

United Press International

Sinclair Lewis, first American to win the Nobel Prize for Literature, photographed with his wife, Dorothy Thompson, enroute to Stockholm in 1930

as it was when it had but 40 million; that in an industrial plant with 10,000 employees, the relationship between the worker and the manager is still as neighborly and uncomplex as in a factory of 1840, with 5 employees; that the relationships between father and son, between husband and wife, are precisely the same in an apartment in a thirty-story palace today, with three motor cars awaiting the family below and five books on the library shelves and a divorce imminent in the family next week, as were those relationships in a rose-veiled, five-room cottage in 1880; that, in fine, America has gone through the revolutionary change from rustic colony to world empire without having in the least altered the bucolic and puritanic simplicity of Uncle Sam.

I am, actually, extremely grateful to the fishing Academician for having somewhat condemned me. For since he is a leading member of the American Academy of Arts and Letters, he has released me, has given me the right to speak as frankly of that Academy as he has spoken of me. And in any honest study of American intellectualism today, that curious institution must be considered.

Before I consider the Academy, however, let me sketch a fantasy which has pleased me the last few days in the unavoidable idleness of a rough trip on the Atlantic. I am sure that you know, by now, that the award to me of the Nobel Prize has by no means been altogether popular in America. Doubtless the experience is not new to you. I fancy that when you gave the award even to Thomas Mann, whose *Zauberberg* seems to me to contain the whole of intellectual Europe, even when you gave it to Kipling, whose social significance is so profound that it has been rather authoritatively said that he created the British Empire, even when you gave it to Bernard Shaw, there were countrymen of those authors who complained because you did not choose another.

And I imagined what would have been said had you chosen some American other than myself. Suppose you had taken Theodore Dreiser.

Now to me, as to many other American writers, Dreiser more than any other man, marching alone, usually unappreciated, often hated, has cleared the trail from Victorian and Howellsian timidity and gentility in American fiction to honesty and boldness and passion of life. Without his pioneering, I doubt if any of us could, unless we liked to be sent to jail, seek to express life and beauty and terror.

My great colleague Sherwood Anderson has proclaimed this leadership of Dreiser. I am delighted to join him. Dreiser's great first novel, *Sister Carrie*, which he dared to publish thirty long years ago and which I read twenty-five years ago, came to housebound and airless America like a great, free, Western wind, and to our stuffy domesticity gave us the first fresh air since Mark Twain and Whitman.

Yet had you given the Prize to Mr. Dreiser, you would have heard groans from

America; you would have heard that his style — I am not exactly sure what this mystic quality "style" may be, but I find the word so often in the writings of minor critics that I suppose it must exist — you would have heard that his style is cumbersome, that his choice of words is insensitive, that his books are interminable. And certainly respectable scholars would complain that in Mr. Dreiser's world men and women are often sinful and tragic and despairing, instead of being forever sunny and full of song and virtue, as befits authentic Americans.

And had you chosen Mr. Eugene O'Neill, who has done nothing much in American drama save to transform it utterly, in ten or twelve years, from a false world of neat and competent trickery to a world of splendor and fear and greatness, you would have been reminded that he has done something far worse than scoffing — he has seen life as not to be neatly arranged in the study of a scholar but as a terrifying, magnificent, and often quite horrible thing akin to the tornado, the earthquake, the devastating fire.

And had you given Mr. James Branch Cabell the Prize, you would have been told that he is too fantastically malicious. So would you have been told that Miss Willa Cather, for all the homely virtue of her novels concerning the peasants of Nebraska, has in her novel, *The Lost Lady*, been so untrue to America's patent and perpetual and possibly tedious virtuousness as to picture an abandoned woman who remains, nevertheless, uncannily charming even to the virtuous, in a story without any moral; that Mr. Henry Mencken is the worst of all scoffers; that Mr. Sherwood Anderson viciously errs in considering sex as important a force in life as fishing; that Mr. Upton Sinclair, being a Socialist, sins against the perfectness of American capitalistic mass production; that Mr. Joseph Hergesheimer is un-American in regarding graciousness of

manner and beauty of surface as of some importance in the endurance of daily life; and that Mr. Ernest Hemingway is not only too young but, far worse, uses language which should be unknown to gentlemen; that he acknowledges drunkenness as one of man's eternal ways to happiness, and asserts that a soldier may find love more significant than the hearty slaughter of men in battle.

Yes, they are wicked, these colleagues of mine; you would have done almost as evilly to have chosen them as to have chosen me; and as a Chauvinistic American — only, mind you, as an American of 1930 and not of 1880 — I rejoice that they are my countrymen and countrywomen, and that I may speak of them with pride even in the Europe of Thomas Mann, H. G. Wells, Galsworthy, Knut Hamsun, Arnold Bennett, Feuchtwanger, Selma Lagerlöf, Sigrid Undset, Verner von Heidenstam, D'Annunzio, Romain Rolland.

It is my fate in this paper to swing constantly from optimism to pessimism and back, but so is it the fate of anyone who writes or speaks of anything in America — the most contradictory, the most depressing, the most stirring, of any land in the world today.

Thus, having with no muted pride called the roll of what seem to me to be great men and women in American literary life today, and having indeed omitted a dozen other names of which I should like to boast were there time, I must turn again and assert that in our contemporary American literature, indeed in all American arts save architecture and the film, we — yes, we who have such pregnant and vigorous standards in commerce and science — have no standards, no healing communication, no heroes to be followed nor villains to be condemned, no certain ways to be pursued and no dangerous paths to be avoided.

The American novelist or poet or dramatist or sculptor or painter must work alone, in confusion, unassisted, save by his own integrity.

That, of course, has always been the lot of the artist. The vagabond and criminal François Villon had certainly no smug and comfortable refuge in which elegant ladies would hold his hand and comfort his starveling soul and more starved body. He, veritably a great man, destined to outlive in history all the dukes and puissant cardinals whose robes he was esteemed unworthy to touch, had for his lot the gutter and the hardened crust.

Such poverty is not for the artist in America. They pay us, indeed, only too well; that writer is a failure who cannot have his butler and motor and his villa at Palm Beach, where he is permitted to mingle almost in equality with the barons of banking. But he is oppressed ever by something worse than poverty — by the feeling that what he creates does not matter, that he is expected by his readers to be only a decorator or a clown, or that he is good-naturedly accepted as a scoffer whose bark probably is worse than his bite and who probably is a good fellow at heart, who in any case certainly does not count in a land that produces eighty-story buildings, motors by the million, and wheat by the billions of bushels. And he has no institution, no group, to which he can turn for inspiration, whose criticism he can accept and whose praise will be precious to him.

What institutions have we?

The American Academy of Arts and Letters does contain, along with several excellent painters and architects and statesmen, such a really distinguished university president as Nicholas Murray Butler, so admirable and courageous a scholar as Wilbur Cross, and several first-rate writers: the poets Edwin Arlington Robinson and Robert Frost; the free-minded publicist James Truslow Adams; and the novelists Edith Wharton, Hamlin Garland, Owen Wister, Brand Whitlock, and Booth Tarkington.

But it does not include Theodore Dreiser; Henry Mencken; our most vivid critic George Jean Nathan who, though still young, is certainly the dean of our dramatic critics; Eugene O'Neill, incomparably our best dramatist; the really original and vital poets Edna St. Vincent Millay and Carl Sandburg, Robinson Jeffers and Vachel Lindsay and Edgar Lee Masters, whose *Spoon River Anthology* was so utterly different from any other poetry ever published, so fresh, so authoritative, so free from any gropings and timidities that it came like a revelation and created a new school of native American poetry. It does not include the novelists and short-story writers Willa Cather, Joseph Hergesheimer, Sherwood Anderson, Ring Lardner, Ernest Hemingway, Louis Bromfield, Wilbur Daniel Steele, Fannie Hurst, Mary Austin, James Branch Cabell, Edna Ferber, nor Upton Sinclair, of whom you must say, whether you admire or detest his aggressive socialism, that he is internationally better known than any other American artist whosoever, be he novelist, poet, painter, sculptor, musician, architect.

I should not expect any Academy to be so fortunate as to contain all these writers, but one which fails to contain any of them, which thus cuts itself off from so much of what is living and vigorous and original in American letters, can have no relationship whatever to our life and aspirations. It does not represent literary America of today — it represents only Henry Wadsworth Longfellow.

It might be answered that, after all, the Academy is limited to fifty members; that, naturally, it cannot include everyone of merit. But the fact is that while most of our few giants are excluded, the Academy does have room to include three extraordinarily bad poets, two very melodramatic and insignificant playwrights, two gentlemen who are known only because they are university presidents, a man who was thirty years ago known as a rather clever humorous drafts-man, and several gentlemen of whom — I sadly confess my ignorance — I have never heard.

Let me again emphasize the fact — for it is a fact — that I am not attacking the American Academy. It is a hospitable and generous and decidedly dignified institution. And it is not altogether the Academy's fault that it does not contain many of the men who have significance in our letters. Some-times it is the fault of those writers them-selves. I cannot imagine that grizzly bear Theodore Dreiser being comfortable at the serenely Athenian dinners of the Academy, and were they to invite Mencken, he would infuriate them with his boisterous jeering. No, I am not attacking — I am reluctantly considering the Academy because it is so perfect an example of the divorce in Ameri-ca of intellectual life from all authentic stan-dards of importance and reality.

Our universities and colleges, or gymna-sia, most of them, exhibit the same unfortu-nate divorce. I can think of four of them — Rollins College in Florida, Middlebury Col-lege in Vermont, the University of Michi-gan, and the University of Chicago — which has had on its roll so excellent a nov-elist as Robert Herrick, so courageous a critic as Robert Morss Lovett — which have shown an authentic interest in contem-porary creative literature. Four of them. But universities and colleges and musical empo-riums and schools for the teaching of theol-ogy and plumbing and sign painting are as thick in America as the motor traffic. Whenever you see a public building with Gothic fenestration on a sturdy backing of Indiana concrete, you may be certain that it is another university, with anywhere from 200 to 20,000 students equally ardent about avoiding the disadvantage of becom-ing learned and about gaining the social prestige contained in the possession of a B.A. degree.

Oh, socially our universities are close to the mass of our citizens, and so are they in the matter of athletics. A great college foot-ball game is passionately witnessed by 80,000 people, who have paid $5 apiece and motored anywhere from 10 to 1,000 miles for the ecstasy of watching 22 men chase one another up and down a curiously marked field. During the football season, a capable player ranks very nearly with our greatest and most admired heroes — even with Henry Ford, President Hoover, and Colonel Lindbergh.

And in one branch of learning, the sci-ences, the lords of business who rule us are willing to do homage to the devotees of learning. However bleakly one of our trader aristocrats may frown upon poetry or the visions of a painter, he is graciously pleased to endure a Millikan, a Michelson, a Bant-ing, a Theobald Smith.

But the paradox is that in the arts our universities are as cloistered, as far from re-ality and living creation, as socially and ath-letically and scientifically they are close to us. To a true-blue professor of literature in an American university, literature is not something that a plain human being, living today, painfully sits down to produce. No; it is something dead; it is something magi-cally produced by superhuman beings who must, if they are to be regarded as artists at all, have died at least one hundred years be-fore the diabolical invention of the type-writer. To any authentic don, there is some-thing slightly repulsive in the thought that literature could be created by any ordinary human being, still to be seen walking the streets, wearing quite commonplace trousers and coat and looking not so unlike a chauf-feur or a farmer. Our American professors like their literature clear and cold and pure and very dead.

I do not suppose that American universi-ties are alone in this. I am aware that to the dons of Oxford and Cambridge it would seem rather indecent to suggest that Wells and Bennett and Galsworthy and George

Moore may, while they commit the impropriety of continuing to live, be compared to any one so beautifully and safely dead as Samuel Johnson. I suppose that in the Universities of Sweden and France and Germany there exist plenty of professors who prefer dissection to understanding. But in the new and vital and experimental land of America, one would expect the teachers of literature to be less monastic, more human than in the traditional shadows of old Europe.

They are not.

There has recently appeared in America, out of the universities, an astonishing circus called "the New Humanism." Now, of course, "humanism" means so many things that it means nothing. It may infer anything from a belief that Greek and Latin are more inspiring than the dialect of contemporary peasants to a belief that any living peasant is more interesting than a dead Greek. But it is a delicate bit of justice that this nebulous word should have been chosen to label this nebulous cult.

Insofar as I have been able to comprehend them — for naturally in a world so exciting and promising as this today, a life brilliant with Zeppelins and Chinese revolutions and the Bolshevik industrialization of farming and ships and the Grand Canyon and young children and terrifying hunger and the lonely quest of scientists after God, no creative writer would have the time to follow all the chilly enthusiasms of the New Humanists — this newest of sects reasserts the dualism of man's nature. It would confine literature to the fight between man's soul and God, or man's soul and evil.

But, curiously, neither God nor the devil may wear modern dress, but must retain Grecian vestments. Oedipus is a tragic figure for the New Humanists; man, trying to maintain himself as the image of God under the menace of dynamos, in a world of high-pressure salesmanship, is not. And the poor comfort which they offer is that the object of life is to develop self-discipline — whether or not one ever accomplishes anything with this self-discipline. So thus the whole movement results in the not particularly novel doctrine that both art and life must be resigned and negative. It is a doctrine of the blackest reaction introduced into a stirringly revolutionary world.

Strangely enough, this doctrine of death, this escape from the complexities and danger of living into the secure blankness of the monastery, has become widely popular among professors in a land where one would have expected only boldness and intellectual adventure, and it has more than ever shut creative writers off from any benign influence which might conceivably have come from the universities.

But it has always been so. America has never had a Brandes, a Taine, a Goethe, a Croce.

With a wealth of creative talent in America, our criticism has most of it been a chill and insignificant activity pursued by jealous spinsters, ex-baseball reporters, and acid professors. Our Erasmuses have been village schoolmistresses. How should there be any standards when there has been no one capable of setting them up?

The great Cambridge-Concord circle of the middle of the 19th century — Emerson, Longfellow, Lowell, Holmes, the Alcotts — were sentimental reflections of Europe, and they left no school, no influence. Whitman and Thoreau and Poe and, in some degree, Hawthorne, were outcasts, men alone and despised, berated by the New Humanists of their generation. It was with the emergence of William Dean Howells that we first began to have something like a standard, and a very bad standard it was.

Mr. Howells was one of the gentlest, sweetest, and most honest of men, but he had the code of a pious old maid whose greatest delight was to have tea at the vicarage. He abhorred not only profanity and obscenity but all of what H. G. Wells has called "the jolly coarsenesses of life." In his fantastic vision of life, which he innocently conceived to be realistic, farmers and seamen and factory hands might exist, but the farmer must never be covered with muck, the seaman must never roll out bawdy chanteys, the factory hand must be thankful to his good kind employer, and all of them must long for the opportunity to visit Florence and smile gently at the quaintness of the beggars.

So strongly did Howells feel this genteel, this New Humanistic philosophy that he was able vastly to influence his contemporaries, down even to 1914 and the turmoil of the Great War.

He was actually able to tame Mark Twain, perhaps the greatest of our writers, and to put that fiery old savage into an intellectual frock coat and top hat. His influence is not altogether gone today. He is still worshiped by Hamlin Garland, an author who should in every way have been greater than Howells but who, under Howells' influence, was changed from a harsh and magnificent realist into a genial and insignificant lecturer. Mr. Garland is, so far as we have one, the dean of American letters today, and as our dean, he is alarmed by all of the younger writers who are so lacking in taste as to suggest that men and women do not always love in accordance with the prayer book, and that common people sometimes use language which would be inappropriate at a women's literary club on Main Street. Yet this same Hamlin Garland, as a young man, before he had gone to Boston and become cultured and Howellsized, wrote two most valiant and revelatory works of realism, *Main-Travelled Roads* and *Rose of Dutcher's Coolie.*

I read them as a boy in a prairie village in Minnesota — just such an environment as was described in Mr. Garland's tales. They were vastly exciting to me. I had realized in reading Balzac and Dickens that it was possible to describe French and English

common people as one actually saw them. But it had never occurred to me that one might without indecency write of the people of Sauk Centre, Minnesota, as one felt about them. Our fictional tradition, you see, was that all of us in Midwestern villages were altogether noble and happy; that not one of us would exchange the neighborly bliss of living on Main Street for the heathen gaudiness of New York or Paris or Stockholm. But in Mr. Garland's *Main-Travelled Roads,* I discovered that there was one man who believed that Midwestern peasants were sometimes bewildered and hungry and vile — and heroic. And given this vision, I was released; I could write of life as living life.

I am afraid that Mr. Garland would be not pleased but acutely annoyed to know that he made it possible for me to write of America as I see it and not as Mr. William Dean Howells so sunnily saw it. And it is his tragedy, it is a completely revelatory American tragedy, that in our land of freedom, men like Garland, who first blast the roads to freedom, become themselves the most bound.

But, all this time, while men like Howells were so effusively seeking to guide America into becoming a pale edition of an English cathedral town, there were surly and authentic fellows — Whitman and Melville, then Dreiser and James Huneker and Mencken — who insisted that our land had something more than tea-table gentility.

And so, without standards, we have survived. And for the strong young men, it has perhaps been well that we should have no standards. For, after seeming to be pessimistic about my own and much beloved land, I want to close this dirge with a very lively sound of optimism.

I have, for the future of American literature, every hope and every eager belief. We are coming out, I believe, of the stuffiness of safe, sane, and incredibly dull provincialism. There are young Americans today who are doing such passionate and authentic work that it makes me sick to see that I am a little too old to be one of them.

There is Ernest Hemingway, a bitter youth, educated by the most intense experience, disciplined by his own high standards, an authentic artist whose home is in the whole of life; there is Thomas Wolfe, a child of, I believe, thirty or younger, whose one and only novel, *Look Homeward, Angel,* is worthy to be compared with the best in our literary production, a Gargantuan creature with great gusto of life; there is Thornton Wilder, who in an age of realism dreams the old and lovely dreams of the eternal romantics; there is John Dos Passos, with his hatred of the safe and sane standards of Babbitt and his splendor of revolution; there is Stephen Benét, who, to American drabness, has restored the epic poem with his glorious memory of old John Brown; there are Michael Gold, who reveals the new frontier of the Jewish East Side, and William Faulkner, who has freed the South from hoopskirts; and there are a dozen other young poets and fictioneers, most of them living now in Paris, most of them a little insane in the tradition of James Joyce, who, however insane they may be, have refused to be genteel and traditional and dull.

I salute them, with a joy in being not yet too far removed from their determination to give to the America that has mountains and endless prairies, enormous cities and lost far cabins, billions of money and tons of faith, to an America that is as strange as Russia and as complex as China, a literature worthy of her vastness.

15.

Hart Crane: "To Brooklyn Bridge"

The Bridge, Hart Crane's major work, was conceived as an epic of America. In it Crane attempted to convey the energy and complexity of America in time and space and to express an American spirit that would include yet transcend the vulgarity and commercialism of the machine age. For his central and unifying image he chose the Brooklyn Bridge, a structure that he could contemplate from his home in Brooklyn Heights. "To Brooklyn Bridge," which is reprinted below, forms the Proem to The Bridge *and presents a cluster of ideas and moving images that reappear in the body of the poem.* The Bridge *was published in 1930 and won* Poetry *magazine's award for that year.*

Source: *Collected Poems,* Waldo Frank, ed., New York, 1933.

✥ TO BROOKLYN BRIDGE

How many dawns, chill from his rippling rest
The seagull's wings shall dip and pivot him,
Shedding white rings of tumult, building high
Over the chained bay waters Liberty —
Then, with inviolate curve, forsake our eyes

As apparitional as sails that cross
Some page of figures to be filed away;
— Till elevators drop us from our day . . .

I think of cinemas, panoramic sleights
With multitudes bent toward some flashing scene
Never disclosed, but hastened to again,
Foretold to other eyes on the same screen;

And Thee, across the harbor, silver-paced
As though the sun took step of thee, yet left
Some motion ever unspent in thy stride —
Implicitly thy freedom staying thee!

Out of some subway scuttle, cell or loft
A bedlamite speeds to thy parapets,
Tilting there momently, shrill shirt ballooning,
A jest falls from the speechless caravan.

Down Wall, from girder into street noon leaks,
A rip-tooth of the sky's acetylene;
All afternoon the cloud-flown derricks turn . . .
Thy cables breathe the North Atlantic still.

And obscure as that heaven of the Jews,
Thy guerdon . . . Accolade thou dost bestow
Of anonymity time cannot raise:
Vibrant reprieve and pardon thou dost show.

O harp and altar, of the fury fused,
(How could mere toil align thy choiring strings!)
Terrific threshold of the prophet's pledge,
Prayer of pariah, and the lover's cry —

Again the traffic lights that skim thy swift
Unfractioned idiom, immaculate sigh of stars,
Beading thy path — condense eternity:
And we have seen night lifted in thine arms.

Under thy shadow by the piers I waited;
Only in darkness is thy shadow clear.
The City's fiery parcels all undone,
Already snow submerges an iron year . . .

O Sleepless as the river under thee,
Vaulting the sea, the prairies' dreaming sod,
Unto us lowliest sometime sweep, descend
And of the curveship lend a myth to God.

1931

16.

Henry L. Stimson: The United States and the Caribbean

President Hoover and his secretary of state, Henry L. Stimson, abandoned the Wilsonian practice of refusing to recognize revolutionary governments in Latin America, repudiated the (Theodore) Roosevelt Corollary to the Monroe Doctrine, and determined not to interfere in internal Latin-American affairs. This change of heart anticipated the "Good Neighbor Policy" later proclaimed by Franklin D. Roosevelt — the term "good neighbor" having been given currency by Hoover in his pre-inaugural tour of the Caribbean. The speech by Stimson reprinted in part below, "The United States and the Other Republics," was first delivered to the Council of Foreign Relations in New York on February 6, 1931.

Source: U.S. Department of State, Latin American Series, No. 4, Publication No. 156, Washington, 1931.

DURING THE PAST TWO YEARS widespread economic depression and consequent unemployment have brought instability and unrest to many of the countries of the Western Hemisphere. Since March 1929, there have been revolutions in no less than seven Latin-American republics, resulting in the forcible overthrow in six of them of the existing governments. These changes, and the armed contests by which some of them have been accompanied, have presented to the State Department of this country a rapid succession of critical problems for decision. It was inevitable in such a situation that criticism of our decisions should be excited, and it has been.

Therefore, this evening, I shall place before you, from the standpoint of the State Department, a brief statement of the facts as well as of the underlying principles and reasons upon which some of these recent decisions have been based. In particular, I shall discuss the principles by which we have been guided in the recognition of the new governments which have arisen and also the principles which have underlain our action in the regulation of the sale and transportation of arms and munitions to the countries which have been involved in strife. . . .

From the beginning we have made the preservation of individual independence of these nations correspond with our own interest. This was announced in the Monroe

Doctrine and has been maintained ever since. That doctrine, far from being an assertion of suzerainty over our sister republics, was an assertion of their individual rights as independent nations. It declared to the world that this independence was so vital to our own safety that we would be willing to fight for it against an aggressive Europe. The Monroe Doctrine was a declaration of the United States versus Europe — not of the United States versus Latin America.

In taking this position in the Western Hemisphere, our policy has coincided with the basic conception of international law, namely, the equal rights of each nation in the family of nations. The law justly regards this conception as the chief protection of weak nations against oppression. Our people led in the recognition of the independence of those countries with an instinctive readiness which was based upon their sympathy with the doctrine upon which that independence rested. . . .

The very locality where the progress of these republics has been most slow; where the difficulties of race and climate have been greatest; where the recurrence of domestic violence has most frequently resulted in the failure of duty on the part of the republics themselves and the violation of the rights of life and property accorded by international law to foreigners within their territory, has been in Central America, the narrow isthmus which joins the two Americas, and among the islands which intersperse the Caribbean Sea adjacent to that isthmus. That locality has been the one spot external to our shores which nature has decreed to be most vital to our national safety, not to mention our prosperity. It commands the line of the great trade route which joins our Eastern and Western coasts.

Even before human hands had pierced the isthmus with a seagoing canal, that route was vital to our national interest. Since the Panama Canal has become an accomplished fact, it has been not only the vital artery of our coastwise commerce but, as well, the link in our national defense which protects the defensive power of our fleet. One cannot fairly appraise American policy toward Latin America or fully appreciate the standard which it has maintained without taking into consideration all of the elements of which it is the resultant. . . .

The practice of this country as to the recognition of new governments has been substantially uniform from the days of the administration of Secretary of State Jefferson in 1792 to the days of Secretary of State Bryan in 1913. There were certain slight departures from this policy during the Civil War, but they were manifestly due to the exigencies of warfare and were abandoned immediately afterwards. This general policy, as thus observed, was to base the act of recognition not upon the question of the constitutional legitimacy of the new government but upon its *de facto* capacity to fulfill its obligations as a member of the family of nations. This country recognized the right of other nations to regulate their own internal affairs of government and disclaimed any attempt to base its recognition upon the correctness of their constitutional action.

Said Mr. Jefferson in 1792:

> We certainly cannot deny to other nations that principle whereon our own government is founded, that every nation has a right to govern itself internally under what forms it pleases, and to change these forms at its own will; and externally to transact business with other nations through whatever organ it chooses, whether that be a king, convention, assembly, committee, president, or whatever it be. (*Jefferson to Pinckney, Works, Vol. III, p. 500.*)

In these essentials our practice corresponded with the practice of the other nations of the world. . . .

With the advent of President Wilson's administration, this policy of over a century was radically departed from in respect to

The Bettmann Archive

Henry Stimson (left) being congratulated by Frank Kellogg, acting secretary of state, at the time Stimson was appointed to that post in 1929

the Republic of Mexico, and, by a public declaration on March 11, 1913, it was announced that —

> Cooperation (with our sister republics of Central and South America) is possible only when supported at every turn by the orderly processes of just government based upon law, not upon arbitrary or irregular force. We hold, as I am sure that all thoughtful leaders of republican government everywhere hold, that just government rests always upon the consent of the governed, and that there can be no freedom without order based upon law and upon the public conscience and approval. We shall look to make these principles the basis of mutual intercourse, respect, and helpfulness between our sister republics and ourselves. (*Foreign Relations of the United States, 1913, p. 7.*)

Mr. Wilson's government sought to put this new policy into effect in respect to the recognition of the then government of Mexico held by President Victoriano Huerta. Although Huerta's government was in *de facto* possession, Mr. Wilson refused to recognize it, and he sought through the influence and pressure of his great office to force it from power. Armed conflict followed with the forces of Mexico, and disturbed relations between us and that republic lasted until a comparatively few years ago.

In his sympathy for the development of free constitutional institutions among the people of our Latin-American neighbors, Mr. Wilson did not differ from the feelings of the great mass of his countrymen in the United States, including Mr. Jefferson and Mr. Adams, whose statements I have quoted; but he differed from the practice of his predecessors in seeking actively to propagate these institutions in a foreign country by the direct influence of this government and to do this against the desire of the authorities and people of Mexico.

The present administration has refused to follow the policy of Mr. Wilson and has followed consistently the former practice of this government since the days of Jefferson. As soon as it was reported to us, through our diplomatic representatives, that the new governments in Bolivia, Peru, Argentina,

Brazil, and Panama were in control of the administrative machinery of the state, with the apparent general acquiescence of their people, and that they were willing and apparently able to discharge their international and conventional obligations, they were recognized by our government. And, in view of the economic depression, with the consequent need for prompt measures of financial stabilization, we did this with as little delay as possible in order to give those sorely pressed countries the quickest possible opportunities for recovering their economic poise.

Such has been our policy in all cases where international practice was not affected or controlled by preexisting treaty. In the five republics of Central America — Guatemala, Honduras, Salvador, Nicaragua, and Costa Rica — however, we have found an entirely different situation existing from that normally presented under international law and practice. . . . Those countries geographically have for a century been the focus of the greatest difficulties and the most frequent disturbances in their earnest course toward competent maturity in the discharge of their international obligations.

Until some two decades ago, war within and without was their almost yearly portion. No administration of their government was long safe from revolutionary attack instigated either by factions of its own citizens or by the machinations of another one of the five republics. Free elections, the cornerstone upon which our own democracy rests, had been practically unknown during the entire period. In 1907 a period of strife, involving four of the five republics, had lasted almost without interruption for several years.

In that year, on the joint suggestion and mediation of the governments of the United States and Mexico, the five republics met for the purpose of considering methods intended to mitigate and, if possible, terminate the intolerable situation. By one of the conventions which they then adopted, the five republics agreed with one another as follows:

The governments of the high contracting parties shall not recognize any other government which may come into power in any of the five republics as a consequence of a *coup d'état*, or of a revolution against the recognized government, so long as the freely elected representatives of the people thereof, have not constitutionally reorganized the country.

Sixteen years later, in 1923, the same five republics, evidently satisfied with the principle they had thus adopted and desiring to reinforce it and prevent any future evasions of that principle, met again, reenacted the same covenant, and further promised each other that even after a revolutionary government had been constitutionally reorganized by the representatives of the people, they would not recognize it if its president should have been a leader in the preceding revolution or related to such a leader by blood or marriage, or if he should have been a cabinet officer or held some high military command during the accomplishment of the revolution. Some four months thereafter, our own government, on the invitation of these republics, who had conducted their meeting in Washington, announced through Secretary Hughes that the United States would in its future dealings with those republics follow out the same principle which they had thus established in their treaty. Since that time we have consistently adhered to this policy in respect to those five republics.

We followed that policy in Guatemala in the case of a recent revolution in which some fifty-seven people were killed. General Orellano, the leader of the revolt, set himself up as the provisional president of that republic on December 16, 1930. On Dec. 22, 1930, we notified him that in accordance with the policy established by the 1923 treaty he would not be recognized by us. No recognition was granted him by any of the other four republics. Following this, he tendered his resignation and retired from office; and on Jan. 2, 1931, through the constitutional forms provided in the Guatemalan constitution, Señor Reina Andrade was chosen provisional president by the Guatemalan Congress and immediately called a new election for a permanent president. Thereupon, this country and the other four republics recognized the government of Señor Reina Andrade.

Since the adoption by Secretary Hughes, in 1923, of the policy of recognition agreed upon by the five republics in their convention, not one single revolutionary government has been able to maintain itself in those five republics. Twice, once in Nicaragua and once in the case of Guatemala, just described, a revolutionary leader has succeeded in grasping the reins of government for a brief period. But in each case the failure to obtain recognition has resulted in his prompt resignation on account of his inability to borrow money in the international markets.

Several times within the same period a contemplated revolution has been abandoned by its conspirators on the simple reminder by a minister from this country or one of the other republics that, even if they were successful, their government would not be recognized; and undoubtedly in many more cases has the knowledge of the existence of the policy prevented even the preparation for a revolution or *coup d'état.* In every one of these cases the other four republics have made common cause in the efforts of the United States to carry out their policy and maintain stability. When one compares this record with the blood-stained history of Central America before the adoption of the treaty of 1923, I think that no impartial student can avoid the conclusion that the treaty and the policy which it has established in that locality has been productive of very great good.

Of course it is a departure from the regular international practice of our government,

and it undoubtedly contains possible difficulties and dangers of application which we in the State Department are the last to minimize and in case of which, should they arise, this government must reserve its freedom of action. But the distinction between this departure, which was suggested by the five republics themselves and in which we have acted at their earnest desire and in cooperation with them, and the departure taken by President Wilson in an attempt to force upon Mexico a policy which she resented, must be apparent to the most thoughtless student.

A few weeks ago Judge John Bassett Moore, who as counselor of the State Department was a member of Mr. Wilson's administration, criticized Mr. Wilson's departure from the former practice of this country, and he included within his criticism the departure initiated by the treaty of 1923. He did not, however, point out the foregoing radical difference of principle between the two policies, nor the entirely different results which have followed each, and which thus far seem quite to justify the policy of 1923.

Furthermore, it may be noted that one of the dangers which might be apprehended from this policy of recognition adopted by the five Central American republics under the treaty of 1923 has not materialized. One of the most serious evils in Central America has been the fact that throughout the history of those republics, until recently, it has been the habitual practice of the president who held the machinery of government to influence and control the election of his successor. This has tended to stimulate revolution as the only means by which a change of government could be accomplished.

The danger was therefore manifest that this treaty of 1923 might result in perpetuating the autocratic power of the governments which were for the time in possession. As a matter of fact, this has not happened. On the contrary, significant improvement has taken place in election practice. The government of Nicaragua of its own motion has sought and obtained the assistance of the United States in securing free and uncontrolled elections in 1928 and 1930. The government of Honduras, in 1928, without any such assistance, conducted an election which was so free that the party in power was dispossessed by the opposition party; and a similar free election has apparently occurred in 1930.

For nearly one hundred years before 1923, free elections have been so rare in Central America as to be almost unique. Of course, it is too early to make safe generalizations, but it would seem that the stability created by the treaty of 1923 apparently has not tended to perpetuate existing autocracies but, on the contrary, to stimulate a greater sense of responsibility in elections.

I will now pass to the subject of the policy of this government in respect to the export of arms and munitions to countries which are engaged in civil strife. Twice during the present administration, we have had to make important decisions and take important action in respect to this subject. The first of these occasions was in March 1929 when a military insurrection broke out in the Republic of Mexico. This insurrection was of serious nature and extent. It involved disturbances in many of the Mexican provinces and much fighting and bloodshed. Acting under a joint resolution of our Congress, adopted in 1922, this government maintained an embargo upon the exportation of all arms and munitions which might reach the rebels. At the same time, it permitted the sale and itself sold arms and ammunition to the established government of Mexico, with which we were then and had been for a number of years in diplomatic relations. In about three months the insurrection was suppressed, and I think it can be fairly said that it is due in no slight degree to our action in this matter that the feelings of hostility on the part of Mexico to the United States which had existed ever since the intervention of President Wilson against Huerta in 1913 were finally ended and the relations of the two countries became friendly and cordial.

The second occasion was in October 1930 when armed insurrection had broken out against the government of Brazil. In the same way in which we had acted toward Mexico, we permitted that government to purchase arms both from our government and from our nationals in this country; and, when the ambassador of Brazil brought to our attention the fact that arms were being purchased in this country for export to the rebel forces fighting against the recognized government, we placed an embargo against the exportation of such arms. Two days later the government of Brazil suddenly fell, the immediate cause being the revolt of its own garrison in Rio de Janeiro.

In placing the embargo upon the exportation of arms to the Brazilian rebel forces, our government acted under the same joint resolution of our Congress of 1922 and with the same purpose and upon the same policy as had guided our action in the case of Mexico and in other cases where action has been taken under that resolution. That purpose was "to prevent arms and munitions procured from the United States being used to promote conditions of domestic violence" in countries whose governments we had recognized and with which we were in friendly intercourse. This was the purpose and policy as stated by our Congress in the language of the resolution itself. . . .

Under the law of nations the duty of neutrality does not arise until the insurgents have assumed the status of a belligerent power between whom and the mother country other governments must maintain impartiality. This occurs when a condition of belligerency is recognized either by the parent state itself or by the governments of other nations. Such a situation arose in our Civil War when the Confederate States, having occupied exclusively a portion of the territory of the United States and having set up their own capital at Richmond, were recognized as belligerents by the nations of Europe. It has not arisen in any of the recent revolutions of Latin America, whether successful or unsuccessful.

The revolutionists in Brazil had not been recognized as belligerents either by the Brazilian government, by the United States, or by any other nation. Until that happens, under the law and practice of nations, no duty of impartiality arises either on the part of our government or our citizens. Until that time there is only one side toward which, under international law, other nations owe any duty. . . .

Until belligerency is recognized and the duty of neutrality arises, all the humane predispositions toward stability of government, the preservation of international amity, and the protection of established intercourse between nations are in favor of the existing government. This is particularly the case in countries where civil strife has been as frequent, as personal, and as disastrous as it has been in some sections of Central and South America during the past century. The law of nations is not static. It grows and develops with the experience of mankind, and its development follows the line of human predispositions and experiences such as those to which I have referred.

17.

E. E. Cummings: "i sing of Olaf"

"i sing of Olaf" typifies much of E. E. Cummings' poetry: it is manly, it focuses on the inhumanity occasioned by war, and it is obscene, graphic, and nonintellectual. Despite the unconventional appearance of the poem — it lacks, like all of Cummings' work, punctuation marks and capitals — the rhythm and rhyme scheme make it easy to read. "i sing of Olaf" displays the poet's talent for evoking tenderness, anger, and laughter all at the same time, and it is this talent that probably accounts for the fact that Cummings' poems have survived the period of postwar disillusionment and experimentation that shaped his early writing.

Source: *Collected Poems*, New York, 1963.

ஐ I SING OF OLAF

i sing of Olaf glad and big
whose warmest heart recoiled at war:
a conscientious object-or

his wellbelovéd colonel(trig
westpointer most succinctly bred)
took erring Olaf soon in hand;
but — though an host of overjoyed
noncoms(first knocking on the head

him) do through icy waters roll
that helplessness which others stroke
with brushes recently employed
anent this muddy toiletbowl,
while kindred intellects evoke
allegiance per blunt instruments —
Olaf(being to all intents
a corpse and wanting any rag
upon what God unto him gave)

responds,without getting annoyed
"I will not kiss your f.ing flag"

straightway the silver bird looked grave
(departing hurriedly to shave)

but — though all kinds of officers
(a yearning nation's blueeyed pride)
their passive prey did kick and curse
until for wear their clarion
voices and boots were much the worse,
and egged the firstclassprivates on
his rectum wickedly to tease
by means of skilfully applied
bayonets roasted hot with heat —

Olaf(upon what were once knees)
does almost ceaselessly repeat
"there is some s. I will not eat"

our president,being of which
assertions duly notified
threw the yellowsonofabitch
into a dungeon,where he died

Christ(of His mercy infinite)
i pray to see;and Olaf,too

preponderatingly because
unless statistics lie he was
more brave than me:more blond than you.

18.

HERBERT HOOVER: Veto of the Muscle Shoals Bill

The construction of plants for manufacturing fertilizer and nitrates as well as dams to
supply the plants with power had been undertaken in 1918 as a wartime measure along
a 35 mile strip of land called Muscle Shoals on the Tennessee River. After the war
a congressional group headed by Senator George W. Norris of Nebraska urged the
government to complete the project, run the plants, and sell the surplus power. It was
presumed that by selling the surplus power the government could establish lower rates
that private utility companies would be forced to meet. In 1928 a bill authorizing the
government to run the plants passed Congress but was vetoed by President Coolidge.
In 1931 President Hoover vetoed a similar bill. His veto message, which was
delivered to the Senate on March 3, 1931, and is reprinted below in part, summarized
his case against the federal government's participation in business.

Source: *Record*, 71 Cong., 3 Sess., pp. 7046-7048.

I RETURN HEREWITH, without my approval, Senate Joint Resolution 49, to provide for the national defense by the creation of a corporation for the operation of the government properties at and near Muscle Shoals in the state of Alabama; to authorize the letting of the Muscle Shoals properties under certain conditions; and for other purposes.

This bill proposes the transformation of the war plant at Muscle Shoals, together with important expansions, into a permanently operated government institution for the production and distribution of power and the manufacture of fertilizers . . . to provide production and wholesale distribution of surplus power and to give preference to states, municipalities, and cooperative organizations. It further provides that the policy of the government must be to distribute the surplus power equitably among states, counties, and municipalities within transmission distance of Muscle Shoals and provides for the construction of transmission lines to effect this purpose. Such a transmission system for wholesale purposes only is estimated to cost $40 million. If it is proposed to sell power at retail to householders, then there would need be a great increase in the estimates of capital outlay and operation costs for such distribution. . . .

The plants at Muscle Shoals were originally built for a production of nitrates for use in war explosives. I am advised by the War Department that the very large development in the United States by private enterprise in the manufacture of synthetic nitrogen now affords an ample supply covering any possible requirements of war. It is therefore unnecessary to maintain this plant for any such purposes.

This bill provides that the President, for a period of twelve months, may negotiate a lease of the nitrate plants for fertilizer manufacture under detailed limitations, but in failure to make such a lease the bill makes it mandatory upon the government to manufacture nitrogen fertilizers at Muscle Shoals by the employment of existing facilities or by modernizing existing plants or by any other process. I may state at once that the limitations put upon lessees in the bill are such that this provision is of no genuine importance.

Inquiries have been made of the most responsible and experienced concerns that might possibly undertake such lease and they have replied that under the conditions set out in the bill it is entirely impractical for them to make any bid. The leasing provision is therefore of no utility; it may at once be dismissed. In consequence, the project we have to consider under this bill is the manufacture of fertilizers by the federal government.

The Department of Agriculture reports that these plants are now more or less obsolete and that with power at even two mills per kilowatt-hour, with proper charges included, could not produce the products for which they are constructed as cheaply as these products are now being sold in the wholesale markets. Therefore, it would be necessary to modernize the equipment at an unknown cost in millions. There is no evidence as to the costs of nitrogen fertilizers by the newer equipment, and there is therefore no basis upon which to estimate the results to the government from entering upon such a competitive business. It can, however, be stated with assurance that no chemical industry with its constantly changing technology and equipment, its intricate problems of sales and distribution can be successfully conducted by the government. . . .

I am firmly opposed to the government entering into any business the major purpose of which is competition with our citizens. There are national emergencies which require that the government should temporarily enter the field of business, but they must be emergency actions and in matters where the cost of the project is secondary to much higher considerations. There are many localities where the federal government is justified in the construction of great dams and reservoirs, where navigation, flood control, reclamation, or stream regulation are of dominant importance, and where they are beyond the capacity or purpose of private or local government capital to construct. In these cases power is often a by-product and should be disposed of by contract or lease. But for the federal government deliberately to go out to build up and expand such an occasion to the major purpose of a power and manufacturing business is to break down the initiative and enterprise of the American people; it is destruction of equality of opportunity among our people; it is the negation of the ideals upon which our civilization has been based.

This bill raises one of the important is-

sues confronting our people. That is squarely the issue of federal government ownership and operation of power and manufacturing business not as a minor by-product
but as a major purpose. Involved in this
question is the agitation against the conduct
of the power industry. The power problem
is not to be solved by the federal government going into the power business, nor is
it to be solved by the project in this bill.
The remedy for abuses in the conduct of
that industry lies in regulation and not by
the federal government entering upon the
business itself.

I have recommended to the Congress on
various occasions that action should be
taken to establish federal regulation of interstate power in cooperation with state authorities. This bill would launch the federal
government upon a policy of ownership and
operation of power utilities upon a basis of
competition instead of by the proper government function of regulation for the protection of all the people. I hesitate to contemplate the future of our institutions, of
our government, and of our country if the
preoccupation of its officials is to be no longer the promotion of justice and equal opportunity but is to be devoted to barter in
the markets. That is not liberalism, it is degeneration.

This proposal can be effectively opposed
upon other and perhaps narrower grounds.
The establishment of a federal-operated
power business and fertilizer factory in the
Tennessee Valley means federal control
from Washington with all the vicissitudes of
national politics and the tyrannies of remote
bureaucracy imposed upon the people of
that valley without voice by them in their
own resources; the overriding of state and
local government; the undermining of state
and local responsibility. The very history of
this project over the past ten years should
be a complete demonstration of the ineptness of the federal government to administer such enterprise and of the penalties
which the local communities suffer under it.

This bill distinctly proposes to enter the
field of powers reserved to the states. It
would deprive the adjacent states of the
right to control rates for this power, and
would deprive them of taxes on property
within their borders, and would invade and
weaken the authority of local government.

Aside from the wider issues involved, the
immediate effect of this legislation would be
that no other development of power could
take place on the Tennessee River with the
government in that field. That river contains two or three millions of potential
horsepower, but the threat of the subjection
of that area to a competition which under
this bill carries no responsibility to earn interest on the investment or taxes will either
destroy the possibility of private development of the great resources of the river or
alternately impose the extension of this development upon the federal government. It
would appear that this latter is the course
desired by many proponents of this bill.
There are many other objections which can
be raised to this bill, of lesser importance
but in themselves a warranty for its disapproval.

It must be understood that these criticisms are directed to the project as set up in
this bill; they are not directed to the possibilities of a project denuded of uneconomic
and unsound provisions, nor is it a reflection upon the value of these resources.

I sympathize greatly with the desire of
the people of Tennessee and Alabama to
see this great asset turned to practical use.
It can be so turned and to their benefit. I
am loath to leave a subject of this character
without a suggestion for solution. Congress
has been thwarted for ten years in finding
solution by rivalry of private interests and
by the determination of certain groups to
commit the federal government to government ownership and operation of power.

The real development of the resources
and the industries of the Tennessee Valley
can only be accomplished by the people in
that valley themselves. Muscle Shoals can

only be administered by the people upon the ground, responsible to their own communities, directing them solely for the benefit of their communities and not for purposes of pursuit of social theories or national politics. Any other course deprives them of liberty.

I would therefore suggest that the states of Alabama and Tennessee, who are the ones primarily concerned, should set up a commission of their own representatives, together with a representative from the national farm organizations and the Corps of Army Engineers; that there be vested in that commission full authority to lease the plants at Muscle Shoals in the interest of the local community and agriculture generally. It could lease the nitrate plants to the advantage of agriculture. The power plant is today earning a margin over operating expenses. Such a commission could increase this margin without further capital outlay and should be required to use all such margins for the benefit of agriculture.

19.

State-Controlled Apprenticeship in Wisconsin

The first modern American system of apprenticeship training was put into effect in 1915 by the state of Wisconsin, a leader in the field of labor legislation. The term "apprentice" applied to every minor, sixteen years or older, who was to receive instruction in a trade or business in partial recompense for his labor. The indenture agreement had to be written and filed with the Industrial Commission of Wisconsin, and the Commission had the power to change and enforce it. Below is reprinted the Commission's biennial report on the apprenticeship system for the years 1928-1930, which was issued in 1931. In 1937 the U.S. Department of Labor wrote a standard apprenticeship law similar to that used in Wisconsin and urged the states to adopt it.

Source: Industrial Commission of Wisconsin, Biennial Report 1928-1930, Madison, 1931, pp. 45-46.

WISCONSIN'S STATE-CONTROLLED apprenticeship system, the only one of its kind in the country, is designed to establish training programs in the trades for the benefit, not alone of the learner but for the trade generally, and for the good of the public. There is only one public trade school in the state, Wisconsin believing that the place to learn a trade is on the job in industry. Consequently, the state encourages the development of apprenticeship from every angle.

Employers are permitted under the terms of the apprenticeship law to enter into apprenticeship agreements with minors, a copy of each agreement being filed with the Industrial Commission. In these agreements the employer promises to fulfill certain obligations toward the learner, and the apprentice agrees to faithfully serve a full term of training. The Commission in turn supervises the training of apprentices.

Free related technical trade instruction is furnished by the public schools, and apprentices are required to attend 4 hours weekly for a minimum of 400 hours, for which time apprentices are paid by their employers at the same rate of wages as for services on the job. A great many apprentices attend as many as 500 and 600 hours on pay in the course of their apprenticeship, which is an indication that management favors the idea.

In formulating rules and regulations and in promoting apprenticeship generally, the Industrial Commission's policy is to seek the cooperation and advice of those actively engaged in industry. Many addresses are given before state conventions of the various trades and before meetings of city trade organizations. Numerous state and local joint advisory committees, consisting of three or four men representing organized labor and as many representing employers, have been formed for the purpose of closer cooperation and understanding. As a result, Wisconsin's apprenticeship plan is supported by both management and organized labor.

Practically all of the larger employers, principally the metal trades, are doing much more for their apprentices than is expected of them under the terms of the appren-

ticeship law. In addition to sending their apprentices to school for more than the required 400 hours, many employers provide special related instruction in shop classrooms. Instructors, too, work directly with apprentices in the shop, these instructors being hired by the employer. Also, most of the large companies employ apprentice supervisors who have charge of all apprenticeship activities within the plant.

On Aug. 1, 1930, there were 3,350 live apprenticeship contracts on file.

During the past two years, 1,420 new indentures were entered into. During the same period, 654 apprentices completed an average four-year apprenticeship and were given diplomas by the Industrial Commission.

Since 1915, when the present apprenticeship law was adopted, a total of 2,567 indentured apprentices completed their terms of training.

20.

Charles A. Beard: The Myth of Rugged American Individualism

For historian Charles A. Beard the economic collapse that followed the stock market crash of 1929 had proved with finality, if American economic history had not demonstrated it long before, the unworkability of the philosophy of rugged individualism that businessmen and their apologists still clung to even after two years of unprecedented depression. In an article for Harper's *in 1931 that was issued as a pamphlet the following year, he pointed out the dependence business had always had on government control and emphasized the need for national planning. Beard had been a leading Progressive and was to become an ardent defender of the New Deal.*

Source: *The Myth of Rugged American Individualism*, New York, 1932.

"The House of Bishops would be as much at sea in Minneapolis as at Atlantic City." This bit of delicious humor, all too rare in America's solemn assemblies, sparkled at a tense moment in the late conference of the

Episcopalian magnates at Denver when the respective merits of the two cities as future meeting places were under debate. But the real cause of the caustic comment seems to have been a heated discussion, led by the

Honorable George W. Wickersham, over a dangerous proposal to modify, not the Volstead Act but the sacred creed of rugged American individualism.

That contest had been precipitated by the report of a special commission in which occurred these highly inflammatory words: "It is becoming increasingly evident that the conception of society as made up of autonomous, independent individuals is as faulty from the point of view of economic realism as it is from the standpoint of Christian idealism. Our fundamental philosophy of rugged individualism must be modified to meet the needs of a cooperative age." This frightful conclusion flowed from a fact statement which the commission summarized in the following language: "Side by side with such misery and idleness, there are warehouses bursting with goods which cannot be bought; elevators full of wheat while breadlines haunt our cities; carefully protected machinery lying idle, while jobless men throng our streets; money in the banks available at low rates."

These shocking passages Mr. Wickersham read to the assembled delegates with considerable indignation and denied their truth. Then he added an illuminating exposition all his own: "I think this is an expression of a social philosophy that is expressed by the Soviet government of Russia. It is a negation of the whole concept of American civilization. I think it would be a sad day when the American people abandon the principles on which they have grown to greatness." Coming to specifications, he particularly attacked a point in the report, that "compulsory unemployment insurance is feasible." Realizing that Mr. Wickersham was a specialist in individualism, since he was the chief author of a collective report from which each individual signer apparently dissented, the congregated deputies at Denver voted down the proposal that the commission's statement should be taken as "representing the mind of the Church," and substituted a mere pious recommendation that

it should be given "careful consideration" by members of the Church. Such, at least, is the story reported in the press.

This is only one of many straws in the wind indicating a movement to exalt rugged individualism into a national taboo beyond the reach of inquiring minds. From day to day it becomes increasingly evident that some of our economic leaders (by no means all of them) are using the phrase as an excuse for avoiding responsibility, for laying the present depression on "government interference," and for seeking to escape from certain forms of taxation and regulation which they do not find to their interest. If a smoke screen big enough can be laid on the land, our commercial prestidigitators may work wonders — for themselves.

Still more direct evidence confirms this view. For example, in the autumn of 1930, a New York bank published, as a kind of revelation from on high, a slashing attack on "government interference with business," written by that stanch English Whig, Macaulay, a hundred years ago; and a few weeks later one of the leading advertising firms took a whole page in the *New York Times* to blazon forth the creed anew under the captivating head: "Cheer Up! Our Best Times Are Still Ahead of Us!" And the whole gospel was summed up in these words from Macaulay:

> Our rulers will best promote the improvement of the people by strictly confining themselves to their own legitimate duties — by leaving capital to find its most lucrative course, commodities their fair price, industry and intelligence their natural reward, idleness and folly their natural punishment — by maintaining peace, by defending property, by diminishing the price of law, and by observing strict economy in every department of the state. Let the government do this — the people will assuredly do the rest.

In other words, here was put forth in the name of American business, with all the pontifical assurance that characterized Macaulay's shallowest sophistry, the pure creed of historic individualism, and here was served on the government and people of the United States a warning revelation of confident expectations.

A year later, in a release to the press, Mr. Otto Kahn discussed the subject of planning and intimated that the fortunate position of France today is to be ascribed to the fact that the French government interferes less with business than does the government of Germany or Great Britain, with the implication that the United States might profit from this experience. About the same time the Honorable Newton D. Baker made a long address at Williamstown which was evidently designed to show that nothing important could be done in the present crisis by the federal government, except perhaps in the way of tariff reduction by international agreement. And now comes from Chicago the announcement that a number of rugged businessmen are forming a national association to combat government in business, to break up this unholy alliance.

There is not a professional lunching-and-dining fellowship in America that is not now applauding to the echo such ringing cries as "Let Us Alone," "Take Government Out of Business," "Hands Off," "Unburden Capital." With an eye on such straws in the wind, President Hoover publicly states that all notions about planned economy come out of Russia, thus placing such distinguished men as Gerard Swope and Owen D. Young under the horrible Red ban. As one of the high-powered utility propagandists recently explained, the best way to discredit an opponent is to pin a Red tag on him — without reference to his deserts, of course.

II

HENCE IT IS IMPORTANT TO ASK, calmly and without reference to election heats, just what all this means. In what way is the government "in business" and how did it

The Bettmann Archive

Charles Austin Beard, American historian and educator, whose writings in the 1930s focused on the American foreign policy

get there? Here we climb down out of the muggy atmosphere of controversy and face a few stubborn facts. They are entered in the indubitable records of the government of the United States and are as evident as the hills to them that have eyes to see. Let us catalogue a few of them *seriatim* for the first time in the history of this adventure in logomachy.

1. *Government Regulation of Railways, from 1887 to the last Act of Congress.* How did the government get into this business? The general cause was the conduct of railway corporations under the rule of rugged individualism — rebates, pools, stock watering, bankruptcy-juggling, all the traffic will bear, savage rate slashing, merciless competition, and the rest of it. If anyone wants to know the facts, let him read the history of railroading in the sixties, seventies, and early eighties, or, if time is limited, the charming illustrations presented in Charles Francis Adams' *A Chapter of Erie.* And what was the immediate cause of the government's intervention? The insistence of businessmen, that is, shippers, who were harassed and

sometimes ruined by railway tactics, and of farmers, the most rugged of all the rugged individualists the broad land of America has produced.

And the result? Let the gentle reader compare the disastrous railway bankruptcies that flowed from the panic of 1873, including bloodshed and arson, with the plight of railways now, bad as it is. Government regulation is not a utopian success, but it is doubtful whether any of our great businessmen would like to get the government entirely out of this business and return to the magnificent anarchy of Jay Gould's age. President Hoover has not even suggested it.

2. *Waterways.* Since its foundation the government has poured hundreds of millions into rivers, harbors, canals, and other internal improvements. It is still pouring in millions. Some of our best economists have denounced it as wasteful and have demonstrated that most of it does not pay in any sense of the word. But President Hoover, instead of leaving this work to private enterprise, insists on projecting and executing the most elaborate undertakings, in spite of the fact that some of them are unfair, if not ruinous, to railways. Who is back of all this? Businessmen and farmers who want lower freight rates. There is not a Chamber of Commerce on any Buck Creek in America that will not cheer until tonsils are cracked any proposal to make the said creek navigable. Dredging companies want the good work to go on, and so do the concerns that make dredging machinery. Farmers are for it also and they are, as already said, the ruggedest of rugged individuals — so rugged in fact that the vigorous efforts of the Farm Board to instill cooperative reason into them have been almost as water on a duck's back.

3. *The United States Barge Corporation.* Who got the government into the job of running barges on some of its improved waterways? Certainly not the Socialists, but good Republicans and Democrats speaking for the gentlemen listed under 2 above.

4. *The Shipping Business.* The World War was the occasion but not the cause of this departure. For more than half a century the politicians of America fought ship subsidies against businessmen engaged in the shipbuilding and allied industries. At last, under the cover of war necessities, the government went into the shipping business, with cheers from business. Who is back of the huge expenditures for the merchant marine? Businessmen. Who supports huge subsidies under the guise of "lucrative mail contracts," making a deficit in postal finances to be used as proof that the government cannot run any business? Businessmen clamor for these mail subsidies and receive them. Who put the government into the business of providing cheap money for shipbuilding? Businessmen did it.

Those who are curious to know how these things were done may profitably read the sworn testimony presented during the investigation of W. B. Shearer's patriotic labors on behalf of the shipbuilding interests, especially the exhibits showing how money was spent like water "educating" politicians. Who wants Navy officers on half pay to serve on privately owned ships? Businessmen. Who wants the government to keep on operating ships on "pioneer" lines that do not pay? Businessmen. And when the United States Senate gets around to investigating this branch of business, it will find more entertainment than the Trade Commission has found in the utility inquest.

5. *Aviation.* The government is "in" this business. It provides costly airway services free of charge and subsidizes airmail. Who is behind this form of government enterprise? Gentlemen engaged in aviation and the manufacture of planes and dirigibles. Then the government helps by buying planes for national defense. Who is opposed to airmail subsidies? A few despised "politicians."

6. *Canals.* Who zealously supported the construction of the Panama Canal? Shippers on the Pacific Coast who did not like

the railway rates. Also certain important shipping interests on both coasts — all controlled by businessmen. Who insisted that the government should buy the Cape Cod Canal? The businessmen who put their money into the enterprise and found that it did not pay. Then they rejoiced to see the burden placed on the broad back of our dear Uncle Sam.

7. *Highway Building.* Who has supported federal highway aid — the expenditures of hundreds of millions on roads, involving the taxation of railways to pay for ruinous competition? Everybody, apparently, but specifically businessmen engaged in the manufacture and sale of automobiles and trucks. Who proposes to cut off every cent of that outlay? Echoes do not answer.

8. *The Department of Commerce,* its magnificent mansion near the Treasury Department, and its army of hustlers scouting for business at the uttermost ends of the earth. Who is responsible for loading on the government the job of big drummer at large for business? Why shouldn't these rugged individualists do their own drumming instead of asking the taxpayers to do it for them? Businessmen have been behind this enormous expansion, and Mr. Hoover, as secretary of commerce, outdid every predecessor in the range of his activities and the expenditure of public money. Who proposes to take the government out of the business of hunting business for men who ought to know their own business?

9. *The Big Pork Barrel* — appropriations for public buildings, Navy yards, and Army posts. An interesting enterprise for the United States Chamber of Commerce would be to discover a single piece of pork in a hundred years that has not been approved by local businessmen as beneficiaries. When Ben Tillman shouted in the Senate that he intended to steal a hog every time a Yankee got a ham, he knew for whom the speaking was done.

10. *The Bureau of Standards.* Besides its general services, it renders valuable aid to business undertakings. Why shouldn't they do their own investigating at their own expense, instead of turning to the government?

11. *The Federal Trade Commission.* Who runs there for rulings on "fair practices"? Weary consumers? Not often. Principally, businessmen who do not like to be outwitted or cheated by their competitors. If we are rugged individualists, why not let every individualist do as he pleases, without invoking government intervention at public expense?

12. *The Antitrust Acts.* Businessmen are complaining against these laws on the ground that they cannot do any large-scale planning without incurring the risk of prosecution. The contention is sound, but who put these laws on the books and on what theory were they based? They were the product of a clamor on the part of farmers and businessmen against the practices of great corporations. Farmers wanted lower prices. Businessmen of the smaller variety objected to being undersold, beaten by clever tricks, or crushed to the wall by competitors with immense capital. And what was the philosophy behind the Sherman Act and the Clayton Act? Individualism, pure and undefiled. "The New Freedom" as President Wilson phrased it in literary language. "Break up the trusts and let each tub stand on its own bottom." That was the cry among little businessmen. As lawyers put it, in their somber way, "The natural person's liberty should not be destroyed by artificial persons known as corporations created under the auspices of the state." Whether any particular businessman is for or against the antitrust laws depends upon his particular business and the state of its earnings.

13. *The Tariff.* On this tender subject it is scarcely possible to speak soberly. It seems safe to say, however, that if all the businessmen who demand this kind of "interference" — with the right of capital to find its most lucrative course, industry and

intelligence their natural reward, commodities their fair price, and idleness and folly their natural punishment — were to withdraw their support for protection, cease their insistence on it, then the politicians would probably reduce the levy or go over to free trade; with what effect on business no one can correctly predict. At all events there are thousands of businessmen who want to keep the government in the business of protecting their business against foreign competition. If competition is good, why not stand up and take it?

14. *The Federal Farm Board.* This collectivist institution is the product of agrarian agitation, on the part of our most stalwart individualists, the free and independent farmers; but President Hoover sponsored it and signed the bill that created it. Now what is its avowed purpose as demonstrated by the language of the statute, the publications of the Farm Board, and the activities carried out under its auspices? It is primarily and fundamentally intended to stabilize prices and production through cooperative methods.

And what has the Board done? It has encouraged the development of cooperation as distinguished from individualism among farmers; it has financed cooperative associations; it has denounced individualistic farmers who insist on growing as much as they please, and has tried to get them to increase their earnings by a common limitation of production. If the Agricultural Marketing Act means anything, if the procedure of the Farm Board is not a delusion, then cooperation is to be substituted for individualism in agricultural production and marketing. If there is ever to be a rational adjustment of supply to demand in this field, the spirit and letter of President Hoover's measure must be realized through organized action by millions of farmers under federal auspices.

The other alternative is simon-pure individualism: let each farmer produce what he likes, as much of it as he likes, and sell it at any price he can get. But under the happy title "Grow Less — Get More," the Farm Board has given instructions to farmers: "One thing the successful manufacturers learned long ago was that they could not make money when they produced more than they could sell at a profit." The obvious moral is for farmers to get together under government leadership or hang separately.

15. *The Moratorium and Frozen Assets.* The latest form of government interferences with "the natural course" of economy is the suspension of payments due the United States from foreign powers on account of lawful debts and the proposal to give public support to "frozen assets." What was the source of inspiration here? American investment bankers having got themselves into a jam in their efforts to make easy money now demand government assistance. In 1927 one of the most distinguished German economists told the writer of this article that the great game in his country, as in other parts of Europe, was to borrow billions from private bankers in the United States, so that it would ultimately be impossible to pay reparations, the debts due the federal government, *and* then the debts owed to private parties. The expected result? American bankers would then force their government to forgo its claims for the benefit of private operators who wanted to make bankers' commissions and 8 or 10 percent on their money. Well, the game worked. American taxpayers are to be soaked and American bankers are to collect — perhaps.

And what is a "frozen asset"? It is a gaudy name for a piece of paper representing a transaction in which the holder expected to get a larger return than was possible on a prudent, rock-bottom investment. A Hartford, Connecticut, municipal four is not frozen; a holder can get better than par in the present dark hour of Wall Street's sorrows. A 7 percent Western farm mortgage is frozen tight — and ought to be, and the holder frozen with it. So is a Bolivian seven. Why should there be federal interference to save investors from reaping the fruits of their folly and greed? No reason, except that the latter want the government to bring home their cake so that they can eat it. The trouble is that American capital, in finding "its most lucrative course," has fallen into a slough, and if it gets out with its gains intact the government must bring a derrick to hoist it.

III

IN THIS SURVEY OF A FEW leading economic activities of the federal government, the emphasis is not critical; so far as the present argument is concerned, any or all of these functions may be justified with respect to national interest. Indeed it is difficult to find any undertaking of the government which is not supported by some businessmen on the ground of national defense. In the early days of our history, even those statesmen who generally espoused free trade or low tariffs were willing to concede the importance of making the nation independent in the manufacture of munitions of war. And in the latest hour, subsidies to the merchant marine, to aviation, and to waterways development are stoutly defended in the name of preparedness. Transforming a creek into a river navigable by outboard motorboats can be supported by military engineers on the theory that it gives them practice in their art. No; the emphasis here is not critical. The point is that the federal government does not operate in a vacuum, but under impulsion from without; and all of the measures which put the government into business have been supported by rugged individualists — businessmen or farmers or both.

The current tendency to describe the government as a meddling busybody, prying around and regulating for the mere pleasure of taking the joy out of somebody's life, betrays an ignorance of the facts in the case. The government of the United States operates continually in the midst of the most powerful assembly of lobbyists the world has ever seen — the representatives of every business interest that has risen above the level of a corner grocery; and there is not a single form of government interference with business that does not have the approval of one or more of these interests — except perhaps the taxation of incomes for the purpose, among other things, of paying the expenses of subsidizing and regulating business.

For forty years or more there has not been a President, Republican or Democratic, who has not talked against government interference and then supported measures adding more interference to the huge collection already accumulated. Take, for instance, President Wilson. He made his campaign in 1912 on the classical doctrine of individualism; he blew mighty blasts in the name of his new freedom against the control of the government by corporate wealth and promised to separate business and government, thus setting little fellows free to make money out of little business. The heir of the Jeffersonian tradition, he decried paternalism of every kind.

Yet look at the statutes enacted under his benign administration: the trainmen's law virtually fixing wages on interstate railways for certain classes of employees; the shipping board law; the Farm Loan Act; federal aid for highway construction; the Alaskan railway; the Federal Reserve Act; the Water Power Act; and all the rest of the bills passed during his regime. Only the Clayton Antitrust Law can be called individualistic.

No wonder Mr. E. L. Doheny exclaimed to Mr. C. W. Barron that President Wilson was a college professor gone Bolshevist! And why did Democrats who had been saying "the less government the better" operate on the theory that the more government the better? Simply because their mouths were worked by ancient memories and their actions were shaped by inexorable realities.

Then the Republicans came along in 1921 and informed the country that they were going back to normalcy, were determined to take the government out of business. Well, did they repeal a single one of the important measures enacted during the eight years of President Wilson's rule? It would be entertaining to see the Sanhedrim of the United States Chamber of Commerce trying to make out a list of laws repealed in the name of normalcy and still more entertaining to watch that august body compiling a list of additional laws interfering with "the natural course of business" enacted since 1921.

Heirs of the Hamiltonian tradition, the Republicans were not entitled to talk about separating the government from business. Their great spiritual teacher, Daniel Webster, a pupil of Hamilton, had spoken truly when he said that one of the great reasons for framing the Constitution was the creation of a government that could regulate commerce. They came honestly by subsidies, bounties, internal improvements, tariffs, and other aids to business. What was the trouble with them in the age of normalcy? Nothing; they just wanted their kind of government intervention in the "natural course of industry." Evidently, then, there is some confusion on this subject of individualism, and it ought to be examined dispassionately in the light of its history with a view to discovering its significance and its limitations; for there is moral danger in saying one thing and doing another — at all events too long.

IV

HISTORICALLY SPEAKING, there are two schools of individualism: one American, associated with the name of Jefferson, and the other English, associated with the name of Cobden. The former was agrarian in interest, the latter capitalistic. Jefferson wanted America to be a land of free, upstanding farmers with just enough government to keep order among them; his creed was an agrarian creed nicely fitted to a civilization of sailing ships, ox carts, stagecoaches, wooden plows, tallow dips, and homemade bacon and sausages; and since most of the people in the United States, during the first century of their independence, were engaged in agriculture, they thought highly of Jefferson's praise of agriculture and his doctrine of anarchy plus the police constable.

Cobden's individualism was adapted to capitalist England at the middle of the nineteenth century — early industrial England. At that moment his country was the workshop of the world, was mistress of the world market in manufactured commodities, and feared no competition from any foreign country. English capitalists thus needed no protective tariffs and subsidies and, therefore, wanted none. Hence they exalted free trade to the level of a Mosaic law, fixed and eternal. They wanted to employ labor on their own terms and turn working people out to starve when no profitable business was at hand; so they quite naturally believed that any government interference with their right to do as they pleased was "bad." Their literary apologist, Macaulay, clothed their articles of faith in such magnificent rhetoric that even the tiredest businessman could keep awake reading it at night.

Closely examined, what is this creed of individualism? Macaulay defines it beautifully in the passage which the New York bank and our happy advertising agency quoted so joyously. Let the government maintain peace, defend property, reduce the cost of litigation, and observe economy in expenditure — that is all. Do American businessmen want peace all the time, in Nicaragua, for instance, when their undertakings are disturbed? Or in Haiti or Santo Domingo? Property must be defended, of course. But whose property? And what about the cost of litigation and economy in expenditures? If they would tell their hired men in law offices to cut the costs of law, something might happen. As for expenditures, do they really mean to abolish subsidies, bounties, and appropriations-in-aid from which they benefit? Speaking brutally, they do not. That is not the kind of economy in expenditures which they demand; they prefer to cut off a few dollars from the Children's Bureau.

Then comes Macaulay's system of private economy: let capital find its most lucrative course alone, unaided: no government tariffs, subsidies, bounties, and special privileges. That is the first item. Do American businessmen who shout for individualism believe in that? Certainly not. So that much is blown out of the water. Macaulay's next item is: let commodities find their fair price. Do the gentlemen who consolidate, merge, and make price understandings want to allow prices to take their "natural course"? By no means; they are trying to effect combinations that will hold prices up to the point of the largest possible profit. Macaulay's third item is: let industry and intelligence receive their natural reward. Whose industry and intelligence and what industry and intelligence? When these questions are asked, all that was clear and simple dissolves in mist.

Then there is Macaulay's last item: let idleness and folly reap their natural punishment. That was a fundamental specification in the bill of Manchesterism. Malthus made it a law for the economists: the poor are poor because they have so many babies and are improvident; nothing can be done about

it, at least by any government, even though it enforces drastic measures against the spread of information on birth control. Darwin made a natural science of it: biology sanctified the tooth-and-claw struggle of business by proclaiming the eternal tooth-and-claw struggle of the jungle. If the government will do nothing whatever, all people will rise or sink to the level which their industry or idleness, their intelligence or folly commands.

No distinction was made between those who were idle because they could find no work and those who just loved idleness for its own sake — either in slums or mansions. Those who hit bottom and starved simply deserved it. That is the good, sound, logical creed of simon-pure individualism which Herbert Spencer embedded in fifty pounds of printed matter. To him and all his devotees, even public schools and public libraries were anathema: let the poor educate themselves at their own expense; to educate them at public expense is robbery of the taxpayer — that industrious, intelligent, provident person who is entitled to keep his "natural reward."

Do any stalwart individualists believe that simple creed now? Not in England, where Liberals, professing to carry on the Cobden-Bright tradition, vote doles for unemployed working people. Why not let idleness and folly get their natural punishment? Why not, indeed? There must be a reason. Either the individualists betray their own faith, or, as some wag has suggested, they are afraid that they might find themselves hanging to a lantern if they let the idle and the foolish starve, that is, reap the natural punishment prescribed by Macaulay. Nor do American individualists propose to let nature take her course in this country. There is no danger of revolution here; as Mr. Coolidge has said, "we have had our revolution"; yet businessmen agree with the politicians on feeding the hungry. It is true that they seem to be trying to obscure the issues and the facts by talking about the beneficence of private charity while getting most of the dole from public treasuries; but that is a detail. Although our rugged individualists advertise Macaulay's creed, their faith in it appears to be shaky or their courage is not equal to their hopes. Then why should they try to delude themselves and the public?

There is another side to this stalwart individualism that also deserves consideration. Great things have been done in its name, no doubt, and it will always have its place in any reasoned scheme of thinking. Individual initiative and energy are absolutely indispensable to the successful conduct of any enterprise, and there is ample ground for fearing the tyranny and ineptitude of governments. In the days of pioneering industry in England, in our pioneering days when forests were to be cut and mountain fastnesses explored, individualism was the great dynamic which drove enterprise forward. But on other pages of the doom book other entries must be made. In the minds of most people who shout for individualism vociferously, the creed, stripped of all flashy rhetoric, means getting money, simply that and nothing more. And to this creed may be laid most of the shame that has cursed our cities and most of the scandals that have smirched our federal government.

That prince of bosses, Croker, put the individualist creed in its bare logical form when he said that he was working for his own pocket all the time, just as "every man in New York is working for his pocket." Fall, Doheny, and Sinclair were all splendid individualists; they explained that they hoped to make money out of their transactions, even while they covered their operations with the mantle of patriotism — national defense. Tammany judges, Connolly and his iron pipe, Doyle with his split fees, and policemen growing rich on vice are all individualists of the purest brand. W. B. Shearer collecting money from shipbuilding concerns to make a naval scare so that they might increase their profits belongs to the same school.

Britten, bringing a fleet to Montauk Point to boom real estate in which he is interested, does nothing reprehensible under the Manchester creed; his capital is finding "its most lucrative course." Wilder and Bardo, representing shipping interests, when they spend money in Washington "educating" members of Congress, are following the law of the game. They are perfect individualists. The ruinous chaos in coal and oil is to be attributed to the same Darwinian morality. Finally, Al Capone, with his private enterprise in racketeering, is a supreme individualist: he wants no government interference with his business, not even the collection of income taxes; if he is "let alone" he will take care of himself and give some money to soup kitchens besides.

The cold truth is that the individualist creed of everybody for himself and the devil take the hindmost is principally responsible for the distress in which Western civilization finds itself — with investment racketeering at one end and labor racketeering at the other. Whatever merits the creed may have had in days of primitive agriculture and industry, it is not applicable in an age of technology, science, and rationalized economy. Once useful, it has become a danger to society. Every thoughtful businessman who is engaged in management as distinguished from stock speculation knows that stabilization, planning, orderly procedure, prudence, and the adjustment of production to demand are necessary to keep the economic machine running steadily and efficiently. Some of our most distinguished citizens — Owen D. Young, Gerard Swope, Nicholas Murray Butler, and Otto Kahn, for example — have, in effect, warned the country that only by planning can industry avoid the kind of disaster from which we are now suffering; on all sides are signs of its coming — perhaps soon, perhaps late, but inevitably.

And all of them know that this means severe restraints on the anarchy celebrated in the name of individualism. The task before us, then, is not to furbish up an old slogan but to get rid of it, to discover how much planning is necessary, by whom it can best be done, and what limitations must be imposed on the historic doctrine of Manchesterism. And to paraphrase Milton, methinks puissant America, mewing her mighty youth, will yet kindle her undazzled eyes at the full midday beam, purge and unscale her long-abused sight, while timorous and flocking birds, with those that love the twilight, flutter about, amazed at what she means, and in their envious gabble would prognosticate a year of sects and schisms.

21.

Robert M. La Follette, Jr.: Hoover and Unemployment

Through 1931 Hoover hoped to restore prosperity by voluntary means, and except for announcing a tax cut, arranging liberal credit terms for business, and increasing government spending on public works by modest amounts, he took little exceptional executive action. He furthermore vetoed or emasculated anti-depression legislation, all of which he opposed because it was expensive or expanded the role of federal government. Senator Robert M. La Follette, Jr., of Wisconsin, the author of the article reprinted below, was a vigorous advocate of federal action to deal with the Depression. He fought for New York Senator Robert Wagner's measures to stabilize employment, and he became the spokesman in Congress for those who desired to allocate federal funds for direct relief.

Source: *Nation,* July 15, 1931: "The President and Unemployment."

The administration of Herbert Hoover began on March 4, 1929, with his inspiring declaration that "the larger purpose of our economic thought should be to establish more firmly stability and security of business and employment, and thereby remove poverty still further from our borders." Although he acquiesced in the laissez faire philosophy of his immediate predecessors in office by voicing a hope that this purpose would be attained largely through the spontaneous cooperation of individuals, President Hoover added the significant pledge that his administration would "assist and encourage these movements of collective self-help by itself cooperating with them."

For eighteen months, unemployment has been spreading poverty and acute suffering through industrial and agricultural areas alike. No one yet knows when the present economic disaster will be brought to an end. The illusory prosperity and feverish optimism which marked preceding years have given way to fearful economic insecurity and to widespread despair. These eighteen months have revealed the hypocrisy of the President's pledge of cooperation toward the attainment of economic security. The administration's efforts to attain economic security have consisted of attempts to minimize the seriousness of the Depression, of bold assurances that steps which would restore prosperity were about to be taken, and of a woefully unsuccessful program to stimulate private or local agencies to undertake tasks which the administration was determined to shirk.

The utter inadequacy of the President's plan to muddle through the Depression was increasingly evident as time went on. Instead of adopting constructive measures to meet the issues confronting us, the President in his Valley Forge speech of May 30 last abandoned all pretense of economic leadership. He counseled his fellow citizens to await with resignation and individual fortitude the day when good fortune might again bring better economic conditions. Abandoning all thought of controlling the complexities of modern economic society, he urged that we "pin our faith upon the inventiveness, the resourcefulness, the initiative of every one of us."

President Hoover entered office with a widely accepted reputation as an economic expert. For years he had indicated his interest in preventing and mitigating unemployment. After appointment by President Harding in 1921 to the chairmanship of the Conference on Unemployment, Mr. Hoover said: "There is no economic failure so terrible in its import as that of a country possessing a surplus of every necessity of life, in which numbers, willing and anxious to work, are deprived of these necessities. It simply cannot be if our moral and economic system is to survive."

Pledges to bring about security of employment and to "abolish poverty" marked the campaign of 1928. The election of Herbert Hoover, the country was assured, would mean the adoption of constructive and aggressive measures to cope with the problem of unemployment. Three months after the inauguration these pledges were recalled to the President's mind by the head of the Iowa State Federation of Labor, who suggested that a national conference be called to consider the unemployment problem. The President replied that he "hoped that we will be able to take it up when some of the momentarily pressing problems

of the administration are out of the way." These "momentarily pressing problems" continued to dominate the President's attention down to the day on which a stock-market crash warned even the unwary that the nation's economic structure had been undermined.

President Hoover's first recognition of the situation was a reassuring statement, on Oct. 25, 1929, that the country was still "on a sound and prosperous basis." Events soon exploded this theory, and on November 15 the President temporarily avowed a sounder view by saying that "words are not of any great importance in times of economic disturbance; it is action that counts."

Action was to proceed along five fronts. The first involved the maintenance of credit stability and of ample supplies of capital through the Federal Reserve System, a task which the long-established banking organization readily accomplished, especially since it soon became evident that the country had an oversupply rather than a shortage of capital. Other points in the program, including the revival of construction activities, the stimulation of exports, and assistance to agriculture, were defeated by more permanent administration policies which ran in a contrary direction. The fifth point, a reduction of income taxes to reassure business, was jammed through Congress only to demonstrate the hollowness of the administration's glib description of the Depression as merely psychological.

By way of doing something more specific, the President on the same day announced that he called a series of conferences with industrial, financial, and labor leaders, not so much to meet as to "head off an emergency." The eminent gentlemen who visited the White House seemed to agree with the President that no attempt should be made to reduce wages, and pledged increased capital expenditures to maintain employment.

An increasing wave of unemployment soon followed, and the President again declared that it was slight in volume and that it would soon be over. On March 8, 1930, he issued his justly famous statement:

All the evidences indicate that the worst effects of the crash upon employment will have been passed within the next sixty days, with the amelioration of seasonal unemployment, the gaining strength of other forces, and the continued cooperation of the many agencies actively cooperating with the government to restore business and to relieve distress.

On June 4, 1930, the President was waited on by a delegation of bishops, bank presidents, and manufacturers, described by Mr. Amos Pinchot in *The Nation* of Jan. 14, 1931. The President assured the delegation that they must be misinformed concerning the seriousness of the unemployment situation. In Mr. Pinchot's words:

Wide World Photos

Sen. Robert M. La Follette, Jr., from Wisconsin; photographed in 1939

With calm confidence he spoke of the results that were being gained through the conference he had called of great business leaders and of their fine response to his appeal not to curtail the volume of their activities. He showed us, in authoritative style, that every agency of both the federal and state governments was working at top capacity to relieve the situation. "Gentlemen," he said, "you have come six weeks too late."

Ironically enough, it was at this time that the President reached his decision to sign the Hawley-Smoot Tariff Bill, which contributed greatly to the almost complete ruin of our export trade.

Demands that the administration adopt a constructive program became more and more insistent as the fall of 1930 came on. Optimistic statements and announcements of small increases in the volume of federal public works failed to conceal the growth of unemployment, and the protracted drought further enlarged the area of disorganization.

Admission that the unemployment problem had not been met came on Oct. 17, 1930, when President Hoover announced a new series of conferences to draw up more effective plans, on the ground that "as a na-

tion we must prevent hunger and cold to those of our people who are in honest difficulties." The immediate result was the creation of the President's Emergency Committee on Employment, with Col. Arthur Woods as its chairman. The Woods Committee collected information for the President's guidance and made suggestions to private employers and to states and municipalities of ways in which they might alleviate unemployment.

The major public-works expansion program recommended to the President by the Woods Committee, which would have thrown the powerful resources of the federal government into the breach and substantially reduced unemployment, never saw the light of day because of the President's opposition to legislative action and his blind faith that "the spirit of voluntary service" would be strong enough to cope with the problem "in full measure of the need."

Throughout the following session of Congress, from December 1930 until March 1931, the President successfully prevented enactment of more adequate measures to relieve unemployment. Federal assistance to meet the relief of actual distress was blocked through the subserviency of the leaders of a bipartisan majority in the Senate to the influence of large income taxpayers, and through the responsiveness of a majority in the House of Representatives to the pressure of the administration. Instead of an emergency public-works program upon a scale sufficiently great to reduce substantially the volume of unemployment, the administration's emergency public-works program was limited in the main to an appropriation of $116 million, most of which will be available only until September 1.

In harmony with the administration's general attitude toward unemployment, the session ended with the President's pocket veto, based upon untenable grounds, of the Wagner Employment-Exchange Bill, which almost alone among the measures passed by the Seventy-first Congress might have made some permanent contribution toward the alleviation of the evils of unemployment. The virtual disintegration of the Woods Committee, whose members had accepted appointment in the belief that their expert knowledge would receive at least courteous attention from the President, followed within a few weeks. Although the chairman of the committee refused to comment upon his departure from Washington, one of his admirers, Edward A. Filene, remarked that "Colonel Woods is a man of action who refuses to follow a road which leads windingly or not at all to the goal."

A review of the Hoover administration's unemployment policy demonstrates that the President has lacked either the understanding or the courage to press toward the goal of alleviating the distress of the unemployed and of reducing the number out of work. Timidity and disingenuousness have marked the course of the administration at a time when heroic courage and bold frankness were necessary. Vigor and firm leadership have been displayed by the President at times, but only to resist proposals which

would have mitigated suffering but which necessarily involved an additional levy upon wealthy income taxpayers.

No informed person has charged the President with full responsibility for the disaster which overtook the United States in 1929. It was produced by factors which had long been working, although President Hoover, like his predecessors, lacked the vision or the will to control those forces. No one has maintained that the federal government alone could solve all the economic problems which now confront the nation. The failure of President Hoover during his administration is revealed, however, by his attitude toward the measures which would have at least partially ameliorated the unemployment crisis, and which had been under discussion since the unemployment conference over which he presided in 1921. Some of these proposals had again been recommended only a few days before President Hoover's inauguration by the Senate Committee on Education and Labor, which, under the chairmanship of Senator Couzens, had carried on a thorough study of unemployment.

Instead of frankly informing the country concerning the actual state of affairs, the President repeatedly gave out misleading statements. He clung vehemently to his assertions that the Depression would soon be over, and that the number of unemployed was smaller than informed observers had been led to believe.

His Cabinet members for months continued to place the number out of work at 2 million, even after official figures had shown the total to be far greater. Finally, the Woods Committee, in order to obtain a sounder basis for its own guidance, induced the Metropolitan Life Insurance Company to make an independent survey in January 1931, which resulted in an estimate placing the number out of work at more than 5 million. Characteristically, the administration withheld this information until it had been demanded by a resolution of the Senate.

A second and more detailed survey, conducted by the Bureau of the Census early in 1931, showed 6,050,000 persons unemployed. It, too, was withheld by the administration, this time until after the adjournment of Congress had made it impossible to pass relief appropriations. Strange light is cast upon the administration's good faith in this connection by Secretary of Commerce Lamont's announcement in March 1931 that in accordance with a change of administration policy the public would henceforth be given "all the facts." For more than a year, in other words, the facts had been suppressed.

Despite this assurance, unwarranted optimism continues to emanate from the White House. Late in May 1931, the President informed the country that he and his Cabinet had found "many factors they considered favorable." A week later, Fred C. Croxton, vice-chairman of the Woods Committee, felt it necessary to issue a warning that there must be no let-up in relief activities and that almost certainly millions of unemployed would need assistance next winter.

For a hundred years the federal government has granted financial aid to communities temporarily unable to cope with relief problems created by disaster. In spite of his inaugural declaration in favor of cooperation with "movements of self-help," the President devoted much of his energy during the past winter to the defeat of proposals to cooperate with local communities by supplementing out of federal revenues their relief funds, which were rapidly being exhausted. To defend his position, the President drew an arbitrary distinction between "natural" disasters and economic disasters, although the suffering created by the present economic disruption probably far exceeds the burdens imposed by all the "natural" disasters of the last century.

He insisted that relief for the unemployed must be locally and privately financed, although official figures finally disclosed that during 1930, 72 percent of the meager assistance given the unemployed was contributed by local governments and was therefore out of local taxes. The net result of this policy was to throw the burden upon direct, local taxpayers and to relieve the big income taxpayers of their fair share of the relief levy.

Expansion of public works to afford temporary employment in times of depression had been favorably discussed for more than ten years. Appropriations large enough to initiate an effective emergency program were urged by President Hoover's own advisers. He insisted upon a meager appropriation of $116 million. To satisfy the demand for a larger program of public works, he has sponsored misleading statements which lumped expenditures for the purchase of land with expenditures for actual construction, which failed to distinguish between the volume of work normally undertaken prior to the Depression and the amount now under way, which obscured the amount of employment actually afforded, and which combined federal and state outlays.

Senator Wagner's bill setting up a permanent organization to regulate federal public works in accordance with business conditions was enacted only after long delay on the part of administration leaders, and a director to guide its operations is yet to be appointed. Creation of an organization for effective cooperation between federal and state employment offices was proposed in a bill passed by Congress only to be pocket vetoed, after the adjournment, on specious grounds. Instead, the President set up a system of federal employment directors who have already begun to antagonize and disrupt existing state employment offices. Measures to encourage the establishment of employment reserves or to create a national system of employment insurance were ignored by the administration; and when the Senate nevertheless authorized a special committee to consider this problem during the present adjournment, Senator Wagner, who had sponsored the creation of the committee, was deposed from the chairmanship by administration influence.

Other long-range measures — to abolish child labor, to revise the Smoot-Hawley Tariff in order to stimulate export trade, to increase federal income and inheritance taxes to provide funds for an expansion of the government's construction program and to enable it to relieve suffering, and to bring about intelligent planning of our economic life in order to prevent a repetition of the situation into which we drifted — have met with presidential indifference or hostility.

The third winter of unemployment is approaching. Responsibility for the failure of the federal government to provide a program for the relief of distress among millions of our people rests squarely upon President Hoover. The bankruptcy of his leadership in the worst economic crisis in our history reveals the tragic failure of rugged individualism and places the major cost of deflation upon those least able to bear it — the unemployed.

22.

Lotus D. Coffman: Adult Education for the Unemployed

Between the stock market collapse in 1929 and the early months of 1931, the Hoover administration and the business community sought by voluntary measures to tide the nation over what was hoped would be a short recession. Business was not to cut wages or production, and labor was not to strike; but production was gradually cut back, unemployment slowly increased, and wages began to decline. Some Americans felt that the "business as usual" attitude of the administration was incapable of coping with the crisis. Responsibility for action seemed to fall on the states, local communities, and private agencies. One plan for dealing with the problem of growing unemployment was advanced by President Lotus D. Coffman of the University of Minnesota in the following speech delivered in Detroit on February 25, 1931, to the Department of Superintendence of the National Education Association.

Source: *The State University: Its Work and Problems*, Minneapolis, 1934, pp. 148-154.

In this paper I propose to confine myself to a single aspect of the adult education movement. I propose to discuss it as a means of solving the problem of unemployment. Nothing exceeds this in importance just now. The world is more deeply concerned with it than it is with any other single issue. Thousands of panaceas are being offered for the restoration of economic prosperity and the reduction of unemployment. There is no good reason why the schoolmaster should not present his; it cannot be more visionary than those presented by the captains of finance and industry.

Here we are in the midst of the direst

economic debacle the world has ever witnessed. It reaches around the world; it touches all people and affects life on every level. In the United States we are faced with an unparalleled record of business and bank failures. Millions are unemployed. Governmental and charitable agencies are called upon to relieve economic and social conditions.

Our leaders stand before us helpless, advocating for the most part a laissez faire policy. They maintain that if things are left alone they will right themselves soon and that when they have once adjusted themselves we shall enter upon a period of permanent prosperity. They would have us believe that panics will cure themselves. Intelligence, courage, and common sense are to be displaced by optimistic blindness. All this, I think, means that we are suffering from a helpless and misguided leadership. The present disaster and all others like it are an indictment of our civilization. When poverty and misery and unemployment stalk abroad in the midst of plenty, the time has come for an accounting of the leadership that produces such conditions.

With our whole economic structure and the institutions depending upon it, including education, in distress, it is time that we began to look for causes and to seek remedies. For this economic depression is not the last one that will occur; indeed, unless something in the nature of a permanent solution is found, depressions will come with increasing frequency and increasing momentum. It is clear that we have a job to do and that it must be done with foresight and intelligence. Fitful spurts of artificial prosperity only involve us the more deeply in the approaching maelstroms of tomorrow.

But what contribution can adult education make to this problem? A recent survey in Minneapolis, St. Paul, and Duluth showed that approximately 50 percent of the unemployed are forty-five years of age

and over. Many have lost out because of technological conditions resulting from the introduction of machinery; others are of the house-to-house-salesman type for whom there is no longer any need; others have been dropped to reduce overhead when mergers were effected; still others have been displaced by younger men at less salary. What shall we do with this increasing army of men and of women for whom the tide of life is beginning to ebb? Shall we assume that the number must increase and that we must care for them with a government dole? Shall we assume that this situation is merely an inevitable phase of the struggle for progress and that nothing can be done about it? The first of these theories means the impoverishment of the nation and the permanent pauperization of millions of self-respecting persons who are willing to work; while the conclusion that increasing unemployment is a necessary accompaniment of progress and that nothing should be done about it spells communism in the long run.

Recently I listened to a long discussion of this problem by two men prominent in the banking interests of a Midwestern city. The general drift of the conversation was that we have always had unemployed; why worry about them? If they had saved as they should when they had employment, they would not now be objects of charity. Give them as little as possible, these men said; let them suffer; that is the only way that they and their kind will ever learn the lessons they need to know.

These bankers were ignoring one of the simplest and most elemental considerations of economics, which is that no financial depression can ever be solved by perpetuating poverty. They failed to remember that the things men want are protection for their homes, security of position, education for their children, and all the benefits and comforts that science can contribute to their living. These things they are willing to work for; these things they will have even if they have to obtain them in some new way. Communism in its various forms will not be held at bay by negative actions and attempts at government regulation; instead there must be positive action and constructive programs if we are to be spared the consequences of outbreaks of violence. Despair expresses itself in desperate acts. The governments of the world today are at the crossroads. We delude ourselves with the pleasant thought that our own government is so secure that nothing can happen to it, but this is merely a delusion.

In the midst of such a crisis, what shall we do? What can we do? Some say, give pensions to the aged and the unemployed. Certainly pensions for the old would be better in every way than doles for the young. But there is something else that may be tried, and now I come to the point I have had in mind to make. There is no good reason why civilization should not continue to advance; there is no reason why more and more wealth should not be produced; there is no reason why human wants should not be multiplied. More and more, industry and business must provide for those who have been employed long enough to be regarded as permanent employees.

But many types of business and of industry will disappear and others will arise to take their places. There must be a constant inventory of the trends in industry and in business. This is one of the things we have been attempting to do for our region at the University of Minnesota. We have made a study of 450 business establishments. We can tell you which ones are on the upgrade and which ones are on the downgrade. We are of the opinion that we know which will pass out of existence in the next few years, which will hold their own, and which will become stronger. This is valuable information for the young person about to enter upon a career; it is equally valuable for

those men and women now in the employ of decadent industries who will soon be tramping the streets looking hunger in the face unless something constructive is done.

And that is what our university proposes to undertake. We have begun a careful analysis, not of business trends merely but of the social, economic, and educational background of the unemployed. We are giving informational, intelligence, and vocational tests to thousands of such persons. We shall select the casuals from the capables, the stupid and ignorant from the intelligent, the unambitious from the ambitious, those who do not want to work from those who are willing to work.

Then, in cooperation with the officials of the state and of the three largest cities of the state, the university proposes to inaugurate an educational program for those who are capable of profiting by training. This intensive program will be carried on in the closest cooperation with the placement agencies of the state and of the cities. We are gathering together the best students the country affords in the vocational, sociological, and economic fields to assist in mapping out the program and to supervise it while it is under way. We propose to carry this on for two years at least. During that time we hope to show that it is possible to mitigate the problem of unemployment in one area. To put it the other way round, we expect to increase the number of employed, and in so doing to stage for the rest of the country what will in effect be a demonstration of a partial solution of the problem of unemployment. And we believe that the rest of the country can do and should do what we are doing, or think we shall be able to do.

There are, to be sure, those in our midst who say that we should be spending more on feeding the hungry and less on studying the problem. They are the men who have helped to produce the present disaster.

They smile at the impractical dreams of the schoolmaster and continue to spread their propaganda. They are the men who send humanity chasing after ever disappearing and constantly recurring economic rainbows. And the pitiful thing about it all is that many of the sufferers in our present grim world tragedy continue to follow blindly after them. But there are others, and I hope increasing millions, who are thinking of preserving their self-respect, the self-respect of their families, and the institutions of their forebears.

Whether a university can make use of adult education to renew hope among despairing thousands remains to be demonstrated. There seems to be no good reason why it should stand helpless along with the economic leadership that has produced world calamity. Others may seek to prevent the recurrence of the plague that menaces us by enacting legislation, by advocating fewer hours of labor a day, fewer days of work a week, higher wages, and the purchase of more of the goods of life without increasing their cost. But education and educational institutions may do much, by the study and use of adult education, to drive fear and terror from the hearts of those who are caught in the network of industry and do not know how to extricate themselves.

23.

American Emigrants to the Soviet Union

Between March 1930 and March 1931, the number of people unemployed doubled (from 4 to 8 million); and for many of those who retained their jobs, wages as well as hours were cut back. As the United States sank deeper into depression, it began to seem to some Americans that the instability of the capitalist economy and the menace of unemployment had been permanently removed in the Soviet system. In the 1920s and 1930s the Soviet Union scouted abroad for skilled workers and technicians to help fulfill its ambitious industrial goals, and during the Depression years a small minority of Americans responded to the Soviet call. In the United States the scouting agency was the Soviet trade corporation, Amtorg, located in New York. The following news article appeared on October 7, 1931.

Source: *Business Week,* October 7, 1931: "Amtorg Gets 100,000 Bids for Russia's 6,000 Skilled Jobs."

New Yorkers dominate the flow of Americans who have decided, at least for the time being, to cast their lot with the Russians. Pennsylvania, New Jersey, and Illinois show heavy quotas of recruits under the new call for "6,000 skilled workers," and Michigan, Ohio, California, and Massachusetts are well represented.

More than 100,000 applications have been received at the Amtorg's New York office for the 6,000 jobs. One morning's grist of applications last week totaled 280.

All but ten states were represented. Both Alaska and Panama furnished an applicant, and 18 Canadians wanted to "try their luck in Russia."

Nearly one-fourth of the job seekers are from New York state — 73 on this particular morning. Pennsylvania, New Jersey, Ohio, and Illinois fluctuate up and down the list, depending on the type of job open. Pennsylvania offered 28, New Jersey 23, Illinois 21, among the 280 letters checked.

Industrial states naturally supply the largest number of applicants, but others are represented. Iowa, Texas, and Idaho each offered some kind of skilled worker.

Because of the general knowledge that Russia is "industrializing," applicants usually are skilled workers at machine construction, on the railroads, in steel mills, automobile factories, or the building industries. A glance at the qualifications of some of the 280 applicants on this "typical" morning showed that experts in all lines were after work, even if it meant going to Russia and accepting pay in rubles. There were 2 barbers, 1 funeral director, 2 plumbers, 5 painters, 2 cooks, 36 "clerical" workers, 1 service station operator, 9 carpenters, 1 aviator, 58 engineers, 14 electricians, 5 salesmen, 2 printers, 2 chemists, 1 shoemaker, 1 librarian, 2 teachers, 1 cleaner and dyer, 11 automobile mechanics, 1 dentist.

About 85 percent of the applicants are citizens of the United States, though only 40 percent are native-born. The 60 percent foreign-born are largely from Eastern Europe. A few Negroes have applied, but the number is small because the majority are unskilled laborers.

Women form only a small percentage of the applicants, though many wives have decided to accompany their husbands on the new venture. The majority of workers who apply are married and have children.

Three principal reasons are advanced for wanting the position: (1) unemployment; (2) disgust with conditions here; (3) interest in the Soviet experiment. Foreign-born workers practically all state that they intend to remain in the U.S.S.R. Of the engineers, only 10 to 15 percent plan to stay.

The majority of the American workers who have been hired and will be hired in the near future will be placed primarily in the following industrial centers: Stalingrad tractor plant, Kharkov tractor plant, the huge automobile plant at Nizhni Novgorod, the locomotive works at Sormova, the steel works at Magnitogorsk and Kuznetsk, mines in the Kuznetsk region, nonferrous metal plants and mines in the Urals and Kazakstan, and on the railroad lines throughout the country.

"So you've been over in Russia?" said Bernard Baruch, and I answered very literally, "I have been over into the future, and it works."
LINCOLN STEFFENS, *Autobiography*, 1931

View of the New York Stock Exchange on an active day in the late 1920s.

ECONOMIC DISASTER

Herbert Hoover was elected in the midst of unprecedented prosperity; when his administration closed, the economy of the nation was virtually shattered and immobile. The obvious inference is, of course, false. The instability of the economy had been a constant danger from the Harding and Coolidge days, and it was established policy to disregard the "alarmist" warnings of economists and bankers. And, indeed, Hoover broke with policy far enough to attempt to aid the mysterious holdout against prosperity, agriculture. The Agricultural Marketing Act of 1929, though stripped of its more effective — "radical" — measures by Congress, was an attempt to raise farm income. Had there been time to test the Act's effectiveness, the benefits to agriculture would probably have been nullified by the Hawley-Smoot Tariff that raised the protective duties on manufactured items above their already indefensible levels. Official response to the Crash itself was negative, a form of primary disbelief. By January 1932, however, there was enough doubt in the administration and in Congress to allow the creation of the Reconstruction Finance Corporation. But between its reliance on the "trickle-down" theory of wealth, and the relatively miniscule amount of money involved, it had little effect on the disaster. The country was ready for a change; in 1932 Hoover lost to Roosevelt in an election even more lopsided than that of 1928.

(Above) Al Smith, Democratic candidate for President in 1928; (right) cartoon by "Ding" referring to Smith's plan to end Prohibition; (below) Wall Street the day of the Crash, 1929

The campaign of 1928 was undisturbed by issues or by serious debate, for the platforms of the two parties differed hardly at all, and the Progressive Party had disappeared. The election thus became largely a question of personality. Smith lost support in the South and rural areas by being anti-Prohibition and a Catholic; uninterrupted prosperity and force of habit returned the Republican Party to the White House and gave it an overwhelming majority in Congress.

United Press International

Brown Brothers

Brown Brothers

European Picture Service

(Top) Hoover shopping at a dime store during Depression; (center left) "A Most Vicious Circle"; cartoon by Costello in the Albany "News"; (center right) "The Jury Reports"; Talburt in the Washington "Daily News"; (left) jobless parade in Chicago in 1932. Some 13,000 persons participated

(Top) Bonus Army staging a demonstration outside the empty Capitol, 1932; (center) muddy scene at the Bonus Army camp in 1932; (bottom) police acting to break up riots in Washington in 1932

One of the earliest and least justifiable public reactions to the Depression was the Bonus Army's march on Washington in the spring of 1932. Egged on by the American Legion, ever-mindful of the welfare of veterans and, where possible, of the nation, the marchers demanded immediate payment on their bonus certificates. About half the 11,000 men left when ordered to, but the remainder stayed, and the regular Army, under Gen. Douglas MacArthur, was required to rout them in the Battle of Anacostia Flats.

(Top) Hoover orders out the Army to fight the veterans; (center) Gen. Douglas MacArthur, on the left, directing the Army's action against the bonus marchers; (bottom) troops evicting bonus seekers from camps on Pennsylvania Avenue

Police battling hunger strikers at Ford Plant in Dearborn, Mich., 1932

(Above left) John T. McCutcheon's Pulitzer Prize cartoon of 1932; (above right) "Employing an old idea" by Costello; (below) rally conducted by the "unemployed marchers" in Dayton, Ohio

(Above) Unemployed sitting around The Peristyle in Chicago, early 1930s

(Left) Police dispersing group of unemployed who were marching on City Hall in Philadelphia in 1932; (below) bread line at Times Square, New York City, 1932

(Above) Abandoned mail order house in Minneapolis, Minn.; photograph by John Vachon for the Farm Security Administration; (below) closed store of the Amoskeag Mills, Manchester, N.H., 1936

(Above) Unemployed miners in Herrin, Ill.; (below) company houses in a coal town in Floyd County, Ky.; both photographs by Rothstein for FSA

Library of Congress

(Above) Slums in Pittsburgh, Pa., 1938, steel mills in background; (below) eviction in Chicago

Chicago Historical Society

(Above) Homes of the unemployed on Riverside Drive in New York City, 1934; (below) Negro homes in Atlanta, Ga., 1936; photo by Walker Evans

(Above) Uncompleted hotel on the main street of Vincennes, Ind., photo by Arthur Rothstein; (below) men sitting outside hotel in Little Fork, Minn., photo by Russell Lee. Both for FSA

24.

Florence Reece: "Which Side Are You On?"

Florence Reece wrote this famous union song from personal experience. Her husband, Sam, was a union leader in notorious Harlan County, Kentucky, in 1931. As the story goes, Sheriff J. H. Blair and his men came to the house in search of Sam — to beat him up, to jail him, or even to kill him, as Mrs. Reece had good reason to suspect. The sheriff and his men ransacked the house — she was at home with her seven children — and then kept watch outside, waiting for Sam to return. He got word from someone and did not come back for several days. On one of those days of anxious waiting, Mrs. Reece tore a sheet from a wall calendar and wrote the words to "Which Side Are You On?"

Source: *Songs of Work and Freedom*, Edith Fowke and Joe Glazer, eds., New York, 1960.

WHICH SIDE ARE YOU ON?

Come all of you good workers,
Good news to you I'll tell
Of how the good old union
Has come in here to dwell.

Chorus:
Which side are you on?
Which side are you on?
Which side are you on?
Which side are you on?

My daddy was a miner
And I'm a miner's son,
And I'll stick with the union
Till every battle's won.

They say in Harlan County
There are no neutrals there;
You'll either be a union man
Or a thug for J. H. Blair.

Oh, workers, can you stand it?
Oh, tell me how you can.
Will you be a lousy scab
Or will you be a man?

Don't scab for the bosses,
Don't listen to their lies.
Us poor folks haven't got a chance
Unless we organize.

25.

F. Scott Fitzgerald: Echoes of the Jazz Age

F. Scott Fitzgerald at once documented, epitomized, and was adored by the Jazz Age. He was handsome, his wife, Zelda, was beautiful, and together they hosted huge parties and traveled often and easily between Europe and America. After This Side of Paradise *(1920) made him nationally prominent, his writing was in great demand and stories appeared regularly in the* Saturday Evening Post *and* Scribner's. *In 1925, in* The Great Gatsby, *considered his finest novel, Fitzgerald captured the mood of the time as no one else had. The following summing up of that period was published in 1931, by which time Fitzgerald's private fortunes had taken a turn for the worse. His wife confined to an asylum, Fitzgerald ended up writing scripts for Hollywood movies. "Echoes of the Jazz Age" first appeared in* Scribner's *magazine in November 1931 and was later published in the collection called* The Crack-Up.

Source: *Scribner's,* November 1931.

IT IS TOO SOON TO WRITE about the Jazz Age with perspective and without being suspected of premature arteriosclerosis. Many people still succumb to violent retching when they happen upon any of its characteristic words — words which have since yielded in vividness to the coinages of the underworld. It is as dead as were the Yellow Nineties in 1902. Yet the present writer already looks back to it with nostalgia. It bore him up, flattered him, and gave him more money than he had dreamed of, simply for telling people that he felt as they did, that something had to be done with all the nervous energy stored up and unexpended in the War.

The ten-year period that, as if reluctant to die outmoded in its bed, leaped to a spectacular death in October 1929 began about the time of the May Day riots in 1919. When the police rode down the demobilized country boys gaping at the orators in Madison Square, it was the sort of measure bound to alienate the more intelligent young men from the prevailing order.

We didn't remember anything about the Bill of Rights until Mencken began plugging it, but we did know that such tyranny belonged in the jittery little countries of South Europe. If goose-livered businessmen had this effect on the government, then maybe we had gone to war for J. P. Morgan's loans after all.

But, because we were tired of Great Causes, there was no more than a short outbreak of moral indignation, typified by Dos Passos' *Three Soldiers.* Presently we began to have slices of the national cake and our idealism only flared up when the newspapers made melodrama out of such stories as Harding and the Ohio Gang or Sacco and Vanzetti. The events of 1919 left us cynical rather than revolutionary, in spite of the fact that now we are all rummaging around in our trunks wondering where in hell we left the liberty cap — "I know I *had* it" — and the moujik blouse. It was characteristic of the Jazz Age that it had no interest in politics at all.

It was an age of miracles, it was an age

of art, it was an age of excess, and it was an age of satire. A Stuffed Shirt, squirming to blackmail in a lifelike way, sat upon the throne of the United States; a stylish young man hurried over to represent to us the throne of England. A world of girls yearned for the young Englishman; the old American groaned in his sleep as he waited to be poisoned by his wife, upon the advice of the female Rasputin who then made the ultimate decision in our national affairs. But such matters apart, we had things our way at last. With Americans ordering suits by the gross in London, the Bond Street tailors perforce agreed to moderate their cut to the American long-waisted figure and loose-fitting taste, something subtle passed to America, the style of man. During the Renaissance, Francis the First looked to Florence to trim his leg. Seventeenth-century England aped the court of France, and fifty years ago the German Guards officer bought his civilian clothes in London. Gentleman's clothes — symbol of "the power that man must hold and that passes from race to race."

We were the most powerful nation. Who could tell us any longer what was fashionable and what was fun? Isolated during the European War, we had begun combing the unknown South and West for folkways and pastimes and there were more ready to hand.

The first social revelation created a sensation out of all proportion to its novelty. As far back as 1915 the unchaperoned young people of the smaller cities had discovered the mobile privacy of that automobile given to young Bill at sixteen to make him "self-reliant." At first, petting was desperate adventure even under such favorable conditions, but presently confidences were exchanged and the old commandment broke down. As early as 1917 there were references to such sweet and casual dalliance in any number of the *Yale Record* or the *Princeton Tiger*.

But petting in its more audacious manifestations was confined to the wealthier classes — among other young people the old standards prevailed until after the War, and a kiss meant that a proposal was expected, as young officers in strange cities sometimes discovered to their dismay. Only in 1920 did the veil finally fall — the Jazz Age was in flower.

Scarcely had the staider citizens of the republic caught their breaths when the wildest of all generations, the generation which had been adolescent during the confusion of the War, brusquely shouldered my contemporaries out of the way and danced into the limelight. This was the generation whose girls dramatized themselves as flappers, the generation that corrupted its elders and eventually overreached itself less through lack of morals than through lack of taste. May one offer in exhibit the year 1922! That was the peak of the younger generation, for though the Jazz Age continued, it became less and less an affair of youth.

The sequel was like a children's party taken over by the elders, leaving the children puzzled and rather neglected and rather taken aback. By 1923 their elders, tired of watching the carnival with ill-concealed envy, had discovered that young liquor will take the place of young blood, and with a whoop the orgy began. The younger generation was starred no longer.

A whole race going hedonistic, deciding on pleasure. The precocious intimacies of the younger generation would have come about with or without Prohibition — they were implicit in the attempt to adapt English customs to American conditions. (Our South, for example, is tropical and early maturing — it has never been part of the wisdom of France and Spain to let young girls go unchaperoned at sixteen and seventeen.) But the general decision to be amused that began with the cocktail parties of 1921 had more complicated origins.

The word "jazz" in its progress toward

respectability has meant first sex, then dancing, then music. It is associated with a state of nervous stimulation, not unlike that of big cities behind the lines of a war. To many English the War still goes on because all the forces that menace them are still active — Wherefore eat, drink, and be merry, for tomorrow we die. But different causes had now brought about a corresponding state in America — though there were entire classes (people over fifty, for example) who spent a whole decade denying its existence even when its puckish face peered into the family circle. Never did they dream that they had contributed to it. The honest citizens of every class, who believed in a strict public morality and were powerful enough to enforce the necessary legislation, did not know that they would necessarily be served by criminals and quacks, and do not really believe it today.

Rich righteousness had always been able to buy honest and intelligent servants to free the slaves or the Cubans, so when this attempt collapsed, our elders stood firm with all the stubbornness of people involved in a weak case, preserving their righteousness and losing their children. Silver-haired women and men with fine old faces, people who never did a consciously dishonest thing in their lives, still assure each other in the apartment hotels of New York and Boston and Washington that "there's a whole generation growing up that will never know the taste of liquor." Meanwhile their granddaughters pass the well-thumbed copy of "Lady Chatterley's Lover" around the boarding school and, if they get about at all, know the taste of gin or corn at sixteen. But the generation who reached maturity between 1875 and 1895 continue to believe what they want to believe.

Even the intervening generations were incredulous. In 1920 Heywood Broun announced that all this hubbub was nonsense, that young men didn't kiss but told anyhow. But, very shortly, people over twenty-five came in for an intensive education. Let me trace some of the revelations vouchsafed them by reference to a dozen works written for various types of mentality during the decade. We begin with the suggestion that Don Juan leads an interesting life (*Jurgen*, 1919); then we learn that there's a lot of sex around if we only knew it (*Winesburg, Ohio*, 1920), that adolescents lead very amorous lives (*This Side of Paradise*, 1920), that there are a lot of neglected Anglo-Saxon words (*Ulysses*, 1921), that older people don't always resist sudden temptations (*Cytherea*, 1922), that girls are sometimes seduced without being ruined (*Flaming Youth*, 1922), that even rape often turns out well (*The Sheik*, 1922), that glamorous English ladies are often promiscuous (*The Green Hat*, 1924), that in fact they devote most of their time to it (*The Vortex*, 1926), that it's a damn good thing too (*Lady Chatterley's Lover*, 1928), and finally that there are abnormal variations (*The Well of Loneliness*, 1928, and *Sodome and Gomorrhe*, 1929).

In my opinion the erotic element in these works, even *The Sheik* written for children in the key of *Peter Rabbit*, did not one particle of harm. Everything they described, and much more, was familiar in our contemporary life. The majority of the theses were honest and elucidating — their effect was to restore some dignity to the male as opposed to the he-man in American life. ("And what is a 'He-man'?" demanded Gertrude Stein one day. "Isn't it a large enough order to fill out to the dimensions of all that 'a man' has meant in the past? a 'He-man'!") The married woman can now discover whether she is being cheated, or whether sex is just something to be endured, and her compensation should be to establish a tyranny of the spirit, as her mother may have hinted. Perhaps many women found that love was meant to be fun. Anyhow, the objectors lost their tawdry little case, which is one reason why our literature is now the most living in the world.

Contrary to popular opinion the movies of the Jazz Age had no effect upon its morals. The social attitude of the producers was timid, behind the times, and banal — for example, no picture mirrored even faintly the younger generation until 1923, when magazines had already been started to celebrate it and it had long ceased to be news. There were a few feeble splutters and then Clara Bow — in *Flaming Youth;* promptly the Hollywood hacks ran the theme into its cinematographic grave. Throughout the Jazz Age the movies got no farther than Mrs. Jiggs, keeping up with its most blatant superficialities. This was no doubt due to the censorship as well as to innate conditions in the industry. In any case the Jazz Age now raced along under its own power, served by great filling stations full of money.

The people over thirty, the people all the way up to fifty, had joined the dance. We graybeards (to tread down F.P.A.) remember the uproar when, in 1912, grandmothers of forty tossed away their crutches and took lessons in the Tango and the Castle Walk. A dozen years later a woman might pack the Green Hat with her other affairs as she set off for Europe or New York, but Savonarola was too busy flogging dead horses in Augean stables of his own creation to notice. Society, even in small cities, now dined in separate chambers, and the sober table learned about the gay table only from hearsay. There were very few people left at the sober table. One of its former glories, the less sought-after girls who had become resigned to sublimating a probable celibacy, came across Freud and Jung in seeking their intellectual recompense and came tearing back into the fray.

By 1926 the universal preoccupation with sex had become a nuisance. (I remember a perfectly mated, contented young mother asking my wife's advice about "having an affair right away," though she had no one especially in mind, "because don't you think it's sort of undignified when you get much over thirty?") For a while, bootleg Negro records with their phallic euphemisms made everything suggestive, and simultaneously came a wave of erotic plays — young girls from finishing schools packed the galleries to hear about the romance of being a Lesbian and George Jean Nathan protested. Then one young producer lost his head entirely, drank a beauty's alcoholic bath water and went to the penitentiary. Somehow his pathetic attempt at romance belongs to the Jazz Age, while his contemporary in prison, Ruth Snyder, had to be hoisted into it by the tabloids — she was, as *The Daily News* hinted deliciously to gourmets, about "to cook, *and sizzle, AND FRY!*" in the electric chair.

The gay elements of society had divided into two main streams, one flowing toward Palm Beach and Deauville, and the other, much smaller, toward the summer Riviera. One could get away with more on the summer Riviera, and whatever happened seemed to have something to do with art. From 1926 to 1929, the great years of the Cap d'Antibes, this corner of France was dominated by a group quite distinct from that American society which is dominated by Europeans. Pretty much of anything went at Antibes — by 1929, at the most gorgeous paradise for swimmers on the Mediterranean, no one swam anymore, save for a short hangover dip at noon. There was a picturesque graduation of steep rocks over the sea and somebody's valet and an occasional English girl used to dive from them, but the Americans were content to discuss each other in the bar.

This was indicative of something that was taking place in the homeland — Americans were getting soft. There were signs everywhere: we still won the Olympic Games but with champions whose names had few vowels in them — teams composed, like the fighting Irish combination of Notre

Dame, of fresh overseas blood. Once the French became really interested, the Davis Cup gravitated automatically to their intensity in competition. The vacant lots of the Middlewestern cities were built up now — except for a short period in school we were not turning out to be an athletic people like the British after all. The hare and the tortoise.

Of course, if we wanted to, we could be in a minute; we still had all those reserves of ancestral vitality, but one day in 1926 we looked down and found we had flabby arms and a fat pot and couldn't say boop-boop-a-doop to a Sicilian. Shades of Van Bibber! — no utopian ideal, God knows. Even golf, once considered an effeminate game, had seemed very strenuous of late — an emasculated form appeared and proved just right.

By 1927 a widespread neurosis began to be evident, faintly signaled, like a nervous beating of the feet, by the popularity of crossword puzzles. I remember a fellow expatriate opening a letter from a mutual friend of ours, urging him to come home and be revitalized by the hardy, bracing qualities of the native soil. It was a strong letter and it affected us both deeply, until we noticed that it was headed from a nerve sanitarium in Pennsylvania.

By this time contemporaries of mine had begun to disappear into the dark maw of violence. A classmate killed his wife and himself on Long Island, another tumbled "accidentally" from a skyscraper in Philadelphia, another purposely from a skyscraper in New York. One was killed in a speakeasy in Chicago; another was beaten to death in a speakeasy in New York and crawled home to the Princeton Club to die; still another had his skull crushed by a maniac's axe in an insane asylum where he was confined. These are not catastrophes that I went out of my way to look for — these were my friends; moreover, these things happened not during the depression but during the boom.

In the spring of '27, something bright and alien flashed across the sky. A young Minnesotan who seemed to have had nothing to do with his generation did a heroic thing, and for a moment people set down their glasses in country clubs and speakeasies and thought of their old best dreams. Maybe there was a way out by flying, maybe our restless blood could find frontiers in the illimitable air. But by that time we were all pretty well committed; and the Jazz Age continued; we would all have one more.

Nevertheless, Americans were wandering ever more widely — friends seemed eternally bound for Russia, Persia, Abyssinia, and Central Africa. And by 1928 Paris had grown suffocating. With each new shipment of Americans spewed up by the boom, the quality fell off, until toward the end there was something sinister about the crazy boatloads. They were no longer the simple pa and ma and son and daughter, infinitely superior in their qualities of kindness and curiosity to the corresponding class in Europe, but fantastic Neanderthals who believed something, something vague, that you remembered from a very cheap novel. I remember an Italian on a steamer who promenaded the deck in an American Reserve Officer's uniform picking quarrels in broken English with Americans who criticized their own institutions in the bar. I remember a fat Jewess, inlaid with diamonds, who sat behind us at the Russian ballet and said as the curtain rose, "Thad's luffly, dey ought to baint a bicture of it." This was low comedy but it was evident that money and power were falling into the hands of people in comparison with whom the leader of a village Soviet would be a gold mine of judgment and culture. There were citizens traveling in luxury in 1928 and 1929 who, in the distortion of their new condition, had the human value of Pekinese bivalves, cretins, goats. I remember the Judge from some New York district who had taken his daughter to see the Bayeux Tapestries and made a scene in the papers advocating their segregation because one scene was immoral. But in those days life was like the race in *Alice in Wonderland*, there was a prize for everyone.

The Jazz Age had had a wild youth and a heady middle age. There was the phase of the necking parties, the Leopold-Loeb murder (I remember the time my wife was arrested on Queensborough Bridge on the suspicion of being the "Bob-haired Bandit"), and the John Held Clothes. In the second phase such phenomena as sex and murder became more mature, if much more conventional. Middle age must be served and pajamas came to the beach to save fat thighs and flabby calves from competition with the one-piece bathing suit. Finally, skirts came down and everything was concealed. Everybody was at scratch now. Let's go —

But it was not to be. Somebody had blundered and the most expensive orgy in history was over.

It ended two years ago, because the utter confidence which was its essential prop received an enormous jolt and it didn't take long for the flimsy structure to settle earthward. And after two years the Jazz Age seems as far away as the days before the War. It was borrowed time anyhow — the whole upper tenth of a nation living with the insouciance of grand ducs and the casualness of chorus girls. But moralizing is easy now and it was pleasant to be in one's twenties in such a certain and unworried time. Even when you were broke you didn't worry about money, because it was in such profusion around you. Toward the end one had a struggle to pay one's share; it was almost a favor to accept hospitality that required any traveling. Charm, notoriety, mere good manners weighed more than money as a social asset. This was rather splendid but things were getting thinner and thinner as the eternal necessary human values tried to spread over all that expansion.

Writers were geniuses on the strength of one respectable book or play; just as during the War, officers of four months' experience commanded hundreds of men, so there were now many little fish lording it over great big bowls. In the theatrical world extravagant productions were carried by a few second-rate stars, and so on up the scale into politics where it was difficult to interest good men in positions of the highest importance and responsibility, importance and responsibility far exceeding that of business executives but which paid only five or six thousand a year.

Now once more the belt is tight and we summon the proper expression of horror as we look back at our wasted youth. Sometimes, though, there is a ghostly rumble among the drums, an asthmatic whisper in the trombones that swings me back into the early twenties when we drank wood alcohol and every day in every way grew better and better, and there was a first abortive shortening of the skirts, and girls all looked alike in sweater dresses, and people you didn't want to know said "Yes, we have no bananas," and it seemed only a question of a few years before the older people would step aside and let the world be run by those who saw things as they were — and it all seems rosy and romantic to us who were young then, because we will never feel quite so intensely about our surroundings any more.

———◆———

The American people never carry an umbrella. They prepare to walk in eternal sunshine.

ALFRED E. SMITH, 1931

26.

Frederick Lewis Allen: Alcohol and Al Capone

*Prohibition, the "noble experiment," had as its most enduring by-product the
unprecedented increase of organized crime. Frederick Lewis Allen, in
his "informal history of the 1920s," Only Yesterday, discussed the rise of
gangsterism and illicit alcohol in a chapter concerning the era's most notorious
criminal, Al Capone. A portion of the chapter is reprinted below.*

Source: *Only Yesterday*, New York, 1931, pp. 245-269.

IN 1920, WHEN PROHIBITION was very young, Johnny Torrio of Chicago had an inspiration. Torrio was a formidable figure in the Chicago underworld. He had discovered that there was big money in the newly outlawed liquor business. He was fired with the hope of getting control of the dispensation of booze to the whole city of Chicago. At the moment there was a great deal too much competition; but possibly a well-disciplined gang of men handy with their fists and their guns could take care of that, by intimidating rival bootleggers and persuading speakeasy proprietors that life might not be wholly comfortable for them unless they bought Torrio liquor. What Torrio needed was a lieutenant who could mobilize and lead his shock troops.

Being a graduate of the notorious Five Points gang in New York and a disciple of such genial fellows as Lefty Louie and Gyp the Blood (he himself had been questioned about the murder of Herman Rosenthal in the famous Becker case in 1912), he naturally turned to his alma mater for his man. He picked for the job a bullet-headed twenty-three-year-old Neapolitan roughneck of the Five Points gang, and offered him a generous income and half the profits of the bootleg trade if he would come to Chicago and take care of the competition. The young hoodlum came, established himself at Torrio's gambling place, the Four Deuces, opened by way of plausible stage setting an innocent-looking office which contained among its properties a family Bible, and had a set of business cards printed:

ALPHONSE CAPONE

Second Hand Furniture Dealer
2220 South Wabash Avenue

Torrio had guessed right — in fact, he had guessed right three times. The profits of bootlegging in Chicago proved to be prodigious, allowing an ample margin for the mollification of the forces of the law. The competition proved to be exacting: every now and then Torrio would discover that his rivals had approached a speakeasy proprietor with the suggestion that he buy their beer instead of the Torrio-Capone brand, and on receipt of an unfavorable answer had beaten the proprietor senseless and smashed up his place of business. But Al Capone had been an excellent choice as leader of the Torrio offensives; Capone was learning how to deal with such emergencies.

Within three years it was said that the boy from the Five Points had 700 men at his disposal, many of them adept in the use of the sawed-off shotgun and the Thompson submachine gun. As the profits from beer and "alky-cooking" (illicit distilling) rolled in, young Capone acquired more finesse — particularly finesse in the management of politics and politicians. By the middle of the decade he had gained complete control of the suburb of Cicero, had installed his own mayor in office, had posted his agents in the wide-open gambling-resorts and in each of the 161 bars, and had established his personal headquarters in the Hawthorne Hotel. He was taking in millions now. Torrio was fading into the background; Capone was becoming the Big Shot. But his conquest of power did not come without bloodshed. As the rival gangs — the O'Banions, the Gennas, the Aiellos — disputed his growing domination, Chicago was afflicted with such an epidemic of killings as no civilized modern city had ever before seen, and a new technic of wholesale murder was developed.

One of the standard methods of disposing of a rival in this warfare of the gangs was to pursue his car with a stolen automobile full of men armed with sawed-off shotguns and submachine guns; to draw up beside it, forcing it to the curb, open fire upon it — and then disappear into the traffic, later abandoning the stolen car at a safe distance. Another favorite method was to take the victim "for a ride": in other words, to lure him into a supposedly friendly car, shoot him at leisure, drive to some distant and deserted part of the city, and quietly throw his body overboard. Still another was to lease an apartment or a room overlooking his front door, station a couple of hired assassins at the window, and as the victim emerged from the house some sunny afternoon, to spray him with a few dozen machine-gun bullets from behind drawn curtains. But there were also more ingenious and refined methods of slaughter.

Take, for example, the killing of Dion O'Banion, leader of the gang which for a time most seriously menaced Capone's reign in Chicago. The preparation of this particular murder was reminiscent of the kiss of Judas. O'Banion was a bootlegger and a gangster by night, but a florist by day: a strange and complex character, a connoisseur of orchids and of manslaughter. One morning a sedan drew up outside his flower shop and three men got out, leaving the fourth at the wheel. The three men had apparently taken good care to win O'Banion's trust, for although he always carried three guns, now for the moment he was off his guard as he advanced among the flowers to meet his visitors. The middle man of the three cordially shook hands with O'Banion — *and then held on* while his two companions put six bullets into the gangster-florist. The three conspirators walked out, climbed into the sedan, and departed. They were never brought to justice, and it is not recorded that any of them hung themselves to trees in remorse. O'Banion had a first-class funeral, gangster style: a ten-thousand dollar casket, twenty-six truckloads of flowers, and among them a basket of flowers which bore the touching inscription, "From Al."

In 1926 the O'Banions, still unrepentant despite the loss of their leader, introduced another novelty in gang warfare. In broad daylight, while the streets of Cicero were alive with traffic, they raked Al Capone's headquarters with machine-gun fire from eight touring cars. The cars proceeded down the crowded street outside the Hawthorne Hotel in solemn line, the first one firing blank cartridges to disperse the innocent citizenry and to draw the Capone forces to the doors and windows, while from the succeeding cars, which followed a block behind, flowed a steady rattle of bullets, spraying the hotel and the adjoining buildings up and down. One gunman even got out of his car, knelt carefully upon the sidewalk at the door of the Hawthorne, and played one hundred bullets into the lobby

— back and forth, as one might play the hose upon one's garden. The casualties were miraculously light, and Scarface Al himself remained in safety, flat on the floor of the Hotel Hawthorne restaurant; nevertheless, the bombardment quite naturally attracted public attention. Even in a day when bullion was transported in armored cars, the transformation of a suburban street into a shooting gallery seemed a little unorthodox.

The war continued, one gangster after another crumpling under a rain of bullets; not until St. Valentine's Day of 1929 did it reach its climax in a massacre which outdid all that had preceded it in ingenuity and brutality. At half-past ten on the morning of February 14, 1929, seven of the O'Banions were sitting in the garage which went by the name of the S. M. C. Cartage Company, on North Clark Street, waiting for a promised consignment of hijacked liquor. A Cadillac touring car slid to the curb, and three men dressed as policemen got out, followed by two others in civilian dress. The three supposed policemen entered the garage alone, disarmed the seven O'Banions, and told them to stand in a row against the wall. The victims readily submitted; they were used to police raids and thought nothing of them; they would get off easily enough, they expected. But thereupon the two men in civilian clothes emerged from the corridor and calmly mowed all seven O'Banions with submachine gunfire as they stood with hands upraised against the wall. The little drama was completed when the three supposed policemen solemnly marched the two plain-clothes killers across the sidewalk to the waiting car, and all five got in and drove off — having given to those in the wintry street a perfect tableau of an arrest satisfactorily made by the forces of the law!

These killings — together with that of "Jake" Lingle, who led a double life as a reporter for the *Chicago Tribune* and as associate of gangsters, and who was shot to death in a crowded subway leading to the Illinois Central suburban railway station in 1930 — were perhaps the most spectacular of the decade in Chicago. But there were over 500 gang murders in all. Few of the murderers were apprehended; careful planning, money, influence, the intimidation of witnesses, and the refusal of any gangster to testify against any other, no matter how treacherous the murder, met that danger. The city of Chicago was giving the whole country, and indeed the whole world, an astonishing object lesson in violent and unpunished crime. How and why could such a thing happen?

To say that prohibition — or, if you prefer, the refusal of the public to abide by prohibition — caused the rise of the gangs to lawless power would be altogether too easy an explanation. There were other causes: the automobile, which made escape easy, as the officers of robbed banks had discovered; the adaptation to peacetime use of a new arsenal of handy and deadly weapons; the murderous traditions of the Mafia imported by Sicilian gangsters; the inclination of a wet community to wink at the by-products of a trade which provided them with beer and gin; the sheer size and unwieldiness of the modern metropolitan community, which prevented the focusing of public opinion upon any depredation which did not immediately concern the average individual citizen; and, of course, the easy-going political apathy of the times. But the immediate occasion of the rise of gangs was undoubtedly prohibition — or, to be more precise, beer-running. (Beer rather than whisky on account of its bulk; to carry on a profitable trade in beer one must transport it in trucks, and trucks are so difficult to disguise that the traffic must be protected by bribery of the prohibition staff and the police and by gunfire against bandits.)

There was vast profit in the manufacture transportation, and sale of beer. In 1927 according to Fred D. Pasley, Al Capone's biographer, federal agents estimated that the Capone gang controlled the sources of a revenue from booze of something like $60 million a year, and much of this — perhaps most of it — came from beer. Fill a man's pockets with money, give him a chance at a huge profit, put him into an illegal business and thus deny him recourse to the law if he is attacked, and you have made it easy for him to bribe and shoot. There have always been gangs and gangsters in American life and doubtless always will be; there has always been corruption of city officials and doubtless always will be; yet it is ironically true, nonetheless, that the outburst of corruption and crime in Chicago in the nineteen-twenties was immediately occasioned by the attempt to banish the temptations of liquor from the American home.

The young thug from the Five Points, New York, had traveled fast and far since 1920. By the end of the decade he had become as widely renowned as Charles Evans Hughes or Gene Tunney. He had become an American portent. Not only did he largely control the sale of liquor to Chicago's 10,000 speakeasies; he controlled the sources of supply, it was said, as far as Canada and the Florida coast. He had amassed, and concealed, a fortune the extent of which nobody knew; it was said by federal agents to amount to $20 million. He was arrested and imprisoned once in Philadelphia for carrying a gun, but otherwise he seemed above the law. He rode about Chicago in an armored car, a traveling fortress, with another car to patrol the way ahead and a third car full of his armed henchmen following behind; he went to the theater attended by a bodyguard of eighteen young men in dinner coats, with guns doubtless slung under their left armpits in approved gangster fashion; when his sister was married, thousands milled about the church in the snow, and he presented the bride with a nine-foot wedding cake and a special honeymoon car; he had a fine estate at Miami where he sometimes entertained seventy-five guests at a time; and high politicians — and even, it has been said, judges — took orders from him over the telephone from his headquarters in a downtown Chicago hotel. And still he was only thirty-two years old. What was Napoleon doing at thirty-two?

Meanwhile gang rule and gang violence were quickly penetrating other American cities. Toledo had felt them, and Detroit, and New York, and many another. Chicago was not alone. Chicago had merely led the way. . . .

The prohibition problem, the gangster problem, the racket problem: as the Postwar Decade bowed itself out, all of them remained unsolved, to challenge the statesmanship of the nineteen-thirties. Still the rum-running launch slipped across the river, the alky-cooker's hidden apparatus poured forth alcohol, entrepreneurs of the contraband liquor industry put one another "on the spot," "typewriters" rattled in the Chicago streets, automobiles laden with roses followed the gangster to his grave, professional sluggers swung on nonunion workmen, bull-necked gentlemen with shifty eyes called on the tradesman to suggest that he do business with them or they could not be responsible for what might happen, bombs reduced little shops to splintered wreckage; and tabloid readers, poring over the stories of gangster killings, found in them adventure and splendor and romance.

27.

Constance Rourke: Humor and the American Character

The literary critic Constance Rourke believed that the development of a mature American literature required "an imaginative penetration of contemporary life," and that this required a sense of tradition rooted in the national past. It was the task of the critic, she believed, to make the past available to the artist, and this she tried to do in her book American Humor: A Study of the National Character *(1931). The book is a regional and historic survey of popular American humor. A portion of the last chapter, "Round Up," is reprinted below.*

Source: *American Humor*, New York, 1931, pp. 297-302.

Humor has been a fashioning instrument in America, cleaving its way through the national life, holding tenaciously to the spread elements of that life. Its mode has often been swift and coarse and ruthless, beyond art and beyond established civilization. It has engaged in warfare against the established heritage, against the bonds of pioneer existence. Its objective — the unconscious objective of a disunited people — has seemed to be that of creating fresh bonds, a new unity, the semblance of a society and the rounded completion of an American type. But a society has not been palpably defined either in life or in literature. If literature is a gauge, only among expatriates has its strong semblance existed, without genuine roots, and mixed with the tragical. The other social semblance which has come into the common view is that of Main Street.

Nor has a single unmistakable type emerged; the American character is still split into many characters. The comic upset has often relaxed rigidities which might have been more significant if taut; individualism has sometimes seemed to wear away under a prolonged common laughter. The solvent of humor has often become a jaded formula, the comic rebound automatic — "laff that off" — so that only the uneasy habit of laughter appears, with an acute sensitivity and insecurity beneath it as though too much had been laughed away. Whole phases of comedy have become empty; the comic rejoinder has become every man's tool.

From the comic the American has often moved to a cult of the comic. But a characteristic humor has emerged, quiet, explosive, competitive, often grounded in good humor, still theatrical at bottom and full of large fantasy. The note of triumph has diminished as the decades have proved that the land is not altogether an Eden and that defeat is a common human portion. Humor has moved into more difficult areas and has embraced a subtler range of feeling; exaltation of the common American as the national type has been deflated. Yet what must still be called a folk strain has been dominant; perhaps it is still uppermost; the great onset of a Negro art, the influence of Negro music, and popular responses to the more primitive aspects of Negro expression suggest that the older absorption in such elements is unbroken. If the American character is split and many-sided at least a large and shadowy outline has been drawn by the many ventures in comedy.

A consistent native tradition has been formed, spreading over the country, surviving cleavages and dispersals, often growing underground, but rising to the surface like some rough vine. This ruthless effort has produced poetry, not only in the sense that primitive concepts are often poetic but keeping the poetic strain as a dominant strain. Not the realistic sense, which might have been expected of a people who call themselves practical, but the poetic sense of life and of character has prevailed. With all the hasty experiment this tradition has revealed beauty, and wry engaging human twists. It has used subtle idioms, like the quieter Yankee idiom; it has contained the dynamic serenity of Whitman and the sensitive discovering genius of Henry James. With all the explosions its key has often remained low; this tradition has shown an effect of reserve, as if in immediate expression and in its large elements something were withheld, to be drawn upon again. It has produced two major patterns, the rhapsodic and the understated, whose outlines may be traced through the many sequences of popular comedy and through American literature; regional at first, they have passed far beyond the regional.

Clear courses have been drawn, yet these have been full of the vagaries that come from complex experiment. New themes have often been upturned and penetrated only in part. The epical promise has never been completely fulfilled. Though extravagance has been a major element in all American comedy, though extravagance may have its incomparable uses with flights and inclusions denied the more equable view, the extravagant vein in American humor has reached no ultimate expression. The comedy of Rabelais provides a gauge, or that of *Ulysses*. On the other hand little equability has appeared, only a few aspects of social comedy; and emotion remains, as

earlier, submerged, or shaded and subtle and indwelling. T. S. Eliot has voiced an insistent mood.

> Well! and what if she should
>   die some afternoon,
> Afternoon gray and smoky,
>   evening yellow and rose;
> Should die and leave me sitting
>   pen in hand
> With the smoke coming down
>   above the housetops;
> Doubtful, for quite a while
> Not knowing what to feel or if
>   I understand. . . .

Set against this self-consciousness and disillusionment are further primitive elements of American life, showing themselves in the continuance of the cults, in lodges, parades, masquerades, as in earlier years, in shouts like "Hallelujah! I'm a bum!" and in a simple persistent self-portraiture not unlike that to which the American was first given. He still envisages himself as an innocent in relation to other peoples; he showed the enduring conviction during the Great War. He is still given to the rhapsody, the monologue, the tale, in life as in literature. Of late has come one of those absorptions in homely retrospect to which the American mind has periodically been devoted; common and comic characters, pioneers, orators, evangelists, hoboes, hold-up men, have come to the fore with a stream of old story and song, often engaging the same Americans who turn to Eliot or Robinson or Henry James.

These oddly matched aspects of the American character are often at variance. Together or separated, they have found no full and complete expression. Who can say what will bring fulfillment? If this comes it may be conditioned by many undetermined elements in the national life and character, by outside impingements even — since Americans are acutely aware of these — like that which weighed heavily in earlier years, the burden of British opinion. Its effects are still not altogether resolved; it has been noted that the sharp critiques offered in an earlier day by visiting foreigners are now defined by Americans, often as though they had merely borrowed the attitude. The involvement with the older countries is genuine; and the task looms for literature of absorbing traditions of the older world as part of the natural American heritage. The alliances must be instinctive or the fabric will be seamy. In general the American creative mind has lacked the patience and humility to acquire them, or it has been fearful of alienation from American sources.

Against full use of the native tradition many factors are set. That nomadic strain which has run through all American life, deeply influencing the American character, is now accented by the conditions of modern life; and the native character seems to grow more generalized, less specially American. Within the space of a lifetime Henry James saw something of the kind happen; in later years he remarked of the heroine of *Pandora's Box* that she could no longer "pass for quaint or fresh or for exclusively native to any one tract of Anglo-Saxon soil." Yet the main outlines of the American character still persist; American types can be found far from their native habitat and unmistakable in outline, homeless Yankees in Nebraska or frontiersmen in Monte Carlo, and others who may show an erosion due to alien places so that the original grain has grown dim, but who show that grain.

For the creative writer the major problem seems to be to know the patternings of the grain; and these can hardly be discovered in rich color without understanding of the many sequences of the American tradition on the popular side as well as on purely literary levels. The writer must know, as Eliot has said, "the mind of his own country — a mind which he learns in time to be much more important than his own private mind."

A favored explanation for the slow and spare development of the arts in America has lain in stress upon the forces of materialism. But these have existed in every civilization; they have even at times seemed to assist the processes of art. The American failure to value the productions of the artist has likewise been cited; but the artist often seems to need less of critical persuasion and sympathy than an unstudied association with his natural inheritance. Many artists have worked supremely well with little encouragement; few have worked without a rich traditional store from which consciously or unconsciously they have drawn.

The difficult task of discovering and diffusing the materials of the American tradition — many of them still buried — belongs for the most part to criticism; the artist will steep himself in the gathered light. In the end he may use native sources as a point of radical departure; he may seldom be intent upon early materials; but he will discover a relationship with the many streams of native character and feeling. The single writer — the single production — will no longer stand solitary or aggressive but within a natural sequence.

I not only "don't choose to run" but I don't want to leave a loophole in case I am drafted, so I won't "choose." I will say "won't run" no matter how bad the country will need a comedian by that time.

WILL ROGERS, June 28, 1931

Give me the truth. I'll exaggerate it and make it funny.

WILL ROGERS, to his co-workers

1932

28.

OSCAR AMERINGER: Overproduction and Underconsumption

In the winter of 1931-1932, Oscar Ameringer, editor of an Oklahoma City newspaper, toured more than twenty states, observing everywhere the tragic irony of a nation that suffered overproduction and underconsumption at the same time. In February 1932 his observations on the plight of the farmer were reported to a subcommittee of the House Committee on Labor, which was conducting hearings on unemployment. Passages from his testimony are reprinted below.

Source: *Unemployment in the United States, Hearings Before a Subcommittee of the Committee on Labor, House of Representatives,* 72 Congress, 1 Session, Washington, 1932, pp. 97-105.

MY NAME IS OSCAR AMERINGER. I am editor of the *American Guardian* and former editor of the *American Miner.* I live in Oklahoma City, Okla.

I may say that I am a representative of the country at large. During the last four months I have visited more than twenty states in my capacity as a newspaperman and an observer of prevailing conditions. Now, the witnesses that have preceded me have told you about a deplorable condition among the unemployed. They have told you of exhausted city treasuries and exhausted charity funds. They have told you about rising needs and falling incomes. They have told you about mothers being emaciated and not being able to give milk to their offspring. They have told you about infants being fed for months on flour and water. You have heard the young miner from Pennsylvania tell about conditions in his section of the country. You have heard the young miner from the state of West Virginia tell of conditions in his country. Both of these men have served their country trying to make the country safe for democracy.

The governments of their respective states, West Virginia and Pennsylvania, have done all in their power to bring in unions of these men, their only protections, and reduce their wages to a starvation level and, incidentally, make beggars out of World War heroes.

I know these men have told you the truth. And in my former capacity of editor of the *American Miner,* I have received thousands of letters telling of similar and even worse conditions. What they have told you, however, is that their plight could be multiplied by hundreds of thousands.

In the year 1921, the Miners' Union of Illinois was composed of 90,000 men. At the end of 1930 this membership had fallen to 50,000. Of these, 25,000 men were exonerated from the payment of dues on account of unemployment. In this connection it must be remembered that so long as a man works two days for pay — that is two days out of fifteen — he is regarded as employed.

During the last decade some 20,000 families were driven from the coal regions in Illinois alone. Credit and savings had been used long before the stock market crash of 1929. Those who had homes or equities in homes have lost them. What the years of shrinking employment have not devoured, bank failures [have], taking with them not only the meager savings of the most frugal and lucky but also the funds of these unions.

Today there are counties in the once-so-prosperous mining fields of Illinois that do not contain one single bank, as Mr. Keller here will corroborate. In the county Mr. Keller comes from, it is my recollection that there is not a single bank left there. In fact, I do not believe there are any banks left in that coal-mining region. I was in Christian County, and, as I remember, there is not a single one left.

If I had the time I would enumerate some of the causes leading to this disaster involving perhaps 3 million human beings, if we include the coalfields of the Mississippi Valley alone.

Needless to say, the plight of these people is totally undeserved. They are victims of circumstances over which they had no control. Nor can their sufferings be attributed to the so-called acts of God, for while they and many other millions of brother toilers were suffering from the lack of decent necessities of life, food and raw material for clothing were rotting or were destroyed by the millions of tons. . . .

I have visited, as I have said, some twenty states of this wonderfully rich and beautiful country. Here are some of the things I heard and saw:

In the state of Washington I was told that the forest fires raging in that region all summer and fall were caused by unemployed timber workers and bankrupt farmers in an endeavor to earn a few honest dollars as firefighters. The last thing I saw on the night I left Seattle was numbers of women searching for scraps of food in the refuse piles of the principal market of that city. A number of Montana citizens told me of thousands of bushels of wheat left in the fields uncut on account of its low price, that hardly paid for the harvesting. . . .

While I was in Oregon, the *Portland Oregonian* bemoaned the fact that thousands of ewes were killed by the sheep raisers because they did not bring enough in the market to pay the freight on them. And while Oregon sheep raisers fed mutton to the buzzards, I saw men picking for meat scraps in the garbage cans in the cities of New York and Chicago. I talked to one man in a restaurant in Chicago. He told me of his experience in raising sheep. He said that he had killed 3,000 sheep this fall and thrown them down the canyon, because it cost $1.10 to ship a sheep, and then he would get less than $1 for it. He said he could not afford to feed the sheep, and he would not let them starve, so he just cut their throats and threw them down the canyon.

The roads of the West and Southwest teem with hungry hitchhikers. The campfires of the homeless are seen along every railroad track. I saw men, women, and children walking over the hard roads. Most of them were tenant farmers who had lost their all in the late slump in wheat and cotton. Between Clarksville and Russellville, Ark., I picked up a family. The woman was hugging a dead chicken under a ragged coat. When I asked her where she had procured the fowl, first she told me she had found it dead in the road, and then added in grim humor, "They promised me a chicken in the pot, and now I got mine."

In Oklahoma, Texas, Arkansas, and Louisiana I saw untold bales of cotton rotting in he fields because the cotton pickers could not keep body and soul together on 35 cents paid for picking 100 pounds. The farmers' cooperatives who loaned the money to the planters to make the crops allowed the planters $5 a bale. That means 1,500 pounds of seed cotton for the picking of it, which was in the neighborhood of 35 cents a pound. A good picker can pick about 200 pounds of cotton a day, so that the 70 cents would not provide enough pork and beans to keep the picker in the field, so that there is fine staple cotton rotting down there by the hundreds and thousands of tons.

As a result of this appalling overproduction on the one side and the staggering underconsumption on the other side, 70 percent of the farmers of Oklahoma were unable to pay the interests on their mortgages. Last week one of the largest and oldest mortgage companies in that state went into the hands of the receiver. In that and other states we have now the interesting spectacle of farmers losing their farms by foreclosure and mortgage companies losing their recouped holdings by tax sales.

The farmers are being pauperized by the poverty of industrial populations and the industrial populations are being pauperized by the poverty of the farmers. Neither has the money to buy the product of the other, hence we have overproduction and underconsumption at the same time and in the same country.

I have not come here to stir you in a recital of the necessity for relief for our suffering fellow citizens. However, unless something is done for them and done soon, you will have a revolution on hand. And when that revolution comes it will not come from Moscow, it will not be made by the poor Communists whom our police are beading up regularly and efficiently. When the revolution comes it will bear the label "Laid in the U.S.A." and its chief promoters will be the people of American stock. . . .

I do not say we are going to have a revolution on hand within the next year or two, perhaps never. I hope we may not have such; but the danger is here. That is the feeling of our people — as reflected in the letters I have read. I have met these people virtually every day all over the country. There is a feeling among the masses generally that something is radically wrong. They are despairing of political action. They say the only thing you do in Washington is to take money from the pockets of the poor and put it into the pockets of the rich. They say that this government is a conspiracy against the common people to enrich the already rich. I hear such remarks every day.

I never pass a hitchhiker without inviting him in and talking to him. Bankers, even, are talking about that. They are talking in irrational tones. You have more Bolshevism among the bankers today than the hod carriers, I think. It is a terrible situation, and I think something should be done and done immediately. . . .

In conclusion I may add that the temporary business depression that is now in its third winter is deepening daily, and unless the economists whom I have consulted of late are sadly mistaken, the worst is yet to come. And if you have time I will present these reasons in conclusion.

Personally, and as a lifelong student of political economy, I am of the opinion that all this talk about speedy recovery and prosperity being just around the corner is bosh and nonsense. What we are confronted with is not a mere panic like those of 1873 and 1883 but a worldwide economic catastrophe that may spell the end of the capitalistic era — for the cause of it is production for profit instead of production for consumption. The masses cannot buy what they have themselves produced; and unless ways and means are found to make cash customers out of some 20 million of unemployed wage earners and bankrupt farmers, there can be no recovery.

29.

Florence Converse: "Bread Line"

As the Depression moved into its third winter, increasing millions of unemployed (unemployment in March 1932 was estimated at 12,500,000, an increase of 50 percent in one year) were forced to beg for vanishing sources of relief. They met in soup kitchens, breadlines, and the tar-paper cities (sometimes called Hoovervilles) that arose along railroad embankments and in city dumps. Widespread fear existed that from the congregations of the destitute revolution would come. The following selection, "Bread Line," documents that fear. The poem was published at the beginning of 1932.

Source: *Atlantic Monthly*, January 1932.

❦ BREAD LINE

What's the meaning of this queue,
Tailing down the avenue,
Full of eyes that will not meet
The other eyes that throng the street —
The questing eyes, the curious eyes,
Scornful, popping with surprise
To see a living line of men
As long as round the block, and then
As long again? The statisticians
Estimate that these conditions
Have not reached their apogee.
All lines end eventually;
Except of course in theory.
This one has an end somewhere.
End in what? — Pause, there.
What's the meaning in these faces
Modern industry displaces,
Emptying the factory
To set the men so tidily
Along the pavement in a row?
Now and then they take a slow
Shuffling step, straight ahead,
As if a dead march said:
"Beware! I'm not dead."
Now and then an unaverted
Eye bespells the disconcerted
Passer-by; a profile now

And then will lift a beaten brow —
Waiting what? — The Comforter?
The Pentecostal Visitor?
If by fasting visions come,
Why not to a hungry bum?
Idle, shamed, and underfed,
Waiting for his dole of bread,
What if he should find his head
A candle of the Holy Ghost?
A dim and starveling spark, at most,
But yet a spark? It needs but one.
A spark can creep, a spark can run;
Suddenly a spark can wink
And send us down destruction's brink.
It needs but one to make a star,
Or light a Russian samovar.
One to start a funeral pyre,
One to cleanse a world by fire.
What if our breadline should be
The long slow-match of destiny?
What if even now the Holy
Ghost should be advancing slowly
Down the line, a kindling flame,
Kissing foreheads bowed with shame?
Creep, my ember! Blaze, my brand!
The end of all things is at hand.
Idlers in the market place,

Make an end to your disgrace!
Here's a fair day's work for you —
To build a world all over new.
What if our slow-match have caught
Fire from a burning thought?
What if we should be destroyed
By our patient unemployed?
Some of us with much to lose
By conflagration will refuse

To hallow arson in the name
Of Pentecost. We'd rather blame
The Devil, who can always find
For idle hand or empty mind
Work to do at Devil's hire.
The Devil loves to play with fire.
We'd rather blame him — ah, but this
May be just our prejudice.

30.

Social Creed of the Protestant Churches

As the Depression worsened and the administration's inability to cope with it became more evident, public discontent grew. On Labor Day 1931 the Federal Council of Churches issued a statement calling for a complete reconstruction of the economic order and denouncing capitalism as a complete failure. This statement was followed by a revision of the social creed of the churches that set forth specific proposals on economic and social readjustment. The new creed, as promulgated by the Federal Council at its convention in December 1932, is reprinted below.

Source: *Christian Century,* January 4, 1933, p. 34.

The churches should stand for:

1. Practical application of the Christian principle of social well-being to the acquisition and use of wealth, subordination of speculation and the profit motive to the creative and cooperative spirit.

2. Social planning and control of the credit and monetary systems and the economic processes for the common good.

3. The right of all to the opportunity for self-maintenance; a wider and fairer distribution of wealth; a living wage, as a minimum, and above this a just share for the worker in the product of industry and agriculture.

4. Safeguarding of all workers, urban and rural, against harmful conditions of labor and occupational injury and disease.

5. Social insurance against sickness, accident, want in old age, and unemployment.

6. Reduction of hours of labor as the general productivity of industry increases; release from employment at least one day in seven, with a shorter working week in prospect.

7. Such special regulation of the conditions of work of women as shall safeguard their welfare and that of the family and the community.

8. The right of employees and employers alike to organize for collective bargaining and social action; protection of both in the exercise of this right; the obligation of both to work for the public good; encouragement of cooperatives and other organizations among farmers and other groups.

9. Abolition of child labor; adequate pro-

vision for the protection, education, spiritual nurture, and wholesome recreation of every child.

10. Protection of the family by the single standard of purity; educational preparation for marriage, homemaking, and parenthood.

11. Economic justice for the farmer in legislation, financing, transportation, and the price of farm products as compared with the cost of machinery and other commodities which he must buy.

12. Extension of the primary cultural opportunities and social services now enjoyed by urban populations to the farm family.

13. Protection of the individual and society from the social, economic, and moral waste of any traffic in intoxicants and habit-forming drugs.

14. Application of the Christian principle of redemption to the treatment of offenders; reform of penal and correctional methods and institutions, and of criminal court procedure.

15. Justice, opportunity, and equal rights for all; mutual goodwill and cooperation among racial, economic, and religious groups.

16. Repudiation of war, drastic reduction of armaments, participation in international agencies for the peaceable settlement of all controversies; the building of a cooperative world order.

17. Recognition and maintenance of the rights and responsibilities of free speech, free assembly, and a free press; the encouragement of free communication of mind. with mind as essential to the discovery of truth.

31.

Songs of the Hungry

The songs and poems that came out of the Depression are as vivid an index of the feelings of ordinary Americans as all of the statistics and surveys of unemployment, relief programs, and economic distress. The first of the two songs reprinted here, "I Don't Want Your Millions, Mister," was written by Jim Garland, a blacklisted miner from notorious Harlan County, Kentucky, where labor strife was severe during the early 1930s. The second song, "Beans, Bacon, and Gravy," is anonymous; while it reflects the same misery as the first, it does so with less bitterness.

Source: *Songs of Work and Freedom,* Edith Fowke and Joe Glazer, eds., New York, 1960.

I DON'T WANT YOUR MILLIONS, MISTER

I don't want your millions, mister;
I don't want your diamond ring.
All I want is the right to live, mister;
Give me back my job again.

I don't want your Rolls-Royce, mister;
I don't want your pleasure yacht;
All I want is food for my babies;
Give to me my old job back.

We worked to build this country, mister,
While you enjoyed a life of ease;
You've stolen all that we built, mister;
Now our children starve and freeze.

Think me dumb if you wish, mister;
Call me green or blue or red;
This one thing I sure know, mister:
My hungry babies must be fed.

I don't want your millions, mister,
I don't want your diamond ring.
All I want is the right to live, mister;
Give me back my job again.

JIM GARLAND

BEANS, BACON, AND GRAVY

I was born long ago
In eighteen ninety-one,
And I've seen many a panic, I will own.
I've been hungry, I've been cold,
And now I'm growing old,
But the worst I've seen is nineteen thirty-one.

Chorus:
Oh, those beans, bacon, and gravy,
They almost drive me crazy!
I eat them till I see them in my dreams.
When I wake up in the morning
And another day is dawning,
Then I know I'll have another mess of beans.

We all congregate each morning
At the county barn at dawning,
And everyone is happy, so it seems.
But when our work is done
We file in one by one
And thank the Lord for one more mess of beans.

We have Hooverized on butter,
And for milk we've only water,
And I haven't seen a steak in many a day.
As for pies, cakes, and jellies,
We substitute sow-bellies
For which we work the county road each day.

If there ever comes a time
When I have more than a dime,
They will have to put me under lock and key,
For they've had me broke so long
I can only sing this song
Of the workers and their misery.

32.

Adolf A. Berle and Gardiner C. Means: The Corporation and Private Property

The Modern Corporation and Private Property (1932), a collaborative effort by Adolf A. Berle, a lawyer, and Gardiner C. Means, an economist, was one of the most influential economic treatises of its day. "The individualism of Adam Smith's private enterprise," they argued, "has in large measure given way to the collective activity of the modern corporation." The significant difference was in the disappearance of the free market of the classical model, a change that required a shift in emphasis "from analysis in terms of competition to analysis in terms of control." This challenge to the ability of traditional economics to cope with the nation's crisis stirred much controversy. Both authors were later recruited by President Roosevelt; Berle became a member of the "brain trust" and Means served as economic adviser to various agencies.

Source: *The Modern Corporation and Private Property*, New York, 1932, pp. 345, 352-357.

UNDERLYING THE THINKING of economists, lawyers, and businessmen during the last century and a half has been the picture of economic life so skillfully painted by Adam Smith. Within his treatise on the *Wealth of Nations* are contained the fundamental concepts which run through most modern thought. Though adjustments in his picture have been made by later writers to account for new conditions, the whole has been painted in the colors which he supplied. Private property, private enterprise, individual initiative, the profit motive, wealth, competition — these are the concepts which he employed in describing the economy of his time and by means of which he sought to show that the pecuniary self-interest of each individual, if given free play, would lead to the optimum satisfaction of human wants. Most writers of the nine-teenth century built on these logical foundations, and current economic literature is, in large measure, cast in such terms.

Yet these terms have ceased to be accurate, and therefore tend to mislead in describing modern enterprise as carried on by the great corporations. Though both the terms and the concepts remain, they are inapplicable to a dominant area in American economic organization. New terms, connoting changed relationships, become necessary. . . .

Most fundamental to the new picture of economic life must be a new concept of business enterprise as concentrated in the corporate organization. In some measure a concept is already emerging. Over a decade ago, Walter Rathenau wrote concerning the German counterpart of our great corporation:

No one is a permanent owner. The composition of the thousandfold complex which functions as lord of the undertaking is in a state of flux. . . . This condition of things signifies that ownership has been depersonalized. . . . The depersonalization of ownership simultaneously implies the objectification of the thing owned. The claims to ownership are subdivided in such a fashion, and are so mobile, that the enterprise assumes an independent life, as if it belonged to no one; it takes an objective existence, such as in earlier days was embodied only in state and church, in a municipal corporation, in the life of a guild or a religious order. . . . The depersonalization of ownership, the objectification of enterprise, the detachment of property from the possessor, leads to a point where the enterprise becomes transformed into an institution which resembles the state in character.

The institution here envisaged calls for analysis, not in terms of business enterprise but in terms of social organization. On the one hand, it involves a concentration of power in the economic field comparable to the concentration of religious power in the medieval church or of political power in the national state. On the other hand, it involves the interrelation of a wide diversity of economic interests — those of the "owners" who supply capital, those of the workers who "create," those of the consumers who give value to the products of enterprise, and above all those of the control who wield power.

Such a great concentration of power and such a diversity of interest raise the long-sought issue of power and its regulation — of interest and its protection. A constant warfare has existed between the individuals wielding power, in whatever form, and the subjects of that power. Just as there is a continuous desire for power, so also there is a continuous desire to make that power the servant of the bulk of the individuals it affects. The long struggles for the reform of

the Catholic Church and for the development of constitutional law in the states are phases of this phenomenon. Absolute power is useful in building the organization. More slow but equally sure is the development of social pressure demanding that the power shall be used for the benefit of all concerned. This pressure, constant in ecclesiastical and political history, is already making its appearance in many guises in the economic field.

Observable throughout the world, and in varying degrees of intensity, is this insistence that power in economic organization shall be subjected to the same tests of public benefit which have been applied in their turn to power otherwise located. In its most extreme aspect this is exhibited in the communist movement, which in its purest form is an insistence that *all* of the powers and privileges of property, shall be used only in the common interest. In less extreme forms of socialist dogma, transfer of economic powers to the state for public service is demanded. In the strictly capitalist countries, and particularly in time of depression, demands are constantly put forward that the men controlling the great economic organisms be made to accept responsibility for the well-being of those who are subject to the organization, whether workers, investors, or consumers. In a sense the difference in all of these demands lies only in degree. In proportion as an economic organism grows in strength and its power is concentrated in a few hands, the possessor of power is more easily located, and the demand for responsible power becomes increasingly direct.

How will this demand be made effective? To answer this question would be to foresee the history of the next century. We can here only consider and appraise certain of the more important lines of possible development.

By tradition, a corporation "belongs" to

its shareholders, or, in a wider sense, to its security holders, and theirs is the only interest to be recognized as the object of corporate activity. Following this tradition, and without regard for the changed character of ownership, it would be possible to apply in the interests of the *passive* property owner the doctrine of strict property rights. . . . By the application of this doctrine, the group in control of a corporation would be placed in a position of trusteeship in which it would be called on to operate or arrange for the operation of the corporation for the *sole* benefit of the security owners despite the fact that the latter have ceased to have power over or to accept responsibility for the *active* property in which they have an interest. Were this course followed, the bulk of American industry might soon be operated by trustees for the sole benefit of inactive and irresponsible security owners.

In direct opposition to the above doctrine of strict property rights is the view, apparently held by the great corporation lawyers and by certain students of the field, that corporate development has created a new set of relationships, giving to the groups in control powers which are absolute and not limited by any implied obligation with respect to their use. This logic leads to drastic conclusions. For instance, if, by reason of these new relationships, the men in control of a corporation can operate it in their own interests, and can divert a portion of the asset fund of income stream to their own uses, such is their privilege. Under this view, since the new powers have been acquired on a quasi-contractual basis, the security holders have agreed in advance to any losses which they may suffer by reason of such use. The result is, briefly, that the existence of the legal and economic relationships giving rise to these powers must be frankly recognized as a modification of the principle of private property.

If these were the only alternatives, the former would appear to be the lesser of two evils. Changed corporate relationships have unquestionably involved an essential alteration in the character of property. But such modifications have hitherto been brought about largely on the principle that might makes right. Choice between strengthening the rights of passive property owners, or leaving a set of uncurbed powers in the hands of control therefore resolves itself into a purely realistic evaluation of different results. We might elect the relative certainty and safety of a trust relationship in favor of a particular group within the corporation accompanied by a possible diminution of enterprise. Or we may grant the controlling group free rein, with the corresponding danger of a corporate oligarchy coupled with the probability of an era of corporate plundering.

A third possibility exists, however. On the one hand, the owners of passive property, by surrendering control and responsibility over the active property, have surrendered the right that the corporation should be operated in their sole interest; they have released the community from the obligation to protect them to the full extent implied in the doctrine of strict property rights. At the same time, the controlling groups, by means of the extension of corporate powers, have in their own interest broken the bars of tradition which require that the corporation be operated solely for the benefit of the owners of passive property. Eliminating the sole interest of the passive owner, however, does not necessarily lay a basis for the alternative claim that the new powers should be used in the interest of the controlling groups. The latter have not presented, in acts or words, any acceptable defense of the proposition that these powers should be so used. No tradition supports that proposition. The control groups have, rather, cleared the way for the claims of a group far wider than either the owners or the control. They have placed the community in a position to demand that the modern corporation serve not alone the owners or the control but all society.

This third alternative offers a wholly new concept of corporate activity. Neither the claims of ownership nor those of control can stand against the paramount interests of the community. The present claims of both contending parties now in the field have been weakened. . . . It remains only for the claims of the community to be put forward with clarity and force. Rigid enforcement of property rights as a temporary protection against plundering by control would not stand in the way of the modification of these rights in the interest of other groups. When a convincing system of community obligations is worked out and is generally accepted, in that moment the passive property right of today must yield before the larger interests of society.

Should the corporate leaders, for example, set forth a program comprising fair wages, security to employees, reasonable service to their public, and stabilization of business, all of which would divert a portion of the profits from the owners of passive property, and should the community generally accept such a scheme as a logical and human solution of industrial difficulties, the interests of passive property owners would have to give way. Courts would almost of necessity be forced to recognize the result, justifying it by whatever of the many legal theories they might choose. It is conceivable — indeed it seems almost essential if the corporate system is to survive — that the "control" of the great corporations should develop into a purely neutral technocracy, balancing a variety of claims by various groups in the community and assigning to each a portion of the income stream on the basis of public policy rather than private cupidity. . . .

In still larger view, the modern corporation may be regarded not simply as one form of social organization but potentially (if not yet actually) as the dominant institution of the modern world. In every age, the major concentration of power has been based upon the dominant interest of that age. The strong man has, in his time, striven to be cardinal or pope, prince or cabinet minister, bank president or partner in the House of Morgan. During the Middle Ages, the Church, exercising spiritual power, dominated Europe and gave to it a unity at a time when both political and economic power were diffused. With the rise of the modern state, political power, concentrated into a few large units, challenged the spiritual interest as the strongest bond of human society. Out of the long struggle between church and state which followed, the state emerged victorious; nationalist politics superseded religion as the basis of the major unifying organization of the Western world. Economic power still remained diffused.

The rise of the modern corporation has brought a concentration of economic power which can compete on equal terms with the modern state — economic power versus political power, each strong in its own field. The state seeks in some aspects to regulate the corporation, while the corporation, steadily becoming more powerful, makes every effort to avoid such regulation. Where its own interests are concerned, it even attempts to dominate the state. The future may see the economic organism, now typified by the corporation, not only on an equal plane with the state but possibly even superseding it as the dominant form of social organization. The law of corporations, accordingly, might well be considered as a potential constitutional law for the new economic state, while business practice is increasingly assuming the aspect of economic statesmanship.

33.

George Sutherland and L. D. Brandeis: *New State Ice Company* v. *Liebmann*

The great age of judicial review, as it has been called, lasted from 1890 to 1937. During that relatively short period some 69 acts of Congress were invalidated by the Supreme Court as opposed to but 2 in the whole period before the Civil War; and 228 acts of state legislatures were set aside, as opposed to but 20 before 1860. The due process clause of the Fourteenth Amendment was the usual formula used by the Court to disallow state legislation, and that was the precedent cited by Justice Sutherland in his majority opinion in the case presented here. The decision was handed down in March 1932, but it was by no means unanimous, Justice Brandeis providing a notable dissent in which he argued eloquently for the right of government to control business activity for the public welfare. His dissent was written a year before Franklin D. Roosevelt took office, but it nevertheless prefigured the general attitude of the New Deal planners, and at the end of it Brandeis called for the kind of economic and political experimentation that would mark the incoming administration. The Court continued to interpret such experiments with Sutherland's jaundiced eye until 1937, when, in an unprecedented reversal, it began to validate rather than disallow New Deal legislation. The Sutherland and Brandeis opinions are reprinted here in part.

Source: 285 U.S. 262.

Mr. Justice Sutherland. The New State Ice Company, engaged in the business of manufacturing, selling, and distributing ice under a license or permit duly issued by the Corporation Commission of Oklahoma, brought this suit against Liebmann in the Federal District Court for the Western District of Oklahoma to enjoin him from manufacturing, selling, and distributing ice within Oklahoma City without first having obtained a like license or permit from the commission.

The license or permit is required by an act of the Oklahoma legislature. . . . That act declares that the manufacture, sale, and distribution of ice is a public business; that no one shall be permitted to manufacture, sell, or distribute ice within the state without first having secured a license for that purpose from the commission; that whoever shall engage in such business without obtaining the license shall be guilty of a misdemeanor, punishable by fine not to exceed $25, each day's violation constituting a separate offense, and that by general order of the commission, a fine not to exceed $500 may be imposed for each violation. . . .

It must be conceded that all businesses are subject to some measure of public regulation. And that the business of manufacturing, selling, or distributing ice, like that of the grocer, the dairyman, the butcher, or the baker, may be subjected to appropriate regulations in the interest of the public health cannot be doubted; but the question here is whether the business is so charged with a public use as to justify the particular restriction above stated. If this legislative restriction be within the constitutional power of the state legislature, it follows that the license or permit, issued to appellant, constitutes a franchise, to which a Court of Equity will afford protection against one who seeks to carry on the same business without obtaining from the commission a license or permit to do so. . . . In that view, engagement in the business is a privilege to be exercised only in virtue of a public grant, and not a common right to be exercised independently (id.) by any competent person conformably to reasonable regulations equally applicable to all who choose to engage therein. . . .

Here we are dealing with an ordinary business, not with a paramount industry upon which the prosperity of the entire state in large measure depends. It is a business as essentially private in its nature as the business of the grocer, the dairyman, the butcher, the baker, the shoemaker, or the tailor, each of whom performs a service which, to a greater or less extent, the community is dependent upon and is interested in having maintained, but which bears no such relation to the public as to warrant its inclusion in the category of businesses charged with a public use. It may be quite true that in Oklahoma ice is not only an article of prime necessity but indispensable; but certainly not more so than food or clothing or the shelter of a home. And this Court has definitely said that the production or sale of food or clothing cannot be subjected to legislative regulation on the basis of a public use; and that the same is true in respect of the business of renting houses and apartments, except as to temporary measures to tide over grave emergencies. . . .

It has been said that the manufacture of ice requires an expensive plant beyond the means of the average citizen, and that since the use of ice is indispensable, patronage of the producer by the consumer is unavoidable. The same might, however, be said in respect of other articles clearly beyond the reach of a restriction like that here under review. But, for the moment conceding the materiality of the statement, it is not now true, whatever may have been the fact in the past. We know, since it is common knowledge, that today, to say nothing of other means, wherever electricity or gas is available (and one or the other is available in practically every part of the country), anyone for a comparatively moderate outlay may have set up in his kitchen an appliance by means of which he may manufacture ice for himself.

Under such circumstances it hardly will do to say that people generally are at the mercy of the manufacturer, seller, and distributor of ice for ordinary needs. Moreover, the practical tendency of the restriction, as the trial court suggested in the present case, is to shut out new enterprises and thus create and foster monopoly in the hands of existing establishments, against, rather than in aid of, the interest of the consuming public.

Plainly, a regulation which has the effect of denying or unreasonably curtailing the common right to engage in a lawful private business, such as that under review, cannot be upheld consistently with the Fourteenth Amendment. Under that amendment, nothing is more clearly settled than that it is beyond the power of a state, "under the guise of protecting the public, arbitrarily [to] interfere with private business or prohibit lawful occupations or impose unreasonable and unnecessary restrictions upon them." . . .

Stated succinctly, a private corporation here seeks to prevent a competitor from entering the business of making and selling ice. It claims to be endowed with state authority to achieve this exclusion. There is no question now before us of any regulation by the state to protect the consuming public either with respect to conditions of manufacture and distribution or to insure purity of product or to prevent extortion. The control here asserted does not protect against monopoly but tends to foster it. The aim is not to encourage competition

Justices of the Supreme Court at the White House in 1932: (from left) William D. Mitchell, attorney general; Benjamin Cardozo, Harlan Stone, George Sutherland, Willis Van Devanter, Charles E. Hughes, chief justice; Louis Brandeis, Pierce Butler, Owen Roberts, and Thomas D. Thacher, solicitor general

but to prevent it; not to regulate the business but to preclude persons from engaging in it. There is no difference in principle between this case and the attempt of the dairyman under state authority to prevent another from keeping cows and selling milk on the ground that there are enough dairymen in the business; or to prevent a shoemaker from making or selling shoes because shoemakers already in that occupation can make and sell all the shoes that are needed. We are not able to see anything peculiar in the business here in question which distinguishes it from ordinary manufacture and production.

It is said to be recent; but it is the character of the business and not the date when it began that is determinative. It is not the case of a natural monopoly, or of an enterprise in its nature dependent upon the grant of public privileges. The particular requirement before us was evidently not imposed to prevent a practical monopoly of the business, since its tendency is quite to the contrary. Nor is it a case of the protection of natural resources. There is nothing in the product that we can perceive on which to rest a distinction, in respect of this attempted control, from other products in common use which enter into free competition, subject, of course, to reasonable regulations prescribed for the protection of the public and applied with appropriate impartiality.

And it is plain that unreasonable or arbitrary interference or restrictions cannot be saved from the condemnation of that amendment merely by calling them experimental. It is not necessary to challenge the authority of the states to indulge in experimental legislation; but it would be strange and unwarranted doctrine to hold that they may do so by enactments which transcend the limitations imposed upon them by the federal Constitution. The principle is imbedded in our constitutional system that there are certain essentials of liberty with which the state is not entitled to dispense in the interest of experiments. . . .

Mr. Justice Brandeis. Liebmann contends that the manufacture of ice for sale and distribution is not a public business; that it is a private business and, indeed, a common calling; that the right to engage in a common calling is one of the fundamental liberties guaranteed by the due process clause; and that to make his right to engage in that calling dependent upon a finding of public necessity deprives him of liberty and property in violation of the Fourteenth Amendment. Upon full hearing the District Court sustained that contention and dismissed the bill. 42 F. (2d) 913. Its decree was affirmed by the Circuit Court of Appeals. 52 F. (2d) 349. The case is here on appeal. In my opinion, the judgment should be reversed.

First, the Oklahoma statute makes entry into the business of manufacturing ice for sale and distribution dependent, in effect, upon a certificate of public convenience and necessity. Such a certificate was unknown to the common law. It is a creature of the machine age, in which plants have displaced tools and businesses are substituted for trades. The purpose of requiring it is to promote the public interest by preventing waste. Particularly in those businesses in which interest and depreciation charges on plant constitute a large element in the cost of production, experience has taught that the financial burdens incident to unnecessary duplication of facilities are likely to bring high rates and poor service.

There, cost is usually dependent, among other things, upon volume; and division of possible patronage among competing concerns may so raise the unit cost of operation as to make it impossible to provide adequate service at reasonable rates. The introduction in the United States of the certificate of public convenience and necessity marked the growing conviction that under certain circumstances free competition might be harmful to the community and that, when it was so, absolute freedom to enter the business of one's choice should be denied.

Long before the enactment of the Oklahoma statute here challenged, a like requirement had become common in the United States in some lines of business. The certificate was required first for railroads; then for street railways; then for other public utilities whose operation is dependent upon the grant of some special privilege. Latterly, the requirement has been widely extended to common carriers by motor vehicle which use the highways, but which, unlike street railways and electric light companies, are not dependent upon the grant of any special privilege. In Oklahoma the certificate was required, as early as 1915, for cotton gins — a business then declared a public one and, like the business of manufacturing ice, conducted wholly upon private property. . . .

As applied to public utilities, the validity under the Fourteenth Amendment of the requirement of the certificate has never been successfully questioned.

Second, Oklahoma declared the business of manufacturing ice for sale and distribution a "public business"; that is, a public utility. So far as appears, it was the first state to do so. Of course, a legislature cannot by mere legislative fiat convert a business into a public utility. . . . But the conception of a public utility is not static. The welfare of the community may require that the business of supplying ice be made a public utility as well as the business of supplying water or any other necessary commodity or service. If the business is, or can be made, a public utility, it must be possible to make the issue of a certificate a prerequisite to engaging in it.

Whether the local conditions are such as to justify converting a private business into a public one is a matter primarily for the determination of the state legislature. Its determination is subject to judicial review; but the usual presumption of validity attends the enactment. The action of the state must be held valid unless clearly arbitrary, capricious, or unreasonable. . . . Whether the grievances are real or fancied, whether the remedies are wise or foolish, are not matters about which the Court may concern itself. . . . A decision that the legislature's belief of evils was arbitrary, capricious, and unreasonable may not be made without enquiry into the facts with reference to which it acted.

Third, Liebmann challenges the statute — not an order of the Corporation Commission. If he had applied for a license and been denied one, we should have been obliged to enquire whether the evidence introduced before the Commission justified it in refusing permission to establish an additional ice plant in Oklahoma City. As he did not apply but challenges the statute itself, our enquiry is of an entirely different nature. Liebmann rests his defense upon the broad claim that the federal Constitution gives him the right to enter the business of manufacturing ice for sale even if his doing so be found by the properly constituted authority to be inconsistent with the public welfare. He claims that, whatever the local conditions may demand, to confer upon the Commission power to deny that right is an unreasonable, arbitrary, and capricious restraint upon his liberty.

The function of the Court is primarily to determine whether the conditions in Oklahoma are such that the legislature could not reasonably conclude (1) that the public welfare required treating the manufacture of ice for sale and distribution as a "public business"; and (2) that in order to ensure to the inhabitants of some communities an adequate supply of ice at reasonable rates, it was necessary to give the Commission power to exclude the establishment of an additional ice plant in places where the community was already well served. Unless the Court can say that the federal Constitution confers an absolute right to engage anywhere in the business of manufacturing ice for sale, it cannot properly decide that the legislators acted unreasonably without first ascertaining what was the experience of Oklahoma in respect to the ice business. . . .

In considering these matters we do not, in a strict sense, take judicial notice of them as embodying statements of uncontrovertible facts. Our function is only to determine the reasonableness of the legislature's belief in the existence of evils and in the effectiveness of the remedy provided. In performing this function we have no occasion to consider whether all the statements of fact which may be the basis of the prevailing belief are well-founded; and we have, of course, no right to weigh conflicting evidence. . . .

Fourth, can it be said in the light of these facts that it was not an appropriate exercise of legislative discretion to authorize the Commission to deny a license to enter the business in localities where necessity for another plant did not exist? The need of some remedy for the evil of destructive competition, where competition existed, had been and was widely felt. Where competition did not exist, the propriety of public regulation had been proven. Many communities were not supplied with ice at all.

The particular remedy adopted was not enacted hastily. The statute was based upon a long-established state policy recognizing the public importance of the ice business, and upon seventeen years' legislative and administrative experience in the regulation of it. The advisability of treating the ice business as a public utility and of applying to it the certificate of convenience and necessity had been under consideration for many years. Similar legislation had been enacted in Oklahoma under similar circumstances with respect to other public services.

The measure bore a substantial relation to the evils found to exist. Under these circumstances, to hold the act void as being unreasonable, would, in my opinion involve the exercise not of the function of judicial review but the function of a super-legislature. If the act is to be stricken down, it must be on the ground that the federal Constitution guarantees to the individual the absolute right to enter the ice business, however detrimental the exercise of that right may be to the public welfare. Such, indeed, appears to be the contention made.

Fifth, the claim is that manufacturing ice for sale and distribution is a business inherently private, and, in effect, that no state of facts can justify denial of the right to engage in it. To supply oneself with water, electricity, gas, ice, or any other article is inherently a matter of private concern. So also may be the business of supplying the same articles to others for compensation. But the business of supplying to others, for compensation, any article or service whatsoever may become a matter of public concern. Whether it is or is not depends upon the conditions existing in the community affected.

If it is a matter of public concern, it may be regulated, whatever the business. The public's concern may be limited to a single feature of the business, so that the needed protection can be secured by a relatively slight degree of regulation. Such is the concern over possible incompetence, which dictates the licensing of dentists *(Dent* v. *West Virginia)* . . . or the concern over possible dishonesty, which led to the licensing of auctioneers or hawkers. . . . On the other hand, the public's concern about a particular business may be so pervasive and varied as to require constant detailed supervision and a very high degree of regulation. Where this is true, it is common to speak of the business as being a "public" one, although it is privately owned. It is to such businesses that the designation "public utility" is commonly applied; or they are spoken of as "affected with a public interest." . . .

A regulation valid for one kind of business may, of course, be invalid for another; since the reasonableness of every regulation is dependent upon the relevant facts. But so far as concerns the power to regulate, there is no difference in essence between a business called private and one called a public utility or said to be "affected with a public interest." Whatever the nature of the business, whatever the scope or character of the regulation applied, the source of the power invoked is the same. And likewise the con-

stitutional limitation upon that power. The source is the police power. The limitation is that set by the due process clause, which, as construed, requires that the regulation shall be not unreasonable, arbitrary or capricious; and that the means of regulation selected shall have a real or substantial relation to the object sought to be obtained.

The notion of a distinct category of business "affected with a public interest," employing property "devoted to a public use," rests upon historical error. The consequences which it is sought to draw from those phrases are belied by the meaning in which they were first used centuries ago, and by the decision of this Court, in *Munn* v. *Illinois,* 94 U.S. 113, which first introduced them into the law of the Constitution. In my opinion, the true principle is that the state's power extends to every regulation of any business reasonably required and appropriate for the public protection. I find in the due process clause no other limitation upon the character or the scope of regulation permissible.

Sixth, it is urged specifically that manufacturing ice for sale and distribution is a common calling; and that the right to engage in a common calling is one of the fundamental liberties guaranteed by the due process clause. To think of the ice-manufacturing business as a common calling is difficult, so recent is it in origin and so peculiar in character. Moreover, the Constitution does not require that every calling which has been common shall ever remain so. The liberty to engage in a common calling, like other liberties, may be limited in the exercise of the police power.

The slaughtering of cattle had been a common calling in New Orleans before the monopoly sustained in *Slaughter-House Cases,* 16 Wall 36, was created by the legislature. Prior to the Eighteenth Amendment selling liquor was a common calling, but this Court held it to be consistent with the due process clause for a state to abolish the calling . . . or to establish a system limiting the number of licenses. . . . Every citizen has the right to navigate a river or lake, and may even carry others thereon for hire. But the ferry privilege may be made exclusive in order that the patronage may be sufficient to justify maintaining the ferry service. . . .

It is settled that the police power commonly invoked in aid of health, safety, and morals extends equally to the promotion of the public welfare. The cases just cited show that, while, ordinarily, free competition in the common callings has been encouraged, the public welfare may at other times demand that monopolies be created. Upon this principle is based our whole modern practice of public utility regulation. It is no objection to the validity of the statute here assailed that it fosters monopoly. That, indeed, is its design. The certificate of public convenience and invention is a device — a recent social-economic invention — through which the monopoly is kept under effective control by vesting in a commission the power to terminate it whenever that course is required in the public interest.

To grant any monopoly to any person as a favor is forbidden even if terminable. But where, as here, there is reasonable ground for the legislative conclusion that in order to secure a necessary service at reasonable rates it may be necessary to curtail the right to enter the calling, it is, in my opinion, consistent with the due process clause to do so, whatever the nature of the business. The existence of such power in the legislature seems indispensable in our ever changing society.

It is settled by unanimous decisions of this Court that the due process clause does not prevent a state or city from engaging in the business of supplying its inhabitants with articles in general use when it is believed that they cannot be secured at reasonable prices from the private dealers. Thus, a city may, if the local law permits, buy and sell at retail coal and wood . . . or gasoline. . . . And a state may, if permitted by its own constitution, build and operate warehouses, elevators, packinghouses, flour mills or other factories. . . .

As states may engage in a business because it is a public purpose to assure to their inhabitants an adequate supply of necessary articles, may they not achieve this public purpose, as Oklahoma has done, by exercising the lesser power of preventing single individuals from wantonly engaging in the business and thereby making impossible a dependable private source of supply? As a state so entering upon a business may exert the taxing power all individual dealers may be driven from the calling by the unequal competition. If states are denied the power to prevent the harmful entry of a few individuals into a business, they may thus, in effect, close it altogether to private enterprise.

Seventh, the economic emergencies of the past were incidents of scarcity. In those days it was preeminently the common callings that were the subjects of regulation. The danger then threatening was excessive prices. To prevent what was deemed extortion, the English Parliament fixed the prices of commodities and of services from time to time during the four centuries preceding the Declaration of Independence. Like legislation was enacted in the Colonies; and in the states, after the Revolution.

When the first due process clause was written into the federal Constitution, the price of bread was being fixed by statute in at least two of the states, and this practice continued long thereafter. Dwelling houses when occupied by the owner are preeminently private property. From the foundation of our government those who wished to lease residential property had been free to charge to tenants such rentals as they pleased. But for years after the World War had ended, the scarcity of dwellings in the city of New York was such that the state's legislative power was invoked to ensure reasonable rentals. The constitutionality of the statute was sustained by this Court. . . .

Eighth, the people of the United States

are now confronted with an emergency more serious than war. Misery is widespread in a time not of scarcity but of overabundance. The long-continued depression has brought unprecedented unemployment, a catastrophic fall in commodity prices, and a volume of economic losses which threatens our financial institutions. Some people believe that the existing conditions threaten even the stability of the capitalistic system. Economists are searching for the causes of this disorder and are reexamining the bases of our industrial structure. Businessmen are seeking possible remedies. Most of them realize that failure to distribute widely the profits of industry has been a prime cause of our present plight. But rightly or wrongly, many persons think that one of the major contributing causes has been unbridled competition.

Increasingly, doubt is expressed whether it is economically wise or morally right that men should be permitted to add to the producing facilities of an industry which is already suffering from overcapacity. In justification of that doubt, men point to the excess capacity of our productive facilities resulting from their vast expansion without corresponding increase in the consumptive capacity of the people. They assert that through improved methods of manufacture, made possible by advances in science and invention and vast accumulation of capital, our industries had become capable of producing from 30 to 100 percent more than was consumed even in days of vaunted prosperity; and that the present capacity will, for a long time, exceed the needs of business.

All agree that irregularity in employment — the greatest of our evils — cannot be overcome unless production and consumption are more nearly balanced. Many insist there must be some form of economic control. There are plans for proration. There are many proposals for stabilization. And some thoughtful men of wide business experience insist that all projects for stabilization and proration must prove futile unless, in some way, the equivalent of the certificate of public convenience and necessity is made a prerequisite to embarking new capital in an industry in which the capacity already exceeds the production schedules.

Whether that view is sound nobody knows. The objections to the proposal are obvious and grave. The remedy might bring evils worse than the present disease. The obstacles to success seem insuperable. The economic and social sciences are largely uncharted seas. We have been none too successful in the modest essays in economic control already entered upon. The new proposal involves a vast extension of the area of control. Merely to acquire the knowledge essential as a basis for the exercise of this multitude of judgments would be a formidable task; and each of the thousands of these judgments would call for some measure of prophecy. Even more serious are the obstacles to success inherent in the demands which execution of the project would make upon human intelligence and upon the character of men. Man is weak and his judgment is at best fallible.

Yet the advances in the exact sciences and the achievements in invention remind us that the seemingly impossible sometimes happens. There are many men now living who were in the habit of using the age-old expression: "It is as impossible as flying." The discoveries in physical science, the triumphs in invention attest the value of the process of trial and error. In large measure, these advances have been due to experimentation. In those fields experimentation has, for two centuries, been not only free but encouraged. Some people assert that our present plight is due, in part, to the limitations set by courts upon experimentation in the fields of social and economic science, and to the discouragement to which proposals for betterment there have been subjected otherwise.

There must be power in the states and the nation to remold, through experimentation, our economic practices and institutions to meet changing social and economic needs. I cannot believe that the framers of the Fourteenth Amendment, or the states which ratified it, intended to deprive us of the power to correct the evils of technological unemployment and excess productive capacity which have attended progress in the useful arts.

To stay experimentation in things social and economic is a grave responsibility. Denial of the right to experiment may be fraught with serious consequences to the nation. It is one of the happy incidents of the federal system that a single courageous state may, if its citizens choose, serve as a laboratory, and try novel social and economic experiments without risk to the rest of the country.

This Court has the power to prevent an experiment. We may strike down the statute which embodies it on the ground that, in our opinion, the measure is arbitrary, capricious, or unreasonable. We have power to do this because the due process clause has been held by the Court applicable to matters of substantive law as well as to matters of procedure. But in the exercise of this high power, we must be ever on our guard lest we erect our prejudices into legal principles. If we would guide by the light of reason, we must let our minds be bold.

34.

Malcolm Cowley: The Flight of the Bonus Army

Throughout June of 1932 the so-called Bonus Army, composed of some 15,000 World War I veterans, congregated in Washington with their wives and children to pressure Congress for legislation to make funds scheduled to be paid the veterans in 1945 available immediately. They moved into abandoned shacks below the Capitol and set up shanties along the Anacostia River. The bonus bill was defeated, and many of the veterans left for home discouraged. The rest were driven away by the U.S. Army after weeks of restlessness and threats of turbulence. A second Bonus Army came in May 1933 and this time was greeted by Mrs. Roosevelt and presidential assistant Louis Howe. Although, again, no bonus legislation was passed, Congress did create the Civilian Conservation Corps, in which many of the veterans were able to find work. The selection below, by Malcolm Cowley in August 1932, tells of the evacuation and disintegration of the 1932 march.

Source: *New Republic*, August 17, 1932.

WHEN THE VETERANS of the Bonus Army first tried to escape, they found that the bridges into Virginia were barred by soldiers and the Maryland roads blocked against them by state troopers. They wandered from street to street or sat in ragged groups, the men exhausted, the women with wet handkerchiefs laid over their smarting eyes, the children waking from sleep to cough and whimper from the tear gas in their lungs. The flames behind them were climbing into the night sky. About four in the morning, as rain began to fall, they were allowed to cross the border into Maryland, on condition that they move as rapidly as possible into another state.

The veterans were expected to disperse to their homes — but most of them had no homes, and they felt that their only safety lay in sticking together. Somehow the rumor passed from group to group that the mayor of Johnstown had invited them to his city. And they cried, as they rode toward Pennsylvania or marched in the dawn twilight along the highways, "On to Johnstown."

Their shanties and tents had been burned, their personal property destroyed, except for the few belongings they could carry on their backs; many of their families were separated, wives from husbands, children from parents. Knowing all this, they still did not appreciate the extent of their losses. Two days before, they had regarded themselves, and thought the country regarded them, as heroes trying to collect a debt long overdue. They had boasted about their months or years of service, their medals, their wounds, their patriotism in driving the Reds out of their camp; they had nailed an American flag to every hut. When threatened with forcible eviction, they answered that no American soldier would touch them: hadn't a detachment of Marines (consisting, some said, of twenty-five or thirty men, though others claimed there were two whole companies) thrown down its arms and refused to march against them?

But the infantry, last night, had driven them out like so many vermin. Mr. Hoover had announced that "after months of patient indulgence, the government met overt lawlessness as it always must be met if the cherished processes of self-government are to be preserved." Mr. Hoover and his subordinates, in their eagerness to justify his action, were about to claim that the veterans were Red radicals, that they were the dregs of the population, that most of them had criminal records and, as a final insult, that half of them weren't veterans at all.

They would soon discover the effect of these official libels. At Somerset, on the Lincoln Highway, some of them asked for food. "We can't give you any," said a spokesman for the businessmen. "The President says that you're rebels — don't you understand? You're all outlaws now." A veteran's wife and children were refused admission to a hotel, even though they offered to pay for a room in advance. At Johnstown, the wealthier citizens were dismayed to hear of their arrival. Possibly half the workmen in the city were unemployed; a fifth or a sixth of the population was in need of charity. Ten thousand hungry people were a threat in themselves, but the editor of the Johnstown *Tribune* was about to conjure up new terrors. He wrote:

> Johnstown faces a crisis. It must prepare to protect itself from the Bonus Army concentrating here at the invitation of Mayor Eddie McCloskey. . . .
>
> In any group of the size of the Bonus Army, made up of men gathered from all parts of the country, without discipline, without effective leadership in a crisis, without any attempt on the part of those leaders to check up the previous records of the individuals who compose it, there is certain to be a mixture of undesirables — thieves, plug-uglies, degenerates. . . . The community must protect itself from the criminal fringe of the invaders.
>
> Booster clubs, community organizations of every sort, volunteer organizations if no sectional group is available should get together in extraordinary sessions and organize to protect property, women, and possibly life.
>
> It is no time for halfway measures. . . .

The heroes of 1918, now metamorphosed into "thieves, plug-uglies, degenerates," were preparing to gather in the outskirts of the city, in the campsite offered them at Ideal Park. And the leading citizens, aided by the state police, were planning to use any means short of violence to keep them from reaching it. Mr. Hoover's proclamation had done its work.

At Jennerstown is a barracks of the Pennsylvania State Police, looking for all the world like a fashionable roadhouse. In front of the barracks is a traffic light. The road ahead leads westward over Laurel Hill and Chestnut Ridge; the right-hand road leads nineteen miles northward into Johnstown. It was the task of the state troopers to keep the Bonus Army moving west over the mountains, toward Ligonier and the Ohio border.

In half an hour on Saturday morning, I saw more than a thousand veterans pass through Jennerstown — that is, more than fifty trucks bearing an average of twenty men apiece. Later I was told that the procession continued at irregular intervals until Sunday evening. The troopers would wait at the intersection, twenty men on their motorcycles like a school of swift gray sharks, till they heard that a convoy was approaching; then they would dart off to meet it in a cloud of dust and blue gasoline smoke, with their hats cutting the air like so many fins. One of the troopers stayed behind to manipulate the traffic light. As the trucks came nearer, he would throw a switch that changed it into a mere yellow blinker, so that all of them could shoot past the intersection without slackening speed. They were full of ragged men, kneeling, standing unsteadily, clinging to the sideboards; there was no room to sit down. Behind each truck rode a trooper, and there were half a dozen others mingled with the crowd that watched from in front of a filling station.

The contrast between these homeless veterans, hatless, coatless, unshaven, half-starved — most of them hadn't eaten or slept for thirty-six hours, a few hadn't had so much as a drink of water — and the sleekly uniformed, smug, well-nourished troopers who were herding them past their destination, produced a sharp effect on the crowd of backwoods farmers, who otherwise cared little about the Bonus March.

"Hey, buddies," they shouted, "turn right, turn right. Johnstown" — pointing northward — "Johnstown." The hungry men smiled and waved at them uncomprehendingly.

But a few had seen that something was wrong, that they were being carried beyond their meeting place. They tried to pass the word from truck to truck, above the roar of the motors. As they went bowling through the level village street, there was no way of escape; but just beyond Jennerstown, the road climbs steeply up Laurel Hill; the drivers shifted into second gear — and promptly lost half their passengers. The others, those who received no warning or let themselves be cowed by the troopers, were carried westward. The following week I met a New York veteran who hadn't escaped from the convoy till it passed the Ohio line. A Negro from Washington, a resident of the city for thirty years — he wasn't a Bonus marcher at all, but made the mistake of walking through Anacostia in his shirt sleeves — was arrested, piled into a truck, and carried all the way to Indianapolis before he managed to tell his story to a reporter.

As for the veterans who escaped at Jennerstown, they lay by the roadside utterly exhausted. Their leaders had been arrested, dispersed, or else had betrayed them; their strength had been gnawed away by hunger or lack of sleep; they hoped to reunite and recuperate in a new camp, but how to reach it they did not know. For perhaps twenty minutes, they dozed there hopelessly. Then — and I was a witness of this phenomenon — a new leader would stand forth from the ranks. He would stop a motorist, learn the road to Johnstown, call the men together, give them their instructions — and the whole group would suddenly obey a self-imposed discipline. As they turned northward at the Jennerstown traffic light, one of them would shout, "We're going back!" and perhaps half a dozen would mumble in lower voices, "We're gonna get guns and go back to Washington."

Mile after mile we passed the ragged line

Washington police chief, Major Pelham Glassford, inspecting the camp of the Bonus Army during 1932

as we too drove northward to the camp at Ideal Park. We were carrying two of the veterans, chosen from a group of 300 by a quick informal vote of their comrades. One was a man gassed in the Argonne and tear-gassed at Anacostia; he breathed with an effort, as if each breath would be his last. The other was a man with family troubles; he had lost his wife and six children during the retreat from Camp Marks and hoped to find them in Johnstown. He talked about his service in France, his three medals, which he refused to wear, his wounds, his five years in a government hospital. "If they gave me a job," he said, "I wouldn't care about the Bonus."

The sick man, as we passed one group of veterans after another, pointed northward and said in an almost inaudible voice, "This way, comrades, this way. Comrades, this way," till his head fell back and he lapsed into a feverish sleep.

It seemed the ragged line would never end. Here the marchers were stumbling under the weight of their suitcases and blanket rolls, here they were clustered round a farmhouse pump, here a white man was sharing the burden of a crippled Negro, here white and Negro together were snoring in a patch of shade. The road curled downward into the valley where Johnstown swelters between steep hills. On either side of us were fields of golden grain, cut and stacked for the threshers; a moment later we were winding through a forest. It was a landscape not unlike the high hills north of the River Aisne. In that other country, fifteen years before, I had seen gaunt men coming out of the trenches half-dead with fatigue, bending under the weight of their equipment. The men on the Johnstown road that day were older, shabbier, but somehow more impressive: they were volunteers, fighting a war of their own. "And don't forget it, buddy," one of them shouted as the car slowed down, "we've enlisted for the duration."

At Ideal Park, where the new camp was being pitched, there was the same determination, combined with a hysteria caused by sudden relief from tension. A tall man with a tear-streaked face was marching up and down. "I used to be a hundred-percenter," he said, "but now I'm a Red radical. I had an American flag, but the damned tin soldiers burned it. Now I don't ever want to see a flag again. Give me a gun and I'll go back to Washington" — "That's right, buddy," said a woman looking up from her two babies, who lay on a dirty quilt in the sun. A cloud of flies hovered above them. Another man was reading the editorial page of a Johnstown paper. He shouted, "Let them come here and mow us down with machine guns. We won't move this time" — "That's right, buddy," said the woman again. A haggard face — eyes bloodshot, skin pasty white under a three days' beard — suddenly appeared at the window of our car. "Hoover must die," said the face ominously. "You know what this means?" a man shouted from the other side. "This means revolution." — "Yes, you're damned right it means revolution."

But 1,000 homeless veterans, or 50,000, don't make a revolution. This threat would pass and be forgotten, like the other threat that was only half-concealed in the Johnstown editorial. Next day the Bonus leaders would come, the slick guys in leather puttees; they would make a few speeches and everything would be smoothed over. They would talk of founding a new Fascist order of khaki shirts, but this threat, too, can be disregarded: a Fascist movement, to succeed in this country, must come from the middle classes and be respectable. No, if any revolution results from the flight of the Bonus Army, it will come from a different source, from the government itself. The army in time of peace, at the national capital, has been used against unarmed citizens — and this, with all it threatens for the future, is a revolution in itself.

35.

George Soule: Are We Going To Have a Revolution?

There was much talk during the early years of the Depression about the possibility of a revolution in America. Actually, very little of it originated with the poor and unemployed; instead, most of it came from disaffected and disillusioned intellectuals, many of whom had moved sharply to the left since 1929, and from the rich, who, of course, had the most to lose. A few occurrences like the veterans' bonus march of 1932 seemed to lend plausibility to the fear that a revolt of the masses was brewing. Noted economic historian George Soule analyzed the symptoms of revolution in an article published in August 1932, part of which appears here.

Source: *Harper's,* August 1932.

If you want to hear discussions of the future revolution in the United States, do not go to the breadlines and the mill towns, but to Park Avenue and Wall Street, or to the gatherings of young literary men. Well-fed people will anxiously inquire when you think the revolution is coming. They will admit in a large way that profits must be abolished and that some form of Communism might be desirable. In the next breath they may express doubt whether the Democrats can muster enough votes to defeat Mr. Hoover for reelection, or they may oppose moderate reforms like unemployment insurance, or may support the sales tax, which transfers burdens from the rich to the poor. Nevertheless, they vaguely expect profound changes.

But you will find that searching for actual flesh-and-blood revolutionary proletarians is a thankless task. Most of those who really suffer from the depression are, according to the best-informed reports, simply stricken dumb by it. Like the Republican administration, they are awaiting nothing more drastic than the return of prosperity.

The strange inertia of those who would benefit most by a revolution and, therefore, it is supposed, will create it, is a subject for frequent remark. When an economist heard that the son of a prominent banker had become a Communist, he replied that he would be more impressed if the son of a prominent workman had become a Communist. As a matter of fact, if one can believe the reports of the party membership drives in the *Daily Worker,* converts are numbered by dozens or at most hundreds rather than by thousands or hundreds of thousands. There are a few strikes and riots, to be sure, but why are there not more? The unemployed number between eight and ten million.

A man in close touch with workers' movements of all sorts received a telephone call not long ago from the chairman of a committee engaged in raising money for unemployment relief. "Our funds are running low," said this gentleman, "and we are having difficulty in collecting more. I think it would help if a good scare were thrown into our contributors. They don't realize how desperate the situation is. Can't we have a bread riot?"

"Well, I'll see what I can do by consulting my Communist friends."

"Oh, that won't do at all," was the reply.

"Everybody expects the Communists to riot, with or without cause. What we need is an unmistakable expression of resentment and desperation, a real mass movement."

"In that case, I'm afraid I can't help you. The masses are in a desperate condition all right, but unfortunately there is no sign that they feel the slightest resentment. They just sit at home and blame prohibition."

This distressing lack of authentic bread riots may shortly be supplied when relief funds run out, as it is almost certain that they will. But bread riots do not necessarily mean revolution. People may smash windows because they are hungry without wanting a governmental overturn or knowing how to bring it about. As far back as the 1870s, mobs of unemployed men looted shops and burned railroad stations; in fact, they frightened substantial citizens so much that the movement to build armories and recruit state militia was set under way. For the first time in the history of this country, the idea was born that troops might be necessary as a protection for wealth against a propertyless class. But we did not come within hailing distance of a revolution, and the passing of the crisis left scarcely a trace of any organized radical movement.

The most solid recent gains of the revolutionary faith have taken place among the intellectuals. So marked has been the drift of writers toward the left that it has been discussed at length in the critical reviews. These persons, who are, with few exceptions, of middle-class origin and training, have identified themselves emotionally with the worker. Not, however, with the American worker as he actually is and thinks, in the great average, but as he ought to be and ought to think, according to revolutionary theory. The worker, in this sense, is not a concrete or representative person but an abstraction, a Platonic ideal. The workers may not be conscious of the class struggle, but that makes no difference to these intellectuals; the class struggle is there just the same, and the workers are unconscious of it only because their minds have been poisoned by bourgeois ideology. Given the right leadership and education, they will respond.

This intellectual zeal sometimes lays itself open to ridicule. An ardent young college instructor, a recent convert, who, so far as is known, never was dependent on the wages of daily labor for his sustenance, yet wrote that an argument by another in behalf of a labor cause could not be sincere because the author of the argument was a "bourgeois intellectual." An ironic letter to a literary column revealed the practical dilemma of these revolutionaries. They had justifiably made up their minds, the letter stated, that capitalists could not be relied upon to change the existing order. The measures proposed by the moderate reformers who did not contemplate a revolution were, therefore, unworthy of support. It was also obvious that labor was not prepared to revolt. Why, then, did not the writers form a party of their own to fight both capital and labor? . . .

It would be easy . . . to dismiss the whole subject with a superior smirk, to join the humorous writers of the respectable press in kidding the parlor-pinks. But that is not, I think, either a just or a sound conclusion from these observations. The revolt of the intellectuals has a more valid meaning than it would have if one accepted all their phrases and assumptions at face value. Of course they are not proletarians and cannot become proletarians. The revolution to which they look forward probably is not imminent. The class struggle does not at this moment threaten to split the American people and lead to a triumph of the downtrodden workers. But the mistake may not lie in the intellectuals' sense of the needs of modern society or its main drift. The mistake may reside in their beliefs as to the exact course which revolution is to take and in their timing of the process. I believe that, in one sense of the word, we are veritably

in the midst of a great social revolution. But a hardboiled look at the facts indicates that the prevalent popular beliefs about what a revolution is and how it comes about are naive and unscientific.

II

THESE POPULAR BELIEFS — held, apparently, both by the literary radicals and by the Park Avenue conservatives — may be briefly summarized as follows:

1. Capitalism may soon come to an end by a final collapse.

2. A revolution is a violent overturn of political government.

3. Nothing is essentially changed, or can be changed, before this overturn; after it a brand new order is suddenly set up.

4. The revolution is brought about by rioting mobs who overrun the capital and loot and massacre; there are barricades in the streets, and the air is noisy with gunfire.

5. The riots and mobs result from the discontent of an oppressed class, whose misery is so profound that it is driven to revolt. Actual starvation is the usual motive for revolution.

Every one of these beliefs is almost completely unfounded. A mental picture of revolution based only on these assumptions is sure to be misleading.

First let us examine the collapse of capitalism. This is a vague term. Precisely what is meant by it? The closing of banks? The inability to get money with which to buy goods? Wholesale bankruptcies and defaults? Vanishing of capital values through the shrinking of trade and the disappearance of profits? Widespread unemployment? Starvation?

There is not one of these phenomena which has not occurred in previous depressions. In 1907 all banks were closed for days and nobody could get a check cashed. We have had numerous financial panics in which, for a time, no new money at all was invested, and the rates for even collateral loans rose to prohibitive heights. Failures, shrinkage of trade, unemployment — these are the common marks of hard times.

Our unsystematic system always fails to work when we have a crisis. Perhaps the difference is one of degree. The system may not be in danger when the curve of economic activity sinks 20 percent or 30 percent. But perhaps at, say, a decline of 47 percent, it will pitch over into the abyss. In order to make the argument conclusive, let us imagine that the drop of the curve will be 100 percent. All businesses shut down, all railroads stop running, all banks are closed. All stocks and bonds, all deeds to real estate become worthless. Everybody is unemployed, nobody has a cent of income. What would happen?

What would happen would depend, not on exterior conditions but upon what was in people's minds. If they were still imbued with habits of trading, of individualistic competition, of accumulation, they would immediately start to rebuild capitalism. . . .

If, on the other hand, enough energetic leaders had developed ideas and habits of cooperation, of placing the common welfare ahead of the individual, and if the collapse and prospective rebuilding of capitalism involved so much suffering that large bodies of people were willing to follow these socially minded persons, another system might be set up. The stores of materials, the factories, and land could be taken over for the community, private ownership of capital could be forbidden, and everybody could be set to work making goods to be distributed more or less equally.

Capitalism is not going to collapse. It *did* collapse in the fall of 1929. It has collapsed many times before — 1921, 1893, 1873, for instance. The point is that a collapse of capitalism does not necessarily lead to a revolutionary change. The revolution depends on what is in men's minds and habits. Capitalism fails, in some degree, every

time we have a depression. It is rebuilt every time we come out of one. The whole building does not crash down in dust and splinters, to be sure, but parts of the roof give way, walls sag and crumble, foundations rot. Whether we replace them or abandon the old structure and erect a new building depends on something more profound than the chronic unworkability of individualism in production and distribution. Kreugers may commit suicide, railroad companies may go into receivership, banks may close. But that does not mean that new Kreugers, new railroad companies, and new banks may not eventually take their places, and carry on in essentially the same way.

Nor is it true that a revolution is a sudden, violent overturn of political government. That is, the kind of revolution the intellectuals really are talking about is not that. . . . A true revolution takes many years, even generations, in the making. There is no more fallacious trick of speech than that which opposes revolution to evolution, and argues that we can choose the one or the other. Revolution, in a better sense, is merely a name for a single cycle in the long evolutionary process. . . .

III

THERE ARE CERTAIN SYMPTOMS by observation of which we may guess how far advanced this process is. Revolutions are, like every other phenomenon of human behavior, extremely irregular in detail, and precise schedules of revolutionary time and succession cannot be laid out on the basis of our limited experience and partial study. Nevertheless, certain tentative generalizations may be made.

An early symptom is the oppression of certain large classes by other classes. Some groups benefit from the existing regime far more than others; those who benefit least may at times be actively injured by it. This

state of affairs is not the exclusive characteristic of any one social order. People sometimes loosely identify oppression with autocracy, or feudalism, or dictatorship, or
capitalism. But each of these systems, under
the circumstances proper to it, has its reason
for being in the greatest feasible welfare and
security of the community as a whole. Oppression of a large class indicates the beginning of the end of a system; it is not the
characteristic of any one system throughout
its whole life. . . .

A symptom of approaching change which
has not been absent in any revolutionary
era is the disaffection of the intellectuals.
This begins early in the process; it grows as
unrest develops; eventually the more influential writers and teachers have shifted their
loyalties from the existing order, if not to a
new class, at least to a new range of social
ideas. In a normally functioning regime it is
the job of the intellectuals to pass on the
sanctioned traditions, to enrich, embroider,
and develop them, to celebrate existing
faith. They connect the future with the past.
But when their leaders begin to feel ill at
ease, to strike out in new directions, it is a
sign that the old order is moribund. . . .

The intellectuals almost never agree with
one another; they are unable to foresee in
detail what is going to happen and why and
when; but they do attack the injustices that
exist, they expose the corruptions and ridicule the absurdities of the ruling classes,
they throw out the ideas and phrases about
which new faiths cohere.

The progress of a typical revolution may
thus be crudely divided into the following
steps. These steps are not strictly successive;
some go on simultaneously with others.

The development of wide disparities
of wealth and power

Blind, sporadic, and unsuccessful
protests from the oppressed classes

Stern and efficient repression of
discontent

A long process of widespread
disillusionment

A long process of criticism, ridicule,
and reformulation of ideas by
intellectuals

Loss of faith in themselves and their
institutions by many in the ruling
classes

Rise in welfare and power of the
oppressed classes

Reforms from above

Accession to power of moderate
revolutionaries

Last of all, what is usually called
revolution — violence and
dictatorship
by an extremist minority — perhaps
to be followed by temporary
reactions.

The final developments do not always occur. They did not occur, for instance, in the
American Revolution: the moderates remained in power and established a stable
government. . . .

IV

IF THERE IS TRUTH in this analysis, it is not
strange that while the masses in the United
States now appear to be inert and nonrevolutionary, there are revolutionary fears in
high places, and the chief vocal opposition
to the existing regime comes from a few
writers and technical experts. This is precisely what we should expect. Ideas of revolutionary implication are bound to arise first

among the best educated and those near to power, not among those who are in the depths of penury and hopelessness.

Acknowledging that prediction in this field can have no pretension to scientific assurance and that the unexpected may always occur, let us fancifully lay out — on the basis of what has usually happened in the past — the probable course of any future overturn of capitalism in this country. It will presumably take some such form as this.

First, there will in the course of time be many riots, strikes, and demonstrations, not for the most part revolutionary in purpose but prompted by immediate conditions. These will be firmly suppressed by groups who have supreme faith in the traditional forms of "Americanism." They will not produce a revolution.

Meanwhile those who deal in ideas will increasingly express dislike of the existing culture and will expose and ridicule its outstanding figures. They will build up new conceptions of the right way to conduct affairs. Not all intellectuals will do this, but those who do will gain a larger and larger following. This process will be, as it has been in the past, spasmodic. It will grow rapidly at some times and will falter at others. But, over a long period, it will make headway. It will eventually provide a body of new ideas, sanctioned not solely or even mainly by insecure proletarians but by a large body of cultivated, comparatively well-to-do Americans.

The most efficient advocates of the new order will not be unwashed day laborers from the steel mills but white-collared citizens of Main Street. There will be general acknowledgment, except among a few capitalists, corporation presidents, politicians, members of patriotic societies, and the more densely ignorant strata, that a society governed by competition, unchecked private acquisition of wealth, and lack of intelligent foresight and planning, is injurious, ridiculous, and outmoded.

Reforms will be made which will increase the power and wealth of the potential governors of a new society and of the classes with which they are allied. The importance of the business executive (divorced from ownership and profits), of the technician, of the management engineer, of the practical social scientist, will be greatly enhanced in industry, finance, and politics. Organized farmers and organized labor will achieve greater recognition than in the past, and in cooperation with active management will force the adoption of measures of planning and control which will improve their status. Their leaders will become really influential.

The result of these reforms will be, not to satisfy the rising classes and leaders but to make them more radical and active. We had a taste of this development just after the war, when organized labor and the organized farmers had become more powerful than ever before, when unemployment had virtually disappeared, and the farmers were really making money and when movements for government ownership of railways and other economic and political changes made real though temporary headway. The vigorous agitation for the Plumb Plan in 1919 was a result, not of the desperate condition of railway labor but of its growing power.

Corruption and incompetence among the traditional powers of government and finance will become more prevalent and injurious than ever. These powers will be sustained less than at present by faith in their legitimacy and necessity, and more by cynical clutching for immediate advantage, stupid assertion of outworn dogma, and ineffectual efforts at repression of the rising forces. Their elements of strength and intelligence will be drained away by the new movements.

Abuses and confusion will finally produce a crisis which will lead the newly powerful classes and leaders to move actively for more thoroughgoing changes than have previously been made. Almost nobody will believe that the old regime can or will do what is necessary. A shift in the governing powers will take place — probably by constitutional means. Then, and only then, will begin the critical period when the capacity of the more moderate reformers who have gained power will be tested, and when it will be decided whether the irreconcilable revolutionaries will gain the ascendancy.

On the basis of this prediction, it looks as if we had begun to float on a revolutionary tide but were still far from its flood. Prophecy of this sort, as I have already said, is extremely uncertain. Nobody can tell how rapidly the current may flow around the next headland. All one can do is to chart the course which it has generally followed in the past. But of one thing I am sure. As long as people wait for the downtrodden and the hopeless to produce a revolution, the revolution is far away. Revolutions are made, not by the weak, the unsuccessful, or the ignorant, but by the strong and the informed. They are processes, not merely of decay and destruction but of advance and building. An old order does not disappear until a new order is ready to take its place.

36.

Franklin D. Roosevelt: Commonwealth Club Address

If Franklin D. Roosevelt's presidential campaign of 1932 often seemed a maze of inconsistencies, it is probably because the candidate, surrounded by advisers pleading a special approach, had arrived at no clear-cut view of what action he would take if elected. Upset by the low intellectual tenor of the campaign, some of Roosevelt's advisers enjoined him to take advantage of the sophisticated audience that he would confront on September 23 at the Commonwealth Club of San Francisco and deliver a major address. Roosevelt acquiesced, and Adolf A. Berle wrote a speech on short notice. Reputedly, Roosevelt did not have a chance even to read the speech before he delivered it, and the speech is more expressive of Berle than of Roosevelt at that time. Nonetheless, it is a unique and remarkable forecast of New Deal thought and action.

Source: *New York Times*, September 24, 1932.

I want to speak not of politics but of government. I want to speak not of parties but of universal principles. They are not political, except in that large sense in which a great American once expressed a definition of politics — that nothing in all of human life is foreign to the science of politics.

I do want to give you, however, a recollection of a long life spent for a large part in public office. Some of my conclusions and observations have been deeply accentuated in these past few weeks. I have traveled far — from Albany to the Golden Gate. I have seen many people and heard many things, and today, when in a sense my journey has reached the halfway mark, I am glad of the opportunity to discuss with you what it all means to me.

Sometimes, my friends, particularly in years such as these, the hand of discouragement falls upon us. It seems that things are in a rut — fixed, settled — that the world has grown old and tired and very much out of joint. This is the mood of depression, of dire and weary depression. But then we look around us in America, and everything tells us that we are wrong. America is new. It is in the process of change and development. It has the great potentialities of youth, and particularly is this true of the great West, and of this coast, and of California.

I would not have you feel that I regard this in any sense a new community. I have traveled in many parts of the world, but never have I felt the arresting thought of the change and development more than here, where the old, mystic East would seem to be near to us, where the currents of life and thought and commerce of the whole world meet us. This factor alone is sufficient to cause man to stop and think of the deeper meaning of things when he stands in this community.

But more than that, I appreciate that the membership of this club consists of men who are thinking in terms beyond the immediate present, beyond their own immediate tasks, beyond their own individual interest. I want to invite you, therefore, to consider with me in the large, some of the relationships of government and economic life that go deep into our daily lives, our happiness, our future, and our security.

The issue of government has always been whether individual men and women will have to serve some system of government or economics, or whether a system of government and economics exists to serve individual men and women. This question has persistently dominated the discussions of government for many generations. On questions relating to these things, men have differed, and for time immemorial it is probable that honest men will continue to differ.

The final word belongs to no man; yet we can still believe in change and in progress. Democracy, as a dear old friend of mine in Indiana, Meredith Nicholson, has called it, is a quest, a never-ending seeking for better things, and in the seeking for these things and the striving for them, there are many roads to follow. But, if we map the course of these roads, we find that there are only two general directions.

When we look about us, we are likely to forget how hard people have worked to win the privilege of government. The growth of the national governments of Europe was a struggle for the development of a centralized force in the nation, strong enough to impose peace upon ruling barons. In many instances the victory of the central government, the creation of a strong central government, was a haven of refuge to the individual. The people preferred the master far away to the exploitation and cruelty of the smaller master near at hand.

But the creators of national government were perforce ruthless men. They were often cruel in their methods, but they did strive steadily toward something that society needed and very much wanted, a strong central state able to keep the peace, to stamp out civil war, to put the unruly nobleman in his place, and to permit the bulk of individuals to live safely. The man of ruthless force had his place in developing a pioneer country, just as he did in fixing the power of the central government in the development of the nations. Society paid him well for his services and its development. When the development among the nations of Europe, however, had been completed, ambition and ruthlessness, having served their term, tended to overstep their mark.

There came a growing feeling that government was conducted for the benefit of a few who thrived unduly at the expense of all. The people sought a balancing — a limiting force. There came gradually, through town councils, trade guilds, national parliaments, by constitution and by popular participation and control, limitations on arbitrary power. Another factor that tended to limit the power of those who ruled was the rise of the ethical conception that a ruler bore a responsibility for the welfare of his subjects.

The American colonies were born in this struggle. The American Revolution was a turning point in it. After the Revolution the struggle continued and shaped itself in the public life of the country. There were those who, because they had seen the confusion which attended the years of war for American independence, surrendered to the belief that popular government was essentially dangerous and essentially unworkable. They were honest people, my friends, and we cannot deny that their experience had warranted some measure of fear. The most brilliant, honest, and able exponent of this point of view was Hamilton. He was too impatient of slow-moving methods. Fundamentally he believed that the safety of the republic lay in the autocratic strength of its government, that the destiny of individuals was to serve that government, and that fundamentally a great and strong group of central institutions, guided by a small group of able and public spirited citizens, could best direct all government.

But Mr. Jefferson, in the summer of 1776, after drafting the Declaration of Independence, turned his mind to the same problem and took a different view. He did not deceive himself with outward forms. Government to him was a means to an end, not an end in itself; it might be either a refuge and a help or a threat and a danger, depending on the circumstances. We find him carefully analyzing the society for which he was to organize a government.

We have no paupers. The great mass of our population is of laborers, our rich who cannot live without labor, either manual or professional, being few and of moderate wealth. Most of the laboring class possess property, cultivate their own lands, have families, and from the demand for their labor are enabled to exac from the rich and the competent such prices as enable them to feed abundantly clothe above mere decency, to labor moderately, and raise their families.

These people, he considered, had two sets of rights, those of "personal competency" and those involved in acquiring and possessing property. By "personal competency" he meant the right of free thinking, freedom of forming and expressing opinions, and freedom of personal living, each man according to his own lights. To insure the first set of rights, a government must so order its functions as not to interfere with the individual. But even Jefferson realized that the exercise of the property rights might so interfere with the rights of the individual that the government, without whose assistance the property rights could not exist, must intervene, not to destroy individualism but to protect it.

You are familiar with the great political duel which followed; and how Hamilton and his friends, building toward a dominant centralized power, were at length defeated in the great election of 1800 by Mr. Jefferson's party. Out of that duel came the two parties, Republican and Democratic, as we know them today.

So began, in American political life, the new day, the day of the individual against the system, the day in which individualism was made the great watchword of American life. The happiest of economic conditions made that day long and splendid. On the Western frontier, land was substantially free. No one, who did not shirk the task of earning a living, was entirely without opportunity to do so. Depressions could, and did, come and go; but they could not alter the fundamental fact that most of the people lived partly by selling their labor and partly by extracting their livelihood from the soil, so that starvation and dislocation were practically impossible. At the very worst there was always the possibility of

United Press International

Franklin Roosevelt campaigning in Georgia in 1932

climbing into a covered wagon and moving West, where the untilled prairies afforded a haven for men to whom the East did not provide a place. So great were our natural resources that we could offer this relief, not only to our own people but to the distressed of all the world; we could invite immigration from Europe and welcome it with open arms. Traditionally, when a depression came, a new section of land was opened in the West; and even our temporary misfortune served our manifest destiny.

It was in the middle of the 19th century that a new force was released and a new dream created. The force was what is called the Industrial Revolution, the advance of steam and machinery and the rise of the forerunners of the modern industrial plant. The dream was the dream of an economic machine, able to raise the standard of living for everyone; to bring luxury within the reach of the humblest; to annihilate distance by steam power and later by electricity, and to release everyone from the drudgery of the heaviest manual toil. It was to be expected that this would necessarily affect government. Heretofore, government had

merely been called upon to produce conditions within which people could live happily, labor peacefully, and rest secure. Now it was called upon to aid in the consummation of this new dream. There was, however, a shadow over the dream. To be made real, it required use of the talents of men of tremendous will and tremendous ambition, since by no other force could the problems of financing and engineering and new developments be brought to a consummation.

So manifest were the advantages of the machine age, however, that the United States fearlessly, cheerfully, and, I think, rightly, accepted the bitter with the sweet. It was thought that no price was too high to pay for the advantages which we could draw from a finished industrial system. The history of the last half century is accordingly in large measure a history of a group of financial Titans, whose methods were not scrutinized with too much care and who were honored in proportion as they produced the results, irrespective of the means they used.

The financiers who pushed the railroads to the Pacific were always ruthless, often wasteful, and frequently corrupt; but they did build railroads, and we have them today. It has been estimated that the American investor paid for the American railway system more than three times over in the process; but, despite this fact, the net advantage was to the United States. As long as we had free land; as long as population was growing by leaps and bounds; as long as our industrial plants were insufficient to supply our own needs, society chose to give the ambitious man free play and unlimited reward provided only that he produced the economic plant so much desired.

During this period of expansion, there was equal opportunity for all and the business of government was not to interfere but to assist in the development of industry. This was done at the request of businessmen themselves. The tariff was originally imposed for the purpose of "fostering our infant industry," a phrase I think the older among you will remember as a political issue not so long ago. The railroads were subsidized, sometimes by grants of money, oftener by grants of land; some of the most valuable oil lands in the United States were granted to assist the financing of the railroad which pushed through the Southwest. A nascent merchant marine was assisted by grants of money, or by mail subsidies, so that our steamshipping might ply the seven seas.

Some of my friends tell me that they do not want the government in business. With this I agree; but I wonder whether they realize the implications of the past. For while it has been American doctrine that the government must not go into business in competition with private enterprises, still it has been traditional, particularly in Republican administrations, for business urgently to ask the government to put at private disposal all kinds of government assistance. The same man who tells you that he does not want to see the government interfere in business — and he means it, and has plenty of good reasons for saying so — is the first to go to Washington and ask the government for a prohibitory tariff on his product. When things get just bad enough, as they did two years ago, he will go with equal speed to the United States government and ask for a loan; and the Reconstruction Finance Corporation is the outcome of it. Each group has sought protection from the government for its own special interests, without realizing that the function of government must be to favor no small group at the expense of its duty to protect the rights of personal freedom and of private property of all its citizens.

In retrospect we can now see that the turn of the tide came with the turn of the century. We were reaching our last frontier; there was no more free land and our industrial combinations had become great uncontrolled and irresponsible units of power within the state. Clear-sighted men saw with fear the danger that opportunity would no longer be equal; that the growing corporation, like the feudal baron of old, might threaten the economic freedom of individuals to earn a living. In that hour, our antitrust laws were born. The cry was raised against the great corporations.

Theodore Roosevelt, the first great Republican Progressive, fought a presidential campaign on the issue of "trust busting" and talked freely about malefactors of great wealth. If the government had a policy it was rather to turn the clock back, to destroy the large combinations and to return to the time when every man owned his individual small business. This was impossible; Theodore Roosevelt, abandoning the idea of "trust busting," was forced to work out a difference between "good" trusts and "bad" trusts. The Supreme Court set forth the famous "rule of reason" by which it seems to have meant that a concentration of industrial power was permissible if the method by which it got its power, and the use it made of that power, was reasonable.

Woodrow Wilson, elected in 1912, saw the situation more clearly. Where Jefferson had feared the encroachment of political power on the lives of individuals, Wilson knew that the new power was financial. He saw, in the highly centralized economic system, the despot of the 20th century, on whom great masses of individuals relied for their safety and their livelihood, and whose irresponsibility and greed (if it were not controlled) would reduce them to starvation and penury. The concentration of financial power had not proceeded as far in 1912 as it has today; but it had grown far enough for Mr. Wilson to realize fully its implications.

It is interesting, now, to read his speeches. What is called "radical" today (and I have reason to know whereof I speak) is mild compared to the campaign of Mr. Wilson. "No man can deny," he said,

> that the lines of endeavor have more and more narrowed and stiffened; no man who knows anything about the development of industry in this country can have failed to observe that the larger kinds of credit are more and more difficult to obtain unless you obtain them upon terms of uniting your efforts with those who already control the industry of the country, and nobody can fail to observe that every man who tries to set himself up in competition with any process of manufacture which has taken place under the control of large combinations of capital will presently find himself either squeezed out or obliged to sell and allow himself to be absorbed.

Had there been no World War — had Mr. Wilson been able to devote eight years to domestic instead of to international affairs — we might have had a wholly different situation at the present time. However, the then distant roar of European cannon, growing ever louder, forced him to abandon the study of this issue. The problem he saw so clearly is left with us as a legacy; and no one of us on either side of the political controversy can deny that it is a matter of grave concern to the government.

A glance at the situation today only too clearly indicates that equality of opportunity as we have known it no longer exists. Our industrial plant is built; the problem just now is whether under existing conditions it is not overbuilt. Our last frontier has long since been reached, and there is practically no more free land. More than half of our people do not live on the farms or on lands and cannot derive a living by cultivating their own property. There is no safety valve in the form of a Western prairie to which those thrown out of work by the Eastern economic machines can go for a new start. We are not able to invite the immigration from Europe to share our endless plenty. We are now providing a drab living for our own people.

Our system of constantly rising tariffs has at last reacted against us to the point of closing our Canadian frontier on the North, our European markets on the East, many of our Latin-American markets to the South, and a goodly proportion of our Pacific markets on the West, through the retaliatory tariffs of those countries. It has forced many of our great industrial institutions which exported their surplus production to such countries, to establish plants in such countries, within the tariff walls. This has resulted in the reduction of the operation of their American plants and opportunity for employment.

Just as freedom to farm has ceased, so also the opportunity in business has narrowed. It still is true that men can start small enterprises, trusting to native shrewdness and ability to keep abreast of competitors; but area after area has been preempted altogether by the great corporations, and even in the fields which still have no great concerns, the small man starts under a handicap. The unfeeling statistics of the past three decades show that the independent businessman is running a losing race. Perhaps he is forced to the wall; perhaps he cannot command credit; perhaps he is "squeezed out," in Mr. Wilson's words, by highly organized corporate competitors, as your corner groceryman can tell you.

Recently, a careful study was made of the concentration of business in the United States. It showed that our economic life was dominated by some 600-odd corporations who controlled two-thirds of American industry. Ten million small businessmen divided the other third. More striking still, it appeared that if the process of concentration goes on at the same rate, at the end of another century we shall have all American industry controlled by a dozen corporations, and run by perhaps 100 men. But plainly, we are steering a steady course toward economic oligarchy, if we are not there already.

Clearly, all this calls for a reappraisal of values. A mere builder of more industrial plants, a creator of more railroad systems, an organizer of more corporations is as likely to be a danger as a help. The day of the great promoter or the financial Titan, to whom we granted anything if only he would build or develop, is over. Our task now is not discovery or exploitation of natural resources, or necessarily producing more goods. It is the soberer, less dramatic business of administering resources and plants already in hand, of seeking to reestablish foreign markets for our surplus production, of meeting the problem of underconsumption, of adjusting production to consumption, of distributing wealth and products more equitably, of adapting existing economic organizations to the service of the people. The day of enlightened administration has come.

Just as in older times the central government was first a haven of refuge and then a threat, so now, in a closer economic system, the central and ambitious financial unit is no longer a servant of national desire, but a danger. I would draw the parallel one step further. We did not think because national government had become a threat in the 18th century that therefore we should abandon the principle of national government. Nor today should we abandon the principle of strong economic units called corporations merely because their power is susceptible of easy abuse. In other times we dealt with the problem of an unduly ambitious central government by modifying it gradually into a constitutional democratic government. So today we are modifying and controlling our economic units.

As I see it, the task of government in its relation to business is to assist the development of an economic declaration of rights, an economic constitutional order. This is the common task of statesman and businessman. It is the minimum requirement of a more permanently safe order of things.

Happily, the times indicate that to create such an order not only is the proper policy of government but it is the only line of safety for our economic structures as well. We know, now, that these economic units cannot exist unless prosperity is uniform, that is, unless purchasing power is well distributed throughout every group in the nation. That is why even the most selfish of corporations for its own interest would be glad to see wages restored and unemployment ended and to bring the Western farmer back to his accustomed level of prosperity and to assure a permanent safety to both groups. That is why some enlightened industries themselves endeavor to limit the freedom of action of each man and business group within the industry in the common interest of all; why businessmen everywhere are asking a form of organization which will bring the scheme of things into balance, even though it may in some measure qualiy the freedom of action of individual units within the business.

The exposition need not further be elaborated. It is brief and incomplete, but you will be able to expand it in terms of your own business or occupation without difficulty. I think everyone who has actually entered the economic struggle — which means everyone who was not born to safe wealth — knows in his own experience and his own life that we have now to apply the earlier concepts of American government to the conditions of today.

The Declaration of Independence discusses the problem of government in terms of a contract. Government is a relation of give and take, a contract, perforce, if we would follow the thinking out of which it grew. Under such a contract, rulers were accorded power, and the people consented to that power on consideration that they be accorded certain rights. The task of statesmanship has always been the redefinition of these rights in terms of a changing and growing social order. New conditions impose new requirements upon government and those who conduct government.

I held, for example, in proceedings before me as governor, the purpose of which was the removal of the sheriff of New York, that under modern conditions it was not enough for a public official merely to evade the legal terms of official wrongdoing. He owed a positive duty as well. I said in substance that if he had acquired large sums of money, he was, when accused, required to explain the sources of such wealth. To that extent this wealth was colored with a public interest. I said that public servants should, even beyond private citizens, in financial matters be held to a stern and uncompromising rectitude.

I feel that we are coming to a view through the drift of our legislation and our public thinking in the past quarter century that private economic power is, to enlarge

an old phrase, a public trust as well. I hold that continued enjoyment of that power by any individual or group must depend upon the fulfillment of that trust. The men who have reached the summit of American business life know this best; happily, many of these urge the binding quality of this greater social contract. The terms of that contract are as old as the republic and as new as the new economic order.

Every man has a right to life; and this means that he has also a right to make a comfortable living. He may by sloth or crime decline to exercise that right; but it may not be denied him. We have no actual famine or dearth; our industrial and agricultural mechanism can produce enough and to spare. Our government, formal and informal, political and economic, owes to everyone an avenue to possess himself of a portion of that plenty sufficient for his needs, through his own work.

Every man has a right to his own property; which means a right to be assured, to the fullest extent attainable, in the safety of his savings. By no other means can men carry the burdens of those parts of life which, in the nature of things, afford no chance of labor: childhood, sickness, old age. In all thought of property, this right is paramount; all other property rights must yield to it. If, in accord with this principle, we must restrict the operations of the speculator, the manipulator, even the financier, I believe we must accept the restriction as needful, not to hamper individualism but to protect it.

These two requirements must be satisfied, in the main, by the individuals who claim and hold control of the great industrial and financial combinations which dominate so large a part of our industrial life. They have undertaken to be, not businessmen but princes — princes of property. I am not prepared to say that the system which produces them is wrong. I am very clear that they must fearlessly and competently assume the responsibility which goes with the power.

So many enlightened businessmen know this that the statement would be little more than a platitude, were it not for an added implication. This implication is, briefly, that the responsible heads of finance and industry, instead of acting each for himself, must work together to achieve the common end. They must, where necessary, sacrifice this or that private advantage; and in reciprocal self-denial must seek a general advantage. It is here that formal government — political government, if you choose — comes in.

Whenever in the pursuit of this objective the lone wolf, the unethical competitor, the reckless promoter, the Ishmael or Insull whose hand is against every man's, declines to join in achieving an end recognized as being for the public welfare and threatens to drag the industry back to a state of anarchy, the government may properly be asked to apply restraint. Likewise, should the group ever use its collective power contrary to the public welfare, the government must be swift to enter and protect the public interest.

The government should assume the function of economic regulation only as a last resort, to be tried only when private initiative, inspired by high responsibility, with such assistance and balance as government can give, has finally failed. As yet there has been no final failure, because there has been no attempt; and I decline to assume that this nation is unable to meet the situation.

The final term of the high contract was for liberty and the pursuit of happiness. We have learned a great deal of both in the past century. We know that individual liberty and individual happiness mean nothing unless both are ordered in the sense that one man's meat is not another man's poison. We know that the old "rights of personal competency," the right to read, to think, to speak, to choose, and live a mode of life

must be respected at all hazards. We know that liberty to do anything which deprives others of those elemental rights is outside the protection of any compact; and that government in this regard is the maintenance of a balance, within which every individual may have a place if he will take it; in which every individual may find safety if he wishes it; in which every individual may attain such power as his ability permits, consistent with his assuming the accompanying responsibility.

All this is a long, slow task. Nothing is more striking than the simple innocence of the men who insist, whenever an objective is present, on the prompt production of a patent scheme guaranteed to produce a result. Human endeavor is not so simple as that. Government includes the art of formulating a policy and using the political technique to attain so much of that policy as will receive general support; persuading, leading, sacrificing, teaching always, because the greatest duty of a statesman is to educate. But in the matters of which I have spoken, we are learning rapidly, in a severe school. The lessons so learned must not be forgotten, even in the mental lethargy of a speculative upturn. We must build toward the time when a major depression cannot occur again; and if this means sacrificing the easy profits of inflationist booms, then let them go; and good riddance.

Faith in America, faith in our tradition of personal responsibility, faith in our institutions, faith in ourselves demand that we recognize the new terms of the old social contract. We shall fulfill them, as we fulfilled the obligation of the apparent utopia which Jefferson imagined for us in 1776, and which Jefferson, Roosevelt, and Wilson sought to bring to realization. We must do so, lest a rising tide of misery, engendered by our common failure, engulf us all. But failure is not an American habit; and in the strength of great hope we must all shoulder our common load.

37.

Unemployment as a National Problem

The critical year of the Depression was 1932. More than 12 million people were unemployed; and as the year wore on with little evidence that the federal government could cope with the situation, signs of resentment and bitterness against the remaining wealthy of the land began to appear. President Hoover concentrated his efforts on aid to business through the Reconstruction Finance Corporation and resisted appeals for federal aid for the unemployed. Finally acknowledging the extent of their plight, he approved the Emergency Relief and Construction Act in July 1932, but the amounts of money made available were hopelessly inadequate. The failure of the relief act was the subject of Fortune's *leading article in September 1932. The article is reprinted here in part.*

Source: *Fortune,* September 1932: "No One Has Starved."

DULL MORNINGS LAST WINTER the sheriff of Miami, Florida, used to fill a truck with homeless men and run them up to the county line. Where the sheriff of Fort Lauderdale used to meet them and load them into a second truck and run them up to *his* county line. Where the sheriff of Saint Lucie's would meet them and load them into a third truck and run them up to *his* county line. Where the sheriff of Brevard County would *not* meet them. And whence they would trickle back down the roads to Miami. To repeat.

It was a system. And it worked. The only trouble was that it worked too well. It kept the transients transient and it even increased the transient population in the process. But it got to be pretty expensive, one way or another, if you sat down and figured it all out — trucks and gas and time and a little coffee. . . .

That was last winter.

Next winter there will be no truck. And there will be no truck, not because the transients will have disappeared from Miami: if anything, there will be more blistered Fords with North Dakota licenses and more heel-worn shoes with the Boston trademark rubbed out next winter than there were last. But because the sheriff of Miami, like the President of the U.S., will next winter think of transients and unemployed miners and jobless mill workers in completely different terms.

The difference will be made by the Emergency Relief Act. Or rather by the fact that the Emergency Relief Act exists. For the act itself with its $300 million for direct relief loans to the states is neither an adequate nor an impressive piece of legislation. But the passage of the Act, like the green branch which young Mr. Ringling used to lay across the forks of the Wisconsin roads for his circus to follow, marks a turning in American political history. And the beginning of a new chapter in American unemployment relief. It constitutes an open and legible acknowledgment of governmental responsibility for the welfare of the victims of industrial unemployment. And its ultimate effect must be the substitution of an ordered, realistic, and intelligent relief program for the wasteful and uneconomic methods (of which the Miami truck is an adequate symbol) employed during the first three years of the depression.

There can be no serious question of the failure of those methods. For the methods were never seriously capable of success. They were diffuse, unrelated, and unplanned. The theory was that private charitable organizations and semi-public welfare groups, established to care for the old and the sick and the indigent, were capable of caring for the casuals of a worldwide economic disaster. And the theory in application meant that social agencies manned for the service of a few hundred families, and city shelters set up to house and feed a handful of homeless men, were compelled by the brutal necessities of hunger to care for hundreds of thousands of families and whole armies of the displaced and the jobless. And to depend for their resources upon the contributions of communities no longer able to contribute, and upon the irresolution and vacillation of state legislatures and municipal assemblies long since in the red on their annual budgets. The result was the picture now presented in city after city and state after state — heterogeneous groups of official and semiofficial and unofficial relief agencies struggling under the earnest and untrained leadership of the local men of affairs against an inertia of misery and suffering and want they are powerless to overcome.

But the psychological consequence was even worse. Since the problem was never honestly attacked as a national problem, and since the facts were never frankly faced as facts, people came to believe that American unemployment was relatively unimportant. They saw little idleness and they therefore believed there was little idleness. It is possible to drive for blocks in the usual shopping and residential districts of New York and Chicago without seeing a breadline or a food station or a hungry mob or indeed anything else much more exciting than a few casuals asleep on a park bench. And for that reason, and because their newspapers played down the subject as an additional depressant in depressing times, and because they were bored with relief measures anyway, the great American public simply ignored the whole thing. They would still ignore it today were it not that the committee hearings and the congressional debate and the presidential veto of relief bills this last June attracted their attention. And that the final passage of the Emergency Relief and Construction Act of 1932 has committed their government and themselves to a policy of affirmative action which compels both it and them to know definitely and precisely what the existing situation is.

It should be remarked at this point that nothing the federal government has yet done or is likely to do in the near future constitutes a policy of *constructive* action. Unemployment basically is not a social disease but an industrial phenomenon. The natural and inevitable consequence of a machine civilization is a lessened demand for human labor. (An almost total elimination of human labor in plowing, for example, is now foreseeable.) And the natural and inevitable consequence of a lessened demand for human labor is an increase of idleness. Indeed the prophets of the machine age have always promised an increase of idleness, under the name of leisure, as one of the goals of industry. A constructive solution of unemployment therefore means an industrial solution — a restatement of industrialism which will treat technological displacement not as an illness to be cured but as a goal to be achieved — and achieved with the widest dispensation of benefits and the least incidental misery.

But the present relief problem as focused by the federal act is not a problem of ultimate solutions but of immediate palliatives.

One does not talk architecture while the house is on fire and the tenants are still inside. The question at this moment is the pure question of fact. Having decided at last to face reality and do something about it, what is reality? How many men are unemployed in the U.S.? How many are in want? *What are the facts?*

TWENTY-FIVE MILLIONS

THE FOLLOWING MINIMAL STATEMENTS may be accepted as true — with the certainty that they underestimate the real situation:

1. Unemployment has steadily increased in the U.S. since the beginning of the depression and the rate of increase during the first part of 1932 was more rapid than in any other depression year.

2. The number of persons totally unemployed is now at least 10 million.

3. The number of persons totally unemployed next winter will, at the present rate of increase, be 11 million.

4. Eleven million unemployed means better than one man out of every four employable workers.

5. This percentage is higher than the percentage of unemployed British workers registered under the compulsory insurance laws (17.1 percent in May 1932, as against 17.3 percent in April and 18.4 percent in Jan.) and higher than the French, the Italian, and the Canadian percentages, but lower than the German (43.9 percent of trade unionists in April 1932) and the Norwegian.

6. Eleven million unemployed means 27,500,000 whose regular source of livelihood has been cut off.

7. Twenty-seven and a half million without regular income includes the families of totally unemployed workers alone. Taking account of the numbers of workers on part time, the total of those without adequate income becomes 34 million, or better than a quarter of the entire population of the country.

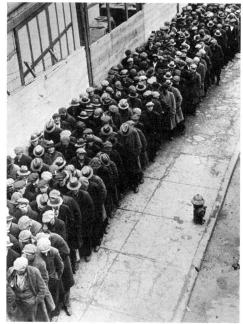

United Press International

View of breadline in New York City during the early 1930s

8. Thirty-four million persons without adequate income does not mean 34 million in present want. Many families have savings. But savings are eventually dissipated and the number in actual want tends to approximate the number without adequate income. How nearly it approximates it now or will next winter no man can say. But it is conservative to estimate that the problem of next winter's relief is a problem of caring for approximately 25 million souls. . . .

The director of the President's Organization on Unemployment Relief, Mr. Walter S. Gifford of the American Telephone & Telegraph Co., was forced to acknowledge before a subcommittee of the Senate in January 1932 that he did not know, nor did his organization know, how many persons were out of work and in need of assistance in the U.S., nor even how many persons were actually receiving aid at the time of his testimony. And more recently the commissioner of Labor Statistics, Mr. Ethelbert Stewart, generally recognized as the government's foremost authority on unemployment, has been allowed to lose his office at the most critical period in American unemployment history because, according to press accounts, the secretary of labor, Mr. Doak, was irritated by the commissioner's correction of one of his over-optimistic statements.

Fortunately, however, the more important estimators agree among themselves and the total of 25 million may fairly be accepted.

But it is impossible to think or to act in units of 25 million human beings. Like the casualty lists of the British War Office during the Battle of the Somme, they mean nothing. They are at once too large and too small. A handful of men and women and children digging for their rotten food in the St. Louis dumps are more numerous, humanly speaking, than all the millions that ever found themselves in an actuary's column. The 25 million only become human in their cities and their mill towns and their mining villages. And their situation only becomes comprehensible in terms of the relief they have already received.

That is to say that the general situation can only be judged by the situation in the particular localities. But certain generalizations are possible. Of which the chief is the broad conclusion that few if any of the industrial areas have been able to maintain a minimum decency level of life for their unemployed. Budgetary standards as set up by welfare organizations, public and private, after years of experiment, have been discarded. Food only, in most cases, is provided, and little enough of that. Rents are seldom paid. Shoes and clothing are given in rare instances only. Money for doctors and dentists is not to be had. And free clinics are filled to overflowing. Weekly allowances per family have fallen as low as $2.39 in New York with $3 and $4 the rule in most cities and $5 a high figure. And even on these terms funds budgeted for a twelve-month period have been exhausted in three or four. While city after city has been compelled to abandon a part of its dependent population.

"We are merely trying to prevent hunger and exposure," reported a St. Paul welfare head last May. And the same sentence would be echoed by workers in other cities with such additions as were reported at the same time from Pittsburgh where a cut of 50 percent was regarded as "inevitable," from Dallas where Mexicans and Negroes were not given relief, from Alabama where discontinuance of relief in mining and agricultural sections was foreseen, from New Orleans where no new applicants were being received and 2,500 families in need of relief were receiving none, from Omaha where two-thirds of the cases receiving relief were to be discontinued, from Colorado where the counties had suspended relief for lack of funds . . . from Scranton . . . from Cleveland . . . from Syracuse. . . . But the individual localities present their own picture:

NEW YORK CITY

ABOUT 1 MILLION out of the city's 3,200,000 working population are unemployed. Last April 410,000 were estimated to be in dire want. Seven hundred and fifty thousand in 150,000 families were receiving emergency aid, while 160,000 more in 32,000 families were waiting to receive aid not then available. Of these latter families — families which normally earn an average of $141.50 a month — the average income from all sources was $8.20. Of families receiving relief, the allowance has been anything from a box of groceries up to $60 a month. In general, New York relief, in the phrase of Mr. William Hodson, executive director of the New York Welfare Council, has been on "a disaster basis." And the effects have been disaster effects. It is impossible to estimate the number of deaths in the last year in which starvation was a contributing cause. But 95 persons suffering directly from starvation were admitted to the city hospitals in 1931, of whom 20 died; and 143 suffering from malnutrition, of whom 25 died. While visiting nurses and welfare workers report a general increase in malnutrition, and the clinics and medical relief agencies are so overcrowded they can give adequate relief to no one, although 75 percent of persons applying to one relief agency had some form of illness.

Housing is, of course, with the general lowering of standards and the doubling-up of families, worse even than it was during the boom. Relief expenditures for 1930 were something over $6 million; for 1931, more than $25 million; and for the first four months of 1932 over $20 million or $5 million per month. But large as this latter figure is, it must be compared with the wage and salary loss by reason of unemployment, which is at least $100 million per month. The need, even with static unemployment figures, is cumulative, and $75 million for the next twelve months is a low estimate. . . .

DETROIT

Relief in Detroit was originally upon a boom-time, boom-extravagance basis with gross incompetence in the administration of funds, an embezzlement of $207,000, and doles of silk stockings and cosmetics. The resultant imminent bankruptcy forced a contraction of expenditures, and relief in May 1932, with a greatly increased need, was only $859,925 as against $2,088,850 in Jan. 1931. There were 223,000 unemployed last Nov. in the city and 410,000 in the state. In Jan. the city was caring for 48,000 distressed families. This number was cut to 22,000 in April and relief was given at the rate of 15 cents per day per person. In July, under pressure of further shortage, a further cut of 5,000 families totaling 20,000 persons was determined. Aid was to be denied to able-bodied persons who had been public charges for a year or more whether work was available for them or not, and childless couples and small families with no definite ties in Detroit were to be forced to leave the city. The resultant relief roll was expected to be 17,757 families, of whom 7,000 were dependent because of age or illness. The great majority on relief are laborers, but Detroit also carries or has carried 45 ministers, 30 bank tellers, lawyers, dentists, musicians, and "two families after whom streets are named." Riots, chiefly employment riots, have been fairly common, with bloodshed in at least one. And enormous breadlines and the like are daily sights. No adequate statistics on public health in Detroit exist but it may safely be assumed to be at least as low as New York's.

CHICAGO

Unemployed in Chicago number somewhere between 660,000 and 700,000, or 40 percent of its employable workers, while the number for the state at large is about 1 in 3 of the gainfully employed. About 100,000 families have applied down to July for relief in Cook County. The minimum relief budget has been $2.40 per week for an adult and $1.50 per week for a child for food, with $22 to $23 per month to a family. But these figures have since been cut to $2.15 weekly for a man, $1.10 for a child. And persons demanding relief must be completely destitute to receive it. Rents are not paid by the relief agencies and housing is, in certain sections, unspeakably bad. While the situation of city employees is tragic. Teachers in May 1932 had had only five months cash for the last thirteen months, 3,177 of them had lost $2,367,000 in bank failures, 2,278 of them had lost $7,800,000 in lapsed policies, 805 had borrowed $232,000 from loan sharks at rates adding up to 42 percent a year, and 759 had lost their homes. (The city at one time undertook to sell for tax default the houses of its employees unable to pay taxes because of its own default in wages.) . . .

TEXTILES AND MINES

OBVIOUSLY, HOWEVER, urban figures give an incomplete picture of the whole industrial situation, for they do not include such areas as the industrial area of New Jersey. In Passaic County, for example, 23,749 persons, heads of families, representing 90,699 of the county's 300,000 population, have applied for relief. The authorities have been forced to pick 12,171 families, about half, and give them relief amounting to about $9 a month per family. And in Paterson 8,500 of the registered 12,000 unemployed are without relief of any kind. Moreover, the situation in the textile areas of the state is complicated by the fact that certain employers have taken advantage of the necessity of their employees to reestablish sweatshop conditions. Under such circumstances the employed as well as the unemployed become a burden upon the community.

But elsewhere in the textile mill towns even the pretense of a living wage has been dropped. North Carolina has 100,000 unemployed textile workers with another 100,000 on the payrolls of closed plants, most of whom are begging on the roads, having long ago exhausted their savings from the low wage paid them before the depression. And those employed on part time are hardly better off since the full-time wage now averages about $6.50. In Georgia, in the Piedmont Mill Village of Egan Park, fifteen families have banded together to keep alive on a total weekly income of $10. And similar stories come from other towns in the region. While some of the small steel towns are almost as badly off. At Donora, Pennsylvania, there were in March 277 regular workers out of a population of 13,900 while 2,300 others performed "made work" at $3.50 per week and 2,000 others "seem to have disappeared." . . .

The story of factory unemployment is, however, only part of the story. In *agriculture* and in *mining*, particularly soft-coal mining, the depression is not in its fourth year but in its eighth or tenth or twelfth. It is estimated that there is a destitute coal-mining population of 1,200,000 souls dependent upon some 240,000 unemployed and distressed bituminous miners, most of whom live in six states in regions where coal mining is the only important enterprise, where merchants are bankrupt, banks closed, schools without funds, and once wealthy residents in actual want. And this situation is of many years' standing, for even in the boom years of 1928 and 1929 the industry as a whole lost a total of $41 million. The American Friends Service Committee, which has worked with children in Kentucky, West Virginia, and Williamson and Franklin counties, Illinois, estimates that of the 500,000 soft-coal workers making a living in 1928 only 300,000 are now employed and on wages often as low as $8 a week. Over the entire area from 20 percent to 99 percent of the children are found to be underweight and the probability is that 20,000 children and 20,000 adults will shortly be in actual and pressing want.

Kentucky conditions have been well aired as a result of the fascist policy pursued by the local authorities, particularly in Harlan County. Miners in that county who work at all work one to one and a half days a week with payment in scrip from which the company deducts an average of $11.80 monthly for rent, medical attention, powder and caps, and insurance. To pay this deduction, a man must mine forty-five tons a month, which means that he must work nine days. Most of them work a total of six days and the result is a load of debt with no balance for food. As a consequence, pellagra — a deficiency disease of the nerve centers finally causing insanity — is common. In Pineville, Kentucky, 157 children are fed one meal a day at a soup kitchen — the meal consisting of boiled potatoes, boiled beans, and cornbread, an ideal pellagra-breeding diet.

Most of the miners attempt to farm but the land is poor and jars for canning are too expensive for a community in which cash is practically nonexistent. Moreover, there was last year a severe drought in this district, and a great many miners' crops were destroyed by sun and pests — a fact which must be compared with the September 1931 statement of Executive Director Croxton of the President's Organization on Unemployment Relief to the effect that the unemployment situation in West Virginia and Kentucky would be alleviated by the "bountiful crops."

The state of Franklin and Williamson counties in Illinois is, if anything, worse. All mines in the counties were closed by April 1932. A cross-section of twelve homes in the town of Benton showed no money, worn-out clothing, houses bare of "unnecessary" furniture, dishes made of flour, emaciated parents, undernourished children, unpaid rentals, and an average family indebtedness for groceries and doctors' bills of $300. Twenty-five thousand persons in the two counties were either in want last spring or rapidly approaching it.

Other coal-mining states are in the same condition. There were 20,000 distressed miners in Ohio in February 1932. In Pennsylvania last winter there were 60,000 in distress, many small communities were half-deserted, one day's work a month was the frequent rule, undernourishment and malnutrition were common, and school children were stupid and sleepy with hunger. In West Virginia the number of distressed miners was about 30,000, thousands of men and women lived in tents, many children were eating every other day, prostitution among young girls was increasing, dysen-

tery and pellagra were common diseases, and 15,000 men in Logan County alone were working twelve to eighteen hours a day without extra pay. In Arizona 200 miners' families in utter destitution were living under one of the bridges of the Salt River.

So it goes from one city to another and out into the mill towns and the mine villages and on beyond into the farms where the hides of a carload of cattle will hardly buy a pair of shoes and alfalfa costing $12 a ton to raise sells at $2.50 and the tractors rust in the fields. The difficulty with such facts is that in mass they cease to have meaning. And the reiteration of the statement that hundreds of thousands of people have faced or are facing starvation with inadequate doles to support them merely produces skepticism. "They haven't starved yet," remarks the reader. "They get along somehow."

It is true they get along somehow. But just how they get along is another matter. There were eleven days in Philadelphia last April when private funds had run out and public funds were not yet available. During that period, the relief organizations studied ninety-one families to see just how people get along under those circumstances. They found out. One woman borrowed 50 cents, bought stale bread at 3½ cents a loaf, and the family lived on it for eleven days. Another put the last food order into soup stock and vegetables and made a soup. When a member of the family was hungry, he ate as little as he could. Another picked up spoiled vegetables along the docks and, except for three foodless days, the family ate them. Another made a stew with her last food order, which she cooked over and over daily to keep it from spoiling. Another family lived on dandelions. Another on potatoes. Another had no food for two and one-half days. And one in ten of the women were pregnant and one in three of the children of nursing age. And they "got along."

TREK

SUCH IS THE PROBLEM created by three years of increasing unemployment and two years of hand-to-mouth relief: city after city attempting to feed a half or a third or a quarter of its citizens upon gifts made from the reduced earnings, or from taxes levied on the over-appraised homes of the other half or the other two-thirds or the other three-quarters; city after city maintaining the lives but not the health of its unemployed on a survival ration; city after city where the whole mechanism of relief has failed or is about to fail or has survived only by abandoning a major part of its task; and beyond the cities the mill towns and the coal mines and the cropper farms where relief is merely a name.

But the depression, along with its misery, has produced its social curiosities, not the least of which is the wandering population it has spilled upon the roads. Means of locomotion vary but the objective is always the same — somewhere else. No one has yet undertaken to estimate the number of hitchhikers whose thumbs jerk onward along the American pike, nor the number of spavined Fords, dragging destitute families from town to town in search of a solvent relative or a generous friend. But the total migratory population of the country has been put at 600,000 to 1 million. The Pacific Coast, the Southwest, and the Atlantic South are the habitat of the larger groups. Los Angeles once had over 70,000 with a daily influx of 1,500 more, while the state of California reported an increase of 311.8 percent in the monthly average of meals served to homeless men in early 1931 as compared with early 1929. And 365 vagrant boys running from fourteen to twenty and including college students, high-school students, and eighth-graders applied to the Salt Lake Salvation Army and the Salt Lake County Jail for shelter between May 15 and June 15, 1932. Many of them were homeless, destitute children of families broken up by unemployment. And save for the fact that almost all of them were traveling alone or with one companion, and that most of them wanted work, they suggested with an uncomfortable accuracy the vagrant children who haunted the Russian railway stations after the October Revolution.

The presence of these wandering groups is curious and significant. It has long been recognized that the population of the U.S. was becoming increasingly migratory in character. But it was not until the depression that the meaning of the phenomenon was made clear. When millions of people have no relation to the land and are able at the same time to find cheap transportation, the effect of an economic crisis is not to fix them in one place but to drive them elsewhere. And the consequence, as regards these groups, is a complete failure of local relief. The destitute families of the Fords and the homeless men of the flat cars are entitled to relief in no city. As the history of the Bonus Expeditionary Force after its ouster from Washington makes clear. . . .

SUCH, BROADLY SPEAKING, are the facts of unemployment relief in the late summer of 1932. Ahead, whether the depression "ends" this fall or not, is the problem of caring for some 25 million souls through what may prove to be one of the most difficult winters of the republic's history. Behind are three years of muddled purpose, insufficient funds, and unscientific direction. Across the threshold lies a new federal policy and a formal acceptance of the issue. The immediate consequences, to be counted next spring, will depend upon the intelligence with which the adequate forces of the country are administered. The ultimate consequences and the final solution will depend upon American industry. And for that reason the present agitation for the thirty-hour week which began in industry and which is backed by industry is perhaps the most important single development of the depression.

RURAL DEPRESSION

The war years had been a time of unwonted prosperity for American farmers. The increased demands for their products coupled with prices boosted by the war economy had come just at a time when agricultural methods and equipment were changing over to the mechanized system. The result was a huge increase in production, in terms of both yield and acreage, and an optimistic wave of extension. With the end of the war, and particularly with the general economic depression of 1920-21, agriculture found itself suddenly overextended. Over-production, in peacetime terms, and falling prices — the prices of many major commodities dropped by half or more between 1919 and 1921 — plunged agriculture into its own depression that was to last until the next war. Hampered by the pointlessly high tariffs of the industrial-bloc Republicans, by the unstable economy of post-Versailles Europe, and by Congress' habitually hysterical application of the word "socialistic" to proposed corrective legislation, farm income dropped continuously. Farm mortgages and farm tenancy hit all-time highs. As a background to the industrial boom and urban prosperity of the times, however, the deteriorating rural situation was easily and usually overlooked.

(Above) Lounging along the main street of Childersburg, Ala., photo by John Delano; (below) idling in front of the courthouse in Compton, Ky. on court day; both photos for the FSA

(Left) Man killed when troops broke up lynch mob in Shelbyville, Tenn.; Huey Long, whose populist demagoguery during the Depression brought him national attention and unchallenged power in Louisiana; (below) striking textile workers picketing Sargent Mills, Newman, Ga.

(Above) Housing on a Farm Security Administration project outside Schriever, La., photographed by Wolcott in 1940; (below) Negroes attending an FSA project meeting in Marshall, Tex., 1937

Little was done to alleviate the agricultural depression until the New Deal period. The Agricultural Marketing Act of 1929 was much too late to accomplish anything; the crash in October caught farmers with unsold harvests, with debts, and often with now worthless stock certificates. The small efforts at securing mortgages through government corporations had no effect whatever on tenant farmers who by 1930 constituted 42 percent of all farmers.

(Top) Neshoba County, Miss., businessmen at an FSA meeting; (right) South Dakota farmers working on an irrigation project sponsored by WPA, 1936; (bottom) men working on a flood control project along the lower Mississippi River

(Above) A leading citizen of Wendell, N.C., in his domain; (below) card players passing the time on the courthouse lawn in Yanceyville, N.C.; both photos by Wolcott for the FSA

(Above) Longshoremen on the cotton docks, Houston, Texas, photo by Russell Lee; (below) workers in a Georgia turpentine forest, photo by Dorothea Lange. Both photos for the FSA

(Above) The town square in Camden, Tennessee, 1935; (below) men without work passing the time in Maynardville, Tennessee. Both photographs by Ben Shahn for the Farm Security Administration

(Above) Evicted sharecroppers along U.S. 60 in New Madrid County, Missouri, photo by Arthur Rothstein; (below) Mississippi sharecroppers' cabins, photo by Dorothea Lange, both for FSA

(Above) Negro woman planning to leave Georgia to live with her children in Memphis, Tennessee; (below) farmer in the market at Weatherford, Texas

38.

Franklin D. Roosevelt: Call for Federal Responsibility

"What do the people of America want more than anything else?" Franklin D. Roosevelt asked in his unprecedented speech before the Democratic Convention in Chicago that had just nominated him the presidential candidate. "Work and security. . . . They are the spiritual values, the true goal toward which our efforts of reconstruction should lead." Roosevelt had entered politics with the conviction that government was responsible for its citizens' welfare. As governor of New York he had sponsored the Temporary Emergency Relief Administration that undertook relief and public works. In September 1931 it was the first agency of its kind in the nation. Roosevelt's campaign address of October 13, 1932, a portion of which appears here, explained further his views on social legislation.

Source: FDR, I, pp. 786-795.

THE FIRST PRINCIPLE I would lay down is that the primary duty rests on the community, through local government and private agencies, to take care of the relief of unemployment. But we then come to a situation where there are so many people out of work that local funds are insufficient.

It seems clear to me that the organized society known as the State comes into the picture at this point. In other words, the obligation of government is extended to the next higher unit.

I practise what I preach. In 1930 the state of New York greatly increased its employment service and kept in close touch with the ability of localities to take care of their own unemployed. But by the summer of 1931 it became apparent to me that actual state funds and a state-supervised system were imperative.

I called a special session of the legislature, and they appropriated a fund of $20 million for unemployment relief, this fund to be reimbursed to the state through the doubling of our income taxes. Thus the state of New York became the first among all the states to accept the definite obligation of supplementing local funds where these local funds were insufficient.

The administration of this great work has become a model for the rest of the country. Without setting up any complex machinery or any large overhead, the state of New York is working successfully through local agencies, and, in spite of the fact that over a million people are out of work and in need of aid in this one state alone, we have so far met at least the bare necessities of the case.

This past spring the legislature appropriated another $5 million, and on November 8 the voters will pass on a $30 million bond issue to tide us over this winter and at least up to next summer. . . .

I am very certain that the obligation extends beyond the states and to the federal government itself, if and when it becomes apparent that states and communities are unable to take care of the necessary relief work.

It may interest you to have me read a short quotation from my message to the legislature in 1931:

What is the State? It is the duly constituted representative of an organized society of human beings, created by them for their mutual protection and well-being. One of the duties of the State is that of caring for those of its citizens who find themselves the victims of such adverse circumstances as make them unable to obtain even the necessities of mere existence without the aid of others.

In broad terms, I assert that modern society, acting through its government, owes the definite obligation to prevent the starvation or the dire want of any of its fellowmen and women who try to maintain themselves but cannot. To these unfortunate citizens aid must be extended by the government, not as a matter of charity but as a matter of social duty.

That principle which I laid down in 1931, I reaffirm. I not only reaffirm it, I go a step further and say that where the State itself is unable successfully to fulfill this obligation which lies upon it, it then becomes the positive duty of the federal government to step in to help.

In the words of our Democratic national platform, the federal government has a "continuous responsibility for human welfare, especially for the protection of children." That duty and responsibility the federal government should carry out promptly, fearlessly, and generously.

It took the present Republican administration in Washington almost three years to recognize this principle. I have recounted to you in other speeches, and it is a matter of general information, that for at least two years after the crash, the only efforts made by the national administration to cope with the distress of unemployment were to deny its existence.

When, finally, this year, after attempts at concealment and minimizing had failed, it was at last forced to recognize the fact of suffering among millions of unemployed, appropriations of federal funds for assistance to states were finally made.

I think it is fair to point out that a complete program of unemployment relief was on my recommendation actually under way in the state of New York over a year ago and that in Washington relief funds in any large volume were not provided until this summer, and at that they were pushed through at the demand of Congress rather than through the leadership of the President of the United States.

At the same time, I have constantly reiterated my conviction that the expenditures of cities, states, and the federal government must be reduced in the interest of the nation as a whole. I believe that there are many ways in which such reduction of expenditures can take place, but I am utterly unwilling that economy should be practised at the expense of starving people.

We must economize in other ways, but it shall never be said that the American people have refused to provide the necessities of life for those who, through no fault of their own, are unable to feed, clothe, and house themselves. The first obligation of government is the protection of the welfare and well-being, indeed the very existence, of its citizens. . . .

The next question asks my attitude toward appropriations for public works as an aid to unemployment. I am perfectly clear as to the principles involved in this case also.

From the long-range point of view it would be advisable for governments of all kinds to set up in times of prosperity what might be called a nest egg to be used for public works in times of depression. That is a policy which we should initiate when we get back to good times.

But there is the immediate possibility of helping the emergency through appropriations for public works. One question, however, must be answered first because of the simple fact that these public works cost money.

We all know that government treasuries, whether local or state or federal, are hard put to it to keep their budgets balanced; and, in the case of the federal Treasury, thoroughly unsound financial policies have made its situation not exactly desperate but at least threatening to future stability if the policies of the present administration are continued.

All public works, including federal, must be considered from the point of view of the ability of the government Treasury to pay for them. There are two ways of paying for public works. One is by the sale of bonds. In principle, such bonds should be issued only to pay for self-sustaining projects or for structures which will without question have a useful life over a long period of years. The other method of payment is from current revenues, which in these days means in most cases added taxes. We all know that there is a very definite limit to the increase of taxes above the present level.

From this point, therefore, I can go on and say that, if funds can be properly provided by the federal government for increased appropriations for public works, we must examine the character of these public works. I have already spoken of that type which is self-sustaining. These should be greatly encouraged. The other type is that of public works which are honestly essential to the community. Each case must rest on its own merits.

It is impossible, for example, to say that all parks or all playgrounds are essential. One may be and another may not be. If a school, for instance, has no playground, it is obvious that the furnishing of a playground is a necessity to the community. But if the school already has a playground and some people seek merely to enlarge it, there may be a very definite question as to how necessary that enlargement is.

Let me cite another example. I am much interested in providing better housing accommodations for the poor in our great cities. If a slum area can be torn down and new modern buildings put up, I should call that almost a human necessity; but, on the other hand, the mere erection of new buildings in some other part of the city while allowing the slums to remain raises at once

a question of necessity. I am confident that the federal government working in cooperation with states and cities can do much to carry on increased public works and along lines which are sound from the economic and financial point of view.

Now I come to another question. I am asked whether I favor a system of unemployment insurance reserves made compulsory by the states, supplemented by a system of federally coordinated state employment offices to facilitate the reemployment of jobless workers.

The first part of the question is directly answered by the Democratic platform, which advocates unemployment insurance under state laws.

This is no new policy for me. I have advocated unemployment insurance in my own state for some time, and, indeed, last year six Eastern governors were my guests at a conference which resulted in the drawing up of what might be called an ideal plan of unemployment insurance.

This type of insurance is not a cure-all, but it provides at least a cushion to mitigate unemployment in times of depression. It is sound if, after starting it, we stick to the principle of sound insurance financing. It is only where governments, as in some European countries, have failed to live up to these sound principles that unemployment insurance has been an economic failure.

As to the coordinated employment offices, I can only tell you that I was for the bills sponsored by Senator Wagner of my own state and passed by the Congress. They created a nationally coordinated system of employment offices operated by the individual states with the advisory cooperation of joint boards of employers and employees.

To my very great regret this measure was vetoed by the President of the United States. I am certain that the federal government can, by furnishing leadership, stimulate the various states to set up and coordinate practical, useful systems.

39.

HERBERT HOOVER: Against the Proposed New Deal

President Hoover attributed the Depression to forces that bore on the United States from without, not to weaknesses in the American system itself. He had originally intended to conduct a limited campaign for reelection; but as Roosevelt's intentions to alter the economic system became increasingly apparent, he was stirred to political battle. Hoover was constantly on the defensive during the campaign, celebrating the virtues of individualism and voluntary cooperation while charging that Roosevelt's promised New Deal was based on "the same philosophy of government which has poisoned all Europe." Hoover's speech at Madison Square Garden in New York City on October 31, 1932, is reprinted here in part. Like all of his speeches, it was written by Hoover himself.

Source: *The State Papers and Other Public Writings of Herbert Hoover*, William S. Myers, ed., Garden City, N.Y., 1934, Vol. II, pp. 408-413.

THIS CAMPAIGN IS MORE than a contest between two men. It is more than a contest between two parties. It is a contest between two philosophies of government.

We are told by the opposition that we must have a change, that we must have a new deal. It is not the change that comes from normal development of national life to which I object but the proposal to alter the whole foundations of our national life which have been builded through generations of testing and struggle, and of the principles upon which we have builded the nation. The expressions our opponents use must refer to important changes in our economic and social system and our system of government, otherwise they are nothing but vacuous words. And I realize that in this time of distress many of our people are asking whether our social and economic system is incapable of that great primary function of providing security and comfort of life to all of the firesides of our 25 million homes in America, whether our social system provides for the fundamental development and progress of our people, whether our form of government is capable of originating and sustaining that security and progress.

This question is the basis upon which our opponents are appealing to the people in their fears and distress. They are proposing changes and so-called new deals which would destroy the very foundations of our American system.

Our people should consider the primary facts before they come to the judgment — not merely through political agitation, the glitter of promise, and the discouragement of temporary hardships — whether they will support changes which radically affect the whole system which has been builded up by 150 years of the toil of our fathers. They should not approach the question in the despair with which our opponents would clothe it.

Our economic system has received abnormal shocks during the past three years, which temporarily dislocated its normal functioning. These shocks have in a large sense come from without our borders, but I say to you that our system of government has enabled us to take such strong action as to prevent the disaster which would otherwise have come to our nation. It has enabled us further to develop measures and programs which are now demonstrating their ability to bring about restoration and progress.

We must go deeper than platitudes and emotional appeals of the public platform in the campaign if we will penetrate to the full significance of the changes which our opponents are attempting to float upon the wave of distress and discontent from the difficulties we are passing through. We can find what our opponents would do after searching the record of their appeals to discontent, group and sectional interest. We must search for them in the legislative acts which they sponsored and passed in the Democratic-controlled House of Representatives in the last session of Congress. We must look into measures for which they voted and which were defeated. We must inquire whether or not the presidential and vice-presidential candidates have disavowed these acts. If they have not, we must conclude that they form a portion and are a substantial indication of the profound changes proposed.

And we must look still further than this as to what revolutionary changes have been proposed by the candidates themselves.

We must look into the type of leaders who are campaigning for the Democratic ticket, whose philosophies have been well known all their lives, whose demands for a change in the American system are frank and forceful. I can respect the sincerity of these men in their desire to change our form of government and our social and economic system, though I shall do my best tonight to prove they are wrong. I refer particularly to Senator Norris, Senator La Follette, Senator Cutting, Senator Huey Long, Senator Wheeler, William R. Hearst, and other exponents of a social philosophy different from the traditional American one. Unless these men feel assurance of support to their ideas, they certainly would not be supporting these candidates and the Democratic Party. The seal of these men indicates that they have sure confidence that they will have voice in the administration of our government.

I may say at once that the changes proposed from all these Democratic principals and allies are of the most profound and penetrating character. If they are brought about, this will not be the America which we have known in the past.

Let us pause for a moment and examine the American system of government, of social and economic life, which it is now proposed that we should alter. Our system is the product of our race and of our experience in building a nation to heights unparalleled in the whole history of the world. It is a system peculiar to the American people. It differs essentially from all others in the world. It is an American system.

It is founded on the conception that only through ordered liberty, through freedom to the individual, and equal opportunity to the individual will his initiative and enterprise be summoned to spur the march of progress.

It is by the maintenance of equality of opportunity and therefore of a society absolutely fluid in freedom of the movement of its human particles that our individualism departs from the individualism of Europe. We resent class distinction because there can be no rise for the individual through the frozen strata of classes, and no stratification of classes can take place in a mass livened by the free rise of its particles. Thus in our ideals the able and ambitious are able to rise constantly from the bottom to leadership in the community.

This freedom of the individual creates of itself the necessity and the cheerful willingness of men to act cooperatively in a thousand ways and for every purpose as occasion arises; and it permits such voluntary cooperations to be dissolved as soon as they have served their purpose, to be replaced by new voluntary associations for new purposes.

There has thus grown within us, to gigantic importance, a new conception. That is, this voluntary cooperation within the community. Cooperation to perfect the social organization; cooperation for the care of those in distress; cooperation for the advancement of knowledge, of scientific research, of education; for cooperative action in the advancement of many phases of economic life. This is self-government by the people outside of government; it is the most powerful development of individual freedom and equal opportunity that has taken place in the century and a half since our fundamental institutions were founded.

It is in the further development of this cooperation and a sense of its responsibility that we should find solution for many of our complex problems, and not by the extension of government into our economic and social life. The greatest function of government is to build up that cooperation, and its most resolute action should be to deny the extension of bureaucracy. We have developed great agencies of cooperation by the assistance of the government which promote and protect the interests of individuals and the smaller units of business. The Federal Reserve System, in its strengthening and support of the smaller banks; the Farm Board, in its strengthening and support of the farm cooperatives; the Home Loan Banks, in the mobilizing of building and loan associations and savings banks; the Federal Land Banks, in giving independence and strength to land mortgage associations; the great mobilization of relief to distress, the mobilization of business and industry in measures of recovery, and a score of other activities are not socialism — they are the essence of protection to the development of free men.

The primary conception of this whole American system is not the regimentation of men but the cooperation of free men. It is founded upon the conception of responsibility of the individual to the community, of the responsibility of local government to the state, of the state to the national government.

It is founded on a peculiar conception of self-government designed to maintain this equal opportunity to the individual, and through decentralization it brings about and maintains these responsibilities. The centralization of government will undermine responsibilities and will destroy the system.

Our government differs from all previous conceptions, not only in this decentralization but also in the separation of functions between the legislative, executive, and judicial arms of government, in which the independence of the judicial arm is the keystone of the whole structure.

It is founded on a conception that in times of emergency, when forces are running beyond control of individuals or other cooperative action, beyond the control of local communities and of states, then the great reserve powers of the federal government shall be brought into action to protect the community. But when these forces have ceased, there must be a return of state, local, and individual responsibility.

The implacable march of scientific discovery with its train of new inventions presents every year new problems to government and new problems to the social order. Questions often arise whether, in the face of the growth of these new and gigantic tools, democracy can remain master in its own house, can preserve the fundamentals of our American system. I contend that it can; and I contend that this American system of ours has demonstrated its validity and superiority over any other system yet invented by human mind.

It has demonstrated it in the face of the greatest test of our history — that is the emergency which we have faced in the past three years.

When the political and economic weakness of many nations of Europe, the result of the World War and its aftermath, finally culminated in collapse of their institutions, the delicate adjustment of our economic and social life received a shock unparalleled in our history. No one knows that better than you of New York. No one knows its causes better than you. That the crisis was so great that many of the leading banks sought directly or indirectly to convert their assets into gold or its equivalent with the result that they practically ceased to function as credit institutions; that many of our citizens sought flight for their capital to other countries; that many of them attempted to hoard gold in large amounts. These were but indications of the flight of confidence and of the belief that our government could not overcome these forces.

Yet these forces were overcome — perhaps by narrow margins — and this action demonstrates what the courage of a nation can accomplish under the resolute leadership in the Republican Party. And I say the Republican Party, because our opponents, before and during the crisis, proposed no constructive program; though some of their members patriotically supported ours. Later on the Democratic House of Representatives did develop the real thought and ideas of the Democratic Party, but it was so destructive that it had to be defeated, for it would have destroyed, not healed.

In spite of all these obstructions, we did succeed. Our form of government did prove itself equal to the task. We saved this nation from a quarter of a century of chaos and degeneration, and we preserved the savings, the insurance policies, gave a fighting chance to men to hold their homes. We saved the integrity of our government and the honesty of the American dollar. And we installed measures which today are bringing back recovery. Employment, agriculture, business — all of these show the steady, if slow, healing of our enormous wound.

I therefore contend that the problem of today is to continue these measures and policies to restore this American system to its normal functioning, to repair the wounds it has received, to correct the weaknesses and evils which would defeat that system. To enter upon a series of deep changes, to embark upon this inchoate new deal which has been propounded in this campaign, would be to undermine and destroy our American system.

[It is] *dangerous to change parties in mid-Depression.*
> DAVID LAWRENCE, advising the readers of his column to vote for Hoover, 1932

Don't Swap Barrels Going Over Niagara.
> Slogan ascribed ironically to the Republicans during Roosevelt-Hoover campaign, 1932. It refers, of course, to the time-honored Republican slogan, "Don't Switch Horses in Midstream" (Lincoln first to use it).

40.

Henry Ford: Advice to the Unemployed

"Better business will come," Roger W. Babson, the financial statistician, was quoted as saying in 1932, "when the unemployed change their attitude toward life." This sentiment, or variations on it, was not uncommon among businessmen during the Depression. Poverty and unemployment, they felt, were the fault of the poor, and large-scale relief programs would only weaken the moral fiber of the poor and stimulate an unwillingness to work. Some businessmen conceded that the economy needed government aid to get things going again; but once prosperity was restored at the top, it would trickle down to the lower levels of society. The following advice to the nearly 13 million unemployed and their families in June 1932 came from Henry Ford.

Source: *Literary Digest*, June 11, 1932.

I HAVE ALWAYS HAD TO WORK, whether anyone hired me or not. For the first forty years of my life, I was an employee. When not employed by others, I employed myself. I found very early that being out of hire was not necessarily being out of work. The first means that your employer has not found something for you to do; the second means that you are waiting until he does.

We nowadays think of work as something others find for us to do, call us to do, and pay us to do. No doubt our industrial growth is largely responsible for that. We have accustomed men to think of work that way.

In my own case, I was able to find work for others as well as myself. Outside my family life, nothing has given me more satisfaction than to see jobs increase in number and in profit to the men who handle them. And, beyond question, the jobs of the world today are more numerous and profitable in wages than they were even eighteen years ago.

But something entirely outside the workshops of the nation has affected this hired employment very seriously. The word "unemployment" has become one of the most dreadful words in the language. The condition itself has become the concern of every person in the country.

When this condition arrived, there were just three things to be done. The first, of course, was to maintain employment at the maximum by every means known to management. Employment — hire — was what the people were accustomed to; they preferred it; it was the immediate solution of the difficulty. In our plants we used every expedient to spread as much employment over as many employees as was possible. I don't believe in "make work" — the public pays for all unnecessary work — but there are times when the plight of others compels us to do the human thing even though it be but a makeshift; and I am obliged to admit that, like most manufacturers, we avoided layoffs by continuing work that good busiless judgment would have halted. All of our nonprofit work was continued in full force and much of the shop work. There were always tens of thousands employed — the lowest point at Dearborn was 40,000 — but there were always thousands unemployed or so meagerly employed that the situation was far from desirable.

When all possible devices for providing employment have been used and fall short, there remains no alternative but self-help or charity.

I do not believe in routine charity. I think it a shameful thing that any man should have to stoop to take it, or give it. I do not include human helpfulness under the name of charity. My quarrel with charity is that it is neither helpful nor human. The charity of our cities is the most barbarous thing in our system, with the possible exception of our prisons. What we call charity is a modern substitute for being personally kind, personally concerned, and personally involved in the work of helping others in difficulty. True charity is a much more costly effort than money-giving. Our donations too often purchase exemption from giving the only form of help that will drive the need for charity out of the land.

Our own theory of helping people has been in operation for some years. We used to discuss it years ago — when no one could be persuaded to listen. Those who asked public attention to these matters were ridiculed by the very people who now call most loudly for someone to do something.

Our own work involves the usual emergency relief, hospitalization, adjustment of debt, with this addition — we help people to alter their affairs in commonsense accordance with changed conditions, and we have an understanding that all help received should be repaid in reasonable amounts in better times. Many families were not so badly off as they thought; they needed guidance in the management of their resources and opportunities. Human nature,

of course, presented the usual problems. Relying on human sympathy many develop a spirit of professional indigence. But where cooperation is given, honest and self-respecting persons and families can usually be assisted to a condition which is much less distressing than they feared.

One of our responsibilities, voluntarily assumed — not because it was ours but because there seemed to be no one else to assume it — was the care of a village of several hundred families whose condition was pretty low. Ordinarily, a large welfare fund would have been needed to accomplish anything for these people. In this instance, we set the people at work cleaning up their homes and backyards, and then cleaning up the roads of their town, and then plowing up about 500 acres of vacant land around their houses. We abolished everything that savored of "handout" charity, opening instead a modern commissary where personal I O U's were accepted, and a garment-making school, and setting the cobblers and tailors of the community to work for their neighbors. We found the people heavily burdened with debt, and we acted informally as their agents in apportioning their income to straighten their affairs. Many families are now out of debt for the first time in years. There has appeared in this village, not only a new spirit of confidence in life but also a new sense of economic values and an appreciation of economic independence which we feel will not soon be lost.

None of these things could have been accomplished by paying out welfare funds after the orthodox manner. The only true charity for these people was somehow to get under their burdens with them and lend them the value of our experience to show them what can be done by people in their circumstances.

Our visiting staff in city work has personally handled thousands of cases in the manner above described. And while no one institution can shoulder all the burden, we feel that merely to mitigate present distress is not enough — we feel that thousands of families have been prepared for a better way of life when the wheels of activity begin turning again.

But there is still another way, a third way, so much better than the very best charitable endeavor that it simply forbids us to be satisfied with anything less. That is the way of Self-Help.

41.

Teachers in the Depression

The following testimony of May 9, 1932, by Irvin A. Wilson, president of the Chicago Principals Club, reveals the plight of the Chicago schoolteachers in the early years of the Depression. The financial difficulties, unrelieved by the city government, threatened to close down the public school system. It was nearly ten years before the teachers received their back pay.

Source: *Federal Cooperation in Unemployment Relief, Hearing Before a Subcommittee of the Committee on Manufactures, U.S. Senate,* 72 Congress, 1 Session, Washington, 1932, pp. 48-51.

Senator Costigan. What is your name?

Mr. Wilson. Irvin A. Wilson.

Senator Costigan. Are you president of the Chicago Principals Club?

Mr. Wilson. I am president of the Chicago Principals Club, and am here officially representing that organization.

Senator Costigan. Have you a statement for the committee?

Mr. Wilson. I have no statement. I will speak from notes, Mr. Chairman.

Senator Costigan. Please proceed.

Mr. Wilson. In the first place, gentlemen of the committee, the credit of the Chicago Board of Education has completely collapsed. The taxes which are now in process of collection on the penalty date, which was the 1st of June, were collected only to the extent of less than 50 percent.

Senator Wheeler. You say the financial structure has completely collapsed. How much of that has been due to the misapplication of funds by those in charge of the School Board, if any?

Mr. Wilson. I should say a very small part of it from that standpoint alone. . . In a period of two years no taxes whatever have been collected, and we have been borrowing money for the last several years at least a year ahead, and for the last three or four years, two years ahead in order to meet expenses.

Senator Wheeler. One hears so much these days about the corruption and crookedness of city officials and school boards that I was wondering as to the making of money of those interested in school boards on private contracts — I was wondering how much, if any, you had knowledge of in Chicago; just in a general way, without specific instances, has there been much of that?

Mr. Wilson. The schools have recently been surveyed by Dr. George D. Strayer, of Columbia University, and in his survey report just submitted to the Board of Education this week, he makes several recommendations for economy in the Board of Education, and the Board of Education already ahead of that survey put into operation a great many economies under the present stress period of financial depression.

Senator Wheeler. I hope an aroused public opinion will come about in Chicago and other large cities that are suffering from lack of funds against these thieving public officials who have been responsible to some extent, at least, in breaking down the finances of the cities, counties, and states of our country.

Mr. Wilson. I want to address myself, gentlemen, to two or three things. In the middle of February the Chicago Principals Club, in order to acquaint the people of Chicago with the critical financial situation facing the school people, sent a questionnaire to each of the 14,000 teachers in the city. We had replies from 263 of the city's schools and from 6,315 teachers, covering their own financial situation, beginning with the 1st of last May, when salaries ceased to come through on time. Over the period of the last thirteen months the Chicago school system has paid in cash to school employees only five months out of thirteen.

Senator Costigan. When you refer to the 1st of last May, what year have you in mind? Is that of this year?

Mr. Wilson. The 1st of May, 1931.

These are some of the results we have on the questionnaire. The teachers of Chicago, 3,177 of those teachers out of 6,315 reported a total loss of $2,367,000 in bank failures. Two thousand eight hundred and sixty-nine of those teachers reported a loss of time of $621,293 because of personal illness, this at a time when salaries were not forthcoming.

Senator Wheeler. How many lost money by investing in the Insull Securities Co. in Chicago?

Mr. Wilson. I imagine a large number of them did that. Two thousand two hundred and seventy-eight reported losses to the extent of $7,800,000, by lapsed life insurance policies, as the result of this critical financial situation. Seven hundred and fifty-nine lost

their homes, lost an equity in the homes which they were buying. There were large amounts due on rent and food, doctors' and dentists' bills, and all those things.

Insurance companies have loaned teachers at Chicago, on their policies, $1,128,000. Many of the teachers had been forced to allow their life insurance policies to lapse. Eight hundred and five teachers reported having gone to what we call the loan sharks and procured money to the extent of $232,000, and were therefore paying an interest rate equal to a maximum of 42 percent a year on that.

I want to say to you that the situation of the Chicago schoolteachers has been critical for the past year. A year ago we went into the summer vacation period with two months' back salary unpaid. This year, unless something unexpected happens in the next few days, we will go into the summer vacation with six months' unpaid salaries.

Twenty million dollars today is owing the teachers, 14,000 teachers, of Chicago. That is an average of $1,400 for each teacher in the Chicago school system that that community owes to the teachers. If every citizen in the United States were assessed an equal tax, that would bring in the stupendous total of $150,000,000,000, enough to operate the entire public school system of the United States of America for three-quarters of a century.

I say to you that we have reached the breaking point. I believe that it is impossible for the Chicago school situation to go on as it is without some form of relief. We cannot see any relief immediately ahead in the city. We are appealing to you as representatives of the United States government, because we believe that education is fundamental to the preservation of the ideals of this nation.

We are certain that anything that wrecks, cripples the school system of this nation cannot but have an effect upon the citizenship in all times. We believe the second largest city in the country, with such a school situation that we are certain is absolutely unique and tremendously dangerous, tremendously serious; we believe that that situation if permitted to continue will finally result in but one thing, the complete collapse of the Chicago public school system, which would be a blot upon the good name, not only of that city but upon the records of this nation.

We believe that education and citizenship must go hand in hand. We believe that anything that interferes with the proper carrying out of the educational system of this nation will finally have its effect upon the citizenship and upon the state as a whole.

This we believe to be a real crisis, a crisis that demands the most expert thinking, the most expert acting, and the most expert remedy. We are, therefore, appealing to you wholly on the ground that the United States of America cannot afford to permit 500,000 boys and girls to remain out upon the streets of the second largest city in this nation. We are certain that is imminent unless some relief comes, and comes immediately.

Certainly the ideals of America support public education. We believe that that city of ours is supporting public education. We are willing to make any sacrifice, and we have made all sacrifices in order that the schools of that city be kept open during the past year.

Senator Costigan. Mr. Wilson, the problem of the boys on the street is further complicated, is it not, because many of them belong to families the members of which have long been and still are unemployed?

Mr. Wilson. Absolutely. That is a very, very important point in connection with that.

Senator Wheeler. What has the appeal been to the bankers out there to take up these warrants?

Mr. Wilson. The warrants which are now given to teachers — I have a half of one month's salary in my pocket at the present time that I have not been able to dispose of, that I would have to dispose of, if I were putting it on the market today, at 12 to 20 percent discount. That is the answer of the bankers.

Senator Wheeler. Will the bankers take these warrants?

Mr. Wilson. The bankers will not take the warrants at all. You have to sell them through private investment companies.

Senator Wheeler. They will not take them at all?

Mr. Wilson. Not at the present time.

Senator Wheeler. Why will they not take them? What is the excuse they will not take them, the reason for it?

Mr. Wilson. Very largely because of the muddle the tax situation is in, out of which we have not emerged in Chicago.

Senator Wheeler. But eventually it seems to me the city of Chicago, certainly the people of the city of Chicago, are not going to let the complete city government collapse there.

I want to remind you that the Congress of the United States has passed a reconstruction bill for the purpose of helping the bankers of the country. We have passed the Glass-Steagall Bill for the purpose of helping the bankers of the country, and to keep the banks open, and we have passed other legislation, all of it with the idea of helping the big banks of the country, and it seems to me that when a community is in the situation that you have described, that at least there ought to be patriotism enough among your bankers in Chicago to take up these warrants and keep it going until such time as your tax muddle is straightened out.

Mr. Wilson. Of course, as a matter of fact, over the last several years the bankers have carried the situation completely, but when this so-called tax strike came on, and with less than 50 percent of the taxes due, and on which the penalty date began June 1, with less than 50 percent of those taxes paid, the bankers find it impossible to carry the situation longer.

1933

42.

Senate Hearings on Federal Aid for Unemployment Relief

The following testimony was presented in January 1933 to a subcommittee of the Senate Committee on Manufactures that was conducting hearings on a bill to provide for cooperative action by the states and the federal government for relief of unemployment. The two witnesses represented here were Donald R. Richberg, later an assistant to Hugh Johnson in the National Recovery Administration (NRA), and Sumner H. Slichter, professor of business economics at Harvard. That the federal government was going to have a larger role in national economic matters was recognized by everyone even before President Roosevelt took office in March, but the remarks of Richberg and Slichter, taken together, indicate the considerable divergence of opinion in the country with regard to what the federal role should be. The testimony of both men is reprinted in part.

Source: *Federal Aid for Unemployment Relief, Hearings Before a Subcommittee of the Committee on Manufactures, U.S. Senate,* 72 Congress, 2 Session, Washington, 1933, Pt. 1, pp. 124-130, 447-456.

SUMNER H. SLICHTER:
National Assistance and
Decentralized Control

Professor Slichter. My name is Sumner H. Slichter, and I am Professor of Business Economics, Harvard Business School.

The Chairman. The committee would be grateful to you, Doctor Slichter, if you would, in your own way, comment upon the economic consequences and implications of the unemployment problem. We will then ask you any questions that occur to us.

Professor Slichter. Mr. Chairman, the need for national assistance, by this time, has become so self-evident that it would seem to me to be a waste of your time for me to offer anything along that line.

The Chairman. Unfortunately, however, we do not find that to be the generally accepted opinion.

Professor Slichter. The tax base of the local communities is a somewhat narrow one. About nine-tenths of their income is derived from real-estate taxation, and the difficulty, or one of the difficulties, with that base is that a man is liable for taxes simply because he owns the title to the real estate, quite regardless of whether or not he has any income from the real estate.

Senator Costigan. Or able to pay it?

Professor Slichter. Yes, or from any other source.

The result one could predict without much difficulty is a steadily rising ratio of delinquent taxes throughout the country. In fact, delinquency ratios of from 20 to 30 percent are not unusual.

The income from real estate, itself, of course, has gone down. It is one of the slower incomes to fall; but it is a fairly conservative generalization, I should say, to estimate that the rentals, in most places, are down about 20 percent, in some cases more, and in some cases less.

Of course, the real-estate owner bears a double burden in the case of unemployment, because it is almost the universal rule that relief agencies do not pay rent, except on eviction, and then they only pay for a month or two. In other words, there is a more or less national moratorium on rents, insofar as the unemployed are concerned.

The older the Depression gets, the more unsatisfactory becomes this narrow base of public revenue. The private agencies have been compelled to conserve their resources and to withdraw from the strictly unemployment field. They started out to help out the unemployed, more or less, but the burden became too great; and in order to conserve the permanent part of their work, they had to withdraw.

I made a compilation not long ago of some Community Chest drives for 1932 and 1933, and this covers forty-four cities. In 1932, the Community Chests in these cities raised about $24.9 million. This goal for 1933 is $23.1 million. That, of course, means that the burden on public relief funds is increasing.

I have gone through the bill, and I have one or two questions which have come to my mind. They do not bear on the principle of national assistance, but they do bear upon some of the administrative features of the bill.

It is proposed that the chief executive officer of the board should be the chief of the Children's Bureau. Is it not unwise to designate the executive officer of the board which it is proposed to create? The board would have the responsibility of disbursing $500 million, and the members who have that responsibility should also have the responsibility of selecting their executive officer.

Senator Costigan. You believe that experience in administering relief, however should be a factor, however, in the choice of the executive officer of such a board?

Professor Slichter. Yes; it would seem proper to designate, in general terms, what qualifications the executive officer of the board should have; but the selection of the particular person, it seems to me, should be left to those who have the administration of the $500 million. The fund is divided into two parts and ——

Senator Costigan. Nothing you are saying is to be interpreted in terms of criticism of the chief of the Children's Bureau?

Professor Slichter. Far from it. I am simply discussing general principles.

The bill, as drafted, provides that part of the appropriation shall be distributed on the basis of the population of the states, but that "no state shall receive more than two-thirds of the amount made available by it or its subdivisions." Now, if I interpret this correctly, the cities of a state and the private agencies might be making available $10 million, and the state would then have the right, assuming its population were sufficient, to receive up to $6,667,000 under the bill. Under these conditions, it seems to me that there is danger that some states might make no appropriations at all. In other words, some states might fall back on this federal aid, obtained because the cities and charitable organizations within the state made appropriations.

That would be unfortunate, not primarily because the states should be such an important source of help but because, in order to get the best administration through the states' machinery, some of the money should be the states' money. Consequently, I venture the suggestion that the states be required, in order to share in the appropriation on the basis of population, to make reasonable appropriations of their own funds.

After all, I think only eight states have made appropriations. These eight include some of the largest industrial states, such as the states of New York, New Jersey, Pennsylvania, and Illinois, but on the whole, the states have been the most delinquent bodies in helping the unemployment relief in the country; and if the proper administrative machinery is to be created, the states must help provide it. In order for that machinery to function most effectively the states should be spending some of their own money.

On page 10, in line 17, it is provided:

> That no such allocation shall be made to any state, unless the board is satisfied that the state or its political subdivisions have made reasonable efforts within their resources to provide for the emergency relief expenditures.

"Any state or its political subdivisions!" The question arose in my mind when I read that whether it would not be desirable to replace "or" with "and," because the political subdivisions may be making reasonable efforts, yet the state itself may be doing little or nothing. That would be safeguarded by the change of the one word.

Senator Costigan. Doctor Slichter, have you considered the possibility that the constitutional clauses may interfere with a state's inability to pledge its credit for direct relief, or that certain states may be in that situation? In that event, would you be unwilling to have relief given in case of need to the people within the boundaries of such states?

Professor Slichter. No; that would perhaps require a specific clause to exempt the state from the handicap of its own constitution.

But it is true that a number of states have been slow in moving to the assistance of their people; and as I said a few moments ago, I am not primarily interested in seeing the states appropriate huge sums, but I am interested in seeing them spend some of their own money, because, if we are going to make our dole system the best in the world instead of the worst in the world, we have to do it through building the most effective possible administrative agencies, and the states must feel that it is not just a gift from the federal government which they are spending but something of their own also. . . .

The Chairman. If I get your point, Doctor Slichter, it is that this should be based upon the principle of joint cooperation between the federal government and the states, such as we have had in connection with other federal-aid projects — a matching of funds and a participation in administrative function by both state and federal governments?

Professor Slichter. Yes; the unemployment problem is so far-flung and it varies so greatly in the different parts of the country that some decentralization of the overseeing machinery is necessary, and that machinery ought not to get its money solely from Washington. Yet it seems to me, as the bill stands, there is the possibility of a state, which had done nothing, receiving, under the two-thirds provision, a really substantial sum simply because some of its cities have done a great deal. . . .

As the Depression grows older, the proportion of men who have had no work for a considerable period of time is becoming quite large. A recent survey made by Mr. Croxton in Buffalo indicates that about one-third of the unemployed have had no work for two years or more, and that about three-fifths, or slightly more than one-half, had had no work for a year or more.

Now, this raises, it seems to me, a grave question with respect to the absorption of the unemployed when a revival in business occurs.

The practice of spreading work has been widespread during the Depression, and that means that a considerable increase in production could be handled with relatively little hiring of men off the streets. . . . Now, if an increased demand for goods occurs, is it not important that an organized effort be made to spread as many of those new jobs among the men who now have none? I am not a constitutional lawyer, but it would seem to me that for the period of the emergency, at any rate, the federal government would have authority to compel a spreading of the work. You cannot compel employers to give jobs which do not exist, but can not they be compelled to spread such work as may exist? Might it not be desirable also to give the body which is to administer the federal aid also authority to compel spreading of the work?

Of course, the administrative problem is a difficult one, because the situation in no two industries is alike, and it is changing from time to time. So the sensible way to solve that problem would seem to me to be to authorize the board to establish committees within the industries, which should determine what, in the light of the employment situation, are reasonable working hours for the men — not for the plants but for the men; and to make the orders of these committees, constituted under the general direction of this administrative board — to make those orders enforceable, subject to appeal, of course. . . .

Senator Costigan. You have in view primarily spreading the work rather than increasing the burden on the present workers?

Professor Slichter. Yes.

Senator Costigan. Spreading the work to the new employees rather than adding to the hours of work of those who are already employed, when the work begins to revive?

Professor Slichter. The arrangement as here proposed is an exceedingly flexible one, because the situation in the different industries is so different. It might be necessary, in some industries, to let the worker's hours increase substantially before bringing in additional men from the streets. In one industry, such as steel, where 15 percent operations have prevailed, it might be necessary to let the hours be doubled. But that is the reason for separate committees in the different industries — let each one take account of the situation and decide what seems to be reasonable.

That would not make the ideal solution, but it is better than letting what happened this fall in the textile industries happen again, when the working hours of a few people went up to seventy or more hours per week.

II.

Donald R. Richberg: The Need for a Planned Economy

Mr. Richberg. My name is Donald R. Richberg, counsel for the Railway Labor Executives Association. I am speaking in behalf of the association which represents the twenty-one standard railroad labor organizations. I do not think it is necessary, probably, to go into any details concerning the membership of that association. . . .

In giving wholehearted support to this bill the railway employees . . . must . . . make clear their position, that this is only a pitifully small measure of relief to meet unavoidable demands and to alleviate acute distress. We would point out that Congress must not be satisfied merely with assisting public and private relief agencies to prevent wholesale starvation and intolerable physical distress. The object of federal relief should not be merely to prevent masses of the people from choosing between suicide and revolution.

Now, this is our position, which I feel should be made very clear in this case in connection with our wholehearted support of this bill, [which] is urgently needed, knowing the distressing conditions existing throughout the country and the absence of any very adequate relief — and by "adequate" I refer to the extent to which it goes. We want to make our position in the handling of this practical problem quite clear.

First, to limit federal relief to emergency aid for the destitute is to carry on a policy of gradually pauperizing the nation. The persistent reduction of the living standards of more than one-fourth of our population to mere subsistence is creating an army of submerged workers who, by competitive labor, will drag the entire body of manual workers down to lower and lower levels.

I want to give a very unpleasant example of that which has come to my attention in the last few days, without particularizing to attack a particular railroad. But one of the great railroad systems of this country, because they can obtain labor now for 90 cents a day, is using labor on that wage scale for construction purposes, although they ordinarily handle their maintenance-of-way work with their maintenance-of-way forces. The maintenance-of-way forces, men who get the enormous sum of 35 cents an hour, are too expensive for the economy of railroad purposes; therefore, this particular railroad is building new construction work with labor paid at the rate of 90 cents a day.

There are many instances of this sort of the driving down of the level of living by this constant competition of low-paid labor.

I might give another example that we have had a great deal of difficulty with, and that is, for example, in the Pullman service. In order to save the wages of Pullman conductors, the Pullman Co. is adopting, as an emergency measure, putting Pullman porters in charge of cars instead of conductors,

because, by doing that, they have only to add $5 a month to the wages of the Pullman porter. Therefore, you have substituted an underpaid porter, supported largely by tips, for a previously self-supporting individual.

Those are just two examples that came particularly to my attention. In regard to the employment of cheap labor on the railroads, the instances I have named are not exceptional.

The Chairman. Are you apprehensive that the conditions may be extended and become more aggravated?

Mr. Richberg. That is perfectly evident, and if you consider the possible transfer of work from the shops of railroads to outside contractors who may not be required to maintain a respectable wage scale, all we have to do is to go back to 1921, when that became almost the universal practice of the railroads of the country, to contract out the work and thus evade the wage scales they were paying, by agreements, to their employees. We know from sad and very bitter experience just how this competition of underpaid labor breaks down the whole wage scale.

The result is that the fiber of the nation is being steadily weakened; self-respect, courage, and initiative are being destroyed in millions of homes by years of idleness, malnutrition, and despair. We must check this national degradation at any cost. To continue present industrial competition in reducing the standards of American living, and present competition in reducing the standards of charitable relief — and I think you have a great deal of testimony on that — and present competition in reducing quality or quantity of necessary public services is simply to engage in competitive suicide. That we are engaged in it, anyone can see; and certainly we are getting a demonstration of what it means in this country today.

Second, it has been demonstrated to be

futile to utilize national credit and to mortgage the future in order to try to support, temporarily, property values which can only be supported by employed workers earning decent livelihoods on the farms, and the cities, and on the highways.

If time permitted and I had the ability, I could expand that particular proposition into a volume. It seems to me that is one thing that has been made overwhelmingly clear during the years of the Depression. You cannot maintain property values and security values except by maintaining the earnings of the workers. Out of the earnings of the workers must be taken the interest paid on capital and all the returns that create property values; and when you are constantly cutting down the earnings of the workers, you are cutting down property values, and you cannot maintain them by constantly borrowing money to maintain interest payments. It is a hopeless proposition, and I think all of the operations of the government have demonstrated that it is hopeless. Huge sums of money have been loaned the railroads in order to protect their financial situation, but what is the result? With declining revenue, they are getting into worse and worse condition all the time, and all that is happening is that they are sinking deeper and deeper into the mire of debt.

Third, our national credit should be used to mobilize, and to bring about the utilization of, our natural resources, our manpower, and our industrial facilities so as to provide compensatory employment for all those capable of self-support.

Fourth, while not advocating the permanent socialization of business or property, we believe that an emergency governmental control is now as essential to the national welfare as it would be in a time of war. In other words, we see no way of checking this constant competition for lower standards and the constant degradation of the

standard of living except by a governmental control to establish common standards. It is exactly the same type of problem I have been testifying to this morning before a subcommittee of the Committee on Interstate Commerce in the way of pensions. One railroad cannot maintain a decent system of pensions unless its competitors maintain it. If one railroad throws out upon the public its unemployed in old age ——

The Chairman. It throws that cost on society.

Mr. Richberg. Yes; and someone must bear it, and such a railroad is in unfair competition with the railroad attempting to meet the problem.

Senator Cutting. How far would you extend governmental control of that kind?

Mr. Richberg. Practically as far as necessary to put the employees to work by whatever means were necessary. In a word, it seems to me that, by a concerted, national effort, such a mobilization as we have had in time of war, it would not be at all impossible by the utilization of government credit to put factories into operation to bring the unemployed industrial workers back to work, to bring the products of the farm to those workers, and, by bringing up the prices of commodities on the farms so that a decent living would be had by the agricultural workers, to bring about that exchange of products, the lack of which at the present time seems to indicate the absolute insanity of the whole system.

Of course, we have talked much during the last few years about the absurdity of surpluses on the farms, surplus productive power in the factories, and surplus transportation facilities, and no ability to put these people to work — but we have made no concerted effort to do so.

Senator Cutting. You realize there is, of course, a strong urge for governmental retrenchment at this time?

Mr. Richberg. There is.

Senator Costigan. Not only that, we have not succeeded in bringing the surplus food and the unemployed people together.

Mr. Richberg. We absolutely have not; and it is difficult for me to understand that particular policy — I can understand the necessity for the elimination of waste and duplication of effort, but I cannot understand the policy of throwing out of employment hundreds and thousands of workers and then turning around and appropriating money to help meet the problem of the unemployed. I am frankly out of sympathy with the proposals of some of these "economy" organizations.

Senator Cutting. Do you not think at times it is necessary for the government to extend its activities?

Mr. Richberg. It is necessary for the government to extend its activities; and just as in time of war you issue bonds and borrow against the future to protect the future of the nation, so if you cannot raise, by taxation, the funds to carry through such a program, you can raise it by borrowing against the future. Of course, the minute you start the wheels of machinery moving, the minute commodity prices begin to rise, the entire taxation problem you are discussing begins to disappear, because then the sources of government revenue open up.

Senator Cutting. In other words, it would be easier to balance the budget in years of prosperity than in years of depression?

Mr. Richberg. Absolutely.

Senator Costigan. And the raising of funds in the manner you suggest does not really involve unbalancing the budget?

Mr. Richberg. As far as I can see, it will be impossible for us to balance the budget as long as we are going downhill. I do not believe it is possible to balance a budget while sliding downhill. Your revenues are diminishing and you cannot increase your economy without accentuating the speed of the descent.

Senator Costigan. A bond issue is not properly chargeable against the budget, is it?

Mr. Richberg. That is not my understanding of it. It is not a means of raising revenue. It surely is not the method in normal accounting. If you think of it in a broader way and think of it as the raising of capital for the benefit of the whole nation for the future, any such expenditures should not be charged as current expenditures.

Fifth, the last point I have listed is that we advocate a civil mobilization under civil authority to organize our resources for national defense against the destructiveness of present uncontrolled economic forces. The kindergarten arguments of those in high places, who are still waiting for economic disease to cure itself, merit only contempt. Frankly, I cannot differentiate between a great economic crisis such as we are facing, or a vast epidemic, or anything of that sort, and the menace of war.

Public physicians who urged us to let an epidemic run its course would be universally condemned. Economic illness is primarily man-made and can be cured by the use of human intelligence or aggravated by human timidity and folly. I do not pretend to be an economist in the sense of one having a series of university degrees in such subjects to my credit, but I have long been a student of political economy and a student of the law, and it seems to me quite obvious that our economic conditions are all manmade. This is a kind of social structure and business structure which we have built up in which we live. It is not a creation of Providence — something found in the world; it is not a natural product; it is manmade and, if it is not working correctly, it is subject to correction by the men who made it.

The idea of saying that the system is going badly and therefore we must wait until it begins to go rightly is a type and kind of logic I cannot follow. It is simply our own system that is not going rightly. It is as though a man whose office gets in such a mess that he cannot do business should then sit down and say, "If I wait long enough it will straighten itself out and everything will be all right."

That is the whole situation, as I see it, in regard to our economic conditions. We created society and created, by law, the corporate forms of activities which permit this tremendous mass organization of our resources and therefore permit mass destructive policies. All these factors in our system are man-created and certainly the remedy for them lies in new systems ——

Senator Costigan. In your last statement, do you want to go on record as favoring a nationally planned economy?

Mr. Richberg. A nationally planned economy is the only salvation of our present situation and only hope for the future in the complications of modern life.

To conclude what I have to say, definitely in behalf of the organizations I represent, I want to say that we endorse this bill to provide for the relief of immediate and acute distress in the hope that, through such relief, opportunity may be given, even at this late hour, for the development of a program of economic recovery by public officials who have faith in planning for recovery. I say "at this late hour" because of assuming that we still have an opportunity to plan in the midst of order and comparative social regularity.

We trust that such a program may be devised in confidence; that it will not be sabotaged by those who administer it — which I think is a very important part of the program. We hope that such a program may

be made effective before too large a percentage of the people have been starved into either hopeless resignation or desperate revolt.

I would like to say there that the menace, as much as any other, to the future is not merely the danger of revolt but the danger of destruction of character and confidence and faith of the people until they are unable to adopt and carry forward real programs for their salvation.

The patience of the American people with leaders who are either unable or unwilling to lead has been astounding; but it cannot be everlasting. There are many signs that if the lawfully constituted leadership does not soon substitute action for words, a new leadership, perhaps unlawfully constituted, will arise and act. We commend this bill as a better means of preserving law and order than machine guns and tear gas.

I would like to say, in amplification of what I said concerning leadership, that I am not referring merely to political leadership. I am referring to industrial leadership and I am referring particularly to the field of labor leadership; in other words, there is a demand in every avenue of life today for a leadership that will really lead.

The present leadership is a result of the system which has built up what we call lawfully constituted authority, but we find everywhere that the system is breaking down and showing cracks and there is a rise of irregularly constituted leaders. You see that demonstrated in the tax strikes; in the efforts to prevent foreclosure of farm mortgages. We can find that exactly in the same way in labor organizations where internal rifts develop. In every avenue of our public life I think that condition is developing.

It is common sense to take a method and try it. If it fails, admit it frankly and try another. But above all, try something.

FRANKLIN D. ROOSEVELT, speech during campaign, 1932

43.

Franklin D. Roosevelt: First Inaugural Address

In his acceptance speech after being nominated by the Democrats, Roosevelt had pledged himself to a "new deal" for the American people. The phrase was seized upon by the press and immediately became the unofficial designation of the Roosevelt program. The New Deal era was launched on March 4, 1933, the day that Roosevelt was inaugurated. His first inaugural address was delivered from the east front of the Capitol to a crowd estimated at nearly 100,000 persons, and the new President's promise that the executive power would, if necessary, be used to wage war on the Depression as if it were an enemy invasion drew the loudest applause. The ensuing three months — the "Hundred Days" — witnessed the most extensive program of economic reform ever passed by Congress in a like period.

Source: *Record*, 73 Cong., Special Sess. of the Senate, pp. 5-6.

I AM CERTAIN THAT my fellow Americans expect that on my induction into the presidency I will address them with a candor and a decision which the present situation of our nation impels. This is preeminently the time to speak the truth, the whole truth, frankly and boldly. Nor need we shrink from honestly facing conditions in our country today. This great nation will endure as it has endured, will revive and will prosper.

So, first of all, let me assert my firm belief that the only thing we have to fear is fear itself — nameless, unreasoning, unjustified terror which paralyzes needed efforts to convert retreat into advance. In every dark hour of our national life a leadership of frankness and vigor has met with that understanding and support of the people themselves which is essential to victory. I am convinced that you will again give that support to leadership in these critical days.

In such a spirit on my part and on yours we face our common difficulties. They concern, thank God, only material things. Values have shrunken to fantastic levels; taxes have risen; our ability to pay has fallen; government of all kinds is faced by serious curtailment of income; the means of exchange are frozen in the currents of trade; the withered leaves of industrial enterprise lie on every side; farmers find no markets for their produce; the savings of many years in thousands of families are gone.

More important, a host of unemployed citizens face the grim problem of existence, and an equally great number toil with little return. Only a foolish optimist can deny the dark realities of the moment.

Yet our distress comes from no failure of substance. We are stricken by no plague of locusts. Compared with the perils which our forefathers conquered because they believed and were not afraid, we have still much to be thankful for. Nature still offers her bounty, and human efforts have multiplied it. Plenty is at our doorstep, but a generous use of it languishes in the very sight of the supply. Primarily this is because the rulers of the exchange of mankind's goods have failed, through their own stubbornness and their own incompetence, have admitted their failure, and abdicated. Practices of the unscrupulous money changers stand indicted in the court of public opinion, rejected by the hearts and minds of men.

True they have tried, but their efforts have been cast in the pattern of an outworn tradition. Faced by failure of credit, they have proposed only the lending of more money. Stripped of the lure of profit by which to induce our people to follow their false leadership, they have resorted to exhortations, pleading tearfully for restored confidence. They know only the rules of a generation of self-seekers. They have no vision, and when there is no vision the people perish.

The money changers have fled from their high seats in the temple of our civilization. We may now restore that temple to the ancient truths. The measure of the restoration lies in the extent to which we apply social values more noble than mere monetary profit.

Happiness lies not in the mere possession of money; it lies in the joy of achievement, in the thrill of creative effort. The joy and moral stimulation of work no longer must be forgotten in the mad chase of evanescent profits. These dark days will be worth all they cost us if they teach us that our true destiny is not to be ministered unto but to minister to ourselves and to our fellowmen.

Recognition of the falsity of material wealth as the standard of success goes hand in hand with the abandonment of the false belief that public office and high political position are to be valued only by the standards of pride of place and personal profit; and there must be an end to a conduct in banking and in business which too often has given to a sacred trust the likeness of callous and selfish wrongdoing. Small wonder

that confidence languishes, for it thrives only on honesty, on honor, on the sacredness of obligations, on faithful protection, on unselfish performance; without them it cannot live.

Restoration calls, however, not for changes in ethics alone. This nation asks for action, and action now.

Our greatest primary task is to put people to work. This is no unsolvable problem if we face it wisely and courageously. It can be accomplished in part by direct recruiting by the government itself, treating the task as we would treat the emergency of a war, but, at the same time, through this employment, accomplishing greatly needed projects to stimulate and reorganize the use of our natural resources.

Hand in hand with this we must frankly recognize the overbalance of population in our industrial centers and, by engaging on a national scale in a redistribution, endeavor to provide a better use of the land for those best fitted for the land. The task can be helped by definite efforts to raise the values of agricultural products and with this the power to purchase the output of our cities. It can be helped by preventing realistically the tragedy of the growing loss through foreclosure of our small homes and our farms. It can be helped by insistence that the federal, state, and local governments act forthwith on the demand that their cost be drastically reduced. It can be helped by the unifying of relief activities which today are often scattered, uneconomical, and unequal. It can be helped by national planning for and supervision of all forms of transportation and of communications and other utilities which have a definitely public character. There are many ways in which it can be helped, but it can never be helped merely by talking about it. We must act and act quickly.

Finally, in our progress toward a resumption of work, we require two safeguards against a return of the evils of the old order: there must be a strict supervision of all banking and credits and investments; there must be an end to speculation with other people's money, and there must be provision for an adequate but sound currency.

These are the lines of attack. I shall presently urge upon a new Congress in special session detailed measures for their fulfillment, and I shall seek the immediate assistance of the several states.

Through this program of action we address ourselves to putting our own national house in order and making income balance outgo. Our international trade relations, though vastly important, are in point of time and necessity secondary to the establishment of a sound national economy. I favor as a practical policy the putting of first things first. I shall spare no effort to restore world trade by international economic readjustment, but the emergency at home cannot wait on that accomplishment.

The basic thought that guides these specific means of national recovery is not narrowly nationalistic. It is the insistence, as a first consideration, upon the interdependence of the various elements in and parts of the United States — a recognition of the old and permanently important manifestation of the American spirit of the pioneer. It is the way to recovery. It is the immediate way. It is the strongest assurance that the recovery will endure.

In the field of world policy I would dedicate this nation to the policy of the good neighbor — the neighbor who resolutely respects himself and, because he does so, respects the rights of others — the neighbor who respects his obligations and respects the sanctity of his agreements in and with a world of neighbors.

If I read the temper of our people correctly, we now realize as we have never realized before our interdependence on each other; that we cannot merely take but we must give as well; that if we are to go forward, we must move as a trained and loyal army willing to sacrifice for the good of a common discipline, because without such discipline no progress is made, no leadership becomes effective. We are, I know, ready and willing to submit our lives and property to such discipline, because it makes possible a leadership which aims at a larger good. This I propose to offer, pledging that the larger purposes will bind upon us all as a sacred obligation, with a unity of duty hitherto evoked only in time of armed strife.

With this pledge taken, I assume unhesitatingly the leadership of this great army of our people dedicated to a disciplined attack upon our common problems.

Action in this image and to this end is feasible under the form of government which we have inherited from our ancestors. Our Constitution is so simple and practical that it is possible always to meet extraordinary needs by changes in emphasis and arrangement without loss of essential form. That is why our constitutional system has proved itself the most superbly enduring political mechanism the modern world has produced. It has met every stress of vast expansion of territory, of foreign wars, of bitter internal strife, of world relations.

It is to be hoped that the normal balance of executive and legislative authority may be wholly adequate to meet the unprecedented task before us. But it may be that an unprecedented demand and need for undelayed action may call for temporary departure from that normal balance of public procedure.

I am prepared under my constitutional duty to recommend the measures that a stricken nation in the midst of a stricken world may require. These measures, or such other measures as the Congress may build out of its experience and wisdom, I shall seek, within my constitutional authority, to bring to speedy adoption.

But in the event that the Congress shall fail to take one of these two courses, and in the event that the national emergency is still critical, I shall not evade the clear course of duty that will then confront me. I shall ask the Congress for the one remaining instrument to meet the crisis — broad executive power to wage a war against the emergency, as great as the power that would be given to me if we were in fact invaded by a foreign foe.

For the trust reposed in me I will return the courage and the devotion that befit the time. I can do no less.

We face the arduous days that lie before us in the warm courage of national unity; with the clear consciousness of seeking old and precious moral values; with the clean satisfaction that comes from the stern performance of duty by old and young alike. We aim at the assurance of a rounded and permanent national life.

We do not distrust the future of essential democracy. The people of the United States have not failed. In their need they have registered a mandate that they want direct, vigorous action. They have asked for discipline and direction under leadership. They have made me the present instrument of their wishes. In the spirit of the gift I take it.

In this dedication of a nation we humbly ask the blessing of God. May He protect each and every one of us. May He guide me in the days to come.

44.

Business Stability and Government Regulation

One of the most important matters on the agenda for the special session of Congress during the "Hundred Days" following March 4, 1933, was industrial recovery. The administration wanted a program of control and coordination that would stimulate production, protect the interests of labor, and promote public works where necessary. On May 10, the day the following editorial appeared in Business Week, *President Roosevelt told his advisers responsible for drafting industrial legislation to lock themselves in a room until the job was done. The resulting bill was the National Industrial Recovery Act, which was passed on June 13 and signed three days later.*

Source: *Business Week,* May 10, 1933: "Toward Stability."

TWO MAIN CONCLUSIONS EMERGE from the wide discussion of the revolutionary proposal to set up governmental control of industry on a scale never before seriously proposed in the United States.

The first is that there is a surprising unanimity among businessmen in favor of the general theory. The second, that every businessman believes it would be extraordinarily difficult to set up regulations for his particular industry.

The American businessman at this moment is utterly weary of the ruthless competitive struggle. It has been too much for him; he has survived so far, but he is spent. He is willing, he feels just now, to surrender some part of his freedom of action to achieve a degree of stability.

Reduced to lowest terms, his support of the general idea is based on the thought that he would be willing to pay higher wages for shorter hours if he could be assured that every competitor would be on the same footing and if he could be sure a fair price level would be enforced. On the higher plane, he recognizes the broad truth that business exists for the satisfaction of human needs; essentially it has no other excuse for being. Among the greatest of human needs is safety, stability of employment and of earnings. But what can one business concern do of itself, and alone? Again the need for protection from the unscrupulous.

There is general agreement among the leading businessmen who have appeared before the congressional hearings that something must be done to regulate hours, pay, production, and prices. Even more convincing are the results of a questionnaire conducted by Cornell. Most of the leading businessmen questioned felt that the times demand a drastic reorganization designed to reduce to a minimum the effects of the business cycle, to increase the stability of employment, and to insure adequate purchasing power. A minimum wage is necessary to prevent the unscrupulous from exploiting labor. Any plan devised to reach these ends must have in mind raising the standard of living of the country as a whole.

But, and this brings us back to the beginning, the incredible complexity of our industrial structure creates myriad special problems. It seems impossible to conceive of general legislation rigid enough to achieve the desired ends, flexible enough to meet thousands of special cases.

It is to be feared that because of these detailed objections, the Black Bill may be rejected — which will be no loss — and nothing put in its place, which will be a real tragedy.

Tremendous issues are before this special session of Congress. There is too much to be done. Some things must be postponed. But no issue can be much more important than this one. The administration believes it can launch a business recovery. If it does not at the very inception of recovery lay plans for its control, we predict that we shall run straight through wild boom to ghastly depression with a speed hitherto unprecedented.

It will take some pains to work out details. But the solution is not impossible and it is worth all the pains and time it may cost. Let industry formulate its own codes of practice. Each industry knows its own special needs, its own problems. Let the government supervise these self-formulated codes: first, to see that they are fair to the public; second, to see that they are enforced on the unscrupulous fringe who will never cooperate voluntarily with the majority, and who, under the present system of free competition, can undo the progressive work of all the rest.

Limit this, if you like, to the period of the emergency. Once tried we predict the system never will be abandoned.

The brains trust.
JAMES M. KIERAN, in a conversation with Franklin D. Roosevelt, Aug. 1932, referring to the intellectuals who were flocking to the Roosevelt campaign banner. The newspapers converted the phrase, which has been attributed to others, to "brain trust."

45.

Franklin D. Roosevelt: Progress of the Recovery Program

*In addition to his regular news conferences with the press, President Roosevelt kept
the American people informed of public policy by radio in what came to be known as
Fireside Chats. He regarded these broadcasts as instruments of public education
in national affairs as well as a way of enlisting support for his program. The following
selection is the third of the Fireside Chats and was delivered July 24, 1933, to sum
up the legislation of the "Hundred Days" and to launch the Blue Eagle program. This
endeavor, under the supervision of Hugh S. Johnson, head of the National Recovery
Administration (NRA), was designed to enlist popular support for the NRA and to get as
many businesses as possible involved in its cooperative program; cooperating stores
and businesses displayed the Blue Eagle emblem.*

Source: FDR, II, pp. 295-303.

FOR MANY YEARS the two great barriers to a normal prosperity have been low farm prices and the creeping paralysis of unemployment. These factors have cut the purchasing power of the country in half. I promised action. Congress did its part when it passed the Farm and the Industrial Recovery acts. Today we are putting these two acts to work and they will work if people understand their plain objectives.

First, the Farm Act: It is based on the fact that the purchasing power of nearly half our population depends on adequate prices for farm products. We have been producing more of some crops than we consume or can sell in a depressed world market. The cure is not to produce so much. Without our help the farmers cannot get together and cut production, and the Farm Bill gives them a method of bringing their production down to a reasonable level and of obtaining reasonable prices for their crops. I have clearly stated that this method is in a sense experimental, but so far as we have gone we have reason to believe that it will produce good results.

It is obvious that if we can greatly increase the purchasing power of the tens of millions of our people who make a living from farming and the distribution of farm crops, we shall greatly increase the consumption of those goods which are turned out by industry.

That brings me to the final step — bringing back industry along sound lines.

Last autumn, on several occasions, I expressed my faith that we can make possible by democratic self-discipline in industry general increases in wages and shortening of hours sufficient to enable industry to pay its own workers enough to let those workers buy and use the things that their labor produces. This can be done only if we permit and encourage cooperative action in industry, because it is obvious that without united action a few selfish men in each competitive group will pay starvation wages and insist on long hours of work. Others in that group must either follow suit or close up shop. We have seen the result of action of that kind in the continuing descent into the economic hell of the past four years.

There is a clear way to reverse that process: If all employers in each competitive group agree to pay their workers the same wages — reasonable wages — and require the same hours — reasonable hours — then higher wages and shorter hours will hurt no employer. Moreover, such action is better for the employer than unemployment and low wages, because it makes more buyers for his product. That is the simple idea which is the very heart of the Industrial Recovery Act.

On the basis of this simple principle of everybody doing things together, we are starting out on this nationwide attack on unemployment. It will succeed if our people understand it — in the big industries, in the little shops, in the great cities, and in the small villages. There is nothing complicated about it and there is nothing particularly new in the principle. It goes back to the basic idea of society and of the nation itself that people acting in a group can accomplish things which no individual acting alone could even hope to bring about.

Here is an example. In the Cotton Textile Code and in other agreements already signed, child labor has been abolished. That makes me personally happier than any other one thing with which I have been connected since I came to Washington. In the textile industry — an industry which came to me spontaneously and with a splendid cooperation as soon as the Recovery Act was signed — child labor was an old evil. But no employer acting alone was able to wipe it out. If one employer tried it, or if one state tried it, the costs of operation rose so high that it was impossible to compete with the employers or states which had failed to act. The moment the Recovery Act was passed, this monstrous thing which neither opinion nor law could reach through years of effort went out in a flash. As a British editorial put it, we did more under a Code in one day than they in England had been able to do under the common law in

eighty-five years of effort. I use this incident, my friends, not to boast of what has already been done but to point the way to you for even greater cooperative efforts this summer and autumn.

We are not going through another winter like the last. I doubt if ever any people so bravely and cheerfully endured a season half so bitter. We cannot ask America to continue to face such needless hardships. It is time for courageous action, and the Recovery Bill gives us the means to conquer unemployment with exactly the same weapon that we have used to strike down child labor.

The proposition is simply this: If all employers will act together to shorten hours and raise wages, we can put people back to work. No employer will suffer, because the relative level of competitive cost will advance by the same amount for all. But if any considerable group should lag or shirk, this great opportunity will pass us by and we shall go into another desperate winter. This must not happen.

We have sent out to all employers an agreement which is the result of weeks of consultation. This agreement checks against the voluntary codes of nearly all the large industries which have already been submitted. This blanket agreement carries the unanimous approval of the three boards which I have appointed to advise in this, boards representing the great leaders in labor, in industry, and in social service. The agreement has already brought a flood of approval from every state and from so wide a cross-section of the common calling of industry that I know it is fair for all. It is a plan — deliberate, reasonable, and just — intended to put into effect at once the most important of the broad principles which are being established, industry by industry, through codes. Naturally, it takes a good deal of organizing and a great many hearings and many months to get these codes perfected and signed, and we cannot wait for all of them to go through. The blanket agreements, however, which I am sending to every employer will start the wheels turning now, and not six months from now.

There are, of course, men, a few men, who might thwart this great common purpose by seeking selfish advantage. There are adequate penalties in the law, but I am now asking the cooperation that comes from opinion and from conscience. These are the only instruments we shall use in this great summer offensive against unemployment. But we shall use them to the limit to protect the willing from the laggard and to make the plan succeed.

In war, in the gloom of night attack, soldiers wear a bright badge on their shoulders to be sure that comrades do not fire on comrades. On that principle, those who cooperate in this program must know each other at a glance. That is why we have provided a badge of honor for this purpose, a simple design with a legend, "We do our part," and I ask that all those who join with me shall display that badge prominently. It is essential to our purpose.

Already all the great, basic industries have come forward willingly with proposed codes, and in these codes they accept the principles leading to mass reemployment. But, important as is this heartening demonstration, the richest field for results is among the small employers, those whose contribution will be to give new work for from one to ten people. These smaller employers are indeed a vital part of the backbone of the country, and the success of our plan lies largely in their hands.

Already the telegrams and letters are pouring into the White House — messages from employers who ask that their names be placed on this special Roll of Honor. They represent great corporations and companies, and partnerships and individuals. I ask that even before the dates set in the agreements which we have sent out, the employers of the country who have not already done so — the big fellows and the little fellows — shall at once write or telegraph to me personally at the White House, expressing their intentions of going through with the plan. And it is my purpose to keep posted in the post office of every town a Roll of Honor of all those who join with me.

I want to take this occasion to say to the twenty-four governors who are now in conference in San Francisco that nothing thus far has helped in strengthening this great movement more than their resolutions adopted at the very outset of their meeting, giving this plan their instant and unanimous approval, and pledging to support it in their states.

To the men and women whose lives have been darkened by the fact or the fear of unemployment, I am justified in saying a word of encouragement because the codes and the agreements already approved, or about to be passed upon, prove that the plan does raise wages and that it does put people back to work. You can look on every employer who adopts the plan as one who is doing his part, and those employers deserve well of everyone who works for a living. It will be clear to you, as it is to me, that while the shirking employer may undersell his competitor, the saving he thus makes is made at the expense of his country's welfare.

While we are making this great common effort there should be no discord and dispute. This is no time to cavil or to question the standard set by this universal agreement. It is time for patience and understanding and cooperation. The workers of this country have rights under this law which cannot be taken from them, and nobody will be permitted to whittle them away, but, on the other hand, no aggression is now necessary to attain those rights. The whole country will be united to get them for you. The principle that applies to the employers applies to the workers as well, and I ask you workers to cooperate in the same spirit.

When Andrew Jackson, "Old Hickory,"

died, someone asked, "Will he go to heaven?" and the answer was, "He will if he wants to." If I am asked whether the American people will pull themselves out of this depression, I answer, "They will if they want to." The essence of the plan is a universal limitation of hours of work per week for any individual by common consent and a universal payment of wages above a minimum, also by common consent. I cannot guarantee the success of this nationwide plan, but the people of this country can guarantee its success.

I have no faith in "cure-alls" but I believe that we can greatly influence economic forces. I have no sympathy with the professional economists who insist that things must run their course and that human agencies can have no influence on economic ills. One reason is that I happen to know that professional economists have changed their definition of economic laws every five or ten years for a very long time, but I do have faith, and retain faith, in the strength of the common purpose and in the strength of unified action taken by the American people.

That is why I am describing to you the simple purposes and the solid foundations upon which our program of recovery is built. That is why I am asking the employers of the nation to sign this common covenant with me — to sign it in the name of patriotism and humanity. That is why I am asking the workers to go along with us in a spirit of understanding and of helpfulness.

46.

Nathaniel Peffer: A Warning to America

Despite the protests issued by the League of Nations and the declared refusal of the United States to recognize any change in the status quo in the Far East, Japanese forces systematically pursued the invasion of Manchuria they had begun in September 1931. In February 1932 Japan signaled its complete control of the province by declaring the independence of Manchuria (nominally part of China) and recognizing the puppet state of Manchoukuo and, in March 1933, gave notice of its intent to retire from the League. In the face of this determined aggression, the elaborate international peace-keeping machinery of the 1920s broke down. The meaning that events in Manchuria had for the future of the United States was analyzed by Nathaniel Peffer in an article published in February 1933 and reprinted here in part.

Source: *Harper's,* February 1933: "Manchuria: A Warning to America."

A YEAR HAS PASSED since Japan's absorption of Manchuria presented the most serious threat to world peace since 1918, and the first concrete test of all the hopes, plans, and devices contrived for the prevention of war. It is time to take a reckoning.

Two items stand out in such a reckoning.

First, America, while clinging to the fiction of isolation from Europe, has become definitely, alarmingly, and perhaps inextricably involved in Asia.

Second, the promise of control of war by

international machinery has proved illusive. For, despite the concurrent ceremonials of League of Nations meetings, international commissions, invocations of peace pacts, and "the technic of peace by conference," Japan has acted as it would have acted before 1914. It wanted Manchuria and has taken it. The League of Nations and the Kellogg Pact might as well not have been.

It is not my intention here to discuss questions of Far Eastern international politics or the Manchurian controversy. They have been sufficiently aired, and the issue has now passed far beyond their intrinsic importance. Nor do I wish to labor the obvious point that the League has failed. For the point is not so much that the League has failed as that it never had a chance to succeed. And in this point lies the innermost truth of the Manchurian controversy, of the whole Far Eastern question, and of all international relations, for that matter. The larger significance of the Manchurian episode and its aftermath is just this, that it is the perfect laboratory specimen of how international conflicts are made, how not to attempt to unmake them, and also how they might be averted if we were willing to pay the price. What it shows is that peace cannot be achieved through mechanisms, that there can be no peace so long as the causes of war remain — that is, so long as nations strive for objects which can be attained only by the use of armed force.

This truth, platitudinous and commonly ignored, has never been more completely ignored than in the last year. Underlying all the organized efforts to deal with the Manchurian affair — and never before has so conscious and systematic an effort been made to deal with an international dispute — has been the premise that this was a "crisis," to be "settled" by bringing about a cessation of fighting and a compromise between the disputants, after which peace would be secure. There has been no disposition to face the conditions in the Far East which produce conflicts like this one, which have produced them before, and will do so again unless they are changed.

The Manchurian affair has been treated as an event isolated in time and space, as beginning in 1931, restricted to a region north of the Great Wall of China, and concerning only Japan and China, whereas, in fact, it has roots running back almost a hundred years and extending to Europe and North America. It is the latest phase of an old struggle and can be understood only in its setting.

This struggle has two aspects, which are interrelated. The first is between China and all the powers which have appropriated parts of its territory, acquired special privileges on its soil, and otherwise nullified its sovereignty. The issue is whether China will regain its independence or remain the spoils of high politics. The second is among those powers for the exclusive right to dominate China. The stake is the profits from China's material development. . . .

For Japan the question is not so simple as whether it shall keep Manchuria or China shall have it back. It is whether Japan shall keep Manchuria or China shall have it back or some other power shall take it. The Japanese came to their second maturity in the harsh and ugly world of the end of the nineteenth century, a world in which the strong took what they could wherever they could. Japan was itself for a generation the victim of the same process to which China was subjected, and if it escaped China's fate, the explanation is partly in its own miraculous effort but mainly in the happy accident that it was near China and China was the bigger prize. To the rival aspirants for Eastern empire, Japan was by comparison small pickings. Moreover, Japan watched the relentless approach of the dismemberment of China — until given pause by the outbreak of the World War — knowing that whatever power appropriated the largest share would have a weapon against Japan itself.

Out of the fear begotten by that threat it had to fight Russia in 1904. A definite psychology was formed in the mind of the Japanese. They cannot believe that relinquishment of Manchuria necessarily means its retention by China. They cannot believe that 1914 was more than an interruption. And they may be right. It may be that a new international ethic was born of the lessons of the war and that the race for empire has been abandoned in the East; and it may be that the Great Powers are only winded and that when they recover their wind the race will be resumed, each spurred now by the redoubled need for foreign markets. If the latter be true, then obviously it would be fatal for Japan not to take advantage of their exhaustion and consolidate its position of mastery when it can. And thus may be explained the motives of Japan's aggressive policy since the Twenty-one Demands of 1915 and its obduracy before world opinion since 1931. Thus may be explained the failure of the League's intervention into the Manchurian conflict and Japan's rejection of the Lytton Report.

The League did not fail, however. It did not try. From the first hastily convoked meeting of the Council to the formal debates on the Lytton Report, it never took cognizance of considerations such as have just been outlined. And without facing them, any attempt to deal with the Far East was unreal. It did not touch the root causes of the conflict it was trying to stop. It dealt only with effects. To have gone to the underlying causes might have been unpleasant, since it would have put others besides Japan on the defensive; but without doing so there was no hope of restoring peace in the Far East. The conflict could not be prevented or stopped, because it had been set by the operation of the causes. At the best this particular incident could be arrested and the

basic conflict left to be resumed by a similar incident later. As it happened, not even the incident was arrested. Japan proceeded according to plan, absorbed Manchuria, and set up a fictive state called Manchoukuo as a transition to eventual annexation. The incident could be called closed except for the entrance of one factor — the American government. The United States intervened.

II

WHEN THE BALANCE OF ALL THE FORCES working on history in the Far East is taken, the resultant will be found to be the definitive entry of the United States into the East. The United States has not only intervened but made unequivocal commitments and thereby, with or without deliberate intent, moved to a new position in world affairs. The pronouncements of the American government with reference to Manchuria, so glibly hailed by liberals, will constitute, unless revoked, a pledge and policy no less binding than the Monroe Doctrine but infinitely harder to effectuate. They will embroil us in the most inflammable area in the world; make us the protagonist of the status quo in a region where the status quo is inherently unstable; enroll us as a partisan in a congeries of crusty international feuds, and, unless revoked, will have a more positive influence on the course of our history than the Monroe Doctrine, since they concern a part of the world more contested than South America and state a position less easy to defend. And of this fact the American people remain singularly unaware and wholly uncritical.

Mr. Stimson, as secretary of state, has formally announced, not once but twice, that the American government does not recognize what has taken place in Manchuria. He has said that the American government will not recognize political changes brought about by force in contravention of the Kellogg Pact, and by more than inference has so classified the changes in Manchuria. In his studied words before the Council on Foreign Relations in New York he explicitly characterized the formation of the new state of Manchoukuo under the aegis of Japan as "fruits of aggression." Mr. Stimson has not said, however, how the American government will implement its declaration.

Unfortunately the occasion will arise when this will have to be determined. It cannot be evaded. Either all the events since September 1931 are nullified and Manchuria returns to the status it then occupied, or Manchuria remains Manchoukuo, a fiction for Japanese hegemony. The American government says Manchuria is still a part of China; Japan says it is Manchoukuo, an independent state under Japanese advisers. There is no possibility of evasion or compromise. It must be one or the other, and the concrete test will come. . . .

Saving only the possibility of an economic catastrophe, Japan will not yield. That can be said with dogmatic certainty. Since Japan won South Manchuria from Russia, there has been no time when it has not stood ready to fight to extinction to defend its position. On that point there is no division within Japan. There are no Japanese who would not support the government on Manchuria. The so-called Japanese liberals, of whom so much is made by certain elements in America, are a creation of the imagination of finely tempered but innocent Americans who go junketing about the world on goodwill tours and believe what they hear at banquets and stage-set laymen's conferences. As we understand the word "liberal," there are few Japanese liberals, if any. Such as are liberal are without influence. Those commonly designated as liberal are semi-official apologists. The Japanese people will support their government on Manchuria. Against the United States they will support it on anything.

For the United States it will be awkward to yield. For one thing, its prestige is now engaged. More important, the American government has not acted out of caprice or impulse. It has brought into the open a tendency latent for a generation, though but dimly felt and to the American people unknown. With Europe, with which we have racial kinship, cultural affinity, common historical origins and evolution, and economic relations so close that a bank failure on the Danube causes shoe factories in Missouri to go into bankruptcy — with Europe we will not be "involved." But we leap to defiance over the Manchurian plains of Asia, straight into "entanglement" in an area which has produced more wars in the last hundred years than Europe. Our trade there is trifling, our vested interest negligible, our residents there could be housed in a hotel of moderate size.

Why, then? It is not our present material stake that draws us. What is it? Nor is this entirely new. For a generation we have been moving in the same direction. For twenty years we have stood squarely in the way of Japan's aggrandizement. Where Japan has been obstructed, as it has been in China, in Manchuria, and in Siberia, the obstruction has been of American making. Whether or not Japan's grandiose dreams imperil world security is another matter. They do, of course, but that is irrelevant in this connection. The point is that America, 4,000 miles away and without any tangible interest at stake, takes upon itself the burden of the defense of the status quo, deliberately giving the challenge to a militant, determined power. Why?

Can it be that America has a manifest destiny? Is there some mystic drive that impels us ever westward? As soon as the first settlements had been cleared, we started toward the Pacific, reached it, leaped half across to the Hawaiian Islands, and then all the way across to the Philippines. Immediately, then, our interest in China lifted, and Secretary Hay spoke for the Open Door. Is there in the restless American spirit the unexpressed, inarticulate conviction that Asia is our oyster, ours to open and ours to pluck the pearl? Is that what motivates the otherwise unexplainable determination of our government in the Far East? Have we a destiny, and incidentally do the American people know it, and are they prepared to pay the price that national destinies exact?

These are the questions that are being asked in the Far East and elsewhere, everywhere, in fact, more than in America. Most of all they are being asked in Japan. The cardinal point of reference for Japan's foreign policy is America. China is its theater of action, but toward America is its polarization. When Japanese who think of the political future of their country look out on their world they face America: *voilà l'ennemi.* It is not the attempted restraint by the League of Nations that has aroused Japanese resentment since the beginning of the Manchurian affair; it is the succession of pronouncements by the American government. It is not the League that is held to blame for the strictures on Japan emanating from Geneva, but America for having goaded the League to action. And in that position there is some reason, for Great Britain and France plainly have come as reluctant judges and more reluctant prosecutors.

America and Japan stand at deadlock on Manchuria. Japan will not yield. If America yields it will be for the first time on any important measure of foreign policy on which it has taken a positive stand, and it will be on something, moreover, that lies deeper than prestige or present material interest. What then? By every historical analogy, by all political precedent, Japan and America are today where England and Germany were in, say, 1907. If they drift, if the forces now making are allowed to gather, then by every precedent they will come to

the same culmination. If we really are concerned about world peace we shall not worry ourselves about machinery and treaties and conferences and commissions. We shall face this fact and deal with it in time.

III

CONCRETELY, THERE ARE TWO POSSIBLE courses of action. One is for the American people — not one in five of whom can place Manchuria on a map without search — to ask themselves whether Manchuria means enough to them to risk their fortunes, their future, and the lives of their sons on its disposition. And more is involved than a single war. America would then be caught in a welter of rivalries in what would be worse than the Balkans and from which a succession of wars would result. For no one can be so credulous as to believe that if America should go to war with Japan over Manchuria and win — as it will, by reason of greater economic resources, though only after a long war — it will then return Manchuria to China as before 1931. Instead, it will keep hegemony over Manchuria itself. It will have to; and it will want to. And it will inherit all the resentments, jealousies, and hostilities now Japan's.

If the American people believe that Manchuria means enough for them to be willing to face this prospect, they will let their government proceed on its course and stand behind it, as the Japanese people do theirs. If not, they will consolidate public opinion to bring pressure on their government to withdraw from positions which expose them to risks they are unwilling to take. But this is a counsel of perfection — or of despair. There is no instrument by which democracies can control their foreign affairs. The public does not initiate or deliberate and then give its government mandates for action. Men in governments make commitments, and then it is a point of honor as well as duty to stand by the government. None asks then whether the individuals or groups in office made their commitments with wisdom and with the consent of the governed. By then the hostage of patriotism has been given.

The second course of action is to do as the League of Nations did not attempt to do. That is for the Great Powers to face the causes of conflict in the Far East and eradicate them. Fundamentally there is no other course. . . .

There can be no peace in the Far East so long as there are rival ambitions for mastery of China. There can be no peace unless those ambitions are slaked or renounced. The first can come only as the consummation of a succession of wars. There is no alternative but the second. What we can do constructively is not wait for the next eruption and then attempt to deal with it isolated from the conditions which gave rise to it, but act in advance by way of prevention. If our desire for peace is truthfully measured by the implications of the Covenant of the League and the Kellogg Pact, the powers will formally meet and lay down the foundations of peace in the Far East by first tearing down the international system built up since relations were established with China in 1842. They will do more than indite amiable generalities of self-denying ordinances as they did at the Washington Conference. They will implement them. They will give tokens of good faith. . . .

A situation generations in the making cannot be unmade by resolving. But it will take equally long no matter when we begin. Had we honestly faced the causes of international rancors in the Far East at the Washington Conference in 1921 we might have prevented the outbreak in 1931. If we start now, we may not attain the consummation of our hopes until 1951. If we wait until 1941, we shall not attain it until 1961 — provided there is not war in the meantime. A long time will be required; also it will be costly. From that, too, there is no escape. The choice is only between loss voluntarily accepted and the loss imposed by the destruction of war. The rampages of the nineteenth-century conquerors must be paid for. Before there can be a new international society there must be a drastic writing off of old social losses.

There is no easy road to peace. The liberal reliance on treaties and international machinery is part of the deep-seated American faith in mechanical contrivances in all human situations. Peace cannot be had by wishing. If we want peace we must pay for it. We may not get it then. The momentum for war in the East, long gathered, is swift and powerful. But if we get peace at all, it will be only by paying. For America just now the stake is big and worth a risk.

———◆———

[Hitler] states that he could not, for anything in the world, live in a country like the U.S.A., whose conceptions of life are inspired by the most grasping commercialism and which does not love any of the loftiest expressions of the human spirit such as music.

Count Ciano, *Diplomatic Papers*

47.

Franklin D. Roosevelt: Recognition of Soviet Russia

Relations between America and the Soviet Union had been strained ever since the Archangel expedition of 1918, in which the United States had supported efforts of the deposed "White" Russians to regain their power. The United States had never formally recognized the Revolution, and all communication between the two countries had been carried on via third parties. However, stimulated both by pressures from American exporters and by a desire to have a friend in the Soviet Union in the face of growing German and Japanese aggression, President Roosevelt determined soon after his inauguration to recognize the Communist regime. On the night of November 16, 1933, Maxim Litvinov, the Soviet representative, and Roosevelt exchanged a series of letters, two of which are reprinted here. The Soviets agreed not to engage in any subversive activities in the United States, to grant religious freedom and legal protection to Americans living in Russia, and to negotiate the settlement of outstanding debts. Although subsequent events put the matter in a different light, recognition was widely acclaimed and supported at the time.

Source: FDR, II, pp. 471-472, 474-475.

I.

First Letter to Mr. Litvinov

I AM VERY HAPPY to inform you that as a result of our conversations the government of the United States has decided to establish normal diplomatic relations with the government of the Union of Soviet Socialist Republics and to exchange ambassadors.

I trust that the relations now established between our peoples may forever remain normal and friendly, and that our nations henceforth may cooperate for their mutual benefit and for the preservation of the peace of the world.

II.

Second Letter to Mr. Litvinov

I AM GLAD TO HAVE RECEIVED the assurance expressed in your note to me of this date that it will be the fixed policy of the government of the Union of Soviet Socialist Republics:

1. To respect scrupulously the indisputable right of the United States to order its own life within its own jurisdiction in its own way and to refrain from interfering in any manner in the internal affairs of the United States, its territories, or possessions.

2. To refrain and to restrain all persons in government service and all organizations of the government or under its direct or indirect control, including organizations in receipt of any financial assistance from it, from any act overt or covert liable in any way whatsoever to injure the tranquillity, prosperity, order, or security of the whole or any part of the United States, its territories, or possessions, and, in particular, from any act tending to incite or encourage armed intervention, or any agitation or propaganda having as an aim the violation of the territorial integrity of the United

States, its territories, or possessions, or the bringing about by force of a change in the political or social order of the whole or any part of the United States, its territories, or possessions.

3. Not to permit the formation or residence on its territory of any organization or group — and to prevent the activity on its territory of any organization or group, or of representatives or officials of any organization or group — which makes claim to be the government of, or makes attempt upon the territorial integrity of, the United States, its territories, or possessions; not to form, subsidize, support, or permit on its territory military organizations or groups having the aim of armed struggle against the United States, its territories, or possessions, and to prevent any recruiting on behalf of such organizations and groups.

4. Not to permit the formation or residence on its territory of any organization or group — and to prevent the activity on its territory of any organization or group, or of representatives or officials of any organization or group — which has as an aim the overthrow or the preparation for the overthrow of, or the bringing about by force of a change in, the political or social order of the whole or any part of the United States, its territories or possessions.

It will be the fixed policy of the Executive of the United States within the limits of the powers conferred by the Constitution and the laws of the United States to adhere reciprocally to the engagements above expressed.

48.

Henry A. Wallace: Declaration of Interdependence

Farmers, who had not known good times even during the prosperity of the 1920s, were reduced to severe straits by 1933. Overproduction, low prices, high costs, and increased indebtedness burdened nearly every farmer. On May 10, 1933, Congress passed the Agricultural Adjustment Act, which was designed to restore the balance between the agricultural and industrial sectors of the economy by limiting farm production and relieving the burden of farm mortgages. On May 13 Secretary of Agriculture Henry A. Wallace went on the radio with what he called a declaration of interdependence to explain the adminstration's intent with regard to the new farm bill. A portion of his radio address is reprinted here.

Source: Library of Congress, Wallace Papers.

THE NEW FARM ACT signed by President Roosevelt yesterday comprises twenty-six pages of legal document, but the essence of it can be stated simply. It has three main parts. The word "adjustment" covers all three.

First, the administration is empowered to adjust farm production to effective demand as a means of restoring the farmer's purchasing power. The secretary of agriculture is charged to administer this adjustment and to direct, at the same time, an effort to reduce those wastes of distribution which now cause food to pile up, unused, while people go hungry a hundred miles away.

Second is an accompanying authorization

to refinance and readjust farm mortgage payments. . . .

In the third part of the act, the power for controlled inflation is delegated to the President, and this too signifies adjustment — adjustment of currency and credit to our changed needs. My own responsibility, however, as secretary of agriculture is solely with the first part of the act.

It should be made plain at the outset that the new Farm Act initiates a program for a general advance in buying power, an advance that must extend throughout America, lightening the way of the people in city and country alike. We must lift urban buying power as we lift farm prices. The Farm Act must not be considered an isolated advance in a restricted sector; it is an important part of a large-scale, coordinated attack on the whole problem of depression.

If enough people will join in the wide and swift adjustments that this act proposes, we can make it work. I say *if* because this act is not a hand-out measure. It does provide new governmental machinery which can be used by all who labor to grow and to bring us food and fabrics, to organize, to put their businesses in order, and to make their way together out of a wilderness of economic desolation and waste.

But the machinery will not work itself. The farmers and the distributors of foodstuffs must use it and make it work. The government can help map lines of march and can see that the interest of no one group is advanced out of line with the interest of all. But government officials cannot and will not go out and work for private businesses. A farm is a private business; so is a farmers' cooperative; and so are all the great links in the food-distributing chain. Government men cannot and will not go out and plow down old trails for agriculture or build for the distributing industries new roads out of the woods. The growers, the processors, the carriers and sellers of food must do that for themselves.

Following trade agreements, openly and democratically arrived at, with the consumer at all times represented and protected from gouging, these industries must work out their own salvation. They must put an end to cutthroat competition and wasteful disorder. The Emergency Adjustment Act makes it lawful and practical for them to get together and do so. It provides for a control of production to accord with actual need and for an orderly distribution of essential supplies.

In the end, we envision programs of planned land use, and we must turn our thought to this end immediately; for many thousands of refugees from urban pinch and hunger are turning, with little or no guidance, to the land. A tragic number of city families are reoccupying abandoned farms, farms on which born farmers, skilled, patient, and accustomed to doing with very little, were unable to make a go of it. In consequence of this backflow there are now 32 million people on the farms of the United States, the greatest number ever recorded in our history. Some of those who have returned to farming will find their place there, but most of them, I fear, will not.

I look to a day when men and women will be able to do in the country the work that they have been accustomed to do in the city; a day when we shall have more industrial workers out in the open where there is room to live. I look to a decentralization of industry; and hope that out of this Adjustment Act will come, in time, a resettlement of America. But in this respect we shall have to make haste slowly. We do not need any more farmers out in the country now. We do need more people there with some other means of livelihood, buying, close at hand, farm products; enriching and making more various the life of our open-country and village communities.

In adjusting our production of basic foods and fabrics, our first need is to plant and send to market less wheat, less cotton, less corn, fewer hogs, and less of other basic crops whereof already we have towering surpluses, with no immediate prospect of clearance beyond the sea. The act authorizes the secretary of agriculture to apply excise taxes on the processing of these products and to pay the money thus derived to farmers who agree to enter upon programs of planned production, and who abide by that agreement. There are increasing possibilities that by trade agreements we may be able on certain crops or livestock products to arrive at a balanced abundance without levying a tax on the product at any point. In no case will taxes be levied on products purchased for the unemployed.

What it amounts to is an advance toward higher prices all along the line. Current proposals for government cooperation with industry are really at one with this Farm Act. Unless we can get reemployment going, lengthen payrolls, and shorten breadlines, no effort to lift prices can last very long. Our first effort as to agriculture will be to seek markets and to adjust production downward, with safe margins to provide enough food for all. This effort we will continue until such time as diminishing stocks raise prices to a point where the farmer's buying power will be as high as it was in the prewar years, 1909 to 1914.

The reason that we chose that period is because the prices farmers got for their crops in those years and the prices they paid for manufactured goods and urban services most nearly approached an equitable relationship. There was thus a balance between our major producing groups. At that time there was not the terrific disparity between rural and urban purchasing power which now exists and which is choking the life out of all forms of American business.

We do not propose to reduce agricultural production schedules to a strictly domestic basis. Our foreign trade has dwindled to a mere trickle; but we still have some foreign customers for farm products; we want to keep that trade, if possible, and to get more foreign trade, if we can. The immediate job, as I see it now, is to organize American agriculture to reduce its output to domestic need, plus that amount which we can export at a profit.

If, within a year or so, it happens that the world tide turns and world trade revives, we still can utilize to excellent advantage our crop adjustment and controlled distribution setup. We can find out how much they really want over there, and at what price; and then we can take off the brakes and step on the gas a little at a time, deliberately, not recklessly and blindly, as we have in times past. We can speed up just enough to meet that demand for our products which will return a decent price.

The first sharp downward adjustment is necessary because during the past years we have defiantly refused to face an overwhelming reality. In consequence, changed world conditions bear down on us so heavily as to threaten our national life. In the years immediately before the war, our agriculture was tending toward a domestic basis of production. The war rushed us out upon the markets of the world. Fifty million acres of Europe, not counting Russia, went out of cultivation. Food prices rose. A new surge of pioneers strode forth upon those high and dusty plains once called the Great American Desert and found that they could grow wheat there. Throughout the country, sod was broken. America entered the war. American farmers stepped out to serve the nation as American boys stepped up in answer to the call. Before the surge was over, we had put to the plow a vast new area. To replace the 50 million lost acres of Europe, America had added 30 million acres to its tilled domain and thrown its whole farm plant into high gear. . . .

The oversupplied situation began as a result of the war. As early as 1920 American agriculture was served notice that martial adventures must be paid for afterward, through the nose. The agricultural deflation was well under way by 1923; half of Montana's wheat farmers had by that time lost their farms. In 1929, the agricultural deflation became a plunge. Today, agriculture is twice as much deflated as general industry; and its prices are down 40 percent below the level of prices in general.

Ever since 1920, hundreds of thousands of farm families have had to do without civilized goods and services which in normal times they were glad and eager to buy. Since 1929, millions of farm people have had to patch their garments, store their cars and tractors, deprive their children of educational opportunities, and cease, as farmers, to improve their practices and their property. They have been forced to let their homes and other buildings stand bare and unpainted, eaten by time and the weather. They have been driven toward peasant, or less than peasant, standards; they have been forced to adopt frontier methods of bare sustenance at a time when in the old surging, unlimited sense of the word we have no longer a frontier.

When the farmer gets higher prices, he will start spending. He will have to. He needs things. He needs new shoes and clothing for all the family so that his children can go to school in any weather with dry feet, protected bodies, and a decent American feeling of equality and pride. . . .

To reorganize agriculture, cooperatively, democratically, so that the surplus lands on which men and women now are toiling, wasting their time, wearing out their lives to no good end shall be taken out of production — that is a tremendous task. The adjustment we seek calls, first of all, for a mental adjustment, a willing reversal of driving, pioneer opportunism and ungoverned laissez-faire. The ungoverned push of rugged individualism perhaps had an economic justification in the days when we had all the West to surge upon and conquer; but this country has filled up now and

grown up. There are no more Indians to fight. No more land worth taking may be had for the grabbing. We must experience a change of mind and heart.

The frontiers that challenge us now are of the mind and spirit. We must blaze new trails in scientific accomplishment, in the peaceful arts and industries. Above all, we must blaze new trails in the direction of a controlled economy, common sense, and social decency. . . .

This Farm Act differs from the partway attacks on the problems that have been launched in the past. This act provides for controlled production. Without that, no price-lifting effort can possibly work; because if there is no control of acreage, the better price increases the next year's planting and the greater harvest wrecks the price.

For example, I would call to your attention that Chicago wheat is 13 cents above Liverpool, whereas ordinarily it is 15 cents below. We are 28 cents out of line with our customary export situation because the new wheat crop is 250 million bushels below normal. It is obvious, therefore, that with ordinary weather conditions next winter and spring we can easily have a crop which will result in prices again being 15 cents below Liverpool in this country. I am saying this because I do not want the wheat farmers of this country to live too long in a fool's paradise. . . .

Our immediate job is to decide what products to concentrate on, what methods of production adjustment to employ on them, to determine to what extent marketing agreements can be useful, and to appraise the necessity for and rates of processing taxes.

To help us in these determinations, as rapidly as possible, we shall have here in Washington representatives of agriculture and representatives of the processing and distributing trades. These men and women will take part in commodity conferences, and in the light of their technical knowledge will suggest which of the several plans of attack will work best for different crops and regions. Bearing their recommendations in mind, we shall decide just what action to take and when to take it. As each decision is made, we shall get it out directly and publicly to the farmers affected and launch organization efforts throughout the nation.

As President Roosevelt indicated at Topeka last September, the right sort of farm and national relief should encourage and strengthen farmer cooperation. I believe we have in this new law the right sort of stimulus to that end.

I want to say, finally, that unless, as we lift farm prices, we also unite to control production, this plan will not work for long. And the only way we can effectively control production for the long pull is for you farmers to organize, and stick, and do it yourselves. This act offers you promise of a balanced abundance, a shared prosperity, and a richer life. It will work if you will make it yours, and *make* it work.

I hope that you will come to feel in time, as I do now, that the rampageous individualist who signs up for adjustment and then tries to cheat is cheating not only the government but his neighbors. I hope that you will come to see in this act, as I do now, a Declaration of Interdependence; a recognition of our essential unity and of our absolute reliance one upon another.

49.

Chester C. Davis: Planned Harvests

The problems involved in the implementation of the Agricultural Adjustment Act were enormously complex, owing not only to the great number of farmers and the wide diversity of crops but also to a conflict within the nation and the agency itself (the AAA) over the ultimate aims of the program. The AAA had a ready-made staff in county agents supplied by already existing extension services and by the land-grant colleges, but it had difficulty in determining an overall policy. Chester Davis replaced George Peek as director of the AAA in December 1933. Davis' views on the troublesome question of production controls were expressed in "Toward Planned Harvests," part of which is reprinted here.

Source: *Review of Reviews and World's Work*, December 1933.

THERE ARE 52 MILLION square miles of land on the face of this earth. Figuring out mountains, the polar regions, absolute desert, unsuitable soils, and so on, we find that 5½ million acres might be sown, for instance, to wheat; and that less than a half-million square miles is actually so sown now throughout the world. North America, Europe, and Asia, alone, each has at least

1½ million square miles which *might* be sown to wheat.

Fundamental in the situation is the fact that the land resources of the United States exceed those of all Europe, excluding Soviet Russia, and are of a similar magnitude to those of China plus India; whereas the population of the United States is about 125 million, as compared with 350 million in

Europe, excluding Russia, and probably 800 million in China and India. And throughout the world the average man can eat only about so much food in the aggregate.

In the years immediately before the war, agriculture in the United States was tending toward a domestic basis of production. The war led to distorted plantings and raced us onto the markets of the world.

Fifty million acres of Europe, not counting Russia, went out of cultivation. The nations called for food. When this country entered the war, patriotic pressure was added to the lure of soaring prices. A new surge of pioneers built sod shelters on high and dusty drylands and found that wheat sown deep with the drill furrows sidewise to the south wind would generally make a crop. Throughout the country sod was broken. To replace the 50 million lost acres of Europe, America added 30 million acres to its tilled domain and threw its whole farm plant into high gear.

The war ended with Europe deeply in debt to us; and since we would not, generally speaking, take goods from her, there was no real hope of her paying these debts. We should have seen the handwriting on the wall and started then and there to retire our wartime emergency acreages of wheat, cotton, and other export crops; but we did not. In order to keep on triumphantly expanding, we loaned Europe still more money to buy our crops and goods.

We kept this up for something more than ten years. When we got tired of throwing good money after bad, Europe quit buying. By that time she was back in stride agriculturally, passionately nationalistic, strongly inclined to "live at home." Farm prices plunged to the lowest levels in American history. Last winter we experienced the hideous dilemma of the largest food surpluses and the longest breadlines anywhere on earth.

I shall not describe here, step by step, our developing efforts to correct this fantastic situation. The barest outline will suffice. In 1927, Dr. W. J. Spillman of the United States Department of Agriculture published a book called *Balancing the Farm Output.* In this book he suggested an induced reduction of crop acreages, farm by farm. M. L. Wilson, Dr. John D. Black, and others tried in the years that followed to simplify the Spillman scheme somewhat. It came to be known as the voluntary domestic allotment plan. In essence, it calls for an adjustment payment to cooperating farmers, by the government, on the domestically consumed part of the crop, and an orderly cooperative adjustment of acreage pro-rata.

The voluntary domestic allotment plan was originally presented to Congress in July 1932, in the Hope-Norbeck Bill. The bill failed of hearing but evoked wide interest within our borders and without. Shortly after that, Governor Roosevelt, in his campaign speech at Topeka, committed himself to the principle of bringing about a better balance between supply and demand of exportable agricultural commodities and indicated special interest in this allotment plan.

The Farm Act, passed by the Congress on May 10 last, gave the secretary of agriculture and an adjustment administrator, representing the President, broad permissive powers to induce active agricultural planning among the farmers themselves. The Agricultural Adjustment Administration was set up in the Department of Agriculture. George N. Peek of Illinois, who throughout the twelve years of American agriculture's post-war depression, had fought for better farm prices and a better balance between rural and urban spending power, was named chief administrator.

The attack of the Agricultural Adjustment Administration upon surplus plantings of wheat, corn, cotton, and tobacco is essentially the domestic allotment plan fortified by provision for a variety of other necessary adjustments. The act provides for an adjustment of debts and authorizes an adjusted dollar, if need be. It allows auxiliary maneuvers to clear surpluses from the top of the pile, as well as from direct attack from underneath in the soundest manner possible — not planting them. Our recent relief purchases of butter, the induced export of Northwestern wheat, and present efforts to feed other surpluses direct to the unemployed are examples of auxiliary maneuvers.

Devices of this nature are of dubious value if employed alone. The operation, if successful, raises prices temporarily. The raised price induces a greater sowing. The great sowing wrecks the price. But if under your entire structure of farm prices you put a solid basis of controlled sowing and planned national harvests, then stabilization and induced exports, within the limits of well-defined world agreements, become not only defensible but promising means of meeting temporary emergencies. In the future we shall probably employ stabilization and induced shipments to level off regional and national crop excesses and deficiencies due to the weather, from year to year.

In this article I wish to speak principally of our foundation effort: a voluntary, cooperative control of volume output, organized from the ground up and conducted principally by the farmers themselves. But the fact that this cooperation is induced by processing taxes, which redistribute buying power to people at the grass roots, long deprived; and the fact that we are attacking not only disorganized food production, but disorganized distribution should at least be mentioned.

Agriculture first felt the present depression in 1920. With agriculture prostrate at the end of 1932, and with the cities sharing in the depression, at last, many distribution margins remained as wide as in 1929. Between 1929 and 1933 city incomes fell one-third; farm income, already low, fell two-thirds; but distribution spreads stayed wide. It is informing to note that of the fifteen leading corporations in point of earnings in 1932, nine dealt in food or tobacco.

Industry and the distribution trades in general, like agriculture in general, are overextended, sprawling, struggling more or less helplessly amid insane duplications of effort and blind, destructive competition. Unlike agriculture, industry and the distributing trades have been putting too little money into prices for raw materials and into wages. Wealth has become overcentralized, too narrowly circulated. Business has stacked up too much of a pile in excess plant, dividends, and interest payments. The New Deal proposes, for the sake of all, that money be put forth more freely in farm prices and city wages, to breed again. The great effort is to start money moving from the bottom up, and to reorganize both production and distribution so as to avoid recurring economic paralysis which, under laissez faire, has been the price of progress.

In the field of agricultural distribution, we have chosen at first to move rather slowly, feeling our way. The act gives us mandate to seek, first, more orderly distribution by marketing agreements voluntarily entered into by the trades. If voluntary agreements do not suffice, we can issue revokable licenses. By voluntary agreement we have obtained from the leading tobacco companies a farm price on flue-cured tobacco 40 percent above the figure that was being paid them when the governors of certain Southern states were closing markets last summer.

Milk, which provides about a quarter of all American farm income, presents production and distribution problems that have given us much concern. The situation is enormously complicated and varies widely by regions. Only recently have we succeeded in getting marketing agreements that give the farmer more money without running up the price to the consumer. We shall proceed in that direction, using the power to license wherever necessary; but we shall never put the milk business on a satisfactory basis until we introduce decisive measures of production control.

Production adjustment efforts so far have been directed against the crops of which, in consequence of closing European markets, we have towering export surpluses. We have had to work fast, taking these crops as they came along. Time so forced our hand on cotton that we had to take it out as it ripened. I hope we shall never again have to destroy part of a standing crop, but the urgency was so great in the South this year that our emergency campaign there was justified. Another year of 5-cent cotton would stifle the whole program of national recovery. We are lending 10 cents a pound on cotton now.

We took out 10½ million acres of ripening cotton, a quarter of the 1933 crop, and seeded $110 million in new spending power in the cotton South. It was rough work, but the crisis in the South has eased. The plows of those cotton farmers struck at the roots of their trouble and turned those roots to the sky. Now we are launching a program to plant not the usual 40 million acres but only 25 million for 1934 harvest.

This year's wheat campaign was more thoroughly organized. There was time. With world accord, we have signed about four-fifths of America's commercial wheat acreage for a three-year acreage adjustment, with a 15 percent pro-rata reduction in 1934. In 1,450 counties more than a half-million wheat growers have formed county wheat production control associations to administer this huge cooperative undertaking from the ground up. We shall displace 8 million acres from American wheatlands in 1934, and distribute around $100 million in adjustment payments.

Because of the intricate interrelation of corn and hog prices, the $350 million adjustment program that we now are launching in the Corn Belt is beset with peculiar difficulties. The rough stab that we were forced to take at the problem last summer, with an induced slaughter of little pigs and sows, was a stopgap at best. The present plan attacks the base of the difficulty by the sounder means of agrarian birth control. We are striving now for permanent effect. Somewhere between 10 and 15 million acres now planted to corn are surplus acres. We shall seek to reduce corn planting about one-fifth and hog farrowing about one-quarter in the next three years.

Let me say at this point that all our plans are elastic. If an unforeseen world condition should require us to increase rather than to decrease agricultural output, our newly mobilized production control machinery could immediately be turned the other way, with a premium put upon expanding, not upon restricting, acreage.

Fifteen million acres less cotton next year, 8 million acres taken out of wheat, 10 million or more acres no longer given over to surplus cornland: these figures begin to mount up. Add minor displacements of tobacco and rice acreage already agreed upon, the figure exceeds 33 million acres, more than the entire cultivated area of Japan proper, taken out of key crops — and turned to other uses.

To what other uses? That is a pressing question nowadays, not only here in Washington but on every farm in the land. You cannot move one piece on the vast agricultural checkerboard without altering in the end the entire design. One move compels another.

The land taken out of cotton, wheat, corn, and tobacco is being fallowed and rested, or sown, speaking generally, to noncompetitive, soil-building crops. That generally means grass. The dairymen are inclined to resist the tendency (mistakenly, I believe, as dairy cows are preeminently efficient in transforming grass into proteins); but the tendency of our present programs seems increasingly back in the direction we came from far too hastily — back to grass.

There are many reasons for this. The land needs a rest. The people who have overworked it need rest also. Women and children of the farm family especially have been driven often far too hard without reward. Grassland culture is less laborious, and life upon grasslands is pleasanter than life in a skinned, high-pressure farming area, as a rule. Land in grass does not wash away. But the most immediate and pressing cause of retreat from high-pressure farming toward a more pastoral, yet modern, economy is this: It takes three or four times as much land to feed a cow on grass as it does to grow grain and feed high-pressure feed mixtures. Livestock on grass, with supplemental rations, will not produce as much of meat or milk as livestock pressed into high production by grain feeding. But we have too much milk and meat as it is; and food produced on a grassland economy over wider areas is much more cheaply produced.

The open country is not only a place to grow things; it is a place to live; and much land pleasant to live upon is unfit to farm. As we put our lands in order from the standpoint of economical production, we shall gradually accomplish also a reordering of all America as a place to live. Not only crops will move; people will move; and we shall see, I think, a widespread intermingling of those ways of life we now think of separately as rural and urban. The decentralization experiments now being conducted by M. L. Wilson look in that direction. The workers will be sustained by decentralized industries and live in the open country in homes of their own.

It is not my purpose here to consider the remote probabilities to which we stand committed, having embarked upon changed and sweeping policies of planned land use.

Thus far we have made acreage cuts pro-rata, on the basis of existing plantings. Anyone who has ever considered the question knows that in time we must push on from there to more selective adjustments. A recent announcement from the White House gives an idea of the direction these adjustments must take. The President has said that as rapidly as good new lands are brought into cultivation by drainage or irrigation a correspondingly productive area will be taken out of cultivation and kept out.

This will not mean bringing an acre in and taking an acre out. An acre (or area) of rich new land brought in may mean three or more acres of unproductive farming areas retired to suitable use.

"Meantime," as R. G. Tugwell has written,

> it is not merely a fond, pastoral hope to say that we are marching, without changing base, toward a land of greener fields and bluer streams. For reasons wholly practical, our trend is from cultivated crops to meadows, lawns, and pastures and the steps we are taking to prevent erosion will tend to clear our running streams.
>
> Quite as important in another way is a renewal in modern terms of an old American dream — that citizens should be given access to this soil and allowed in their various ways to live in peace and security in homes of their own. These are aims, at least, which make profoundly stirring our crop adjustment program, our experiments in decentralization, our dream of a New America — a land in order, wisely used, with the hills green and the streams blue.

The government is mainly an expensive organization to regulate evildoers, and tax those who behave; government does little for fairly respectable people except annoy them.

EDGAR W. HOWE, *Notes for My Biographer*

50.

Ralph Borsodi: The Family as a Unit of Production

*During the Depression the population flow from the country to the city was temporarily
reversed. A back-to-the-land movement was officially sanctioned, and a $25 million
appropriation for the establishment of self-sustaining homestead communities, including
some light industry, was written into the National Industrial Recovery Act. The
movement had a strong advocate and pioneer in Ralph Borsodi, who in the 1920s had
left the city with his family and later served as an adviser to a homestead community in
Dayton, Ohio. Borsodi's experiments in rural living were recorded in his book*
Flight from the City *(1933). Chapter One is reprinted below.*

Source: *Flight from the City,* Suffern, N.Y., 1947, pp. 1-17.

n 1920 the Borsodi family — my wife,
two small sons, and myself — lived in a
rented home. We *bought* our food and
clothing and furnishings from retail stores.
We were *dependent* entirely upon my income from a none too certain white-collar
job.

We lived in New York City — the metropolis of the country. We had the opportunity to enjoy the incredible variety of
foodstuffs which pour into that great city
from every corner of the continent; to live
in the most luxurious apartments built to
house men and women in this country; to
use the speedy subways, the smart restau-
rants, the great office buildings, the libraries,
theaters, public schools — all the thousand
and one conveniences which make New
York one of the most fantastic creations in
the history of man. Yet in the truest sense,
we could not enjoy any of them.

How could we enjoy them when we
were financially insecure and never knew
when we might be without a job; when we
lacked the zest of living which comes from
real health and suffered all the minor and

sometimes major ailments which come from
too much excitement, too much artificial
food, too much sedentary work, and too
much of the smoke and noise and dust of
the city; when we had to work just as hard
to get to the places in which we tried to
entertain ourselves as we had to get to the
places in which we worked; when our lives
were barren of real beauty — the beauty
which comes only from contact with nature
and from the growth of the soil, from flowers and fruits, from gardens and trees, from
birds and animals?

We couldn't. Even though we were able
for years and years, like so many others, to
forget the fact — to ignore it amid the host
of distractions which make up city life.

And then in 1920, the year of the great
housing shortage, the house in which we
were living was sold over our heads. New
York in 1920 was no place for a houseless
family. Rents, owing to the shortage of
building which dated back to the World
War, were outrageously high. Evictions
were epidemic — to enable rapacious land-
lords to secure higher rents from new ten-

ants — and most of the renters in the city seemed to be in the courts trying to secure the protection of the Emergency Rent Laws. We had the choice of looking for an equally endurable home in the city, of reading endless numbers of classified advertisements, of visiting countless real-estate agents, of walking weary miles and climbing endless flights of steps in an effort to rent another home, or of flight from the city. And while we were trying to prepare ourselves for the struggle with this typical city problem, we were overcome with longing for the country — for the security, the health, the leisure, the beauty we felt it must be possible to achieve there. Thus we came to make the experiment in living which we had often discussed but which we had postponed time and again because it involved so radical a change in our manner of life.

Instead, therefore, of starting the irritating task of house and apartment hunting, we wrote to real-estate dealers within commuting distance of the city. We asked them for a house which could be readily remodeled; a location near the railroad station because we had no automobile; five to ten acres of land with fruit trees, garden space, pasturage, a woodlot, and, if possible, a brook; a location where electricity was available, and, last but not least, a low purchase price. Even if the place we could afford only barely complied with these specifications, we felt confident that we could achieve economic freedom on it and a degree of comfort we never enjoyed in the city. All the other essentials of the good life, not even excepting schooling for our two sons, we decided we could produce for ourselves if we were unable to buy in a neighborhood which already possessed them.

We finally bought a place located about an hour and three-quarters from the city. It included a small frame house, one and a half stories high, containing not a single modern improvement — there was no plumbing, no running water, no gas, no electricity, no steam heat. There was an old barn and a chicken house which was on the verge of collapse, and a little over seven acres of land. There was a little fruit in the orchard — some apples, cherries, and plums, but of the apples at least there were plenty. . . . Yet "Sevenacres," as we called the place, was large enough for our initial experiment. Four years later we were able to select a more suitable site and begin the building of the sort of home we really wanted.

We began the experiment with three principal assets, courage — foolhardiness, our city friends called it; a vision of what modern methods and modern domestic machinery might be made to do in the way of eliminating drudgery, and the fact that my wife had been born and had lived up to her twelfth year on a ranch in the West. She, at least, had had childhood experience of life in the country.

But we had plenty of liabilities. We had little capital and only a modest salary. We knew nothing about raising vegetables, fruit, and poultry. All these things we had to learn. While I was a handy man, I had hardly ever had occasion to use a hammer and saw (a man working in an office rarely does), and yet if our experiment was to succeed it required that I should make myself a master of all trades. We cut ourselves off from the city comforts to which we had become so accustomed without the countryman's material and spiritual compensations for them.

We went to the country with nothing but our city furniture. We began by adding to this wholly unsuitable equipment for pioneering an electric range. This was the first purchase in the long list of domestic machines with which we proposed to test our theory that it was possible to be more comfortable in the country than in the city, with security, independence, and freedom to do the work to which we aspired thrown in for good measure.

Discomforts were plentiful in the beginning. The hardships of those early years are now fading into a romantic haze, but they were real enough at the time. A family starting with our handicaps had to expect them. But almost from the beginning there were compensations for the discomforts.

Before the end of the first year, the year of the depression of 1921, when millions were tramping the streets of our cities looking for work, we began to enjoy the feeling of plenty which the city dweller never experiences. We cut our hay; gathered our fruit; made gallons and gallons of cider. We had a cow, and produced our own milk and butter, but finally gave her up. By furnishing us twenty quarts of milk a day, she threatened to put us in the dairy business. So we changed to a pair of blooded Swiss goats. We equipped a poultry yard, and had eggs, chickens, and fat roast capons. We ended the year with plenty, not only for our own needs but for a generous hospitality to our friends — some of whom were out of work — a hospitality which, unlike city hospitality, did not involve purchasing everything we served our guests.

To these things which we produced in our first year, we have since added ducks, guineas, and turkeys; bees for honey; pigeons for appearance; and dogs for company. We have in the past twelve years built three houses and a barn from stones picked up on our place; we weave suitings, blankets, carpets, and draperies; we make some of our own clothing; we do all of our own laundry work; we grind flour, cornmeal, and breakfast cereals; we have our own workshops, including a printing plant; and we have a swimming pool, tennis court, and even a billiard room.

In certain important respects our experiment was very different from the ordinary back-to-the-land adventure. We quickly abandoned all efforts to raise anything to sell. After the first year, during which we raised some poultry for the market, this became an inviolable principle. We produced only for our own consumption. If we found it difficult to consume or give away any surplus, we cut down our production of that particular thing and devoted the time to producing something else which we were then buying. We used machinery wherever we could, and tried to apply the most approved scientific methods to small-scale production. We acted on the theory that there was always some way of doing what we wanted to do, if we only sought long enough for the necessary information, and that efficient machinery would pay for itself in the home precisely as it pays for itself in the factory.

The part which domestic machinery has played in making our adventure in homesteading a success cannot be too strongly emphasized. Machinery enabled us to eliminate drudgery; it furnished us skills which we did not possess, and it reduced the costs of production both in terms of money and in terms of labor. Not only do we use machines to pump our water, to do our laundry, to run our refrigerator — we use them to produce food, to produce clothing, to produce shelter.

Some of the machines we have purchased have proved unsatisfactory — something which is to be expected since so little real thought has been devoted by our factory-dominated inventors and engineers to the development of household equipment and domestic machinery. But taking the machines and appliances which we have used as a whole, it is no exaggeration to say that we started our quest of comfort with all the discomforts possible in the country, and, because of the machines, we have now achieved more comforts than the average prosperous city man enjoys.

What we have managed to accomplish is the outcome of nothing but a conscious determination to use machinery for the purpose of eliminating drudgery from the home and to produce for ourselves enough of the essentials of living to free us from the thralldom of our factory-dominated civilization.

What are the social, economic, political, and philosophical implications of such a type of living? What would be the consequence of a widespread transference of production from factories to the home?

If enough families were to make their homes economically productive, cash-crop farmers specializing in one crop would have to abandon farming as a business and go back to it as a way of life. The packinghouses, mills, and canneries, not to mention the railroads, wholesalers, and retailers, which now distribute agricultural products would find their business confined to the production and distribution of exotic foodstuffs. Food is our most important industry. A war of attrition, such as we have been carrying on all alone, if extended on a large enough scale, would put the food industry out of its misery, for miserable it certainly is, all the way from the farmers who produce the raw materials to the men, women, and children who toil in the canneries, mills, and packinghouses, and in addition reduce proportionately the congestion, adulteration, unemployment, and unpleasant odors to all of which the food industry contributes liberally.

If enough families were to make their homes economically productive, the textile and clothing industries, with their low wages, seasonal unemployment, cheap and shoddy products, would shrink to the production of those fabrics and those garments which it is impractical for the average family to produce for itself.

If enough families were to make their homes economically productive, undesirable and nonessential factories of all sorts would disappear and only those which would be desirable and essential, because they would be making tools and machines, electric-light bulbs, iron and copper pipe, wire of all kinds, and the myriad of things which can best be made in factories, would remain to furnish employment to those benighted human beings who prefer to work in factories.

Domestic production, if enough people turned to it, would not only annihilate the undesirable and non-essential factory by depriving it of a market for its products; it would do more. It would release men and women from their present thralldom to the factory and make them masters of machines instead of servants to them; it would end the power of exploiting them which ruthless, acquisitive, and predatory men now possess; it would free them for the conquest of comfort, beauty and understanding.

The dyed-in-the-wool New Yorker professes to hate the city of his adoption. Yet he would not live anywhere else. The furore of its high pressure living gets into the blood. The famous George M. Cohan, the actor, used to carol: "When you are away from old Broadway you are only camping out." That is the New Yorker's credo.

O. O. McINTYRE

51.

Learned Hand: The Judge's Freedom Before the Law

The address reprinted here (originally titled "How Far Is a Judge Free in Rendering a Decision?") was broadcast to the nation over CBS on May 14, 1933. Its author, Judge Learned Hand, was a member of the U.S. Court of Appeals for the Second Circuit (New York, Connecticut, and Vermont), where he became chief judge in 1939. Under his guidance the Court was one of the most respected in the country, and many of his decisions had almost as much authority as those of Supreme Court justices. Judge Hand's conception of the limitations on the judicial function, as expressed in this address, placed him in the same legal tradition as that of his friend and mentor Oliver Wendell Holmes, Jr.

Source: *How Far Is a Judge Free in Rendering a Decision?*, Chicago, 1933, pp. 1-6.

I HAVE CHOSEN as a subject tonight how far a judge is free in rendering a decision, because I know that in many people's minds there is much confusion about it. To some it seems that a judge ought to look to his conscience and follow its dictates; he ought not to be bound by what they call technical rules having no relation to natural right and wrong. Others wish him to observe very strictly what they consider the law, reading it as though it were all to be found in written words, and never departing from the literal meaning. They demand this of him because they say, and rightly, that he ought not to usurp the power of government, and they believe that to exercise his own judgment as to the justice of the cause would be just such a usurpation. I believe that neither side is right, and, although I am afraid that the subject will seem abstract and dry, still it is important, and it is well for us to try to come to some understanding about it. The first thing is to find out what we mean by law.

Legal philosophers have disputed for more than 2,000 years about what law means. Some have thought that it includes the customs or usages which are generally current in a society; others have held that it should be limited to those rules which will be enforced by the government. The question is perhaps one of words, but as I am speaking of civilized modern society, it will be more convenient to use the word in the second sense. Law does not mean then whatever people usually do, or even what they think to be right. Certainly it does not mean what only the most enlightened individuals usually do or think right. It is the conduct which the government, whether it is a king or a popular assembly, will compel individuals to conform to, or to which it will at least provide forcible means to secure conformity. If this is true, there must be some way to learn what is this conduct. The law is the command of the government, and it must be ascertainable in some form if it is to be enforced at all.

The only way in which its will can be put is in words, and in modern and civilized societies these are always written. They are in the form of statutes enacted formally, or they are in books which report what has been decided before by judges whom the government gave power to decide. There is no inevitable reason why that should be law which has been decided before, and in many countries this is not true. But it is true in ours, as it is in most countries which Englishmen settled and where English speech prevails. Perhaps it ought not to be, but it is. In all civilized, and for that matter in practically all uncivilized, countries, there are judges who are charged with the duty of saying what the law means, that is, what the government has in fact commanded. When these judges have spoken, the force behind the law will be used.

It seems a simple matter, especially when the law is written down in a book with care and detail, just to read it and say what is its meaning. Perhaps this could be made as easy as it seems if the law used language coined expressly for its purposes, like science or mathematics or music. But that would be practically undesirable, because while the government's commands are to be always obeyed, still they should include only what is generally accepted as just or convenient or usual, and should be stated in terms of common speech, so that they may be understood by those who must obey and may not appear foreign to their notions of good or sensible conduct. Besides, even if the law had a language of its own, it could not provide for all situations which might come up.

Nobody is so gifted with foresight that he can divine all possible human events in advance and prescribe the proper rule for each. Take, for example, a collision between two motorcars. There is no way of saying beforehand exactly what each driver should do or should not until all the circumstances of the particular case are known. The law leaves this open with the vague command to each that he shall be careful. What being

careful means, it does not try to say; it leaves that to the judge, who happens in this case to be a jury of twelve persons, untrained in the law. That is a case where the appeal is almost entirely to the conscience of the tribunal.

The judge must therefore find out the will of the government from words which are chosen from common speech and which had better not attempt to provide for every possible contingency. How does he in fact proceed? Although at times he says and believes that he is not doing so, what he really does is to take the language before him, whether it be from a statute or from the decision of a former judge, and try to find out what the government, or his predecessor, would have done if the case before him had been before them. He calls this finding the intent of the statute or of the doctrine.

This is often not really true. The men who used the language did not have any intent at all about the case that has come up; it had not occurred to their minds. Strictly speaking, it is impossible to know what they would have said about it, if it had. All they have done is to write down certain words which they mean to apply generally to situations of that kind. To apply these literally may either pervert what was plainly their general meaning, or leave undisposed of what there is every reason to suppose they meant to provide for. Thus, it is not enough for the judge just to use a dictionary. If he should do no more, he might come out with a result which every sensible man would recognize to be quite the opposite of what was really intended; which would contradict or leave unfulfilled its plain purpose.

Thus, on the one hand, he cannot go beyond what has been said because he is bound to enforce existing commands and only those; on the other, he cannot suppose that what has been said should clearly frustrate or leave unexecuted its own purpose. This is his frequent position in cases that are not very plain; that is to say, in the greater number that arise. As I have said, there are two extreme schools, neither one of which is really willing to apply its theory consistently, usually applying it when its interests lie along the path it advocates.

One school says that the judge must follow the letter of the law absolutely. I call this the dictionary school. No matter what the result is, he must read the words in their usual meaning and stop where they stop. No judges have ever carried on literally in that spirit, and they would not be long tolerated if they did. Nobody would in fact condemn the surgeon who bled a man in the street to cure him because there was a law against drawing blood in the streets. Everyone would say that the law was only meant to prevent street fighting and was not intended to cover such a case; that is, that the government which passed that law, although literally it used words which covered the case, did not in fact forbid necessary assistance to sick people. An obviously absurd extreme of that school was where a guilty man escaped because the indictment left out the word "the," alleging that what he did was "against the peace of state," instead of "against the peace of *the* state." The statute had said that to convict a man the indictment must read like that, but the statute did not mean every syllable it contained.

It is easy to seize on such instances and say that judges are always too literal and that what is needed are men of more common sense. Men of common sense are always needed, and judges are by no means always men of common sense. They are quite like the rest of us. But it is also easy to go wrong if one gives them too much latitude. The other school would give them almost complete latitude. They argue that a judge should not regard the law; that this has never really been done in the past, and that to attempt ever to do it is an illusion.

He must conform his decision to what honest men would think right, and it is better for him to look into his own heart to find out what that is.

As I have already said, in a small way some such process is inevitable when one is interpreting any written words. When a judge tries to find out what the government would have intended which it did not say, he puts into its mouth things which he thinks it ought to have said, and that is very close to substituting what he himself thinks right. Let him beware, however, or he will usurp the office of government, even though in a small way he must do so in order to execute its real commands at all.

In our country we have always been extremely jealous of mixing the different processes of government, especially that of making law, with that of saying what it is after it has been made. This distinction, if I am right, cannot be rigidly enforced; but like most of those ideas, which the men who made our constitutions believed in, it has a very sound basis as a guide, provided one does not try to make it into an absolute rule, like driving to the right. They wanted to have a government by the people, and they believed that the only way they could do it was by giving the power to make laws to assemblies which the people chose, directly or at second hand. They believed that such assemblies would express the common will of the people who were to rule.

Never mind what they thought that common will was; it is not so simple as it seems to learn just what they did mean by it, or what anybody can mean. It is enough that they did not mean by it what any one individual, whether or not he was a judge, should think right and proper. They might have made the judge the mouthpiece of the common will, finding it out by his contacts with people generally; but he would then have been ruler, like the Judges of Israel. Still, they had to leave him scope in which he in a limited sense does act as if he were the government, because, as we have seen, he cannot otherwise do what he is required to do. So far they had to confuse lawmaking with law interpreting.

But the judge must always remember that he should go no further than he is sure the government would have gone had it been faced with the case before him. If he is in doubt, he must stop, for he cannot tell that the conflicting interests in the society for which he speaks would have come to a just result, even though he is sure that he knows what the just result should be. He is not to substitute even his juster will for theirs; otherwise it would not be the common will which prevails, and to that extent the people would not govern.

So you will see that a judge is in a contradictory position; he is pulled by two opposite forces. On the one hand, he must not enforce whatever he thinks best; he must leave that to the common will expressed by the government. On the other, he must try as best he can to put into concrete form what that will is, not by slavishly following the words but by trying honestly to say what was the underlying purpose expressed. Nobody does this exactly right; great judges do it better than the rest of us.

It is necessary that someone shall do it if we are to realize the hope that we can collectively rule ourselves. And so, while it is proper that people should find fault when their judges fail, it is only reasonable that they should recognize the difficulties. Perhaps it is also fair to ask that before the judges are blamed they shall be given credit of having tried to do their best. Let them be severely brought to book, when they go wrong, but by those who will take the trouble to understand.

52.

John M. Woolsey: *U.S.* v. *One Book Called* Ulysses

James Joyce's masterpiece, Ulysses, *had been published in Paris in 1922, but its importation into the United States had been banned under the Tariff Act of 1890, which authorized customs officials to confiscate "obscene" books. Joyce's New York publishers sued to have the ban lifted, and in a landmark decision in 1933 Judge John M. Woolsey upheld their plea. The decision, reprinted here, is notable for the clarity with which it defines obscenity in literary works — and also for the healthy respect expressed by Judge Woolsey for the maturity of the American reading public. The decision was handed down in the U.S. District Court (New York) on December 6.*

Source: 5 F. Supp. 182.

The motion for a decree dismissing the libel herein is granted, and, consequently, of course, the government's motion for a decree of forfeiture and destruction is denied.

Accordingly, a decree dismissing the libel without costs may be entered herein.

I. The practice followed in this case is in accordance with the suggestion made by me in the case of *United States* v. *One Book, Entitled "Contraception"* (D.C.) 51 F. (2d) 525, and is as follows:

After issue was joined by the filing of the

claimant's answer to the libel for forfeiture against *Ulysses*, a stipulation was made between the United States Attorney's office and the attorneys for the claimant providing:

1. That the book *Ulysses* should be deemed to have been annexed to and to have become part of the libel just as if it had been incorporated in its entirety therein.

2. That the parties waived their right to a trial by jury.

3. That each party agreed to move for decree in its favor.

4. That on such cross-motions the court might decide all the questions of law and fact involved and render a general finding thereon.

5. That on the decision of such motions the decree of the court might be entered as if it were a decree after trial.

It seems to me that a procedure of this kind is highly appropriate in libels such as this for the confiscation of books. It is an especially advantageous procedure in the instant case because, on account of the length of *Ulysses* and the difficulty of reading it, a jury trial would have been an extremely unsatisfactory, if not an almost impossible method of dealing with it.

II. I have read *Ulysses* once in its entirety and I have read those passages of which the government particularly complains several times. In fact, for many weeks, my spare time has been devoted to the consideration of the decision which my duty would require me to make in this matter.

Ulysses is not an easy book to read or to understand. But there has been much written about it, and in order properly to approach the consideration of it it is advisable to read a number of other books which have now become its satellites. The study of *Ulysses* is, therefore, a heavy task.

III. The reputation of *Ulysses* in the literary world, however, warranted my taking such time as was necessary to enable me to satisfy myself as to the intent with which the book was written, for, of course, in any case where a book is claimed to be obscene it must first be determined whether the intent with which it was written was what is called, according to the usual phrase, "pornographic," that is, written for the purpose of exploiting obscenity.

If the conclusion is that the book is pornographic, that is the end of the inquiry and forfeiture must follow. But in *Ulysses*, in spite of its unusual frankness, I do not detect anywhere the leer of the sensualist. I hold, therefore, that it is not pornographic.

IV. In writing *Ulysses*, Joyce sought to make a serious experiment in a new, if not wholly novel, literary genre. He takes persons of the lower middle class living in Dublin in 1904 and seeks, not only to describe what they did on a certain day early in June of that year as they went about the city bent on their usual occupations but also to tell what many of them thought about the while.

Joyce has attempted — it seems to me, with astonishing success — to show how the screen of consciousness with its ever-shifting kaleidoscopic impressions carries, as it were on a plastic palimpsest, not only what is in the focus of each man's observation of the actual things about him but also in a penumbral zone residua of past impressions, some recent and some drawn up by association from the domain of the subconscious. He shows how each of these impressions affects the life and behavior of the character which he is describing.

What he seeks to get is not unlike the result of a double or, if that is possible, a multiple exposure on a cinema film, which would give a clear foreground with a background visible but somewhat blurred and out of focus in varying degrees.

To convey by words an effect which obviously lends itself more appropriately to a graphic technique, accounts, it seems to me, for much of the obscurity which meets a reader of *Ulysses*. And it also explains another aspect of the book, which I have further to consider, namely, Joyce's sincerity and his honest effort to show exactly how the minds of his characters operate.

If Joyce did not attempt to be honest in developing the technique which he has adopted in *Ulysses*, the result would be psychologically misleading and thus unfaithful to his chosen technique. Such an attitude would be artistically inexcusable.

It is because Joyce has been loyal to his technique and has not funked its necessary implications, but has honestly attempted to tell fully what his characters think about, that he has been the subject of so many attacks and that his purpose has been so often misunderstood and misrepresented. For his attempt sincerely and honestly to realize his objective has required him incidentally to use certain words which are generally considered dirty words and has led at times to what many think is a too poignant preoccupation with sex in the thoughts of his characters.

The words which are criticized as dirty are old Saxon words known to almost all men and, I venture, to many women, and are such words as would be naturally and habitually used, I believe, by the types of folk whose life, physical and mental, Joyce is seeking to describe. In respect of the recurrent emergence of the theme of sex in the minds of his characters, it must always be remembered that his locale was Celtic and his season spring.

Whether or not one enjoys such a technique as Joyce uses is a matter of taste on which disagreement or argument is futile, but to subject that technique to the standards of some other technique seems to me to be little short of absurd. Accordingly, I hold that *Ulysses* is a sincere and honest book, and I think that the criticisms of it are entirely disposed of by its rationale.

V. Furthermore, *Ulysses* is an amazing *tour de force* when one considers the success which has been in the main achieved with such a difficult objective as Joyce set for himself. As I have stated, *Ulysses* is not an easy book to read. It is brilliant and dull, intelligible and obscure, by turns. In many places it seems to me to be disgusting, but although it contains, as I have mentioned above, many words usually considered dirty, I have not found anything that I consider to be dirt for dirt's sake. Each word of the book contributes like a bit of mosaic to the detail of the picture which Joyce is seeking to construct for his readers.

If one does not wish to associate with such folk as Joyce describes, that is one's own choice. In order to avoid indirect contact with them, one may not wish to read *Ulysses*; that is quite understandable. But when such a great artist in words, as Joyce undoubtedly is, seeks to draw a true picture of the lower middle class in a European city, ought it to be impossible for the American public legally to see that picture?

To answer this question it is not sufficient merely to find, as I have found above, that Joyce did not write *Ulysses* with what is commonly called pornographic intent, I must endeavor to apply a more objective standard to his book in order to determine its effect in the result, irrespective of the intent with which it was written.

VI. The statute under which the libel is filed only denounces, insofar as we are here concerned, the importation into the United States from any foreign country of "any obscene book." Section 305 of the Tariff Act of 1930, Title 19 United States Code, Section 1305 (19 USCA, Section 1305). It does not marshal against books the spectrum of condemnatory adjectives found, commonly, in laws dealing with matters of this kind. I am, therefore, only required to determine whether *Ulysses* is obscene within the legal definition of that word.

The meaning of the word "obscene" as legally defined by the courts is: Tending to stir the sex impulses or to lead to sexually impure and lustful thoughts. . . . Whether a particular book would tend to excite such impulses and thoughts must be tested by the court's opinion as to its effect on a person with average sex instincts — what the French would call *l'homme moyen sensuel* — who plays, in this branch of legal inquiry, the same role of hypothetical reagent as does the "reasonable man" in the law of torts and "the man learned in the art" on questions of invention in patent law.

The risk involved in the use of such a reagent arises from the inherent tendency of the trier of facts, however fair he may intend to be, to make his reagent too much subservient to his own idiosyncrasies. Here, I have attempted to avoid this, if possible, and to make my reagent herein more objective than he might otherwise be, by adopting the following course:

After I had made my decision in regard to the aspect of *Ulysses,* now under consideration, I checked my impressions with two friends of mine who in my opinion answered to the above-stated requirement for my reagent. These literary assessors — as I might properly describe them — were called on separately, and neither knew that I was consulting the other. They are men whose opinion on literature and on life I value most highly. They had both read *Ulysses,* and, of course, were wholly unconnected with this cause.

Without letting either of my assessors know what my decision was, I gave to each of them the legal definition of obscene and asked each whether in his opinion *Ulysses* was obscene within that definition. I was interested to find that they both agreed with my opinion: That reading *Ulysses* in its entirety, as a book must be read on such a test as this, did not tend to excite sexual impulses or lustful thoughts, but that its net effect on them was only that of a somewhat tragic and very powerful commentary on the inner lives of men and women.

It is only with the normal person that the law is concerned. Such a test as I have described, therefore, is the only proper test of obscenity in the case of a book like *Ulysses* which is a sincere and serious attempt to devise a new literary method for the observation and description of mankind.

I am quite aware that owing to some of its scenes *Ulysses* is a rather strong draft to ask some sensitive, though normal, persons to take. But my considered opinion, after long reflection, is that, while in many places the effect of *Ulysses* on the reader undoubtedly is somewhat emetic, nowhere does it tend to be an aphrodisiac.

Ulysses may, therefore, be admitted into the United States.

Literature is news that stays news.

EZRA POUND, *How to Read*

53.

E. B. White: "I Paint What I See"

*Rockefeller Center, a complex of business buildings constructed during the 1930s
on cleared slumlands in New York City, was designed as a unit and was considered
a model of modern urban planning. The buildings were lavishly decorated, and
Diego Rivera, the radical Mexican painter, was commissioned to do a mural for one
of the lobbies. Rivera was already the subject of controversy owing to a mural
painted in 1932 for the Detroit Institute of Fine Arts, and his mural for Rockefeller
Center, titled "Man at the Crossroads," got him into even deeper water. The main
trouble was that it included a portrait of Lenin, which, combined with the fact that
during the Depression years it was hard to rent the finished offices, strained the
relations between Rivera and the Rockefeller family. E. B. White's poem, reprinted
here, describes the dispute as it manifested itself during 1933; but in fact White's
last stanza is somewhat optimistic, for the mural was eventually removed and
reconstituted at the Palace of Fine Arts in Mexico City. Rockefeller Center was
filled to capacity after the war broke out in Europe in 1939.*

Source: *The Fox of Peapack*, New York, 1933.

I PAINT WHAT I SEE

A Ballad of Artistic Integrity

"What do you paint, when you paint a
      wall?"
    Said John D.'s grandson Nelson.
"Do you paint just anything there at all?
"Will there be any doves, or a tree in fall?
"Or a hunting scene, like an English hall?"

      "I paint what I see," said Rivera.

"What are the colors you use when you
      paint?"
    Said John D.'s grandson Nelson.
"Do you use any red in the beard of a
      saint?
"If you do, is it terribly red, or faint?
"Do you use any blue? Is it Prussian?"

      "I paint what I paint," said Rivera.

"Whose is that head that I see on my
      wall?"
    Said John D.'s grandson Nelson.
"Is it anyone's head whom we know, at all?
"A Rensselaer, or a Saltonstall?
"Is it Franklin D.? Is it Mordaunt Hall?
"Or is it the head of a Russian?"

      "I paint what I think," said Rivera.

*"I paint what I paint, I paint what I see,
    "I paint what I think," said Rivera,
"And the thing that is dearest in life to me
"In a bourgeois hall is Integrity;
    "However . . .
"I'll take out a couple of people drinkin'
"And put in a picture of Abraham Lincoln,
"I could even give you McCormick's reaper
"And still not make my art much cheaper.
"But the head of Lenin has got to stay
"Or my friends will give me the bird today
"The bird, the bird, forever."*

"It's not good taste in a man like me,"
  Said John D.'s grandson Nelson,
"To question an artist's integrity
"Or mention a practical thing like a fee,
"But I know what I like to a large degree
  "Though art I hate to hamper;
"For twenty-one thousand conservative bucks
"You painted a radical. I say shucks,
  "I never could rent the offices —

"The capitalistic offices.
"For this, as you know, is a public hall
"And people want doves, or a tree in fall,
"And though your art I dislike to hamper,
"I owe a *little* to God and Gramper,
  "And after all,
  "It's *my* wall . . ."

    "We'll see if it is," said Rivera.

54.

Robert Morss Lovett: A Century of Progress?

*Forty years after the World's Columbian Exposition that had celebrated (in 1893) the
400th anniversary of the discovery of America, Chicago threw open its doors
to a second international exposition, "A Century of Progress," celebrating the
centennial of the incorporation of the city in 1833. The new world's fair came at a
difficult time not only for the nation but also for Chicago, which, along with its
pressing economic troubles, had a reputation for organized crime, official corruption,
racketeering, and gang wars. Its glittering Midway may have made some difference
in the city's "image," but the fair's promise — or pretense — of prosperity "just
around the corner" came in for a good deal of criticism. The title of the fair itself
led commentators to speculate on the history of those eventful hundred years, and to
ask, as Robert Morss Lovett did in the article of which a portion is reprinted here,
whether much progress had really been made since 1833.*

Source: *Current History*, January 1934: "Progress — Chicago Style."

The century of Chicago's history is divided by events of which the two world's fairs are not the least significant. The Columbian Exposition marked the close of a period during which the city retained some of the aspects of a frontier boom town, a period of speculation and sporting, of easy money, easy manners, easy morals. The fair of 1893 was part of a concerted movement toward what was vaguely called culture, of which the Chicago Symphony Orchestra, the Art Institute, the university, and the architectural genius which brought forth the Auditorium, the Monadnock, and the Field

wholesale building were evidence. American humor made merry with the theme of Chicago's energetic pursuit of culture, but the achievement was nevertheless real. In other respects the transition from an overgrown Western village to a modern metropolis was less fortunate. In both characters Chicago showed its usual tendency toward exaggeration. . . .

Among many aspects of progress presented, that in the use of propaganda was the one most fully illustrated by the [1933] fair and its concessions. The architecture was the first great advertisement. If it was the purpose of the architects to make the fair talked about, they succeeded. Visitors entering the city by the Illinois Central were intrigued by the grotesque shapes and crude colors of the buildings rising from shore and islands drawn up by sand suckers from the bottom of the lake. No greater contrast can be imagined than that between the chaste, classical architectural forms, white as Greek statues, of the fair of 1893 and the violently cubistic structures in the motley colors of the clown which were their successors.

The contrast is significant of a change in civilization. Culture was the ambition of the late nineteenth century, a pursuit of perfection by seeking the best that had been done in the world, which led to a concept of classical unity. Technology has replaced culture as the motive of the present century. . . .

The central theme of the [1933] exposition was the growth of science and its application to industry and the arts of life. The development of the basic sciences — mathematics, physics, chemistry — was skillfully shown. Among the applications of science, chief emphasis was laid upon communication — the telephone, radio, the timid beginnings of television, the ocean liner, the railroad, the automobile. In striking contrast to these technical marvels, however, the most popular exhibit was that illustrating the human reproductive process — a series of jars in which were shown specimens of the human embryo in various stages of development. Guards in the Hall of Science stated that more people asked to be directed to this exhibit than to any other, and that at least four out of five visitors saw it in spite of the small space, which necessitated tedious waiting in line. Supplementing this were the exhibits of the Mayo Institute illustrating the progress of medicine and surgery, and the dental exhibits. The attention given these seemed to point to an obscure recognition of the fact that

life is more than meat and the body more than that which sustains it.

The chief disappointment in connection with the fair as a record of progress lay in the obscuring of this cardinal truth. Fundamental to civilization, the most important exhibit was a huge diorama which portrayed the gathering of water into reservoirs, whence streams issued to spin turbines and set a current racing across the country to light farms, mines, and quarries, to move trains, and awaken to life cities with their homes, skyscrapers, stores, and factories. It exemplified the enormous difference between the machine age and the power age, between the industrial revolution and the technological. It reminded one that the machine by itself is a tool, an extension of the human hand, and that the possession of power in cheap and accessible form makes possible the unlimited exercise of human ingenuity to convert this machine into a thing of independent life, automatic, self-regulating, self-renewing. One wondered how many of the spectators who gazed on this exhibit saw its anticipation of a time when the functional need for man would be as limited as that for the horse, and their present lives as meaningless. The basic theme of the fair as expressed officially was "the achievements of science and their application through industry to the creation of a larger life for mankind." The achievements of science were there in abundance, and their applications; but where, one was moved to ask, was the evidence of the larger life for mankind, or even the promise of it? . . .

If the progress here claimed for social science seemed at times illusory, the lack of vision toward the society of the future was even more marked. That this society will be obliged to take account of more than one class is evident, but so far as the social exhibits of the Century of Progress were conceived, the working class might not exist. A conspicuous omission was in the matter of popular housing. There were examples of houses of steel, of glass, of concrete, but none of model tenements. There were hundreds of appliances for household comfort, all of them beyond the means of the poor. The fair appealed largely to the middle class, and its exhibits emphasized the technical progress from which this class has gained so much in comfort and spiritual satisfaction. In this rendering of the century of progress, the problem of poverty did not exist. . . .

A conspicuous lapse from progress appeared in the amusements offered to a public which must address itself in the future to the problem of the use of leisure. Nothing more pitifully banal could be imagined than the sideshows of the Midway. There was the old Battle of Gettysburg, and a new Pantheon glorifying the recent World War and the statesmen and soldiers who directed it. There was Ripley's Odditorium with our old friends the ossified man, the Negro who crams four golf balls into his mouth, the armless wonder who shaves himself with his toes. The chief source of entertainment, however, was the female form. In the Streets of Paris it was shown under water, diminished to inches by a clever arrangement of mirrors, and again through the pretense of a sketching class, the audience being perfunctorily supplied with pencils and paper.

The most notorious of all nudities was procured by means of the fan dance. This was a novelty in Earl Carroll's Vanities some years ago, revived for this occasion by Faith Bacon. It was an experience to sit in the great auditorium of the concession labeled Hollywood, among an audience of perfectly respectable Middle Western, middle-class, middle-aged people, all palpitating for the divine moment when the two fans were held aloft and the naked body was fully revealed. No one could deny the beauty of the spectacle, but one doubted whether the audience was entirely composed of beauty seekers. The dance was reproduced at the Streets of Paris by one Sally Rand, whose arrest, trial, and sentence to a year's imprisonment was the chief publicity stunt pulled during the entire exposition. Soon, every dancing show had its fan dance, and the language of the barkers inviting the public to witness it became luridly vulgar. . . .

The name "Century of Progress" committed the sponsors of the enterprise to an idealistic interpretation of the world. It was not their fault that they were in a measure betrayed by events, nor can they be blamed for putting the best face possible upon the matter. Nevertheless, the total effect of the fair was to raise more insistently the question — progress toward what? If the accelerated advance of technology, the increase of control over natural forces, is to lead to nothing better than a civilization of which the highest aspect is to be found in material comfort for a class which can afford it, and the lowest in the crass vulgarity of its recreations, it may be doubted whether the triumph was worth celebrating. The enormous irony of the Century of Progress was to be appreciated in the unescapable contrast between the combination of natural beauty of lake, island, lagoons, with lavish architectural decoration and brilliant illumination, against the imposing skyline of the city's facade and the sordid background of civic life in which official corruption was never more arrogant nor human misery more appalling. Spengler would surely have found here an instance of the fantastic exhibitionism with which civilizations are prone to bear witness to their decline.

It's easy to build a philosophy. It doesn't have to run.
CHARLES F. KETTERING

1934

55.

Abrogation of the Platt Amendment

*In the treaty with Cuba of May 29, 1934, that part of the so-called Platt Amendment of
1903 that gave the United States the right to intervene in Cuba's internal affairs was
abrogated, but the right to retain a naval station at Guantánamo Bay was, significantly,
retained. The new agreement was reached with the government of Carlos Mendieta
that had come to power with the indirect aid of the Roosevelt administration, after
a protracted Cuban revolution. The treaty was in keeping both with the avowed aims
of Roosevelt's Good Neighbor Policy and a declaration, drawn up at the Seventh
International Conference of American States on December 26, 1933, that no state has
the right to intervene in the internal or external affairs of another. The five articles
of the treaty are reprinted here.*

Source: *Statutes*, XLVIII, Pt. 2, pp. 1682-1684.

ARTICLE I

The Treaty of Relations which was concluded between the two contracting parties
on May 22, 1903, shall cease to be in force,
and is abrogated from the date on which
the present Treaty goes into effect.

ARTICLE II

All the acts effected in Cuba by the
United States of America during its military
occupation of the island, up to May 20,
1902, the date on which the Republic of
Cuba was established, have been ratified
and held as valid; and all the rights legally
acquired by virtue of those acts shall be
maintained and protected.

ARTICLE III

Until the two contracting parties agree to
the modification or abrogation of the stipulations of the agreement in regard to the
lease to the United States of America of
lands in Cuba for coaling and naval stations
signed by the president of the Republic of
Cuba on February 16, 1903, and by the
President of the United States of America
on the 23rd day of the same month and
year, the stipulations of that agreement with
regard to the naval station of Guantánamo
shall continue in effect. The supplementary
agreement in regard to naval or coaling stations signed between the two governments
on July 2, 1903, also shall continue in effect
in the same form and on the same condi-

tions with respect to the naval station of Guantánamo. So long as the United States of America shall not abandon the said naval station of Guantánamo or the two governments shall not agree to a modification of its present limits, the station shall continue to have the territorial area that it now has, with the limits that it has on the date of the signature of the present Treaty.

ARTICLE IV

If at any time in the future a situation should arise that appears to point to an outbreak of contagious disease in the territory of either of the contracting parties, either of the two governments shall, for its own protection, and without its act being considered unfriendly, exercise freely and at its discretion the right to suspend communications between those of its ports that it may designate and all or part of the territory of the other party, and for the period that it may consider to be advisable.

ARTICLE V

The present Treaty shall be ratified by the contracting parties in accordance with their respective constitutional methods; and shall go into effect on the date of the exchange of their ratifications, which shall take place in the city of Washington as soon as possible.

56.

WALTER LIPPMANN: The Limits of Self-Reliance

The illusions of the past died hard, even in the Depression. One still heard talk of the essential vitality of laissez faire capitalism and of the spirit of individualism. In the following newspaper column, Walter Lippmann dealt with the myth of the self-reliant farmer in an age of industrial technology and worldwide commerce. The column was published on June 5, 1934.

Source: *The Essential Lippmann,* Clinton Rossiter and James Lare, eds., New York, 1963, pp. 145-146.

WHILE NO ONE WILL GRUDGE RELIEF in the emergency, the question is bound to be raised in many minds as to how far the government can and should go in assuming the burdens caused by natural and by man-made calamities. The traditional view is, of course, that farmers must take the weather as it comes; relying not at all upon government devices, they become the self-reliant, independent stock from which the nation renews its vitality. In this view a paternalistic policy for the farmer is undesirable, not so much because it costs money but because it softens him as an individual.

There are few persons who would not feel that, while there is something in this view, it is infected with a kind of moral blindness. Is the modern American farmer the same kind of farmer around whom there has grown the ideal of complete self-reliance? The traditional view is an ancient one based upon the experience of farmers working their own land for their own needs and for a neighboring community. But the wheat farmer in the Dakotas and Kansas and Nebraska does not live that kind of life. He produces for a world market and he supplies his own needs out of a world market. He is no longer even approximately self-sufficient. Can he then be expected to be wholly self-reliant?

In earlier days if his crop was bad, he suffered and accepted his lot. But today if his crop is bad, his competitor in another region makes a big profit. In earlier days, because he supplied his principal needs at home or in the neighborhood, his standard of life was relatively independent of the consequences of political and economic policies. Today, his real income fluctuates spectacularly due to causes which he cannot control by his own prudence, thrift, or industry.

These are the underlying reasons why we now recognize that to protect the farmer against great natural calamities or economic convulsions is a social duty. If he is to be self-reliant, he must be more or less self-sufficient; insofar as he is not, he must either be led back to self-sufficiency or insured against those forces of nature and of society which self-reliance alone cannot deal with.

The difficult aspect of the matter is to know where to draw the line and then to have the political courage to draw it. The farmer, being only human, will expect more protection than society can afford or than he is really entitled to have. But the rule which ought to govern in these affairs is reasonably clear, however hard it may be to apply it in many particular cases. Taking into consideration its resources in the light of its obligations to other groups in the nation, society ought to attempt to insure men against those risks which a reasonably prudent man cannot be expected to avert or to deal with singlehanded. . . .

If the virtues and values of individualism and self-reliance are to be preserved, we must not put upon the individual person burdens that are greater than he can by self-reliance carry. This is the surest way to kill individualism: by making it intolerable. In the misery of the past few years the individual burden has been greater than individuals could carry. That is why the very word "individualism," though it is the name of a noble conception of life, has suddenly fallen into such disrepute. To restore men's faith in it, and all that it means in the preservation of liberty and of the free growth of the human spirit, individualism has to be made safe for reasonably prudent men.

For that reason it can be said that those who are laboring to distribute justly the social risks of our immensely complicated society are the true defenders of individual liberty against the diseases of paternalism and the dangers of tyranny.

It may be that the race is not always to the swift, nor the battle to the strong — but that's the way to bet. Nothing between humans is one to three. In fact, I long ago came to the conclusion that all life is six to five against.
DAMON RUNYON

Dorothea Lange · Library of Congress

FROM RELIEF TO WAR

As the Thirties advanced, international problems slowly diverted attention from the domestic New Deal policies that had been the center of attraction — and of phobic reaction — since 1932. Predictably, Roosevelt's foreign policy ideas drew sharp criticism from several directions, often from the same sources responsible for the less rational attacks on the New Deal. The Congress was not so pliable on matters of foreign policy as it had been on domestic matters, and, considering America's participation in World War I to have been a mistake

caused by an insistence on neutrality rights and freedom of the seas, it attempted to stave off another war by taking a strong isolationist stand. The three neutrality acts passed between 1935 and 1937 stood directly in the way of the aid needed by China, Britain, and France. The acts were first circumvented, as in the case of the non-war between Japan and China, and finally repealed when the near-desperation of Britain and France required immediate action. The resulting minimal cash-and-carry policy held until 1940.

Brown Brothers

Brown Brothers

(Above) "Now Comes the Hard Part of the Act!"; cartoon by Gale in the Los Angeles "Times" in 1933. (Left) Roosevelt (seated right) reading returns on election night, 1932, with his campaign manager James Farley (seated left) and Louis McHenry Howe, close adviser to the President

(Left) Nancy Cook and Mrs. Roosevelt tack sign to the door of their shop in support of the National Recovery Administration's program; (below) Harry Hopkins and Harold Ickes at a conference on the relief problem, 1933

UPI—Compix

UPI—Compix

The unified governmental attack on laissez faire capitalism that the New Deal represented was simply a broad, rational articulation of the trend begun by the Interstate Commerce Act of 1887. The year 1935 is often taken as a turning point between a "first" and a "second" New Deal; the NRA and the AAA were voided by the Supreme Court in 1935-36, and the emphasis in government action turned from immediate relief to long-term planning and security. New Deal economic supervision merged into the demand for planning that was to be made by World War II.

(Top) Men working on a Civil Works Administration project in Central Park Zoo, New York City. Roosevelt created the CWA in the winter of 1933-34 to provide an immediate relief program until the Public Works Administration was in operation. (Center) Frances Perkins, secretary of labor under Roosevelt and the first woman to serve in the Cabinet. (Bottom) Strikers battling police in Toledo, Ohio, during labor unrest of 1934

(Above) German President Paul von Hindenburg being greeted at the Tannenberg Festival. Behind him on the right are Hitler and Goering. (Below) Hitler participating in a Nazi parade in Munich

Demonstration by Hitler youth spelling "Saar," one of Hitler's first territorial demands

(Bottom left) Anthony Eden and John Simon meet with Hitler in 1935; (below) Nazi troops reoccupy Dusseldorf in the Rhineland in 1936

Hitler and his Fascist cohorts gained their strength from three major sources: the inequities of Versailles, the general and almost frantic desire of most nations to avoid war, and the nearly total breakdown of international cooperation. The failure of Britain, France, and the U.S. to oppose consistently Fascist expansion lost the Rhineland, Austria, Czechoslovakia, Ethiopia, Albania, and Spain. Only the Russo-German Pact and the subsequent partition of Poland solidified the Allied stand.

Japanese machine-gunners set up their guns on the top of a building in a Chinese city

GR-R-R-R-R-R-R!

WOOF

HE'S ONE
OF THE
FIERCEST
WATCH-DOGS
IN THE
NEIGHBORHOOD -

LEAGUE
OF
NATIONS

— UNTIL DANGER
COMES AROUND.

LEAGUE
ACTION

MANCHURIAN
WAR
DANGER

(Above) "A Peculiar Breed"; anti-League of Nations cartoon by Orr in the Chicago "Tribune," 1931;
(below) Japanese troops entering Peiping in 1937

Ethiopian cavalry preparing for action against the Italian army in the summer of 1935

Hitler and Mussolini had been greatly encouraged by Japan's successful flouting of the League of Nations and of numerous treaties. On a flimsy pretext, Japanese forces had occupied Manchuria in 1931-32 and set up the puppet state of Manchoukuo. The League's total inability to deal with the situation served to promote further aggression in both Asia and Europe. Japan proceeded against China in 1937, and then moved on into Indochina and the Malay Peninsula. The Russo-German Pact further bolstered Japan's confident drive to establish exclusive hegemony in Asia, while Japanese actions diverted attention from much of the maneuvering of the European Axis.

(Right) Haile Selassie at the League of Nations; **(below)** victorious Italian troops in Ethiopia

(Above) Rally in Madison Square Garden, New York, attended by 20,000 Nazi sympathizers in 1934

(Below left) "A Knot-Hole View"; cartoon by Cassel in the Brooklyn "Daily Eagle"; (below right) isolationist Senators William Borah and Hiram Johnson, who kept America out of the World Court, 1935

THE LEAGUE OF NATION'S
BATTLE FOR LIFE

The Red Scare of 1920 had long since died down, but the potential for a recurrence of this peculiarly American phobia remained. The liberalism of the New Deal incurred the consistent wrath of professionals like William Randolph Hearst, and there was some concern among the more stolidly right-wing Congressmen over the leading edge of New Dealism. Exclusion and deportation bills were introduced but defeated. In 1938 a Special Committee to Investigate Un-American Activities was established under Representative Martin Dies of Texas; though it looked into Fascist activities to some degree, the committee's primary interest was Communist subversion.

(Top) American Inquiry Commission, headed by Clarence Darrow, hears testimony about the build-up of concentration camps in Nazi Germany in 1934; (center) cartoon in "The Washington Star." In 1938, an election year, Roosevelt's dislike for the Dies Committee led him to issue a public criticism when the committee implied that Communist sympathies were the basis for Governor Murphy's liberal attitude toward Michigan's labor movement; (bottom) protest meeting by 10,000 Communists in Union Square, New York

Alf Landon, Republican candidate for President, campaigning in Springfield, Ill., in 1936

Dissatisfaction with Roosevelt's policies in 1937 is shown by these cartoons: (Below) "Ominous Rumblings in Old Vesuvius" by Lewis in the "Milwaukee Journal"; (right) "To Furnish the Supreme Court Practical Assistance" by Elderman

Left) "What Helps Business Helps You"; (right)
Lewis addresses textile workers; (center) Stickle and
Reuther, beaten by anti-union Ford workers; (bot-
tom) Chicago police battle strikers in 1937

Organized labor, which had faltered during prosperity, was revitalized by the Depression. Led by John L. Lewis and others, the
Committee for Industrial Organization was
formed in 1935 within the somnolent AF of L
to promote unionism in mass industries. The
CIO member unions were expelled from the
AF of L in 1936 but continued the drive; by
1937 the major steel and automobile companies had agreed to CIO organization.

Robert Capa from Magnum

(Above) Loyalist infantryman falls, fatally wounded, during the fighting in 1936; (left) fighting in the Alcazar of Toledo during the Civil War

Georges Reisner from Black Star

Robert Capa from Magnum

(Below) "Nowhere is there safety for anyone in this war." Residents of a Spanish town keep a wary eye out for possible aerial attack

Dead Loyalist fighters after the Battle of Teruel, 1938

After a long period of political unrest marked by strikes and rebellions, the liberal-reform government of the Spanish republic was attacked in July 1937 in a full-scale revolution of the Army and other right-wing groups led by Gen. Francisco Franco. The Fascist revolution received prompt and invaluable aid from the Fascist governments of Germany and Italy and became a testing ground for new weaponry and tactics to be used in the conquest of Europe. Franco abstained from the general war in Europe.

The defeated Loyalist Army of Spain, led by French policemen, crosses the border into France

Keystone Press.

European Picture Service

(Above) Hitler in Vienna, March 1938; (left) Chamberlain and Hitler in Munich

Almost the only collective Allied reaction Hitler's policies was the agreement of Fra and Britain to allow Germany to claim a occupy the Sudetenland, a German-speak section of Czechoslovakia. The representati who constructed the 1938 Munich agreem were generally hailed for having boug "peace in our time." In the face of All hopes that he had been satisfied, Hitler tc the remainder of Czechoslovakia six mon later; Italy's seizure of Albania completed wave of unopposed aggression in Europe. attack on Poland in September 1939 finc brought declarations of war from Britain a France.

Hitler tours Asch, first town to be occupied in Sudetenland, which was yielded to the Nazis in 19

Wide World

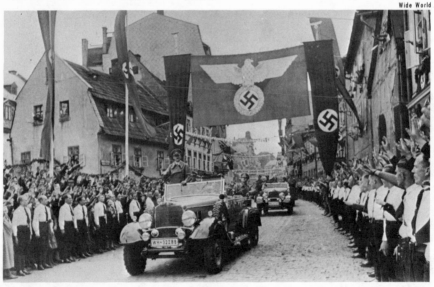

57.

Harry L. Hopkins: 18,000,000 on Relief

When he made the radio address that is reprinted here in part, Harry L. Hopkins was head of the Federal Emergency Relief Administration, one of two agencies instituted by the New Deal to try to cope with unemployment. Hopkins later headed the Works Progress Administration (WPA), in which post he oversaw the spending of billions of dollars in programs to provide jobs for those who could not find them in private industry. According to A. M. Schlesinger, Jr., Hopkins was "a gleeful and unregenerate New Dealer" whose loyalty to his chief was summed up in his remark that "there is a new day, and this is it, and Roosevelt is its leader." During World War II Hopkins was the President's closest and most trusted adviser, and though a sick man he traveled the world on his country's business.

Source: VSD, December 31, 1934, pp. 210-212.

It is a curious thing what a quantity of sickness, coldness, hunger, and barefootedness we are willing to let other men suffer. It literally has no limit. You can hear it in the cautious tone of voice of a man who says, "We'd better be careful or we will have a major disaster." What, might we ask him, would he consider to be a major disaster? Obviously it has nothing to do with numbers. For 18 million persons is a large enough number used in any connection to satisfy most men. Eighteen million men in an army is a large army. Eighteen million sick men is an epidemic larger than any we have ever recorded. Eighteen million criminals would turn the country into a jail. Eighteen million madmen would keep us locked in our rooms in a state of dithering terror. It is a figure large enough so that even in dollars we have to count carefully to know their full purchasing power. For most people large figures are as unusable to their reasoning processes as the astronomer's light-years are to a man with a piece of smoked glass. Yet we can easily roll across our tongues, without a reaction setting up in the heart or mind, the simple statement that 18 million Americans are so poor of this world's goods that they are on relief. . . .

Many of you will say to me that these people like being on relief and that they are better off on relief than they have ever been before. We have heard that one very often. We are told they will not work any more. May I ask you one thing? When you know that a relief budget, for lack of funds, is placed at the very minimum of a family's needs and that in very few places it can take care of rent and that it can hope to do little more than keep body and soul together; and when you realize that this is a nominal budget only, and because we lack funds sometimes families are permitted to receive less than 50 percent of that so-called ideal budget, which is in itself inadequate to life, may I ask you if this is an indictment of relief, that it is said to offer more than life offered before, or is it an indictment of something else?

For myself, I do not call it an indictment of relief. I grant you that examples which you cite of chiseling, racketeering, politics, and laziness may be true, but I also say that we are in a position to know the proportions of these evils, and that it is a fact beyond contradiction that most men do not give up without a struggle that intangible thing they call their independence.

We have lately had a new kind of complaint from a very astute and humorous economist. He asks: "Why are you people in federal relief always apologizing for straight relief, always talking about its being so demoralizing, and such a shameful thing, why are you always saying that as soon as you can, you are going to have work relief for all these people?" (For you know that we harp upon that a good deal in the Relief Administration. We are aware that it costs more in the beginning so we have to fight pretty hard for it.) This economist says: "Of course, you should be apologetic for the amount you give out. The whole matter would be righted and men could hold up their heads again if you gave them $30 a week and called it independent income."

The only trouble with this is that the unemployed themselves want work. We do not have to tell them that not having a job spoils a man for work. They go soft, they lose skill, they lose work habits. But they know it before you and I know it and it is their lives that are being wrecked, not ours. . . .

There are those who tell us that we should not have work relief. They say that straight relief is cheaper. No one will deny this contention. It costs money to put a man to work. Apparently, to the advocates of direct relief, the primary object of relief is to save the government money. The ultimate humane cost to the government never occurs to them of a continued situation through which its citizens lose their sense of independence and strength and their sense of individual destiny. Work for the unemployed is something we have fought for since the beginning of the administration and we shall continue to insist upon it. It

preserves a man's morale. It saves his skill. It gives him a chance to do something socially useful.

Let me say again that we should allow ourselves no smug feelings of charity at this holiday season to know that the federal government is attempting to take care of the actual physical wants of 18 million people. We are merely paying damages for not having had a thought about these things many years ago. We will have to do a great deal of thinking from here out.

I should like to say a word right here about the housing which we have been allowing to stand as the shelter of American citizens. It is evil. It is unnecessary. No civilized nation needs to stand for it. Something has got to be done about housing and something is going to be done. . . .

It is safe to say that poverty in any city is as old as that city and that it has grown in every city from little to big. It is part of its economic nature that poverty is infectious. It is like the old proverb of the shoemaker's children. The children of thousands of unemployed workers in the shoe district of New England are unshod. It would seem that the more you make the more you can't have. It is true that while we have thousands of unemployed cotton textile workers, there are literally hundreds of thousands of beds in the United States that have no sheets and that people sleep on pieces of old carpet placed upon bare springs, or stretch burlap out upon sawdust and lay their babies to sleep on gunny sacks filled with old rags.

I have painted you a very bleak picture. There are the facts with which we have to contend but even though we do not attempt to gloss them over, and it would be idle and even cruel to do so, there is in some ways a more hopeful color in it than any American Christmas has known before. In this country, for the first time, we have a President in the White House whose mind and heart are consecrated to the ending forever of such conditions. It has been one of the outstanding virtues of this administration that it has been willing to uncover the extent of the problem with which it has to deal. It is the motivating force behind the President and his aides to bring about a day when these men and women who have endured so much will come again, or even come, some of them, for the first time, into the inheritance which rightfully belongs to every citizen of the richest country in the world.

And this is not all still in the stage of hope. Much has been accomplished. It lacks some months of being two years since the President undertook a task which was years in preparing. Remember that already at least 3.5 million of unemployed persons have gone back to work. Remember that in spite of the natural seasonal rise of unemployment in winter, and the additional physical needs that people experience in cold weather, and in spite of the fact that depleted family resources have forced newcomers to list themselves upon the relief rolls, there are fewer families on relief at this moment than there were in March 1933. Besides this, new social movements have been begun that will protect and enrich our common life. These good effects are even now at the beginning of a long-time program, substantial enough to be felt. Not only have pledges been made but pledges have been fulfilled.

58.

FRANKLIN D. ROOSEVELT: Relief, Recovery, and Reform

The economy reached its low point in the summer of 1933 and thereafter showed signs of recovering. Between 1933 and 1934 national income rose by about 25 percent and employment increased by more than 2,500,000. In June 1934 the President told Congress that the emergency of the Depression had been met and that government could now turn to charting long-term reforms. Roosevelt reviewed the year past and presented a prospectus for the future in the first "Fireside Chat" of 1934, broadcast to the nation on June 28.

Source: FDR, III, pp. 312-318.

IT HAS BEEN SEVERAL MONTHS since I have talked with you concerning the problems of government. Since January, those of us in whom you have vested responsibility have been engaged in the fulfillment of plans and policies which had been widely discussed in previous months. It seemed to us our duty not only to make the right path clear, but also to tread that path.

As we review the achievements of this session of the Seventy-third Congress, it is made increasingly clear that its task was essentially that of completing and fortifying the work it had begun in March 1933. That was no easy task, but the Congress was equal to it. It has been well said that while there were a few exceptions, this Congress displayed a greater freedom from mere partisanship than any other peacetime Congress since the administration of President Washington himself. The session was distinguished by the extent and variety of legislation enacted and by the intelligence and goodwill of debate upon these measures.

I mention only a few of the major enactments. It provided for the readjustment of the debt burden through the corporate and municipal bankruptcy acts and the Farm Relief Act. It lent a hand to industry by encouraging loans to solvent industries unable to secure adequate help from banking institutions. It strengthened the integrity of finance through the regulation of securities exchanges. It provided a rational method of increasing our volume of foreign trade through reciprocal trading agreements. It strengthened our naval forces to conform with the intentions and permission of existing treaty rights. It made further advances toward peace in industry through the Labor Adjustment Act.

It supplemented our agricultural policy through measures widely demanded by farmers themselves and intended to avert price-destroying surpluses. It strengthened the hand of the federal government in its attempts to suppress gangster crime. It took definite steps toward a national housing program through an act which I signed today designed to encourage private capital in the rebuilding of the homes of the nation. It created a permanent federal body for the just regulation of all forms of communication, including the telephone, the telegraph, and the radio. Finally, and I believe most important, it reorganized, simplified, and made more fair and just our monetary system, setting up standards and policies adequate to meet the necessities of modern economic life, doing justice to both gold and silver as the metal bases behind the currency of the United States.

In the consistent development of our previous efforts toward the saving and safeguarding of our national life, I have continued to recognize three related steps. The first was relief, because the primary concern of any government dominated by the humane ideals of democracy is the simple principle that in a land of vast resources no one should be permitted to starve. Relief was and continues to be our first consideration. It calls for large expenditures and will continue in modified form to do so for a long time to come. We may as well recognize that fact. It comes from the paralysis that arose as the aftereffect of that unfortunate decade characterized by a mad chase for unearned riches, and an unwillingness of leaders in almost every walk of life to look beyond their own schemes and speculations.

In our administration of relief we follow two principles: first, that direct giving shall wherever possible, be supplemented by provision for useful and remunerative work; and second, that where families in their existing surroundings will in all human probability never find an opportunity for full self-maintenance, happiness, and enjoyment, we shall try to give them a new chance in new surroundings.

The second step was recovery, and it is sufficient for me to ask each and every one of you to compare the situation in agriculture and in industry today with what it was fifteen months ago.

At the same time we have recognized the necessity of reform and reconstruction — reform because much of our trouble today and in the past few years has been due to a lack of understanding of the elementary principles of justice and fairness by those in whom leadership in business and finance was placed — reconstruction because new conditions in our economic life as well as old but neglected conditions had to be corrected.

Substantial gains well known to all of you have justified our course. I could cite statistics to you as unanswerable measures of our national progress — statistics to show the gain in the average weekly pay envelope of workers in the great majority of industries — statistics to show hundreds of thousands reemployed in private industries.

Raising the code flag outside the NRA headquarters in New York City, 1934. Mayor La Guardia is in the center foreground

...nd other hundreds of thousands given new employment through the expansion of direct and indirect government assistance of many kinds; although, of course, there are those exceptions in professional pursuits whose economic improvement, of necessity, will be delayed. I also could cite statistics to show the great rise in the value of farm products — statistics to prove the demand for consumers' goods, ranging all the way from food and clothing to automobiles, and of late to prove the rise in the demand for durable goods — statistics to cover the great increase in bank deposits, and to show the scores of thousands of homes and of farms which have been saved from foreclosure.

But the simplest way for each of you to judge recovery lies in the plain facts of your own individual situation. Are you better off than you were last year? Are your debts less burdensome? Is your bank account more secure? Are your working conditions better? Is your faith in your own individual future more firmly grounded?

Also, let me put to you another simple question: Have you as an individual paid too high a price for these gains? Plausible self-seekers and theoretical diehards will tell you of the loss of individual liberty. Answer this question also out of the facts of your own life. Have you lost any of your rights or liberty or constitutional freedom of action and choice? Turn to the Bill of Rights of the Constitution, which I have solemnly sworn to maintain and under which your freedom rests secure. Read each provision of that Bill of Rights and ask yourself whether you personally have suffered the impairment of a single jot of these great assurances. I have no question in my mind as to what your answer will be. The record is written in the experiences of your own personal lives.

In other words, it is not the overwhelming majority of the farmers or manufacturers or workers who deny the substantial gains of the past year. The most vociferous of the doubting Thomases may be divided roughly into two groups: first, those who seek special political privilege; and second, those who seek special financial privilege. About a year ago I used as an illustration the 90 percent of the cotton manufacturers of the United States who wanted to do the right thing by their employees and by the public but were prevented from doing so by the 10 percent who undercut them by unfair practices and un-American standards. It is well for us to remember that humanity is a long way from being perfect and that a selfish minority in every walk of life — farming, business, finance, and even government service itself — will always continue to think of themselves first and their fellow beings second.

In the working out of a great national program which seeks the primary good of the greater number, it is true that the toes of some people are being stepped on and are going to be stepped on. But these toes belong to the comparative few who seek to retain or to gain position or riches or both by some shortcut which is harmful to the greater good.

In the execution of the powers conferred on it by Congress, the administration needs and will tirelessly seek the best ability that the country affords. Public service offers better rewards in the opportunity for service than ever before in our history — not great salaries but enough to live on. In the building of this service there are coming to us men and women with ability and courage from every part of the Union. The days of the seeking of mere party advantage through the misuse of public power are drawing to a close. We are increasingly demanding and getting devotion to the public service on the part of every member of the administration, high and low.

The program of the past year is definitely in operation and that operation month by month is being made to fit into the web of old and new conditions. This process of evolution is well illustrated by the constant changes in detailed organization and method going on in the National Recovery Administration. With every passing month we are making strides in the orderly handling of the relationship between employees and employers. Conditions differ, of course, in almost every part of the country and in almost every industry. Temporary methods of adjustment are being replaced by more permanent machinery and, I am glad to say, by a growing recognition on the part of employers and employees of the desirability of maintaining fair relationships all around.

So also, while almost everybody has recognized the tremendous strides in the elimination of child labor, in the payment of not less than fair minimum wages, and in the shortening of hours, we are still feeling our way in solving problems which relate to self-government in industry, especially where such self-government tends to eliminate the fair operation of competition.

In this same process of evolution we are keeping before us the objectives of protecting, on the one hand, industry against chiselers within its own ranks, and, on the other hand, the consumer through the maintenance of reasonable competition for the prevention of the unfair skyrocketing of retail prices.

But, in addition to this our immediate task, we must still look to the larger future. I have pointed out to the Congress that we are seeking to find the way once more to well-known, long-established but to some degree forgotten ideals and values. We seek the security of the men, women, and children of the nation.

That security involves added means of providing better homes for the people of the nation. That is the first principle of our future program. The second is to plan the use of land and water resources of this country to the end that the means of livelihood of our citizens may be more adequate to meet their daily needs. And, finally, the third principle is to use the agencies of government to assist in the establishment of means to provide sound and adequate protection against the vicissitudes of modern life — in other words, social insurance.

Later in the year I hope to talk with you more fully about these plans.

A few timid people who fear progress will try to give you new and strange names for what we are doing. Sometimes they will call it "Fascism," sometimes "Communism," sometimes "Regimentation," sometimes "Socialism." But, in so doing, they are trying to make very complex and theoretical something that is really very simple.

I believe in practical explanations and in practical policies. I believe that what we are doing today is a necessary fulfillment of what Americans have always been doing — a fulfillment of old and tested American ideals.

Let me give you a simple illustration:

While I am away from Washington this summer, a long-needed renovation of and addition to our White House Office Building is to be started. The architects have planned a few new rooms built into the present all-too-small, one-story structure. We are going to include in this addition and in this renovation modern electric wiring and modern plumbing and modern means of keeping the offices cool in the hot Washington summers. But the structural lines of the old Executive Office Building will remain. The artistic lines of the White House buildings were the creation of master builders when our republic was young. The simplicity and the strength of the structure remain in the face of every modern test. But within this magnificent pattern, the necessities of modern government business require constant reorganization and rebuilding.

If I were to listen to the arguments of some prophets of calamity who are talking these days, I should hesitate to make these alterations. I should fear that while I am away for a few weeks the architects might build some strange new Gothic tower or a factory building or perhaps a replica of the Kremlin or of the Potsdam Palace. But I have no such fears. The architects and builders are men of common sense and of artistic American tastes. They know that the principles of harmony and of necessity itself require that the building of the new structure shall blend with the essential lines of the old. It is this combination of the old and the new that marks orderly peaceful progress, not only in building buildings but in building government itself. Our new structure is a part of and a fulfillment of the old.

All that we do seeks to fulfill the historic traditions of the American people. Other nations may sacrifice democracy for the transitory stimulation of old and discredited autocracies. We are restoring confidence and well-being under the rule of the people themselves. We remain, as John Marshall said a century ago, "emphatically and truly, a government of the people." Our government "in form and in substance . . . emanates from them. Its powers are granted by them, and are to be exercised directly on them, and for their benefits."

Before I close, I want to tell you of the interest and pleasure with which I look forward to the trip on which I hope to start in a few days. It is a good thing for everyone who can possibly do so to get away at least once a year for a change of scene. I do not want to get into the position of not being able to see the forest because of the thickness of the trees.

I hope to visit our fellow Americans in Puerto Rico, in the Virgin Islands, in the Canal Zone, and in Hawaii. And, incidentally, it will give me an opportunity to exchange a friendly word of greeting with the presidents of our sister republics, Haiti and Colombia and Panama.

After four weeks on board ship, I plan to land at a port in our Pacific Northwest, and then will come the best part of the whole trip, for I am hoping to inspect a number of our new great national projects on the Columbia, Missouri, and Mississippi rivers, to see some of our national parks and, incidentally, to learn much of actual conditions during the trip across the continent back to Washington.

While I was in France during the War, our boys used to call the United States "God's country." Let us make it and keep it "God's country."

59.

John Maynard Keynes: Notes on the New Deal

The celebrated English economist, John Maynard Keynes, advocated a system of managed capitalism according to which the virtues of capitalism — among them efficiency, variety, individualism, and freedom — could be preserved, while its defects — mainly the cycle of boom and bust — could be avoided. Government was to manage capitalism by fiscal policy: in times of the cyclical downswing (depression) the government was to stimulate the economy by massive government spending on public works; during the cyclical upswing, the budgetary deficit incurred during the downswing was to be restored, liquidated by increased taxation. In the early 1930s Keynes felt that the survival of the Western social system depended on America's success in combating the Depression. His ideas were to inspire the economic policies of the so-called second New Deal of 1935. Keynes visited President Roosevelt in May 1934, after receiving an honorary degree from Columbia University. The following proposals for action are taken from an article in the New York Times.

Source: *New York Times,* June 10, 1934.

THESE ARE A FEW NOTES on the New Deal by one who has come here on a brief visit of pure inquisitiveness — made under the limitations of imperfect knowledge, but gaining, perhaps, from the detachment of a bird's-eye view.

My purpose is to consider the prospects rather than the past — taking the legislation of this Congress for granted and examining what might be done on the basis thus given. I am in sympathy with most of the social and reforming aims of this legislation; and the principal subject of these notes is the problem of consolidating economic and business recovery.

For this reason, I have not much to say about NRA. I doubt if this measure is either such an advantage to recovery or such a handicap as its advocates and its critics suppose. It embodies some important improvements in labor conditions and for obtaining fair-trade practices. But I agree with the widespread opinion that much of it is objectionable because of its restrictionist philosophy which has a proper place in agricultural adjustment today but not in American industry, and because of its excessive complexity and regimentation.

In particular, it would be advisable to discard most of the provisions to fix prices and to forbid sales below an alleged, but undefinable, cost basis. Nevertheless, its net effect on recovery can easily be overestimated either way.

I find most Americans divided between those who believe that higher wages are good because they increase purchasing power and those who believe that they are bad because they raise costs. But both are right, and the net result of the two opposing influences is to cancel out. The important question is the proper adjustment of relative wage rates. Absolute wage rates are not of primary importance in a country where their effect on foreign trade has been offset by exchange devaluation.

The case for AAA, on the other hand, is much stronger. For the farmer has had to houlder more than his share of the trouble and also has more lasting difficulties ahead of him than industry has. AAA is organizing or the farmer the advisable measure of restriction which industry long ago organized for itself. Thus the task which AAA is attempting is necessary though difficult; whereas some part of what NRA seems to be aiming at is not only impracticable but unnecessary.

I see the problem of recovery, accordingly, in the following light: How soon will normal business enterprise come to the rescue? What measures can be taken to hasten the return of normal enterprise? On what scale, by which expedients, and for how long is abnormal government expenditure advisable in the meantime? For this, I think, is how the administration should view its task.

I see no likelihood that business, of its own initiative, will invest in durable goods on a sufficient scale for many months to come. There are several reasons for this.

In the first place, the important but intangible state of mind, which we call business confidence, is signally lacking. It would be easy to mention specific causes of this, for some of which the administration may be to blame. Probably the most important is the menace of possible labor troubles. But the real explanation, in my judgment, lies deeper than the specific causes. It is to be found in the perplexity and discomfort which the business world feels from being driven so far from its accustomed moorings into unknown and uncharted waters.

The businessman, who may be adaptable and quick on his feet in his own particular field, is usually conservative and conventional in the larger aspects of social and economic policy. At the start he was carried away, like other people, by the prevailing enthusiasm — without being converted at bottom or suffering a sea-change. Thus, he has easily reverted to where he was. He is sulky and bothered; and, with the short memory characteristic of contemporary

man, even begins to look back with longing to the good old days of 1932.

This atmosphere of disappointment, disillusion, and perplexity is nothing to wonder at. I doubt if it could have been avoided without undue concession to conventional ideas. But it is not incurable. The mere passage of time for business to work out its new bearings and recover its equanimity should do much. If the President could convince businessmen that they know the worst, so to speak, and can settle down to adjust themselves to a known situation, that might hasten matters. Above all, the actual experience of gradually improving conditions might work wonders.

In the second place, there are still serious obstacles in the way of reopening the capital market to large-scale borrowing for new investment; particularly, the high cost of borrowing to those who need loans most and the attitude of the finance houses to the Securities Act, though I consider that they should accept the amended act as workable.

Moreover, many types of durable goods are already in sufficient supply, so that business will not be inclined to repair or modernize plant until a stronger demand is being experienced than can be met with existing plant; to which should be added the excessively high cost of building relatively to rents and incomes.

None of these obstacles can be overcome in a day or by a stroke of the pen. The notion that, if the government would retire altogether from the economic field, business, left to itself, would soon work out its own salvation is, to my mind, foolish; and, even if it were not, it is certain that public opinion would allow no such thing. This does not mean that the administration should not be assiduously preparing the way for the return of normal investment enterprise. But this will unavoidably take time. When it comes, it will intensify and maintain a recovery initiated by other means. But it belongs to the second chapter of the story and not to the first.

I conclude, therefore, that, for six months at least, and probably a year, the measure of recovery to be achieved will mainly depend on the degree of the direct stimulus to production deliberately applied by the administration. Since I have no belief in the efficacy for this purpose of the price and wage-raising activities of NRA, this must chiefly mean the pace and volume of the government's emergency expenditure.

Up to last November, such expenditure, excluding refinancing and advances to banks, was relatively small — about $90 million a month. From November onward, the figure rose sharply and, for the first four months of this year, the monthly average exceeded $300 million. The effect on business was excellent. But then came what seems to me to have been an unfortunate decision. The expenditure of the Civil Works Administration was checked before the expenditure of the Public Works Administration was ready to take its place.

Thus, the aggregate emergency expenditure is now declining. If it is going to decline to $200 million monthly, much of the ground already gained will probably be lost. If it were to rise to $400 million monthly, I should be quite confident that a strong business revival would set in by the autumn.

So little divides a retreat from an advance. Most people greatly underestimate the effect of a given emergency expenditure, because they overlook the multiplier — the cumulative effect of increased individual incomes, because the expenditure of these incomes improves the incomes of a further set of recipients and so on. Four hundred million dollars monthly is not much more than 11 percent of the national income; yet it may, directly and indirectly, increase the national income by at least three or four times this amount. Thus the difference between a monthly emergency expenditure of $400 million, financed out of loans and not out of taxation, which would represent a mere redistribution of incomes, and a $100 million expenditure, may be, other things being equal, to increase the national money income by 25 to 30 percent. . . .

This brings me to my agenda for the President:

1. Sufficient appropriations should be obtained before Congress adjourns to provide the necessary ammunition. I believe that this has been obtained.

2. A small office should be set up to collate the spending programs, both realized and prospective, of the various emergency organizations, to compare estimates with results and to report to the President weekly.

3. If the volume or pace of prospective estimates appear to be deficient, the emergency organization should be instructed to report urgently on further available projects. Housing and the railroads appear to offer the outstanding opportunities. The new housing bill is brilliantly conceived, and, if it is operated vigorously, may prove to be a measure of the first importance. Drought relief may be an unexpectedly large factor in the coming months.

4. Meanwhile, active preparations should be on foot to make sure that normal enterprise will take the place of the emergency programs as soon as possible. Much progress has already been made with the problem of remedying the widespread and paralyzing loss of liquidity. But that task must still be carried on.

5. With the Securities Act and the Stock Exchange Act carried into law, the battle is over and the time has come for sincere efforts on both sides to establish cooperative and friendly relations between the commission which will work the acts and the leading financial interests, for it is vital to reopen the capital market.

6. Continuous pressure should be exerted by the Treasury and the Federal Reserve System to bring down the long-term rate of interest. For it assuredly lies in their power, and it is a mistake to suppose that, because the government will be a large borrower, interest rates will rise — inasmuch as the

Treasury's resources in gold and the Reserve System's excess reserves put the market wholly in their hands. . . .

7. To an Englishman the high level of building costs in this country appears to be scandalous, both of building materials and of direct labor. They must be more than 50 percent above, and perhaps double, what they are in England. So long as the volume of work remains as low as it is now, these high costs do not mean high incomes to producers. Thus, no one benefits. It is of the first importance for the administration to take whatever steps are in its power to reduce unit costs in these industries against an undertaking to increase the volume of business sufficiently to maintain and probably to increase actual earnings. This might involve a national program of building working-class houses to rent, which would be, in itself, a great benefit. The measure of recovery now enjoyed in England is largely due to the activity of house building.

8. Either by skill or by good fortune the United States has arrived at what seems to me an excellent currency policy. It was right to devalue. It is right to have a value for the dollar currently fixed in terms of gold. It is prudent to keep a discretionary margin to allow future changes in the gold value of the dollar, if a change in circumstances makes this advisable. But all these measures have been carried fully far enough. Thus there would be no risk, in my judgment, if the President were to make it plain that he has now successfully attained his objects, so far as they can be attained by monetary policy, and that, henceforth, a wise spending policy and a gradual but obstinate attack on high interest rates through the agency of the Federal Reserve System and otherwise will occupy the foreground of the economic program.

9. A word as to the budget. Expenditures fall into three classes: the normal expenditure of administration, relief expenditures, and capital expenditures represented by valuable assets and obligations. The first two classes should, probably, be balanced by revenue by 1936. But it would be a disastrous error, and an instrument of strong deflation, to attempt to cover capital expenditure out of current revenue. At present, the public mind is apt to be confused, because relief and capital expenditure are linked together indiscriminately as emergency expenditure. . . .

If, in conclusion, I may give for what they are worth the impressions of a brief visit to Washington, I believe that there is much devoted and intelligent work in progress there, and that the fittest ideas and the fittest men are tending to survive. In many parts of the world the old order has passed away. But, of all the experiments to evolve a new order, it is the experiment of young America which most attracts my own deepest sympathy. For they are occupied with the task of trying to make the economic order work tolerably well, while preserving freedom of individual initiative and liberty of thought and criticism.

The older generation of living Americans accomplished the great task of solving the technical problem of how to produce economic goods on a scale adequate to human needs. It is the task of the younger generation to bring to actual realization the potential blessings of having solved the technical side of the problem of poverty. The central control which the latter requires involves an essentially changed method and outlook. The minds and energies which have found their fulfillment in the achievements of American business are not likely to be equally well adapted to the further task. That must be, as it should be, the fulfillment of the next generation.

The new men will often appear to be at war with the ideas and convictions of their seniors. This cannot be helped. But I hope that these seniors will look as sympathetically as they can at a sincere attempt — I cannot view it otherwise — to complete, and not to destroy, what they themselves have created.

60.

The Goals of National Planning

In the spring of 1934, as the economy continued to move slowly upward, the Roosevelt administration began to turn from its hastily devised recovery program to the implementation of long-range reforms. The National Resources Board (NRB), established on June 30, 1934, was conceived as a planning commission that was to take stock of the nation's physical and human resources and to devise a program for putting them to beneficial use. However, with the promise of economic recovery, national solidarity broke down, and criticism, especially from conservative quarters, was increasingly voiced. The NRB took pains to emphasize the nonrevolutionary nature of its work, as its report, from which a portion is reprinted below, reveals.

Source: *National Resources Board: A Report on National Planning and Public Works, etc., etc.,* Washington, 1934, pp. 83-85.

PLANNING CONSISTS in the systematic, continuous, forward-looking application of the best intelligence available to programs of common affairs in the public field, as it does to private affairs in the domain of individual activity. In every well-directed home, in every business, in every labor or agricultural group, in every forward-looking organization, social planning goes on continuously, and in the world of government is no exception.

Several considerations are important in looking at plans for planning:

(1) The necessity and value of coordinating our national and local policies, instead of allowing them to drift apart or pull against each other, with disastrous effect.

(2) The value of looking forward in national life, in advance rather than afterward, of preventing the fire rather than putting it out.

(3) The value of basing plans upon the most competent collection and analysis of the facts.

In any case, not all planning is or should be national planning. There is local and state planning, and planning by quasi-public and private agencies and institutions all over the land. The city planning boards thus far chiefly concerned with physical plans and the state planning boards just beginning their work, to say nothing of scores of industrial and other organizations, will continue to develop their special points of view. The centralization of all planning in Washington is not contemplated, and even if possible would not be desirable, since planning is an attitude and practice that must command the confidence and cooperation of wide groups of people to ensure successful operation, must come from the bottom up as well as from the top down, from the circumference as well as the center.

It may reasonably be anticipated that many of the most useful suggestions regarding types of planning will emerge from jurisdictions outside the federal government and outside the governmental group altogether, from detached individuals and associations of individuals, industrial, scientific or otherwise. Planning then does not involve the preparation of a comprehensive blueprint of human activity to be clamped down like a steel frame on the soft flesh of the community by the United States government or by any government.

Second, planning does not involve setting up a fixed and unchangeable system but, on the contrary, contemplates readjustment and revision as new situations and problems emerge. Planning is a continuous process and necessitates the constant reexamination of trends, tendencies, policies, in order to adapt and adjust governmental policies with the least possible friction and loss. The national life is like a moving wave in which a new equilibrium must constantly be found as it sweeps forward. Even physical planning is subject to continuing revision as new factors such as the motor vehicle appear to supersede old ways, while planning, in the broader sense of the term, is likewise subject to change as new inventors come in to disturb older calculations.

Stubborn adherence to an outworn plan is not a mark of intelligence but stupidity, whether in the life of individuals or of nations. Prudence would, of course, dictate that reasonable stability should not be endangered by capricious or arbitrary shift of plans, but would with equal force insist that policies must be promptly modified as emerging trends and new situations necessitate recasting.

Third, it is false and misleading to assert that all planning involves wholesale regimentation of private life. Sound planning, on the contrary, brings about a fresh release of opportunities rather than a narrowing of choice. Street planning and traffic regulation operate for freer use of the highways than unplanned streets and uncontrolled traffic. Laws regulating unfair trade practices release the energies of fair-minded men for other activities than that of guarding against fraud and trickery.

It cannot be forgotten that regimentation is a brutal fact in many private industries now. The modern type of nation was set up in order to break down the old private or semiprivate tyranny over roads, justice, taxation, and to establish public and national control over robber-baron situations that became unendurable. An individual businessman may be absolutely regimented by a ruthless monopoly, just as an individual worker would be helpless against terms dictated by an employer. Over and over again in the United States, as elsewhere, the community has been obliged to intervene to protect the weaker against the insolence and oppression of private citizens who perpetrated injustice and outrage upon their weaker brethren.

Indeed it may be found that some of those who cry "regimentation" when public planning is mentioned foresee interference with their own practices of private regimentation and exploitation of otherwise helpless persons under their private control. Those with special privileges to protect and preserve naturally object to any public planning that may dislodge them from a preferred position where they are able to exact tribute from their fellowmen. This is by no means the only type of opposition to planning, but it is one to which attention must from time to time be directed, since it arises from a type of exploitation from which explosive reaction is most likely to result.

The truth is that it is not necessary or desirable that a central system of planning actually cover all lines of activity or forms of behavior. Such planning overreaches itself. Overcentralized planning must soon begin to plan its own decentralization, for good management is local self-government under a centralized supervision. Thus, wise planning provides for the encouragement of local and personal initiative, realizing that progress may as easily be smothered by overcentralization as by its opposite. Not all government can ever be central government, or all life public life. Experience shows that there must be wide ranges of affairs in which independent criticism, independent judgment, independent initiative is given opportunity for free growth and development in associations as in individuals.

One of the recurring tasks of statesmanship is to cultivate and encourage decentralization. In the excited discussion over this subject, it is often forgotten by both sides that genuine planning really includes planning to preserve and even create noncontrolled free areas of activity. Planning is not an end but a means, a means for better use of what we have, a means for emancipation of millions of personalities now fettered, for the enrichment of human life in ways that will follow individual interest or even caprice. We may plan indeed for fuller liberty and are so planning now.

When men express sincere opposition to all governmental planning, it can only mean a grave misunderstanding of what planning really is, or an opposition to some special detail of planning that seems undesirable, rather than to the general principle.

Wise planning is based on control of certain strategic points in a working system — those points necessary to ensure order, justice, general welfare. It involves continuing reorganization of this system of control points from time to time. The number of controls is never as important as their strategic relations to the operation of the society in which they work. At various times, the community has found it necessary to deal with landowners, with slavery, with the church, with the army, with industrial or labor captains, with racial groups, adjusting control points to meet special situations, and restricting some privileges at one point while releasing other forces and individuals at other points.

It is this shift in the form of planning, the change in strategic planning points, as social and economic conditions change, that leads some to the erroneous conclusion that we have never planned before in America when in point of fact our planning has been continuous and varied as conditions varied.

The essence of successful planning is to find these strategic points as new situations develop, without too great delay and without seizing more points than are necessary for the purpose — or for longer time than

is necessary for the purpose. Insight, sagacity, inventiveness, cooperative spirit are far more important at this point than the club.

Some of these strategic planning points developed in the history of this nation have already been mentioned. In more recent times, national attention has been directed toward land and water utilization, conservation of natural resources, flood control, regulation of public utilities, unfair trade practices; still more recently to the banking and financial structure of the nation, to industrial insecurity, both on the part of worker and investor, to unemployment, to social insurance and welfare problems, to un-American living standards — these among a wide variety of emerging issues of national significance.

In the organization of planning undertakings, the cooperation of the natural and social sciences is of the highest importance. The highest scientific talent of the nation would be available for the purpose of systematic national planning and the government could count upon the cordial and unremitting cooperation of impressive agencies of investigation and exploration already organized to render effective service, such as the American Academy of Science and the Social Science Research Council. The guarantee of such assistance is of deep importance in considering the possibilities of planning.

In the natural science field arise many of the inventions and technologies which, while increasing our possibilities for weal, also make possible much woe if they are not fortunately set in the framework of the social and economic structure. The cooperation of scientists in this field should make possible a wiser and sounder adaptation of technology to economic and social advancement. The cooperation of the social scientists with their research in the field of human behavior should correspondingly facilitate the making and perfecting of social inventions, keeping pace with those in natural science. The memoranda presented by those organizations are impressive in nature and full of promise for technical cooperation in the national planning of the future. . . .

It cannot be too strongly stated that we do not approach the planning of natural and other American resources in any spirit of defeatism. The present emergency may have hastened the growth of systematic planning, but the careful inventory and appraisal of our resources, and the consideration of how we may most effectively utilize these resources, could not in any case have been long delayed after our frontier had been closed and the progress of mechanical invention established as a permanent factor in our civilization.

We do not stand at the broken end of a worn-out road, but look forward down a broad way to another era of American opportunity. Among the nations of the world, America has stood and still stands for discovery, for pioneering across a great continent, for fearless experiment in directions where others had failed, for achievement in mechanism and management, for ready adaptation to new conditions and easy adjustment to new ways of life. When we are resigned to drifting and too weary to plan our own American destiny, then stronger hands and stouter hearts will take up the flag of progress and lead the way out of difficulties into attainment.

61.

Henry A. Wallace: Old and New Frontiers

Henry A. Wallace was raised on an Iowa farm. His father, Henry C. Wallace, had served Harding and Coolidge as secretary of agriculture from 1921 to 1924. In 1928 young Henry repudiated the party of his family to support "Al" Smith. Later, under Roosevelt, he found an atmosphere congenial to his political views and a position — he filled his father's post of secretary of agriculture from 1933 to 1940 — in which to exercise his talents. Wallace's idealism was balanced by a firsthand knowledge of the farmers' problems. One of the most influential supporters of the New Deal, he imparted to the program a moral-religious character and converted many Republicans and conservatives to it. The following selection is taken from the final chapter of New Frontiers, *a book by Wallace published in 1934.*

Source: *New Frontiers,* New York, 1934: "Beyond the Frontier."

When those forty thousand undisciplined slaves, the Children of Israel, left Egypt, it was possible for them to reach their promised land within a few months. But they were not fit to march a straight course, enter and take possession. The older men and women among them thought of everything in terms of the fleshpots of Egypt. Before the promised land could be attained it was necessary for the younger generation, hard-ened by travels in the wilderness, to come to maturity.

We have been forced away from the fleshpots. When our stock market crashed in 1929, it was plain that we would have to abandon them. We, too, know something about a new land and how it may be reached, but we are not yet fit to go in and take possession. Too many of us would like one last round with those fleshpots and golden calves. It may be that many of our younger people have been sufficiently hardened by suffering in our economic wilderness. But all will have to come to a more effective maturity before the new land can be fully possessed. Advance guards sent out to estimate the cost of the march tell us that there are giants in the way.

I am sometimes accused of undue idealism; but I know very well that it will not do to hope too much of the generation of which I am a part. It is simply impossible for us to let go overnight of the habits and beliefs of a lifetime. Younger people, if they will, can easily accomplish changes which seem impossible to older people.

Unfortunately, many of the oncoming generation now in our schools, or idling in our homes, are handicapped by an inheritance of past concepts, bitterly complicated by the present stalemate. They are stirred into potentially menacing forms of protest by the fact that the present world does not seem to want their services. If misled by demagogues and half-baked educators, they may be inclined to assume more and more that the world owes them not only a living but a limousine. Their restlessness and present disillusionment can be fatal or infinitely constructive, depending upon which side they wake up on.

After all, we middle-aged, middle-course people have some hard thinking and many hard jobs to do before we can reasonably expect to arouse our young to hope for an enduring democracy. Talk alone will not lead them to consolidate the position we now strive to hold, and push forward to something better.

The Children of Israel's problems did not come to an end after they had crossed the borders, or even after they had taken possession of their promised land. Their real troubles as a people had then only begun. They had put behind them a vague, nomadic wandering, but they still had to adapt themselves in some measure to the commercial features of the Canaanite civilization. Their old frontier was gone. They had to work on new frontiers. These problems in many respects strikingly modern, provoked the strife and turmoil which resulted in the tremendous literature of the prophets and the historical records contained in Chronicles and Kings. Amos, that farmer-prophet of the hill country of Judah, first raised in dramatic form the problem of social justice, fair treatment of debtors, and balanced prices.

Physically, and in other ways also, the basic structure of our land of yesterday had been torn to pieces. By the raw pioneer rules of first stakes, we have encamped as migrants and have taken greedily and unevenly of its wealth. A few of us, in consequence, have much more than we can comfortably or decently spend or handle; yet most of us have too little for comfort, decency, and hope of a general progress.

We face, moreover, these hard facts: first, the land frontier of the United States is gone. Depression can no longer be solved by shipping the unemployed West. We must learn to live with each other. We have no longer enormous, unexploited natural resources awaiting only the touch of young and vigorous hands to be transformed into fabulous, individual wealth.

Second, the wealth that may be drawn by the shrewdest of a rapidly expanding population is now drawing to an end. In the old days, expanding population, and the million or so of people we received annually from Europe, enlarged certain of our cities so rapidly that tremendous real-estate values were reared. Today, immigration is mostly shut out. Our birthrate is decreasing. It appears that by 1950 our population will probably reach its peak, around a hundred and fifty million people, and then start declining. Our rural areas, especially in the South, furnish most of the present population increase. Most of our cities are growing only insofar as they suck in the surplus population from farms and small towns; and this surplus is falling off.

Third, enormous decentralizing forces are beginning to influence the psychology and eventually the location of many of our city families. Hard roads, trucks, autos, high-line electricity, and the increasing love of city people for good air, sunshine, trees, and natural surroundings, will inevitably result in drawing millions of Americans back into the open.

As we dimly discern these forces which will be at work among us for years to come, we wonder just what, in the new combination, will give to the new life the same unity that our old life obtained, simply as a result of fears and hopes centering in the frontier.

The old frontier was real. There were Indians and fear of foreign conquest. People in the older colonies or states had to stand together against actual perils on the edge of a new civilization.

Their determination to stand together was continually renewed by romantic tales of many unknown kinds of wealth out on the frontier, of precious metals, and fertile valleys, although as a matter of fact, the old frontier was all too often a place of ragged, barbed-wire fences, dusty roads, unpainted shacks. Nevertheless, the hopes and fears that existed in the old frontier furnished a unity to our national life. For a hundred and fifty years we felt it was manifest destiny to push onward, until the Pacific Coast was reached, until all the fertile lands between had been plowed and bound together by railroads and paved highways.

The obvious physical task to which we set ourselves has been accomplished; and in so doing, we have destroyed in large measure the thing which gave us hope and unity as a people.

We now demand a new unity, a new hope. There are many spiritual and mental frontiers yet to be conquered, but they lead in many different directions and our hearts have not yet fully warmed to any one of them. They do not point in an obvious single direction as did that downright physical challenge which, for so many generations, existed on the Western edge of our life. Now we have come to the time when we must search our souls and the relationship of our souls and bodies to those of other human beings.

Can we build up a unified, national cultural life, unique, outstanding, one that will reinforce the cultural life of the entire world? Can we leave something that contributes toward giving life meaning, joy, and beauty for generations to come?

During the sixteenth, seventeenth, eighteenth, and nineteenth centuries, ideas took possession of our fathers and grandfathers which made them resolute hard workers, men of iron, equally good as Indian fighters, pioneer farmers, and captains of industry. They suffered and forged ahead in the world, believing that there was something prophetically worthy in all they did. Progress westward, landward, and wealthward was their continual urge. They exploited not only natural resources but the generations which came after. We glorify these men, grabbers and exploiters that they were, and marvel at their conquests. But they did not know how to live with each other and they did not know how to teach the American nation to live with other nations.

The keynote of the new frontier is cooperation just as that of the old frontier was individualistic competition. The mechanism of progress of the new frontier is social invention, whereas that of the old frontier was mechanical invention and the competitive seizure of opportunities for wealth. Power and wealth were worshiped in the old days. Beauty and justice and joy of spirit must be worshiped in the new.

Many of the most lively, intimate expressions of spirit spring from the joyous, continuous contact of human beings with a particular locality. They feel the age-long spirit of this valley or that hill, each with its trees and rocks and special tricks of weather, as the seasons unfold in their endless charm. If life can be made secure in each community and if the rewards of the different communities are distributed justly, there will flower in every community, not only those who attain joy in daily, productive work well done but also those who paint and sing and tell stories with the flavor peculiar to their own valley, well-loved hill, or broad prairie. And so we think of cooperative communities not merely in a competent commercial sense but also from the standpoint of people who are helping unfold each other's lives in terms of the physical locality and tradition of which they are a part.

In this way, every community can become something distinctly precious in its own right. Children will not try to escape as they grow up. They will look ahead to the possibility of enriching the traditions of their ancestors. They will feel it is a privilege to learn to live with the soil and the neighbors of their fathers. Such communities will be strung like many-colored beads on the thread of the nation and the varied strings of beads will be the glory of the world.

The pettiness of small communities will disappear as their economic disadvantages disappear. The people of small communities, rid of the pettiness which grows of economic fear, will be free to realize that community success may be truly measured only in terms of contribution to a spirit of world unity, even though political and economic ties may be very loose.

In the old days, we could not trust ourselves with joy and beauty because they ran counter to our competitive search for wealth and power. Men of the old days, whether Protestant or Catholic, accepted implicitly the discipline of the Protestant Ethic (see Weber's *The Protestant Ethic and the Spirit of Capitalism*). The men of the new day must have their social discipline comparable in its power with that of the inner drive toward the hard-working, competitive frugality of the old frontier. People may actually work harder than they did on the old frontier, but their motive will be different. They may make and use more mechanical inventions. They may do more to increase the wealth-producing power of the race.

But their efforts will, of necessity, be continually moved by the spirit of cooperative achievement. They will devise ways in which the monetary mechanism can be modified to distribute the rewards of labor more uniformly. They will work with disinterested spirit to modify the governmental and political machinery so that there is a balanced relationship between prices, an even flow of employment, and a far-wider possibility of social justice and social charity.

So enlisted, men may rightfully feel that they are serving a function as high as that of any minister of the Gospel. They will not be Socialists, Communists, or Fascists, but plain men trying to gain by democratic methods the professed objectives of the Communists, Socialists, and Fascists: security, peace, and the good life for all.

In their efforts they will not allow their work to be divided or embittered by the dogma or prejudice of any narrow, superficially logical, political or religious sect.

Some will seek for the fountains of an abundant life in renewed artistic, religious, and scientific inspiration. They will not, I trust, accept the animal view of human nature, put forth by the biologists and the economists of the nineteenth century. Of necessity, they will recognize competitive individualists and competitive nations and deal with them, as the anachronisms they are, treating them kindly, firmly, and carefully.

But the new frontiersman will be continually seeking for his fellows those satisfactions which are mutually enriching. The nature of these satisfactions can only be faintly shadowed now. They exist in a land as strange and far as was America in 1491. In this land of ageless desire we are all striving newcomers. It is not a mushy, sentimental frontier, but one of hard realities, requiring individual and social discipline beyond that of the old frontiers. It lies within us and all about us. A great seer of the human heart who lived nineteen hundred years ago called it the Kingdom of Heaven. He knew that the tiny spark of divine spirit found in each individual could be fanned into an all-consuming flame, an intense passion for fair play, man to man, and man to woman, in the little time that we are here. In the Sermon on the Mount, He spoke of the rules of the Kingdom of Heaven.

The land beyond the new frontier will be conquered by the continuous social inventions of men whose hearts are free from bitterness, prejudice, hatred, greed and fear; by men whose hearts are aflame with the extraordinary beauty of the scientific, artistic and spiritual wealth now before us, if only we reach out confidently, together.

62.

LOUIS ADAMIC: New Americans

Louis Adamic migrated to the United States from a Slavic province in Austria when he was fourteen. He devoted much of his adult life to interpreting and publicizing the problems of immigrants in the United States. The immigrant problem, Adamic believed, was in part a product of the misconception, harbored by the majority of Americans, that they belonged to a pure, white, Anglo-Saxon, Protestant stock. In one publication after another he pointed out the diversity of national backgrounds and cultural traits in what had come to be regarded as the American way of life. "Thirty Million New Americans," published in November 1934, is reprinted here in part.

Source: *Harper's*, November 1934.

WITHIN ITS POPULATION of one hundred and twenty-five million, the United States has today about thirty million citizens — the overwhelming majority of them young citizens — who are the American-born children of immigrant parents of various nationalities: German, Italian, Polish, Czech, Slovak, Serbian, Croatian, Slovenian, Bulgarian, Jewish, Russian, Carpatho-Russian, Ukrainian, Lithuanian, Finnish, Hungarian, Norwegian, Swedish, Danish, Dutch, French, Flemish, Spanish, Portuguese, Rumanian, Armenian, Syrian, Lett, Albanian, Greek, Turkish, and, of course, English, Scotch, and Irish. The country as a whole is but dimly cognizant of this fact, which, in my opinion (held for some time, but lately much strengthened), is of fundamental and urgent importance in our contemporary social and cultural scene. It should perhaps particularly interest those Americans who consider themselves of the old Anglo-Saxon stock; for here is a tremendous new element — what will it do to the old stock? — to the country? — how will it affect the development of civilization and culture, of racial types on this continent? . . .

The chief and most important fact (the only one I shall stress here) about the New Americans is that the majority of them are oppressed by feelings of inferiority in relation to their fellow citizens of older stock, to the mainstream of American life, and to the problem of life as a whole; which, of course, is bad for them as individuals, but, since there are so many of them and their number is still rapidly increasing, even worse for the country.

These feelings of inferiority are to some degree extensions of their parents' feelings of inferiority as immigrants in a country so drastically different from their native lands. The fathers and mothers of these millions of New Americans were naturally at a disadvantage even in the most friendly surroundings, and the surroundings were seldom wholly and continually friendly. As foreigners, in many cases not speaking the English language, they occupied inferior positions in the country's social, economic, and political life. Most of them were workers, performing, by and large, the meanest tasks and receiving meager wages.

All too often, in one form or another, they bumped up against racial or general anti-immigrant prejudice. Old-stock American workers looked askance at them. Many of them lived in the worst sections of their cities and towns, and were called Hunkies or Bohunks, Dagoes or Wops, Polacks or Litvaks, Sheenies or Kikes. They were frequently — and unavoidably — discriminated against. And, in the face of all this, they inevitably felt, as individuals and as members of their immigrant groups, somewhat inferior in their relation to America and to those who occasionally glance at crime and juvenile-delinquency statistics. The surprising thing to me is that there is not more delinquency and crime among the New Americans. And I should add too that the chauvinists mentioned above are not very numerous either. These categories together include perhaps less than five percent of the New Americans.

The majority of the grown-up New Americans just hang back from the mainstream of life in this country, forming a tremendous mass of neutral, politically dead citizenry; while their younger fellow New Americans, boys and girls in their teens (about twelve million of them), now attending public and parochial schools and high schools, show dangerous signs of becoming the same kind of neutral, unstirring citizens, unless something is done about it. There is among them little aggressiveness, little spirit of any sort. Without a vital sense of background, perennially oppressed by the feeling that they are outsiders and thus inferior, they will live outside the mainstream of America's national life. This is especially true of groups which linguistically and culturally are farthest removed from the Anglo-Saxon, and still more of groups which, besides being unrelated to the Anglo-Saxon, are (or till lately have been) suppressed or subject nationalities in Europe.

And these widespread personal inferiority feelings are producing in large sections of this New American element *actual* inferiority in character, mind, and physique. There is no doubt that, by and large, in bodily and other personal qualities, many of the immigrants' children do not favorably compare with their parents. They cannot look one in the eye. They are shy. Their limp handshakes gave me creepy feelings all the way from New York to the Iron Range in Minnesota. Those handshakes symbolized for me the distressing tendency on the part of this vast and growing section of America's population toward characterlessness, lack of force and spirit, and other inferior personal qualities.

From whatever angle one looks at it, this is a serious matter for the New Americans as individuals and for America. Thirty millions — or even twenty millions, a probable number to which most or all of my generalizations here are directly applicable — are a lot of people, and this "second generation" will be (many already are) the fathers and mothers of the third generation, and it is not impossible that in two or three decades more than half of the population of the

United States will be of these new cultural and national strains.

What then should be done — what can be done about it? I think I can make a suggestion.

In going about the country last spring I met several New Americans of whom most of the things I say above are not true. None of them was totally free of personal inferiority feelings (in fact, I find that even very few old-stock Americans are entirely free of them), but they were, nevertheless, fine-looking young men and women, boys and girls, keen and alert, articulate, ambitious, personally charming. Some were still in high school, one or two in college, and doing well as students; in fact, rather better than old-stock American students. Their handshakes were firm and they looked me in the eye. A few had a lively sense of humor which they could apply to themselves. Their laughter had a healthy ring. They knew something of what was going on in the country, in the world.

Some of them, although still very young, seemed to know what they wanted from life. Two or three had literary ambitions. One told me he would try to get into politics "in a big way," by which I understood that the United States Senate was not beyond his gaze; and his name was Wojciezkowski. Another, attending the University of Pittsburgh, thought he might get a job in a steel mill and become a labor leader. In a bleak iron town in Minnesota I met a pretty girl of Slovenian parentage who was the best student in her school, had a vivid personality, and seemed entirely normal in all her attitudes. And so on, and so on. They impressed me as real, solid persons who would be an asset to any country. . . .

During my seven-week trip I met, as I say, scores and scores of these New Americans. Among them were some of the most attractive people I have encountered anywhere. Some of these I already have mentioned. Another was a girl, born and still living in Cleveland, whose father and moth-

er were Slovenians; and there is no doubt in my mind that much of her charm issued from the fact that she was keenly conscious of her parents' native land and culture. . . .

Still another of these exceptional New Americans was a young six-footer of Finnish parentage on the Iron Range in Minnesota. He had never been to Finland, but knew a good deal about the basic cultural qualities of that country from his mother's word-pictures of it, had a fluent command of the Finnish language which did not interfere with his English, knew dozens of Finnish folk ballads and lyrics and sang them well, and had read and re-read in the original the great Finnish epic poem "The Kalevala." He was quietly proud of his people's achievements on the Iron Range both in the mines and on the land, and thought that Minnesota was his country. Despite the bleakness of the region, and the hard life there led by most of the people, especially the Finns, he loved the Iron Range. His people had worked and suffered there for decades and converted great parts of it into farming country, although before they came nobody had thought it could ever be made suitable for anything.

In short, he was conscious of his background; he had a sense of continuity, of being part of a great human experience, which was part of the still greater American adventure. Largely, I think, in consequence of this, a strength of character was discernible in his every move and utterance.

I could give a few more such cases of exceptional New Americans, but that would be, in the main, repeating what I tell of the girl in Cleveland and the boy in Minnesota. All of them — representing, however, but a small minority — were conscious and, in a greater or lesser degree, proud of their racial groups' background in the old countries, and some also of their racial groups' background and history in this country. They had a sense of continuity, a feeling of being a part of something. And they, I think, are the answer to the question: What should be done about the problem sketched in this article?

The answer is that the New Americans, whose inarticulate and otherwise inadequate (through no fault of their own) parents have been unable to give them much along these lines, should be helped to acquire a knowledge of, and pride in, their own heritage; and this help should come, in very large part, from already established and functioning social and cultural institutions and agencies — schools, libraries, settlement and community houses, newspapers, lecture forums, and so on — in cooperation with a central organization which should be formed for the purpose of devising ways to disseminate information about the several racial or national groups represented among the thirty million "second generation" citizens, of studying the problem and working out programs of action for its gradual solution or amelioration, from the point of view of honest, intelligent patriotism — patriotism in the highest, broadest sense of the word which implies concern for the country's future, not in the corrupted or narrow group sense in which it is usually used.

By now it is obvious to many people interested in the problem that it is impossible and, what is more, *undesirable* to make the offspring of Lithuanians or Serbians into Anglo-Saxons; that the aim should be rather to help them become real men and women on the pattern of their own natural cultures. There is no doubt that in the few places where no attempts have been made by "patriotic" old-time Americans to force immigrants' children into the old-stock American mold — as, for instance, in the Bohemian communities in Nebraska and Texas, where Bohemians already are in the fourth generation; in the little city of Hamtramck near Detroit, where the public-school system consistently encourages the large Polish group there to keep its individuality; in O. D. Rölvag's Norwegian settlements in the Northwest; in some of the foreign "colonies" in New York City, notably the Ukrainian one on the Lower East Side; or in several small Polish, Italian, and Finnish rural communities in New England, upstate New York, and elsewhere — the development of character, mentality, and physique in the New American element has been vastly more felicitous than where such attempts have been made.

Social and cultural institutions and agencies in various cities and towns where the problem stares them all in the face wherever they turn already are beginning to do things to help New Americans develop more or less on the pattern of their backgrounds. To give a few examples: In Cleveland the excellent public-library organization, with its scores of branch libraries, has begun to help the New Americans to learn something about themselves, their parents' native lands and their national groups' history in this country, particularly in Cleveland. All three of the big newspapers there have special reporters covering the "foreign sections" of the city, and occasionally print feature articles about the various foreign groups' contribution to the growth and development of Cleveland. Three years in succession now, the *Cleveland Press* has sent to Europe a competent journalist who more or less understands the problem discussed in this article, to write from there "stories" about things in Poland, Lithuania, Czechoslovakia, Hungary, Rumania, and Yugoslavia — things which interest the immigrants from these countries and their American-born children.

Public-school and high-school teachers in Cleveland, as in one or two other cities, whose classes in late years are anywhere from forty to eighty percent "foreign," are becoming eagerly interested in "second-generation problems" which face them in the form of numerous neurotic and backward or "problem" children who, for no apparent reason, burst out crying in the middle of a lesson. Of late teachers nearly everywhere, I am told, have advanced so far that they take the trouble to learn the correct pronunciation of difficult Polish, Yugoslav, Lithuanian, Czech, Finnish, and Slovak names, and to caution the old-stock American boys and girls not to call the New American children Hunkies, Wops, and other such names of derision.

In Pittsburgh, the university, with its colossal new Cathedral of Learning, is developing an educational program or movement for that vicinity which, if carried out with force, courage, and wisdom, is apt to become a great factor in the upbuilding of character, mentality, and physique among the New Americans, who already form well over half of the Pittsburgh metropolitan area's population.

In more than half of the cities and towns which I visited I found the so-called International Institutes, some of them part of the Y.W.C.A., which — with their clubrooms, reading rooms, lectures, social affairs, exhibits of European peasant arts, and printed matter — are beginning to attempt to do something for the second generation, especially the girls. In Flint, Michigan, and in one or two other places, I came upon purely local organizations, some of them officered and run by such exceptional New Americans as I have described above, aiming to help the general run of New Americans to fight their feelings of inferiority.

I came upon professional social workers who were doing elaborate researches in certain phases of the problem and knew a great deal about the local departments thereof. The directors of most of the settlement houses in Pittsburgh, Detroit, Chicago, and Milwaukee were more or less awake to the situation as it existed locally and — in most cases, however, without having any real understanding of it — were also trying to do something about it. The same could be said of various settlement-house workers, teachers, a few ministers, and other agencies elsewhere.

All these efforts or, rather, beginnings of efforts are local, however; usually honest enough but very restricted in scope. The In-

ternational Institutes, for instance, appeal largely to girls. There is no central or national organization interested in the thing as a countrywide problem, which it undoubtedly is, and, as I have tried to show here, a tremendous and important one — important to old-stock Americans and to Americans of the third and fourth generation no less than to these New Americans, and to America as a whole. . . .

I realize, of course, that the problem I sketch above is closely tied up with the socioeconomic system under which we live; that, next to their being more or less strangers here, the worst factors behind the inferiority feelings of these millions of New Americans are poverty and its sister-evil, ignorance, both of them brought over by the immigrants and then fostered by conditions here; and that the cure for most of the second-generation ills lies, ultimately, in the solution of our socioeconomic problem. I doubt, however, whether the latter problem will be quickly and satisfactorily solved in this country if we permit to develop in our population a vast element, running into tens of millions, which is oppressed by acute feelings of inferiority and, largely as a result of those feelings, is becoming actually inferior human material — bewildered, politically neutral, economically unaggressive, prepared to live meekly, slavishly on the dole, and culturally nowhere.

If this element is left alone in the face of its growing economic difficulties and rising prejudice against it on the part of "patriotic" older Americans, there soon will be no help for it. I imagine that hundreds of thousands of New Americans already are hopeless as potential constructive elements in any sort of vital, progressive civilization and culture; and if their number is permitted to increase, they will — let me repeat — profoundly affect the future of this country in a way that no one would want to see it affected.

On the other hand, if something is done about the problem in the spirit of the above general suggestions, I believe that the majority of the New Americans and the generation that they will produce will have an opportunity to become a great body of self-respecting, constructive citizenry; and that, with the diverse racial and cultural backgrounds they inherited from their immigrant parents, they will enrich the civilization and deepen the culture in this New World.

63.

ANONYMOUS: Hollywood Against Upton Sinclair

In 1934 the Democratic Party of California ran the renowned writer and reforming Socialist, Upton Sinclair, for governor. Sinclair promised to "end poverty in California" (the program was commonly referred to as EPIC) by instituting sharply graduated income taxes, establishing self-supporting land colonies for the unemployed, authorizing the state to purchase or rent idle factories for the unemployed to run, and issuing a limited scrip to facilitate the exchange of industrial produce for food. The Republicans, led by movie magnate Louis B. Mayer, conducted a no-holds-barred campaign against Sinclair throughout California. The following article in the New York Times *revealed Hollywood's role in the campaign. Sinclair was defeated by 250,000 votes.*

Source: *New York Times*, November 4, 1934.

THE FULL FORCE of the motion-picture industry, overwhelming in this fabulous city, has been thrown into the crusade to keep Upton Sinclair out of the governor's chair at Sacramento.

Under a plan of campaign accredited generally to Louis B. Mayer, Republican state chairman and head of the Metro-Goldwyn-Mayer Studios, the thirty-odd thousand people employed directly or indirectly in making pictures, as well as the talents and skill of the craft, have been drafted for the final multipartisan assault upon the smiling Socialist who captured the Democratic nomination in the August primaries.

The higher salaried employees of each of the seven major studios have either been assessed or "requested" a day's salary for the campaign fund of Governor Frank F. Merriam, whose Republican candidacy has now become the standard for the "Stop Sin-

clair" forces. All movie workers, high and low, have been called or circularized and either told or "advised" how to vote in the interest of maintenance of their jobs. Merriam literature, buttons, and emblems have been distributed through all the lots.

The city of Los Angeles has turned into a huge movie set, where many newsreel pictures are made every day depicting the feelings of the people against Mr. Sinclair. Equipment from one of the major studios, as well as some of its second-rate players, may be seen at various street intersections or out in the residential neighborhood, "shooting" the melodrama and unconscious comedy of the campaign. Their product can be seen in leading motion-picture houses in practically every city or town of the State.

In one of the "melodramas" recently filmed and shown here in Los Angeles, an interviewer approaches a demure old lady, sitting on her front porch and rocking away in her rocking chair.

"For whom are you voting, Mother?" asked the interviewer.

"I am voting for Governor Merriam," the old lady answers in a faltering voice.

"Why, Mother?"

"Because I want to save my little home. It is all I have left in this world."

In another recent newsreel there is shown a shaggy man with bristling Russian whiskers and a menacing look in his eye.

"For whom are you voting?" asks the interviewer.

"Vy, I am foting for Seenclair."

"Why are you voting for Mr. Sinclair?"

"Vell, his system worked vell in Russia, vy can't it vork here?"

All these "releases" are presented as newsreels.

Another "newsreel" has been made of Oscar Rankin, a colored prizefighter and preacher who is quite a favorite with his race in Los Angeles County. Asked why he was voting for Governor Merriam, he answered that he likes to preach and play the piano and he wants to keep a church to preach in and a piano to play.

Merriam supporters always are depicted as the more worthwhile element of the community, as popular favorites or as substantial businessmen. Sinclair supporters are invariably pictured as the riff-raff. Low paid "bit" players are said to take the leading roles in most of these "newsreels," particularly where dialogue is required. People conversant with movie personnel claim to have recognized in them certain aspirants to stardom.

But even cleverness has faltered at times in the ruthlessness of the anti-Sinclair campaign. A leading newspaper of Los Angeles is reported to have called upon one of the studios for a "still" picture of bums entering the State in response to Sinclair's invitation to the unemployed of the whole country. The picture was quickly furnished and published. The publicity department of another studio immediately recognized the photograph as a scene from a recent cinema. The recognition was made simple because the leading juvenile star on the feature was sitting atop the box car.

The studio managers have stopped at nothing to insure a full vote of their employees for Merriam. They have told them not to put too much stock in the writing genius of the man [Sinclair]. "Out of forty-seven books he has written, not one has ever been filmed," an official is said to have told some of his employees the other day.

At another studio an official called in his scenario writers to give them a bit of "advice" on how to vote. "After all," he is reputed to have told his writers, "what does Sinclair know about anything? He's just a writer."

Stories of this kind can be picked up at every studio provided the teller, who invariably is a Merriam man, can be assured he will not be quoted and provided, too, that he can relate it out of any possible hearing of his associates.

A fun-making film news writer for an Eastern newspaper strolled into the commissary on the Metro-Goldwyn-Mayer lot a few days ago and began distributing Sinclair literature which he had purchased downtown, just to see what would happen. When the high-powered Metro publicity men, to whom he handed the leaflets, saw what they were, they crumpled them up and dropped them as if they were hot. They did not know whether to cram them in their pockets or what to do with them. They pleaded in all seriousness for the news writer not to play such a prank, which might be disastrous to their jobs.

These stories sound fantastic, but they are no more so than the very nature of the class war which is called the Sinclair campaign. It is a humorless, grim affair, made comical by its very lack of humor.

1935

64.

GARDINER C. MEANS: The Making of Industrial Policy

By late 1934 the National Recovery Administration (NRA) was beset by a number of problems that threatened its future usefulness. The issue was basically the extent and goal of national planning: Would the government continue its supervision of the entire economic system, or would it simply aim at recovery by cooperation and coordination? At the end of 1934 economist Gardiner C. Means prepared a report for Congress setting forth the goal of reform. Means's analysis of the economic system was accepted by the New Dealers, but his advocacy of a planned and regulated economy was not widely acclaimed. The report, Industrial Prices and Their Relative Inflexibility, *was submitted to the Senate on January 17, 1935, and is reprinted in part below.*

Source: 74 Congress, 1 Session, Senate Document No. 13, pp. 9-19.

The Basic Cause for the Failure of a Laissez Faire Policy

1. The National Recovery Administration and Agricultural Adjustment Administration were created in response to an overwhelming demand from many quarters that certain elements in the making of industrial policy (including agriculture as an industry) should no longer be left to the market place and the price mechanism but should be placed in the hands of administrative bodies — code authorities, crop control committees, etc. This demand is not only a product of emergency conditions but is also a reflection of more basic dissatisfactions with the results of laissez faire, such as are reflected in the demands for weakening the antitrust laws, strengthening labor organization, intervening to aid the farmers, and for such economic reorganization as will bring the higher standard of living made possible by modern technology.

2. The whole trend of social development both in this country and abroad has been to recognize the failure of a complete laissez faire policy.

3. The basic cause for the failure of a laissez faire policy is to be found in the very same forces which have made possible a high standard of living for all, namely, the gradual, century-long shift from market to

administrative coordination of economic activity, which has resulted in modern industrial organization and modern technology. This shift to administration has brought a new type of competition and inflexible administered prices which disrupt the workings of the market.

4. A century ago the great bulk of economic activity in the United States was conducted on an atomistic basis by individuals or families — as is most of agriculture today — while the actions of the separate individuals were coordinated by the market. The individual produced for sale and his activity was geared to and in part controlled by flexible market prices. Balance between the actions of individuals was maintained — insofar as it was maintained — by the impersonal forces of the market and the law of supply and demand. Through the market, the apparently unrelated activities of individuals were thus made to mesh into a single coordinated whole and industrial policy was made by the market as a result. The policy of laissez-faire has rested on the assumption that the market would continue to make industrial policy and would remain a satisfactory coordinating mechanism.

5. But gradually more and more of economic coordination has been accomplished administratively. Great numbers of individuals have been drawn into large factories or business organizations and their activities have come to be coordinated within the separate enterprises by administrative action. In a single factory the separate activities of thousands of workers are coordinated by the factory management so as to mesh into a single producing organization. Within single corporate enterprises, tens and even hundreds of thousands of individuals have their economic activity coordinated by administrative direction. In 1929 the activity of over 400,000 workers was meshed into a great communication system by the management of the American Telephone & Telegraph Co. Contrast the coordination and balance among this group of workers with that among 400,000 separate farmers whose action in producing more or less of each product is controlled and balanced only by the market. In the first, we have the extreme of administrative coordination; in the second, the extreme of market coordination.

6. The shift from market to administrative coordination has gone so far that a major part of American economic activity is now carried on by great administrative units — our great corporations. More than half of all manufacturing activity is carried on by 200 big corporations, while big corporations dominate the railroad and public-utility fields and play an important role in the fields of construction and distribution.

7. This development of administrative coordination has made possible tremendous increases in the efficiency of industrial production within single enterprises. The large number of workers brought into a single organization has allowed a high degree of subdivision of labor and the use of complicated series of machines so that the volume of production has been expanded way beyond the capacity of the same number of workers operating independently. Organization has made for rapid and extensive development of technology and the improving technology in turn has increased the advantages of administrative coordination. . . .

8. But the very concentration of economic activity which brought increased productivity has by its nature destroyed the free market and disrupted the operations of the law of supply and demand in a great many industries and for the economy as a whole. . . .

9. Evidence of this disruption is to be found in the administrative character and relative inflexibility of price in a great many industries and the fact that, on the whole, prices during the Depression have tended to go down least where the drop in demand has been greatest.

10. The failure of prices to adjust is perfectly familiar to businessmen in nearly every industry. But the implications of this familiar fact for the economy as a whole have not been recognized.

11. In a large part of industry, the market is not equating supply and demand through a flexible price mechanism, but is bringing an adjustment of production to demand at administratively determined prices. Thus, General Motors may set the f.o.b. price of a 1934 Chevrolet at $500 and produce the half million cars demanded at that price, yet be willing and eager to produce and sell a million cars at that price if only there were buyers. . . .

12. The presence of administered prices, while it does not indicate monopoly, does mean that the number of concerns competing in the market has been reduced to the point that the individual concern has a significant power to choose within limits between changing its prices and changing its volume of production or sales. . . . When any small drop in demand occurs, it is in a position to hold its price and reduce its production without losing all its business. As a result it tends to hold up price and reduce volume of production for the industry as a whole.

13. But this means that individuals have a direct power over industrial policy which they exercise in making business policy for their own enterprise.

14. The distinction drawn here between industrial policy and business policy is of the greatest importance.

15. According to laissez-faire principles, industrial policy was supposed to result from the interaction in the market of the business policies of a large number of independent units, no one of which had any significant power. In the truly atomistic economy to which the principles of laissez-faire applied, no individual buyer or seller alone had any significant power over either price or total volume of production for the industry. Prior to AAA, agricultural products, such as wheat and cotton, were produced and marketed under these conditions.

16. Where the number of competing units in a particular industry have been reduced to a relatively small handful, industrial policy is no longer made wholly by the market but in part by individuals. Industrial policy becomes subject to administrative control even though there is no monopoly or collusion between the separate enterprises.

17. But when the businessman has the power to affect industrial policy, he almost necessarily makes wrong industrial decisions. The very position, experience, and training of the businessman which lead him to make the correct decisions on business policy tend to force him to make the wrong decisions on industrial policy in spite of the utmost public spirit which he, as an individual, may seek to exercise. The fact that his decisions are wrong from the point of view of the public interest is no necessary reflection on either his character or his intelligence, but arises from the nature of the situation within which he operates and the functions which he performs.

18. The businessman is expected to make business policy in a way to maximize the profits of his own enterprise. When he has the power to choose between lowering price and lowering production, good business policy frequently requires him, in the presence of falling demand, to hold price and curtail his production, even though this means idle men and idle machines. The amount by which he can count on increasing his sales by lowering price is usually so small that the whole balance of his interest as a businessman points toward a restriction of production. The fact that he can lay off his workers enables him to cut production without having to carry the burden of idle workers as he does that of idle machines.

His interest dictates lowering price only when he is able to squeeze his costs, particularly his labor costs. At best, it is an even choice whether he will choose to maintain profits or minimize losses by seeking a relatively large profit margin on a reduced volume or a small margin on a maintained volume of sales, and in such a situation the easier device, and the one involving the lesser risk, is the device of holding price and accepting curtailed volume. It is only because this holding of prices has become widespread and customary that the term "price chiseler" could be a term of opprobrium in an economy supposed to be coordinated through flexible prices.

19. The net effect of business control over industrial policy is, therefore, to aggravate any fluctuations in economic activity and prevent any necessary readjustments. An initial drop in demand would result, not in price readjustment but in maintained prices and curtailment of production, thus throwing workers and machines out of employment, reducing money income and spending power, and further reducing demand. The inflexible administered prices resulting from the shift from market to administration thus act as a disrupting factor in the economy and could cause an initial small drop in demand to become a national disaster.

20. Only as the businessman was willing to go directly counter to the interests of his enterprise as a profit-making concern and against business tradition would he make the kind of decisions which, if made throughout industry, would keep the economy functioning and would serve the fundamental interests of business itself. If, during the Depression, individual businessmen throughout the economy had been persuaded to lower their prices, thus making decisions which appeared by all the standards available to them to be adverse to their interests, the result would actually have been in their interest since it would have reduced the severity of the breakdown.

21. So long, therefore, as concentration exists and important powers over industrial policy are exercised in the guise of business policy and result in inflexible administered prices, the market cannot be expected to coordinate and balance economic activity under a policy of laissez-faire.

22. Thus, administrative coordination — the very thing that has made modern technology and a high standard of living possible — has destroyed the effectiveness of the market as an overall coordinator by the inflexible administered prices which are inherent in the reduction of competing units it has produced.

23. It is the effects of this failure of the market mechanism which have brought the overwhelming demand from many quarters for governmental intervention in economic matters. This inflexibility has impeded the balancing of trade between nations, disrupted the workings of monetary policy, brought the banking system to its knees, obstructed the full use of human and material resources, disorganized the flow of savings into useful equipment, brought an unbalanced national budget, and greatly increased economic insecurity. . . .

Possible Techniques for
Making Industrial Policy

1. If the NRA and AAA are to develop a partnership technique wherein government and industry are in some way combined to establish the necessary elements of industrial policy, the location and division of power and responsibility in making decisions will importantly affect the likelihood that key decisions will be made "right." Four different methods of distributing responsibility appear to be within the realm of immediate possibility.

(*a*) Decisions could be made by a body (code authority or control committee) made up of businessmen (or farmers) with the government acting as a rubber stamp, reserving its veto power for extreme cases. This is the method which the NRA and, to a lesser extent, the AAA employed for the most part during their first year.

(*b*) The government might undertake to

make these decisions and impose them on industry, using Research and Planning Division to determine what would be "right," perhaps using the code authorities and control committees as channels for carrying out the decisions, supplemented by some method of enforcement.

(c) The code authorities and control committees might constitute a balanced partnership between government and business in which government represented not only the public interest but also the specific interests of other groups in industry, i.e., labor and consumers.

(d) The several interests might jointly be represented in making the key decisions with the government, in possession of all the necessary factual data, exercising a veto power and responsible for seeing that the interactions of the several interests produced a balance in the public interest.

2. A body of businessmen constituting a code authority will almost necessarily make the wrong decisions on industrial policy for their industry for the same reasons that in an individual enterprise power over industrial policy leads to harmful industrial decisions. As has been indicated, this is due not primarily to lack of business foresight and intelligence but to the fact situation with which each industrial authority has to deal. Partly because of the particular interest which the businessmen have in the industrial policy established and partly because the experience and training of businessmen have been primarily in the exercise of business judgment, the decisions on industrial policy inevitably tend to be made in terms of business policy.

The result for each industry is comparable to the result when individual businessmen make elements of industrial policy through their own, strongly situated enterprises. The pressure to create values by establishing higher prices and lower production will persist. In each industry, the only sound business answer to falling demand is to restrict production so as to hold prices.

The fact situation does not allow of any other business decision, even though the business interests of each industry would ultimately be better served if all industries lowered prices in the presence of falling demand. . . .

It is thus apparent that sound industrial policy cannot be expected if left to business groups alone, whether because in making industrial policy they act in their own business interest or simply because they exercise sound business judgment. When the lumber code authority raised prices, thus impeding recovery, it was acting according to sound business policy in the interests of the businessmen in the industry. To blame the lumber code authority for not establishing an effective industrial policy is to place the blame where it does not belong. It should rest on those who would place such a responsibility upon businessmen alone on the assumption that business policy, which aims to create values, and industrial policy, which aims to get things to people, are the same, and that those who are familiar with and interested in the one can be expected to accomplish the other. Only as businessmen failed to act as businessmen and failed to follow their business judgment would their decisions on industrial policy result in a properly functioning economy.

3. If the government took on the whole job of making industrial decisions, it would be better equipped with the information necessary to the making of sound decisions than would anyone else; it is committed to the public interest as the basis for those decisions; and it commands the powers of enforcement.

On the other hand, it is doubtful whether the government could effectively exercise the whole function of making industrial policy without using almost dictatorial methods. It would inevitably become the focus of group pressures vastly more vigorous and disruptive than those now existing; it would expose itself to political attack as dictatorial, and errors in detail would be used against it as political ammunition; industrial policy-making by government itself would call for a very high degree of centralization.

4. The third possibility — joint action of government and business, with the government representing not only the public interest but also the specific interests of labor and consumer groups — would probably provide the most effective available method for getting the interests of the nondominant economic groups represented in the immediate future.

On the other hand, the government would thereby be placed in the position of playing a dual role. In behalf of the public interest it should act as arbiter between conflicting interests; as representative of labor and consumer interests it should play a partisan role. It would be most difficult for the government to perform this partisan role, for it would be constantly under pressure from business, the strongest of the economic interest groups, to act at least equally in its behalf; democratic government rests upon the philosophy that it is an impartial rather than a partisan body; and even if this present administration, or any other particular administration, succeeded in acting on behalf of the nondominant groups, there is neither guarantee nor likelihood that the political commitments of future administrations would permit them so to act.

5. In the fourth possibility, that of having the several interests impinge upon each other under government supervision, the government would be placed in a favorable position to influence the decisions in the direction of the public interest as it would not have to play a partisan role and it would not have to thrust industrial policy upon those who had not shared directly in the making of that policy. Most of the conflict between economic interests would take place between representatives of these interests rather than focusing upon a representative of government.

The introduction of the other interests besides those of business would tend to push the decisions in the direction of the balance of interests which the market is supposed to achieve and whereby it is supposed to produce the optimum functioning of the economy. . . . The pressure from labor representatives to maintain or increase employment and from consumer representatives to lower prices and maintain the fullest use of labor and machines would be set against the businessman's normal tendency to establish higher prices and lower production than the public interest demands.

Thus, in the case of canned peaches, the size of the peach pack was actually decided by a control committee composed of growers and canners, with the secretary of agriculture exercising a veto power over the decision. The figure finally fixed was probably not as large as the public interest demanded. The growers wanted a somewhat larger pack, the canners a smaller pack. Both consumers and picking and canning labor would have been better served by a larger pack. If consumer and labor representatives had also participated in making the decision, it is probable that the size finally set would have been somewhat larger. At the same time, if the consumers and workers had attempted to increase the size of pack too far, the growers would have shifted sides and joined the canners in resisting further increase since too large a pack would have been just as much against their interests as too small a pack.

It would be essential for the consumer interest to be represented as well as those of business and labor, for labor cannot always be relied upon to counteract the inclination of business to create value by restricting production. Too often labor representatives, by focusing their attention on the division of the spoils, would be persuaded to join business in using the scarcity technique in return for higher money wages. This is indicated by the experience of some of the German cartels in which business and labor combined to exploit the consumers — *i.e.,* the owners and workers in other industries — and of some American cities where organized labor and organized business in the building industry have combined for similar exploitation. The inclusion of consumer representatives along with those of business and labor would insure a direct pressure for the full use of resources.

The chief disadvantages of such a set-up would be: (1) that the diverse interests are not equally strong as pressure groups, so that the greater and more effective organization of business would make business interests still dominant; and (2) that the veto power in the hands of the government and the necessity of getting agreement on the part of conflicting groups may lead to stalemates in particular situations — a disadvantage which might also present itself if the government represented the nondominant groups in a partnership with business.

6. Whichever method of determining the key elements of industrial policy is adopted, problems distinctive to each solution must be met.

(a) If the government is to do the whole job, an effective enforcement machinery must be developed; it would be essential to secure public acceptance of the idea that government should exercise such power over industry; the problems inherent in centralization would have to be solved. The direct impact of conflicting groups upon the government could be minimized by the creation of an advisory body for each industry within which the conflicting interests were represented.

(b) If the government is to represent the nondominant economic groups, the problem becomes that of pitting the political power of these groups against the economic power of the business group. This would call for a definite realignment of political parties on the basis of economic interests.

(c) If the interests are to impinge on each other, labor and consumer interests must be strengthened as pressure groups, presumably through the building up of their organizations. Such organizations would gain a status which they do not now have by being given a constructive role to play in the making of industrial policy, and the government might properly take positive steps to encourage their growth, just as it did in the case of business organizations in the first year of NRA and in the case of farmers through the encouragement of farm cooperatives and the farm-extension service. As the interest groups became more nearly equal in power, their decisions would tend increasingly to be in the public interest.

The danger of stalemate is inherent in any solution which contains the element of democracy and which avoids both a positive dictatorship and the complete atomization of industry necessary to make laissez-faire operate effectively. By shifting the major emphasis in industrial relations from the division of the spoils to making the economic machine work — a shift which is basic to the whole technique here described — a chief reason for stalemate would automatically be removed.

7. The choice among these possible ways of determining key elements of industrial policy should be made with reference to the basic requirements for a satisfactory American program. It should be geared to the conditions established by modern technology; it should leave existing economic and governmental organization intact as far as possible; it should provide the minimum centralization compatible with necessary coordination and avoid as far as possible bureaucracy and political influence; it should secure industrial decisions in the direction of the optimum use of human and material resources and a balance of economic interest among various groups; it should meet the traditional American demands for liberty, opportunity, and democracy as far as the need to provide security will permit, and it must be compatible with the Constitution.

65.

Hugh S. Johnson: The New Deal Experiment

General Hugh S. Johnson had served on the War Industries Board during World War I and from that experience had concluded that a planned economy was suited to peace as well as to war. In 1933 he helped to frame the National Industrial Recovery Act and became the first director of its executive agency, the NRA. He hoped in time to bring the departments of labor and commerce under the agency's control. Johnson was retired in the fall of 1934 — his fluctuating temperament was wearing his associates down — and thereafter wrote a book, The Blue Eagle from Egg to Earth *(1935), from which the following selection is taken. The "Blue Eagle" had become, under Johnson's direction, the symbol of the NRA.*

Source: *The Blue Eagle from Egg to Earth*, Garden City, N.Y., 1935, pp. 158-188.

THERE IS SOMETHING about this depression that doesn't speak well for what we call our common sense. We have suffered for five years. And for what? The fields are just as green and fruitful, the skies are just as blue as they were in the 1929 boom, when everybody was going to get rich and poverty was to be no more in the land. The birds and the beasts seem to be faring about as well as ever — except those in care of men — and, so far as one can see just riding through, there is nothing much the matter with the country — until we get to the Lords of Creation — the vaunted human race.

If we saw a squirrel starving to death in a knothole in his nut-filled hollow tree, we wouldn't believe it. And yet here are 125,000,000 people — granaries full, factories shut — but with millions of workers idle and hungry and shabby and afraid of the future and of everything and everybody about them — and money galore in banks and depositories. It just doesn't make sense. It is too much like a dark huddle of jungle savages dying, by swarms, of Asiatic cholera, because nobody ever told them to wash their hands before eating. It is a shocking thing.

Although tariffs and selective taxes and Adamson Acts and many other devices affect the natural laws of supply and demand, yet during the depression and up to March 4, 1933, few legislative steps were tried and the argument was, "Let things alone and they will get all right because they always did, and because you cannot interfere with natural laws." That is the same philosophy that kills the savages. It is the philosophy that opposes vaccination for smallpox or the use of a parachute when you jump out of a balloon. We can and do daily interfere with natural laws. It is fair to say that if we had let things alone for a few weeks longer we *would* have had to call somebody in — the undertaker and the riot squad.

We have mechanized our industries and specialized our people. Families are no longer self-contained, economic units that can be put on wheels and trundled into a new environment to start things over again. Our nineteenth century safety valve of cheap or free new lands and a constantly expanding country has ceased to exist. The old order of our frontier days is gone forever and by no man's designing. All this had brought benefits, but it has also brought great griefs. The roaring, clacking engine of our industry and commerce has become a vast and highly active machine of which no individual is more than an integrated part. Each performs a specialized function.

In most cases living income comes as a matter of determination by a power with whom there is no bargaining in any true sense. The individual worker accepts the wage scales decreed by employers and is thankful, and his separation from the particular ratchet in which he revolves may be a tragedy. At his doorway there is no longer an open road to high adventure in a new and brighter country, and even if there were such a road, his specialization has unfitted him to take it.

In March 1933, we had almost achieved economic collapse. Of the credit and product and hoarded reserve of domestic industry and labor and agriculture (indeed of all our people) *too much had been concentrated on production — too little on distribution and consumption.* The people's financial resources were thus squandered, either through their own unwise investment or the equal madness of their bankers. The results were a grotesque speculative structure of values; an elephantine production and service plant; a creeping paralysis of consumption and employment which began as far back as 1926; a decay of agriculture which began even further back in 1921; and an interior cavity in domestic absorptive and resisting power which started coincident with this diversion and impairment of the proper income of all people, but which was concealed until 1929 by an expansion of all kinds of credit — an expansion like a bubble — the skin of which became so tenuous and thin in 1929 that no power on earth could have saved it.

If you want to know where the consuming power of America went, you need only look around you and see it congealed in icebergs of unnecessary building and unneeded plants — and in the dead leaves of the worthless securities which financed them, and our fatuous foreign loans. Suppose that, instead of so freezing such vast sums a prudent part of them had been distributed in wages and dividends or conserved in cushions of credit invested in more stable securities — does anybody doubt that we would never have suffered this Gethsemane?

But suppose anybody *had* foreseen it all in its precise and exact value as late as 1928 and — seeing it — could have convinced the nation? What could have been done about it as the law then stood? Precisely and exactly nothing — except perhaps to have precipitated an earlier and slightly less violent collapse. Why? Because our law and institutions were such that neither industry, nor labor, nor banking, nor finance could effectively act in unison. . . .

We did not concede that we must try to balance production and consumption and that the best way to increase both is to *push them up together.* The way to do that is to try to balance and correlate the income of great groups. We must not let too much of profit and the people's credit and savings run into unwise speculative obligations of debt for the purpose of increasing production. We should try to direct more of it toward the uses of distribution and consumption, so that farmers and workers and *all* producers can constantly consume more and more in order that there may be more employment, more business, more profit and that the people of this bountiful country can enjoy to the full the fruit of their own labor and the resources which are now locked away from them. We did not act on the principle that *it is the distressed and backward economic areas which topple the structure of prosperity, make depressions, and that the exploitation of any class is a downward drag on the progress of the whole people.*

If we could have perfect balance among all producing segments — agriculture, capital, industry, workers in industry, the services, and the segment engaged in transportation and distribution, there would be almost no limit to our consuming capacity. Of course, that is Utopia and can never be attained. My only point is that all law, all administration, and all popular effort should be directed toward that goal instead of away from that goal. I think that the *essence of the New Deal is to point toward that balance*. I think that the *essence of what preceded the New Deal was to point away from that balance*.

Savage wolfish competition without any direction whatever, has proved to be one of the most destructive forces in our economic life. When it got savage and wolfish enough it began immediately to gnaw upon the living standards of wage and salary earners and hence of farmers, and that happens to include over 85 percent of our population. When times are fabulously good the great prosperity of the few filters down to the many and tends to obscure this tendency. But in normal times, and especially when depression such as that which began five years ago comes upon us like a blight and millions of men begin tramping the streets looking for any kind of work that will afford a crust of bread for their families, the whole aspect changes. . . .

As long ago as 1928, no less a rugged individualist than Herbert Hoover told the nation at Boston that, after increasing our per-man production in industry by 40 percent in a few years, we were producing more than we could consume at home and that we would *have to sell to export* — "*or else*." And that was at a time when we were setting so close to "two cars in every garage" that we were almost ready to call in the carpenters — a time when inflated purchasing power was at its maximum. NRA has taken the position that some *regulation* of new laborsaving devices is advisable, but it has never prohibited new installations. It has said only, "Let's look at them first, and

if the government in consultation with the industry feel that they would now do more harm than good, let's postpone them."

For several years prior to NRA it had been my job for Mr. Baruch to keep in contact with new processes in industry from a purely practical point of view. No man who had lived through those years in that kind of a job could fail to agree with Mr. Hoover's 1928 Boston prophecy — not with his remedy of export trade. . . .

The "economy of plenty" is not plain sailing. We have had it in agriculture ever since the war when, in order to feed our allied friends (who will not now pay even for what they ate — much less for the consequence to us of our efforts for them) we increased our production of cash crops to an astonishing degree. We had plenty with a vengeance when they stopped buying. The theory of the Apostles of Plenty is that that disaster resulting from too much surplus will starve out the surplus-producing acres down to a balance of supply and demand — but in twelve years *it hasn't*.

And if it *did* — what? Must we go through an indefinite period of peonage and destitution while starvation proceeds to balance the account? The farm tragedy in the United States is one of the most sickening chapters in our economic history. We can't sell more bread than people will eat, or make women go back to five and six petticoats to consume our cotton. Production of surplus beyond consumptive requirements has always destroyed price. Destructive price destroys wages which destroys consuming power which again destroys price down to the very depths of the 1933 pit.

Neither is it true in industry that excess productive capacity dries up when bankruptcy overtakes the marginal producer. Somebody simply buys up the ruin at a slaughter price and thus relieved of much of the overhead of interest, depreciation and taxation goes merrily on producing at a new cutthroat price. Why I know one old buggy plant that has been through liquidation over and over again. It still runs and most appropriately it is now making *hearses.*

The Apostles of Plenty must temper their doctrine. The answer is not to produce as much as you can at the lowest cost you can get, especially if that low cost comes out of wages or too abruptly out of employment. That simply starts the descent into the economic Avernus — cut employment, cut consuming power, cut production and so cut employment again. We simply must supervise these trends.

Always the answer is *"balance"* — balance of supply to demand, balance of prices at fair exchange parity throughout the whole economic structure, and balance of benefits among great economic areas. You cannot even move toward this balance in this modern muddle without *some* direction. NRA offers one way to get that supervision in industry just as AAA offers it in agriculture and the various securities and fiscal acts in investment and banking. These statutory makeshifts are not the final answer. Everybody knows that. They are hasty and imperfect. *But* the very heart of the New Deal is the principle of concerted action in industry and agriculture under government supervision looking to a balanced economy as opposed to the murderous doctrine of savage and wolfish competition and rugged individualism, looking to dog-eat-dog and devil take the hindmost. This Utopian balance will never be achieved — there will never be perfection. But every plan should try to achieve it instead of trying to prevent it. . . .

Before the war, American business was a honeycomb of water-tight industrial compartments. Each cell was jealously guarded. There was a maximum of competition and a minimum of cooperation. Ruthless and untempered competition was decreed by the Sherman and Clayton acts. The war changed that. The world went mad. The nations entered a contest to see which could pour the greatest mass of its young manhood and the largest amount of its money

and property into the fire in the shortest space of time. That was the way to win the war.

The old honeycomb machine of the United States couldn't produce things fast enough in this race to destroy everything. We had to scrap it. And in the short period between April 1917 and November 1918, we literally tore it apart and put it together again. On the call of government and under the pressure of patriotism the old individualist battlers royal became an organized squad — all marching toward the sound of the guns.

We did not repeal the Antitrust Acts. *We simply ignored them.* Competitors pooled their resources, their trade secrets, their facilities. Industries organized themselves into groups and figures with the speed and almost the precision of a highly drilled chorus on a musical comedy stage and government took charge of both production and consumption and, to a large extent, prices. It worked. It poured forth such a flood of production for the uses of war as the world had never seen in one country. It won the war.

Woodrow Wilson dispersed the 1918 model Industrial Control Mechanism with a single edict before the year of the Armistice was out. But much of the change in the underlying pattern of trade and industry which had resulted from it remained. The country had learned that cooperation and organization pay. It had learned that high wages and short hours create wider domestic markets — richer than any market to be sought elsewhere in the whole world. It was freely said: "If cooperation can do so much maybe there is something wrong with the old competitive system." . . .

We had supervised cooperation in the war because we had to have it or suffer defeat. There was a "let-us-alone" gang then also, but we swept them into the ashcan and there was no longer any sentiment for the old slogan of "Let-us-alone" because all knew that government intervention was the sole salvation. When that pressure was gone, "Let-us-alone" rebounded into light and became the guiding principle of government administration from the depths of 1921 to the giddy peaks of 1929.

"Let-us-alone" and unhampered individualism worked well enough during the formative days of individual pioneering — nothing else would have worked — but it did not work when we had to meet the war crisis and after-the-war reorganization of trade and industry. It had become a relic of old days and, as things turned out, a very dangerous one.

"Let-us-alone" and every man to himself is one thing when every man can *be* for himself, but it is a very different thing when progress has organized it out of existence but statutes still retain it.

At the adoption of the Constitution almost everybody worked for himself — the boot and shoe industry was the village cobbler, the textile industry was the housewife and the weaver, the steel industry was the forge and the smithy, the electric light industry was the candlemaker, and so forth through the whole gamut. In such a scene we invented the doctrine of rugged individualism. . . .

There is now much talk about the desirability of a return to the good old Antitrust Acts and the safety of the Federal Trade Commission. They talk about the mild control of NRA as encouraging monopoly, oppressing small enterprise, and thus threatening people with economic serfdom. . . . *NRA will have to move on a broad front and at terrific speed if it can beat that record of the destruction of individual enterprise made under the full force of the Antitrust Acts, the negative powers of the Federal Trade Commission, and the most active business period in our history.*

It is black on the record that the unchecked competitive plan under the Antitrust Acts was destroying small enterprise of every kind at a most astonishing rate. It is a shorter record but equally certain the NRA has exactly reversed this killing process.

Competition down to reasonable cost is still as free as air but the public does not want and cannot afford competition of bankrupt stocks and it is now protected against the flim-flam of being enticed into a store by a window display of some popular product being sold for half its cost and then inveigled into buying other things at a good fat profit. There is a curious, almost maddening, confusion in terms when superficial observers begin using the words "monopoly," "price fixing," "antitrust acts," etc.

The Antitrust Acts prohibit combinations in restraint of trade. But NRA specifically permits such combinations with government sanction and supervision. *There is not one single Code that is not a combination in restraint of trade,* and if Codes are not permitted so to restrain trade then NIRA ought to be repealed tomorrow. It doesn't mean a thing.

But both NIRA and the Antitrust Acts do prohibit monopoly — there is no question about that. The only real question that has been raised comes from the assertion that price agreements and combinations in restraint of trade *are of themselves* monopolistic. *That is the very heart of the question that plagues NRA.*

Of course price control *can* be used as a weapon of monopoly. It has frequently been so used and that use of it was the very reason for the Antitrust Acts themselves. But that was price control *downward* in an effort to destroy competition and practiced by powerful combinations for the specific and determined purpose of oppressing and wiping out small enterprise and individual initiative, and transforming all business in the country into a gigantic corporate cluster under private control — an unthinkable and intolerable result. No such thing exists or is attempted or could exist or be attempted under any code.

NRA price stabilizations are all for exactly the reverse purpose — to prevent cutthroat and monopolistic price slashing, to maintain small industry, to continue employment, to abolish economic murder. There is only a fragmentary element of cases where this is not true — *i.e.*, cases in which small industries can pay code wages and actually undersell large ones and whenever and as often as this happens relief is given at once. There was never a more ghastly, nonsensical, and destructive anomaly than the charge that price controls under NRA tend toward monopoly. The trend is in precisely the reverse direction. So far as that particular argument is concerned, it is a silly sophistry inimical to the public welfare.

Furthermore, while there is price stabilization in many codes, there is actual price fixing in only three or four cases and in those, such as Bituminous Coal — it was absolutely necessary to support the labor dependent on that industry and to prevent bloody and implacable economic war. That became so apparent and unavoidable during the Bituminous negotiations that I called the President's attention to it and obtained his personal approval to negotiations on that basis.

Of course there are two other aspects of this subject which are rarely mentioned but which are really matter for grave concern. In the first place there are parts of industries which have been built up on *low prices derived from sweated labor* — such as sweatshops, dependents on home piece-work and child labor, and other cases which will be described at another place. When *they* are forced by NRA to pay living wages, they cannot continue to exist. They say, therefore, that NRA *oppresses* them.

But as to this the President, in giving NRA its marching orders, took the bull by the horns. He said that *no industry which depends for existence on less than living wages has a right to continue to exist.* And on that phase of my administration I stand or fall. These were not only my orders — they were also my convictions. I will concede that all the regional differentials under NRA are not scientifically worked out. I know there is a wide field where readjustment is

necessary. But that is no argument for permitting the return of the scandalous labor conditions revealed by NRA.

The second question is *whether the consumer has a right to the lowest prices that any kind of competition can provide.* The Antitrust Acts say yes. NIRA says no. And there is the white-hot center of the dispute. Everybody is a consumer. Nearly everybody depends on *some* enterprise in the competitive field. Consumers are not entitled to low prices achieved by the degradation of human labor and if they were entitled to them they would be fatuous to accept them, because once the principle is admitted it applies to all human labor and all human labor consumes. Nor are consumers wise in seeking the low prices of economic slaughter — especially at a time like this when explosive and disruptive changes in the existing structure throw more and more people out of work.

On all these considerations, NRA came as a blessed alleviation of the dog-eat-dog rule of the Antitrust Acts. This does not mean that there is no competition or even any improper limitation of competition under NRA. It means only that competition must keep its blows above the belt, and that there can be no competition at the expense of decent living. The only price limitations in NRA, outside of three (or at most four) special cases, are limitations against making a practice of selling at less than cost of production for the purpose of destroying competition or of preventing competition based on the degradation of human labor. . . .

The net of all I have just written is to urge that price fixing is not necessarily monopolistic and under NRA it is not monopolistic at all. But there remains the other assertion that *any combination in restraint of trade is monopolistic in and of itself.* . . . If it is, NRA had better be abandoned because *every* code is a combination in restraint of trade. For example, the Petroleum Code's provision to limit production is restraint of trade, limitations on machine hours are restraints, agreements against child labor and sweatshops and in favor of maximum hours and minimum wages are all restraints of trade. So are agreements not to use particular kinds of advertising, or secret rebates, or credit terms which might ruin companies not financed to grant them, and so forth and so on through the infinite variety of NRA code provisions.

But these things are *not* of themselves monopolistic. A monopolistic combination is an easy thing to concoct. But whether a combination is monopolistic or not is a question of fact. Code combinations are not conspiracies of a few companies. They are open to a whole industry on absolutely equal terms to great and little companies. It would be impossible to create a combination of that kind that could be monopolistic. It might be repugnant to consumers' interest or be otherwise objectionable. But the word "industry" comprises *all* competitors in a particular field and if all competitors in an industry operate under the same code rule, that rule could not possibly be monopolistic.

NRA contended that neither price fixing nor fair trade practices authorized by NIRA are under the ban of the Antitrust Acts, unless they are monopolistic or oppressive, *in fact*. Some of NRA's enemies contend that *any* price fixing or *any* combination is inherently monopolistic. That, of course, means that the deliberate Act of Congress known as NIRA is simply a nullity. . . .

But to return to our story — during the whirling, industrial period between the war and the depression, the rapid growth of domestic demand due to post-war higher wages and shorter hours encouraged the creation of bigger and bigger industrial units, greater and greater industrial capacity, and vast profits accrued — not to "little fellows" but on paper, at least, to these great economic clusters. There was economic planning a-plenty but the planning was done by executives of vast corporations.

Even that might have saved us but there were too many plans with no cohesion, coordination, or control and with no regard for industry as a whole, or labor as a whole, or even for the country as a whole, but only for the competitive victory of the particular industrial unit — rugged individualism of gigantic artificial corporate persons, but no rugged individualism of any natural person except in his role as a servant or master within them.

And because, for each of them separately, there was no incentive — nor even any leeway — to do otherwise, they separately plowed so much of gross profit and the people's savings back into increasingly excessive capacity and distributed too little of it as wages and dividends to sustain the buying power of the rich domestic market which the war changes had created on their own doorsteps. They literally starved that market to death.

This has been recently denied and the denial backed by a bristling marshaling of imposing figures showing how little accumulated surplus in industrial balance sheets would have aided consumption if they *had* been distributed. They are entirely beside the point. They neglect to say how much of popular savings and credit was also thus frozen and they came from the "economist" of a bank which was as responsible for as much of this delusion as any.

The biggest and most expensive industrial plant or apartment house or office building in the world is a liability instead of an asset (worth less than zero) unless it can earn money. It can only earn money if it can maintain a profitable market for its product. If there are too many of them in any given market area, none can earn money. In the period of 1922-1929, nonexistent earning power was capitalized by withdrawing or withholding money (consuming power) from the public and freezing it forever into the steel, bricks, and mortar of an astonishing excess capacity-to-produce, in practically every industrial and commercial activity.

The record of this lunacy is too recent and too astonishing for any economist of an affected bank to attack with any statistical abracadabra. It burned the candle at both ends in that it destroyed the consuming power of the American market by congealing it in bricks and mortar at the same moment that it was destroying the earning power of industry itself by overcapacitating its productive facilities. It was sheer, stark madness and it was a direct and inevitable result of the Antitrust legislation.

Take the steel-plow industry as a single example which could be paralleled by a hundred others. There is one plant in Moline, Illinois, which could turn out all the steel plows required by the whole of American Agriculture. Yet that capacity is multiplied no less than ten times in the United States.

Nothing like that could have happened if, during that crazed period, the industries of this country could have taken counsel and united action under governmental sanction and supervision. It happened because they were doomed by the law to unchecked and uncontrolled competition — doomed by the law not to take common counsel, not to regard each industry as a unit, and not to regard the country as an economic integer in which every citizen had an interest and every employer an obligation. They could not have saved themselves because any company that lagged in the fight for a new capacity, constantly increasing production, and the other fellow's market, would go to the wall. The laws of the United States simply said: "Root hog or die — Devil take the hindmost," and the Devil took it all. "The bigger they are, the harder they fall," and this structure first became monstrously big and then fell with a crash that shook the whole world. . . .

You can't have recovery without amending the Antitrust Acts because you must prevent a repetition of 1922-1929. You can't do that without control and you can't have that control under Antitrust legislation. Those Acts have failed in every crisis. They had to be forgotten during the war to enable the country to defend itself. When they came back to memory in 1919, they set the stage for what happened up to 1929. They contributed to the boom and they were helpless in the crash. Without amendment, following the principles of NIRA, they will go on (as they did) to create the very condition of monopoly and erasure of individualism which they were conceived to prevent and in the future, as in the past, they will have to be abandoned in any crisis, economic or military. Unless so amended, they have no place in the mechanized, highly organized, and integrated civilization in which we live. *There is no more vital and fundamental issue before the country than whether we are going to control modern scientific and industrial development to our use or suffer it to our destruction.*

The only forces that *can* control it are industrial self-government under Federal supervision and the only plan that has ever been presented through which that control can be applied is NRA. If we scrap NRA, it will be just like releasing on a roomful of schoolchildren a flock of mechanical maneating Frankensteins — irresistible and ravenous. If we follow and develop and perfect NRA, it will be like harnessing them, putting brains into their brazen skulls and driving them in a powerful team to pull us out of the mud of this morass.

———◆———

It will be red fire at first and dead cats afterwards. This is just like mounting the guillotine on the infinitesimal gamble that the ax won't work.
                    HUGH S. JOHNSON, to friends who congratulated him on his
                    (rumored, later actual) appointment as head of NRA, June
                    1933

66.

Charles Evans Hughes: *A. L. A. Schechter Poultry Corporation et al.* v. *United States*

By the beginning of 1935 a number of cases challenging the constitutionality of New Deal legislation had worked their way up to the Supreme Court. One of the most important of these was Schechter Poultry Corp. v. United States, *otherwise known as the "Sick Chicken Case." The Schechter company had sued the government, claiming that controls exerted over its operations in the state of New York by the National Recovery Administration (NRA) were unconstitutional. In a lower court decision, Judge Learned Hand had thrown out the company's petition, but on an appeal to the Supreme Court it won the case. The decision, by Chief Justice Charles Evans Hughes for a unanimous Court, was handed down on May 27, 1935, a date afterward known as the "Black Monday" of the New Deal. The NRA was invalidated on three grounds: first, that it involved excessive delegation of legislative power to the executive; second, that there was a lack of constitutional authority for such legislation; and, third, that the NRA had been empowered to regulate businesses wholly intrastate in character, which was a misapplication of the commerce clause of the Constitution. The decision, broad in scope, served notice that the administration was in serious trouble in its legislative program. A portion of the opinion is reprinted here.*

Source: 295 U.S. 495.

PETITIONERS IN NO. 854 were convicted in the District Court of the United States for the Eastern District of New York on eighteen counts of an indictment charging violations of what is known as the "Live Poultry Code," and on an additional count for conspiracy to commit such violations. By demurrer to the indictment and appropriate motions on the trial, the defendants contended: (1) that the Code had been adopted pursuant to an unconstitutional delegation by Congress of legislative power; (2) that it attempted to regulate intrastate transactions which lay outside the authority of Congress; and (3) that in certain provisions it was repugnant to the due process clause of the Fifth Amendment. . . .

The "Live Poultry Code" was promulgated under Section 3 of the National In-dustrial Recovery Act. That section . . . authorizes the President to approve "codes of fair competition." Such a code may be approved for a trade or industry upon application by one or more trade or industrial associations or groups if the President finds: (1) that such associations or groups "impose no inequitable restrictions on admission to membership therein and are truly representative"; and (2) that such codes are not designed "to promote monopolies or to eliminate or oppress small enterprises and will not operate to discriminate against them, and will tend to effectuate the policy" of Title I of the act. Such codes "shall not permit monopolies or monopolistic practices."

As a condition of his approval, the President may "impose such conditions (including requirements for the making of reports and the keeping of accounts) for the protection of consumers, competitors, employees, and others, and in furtherance of the public interest, and may provide such exceptions to and exemptions from the provisions of such code as the President in his discretion deems necessary to effectuate the policy herein declared." Where such a code has not been approved, the President may prescribe one, either on his own motion or on complaint. Violation of any provision of a code (so approved or prescribed) "in any transaction in or affecting interstate or foreign commerce" is made a misdemeanor punishable by a fine of not more than $500 for each offense, and each day the violation continues is to be deemed a separate offense.

The "Live Poultry Code" was approved by the President on April 13, 1934. Its divisions indicate its nature and scope. The Code has eight articles entitled (1) purposes, (2) definitions, (3) hours, (4) wages, (5) general labor provisions, (6) administration, (7) trade practice provisions, and (8) general.

The declared purpose is "To effect the policies of Title I of the National Industrial Recovery Act." The Code is established as "a code of fair competition for the live poultry industry of the metropolitan area in and about the city of New York." That area is described as embracing the five boroughs of New York City, the counties of Rockland, Westchester, Nassau, and Suffolk in the state of New York, the counties of Hudson and Bergen in the state of New Jersey, and the county of Fairfield in the state of Connecticut.

The "industry" is defined as including "every person engaged in the business of selling, purchasing for resale, transporting, or handling and/or slaughtering live poultry, from the time such poultry comes into the New York metropolitan area to the time it is first sold in slaughtered form," and such "related branches" as may from

time to time be included by amendment. Employers are styled "members of the industry," and the term "employee" is defined to embrace "any and all persons engaged in the industry, however compensated," except "members."

The Code fixes the number of hours for workdays. It provides that no employee, with certain exceptions, shall be permitted to work in excess of forty (40) hours in any one week, and that no employee, save as stated, "shall be paid in any pay period less than at the rate of fifty (50) cents per hour." The article containing "general labor provisions" prohibits the employment of any person under sixteen years of age, and declares that employees shall have the right of "collective bargaining," and freedom of choice with respect to labor organizations, in the terms of Section 7(a) of the act. The minimum number of employees who shall be employed by slaughterhouse operators is fixed, the number being graduated according to the average volume of weekly sales.

Provision is made for administration through an "industry advisory committee," to be selected by trade associations and members of the industry, and a "code supervisor" to be appointed, with the approval of the committee, by agreement between the secretary of agriculture and the administrator for industrial recovery. The expenses of administration are to be borne by the members of the industry proportionately upon the basis of volume of business, or such other factors as the advisory committee may deem equitable, "subject to the disapproval of the secretary and/or administrator."

The 7th Article, containing "trade practice provisions," prohibits various practices which are said to constitute "unfair methods of competition." The final article provides for verified reports, such as the secretary or administrator may require, "(1) for the protection of consumers, competitors, employees, and others, and in furtherance of the public interest; and (2) for the determination by the secretary or administrator of the extent to which the declared policy of the act is being effectuated by this code." The members of the industry are also required to keep books and records which "will clearly reflect all financial transactions of their respective businesses and the financial condition thereof," and to submit weekly reports showing the range of daily prices and volume of sales for each kind of produce.

The President approved the Code by an executive order in which he found that the application for his approval had been duly made in accordance with the provisions of Title I of the National Industrial Recovery Act, that there had been due notice and hearings, that the Code constituted "a code of fair competition" as contemplated by the act and complied with its pertinent provisions including clauses (1) and (2) of subsection (a) of Section 3 of Title I; and that the Code would tend "to effectuate the policy of Congress as declared in Section 1 of Title I."

The executive order also recited that the secretary of agriculture and the administrator of the National Industrial Recovery Act had rendered separate reports as to the provisions within their respective jurisdictions. The secretary of agriculture reported that the provisions of the Code "establishing standards of fair competition (a) are regulations of transactions in or affecting the current of interstate and/or foreign commerce, and (b) are reasonable"; and also that the Code would tend to effectuate the policy declared in Title I of the act. . . . The report of the administrator for industrial recovery dealt with wages, hours of labor, and other labor provisions.

Of the eighteen counts of the indictment upon which the defendants were convicted, aside from the count for conspiracy, two counts charged violation of the minimum wage and maximum hour provisions of the Code, and ten counts were for violation of the requirement (found in the "trade prac-

tice provisions") of "straight killing." This requirement was really one of "straight" selling. The term "straight killing" was defined in the Code as "the practice of requiring persons purchasing poultry for resale to accept the run of any half coop, coop, or coops, as purchased by slaughterhouse operators, except for culls." The charges in the ten counts, respectively, were that the defendants in selling to retail dealers and butchers had permitted "selections of individual chickens taken from particular coops and half coops."

Of the other six counts, one charged the sale to a butcher of an unfit chicken; two counts charged the making of sales without having the poultry inspected or approved in accordance with regulations or ordinances of the city of New York; two counts charged the making of false reports or the failure to make reports relating to the range of daily prices and volume of sales for certain periods; and the remaining count was for sales to slaughterers or dealers who were without licenses required by the ordinance and regulations of the city of New York.

First, two preliminary points are stressed by the government with respect to the appropriate approach to the important questions presented. We are told that the provision of the statute authorizing the adoption of codes must be viewed in the light of the grave national crisis with which Congress was confronted. Undoubtedly, the conditions to which power is addressed are always to be considered when the exercise of power is challenged. Extraordinary conditions may call for extraordinary remedies. But the argument necessarily stops short of an attempt to justify action which lies outside the sphere of constitutional authority. Extraordinary conditions do not create or enlarge constitutional power.

The Constitution established a national government with powers deemed to be adequate, as they have proved to be both in war and peace, but these powers of the national government are limited by the constitutional grants. Those who act under these grants are not at liberty to transcend the imposed limits because they believe that more or different power is necessary. Such assertions of extra-constitutional authority were anticipated and precluded by the explicit terms of the Tenth Amendment — "The powers not delegated to the United States by the Constitution, nor prohibited by it to the states, are reserved to the states respectively, or to the people."

The further point is urged that the national crisis demanded a broad and intensive cooperative effort by those engaged in trade and industry, and that this necessary cooperation was sought to be fostered by permitting them to initiate the adoption of codes. But the statutory plan is not simply one for voluntary effort. It does not seek merely to endow voluntary trade or industrial associations or groups with privileges or immunities. It involves the coercive exercise of the lawmaking power. The codes of fair competition which the statute attempts to authorize are codes of laws. If valid, they place all persons within their reach under the obligation of positive law, binding equally those who assent and those who do not assent. Violations of the provisions of the codes are punishable as crimes.

Second, the question of the delegation of legislative power. . . . The Constitution provides that "all legislative powers herein granted shall be vested in a Congress of the United States, which shall consist of a Senate and House of Representatives." . . . And the Congress is authorized "To make all laws which shall be necessary and proper for carrying into execution" its general powers. . . . The Congress is not permitted to abdicate or to transfer to others the essential legislative functions with which it is thus vested.

We have repeatedly recognized the necessity of adapting legislation to complex conditions involving a host of details with which the national legislature cannot deal directly. . . . Accordingly, we look to the statute to see whether Congress has overstepped these limitations — whether Congress in authorizing "codes of fair competition" has itself established the standards of legal obligation, thus performing its essential legislative function, or, by the failure to enact such standards, has attempted to transfer that function to others. . . .

In its widest range, "unfair competition," as it has been understood in the law, does not reach the objectives of the codes which are authorized by the National Industrial Recovery Act. The codes may, indeed, cover conduct which existing law condemns, but they are not limited to conduct of that sort. The government does not contend that the act contemplates such a limitation. It would be opposed both to the declared purposes of the act and to its administrative construction.

The Federal Trade Commission Act (Section 5) introduced the expression "unfair methods of competition," which were declared to be unlawful. That was an expression new in the law. Debate apparently convinced the sponsors of the legislation that the words "unfair competition," in the light of their meaning at common law, were too narrow. We have said that the substituted phrase has a broader meaning, that it does not admit of precise definition, its scope being left to judicial determination as controversies arise. . . .

What are "unfair methods of competition" are thus to be determined in particular instances, upon evidence, in the light of particular competitive conditions and of what is found to be a specific and substantial public interest. . . . To make this possible, Congress set up a special procedure. A commission, a quasi-judicial body, was created. Provision was made for formal complaint, for notice and hearing, for appropriate findings of fact supported by adequate evidence, and for judicial review to give assurance that the action of the commission is taken within its statutory authority. . . .

In providing for codes, the National Industrial Recovery Act dispenses with this administrative procedure and with any administrative procedure of an analogous character. But the difference between the code plan of the Recovery Act and the scheme of the Federal Trade Commission Act lies not only in procedure but in subject matter. We cannot regard the "fair competition" of the codes as antithetical to the "unfair methods of competition" of the Federal Trade Commission Act. The "fair competition" of the codes has a much broader range and a new significance. The Recovery Act provides that it shall not be construed to impair the powers of the Federal Trade Commission, but, when a code is approved, its provisions are to be the "standards of fair competition" for the trade or industry concerned, and any violation of such standards in any transaction in or affecting interstate or foreign commerce is to be deemed "an unfair method of competition" within the meaning of the Federal Trade Commission Act. Section 3(b). . . .

The question, then, turns upon the authority which Section 3 of the Recovery Act vests in the President to approve or prescribe. If the codes have standing as penal statutes, this must be due to the effect of the executive action. But Congress cannot delegate legislative power to the President to exercise an unfettered discretion to make whatever laws he thinks may be needed or advisable for the rehabilitation and expansion of trade or industry. . . .

Accordingly, we turn to the Recovery Act to ascertain what limits have been set to the exercise of the President's discretion.

First, the President, as a condition of approval, is required to find that the trade or industrial associations or groups which propose a code, "impose no inequitable restrictions on admission to membership" and are "truly representative." That condition, however, relates only to the status of the initiators of the new laws and not to the permissible scope of such laws.

Second, the President is required to find that the code is not "designed to promote monopolies or to eliminate or oppress small enterprises and will not operate to discriminate against them." And, to this is added a proviso that the code "shall not permit monopolies or monopolistic practices." But these restrictions leave virtually untouched the field of policy envisaged by Section 1, and, in that wide field of legislative possibilities, the proponents of a code, refraining from monopolistic designs, may roam at will and the President may approve or disapprove their proposals as he may see fit. That is the precise effect of the further finding that the President is to make — that the code "will tend to effectuate the policy of this title." While this is called a finding, it is really but a statement of an opinion as to the general effect upon the promotion of trade or industry of a scheme of laws. These are the only findings which Congress has made essential in order to put into operation a legislative code having the aims described in the "Declaration of Policy."

Nor is the breadth of the President's discretion left to the necessary implications of this limited requirement as to his findings. As already noted, the President in approving a code may impose his own conditions, adding to or taking from what is proposed, as "in his discretion" he thinks necessary "to effectuate the policy" declared by the act. Of course, he has no less liberty when he prescribes a code on his own motion or on complaint, and he is free to prescribe one if a code has not been approved.

The act provides for the creation by the President of administrative agencies to assist him, but the action or reports of such agencies, or of his other assistants — their recommendations and findings in relation to the making of codes — have no sanction beyond the will of the President, who may accept, modify, or reject them as he pleases. Such recommendations or findings in no way limit the authority which Section 3 undertakes to vest in the President with no other conditions than those there specified. And this authority relates to a host of different trades and industries, thus extending the President's discretion to all the varieties of laws which he may deem to be beneficial in dealing with the vast array of commercial and industrial activities throughout the country.

Such a sweeping delegation of legislative power finds no support in the decisions upon which the government especially relies. . . .

To summarize and conclude upon this point: Section 3 of the Recovery Act is without precedent. It supplies no standards for any trade, industry, or activity. It does not undertake to prescribe rules of conduct to be applied to particular states of fact determined by appropriate administrative procedure. Instead of prescribing rules of conduct, it authorizes the making of codes to prescribe them. For that legislative undertaking, Section 3 sets up no standards, aside from the statement of the general aims of rehabilitation, correction, and expansion described in Section 1. In view of the scope of that broad declaration, and of the nature of the few restrictions that are imposed, the discretion of the President in approving or prescribing codes, and thus enacting laws for the government of trade and industry throughout the country, is virtually unfettered. We think that the code-making authority thus conferred is an unconstitutional delegation of legislative power.

Third, the question of the application of the provisions of the Live Poultry Code to intrastate transactions. Although the validity of the codes (apart from the question of delegation) rests upon the commerce clause of the Constitution, Section 3(a) is not in terms limited to interstate and foreign commerce. From the generality of its terms, and from the argument of the government at the bar, it would appear that Section 3(a) was designed to authorize codes without that limitation. But under Section 3(f) penalties are confined to violations of a code

provision "in any transaction in or affecting interstate or foreign commerce." This aspect of the case presents the question whether the particular provisions of the Live Poultry Code, which the defendants were convicted for violating and for having conspired to violate, were within the regulating power of the Congress.

These provisions relate to the hours and wages of those employed by defendants in their slaughterhouses in Brooklyn and to the sales there made to retail dealers and butchers.

Were these transactions *"in"* interstate commerce? Much is made of the fact that almost all the poultry coming to New York is sent there from other states. But the code provisions, as here applied, do not concern the transportation of the poultry from other states to New York, or the transactions of the commission men or others to whom it is consigned, or the sales made by such consignees to defendants. When defendants had made their purchases, whether at the West Washington Market in New York City or at the railroad terminals serving the city, or elsewhere, the poultry was trucked to their slaughterhouses in Brooklyn for local disposition. The interstate transactions in relation to that poultry then ended. Defendants held the poultry at their slaughterhouse markets for slaughter and local sale to retail dealers and butchers who in turn sold directly to consumers. Neither the slaughtering nor the sales by defendants were transactions in interstate commerce. . . .

The undisputed facts thus afford no warrant for the argument that the poultry handled by defendants at their slaughterhouse markets was in a *"current"* or *"flow"* of interstate commerce and was thus subject to congressional regulation. The mere fact that there may be a constant flow of commodities into a state does not mean that the flow continues after the property has arrived and has become commingled with the mass of property within the state and is there held solely for local disposition and use. So far as the poultry here in question is concerned, the flow in interstate commerce had ceased. The poultry had come to a permanent rest within the state. It was not held, used, or sold by defendants in relation to any further transactions in interstate commerce and was not destined for transportation to other states. Hence, decisions which deal with a stream of interstate commerce — where goods come to rest within a state temporarily and are later to go forward in interstate commerce — and with the regulations of transactions involved in that practical continuity of movement, are not applicable here. . . .

The instant case is not of that sort. This is not a prosecution for a conspiracy to restrain or monopolize interstate commerce in violation of the Antitrust Act. Defendants have been convicted, not upon direct charges of injury to interstate commerce or of interference with persons engaged in that commerce but of violations of certain provisions of the Live Poultry Code and of conspiracy to commit these violations. Interstate commerce is brought in only upon the charge that violations of these provisions — as to hours and wages of employees and local sales — *"affected"* interstate commerce.

In determining how far the federal government may go in controlling intrastate transactions upon the ground that they "affect" interstate commerce, there is a necessary and well-established distinction between direct and indirect effects. The precise line can be drawn only as individual cases arise, but the distinction is clear in principle. Direct effects are illustrated by the railroad cases. . . . as, *e.g.,* the effect of failure to use prescribed safety appliances on railroads which are the highways of both interstate and intrastate commerce, injury to an employee engaged in interstate transportation by the negligence of an employee engaged in an intrastate movement, the fixing of rates for intrastate transportation which unjustly discriminate against interstate commerce. But where the effect of intrastate

transactions upon interstate commerce is merely indirect, such transactions remain within the domain of state power.

If the commerce clause were construed to reach all enterprises and transactions which could be said to have an indirect effect upon interstate commerce, the federal authority would embrace practically all the activities of the people and the authority of the state over its domestic concerns would exist only by sufferance of the federal government. Indeed, on such a theory, even the development of the state's commercial facilities would be subject to federal control. . . .

The distinction between direct and indirect effects has been clearly recognized in the application of the Antitrust Act. Where a combination or conspiracy is formed, with the intent to restrain interstate commerce or to monopolize any part of it, the violation of the statute is clear. . . . But where that intent is absent, and the objectives are limited to intrastate activities, the fact that there may be an indirect effect upon interstate commerce does not subject the parties to the federal statute, notwithstanding its broad provisions. . . .

The distinction between direct and indirect effects of intrastate transactions upon interstate commerce must be recognized as a fundamental one, essential to the maintenance of our constitutional system. Otherwise, as we have said, there would be virtually no limit to the federal power and for all practical purposes we should have a completely centralized government. We must consider the provisions here in question in the light of this distinction.

The question of chief importance relates to the provisions of the Code as to the hours and wages of those employed in defendants' slaughterhouse markets. It is plain that these requirements are imposed in order to govern the details of defendants' management of their local business. The persons employed in slaughtering and selling in local trade are not employed in interstate commerce. Their hours and wages have no direct relation to interstate commerce. The question of how many hours these employees should work and what they should be paid differs in no essential respect from similar questions in other local businesses which handle commodities brought into a state and there dealt in as a part of its internal commerce. This appears from an examination of the considerations urged by the government with respect to conditions in the poultry trade.

Thus, the government argues that hours and wages affect prices; that slaughterhouse men sell at a small margin above operating costs; that labor represents 50 to 60 percent of these costs; that a slaughterhouse operator paying lower wages or reducing his cost by exacting long hours of work translates his savings into lower prices; that this results in demands for cheaper grade of goods; and that the cutting of prices brings about a demoralization of the price structure. Similar conditions may be adduced in relation to other businesses.

The argument of the government proves too much. If the federal government may determine the wages and hours of employees in the internal commerce of a state because of their relation to cost and prices and their indirect effect upon interstate commerce, it would seem that a similar control might be exerted over other elements of cost also affecting prices, such as the number of employees, rents, advertising, methods of doing business, etc. All the processes of production and distribution that enter into cost would likewise be controlled. If the cost of doing an intrastate business is in itself the permitted object of federal control, the extent of the regulation of cost would be a question of discretion and not of power.

The government also makes the point that efforts to enact state legislation establishing high labor standards have been impeded by the belief that unless similar action is taken generally, commerce will be diverted from the states adopting such standards, and that this fear of diversion has led to demands for federal legislation on the subject of wages and hours. The apparent implication is that the federal authority under the commerce clause should be deemed to extend to the establishment of rules to govern wages and hours in intrastate trade and industry generally throughout the country, thus overriding the authority of the states to deal with domestic problems arising from labor conditions in their internal commerce.

It is not the province of the Court to consider the economic advantages or disadvantages of such a centralized system. It is sufficient to say that the federal Constitution does not provide for it. Our growth and development have called for wide use of the commerce power of the federal government in its control over the expanded activities of interstate commerce and in protecting that commerce from burdens, interferences, and conspiracies to restrain and monopolize it. But the authority of the federal government may not be pushed to such an extreme as to destroy the distinction, which the commerce clause itself establishes, between commerce "among the several states" and the internal concerns of a state. The same answer must be made to the contention that is based upon the serious economic situation which led to the passage of the Recovery Act — the fall in prices, the decline in wages and employment, and the curtailment of the market for commodities. Stress is laid upon the great importance of maintaining wage distributions which would provide the necessary stimulus in starting "the cumulative forces making for expanding commercial activity." Without in any way disparaging this motive, it is enough to say that the recuperative efforts of the federal government must be made in a manner consistent with the authority granted by the Constitution.

We are of the opinion that the attempt through the provisions of the Code to fix the hours and wages of employees of defendants in their intrastate business was not a valid exercise of federal power.

The other violations for which defendants were convicted related to the making of local sales. Ten counts, for violation of the provision as to "straight killing," were for permitting customers to make "selections of individual chickens taken from particular coops and half coops." Whether or not this practice is good or bad for the local trade, its effect, if any, upon interstate commerce was only indirect. The same may be said of violations of the Code by intrastate transactions consisting of the sale "of an unfit chicken" and of sales which were not in ac-

cord with the ordinances of the city of New York. The requirement of reports as to prices and volumes of defendants' sales was incident to the effort to control their intrastate business.

In view of these conclusions, we find it unnecessary to discuss other questions which have been raised as to the validity of certain provisions of the Code under the due process clause of the Fifth Amendment.

On both the grounds we have discussed, the attempted delegation of legislative power and the attempted regulation of intrastate transactions which affect interstate commerce only indirectly, we hold the code provisions here in question to be invalid and that the judgment of conviction must be reversed.

67.

Franklin D. Roosevelt: The Second New Deal

The so-called second New Deal marked the transition from the emergency legislation of 1933 and its aftermath to a trend toward long-term social and economic reconstruction. It began in 1935 but was hampered by a recalcitrant Congress, unfavorable Supreme Court decisions, and differences of opinion among presidential advisers. During this phase of the New Deal the proponents of a planned economy gradually lost ground to those who favored a regulated but competitive free enterprise. President Roosevelt, in his annual message to Congress of January 4, 1935, outlined some of the principles he intended to follow as the second New Deal took shape in his mind. The message is reprinted below.

Source: *Record*, 74 Cong., 1 Sess., pp. 94-97.

WE HAVE UNDERTAKEN a new order of things, yet we progress to it under the framework and in the spirit and intent of the American Constitution. We have proceeded throughout the nation a measureable distance on the road toward this new order. Materially I can report to you substantial benefits to our agricultural population, in-

creased industrial activity, and profits to our merchants. Of equal moment, there is evident a restoration of that spirit of confidence and faith which marks the American character. Let him who, for speculative profit or partisan purpose, without just warrant would seek to disturb or dispel this assurance, take heed before he assumes responsibility for any act which slows our onward steps.

Throughout the world change is the order of the day. In every nation economic problems, long in the making, have brought crises of many kinds for which the masters of old practice and theory were unprepared. In most nations, social justice, no longer a distant ideal, has become a definite goal, and ancient governments are beginning to heed the call.

Thus, the American people do not stand alone in the world in their desire for change. We seek it through tested liberal traditions, through processes which retain all of the deep essentials of that republican form of representative government first given to a troubled world by the United States.

As the various parts in the program begun in the extraordinary session of the Seventy-third Congress shape themselves in practical administration, the unity of our program reveals itself to the nation. The outlines of the new economic order, rising from the disintegration of the old, are apparent. We test what we have done as our measures take root in the living texture of life. We see where we have built wisely and where we can do still better.

The attempt to make a distinction between recovery and reform is a narrowly conceived effort to substitute the appearance of reality for reality itself. When a man is convalescing from illness, wisdom dictates not only cure of the symptoms but also removal of their cause.

It is important to recognize that while we seek to outlaw specific abuses the American objective of today has an infinitely deeper, finer, and more lasting purpose than mere repression. Thinking people in almost every country of the world have come to realize certain fundamental difficulties with which civilization must reckon. Rapid changes — the machine age, the advent of universal and rapid communication, and many other new factors — have brought new problems. Succeeding generations have attempted to keep pace by reforming in piecemeal fashion this or that attendant abuse. As a result, evils overlap and reform becomes confused and frustrated. We lose sight, from time to time, of our ultimate human objectives.

Let us, for a moment, strip from our simple purpose the confusion that results from a multiplicity of detail and from millions of written and spoken words.

We find our population suffering from old inequalities, little changed by past sporadic remedies. In spite of our efforts and in spite of our talk, we have not weeded out the overprivileged and we have not effectively lifted up the underprivileged. Both of these manifestations of injustice have retarded happiness. No wise man has any intention of destroying what is known as the "profit motive," because by the profit motive we mean the right by work to earn a decent livelihood for ourselves and for our families.

We have, however, a clear mandate from the people, that Americans must forswear that conception of the acquisition of wealth which, through excessive profits, creates undue private power over private affairs and, to our misfortune, over public affairs as well. In building toward this end we do not destroy ambition, nor do we seek to divide our wealth into equal shares on stated occasions. We continue to recognize the greater ability of some to earn more than others. But we do assert that the ambition of the individual to obtain for him and his a proper security, a reasonable leisure, and a decent living throughout life is an ambition to be preferred to the appetite for great wealth and great power.

I recall to your attention my message to the Congress last June in which I said, "Among our objectives I place the security of the men, women, and children of the nation first." That remains our first and continuing task; and in a very real sense every major legislative enactment of this Congress should be a component part of it.

In defining immediate factors which enter into our quest, I have spoken to the Congress and the people of three great divisions: first, the security of a livelihood through the better use of the national resources of the land in which we live; second, the security against the major hazards and vicissitudes of life; third, the security of decent homes.

I am now ready to submit to the Congress a broad program designed ultimately to establish all three of these factors of security — a program which because of many lost years will take many future years to fulfill.

A study of our national resources, more comprehensive than any previously made, shows the vast amount of necessary and practicable work which needs to be done for the development and preservation of our national wealth for the enjoyment and advantage of our people in generations to come. The sound use of land and water is far more comprehensive than the mere planting of trees, building of dams, distributing of electricity, or retirement of submarginal land. It recognizes that stranded populations, either in the country or the city, cannot have security under the conditions that now surround them.

To this end we are ready to begin to meet this problem — the intelligent care of population throughout our nation in accordance with an intelligent distribution of the means of livelihood for that population. A definite program for putting people to work, of which I shall speak in a moment, is a component part of this greater program of security of livelihood through the better use of our national resources.

Closely related to the broad problem of livelihood is that of security against the major hazards of life. Here also a comprehensive survey of what has been attempted or accomplished in many nations and in many states proves to me that the time has come for action by the national government. I shall send to you, in a few days, definite recommendations based on these studies. These recommendations will cover the broad subjects of unemployment insurance and old-age insurance, of benefits for children, for mothers, for the handicapped, for maternity care, and for other aspects of dependency and illness where a beginning can now be made.

The third factor — better homes for our people — has also been the subject of experimentation and study. Here, too, the first practical steps can be made through the proposals which I shall suggest in relation to giving work to the unemployed.

Whatever we plan and whatever we do should be in the light of these three clear objectives of security. We cannot afford to lose valuable time in haphazard public policies which cannot find a place in the broad outlines of these major purposes. In that spirit I come to an immediate issue made for us by hard and inescapable circumstance — the task of putting people to work. In the spring of 1933 the issue of destitution seemed to stand apart; today, in the light of our experience and our new national policy, we find we can put people to work in ways which conform to, initiate, and carry forward the broad principles of that policy.

The first objectives of emergency legislation of 1933 were to relieve destitution, to make it possible for industry to operate in a more rational and orderly fashion, and to put behind industrial recovery the impulse of large expenditures in government undertakings. The purpose of the National Industrial Recovery Act to provide work for more people succeeded in a substantial manner within the first few months of its life, and the act has continued to maintain employment gains and greatly improved working conditions in industry.

The program of public works provided for in the Recovery Act launched the federal government into a task for which there was little time to make preparation and little American experience to follow. Great employment has been given and is being given by these works.

More than $2 billion has also been expended in direct relief to the destitute. Local agencies of necessity determined the recipients of this form of relief. With inevitable exceptions the funds were spent by them with reasonable efficiency, and, as a result, actual want of food and clothing in the great majority of cases has been overcome.

But the stark fact before us is that great numbers still remain unemployed. A large proportion of these unemployed and their dependents have been forced on the relief rolls. The burden on the federal government has grown with great rapidity. We have here a human as well as an economic problem. When humane considerations are concerned, Americans give them precedence. The lessons of history, confirmed by the evidence immediately before me, show conclusively that continued dependence upon relief induces a spiritual and moral disintegration fundamentally destructive to the national fiber. To dole out relief in this way is to administer a narcotic, a subtle destroyer of the human spirit. It is inimical to the dictates of sound policy. It is in violation of the traditions of America. Work must be found for able-bodied but destitute workers.

The federal government must and shall quit this business of relief.

I am not willing that the vitality of our people be further sapped by the giving of cash, of market baskets, of a few hours of weekly work cutting grass, raking leaves, or picking up papers in the public parks. We must preserve not only the bodies of the unemployed from destitution but also their self-respect, their self-reliance, and courage and determination. This decision brings me to the problem of what the government

should do with approximately 5 million unemployed now on the relief rolls.

About 1.5 million of these belong to the group which in the past was dependent upon local welfare efforts. Most of them are unable, for one reason or another, to maintain themselves independently — for the most part, through no fault of their own. Such people, in the days before the great depression, were cared for by local efforts — by states, by counties, by towns, by cities, by churches, and by private welfare agencies. It is my thought that in the future they must be cared for as they were before. I stand ready through my own personal efforts and through the public influence of the office that I hold to help these local agencies to get the means necessary to assume this burden.

The security legislation which I shall propose to the Congress will, I am confident, be of assistance to local effort in the care of this type of cases. Local responsibility can and will be resumed; for, after all, common sense tells us that the wealth necessary for this task existed and still exists in the local community, and the dictates of sound administration require that this responsibility be in the first instance a local one.

There are, however, an additional 3.5 million employable people who are on relief. With them the problem is different and the responsibility is different. This group was the victim of a nationwide depression caused by conditions which were not local but national. The federal government is the only governmental agency with sufficient power and credit to meet this situation. We have assumed this task, and we shall not shrink from it in the future. It is a duty dictated by every intelligent consideration of national policy to ask you to make it possible for the United States to give employment to all of these 3.5 million employable people now on relief, pending their absorption in a rising tide of private employment.

It is my thought that, with the exception of certain of the normal public-building operations of the government, all emergency public works shall be united in a single new and greatly enlarged plan. With the establishment of this new system, we can supersede the Federal Emergency Relief Administration with a coordinated authority which will be charged with the orderly liquidation of our present relief activities and the substitution of a national chart for the giving of work.

This new program of emergency public employment should be governed by a number of practical principles:

1. All work undertaken should be useful, not just for a day or a year but useful in the sense that it affords permanent improvement in living conditions or that it creates future new wealth for the nation.

2. Compensation on emergency public projects should be in the form of security payments, which should be larger than the amount now received as a relief dole, but at the same time not so large as to encourage the rejection of opportunities for private employment or the leaving of private employment to engage in government work.

3. Projects should be undertaken on which a large percentage of direct labor can be used.

4. Preference should be given to those projects which will be self-liquidating in the sense that there is a reasonable expectation that the government will get its money back at some future time.

5. The projects undertaken should be selected and planned so as to compete as little as possible with private enterprises. This suggests that if it were not for the necessity of giving useful work to the unemployed now on relief, these projects in most instances would not now be undertaken.

6. The planning of projects would seek to assure work during the coming fiscal year to the individuals now on relief or until such time as private employment is available. In order to make adjustment to increasing private employment, work should be planned with a view to tapering it off in proportion to the speed with which the emergency workers are offered positions with private employers.

7. Effort should be made to locate projects where they will serve the greatest unemployment needs as shown by present relief rolls, and the broad program of the National Resources Board should be freely used for guidance in selection. Our ultimate objective being the enrichment of human lives, the government has the primary duty to use its emergency expenditures as much as possible to serve those who cannot secure the advantages of private capital.

Ever since the adjournment of the Seventy-third Congress, the administration has been studying from every angle the possibility and the practicability of new forms of employment. As a result of these studies I have arrived at certain very definite convictions as to the amount of money that will be necessary for the sort of public projects that I have described. I shall submit these figures in my Budget Message. I assure you now they will be within the sound credit of the government.

The work itself will cover a wide field, including clearance of slums, which for adequate reasons cannot be undertaken by private capital; in rural housing of several kinds, where, again, private capital is unable to function; in rural electrification; in the reforestation of the great watersheds of the nation; in an intensified program to prevent soil erosion and to reclaim blighted areas; in improving existing road systems and in constructing national highways designed to handle modern traffic; in the elimination of grade crossings; in the extension and enlargement of the successful work of the Civilian Conservation Corps; in nonfederal work, mostly self-liquidating and highly useful to local divisions of government; and on many other projects which the nation needs and cannot afford to neglect.

This is the method which I propose to you in order that we may better meet this present-day problem of unemployment. Its greatest advantage is that it fits logically and usefully into the long-range permanent policy of providing the three types of security which constitute as a whole an American plan for the betterment of the future of the American people.

I shall consult with you from time to time concerning other measures of national importance. Among the subjects that lie immediately before us are the consolidation of federal regulatory administration over all forms of transportation; the renewal and clarification of the general purposes of the National Industrial Recovery Act; the strengthening of our facilities for the prevention, detection, and treatment of crime and criminals; the restoration of sound conditions in the public utilities field through abolition of the evil features of holding companies; the gradual tapering off of the emergency credit activities of government, and improvement in our taxation forms and methods.

We have already begun to feel the bracing effect upon our economic system of a restored agriculture. The hundreds of millions of additional income that farmers are receiving is finding its way into the channels of trade. The farmers' share of the national income is slowly rising. The economic facts justify the widespread opinion of those engaged in agriculture that our provision for maintaining a balanced production give at this time the most adequate remedy for an old and vexing problem. For the present, and especially in view of abnormal world conditions, agricultural adjustment with certain necessary improvements in methods should continue.

It seems appropriate to call attention at this time to the fine spirit shown during the past year by our public servants. I cannot praise too highly the cheerful work of the civil-service employees and of those temporarily working for the government. As for those thousands in our various public agencies spread throughout the country who, without compensation, agreed to take over heavy responsibilities in connection with our various loan agencies and particularly in direct relief work, I cannot say too much. I do not think any country could show a higher average of cheerful and even enthusiastic teamwork than has been shown by these men and women.

I cannot with candor tell you that general international relationships outside the borders of the United States are improved. On the surface of things many old jealousies are resurrected, old passions aroused; new strivings for armament and power, in more than one land, rear their ugly heads. I hope that calm counsel and constructive leadership will provide the steadying influence and the time necessary for the coming of new and more practical forms of representative government throughout the world wherein privilege and power will occupy a lesser place and world welfare a greater.

I believe, however, that our own peaceful and neighborly attitude toward other nations is coming to be understood and appreciated. The maintenance of international peace is a matter in which we are deeply and unselfishly concerned. Evidence of our persistent and undeniable desire to prevent armed conflict has recently been more than once afforded. There is no ground for apprehension that our relations with any nation will be otherwise than peaceful. Nor is there ground for doubt that the people of most nations seek relief from the threat and burden attaching to the false theory that extravagant armament cannot be reduced and limited by international accord.

The ledger of the past year shows many more gains than losses. Let us not forget

hat, in addition to saving millions from ut-
er destitution, child labor has been for the
moment outlawed, thousands of homes
aved to their owners, and, most important
of all, the morale of the nation has been
estored. Viewing the year 1934 as a whole,
ou and I can agree that we have a generous measure of reasons for giving thanks.

It is not empty optimism that moves me
o a strong hope in the coming year. We
an, if we will, make 1935 a genuine period
of good feeling, sustained by a sense of purposeful progress. Beyond the material recovery, I sense a spiritual recovery as well.
The people of America are turning as never
before to those permanent values that are
not limited to the physical objectives of life.
There are growing signs of this on every
hand. In the face of these spiritual impulses
we are sensible of the Divine Providence to
which nations turn now, as always, for
guidance and fostering care.

68.

Franklin D. Roosevelt: A Program for Social Security

*Presidential advisers spent much of 1934 considering programs for unemployment
compensation and old-age benefits — important planks in the Democratic platform
of 1932. Unemployment compensation created numerous problems, largely because
of conflict between advocates of a national plan and proponents of state-operated
plans. Old-age insurance, having had no precedent in state legislation, was generally
deemed suitable for a uniform federal program. In the following message to Congress
of January 17, 1935, President Roosevelt presented the administration's proposal
for a social security act. A bill was finally passed on August 14. Like most of
the New Deal legislation, social security was challenged as unconstitutional, but in
May 1937 the Supreme Court upheld the major provisions of the law.*

Source: *Record*, 74 Cong., 1 Sess., pp. 545-546.

IN ADDRESSING YOU on June 8, 1934, I summarized the main objectives of our American program. Among these was, and is, the
security of the men, women, and children
of the nation against certain hazards and vi-
issitudes of life. This purpose is an essential
part of our task. In my annual message to
you I promised to submit a definite program of action. This I do in the form of a
report to me by a Committee on Economic
Security, appointed by me for the purpose
of surveying the field and of recommending
the basis of legislation.

I am gratified with the work of this committee and of those who have helped it:
The Technical Board of Economic Security,
drawn from various departments of the government; the Advisory Council on Economic Security, consisting of informed and pub-
lic-spirited private citizens; and a number of
other advisory groups, including a Committee on Actuarial Consultants, a Medical Advisory Board, a Dental Advisory Committee, a Hospital Advisory Committee, a Public Health Advisory Committee, a Child
Welfare Committee, and an Advisory Committee on Employment Relief. All of those
who participated in this notable task of

planning this major legislative proposal are ready and willing at any time to consult with and assist in any way the appropriate congressional committees and members with respect to detailed aspects.

It is my best judgment that this legislation should be brought forward with a minimum of delay. Federal action is necessary to and conditioned upon the actions of states. Forty-four legislatures are meeting or will meet soon. In order that the necessary state action may be taken promptly, it is important that the federal government proceed speedily.

The detailed report of the committee sets forth a series of proposals that will appeal to the sound sense of the American people. It has not attempted the impossible nor has it failed to exercise sound caution and consideration of all of the factors concerned: the national credit, the rights and responsibilities of states, the capacity of industry to assume financial responsibilities, and the fundamental necessity of proceeding in a manner that will merit the enthusiastic support of citizens of all sorts.

It is overwhelmingly important to avoid any danger of permanently discrediting the sound and necessary policy of federal legislation for economic security by attempting to apply it on too ambitious a scale before actual experience has provided guidance for the permanently safe direction of such efforts. The place of such a fundamental in our future civilization is too precious to be jeopardized now by extravagant action. It is a sound idea — a sound ideal. Most of the other advanced countries of the world have already adopted it, and their experience affords the knowledge that social insurance can be made a sound and workable project.

Three principles should be observed in legislation on this subject. In the first place, the system adopted, except for the money necessary to initiate it, should be self-sustaining in the sense that funds for the payment of insurance benefits should not come from the proceeds of general taxation. Second, excepting in old-age insurance, actual management should be left to the states, subject to standards established by the federal government. Third, sound financial management of the funds and the reserves and protection of the credit structure of the nation should be assured by retaining federal control over all funds through trustees in the Treasury of the United States.

At this time, I recommend the following types of legislation looking to economic security:

First, unemployment compensation.

Second, old-age benefits, including compulsory and voluntary annuities.

Third, federal aid to dependent children through grants to states for the support of existing mother's pension systems and for services for the protection and care of homeless, neglected, dependent, and crippled children.

Fourth, additional federal aid to state and local public-health agencies and the strengthening of the federal Public Health Service. I am not at this time recommending the adoption of so-called health insurance, although groups representing the medical profession are cooperating with the federal government in the further study of the subject, and definite progress is being made.

With respect to unemployment compensation, I have concluded that the most practical proposal is the levy of a uniform federal payroll tax, 90 percent of which should be allowed as an offset to employers contributing under a compulsory state unemployment compensation act. The purpose of this is to afford a requirement of a reasonably uniform character for all states cooperating with the federal government and to promote and encourage the passage of unemployment compensation laws in the states. The 10 percent not thus offset should be used to cover the costs of federal and state administration of this broad system. Thus, states will largely administer unemployment compensation, assisted and guided by the federal government.

An unemployment compensation system should be constructed in such a way as to afford every practicable aid and incentive toward the larger purpose of employment stabilization. This can be helped by the intelligent planning of both public and private employment. It also can be helped by correlating the system with public employment so that a person who has exhausted his benefits may be eligible for some form of public work as is recommended in this report. Moreover, in order to encourage the stabilization of private employment, federal legislation should not foreclose the states from establishing means for inducing industries to afford an even greater stabilization of employment.

In the important field of security for our old people, it seems necessary to adopt three principles — first, noncontributory old-age pensions for those who are now too old to build up their own insurance; it is, of course, clear that for perhaps thirty years to come funds will have to be provided by the states and the federal government to meet these pensions. Second, compulsory contributory annuities, which in time will establish a self-supporting system for those now young and for future generations. Third, voluntary contributory annuities by which

individual initiative can increase the annual amounts received in old age. It is proposed that the federal government assume one-half of the cost of the old-age pension plan, which ought ultimately to be supplanted by self-supporting annuity plans.

The amount necessary at this time for the initiation of unemployment compensation, old-age security, children's aid, and the promotion of public health, as outlined in the report of the Committee on Economic Security, is approximately $100 million.

The establishment of sound means toward a greater future economic security of the American people is dictated by a prudent consideration of the hazards involved in our national life. No one can guarantee this country against the dangers of future depressions, but we can reduce these dangers. We can eliminate many of the factors that cause economic depressions and we can provide the means of mitigating their results. This plan for economic security is at once a measure of prevention and a method of alleviation.

We pay now for the dreadful consequence of economic insecurity — and dearly. This plan presents a more equitable and infinitely less expensive means of meeting these costs. We cannot afford to neglect the plain duty before us. I strongly recommend action to attain the objectives sought in this report.

Soak the Rich.

Denunciation of Franklin D. Roosevelt's tax program, 1935

That Man in the White House.

Uncomplimentary remark applied often to F.D.R. after 1935

69.

Huey Long: Sharing Our Wealth

Of the several demagogues who acquired a national following during the Depression, Huey Long ("Kingfish"), who came to power as the governor of Louisiana, was the most ambitious, the most fascinating, and the most deeply feared. As a United States senator in 1932 he formulated a Share-the-Wealth ("Every Man a King") program to save America, and in 1934 he converted it into a national crusade by establishing a Share-Our-Wealth Society, inviting Americans everywhere to organize local branches. The society, he prophesied, would eventually displace the two major political parties and then elevate him to the presidency. The description of Long's program below is taken from a radio address given by him in January 1935. At the height of his power, Long was shot by an assassin, the son of a man he had vilified, in the capitol building at Baton Rouge, Louisiana, on September 8, 1935.

Source: *Record*, 74 Cong., 1 Sess., pp. 410-412.

President Roosevelt was elected on November 8, 1932. People look upon an elected President as the President. This is January 1935. We are in our third year of the Roosevelt depression, with the conditions growing worse. . . .

We must now become awakened! We must know the truth and speak the truth. There is no use to wait three more years. It is not Roosevelt or ruin; it is Roosevelt's ruin.

Now, my friends, it makes no difference who is President or who is senator. America is for 125 million people and the unborn to come. We ran Mr. Roosevelt for the presidency of the United States because he promised to us by word of mouth and in writing:

1. That the size of the big man's fortune would be reduced so as to give the masses at the bottom enough to wipe out all poverty; and

2. That the hours of labor would be so reduced that all would share in the work to be done and in consuming the abundance mankind produced.

Hundreds of words were used by Mr. Roosevelt to make these promises to the people, but they were made over and over again. He reiterated these pledges even after he took his oath as President. Summed up, what these promises meant was: "Share our wealth."

When I saw him spending all his time of ease and recreation with the business partners of Mr. John D. Rockefeller, Jr., with such men as the Astors, etc., maybe I ought to have had better sense than to have believed he would ever break down their big fortunes to give enough to the masses to end poverty — maybe some will think me weak for ever believing it all, but millions of other people were fooled the same as myself. I was like a drowning man grabbing at a straw, I guess. The face and eyes, the hungry forms of mothers and children, the aching hearts of students denied education were before our eyes, and when Roosevelt promised, we jumped for that ray of hope.

So therefore I call upon the men and women of America to immediately join in our work and movement to share our wealth.

There are thousands of share-our-wealth societies organized in the United States now. We want 100,000 such societies formed for every nook and corner of this country — societies that will meet, talk, and work, all for the purpose that the great wealth and abundance of this great land that belongs to us may be shared and enjoyed by all of us.

We have nothing more for which we should ask the Lord. He has allowed this land to have too much of everything that humanity needs.

So in this land of God's abundance we propose laws, viz.:

1. The fortunes of the multimillionaires and billionaires shall be reduced so that no one person shall own more than a few million dollars to the person. We would do this by a capital levy tax. On the first million that a man was worth, we would not impose any tax. We would say, "All right for your first million dollars, but after you get that rich you will have to start helping the balance of us." So we would not levy any capital levy tax on the first million one owned. But on the second million a man owns, we would tax that 1 percent, so that every year the man owned the second million dollars he would be taxed $10,000. On the third million we would impose a tax of 2 percent. On the fourth million we would impose a tax of 4 percent. On the fifth million we would impose a tax of 8 percent. On the sixth million we would impose a tax of 16 percent. On the seventh million we would impose a tax of 32 percent. On the eighth million we would impose a tax of 64 percent; and on all over the eighth million we would impose a tax of 100 percent.

What this would mean is that the annual tax would bring the biggest fortune down to $3 or $4 million to the person because no one could pay taxes very long in the higher brackets. But $3 to $4 million is enough for any one person and his children

Huey Long, senator from Louisiana, attacking the policies of the New Deal, 1935

and his children's children. We cannot allow one to have more than that because it would not leave enough for the balance to have something.

2. We propose to limit the amount any one man can earn in one year or inherit to $1 million to the person.

3. Now, by limiting the size of the fortunes and incomes of the big men, we will throw into the government Treasury the money and property from which we will care for the millions of people who have nothing; and with this money we will provide a home and the comforts of home, with such common conveniences as radio and automobile, for every family in America, free of debt.

4. We guarantee food and clothing and employment for everyone who should work by shortening the hours of labor to thirty hours per week, maybe less, and to eleven months per year, maybe less. We would have the hours shortened just so much as would give work to everybody to produce enough for everybody; and if we were to get them down to where they were too short, then we would lengthen them again. As long as all the people working can produce enough of automobiles, radios, homes, schools, and theaters for everyone to have that kind of comfort and convenience, then

let us all have work to do and have that much of heaven on earth.

5. We would provide education at the expense of the states and the United States for every child, not only through grammar school and high school but through to a college and vocational education. We would simply extend the Louisiana plan to apply to colleges and all people. Yes; we would have to build thousands of more colleges and employ 100,000 more teachers; but we have materials, men, and women who are ready and available for the work. Why have the right to a college education depend upon whether the father or mother is so well-to-do as to send a boy or girl to college? We would give every child the right to education and a living at birth.

6. We would give a pension to all persons above sixty years of age in an amount sufficient to support them in comfortable circumstances, excepting those who earn $1,000 per year or who are worth $10,000.

7. Until we could straighten things out — and we can straighten things out in two months under our program — we would grant a moratorium on all debts which people owe that they cannot pay.

And now you have our program, none too big, none too little, but every man a king.

We owe debts in America today, public and private, amounting to $252 billion. That means that every child is born with a $2,000 debt tied around his neck to hold him down before he gets started. Then, on top of that, the wealth is locked in a vise owned by a few people. We propose that children shall be born in a land of opportunity, guaranteed a home, food, clothes, and the other things that make for living, including the right to education.

Our plan would injure no one. It would not stop us from having millionaires — it would increase them tenfold, because so many more people could make $1 million if they had the chance our plan gives them. Our plan would not break up big concerns.

The only difference would be that maybe 10,000 people would own a concern instead of 10 people owning it.

But, my friends, unless we do share our wealth, unless we limit the size of the big man so as to give something to the little man, we can never have a happy or free people. God said so! He ordered it.

We have everything our people need. Too much of food, clothes, and houses — why not let all have their fill and lie down in the ease and comfort God has given us? Why not? Because a few own everything — the masses own nothing.

I wonder if any of you people who are listening to me were ever at a barbecue! We used to go there — sometimes 1,000 people or more. If there were 1,000 people, we would put enough meat and bread and everything else on the table for 1,000 people. Then everybody would be called and everyone would eat all they wanted. But suppose at one of these barbecues for 1,000 people that one man took 90 percent of the food and ran off with it and ate until he got sick and let the balance rot. Then 999 people would have only enough for 100 to eat and there would be many to starve because of the greed of just one person for something he couldn't eat himself.

Well, ladies and gentlemen, America, all the people of America, have been invited to a barbecue. God invited us all to come and eat and drink all we wanted. He smiled on our land and we grew crops of plenty to eat and wear. He showed us in the earth the iron and other things to make everything we wanted. He unfolded to us the secrets of science so that our work might be easy. God called: "Come to my feast."

Then what happened? Rockefeller, Morgan, and their crowd stepped up and took enough for 120 million people and left only enough for 5 million for all the other 125 million to eat. And so many millions must go hungry and without these good things God gave us unless we call on them to put some of it back.

The New York Stock Exchange on a quiet day on Wall Street in 1933

ASIDES ON DEPRESSION

The hopes of some and the fears of others notwithstanding, the New Deal was not a revolutionary program. In the beginning, during the Hundred Days, it was hardly a program at all, but a series of loosely related special responses to special problems; it was only later that Keynesian economics provided a theoretical framework upon which to hang the New Deal's multiplicity of alphabetical agencies. Nonetheless, the keynote of the Keynesian approach was also that of the New Deal — preservation rather than revolution. The aim was not to institute state socialism or some equally scarifying specter, but to restore capitalism's viability; the means was to replace ossified practices with a healthy resilience. Thus, the revolution that many foresaw and many actually attempted to lead never began. The people did not rise up nor did they fall down. In general, they simply carried on in whatever manner they could.

(Above) Traffic on Michigan Avenue in Chicago, 1929; (below) Wilshire Boulevard in Los Angeles. The growth of both cities was vastly altered by the automobile

(Above) Group in Montrose, Colorado, watching a World Series scoreboard in 1939

(Left) Policeman aiding a woman battling a winter wind in Chicago in 1929; (below) stock judging at a 4-H Fair in Sublette, Kansas, 1939

(Above) Steel mills standing idle in Chicago in 1930; (below) copper miners in Butte, Mont., photographed by Arthur Rothstein in 1939 for FSA

Above) Oil derricks and producing wells on the grounds of the state capitol building in Oklahoma City suggest the connection between oil and politics in the oil states; (below) the prototype "wheeler-dealer" of Texas mythology; (right) the view in downtown Kilgore, Texas, 1939. All photographs by Russell Lee for the FSA

The Depression did not find everyone equally defenseless. During the 1920s American oil companies, heirs to the Rockefeller tradition and among the richest of corporations, had induced the government to use military threats to protect their holdings in Mexico. In 1926 the oil lobby convinced Congress to raise the dubious oil depletion allowance to 27½ percent, making the government a large partner in expenses but not in profits.

(Above) Offices of the Delta and Pine Land
plantation in Scott, Mississippi

(Above) Two iron ore miners in Jefferson Co.,
Ala.; (right) steelworker in Midland, Pa., 1938;
(below) Negro farmer using a mule-drawn culti-
vator, photographed by Doris Ullman

With most Negroes still involved, on one level or another, in agriculture, the Depression had come early to them; a large percentage were tenants or marginal owners, and this, together with the standard array of discriminatory practices and injustices, served to keep them on the bottom rung as the Depression deepened. Negroes in industry were in a comparable position, at least until the new Committee for Industrial Organization began to organize industrial unions and include Negroes. Generally the first to be dropped from a contracting payroll, Negroes were even held to inferior wages in NIRA codes established for industries with strong Southern connections.

(Top) Aftermath of rioting in Harlem in 1935; (center) New York attorney Leibowitz, second left, conferring with his clients convicted of attacking two white women in Scottsboro, Ala., 1935; (bottom) Father Divine and his followers on an outing designed to offset Depression's bleakness

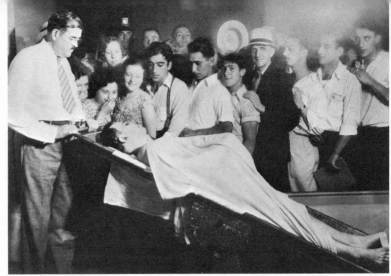

(Top) Crowd viewing the body of John Dillinger at Chicago's county morgue after he was slain in a neighborhood movie theater; (right) Bonnie Parker and Clyde Barrow, bank robbers of the 1930s; (bottom) gangster Al Capone with his son at a Chicago baseball game, 1931

(Top left) Jesse Owens, U.S. track star, winning 100-yard dash at the 1936 Olympic Games in Berlin; (left) Lou Gehrig at a ceremony in his honor at Yankee Stadium, 1939; (above) Chicago Bears' back Bronko Nagurski (with ball) playing in the 1937 championship game; (below) Joe Louis defeats Jimmy Braddock for the heavyweight crown in 1937

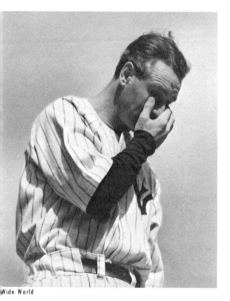

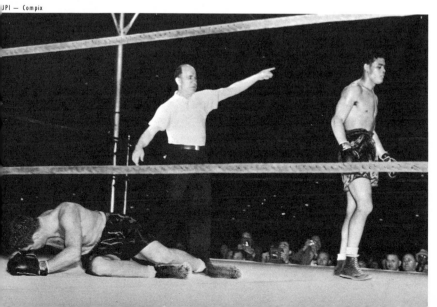

The evolving idiom of jazz, long the soul of black musical expression, came into gradual vogue with white audiences, particularly in the slightly diluted styles of white musicians like Benny Goodman. (Top left) Duke Ellington, genius of the "big band" sound; (top right) W. C. Handy, "Father of the Blues"; (left) "Jelly Roll" Morton. By contrast, Al Jolson's blackface rendering of "Mammy" became increasingly dated, as well as insulting as a racial stereotype

The movies continued through the Depression as more a form of commercial enterprise than as an art form; consequently, they failed to register the social consciousness that was growing in the arts. Movies generally relied on the escape value of adventure, on the personal attractions of the star system, and on their ability, despite the Legion of Decency, to appeal to other than intellectual appetites. Nonetheless, with huge budgets to work with, happy combinations of actors and writers occasionally produced memorable works.

(Top) Scene from ''Little Caesar,'' which was made in 1930 and starred Edward G. Robinson; (right) ''Rasputin and the Empress,'' a 1932 film starring Lionel, Ethel, and John Barrymore; (bottom) Clark Gable, Tully Marshall, Donald Crisp, and Jean Harlow in a 1932 film, ''Red Dust''

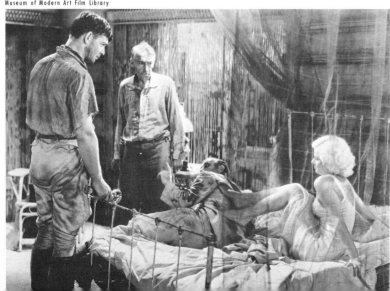

Films and stars of the 1930s: (Top) Chorus number from "The Great Ziegfield"; (center left) W. C. Fields and Freddie Bartholomew in "David Copperfield"; (center right) Wallace Beery as Pancho Lopez in "Bad Man"; (bottom) Claudette Colbert and Clark Gable in a scene from "It Happened One Night"

70.

Lawrence Dennis: American Fascism

American Fascists, if one ignores the often-made charge that Huey Long and his lieutenants belonged in the Fascist camp, were largely without political influence during the 1930s. Nevertheless, the apparent success of Germany and Italy in overcoming the worldwide depression caused a number of Americans to view Fascism as a possible panacea for the country's troubles. One such was Lawrence Dennis, whose glib but clever Is Capitalism Doomed? *(1932) was followed by* The Coming American Fascism *in 1936. Dennis, whose disapproval of capitalist foreign policy (he was in the foreign service in the 1920s) was matched by his low view of business (he abandoned diplomacy for banking), was convinced that capitalism could not survive. Of the alternatives — Communism, Fascism, or chaos — Fascism seemed to him least likely to destroy the social order. "A Portrait of American Fascism," part of which is reprinted here, appeared late in 1935.*

Source: *American Mercury*, December 1935.

THE OBJECTIVE CONDITIONS which may constitute a part of the causation of an American fascism (in all probability called by another name), may be conveniently grouped under three heads: first, the dynamic conflicts of interest; second, the relative breakdown of the political and economic mechanisms which comprise the liberal capitalist system; and third, the logic of sociological rationalization, indicating different social institutions as better means to generally desired ends.

The clash of group interests furnishes a new factor for serious consideration in American life. The Marxists did not discover or invent this factor; it has always been operative in every nation, but the success of capitalism in expansion has both required and assured such a degree of abundance of economic opportunities for all that collisions of group interests have never proved dangerous to the system. If liberal constitution-

al government, however, fails to provide a satisfactory formula for the representation of all legitimate interests and for the harmonious adjustment of their conflicts, that fact alone invalidates the present system, and no appeal to reason or authority can diminish the force of this truth. The question, of course, is whether this is a fact at the present time. Events will have to furnish the conclusive answer.

Today the clash of factions in America is not being reflected in a pitched battle between the attacking proletarian workers and the defending owners and managers, as the Communist analysis would have it. No, the strife is being waged by the minority forces — by the lobbyists and raiders of the public treasury. The liberal constitutional system favors the disorderly play of these groups. They can be more inimical to public order than a fight to the finish between capital and labor, for, presumably, the latter would soon have to end either in a compromise, as has occurred in the past, or in the triumphant emergence of a workers' dictatorship, as happened in Russia, or in a completely successful subjugation of the workers by the victorious owners and managers, as may be said to have occurred in ancient Egypt. If any one of these three conditions comes to pass, an orderly and workable formula is likely to eventuate — whether you like it or not.

But in the conflicts of minority groups acting under the prevailing degree of national or social discipline, kept at a minimum by our constitutional and juridical system, there is likely to result eventually an intolerable degree of chaos, from which a formula like fascism may seem to offer the only remedy. The relevancy of fascism to such a clash would consist chiefly in its bid to make explicit and effective a unique concept of national interest and, of course, to provide the necessary personnel and machinery for realization. It is conceivable that many of our conservatives who are now worried over the dangers of losing liberty under a possible fascism might some day welcome a fascist dictator and a disciplined political party to curb the abuses of constitutional liberties and legal powers now commonly committed by irresponsible minorities. Nor is it unthinkable that many recent Wall Street and Park Avenue converts to states' rights, if given a stiff dose of economic sabotage and antinationalism by some plausible demagogue under the label of states' rights, might make a hasty return to their first love — a strong central government.

The breakdown of the social mechanics of liberal capitalism is too obvious a reason for the triumph of fascism to need much explanation. In this connection it must be remembered that those who have been driven by defeat and frustration to challenge the present system and to follow a leader offering a substitute are not likely to assist in improving a system which they now are attacking. . . .

A third order of conditions which may facilitate the emergence of an American fascism and determine substantially its character may be associated with the idea of instrumental fitness. Every schoolboy knows that the United States has long led the world in technological rationalization, or in scrapping the obsolete and adopting the newest machine or process. When we begin the same sort of rationalization in government and in economic relationships, a social revolution of first magnitude will be under way. Our Constitution and system of government as well as our law of property correspond to eighteenth-century needs, circumstances, and theories. Our federal system with its separation of authority between three branches of government and the delegation of powers to forty-nine separate sovereignties corresponds to the requirements of a compromise among thirteen British colonies which wanted more laissez faire than George III had sense enough to grant them, but which wanted neither to be separate nations nor welded into one America.

Since then, we have had again and again to choose between falling prey to European colonization and exploitation, or becoming a nation. The Civil War, which the Constitution and the Supreme Court precipitated rather than averted, settled the issue of our becoming a nation or becoming Balkanized. The work of political rationalization may be said to have been begun by John Marshall and carried on by Abraham Lincoln. Now it awaits final completion by another American revolution. A fascist upheaval in this country would probably be, among other things, a program of drastic sociological rationalization.

On the purely economic side, the best exposition of the logic of an American fascism has been stated by Berle and Means in their book *The Modern Corporation and Private Property*. Forty-nine percent of all corporate wealth was controlled by 200 corporations in 1929; by the beginning of 1932, the concentration had increased to 55 percent. The significant fact brought out by Messrs. Berle and Means is that under these modern American corporate set-ups, management and ownership are divorced; thus ownership is left without control or effective representation of its interests, and management is given control without practical responsibility either to owners or to the state. These great organizations have all the weaknesses of a state bureaucracy and none of the merits of private capitalism or owner-management. Prices are formed, important decisions are made, economic empires are ruled, not by the play of a free market or in response to freely registered movements of supply and demand but by administrative decisions of dominant bankers and executives of a few hundred large corporations or trusts.

We are not likely to embrace Justice Brandeis' philosophy about the "curse of bigness" for we are too fond of good automobiles at $600 and innumerable other goods and services which only large-scale industry can furnish. As it is, the Supreme Court will not authorize government to control business; the monopolies will not allow supply and demand to control prices, production, and competition; and the whole set-up will not permit the owner of corporate property to safeguard his interests, the consumer to protect himself in the market, labor to guard itself against lockouts, unemployment, and unfair bargaining acts of capital, or management to shelter itself against blackmailing tactics of certain labor organizations. The fascist logic of this situation is a corporate state with a set of mechanisms of group representation and control. Under

these, ownership, management, and labor would represent their interests and exercise their powers subject to effective governmental supervision, thus realizing some scheme of national interest.

At present, liberal critics are constantly exposing the improper acts of big business management and of minority group pressures in coercing political agencies, and in exercising economic powers of government. But well-substantiated as such criticisms usually are, they prove futile. Big business units are inevitable if we are to enjoy cheap automobiles, as well as other important commodities and services. If there is big business, it must exercise governmental functions. And no one can be expected to exercise these powers for private gain under our constitutional and judicial system without committing grave social abuses.

As for minority group pressures, they represent real communities of interest and useful administrative organizations, such as our state subdivisions cannot represent. What possible community of interest is shared by an upstate New York farmer, a Wall Street broker, a Park Avenue bondholder, or an East Side factory worker — except that each has to meet certain obligations to an artificial political subdivision which does not even correspond to the requirements of efficient political and police administration? Minority groups, especially those of economic management, correspond to real needs and exercise real power: if they are not enabled by an appropriate scheme of political and economic organization to represent their interests legally and exercise their powers beneficially, they will do so illegally and antisocially. In short, we have a real government by invisible, improper, irresponsible, and often illegal group pressures, and a visible, proper, legal, and supposedly responsible government which cannot govern but can only allow itself to be manipulated.

71.

HENRY A. WALLACE: Pigs and Pig Iron

The public image of the Agricultural Adjustment Administration (AAA) continued to be associated with the slaughter of pigs and destruction of crops undertaken by the agency in the fall of 1933 to reduce the marketable surplus. (Because the AAA was established after the growing season of 1933 had begun, it could not limit production that year.) Secretary of Agriculture Wallace regretted the necessity for destroying, and even reducing, crops. Nevertheless, he was unwilling to see the farmers produce more until the market for their products increased. The domestic market would expand, Wallace felt, when industries opened up jobs, and the foreign market would expand when the nations abroad could sell more goods to the United States — that is, when the tariffs, still strongly supported by industry, were lowered. These complexities and correlations were discussed by Wallace in the following address over the National Farm and Home Hour, NBC, November 12, 1935.

Source: Library of Congress, Wallace Papers.

PEOPLE ARE STILL INTERESTED in the 6 million pigs that were killed in September of 1933. In letters I have received following these radio talks, the pigs are mentioned more often than any one thing, except potatoes. One letter says:

It just makes me sick all over when I think how the government has killed millions and millions of little pigs, and how that has raised pork prices until today we poor people cannot even look at a piece of bacon.

It is common belief that pork is high today because the little pigs were killed in 1933. As a matter of fact, there is more pork now and the price is lower because these pigs were killed two years ago. Let me tell the story:

For eighteen months before August 1933, farmers had been selling hogs for an average of $3.42 a hundredweight. Such a price was ruinous to farmers. The average hog grower suffered from low hog prices during this period one thousand times more than the average consumer has suffered from high hog prices during the past few months. Hog prices in August of 1933 were intolerably low, and the northwestern Corn Belt was suffering from drought. There was every reason to expect prices to continue low because there had been an increase in the spring pig crop, and because the foreign market, which formerly had absorbed the product of as many as 12 million hogs from this country, had largely disappeared because of tariffs and quotas.

So 6 million little pigs were killed in September of 1933. They were turned into 100 million pounds of pork. That pork was distributed for relief. It went to feed the hungry. Some very small pigs could not be handled as meat by the packers. These were turned into grease and tankage for fertilizer.

If those 6 million pigs had grown up

they would have been marketed in January, February, and March of 1934. They probably would have brought around $2.50 a hundredweight. Instead of that the price of hogs at that time averaged $3.60. In January, February, and March of 1934, the consumers of the United States, in spite of the absence of the little pigs which would have come to market at that time, had their customary quantity of pork. Hogs at $3.60 made it possible for farmers to buy more city products and so put more city people back to work.

If those little pigs had grown up to normal weight they would have eaten about 75 million bushels of corn. The pork made out of these 75 million bushels of corn would have been consumed by August 1934. But that 75 million bushels of corn was not eaten in early 1934. You remember that in 1934 we had the most terrible drought in our history. The corn crop was a billion bushels short. But we had on hand those 75 million bushels of corn. That corn was used to make pork in late 1934 and early 1935. It gave us more pork this year than we would have had without it. Had it been fed in early 1934 the oversupply of pork would have been terrific then and the price would have been $2.50 a hundredweight instead of $3.60. But this year there would have been even fewer hogs and even higher prices than we have had.

As long as we have our program of agricultural adjustment we shall never again need to slaughter little pigs to keep hog prices from going to zero. We have the machinery to furnish consumers a normal, balanced supply.

I suppose it is a marvelous tribute to the humanitarian instincts of the American people that they sympathize more with little pigs which are killed than with full-grown hogs. Some people may object to killing pigs at any age. Perhaps they think that farmers should run a sort of old-folks home for hogs and keep them around indef-

United Press International

Henry Wallace, photographed in his office as he assumed the position of secretary of agriculture

initely as barnyard pets. This is a splendid attitude, but it happens that we have to think about farmers as well as hogs. And above all we must think about consumers and try to get a uniform supply of pork from year to year at a price which is fair to farmer and consumer alike.

The drought of 1934, which cut the supply of feed grain by twice as much as any previous drought, is chiefly responsible for high pork prices today. The slaughter of little pigs in 1933 gave us more pork and lower prices this year than we would have had if they had been allowed to live and eat those 75 million bushels of corn. Those who hold to the contrary are misinformed.

Beef prices are high now because of the same drought. We have never had an AAA production-control program in beef. Thousands of cattle were on the point of starvation in the West in 1934. Should we have allowed them to starve? Because we had the machinery of the Agricultural Adjustment Administration, we were able to step in promptly, buy those cattle, slaughter them and can them. The government has thus been able to distribute hundreds of millions of pounds of meat for relief that would otherwise have been wasted.

Strange to say, I find myself in strong sympathy with the attitude of many folks who held up their hands in horror about the killing of little pigs. I will go further than most of them in condemning scarcity economics. We want an economy of abundance, but it must be balanced abundance of those things we really want.

The pig iron reduction control of the big steel companies in 1933 was in principle one thousand times as damnable as the pig-reduction campaign of 1933. Pig iron production in 1932 was about 20 percent of that in 1929. Pig production in 1933 in pounds was 97 percent of that of 1929. In 1934, pig iron production was 45 percent of that of 1929. Pig production in 1934, the drought year, was 80 percent of that of 1929. In other words, farmers cut pig production 3 percent when steel companies cut pig iron production 80 percent.

That sort of industrial reduction program plowed millions of workers out into the streets. It is because of that industrial-reduction program that we have to spend billions for relief to keep the plowed-out workers from starvation. I hope industry in future reduction programs will not find it desirable to plow millions of workers out of their jobs. People are more important than pigs.

Great corporations should not finance people to attack agricultural adjustment. They are too vulnerable. Instead they should cooperate with agriculture to bring about increased, balanced production of those things which the American people really want at a price which they can afford to pay, but at a price high enough to keep the production coming without undue speculative gain. If industry were as productive as it knows how to be, the increased home market for fruit, vegetables, meat, and dairy products would be truly surprising. But this market cannot come to pass until industry ceases its reduction-control programs. . . .

My attention has been called to a statement by a minister out in the Corn Belt before the district conference of his faith. Concerning the actions of the New Deal he says: ". . . some of them are downright sinful as the destruction of foodstuffs in the face of present want." I have been used to statements of this sort by partisans, demagogues, politicians, and even newspaper columnists. To men of this sort I pay no attention, because I know that their interest in a cause makes it impossible for them to distinguish truth from falsehood. But when a minister of the gospel makes a statement, we expect it to be the truth.

Just what food does he think this administration has destroyed? We would like to know the specific instances. If he is merely referring to acreage control which enabled us to keep out of use in 1935 some 30 million of the 50 million acres which have produced in the past for markets in foreign countries, I would say, "Yes, we are guilty of acreage control and, depending on variations in weather, we shall continue to be until foreign purchasing power is restored by the breaking down of tariff and quota barriers."

We have not destroyed foodstuffs. We do not contemplate destroying them. However, foodstuffs *were* destroyed back in 1932 by farmers who found it profitable to burn their corn for fuel rather than to sell it for 10 cents a bushel (which amounted to $3.33 a ton). It was cheaper for many farmers in the northwest Corn Belt to burn food for fuel at those pitiful prices than to burn coal.

People who believe that we ordered the destruction of food are merely the victims of their prejudices and the misinformation that has been fed to them by interested persons. What we actually did was to stop the destruction of foodstuffs by making it worthwhile for farmers to sell them rather than destroy them.

Agricultural adjustment of the past two years has been a million times as warranted as the industrial reduction policy of the past five years. Why does not the minister attack the industrial reduction which was made possible by corporate and tariff laws? It was this reduction by industry that created the *unemployment* and destroyed the farmers' markets. But really, Mr. Minister, in conformity with the spirit of your sacred calling, might it not be better for all of us to refrain from calling names and instead do what is possible to build up on the part of both agriculture and industry a situation which will result in greatly increased balanced output of those things which we really want?

72.

KENNETH FEARING: "Dirge"

Like many other poets who came to the fore during the Depression, Kenneth Fearing rendered man in a hostile world; he utilized free verse, colloquial phrases, and the familiar clichés of the newspaper and advertising trades to create a bitterly satiric and impersonal social critique. In the following poem, "Dirge," Fearing predicted the dissolution of the American middle class. "Dirge" appeared in a volume by Fearing called Poems, *published in 1935.*

Source: *New and Selected Poems*, Bloomington, Ind., 1956.

☏ DIRGE

1-2-3 was the number he played but to-
    day the number came 3-2-1;
bought his Carbide at 30 and it went
    to 29; had the favorite at Bowie
but the track was slow —

O, executive type, would you like to drive
    a floating power, knee-action, silk-
    upholstered six? Wed a Holly-
    wood star? Shoot the course in
    58? Draw to the ace, king, jack?
O, fellow with a will who won't take
    no, watch out for three cigarettes
    on the same, single match; O,
    democratic voter born in August
    under Mars, beware of liquidated
    rails —

Denouement to denouement, he took a
    personal pride in the certain, cer-
    tain way he lived his own, private
    life,
but nevertheless, they shut off his gas;
    nevertheless, the bank foreclosed;
    nevertheless, the landlord called;
    nevertheless, the radio broke,

And twelve o'clock arrived just once too
    often,
just the same he wore one grey tweed
    suit, bought one straw hat, drank
    one straight Scotch, walked one
    short step, took one long look,
    drew one deep breath,
just one too many,

And wow he died as wow he lived,
  going whop to the office and blooie
    home to sleep and biff got mar-
    ried and bam had children and
    oof got fired,
  zowie did he live and zowie did he die,

With who the hell are you at the corner
    of his casket, and where the hell
    we going on the right-hand silver
    knob, and who the hell cares
    walking second from the end with

an American Beauty wreath from
  why the hell not,

Very much missed by the circulation staff
  of the New York Evening Post;
  deeply, deeply mourned by the
  B.M.T.,

Wham, Mr. Roosevelt; pow, Sears Roebuck; awk, big dipper; bop, summer rain;
    bong, Mr., bong, Mr., bong, Mr., bong.

73.

H. RICHARD NIEBUHR: The Captive Church

With the onset of the Depression, liberal Protestantism lost much of its following. Consolidating a trend that had begun with the First World War, theologians assailed the liberal belief that man was perfectible and the rationalistic belief that all truth could be known. While the search for a new theology led Protestant thinkers down differing paths, most started from the premise that for the church to serve a function it must divorce itself from commitment to economic and political values. The extent to which the church was entangled with the world was pointed out by H. Richard Niebuhr in the essay reprinted in part below. Titled "Toward the Independence of the Church," it appeared in a larger work, The Church Against the World, *that Niebuhr wrote with Wilhelm Pauck and Francis P. Miller.*

Source: *The Church Against the World*, Chicago, 1935, pp. 128-139.

THE CHURCH IS IN BONDAGE to capitalism. Capitalism in its contemporary form is more than a system of ownership and distribution of economic goods. It is a faith and a way of life. It is faith in wealth as the source of all life's blessings and as the savior of man from his deepest misery. It is the doctrine that man's most important activity is the production of economic goods and that all other things are dependent upon this. On the basis of this initial idolatry it develops a morality in which economic worth becomes the standard by which to measure all other values and the economic virtues take precedence over courage, temperance, wisdom and justice, over charity, humility and fidelity. Hence nature, love, life, truth, beauty and justice are exploited or made the servants of the high economic good. Everything, including the lives of workers, is made a utility, is desecrated and ultimately destroyed. Capitalism develops a discipline of its own but in the long run makes for the overthrow of all discipline since the service of its god demands the encouragement of unlimited desire for that which promises — but must fail — to satisfy the lust of the flesh and the pride of life.

The capitalist faith is not a disembodied spirit. It expresses itself in laws and social habits and transforms the whole of civilization. It fashions society into an economic organization in which production for profit becomes the central enterprise, in which the economic relations of men are regarded as their fundamental relations, in which economic privileges are most highly prized, and in which the resultant classes of men are set to struggle with one another for the economic goods. Education and government are brought under the sway of the faith. The family itself is modified by it. The structure of cities and their very architecture is influenced by the religion. So intimate is the relation between the civilization and the faith, that it is difficult to participate in the former without consenting to the latter and becoming entangled in its destructive morality. It was possible for Paul's converts to eat meat which had been offered to idols without compromising with paganism. But the products which come from the altars of this modern idolatry — the dividends, the privileges, the status, the struggle — are of such a sort that it is difficult to partake of them without becoming involved in the whole system of misplaced faith and perverted morality.

No antithesis could be greater than that which obtains between the gospel and capitalist faith. The church has known from the beginning that the love of money is the root of evil, that it is impossible to serve God and Mammon, that they that have riches shall hardly enter into life, that life does not consist in the abundance of things possessed, that the earth is the Lord's and that love, not self-interest, is the first law of life. Yet the church has become entangled

with capitalist civilization to such an extent that it has compromised with capitalist faith and morality and become a servant of the world. So intimate have the bonds between capitalism and Protestantism become that the genealogists have suspected kinship. Some have ascribed the parentage of capitalism to Protestantism while others have seen in the latter the child of the former. But whatever may have been the relation between the modest system of private ownership which a Calvin or a Wesley allowed and the gospel they proclaimed, that which obtains between the high capitalism of the later period and the church must fall under the rule of the Seventh and not of the Fifth Commandment, as a Hosea or a Jeremiah would have been quick to point out.

The entanglement with capitalism appears in the great economic interests of the church, in its debt structure, in its dependence through endowments upon the continued dividends of capitalism, and especially in its dependence upon the continued gifts of the privileged classes in the economic society. This entanglement has become the greater the more the church has attempted to keep pace with the development of capitalistic civilization, not without compromising with capitalist ideas of success and efficiency. At the same time evidence of religious syncretism, of the combination of Christianity with capitalist religion, has appeared. The "building of the kingdom of God" has been confused in many a churchly pronouncement with the increase of church possessions or with the economic advancement of mankind. The church has often behaved as though the saving of civilization and particularly of capitalist civilization were its mission. It has failed to apply to the morality of that civilization the rigid standards which it did not fail to use where less powerful realities were concerned. The development may have been inevitable, nevertheless it was a fall.

The bondage of the church to nationalism

has been more apparent than its bondage to capitalism, partly because nationalism is so evidently a religion, partly because it issues in the dramatic sacrifices of war — sacrifices more obvious if not more actual than those which capitalism demands and offers to its god. Nationalism is no more to be confused with the principle of nationality than capitalism is to be confused with the principle of private property. Just as we can accept, without complaint against the past, the fact that a private property system replaced feudalism, so we can accept, without blaming our ancestors for moral delinquency, the rise of national organization in place of universal empire.

But as the private property system became the soil in which the lust for possessions and the worship of wealth grew up, so the possibility of national independence provided opportunity for the growth of religious nationalism, the worship of the nation, and the lust for national power and glory. And as religious capitalism perverted the private property system, so religious nationalism corrupted the nationalities. Nationalism regards the nation as the supreme value, the source of all life's meaning, as an end-in-itself and a law to itself. It seeks to persuade individuals and organizations to make national might and glory their main aim in life. It even achieves a certain deliverance of men by freeing them from their bondage to self. In our modern polytheism it enters into close relationship with capitalism, though not without friction and occasional conflict, and sometimes it appears to offer an alternative faith to those who have become disillusioned with wealth-worship.

Since the adequacy of its god is continually called into question by the existence of other national deities, it requires the demonstration of the omnipotence of nation and breeds an unlimited lust for national power and expansion. But since the god is limited the result is conflict, war and destruction.

Despite the fact that the nationalist faith becomes obviously dominant only in times of sudden or continued political crisis, it has had constant and growing influence in the West, affecting particularly government and education.

The antithesis between the faith of the church and the nationalist idolatry has always been self-evident. The prophetic revolution out of which Christianity eventually came was a revolution against nationalist religion. The messianic career of Jesus developed in defiance of the nationalisms of Judaism and of Rome. In one sense Christianity emerged out of man's disillusionment with the doctrine that the road to life and joy and justice lies through the exercise of political force and the growth of national power. The story of its rise is the history of long struggle with self-righteous political power. Yet in the modern world Christianity has fallen into dependence upon the political agencies which have become the instruments of nationalism and has compromised with the religion they promote.

The division of Christendom into national units would have been a less serious matter had it not resulted so frequently in a division into nationalistic units. The close relation of church and state in some instances, the participation of the church in the political life in other cases, has been accompanied by a syncretism of nationalism and Christianity. The confusion of democracy with the Christian ideal of life in America, of racialism and the gospel in Germany, of Western nationalism and church missions in the Orient, testify to the compromise which has taken place. The churches have encouraged the nations to regard themselves as messianic powers and have supplied them with religious excuses for their imperialist expansions and aggressions. And in every time of crisis it has been possible for nationalism to convert the major part of the church, which substituted the pagan Baal for the great Jehovah, without being well aware of what it did, and promoted a holy crusade in negation of the cross. The captivity of the church to the world of nationalism does not assume so dramatic a form as a rule, yet the difficulty of Christianity in achieving an international organization testifies to the reality of its bondage.

Capitalism and nationalism are variant forms of a faith which is more widespread in modern civilization than either. It is difficult to label this religion. It may be called humanism, but there is a humanism that, far from glorifying man, reminds him of his limitations the while it loves him in his feebleness and aspiration. It has become fashionable to name it liberalism, but there is a liberalism which is interested in human freedom as something to be achieved rather than something to be assumed and praised. It may be called modernism, but surely one can live in the modern world, accepting its science and engaging in its work, without falling into idolatry of the modern.

The rather too technical term "anthropocentrism" seems to be the best designation of the faith. It is marked on its negative side by the rejection not only of the symbols of the creation, the fall and the salvation of men, but also of the belief in human dependence and limitation, in human wickedness and frailty, in divine forgiveness through the suffering of the innocent. Positively it affirms the sufficiency of man. Human desire is the source of all values. The mind and the will of man are sufficient instruments of his salvation. Evil is nothing but lack of development. Revolutionary second-birth is unnecessary. Although some elements of the anthropocentric faith are always present in human society, and although it was represented at the beginning of the modern development, it is not the source but rather the product of modern civilization. Growing out of the success of science and technology in understanding

and modifying some of the conditions of life, it has substituted veneration of science for scientific knowledge, and glorification of human activity for its exercise.

Following upon the long education in which Protestant and Catholic evangelism had brought Western men to a deep sense of their duty, this anthropocentrism glorified the moral sense of man as his natural possession and taught him that he needed no other law than the one within. Yet, as in the case of capitalism and nationalism, the faith which grew out of modern culture has modified that culture. During the last generations the anthropocentric faith has entered deeply into the structure of society and has contributed not a little to the megapolitanism and megalomania of contemporary civilization.

The compromise of the church with anthropocentrism has come almost imperceptibly in the course of its collaboration in the work of culture. It was hastened by the tenacity of Christian traditionalism, which appeared to leave churchmen with no alternative than one between worship of the letter and worship of the men who wrote the letters. Nevertheless, the compromise is a perversion of the Christian position. The more obvious expressions of the compromise have been frequent but perhaps less dangerous than the prevailing one by means of which Christianity appeared to remain true to itself while accepting the anthropocentric position. That compromise was the substitution of religion for the God of faith.

Man's aspiration after God, his prayer, his worship was exalted in this syncretism into a saving power, worthy of a place alongside science and art. Religion was endowed with all the attributes of Godhead, the while its basis was found in human nature itself. The adaptation of Christianity to the anthropocentric faith appeared in other ways: in the attenuation of the conviction of sin and of the necessity of rebirth, in the substitution of the human claim to immortality for the Christian hope and fear of an afterlife, in the glorification of religious heroes, and in the efforts of religious men and societies to become saviors.

The captive church is the church which has become entangled with this system or these systems of worldliness. It is a church which seeks to prove its usefulness to civilization, in terms of civilization's own demands. It is a church which has lost the distinctive note and the earnestness of a Christian discipline of life and has become what every religious institution tends to become — the teacher of the prevailing code of morals and the pantheon of the social

gods. It is a church, moreover, which has become entangled with the world in its desire for the increase of its power and prestige and which shares the worldly fear of insecurity.

How the church became entangled and a captive in this way may be understood. To blame the past for errors which have brought us to this pass is to indulge in the ancient fallacy of saying that the fathers have eaten sour grapes and the children's teeth are set on edge. The function of the present is neither praise nor blame of the past. It is rather the realization of the prevailing situation and preparation for the next task.

74.

BENNETT CHAMP CLARK: Detour Around War

The first of three Neutrality Acts was passed on August 31, 1935. It was based mainly on two premises: that America did not want to participate, and could avoid participating, in European wars — by 1935 it was obvious to many that a new one was brewing — and that America had been drawn into the previous war to protect manufacturers and bankers. The second premise reflected the findings of the Nye Committee, which in turn had been accepted by the public at large. The provisions of the Neutrality Act were described by Senator Bennett Champ Clark of Missouri in an article published in December 1935, and reprinted here in part. The Second Neutrality Act, passed on February 29, 1936, included only one of the two provisions for which Clark appeals below: it forbade loans to belligerent governments.

Source: *Harper's Monthly*, December 1935.

IS THERE A WAY to keep America out of war?

If there is such a thing as intelligence left in the craniums of mankind, a thing so monstrous as another modern World War must be avoided. There certainly is no moral justification for war between civilized nations. No moralist or philosopher worthy of the name in modern times has ever been able to defend it. The veriest jingo in the

United States does not dare to stand upon any public platform and attempt to justify war as such. The peoples of the whole world abhor it.

Yet it is apparent to any student of international affairs that the postwar era has come to an end, and that the world is once again in that precarious condition in which the bad temper of a dictator, the ineptness of a diplomat, or the crime of a fanatic may let loose irremediable disaster. As these words are being written, early in October, the conflict in Ethiopia has already begun. No one knows how fast or how far it may spread, or whether it may not be merely the first of a series of conflagrations that will roar from continent to continent. But of this we may be sure: If the flames sweep Europe there will be mighty forces presently at work — forces of cunning or desperate diplomacy, of propaganda, of greed, and of thoughtless patriotism — to force us too into the insane debacle to preserve our fancied honor, or freedom of the seas, or "neutral rights."

At present the desire to keep the United States from becoming involved in any war between foreign nations seems practically unanimous among the rank and file of American citizens; but it must be remembered there was an almost equally strong demand to keep us out of the last war. In August 1914, few could have conceived that America would be dragged into a European conflict in which we had no original part and the ramifications of which we did not even understand. Even as late as November 1916, President Wilson was reelected because he "kept us out of war." Yet five months later we were fighting to "save the world for democracy" in the "war to end war."

In the light of that experience, and in the red glow of warfires burning in the old countries, it is high time we give some thought to the hard, practical question of just how we propose to stay out of present and future international conflicts. No one who has made an honest attempt to face the issue will assert that there is an easy answer. But if we have learned anything at all, we know the inevitable and tragic end to a policy of drifting and trusting to luck. We know that however strong is the will of the American people to refrain from mixing in other people's quarrels, that will can be made effective only if we have a sound, definite policy from the beginning.

Such a policy must be built upon a program to safeguard our neutrality. No lesson of the World War is more clear than that such a policy cannot be improvised after war breaks out. It must be determined in advance, before it is too late to apply reason. I contend with all possible earnestness that if we want to avoid being drawn into this war now forming, or any other future war, we must formulate a definite, workable policy of neutral relations with belligerent nations.

Some of us in the Senate, particularly the members of the Munitions Investigation Committee, have delved rather deeply into the matter of how the United States has been drawn into past wars and what forces are at work to frighten us again into the traps set by Mars. As a result of these studies, Senator Nye and I introduced the three proposals for neutrality legislation which were debated so vigorously in the last session of the Congress. A part of that legislative program was battered through both houses in the closing hours of the session late in August; a very vital part of it was held in abeyance.

Senator Nye and I made no claims then, and make none now, that the neutrality proposals will provide an absolute and infallible guarantee against our involvement in war. But we do believe that the United States can stay out of war if it wants to and if its citizens understand what is necessary to preserve our neutrality. We feel that the temporary legislation already passed and the legislation we shall vigorously push at the coming session of the Congress point the only practical way. . . .

As finally passed, the joint resolution on neutrality provides for the prohibition of the exportation of arms, ammunition, and implements of war to belligerent countries; the prohibition of the transportation of arms, ammunition, and implements of war by vessels of the United States for the use of belligerent nations; for the registration and licensing of persons engaged in the manufacturing, exporting, or importing of arms, ammunition and implements of war, at all times; and for the restriction of travel by American citizens on belligerent ships during war. The act is to terminate February 29, 1936. It is a stop-gap only. But it is pointing the way we intend to go.

The President is empowered to enumerate definitely the arms, munitions, and implements of war, the exportation of which is prohibited by this act. On September 27 President Roosevelt made this enumeration in a proclamation, following closely the list submitted to the disarmament conference at Geneva in our government's proposals for international control of the munitions industry. A National Munitions Control Board has been established, composed of the secretaries of state, treasury, war, navy, and commerce, with the administration of the board in the Department of State.

It is contemplated that by November 29, when the act takes effect, the manufacturers and exporters of war implements will all be listed in the office of this board. After that date such materials as are specified may not be exported without a license issued by the board to cover such shipment. This will, obviously, permit the government to prohibit shipments to belligerent nations. The act makes it unlawful for any American vessel to "carry arms, ammunition, or implements of war to any port of the belligerent countries named in such proclamation as being at war, or to any neutral port for transshipment to, or for use in, a belligerent country."

Further provisions of the act empower the President to restrict the use of American ports and waters to submarines of foreign nations in the event such use might disturb our position of neutrality, and to proclaim the conditions under which American citizens on belligerent ships during war must travel entirely at their own risk.

Two provisions from our original program failed to pass: prohibition of loans and credits to belligerent nations, and the application of strict embargoes upon contraband materials other than munitions and war implements. These are the unfinished items of our neutrality proposals. . . .

One is forced to the conclusion that our statesmen and our people knew very little about the forces ready to draw us into war when the conflict broke in Europe in 1914. . . . We should be wiser today! We know much more about both war and neutrality. From all the study of that World War drama, four conclusions stand out in my mind:

1. That a policy based on defense of our so-called neutral rights led us into serious diplomatic controversy with the Allies and the Central Powers, and in the end brought us to a point where we were compelled to choose between surrendering these rights or fighting to defend them. In 1917 we chose to fight.

2. That "national honor" and the "prestige" of the nation are inevitably involved when American ships are sunk on the high seas — even though the owners of these ships and their cargoes are private citizens seeking to profit from other nations' wars. Passions are quickly aroused when American lives are lost — even though the citizens who took passage on belligerent ships knew in advance the risks they ran.

3. That the economic forces set in motion by our huge war trade with the Allies made it impossible to maintain that "true spirit of neutrality" which President Wilson urged upon his fellow citizens at the outbreak of the conflict.

4. That among these economic forces those which involved us most deeply were the huge trade in arms and ammunition and other war materials with the Allies.

I have called the present Neutrality Act a stop-gap. But it has not stopped the activities of our American war-munitions makers anxious for profits from imminent conflicts. Reports from centers of manufacturing and exporting of war implements all tell the same story — there is a boom in war preparations. Chambers of commerce in cities with large war-materials plants proudly report reemployment of skilled munitions makers in large numbers, the stepping up of output to as high as 300 percent, the rushing to completion of new additions to plants. Day-and-night shifts in the brass and copper mills, rising prices and large shipments of these metals, and the acquisition of large capital for immediate wartime-scale production, all indicate that Mars has waved his magic wand in our direction.

Where are these war-implements shipments going? There is no proof that the munitions makers are trying to "beat the embargo" which will prohibit shipments to belligerents after November 29, but it stands to reason they are making hay while the sun shines. Our Munitions Investigation Committee has not had time to look into immediate developments, but it needs no stretch of imagination to contemplate the rich profits that would flow from an Italian-Ethiopian War, with England jumping into the fray against Italy, and other European nations following suit on one side or the other.

And, of course, there's lots of war business right here at home. We have increased our expenditures on our Army and Navy in preparation for another and more dreadful war more rapidly than any European country in the period since the World War. . . .

When the Congress meets in January, facing the expiration of the Neutrality Act on February 29, the battle for a practical policy of neutrality will have to be fought all over again. We who believe that the detour around another devastating war is to be found only in new conceptions of neutrality will fight for the retention of the present legislation and for the passage of the two items left out in the cold at the adjournment of the Congress.

I firmly believe, whatever the status of the Italo-Ethiopian dispute at that time, whatever the position of other European powers as belligerents or as neutrals, that the United States of America cannot turn back to a policy of so-called neutrality that finally pulls us into conflict with one or all the belligerents. Surely it is obvious that the legislation forcing mandatory embargoes upon war materials will serve to check the growth of another vast munitions trade with warring powers and the dangers that follow a swing of our foreign trade in favor of our munitions customers and against those who cannot purchase the munitions. Why shall we contend for embargoes upon contraband articles as well, and prohibition of loans and credits to belligerents? Because it takes these two items to complete any sort of workable neutrality program. If we are in earnest about neutrality we may as well plan to be neutral. . . .

Let us foresee that under conditions of modern warfare everything supplied to the enemy population has the same effect as supplies to the enemy army, and will become contraband. Food, clothing, lumber, leather, chemicals — everything, in fact, with the possible exception of sporting goods and luxuries (and these aid in maintaining civilian "morale") — are as important aids to winning the war as are munitions. Let us foresee, also, that our ships carrying contraband will be seized, bombed from the air, or sunk by submarines. Let us not claim as a right what is an impossibility. The only way we can maintain our neutral rights is to fight the whole world. If we are not prepared to do that we can only pretend to enforce our rights against one side, and go to war to defend them against the other side. We might at least abandon pretense.

On the matter of loans and credits to belligerents, the train of events which pulled us into the World War is equally significant. Correspondence which our Munitions Investigation Committee discovered in the files of the State Department offers illuminating proof that there can be no true neutrality when our nation is allowed to finance one side of a foreign war. One letter, written by Secretary Robert Lansing to President Wilson, dated Sept. 5, 1915, lucidly points out that loans for the Allies were absolutely necessary to enable them to pay for the tremendous trade in munitions, war materials generally, foodstuffs, and the like, or else that trade would have to stop. He declared that the administration's "true spirit of neutrality" must not stand in the way of the demands of commerce. About one month later the first great loan — the Anglo-French loan of $500 million — was floated by a syndicate headed by J. P. Morgan and Company. This company had been the purchasing agents for Allied supplies in the United States since early in 1915. Other loans to the Allied Powers quickly followed.

Our committee is pressing further the investigation of American loans and credits to Allied nations during the World War, and I can say with confidence that in the coming session of the Congress our findings will present irrefutable proof of the influence of the big money lenders and money changers in drawing us into the conflict. One statement needs no proof to intelligent men: You cannot finance one side of a war and remain neutral!

"But, think of the profits!" cry our theorists. "America will never give up her lucrative trade in munitions and necessities of life when war starts!" Mr. Ernest Angell in a recent discussion in *Harper's* asserted: "The American public is not prepared to pay the price of complete abstention from trade with belligerents, and only at that price can neutrality be effectively preserved." . . .

Just who profited from the last war? Labor got some of the crumbs in the form of high wages and steady jobs. But where is labor today, with its 14 million unemployed? Agriculture received high prices for its products during the period of the war and has been paying the price of that brief inflation in the worst and longest agricultural depression in all history. Industry made billions in furnishing the necessities of war to the belligerents and then suffered terrific reaction like the dope addict's morning after. War and depression — ugly, misshapen inseparable twins — must be considered together. Each is a catapult for the other. The present worldwide depression is a direct result of the World War. Every war in modern history has been followed by a major depression.

Therefore, I say, let the man seeking profits from war or the war-torn countries do so at his own risk. . . .

If there are those so brave as to risk getting us into war by traveling in the war zones — if there are those so valiant that they do not care how many people are killed as a result of their traveling — let us tell them, and let us tell the world, that from now on their deaths will be a misfortune to their own families alone, not to the whole nation.

The profiteers and others who oppose any rational neutrality shout: "You would sacrifice our national honor!" Some declare we are about to haul down the American flag, and in a future war the belligerents will trample on our rights and treat us with contempt. Some of these arguments are trundled out by our naval bureaucracy. The admirals, I am told, objected strenuously when the State Department suggested a new policy of neutrality somewhat along these lines.

I deny with every fiber of my being that our national honor demands that we must sacrifice the flower of our youth to safeguard the profits of a privileged few. I deny that it is necessary to turn back the hands of civilization to maintain our national honor. I repudiate any such definition of honor. Is it not time for every lover of our country to do the same thing?

75.

ROBINSON JEFFERS: "Rearmament"

Nothing that occurred in the 1930s, or for that matter in the '40s or '50s, convinced Robinson Jeffers to alter the poetry of doom that he had begun to compose during World War I. Jeffers was fascinated by the way in which his contemporaries were obliviously yet assuredly bringing about their own annihilation. The title of the following poem by Jeffers — "Rearmament" — suggests that the instrument of man's self-destruction was to be war. The poem was published in 1935 in a collection by Jeffers called Solstice; *in the same year Hitler openly announced a massive rearmament program in defiance of the Treaty of Versailles.*

Source: *Solstice*, New York, 1935.

REARMAMENT

These grand and fatal movements toward death: the grandeur of the mass
Makes pity a fool, the tearing pity
For the atoms of the mass, the persons, the victims, makes it seem monstrous
To admire the tragic beauty they build.
It is beautiful as a river flowing or a slowly gathering
Glacier on a high mountain rock-face,
Bound to plow down a forest, or as frost in November,
The gold and flaming death-dance for leaves,
Or a girl in the night of her spent maidenhood, bleeding and kissing.
I would burn my right hand in a slow fire
To change the future . . . I should do foolishly. The beauty of modern
Man is not in the persons but in the
Disastrous rhythm, the heavy and mobile masses, the dance of the
Dream-led masses down the dark mountain.

1936

76.

Louis D. Brandeis: The Ashwander Rules

In one of the few decisions in behalf of the government during the early New Deal period, the Supreme Court (in Ashwander v. TVA) upheld the right of the U.S. government to build dams on rivers that flowed through more than one state. In a concurring opinion, in the course of which he argued that the case should not have been heard by the Court at all, Justice Brandeis enumerated seven general principles, afterwards called the Ashwander Rules, that the Court subsequently relied on in selecting cases for review. The Rules made explicit the long-standing practice of the Court, which avoids questions of constitutionality where there are lesser means of resolving the problem at issue — for example, returning the case to a lower court for a clarification of intent about legislation or reconstruing the issue so as not to raise a constitutional question. In theory, then, the Court presumes the constitutionality of official actions, and the burden of proof always lies with the plaintiff, who, if he wishes to raise a constitutional question, must show that it is unavoidable. The portion of Brandeis' opinion of February 17, 1936, enumerating the Rules appears below.

Source: 297 U.S. 288.

The Court has frequently called attention to the "great gravity and delicacy" of its function in passing upon the validity of an act of Congress, and has restricted exercise of this function by rigid insistence that the jurisdiction of federal courts is limited to actual cases and controversies, and that they have no power to give advisory opinions. On this ground it has in recent years ordered the dismissal of several suits challenging the constitutionality of important acts of Congress. In *Texas* v. *Interstate Commerce Commission*, 258 U.S. 158, 162, the validity of Titles III and IV of the Transportation Act of 1920. In *New Jersey* v. *Sargent*, 269 U.S. 328, the validity of parts of the Federal Water Power Act. In *Arizona* v. *California*, 283 U.S. 423, the validity of the Boulder Canyon Project Act. Compare *United States* v. *West Virginia*, 295 U.S. 463, involving the Federal Water Power Act, and *Liberty Warehouse Co.* v. *Grannis*, 273 U.S. 70, where this Court affirmed the dismissal of a suit to test the validity of a Kentucky statute concerning the sale of tobacco; also *Massachusetts State Grange* v. *Benton*, 272 U.S. 525.

The Court developed, for its own governance in the cases confessedly within its jurisdiction, a series of rules under which it has avoided passing upon a large part of all the constitutional questions pressed upon it for decision. They are:

1. The Court will not pass upon the constitutionality of legislation in a friendly, nonadversary proceeding, declining because to decide such questions "is legitimate only in the last resort, and as a necessity in the determination of real, earnest, and vital controversy between individuals. It never was the thought that, by means of a friendly suit, a party beaten in the legislature could transfer to the courts an inquiry as to the constitutionality of the legislative act." *Chicago & Grand Trunk Ry.* v. *Wellman,* 143 U.S. 339, 345. Compare *Lord* v. *Veazie,* 8 How. 251; *Atherton Mills* v. *Johnston,* 259 U.S. 13, 15.

2. The Court will not "anticipate a question of constitutional law in advance of the necessity of deciding it." *Liverpool, N.Y. & P.S.S. Co.* v. *Emigration Commissioners,* 113 U.S. 33, 39; *Abrams* v. *Van Schaick,* 293 U.S. 188; *Wilshire Oil Co.* v. *United States,* 295 U.S. 100. "It is not the habit of the Court to decide questions of a constitutional nature unless absolutely necessary to a decision of the case." *Burton* v. *United States,* 196 U.S. 283, 295.

3. The Court will not "formulate a rule of constitutional law broader than is required by the precise facts to which it is to be applied." *Liverpool, N.Y. & P.S.S. Co.* v. *Emigration Commissioners, supra.* Compare *Hammond* v. *Schappi Bus Line,* 275 U.S. 164, 169-172.

4. The Court will not pass upon a constitutional question, although properly presented by the record, if there is also present some other ground upon which the case may be disposed of. This rule has found most varied application. Thus, if a case can be decided on either of two grounds — one involving a constitutional question, the other a question of statutory construction or

general law — the Court will decide only the latter. *Siler* v. *Louisville & Nashville R. Co.,* 213 U.S. 175, 191; *Light* v. *United States,* 220 U.S. 523, 538. Appeals from the highest court of a state challenging its decision of a question under the federal Constitution are frequently dismissed because the judgment can be sustained on an independent state ground. *Berea College* v. *Kentucky,* 211 U.S. 45, 53.

5. The Court will not pass upon the validity of a statute upon complaint of one who fails to show that he is injured by its operation. *Tyler* v. *The Judges,* 179 U.S. 405; *Hendrick* v. *Maryland,* 235 U.S. 610, 621. Among the many applications of this rule, none is more striking than the denial of the right of challenge to one who lacks a personal or property right. Thus, the challenge by a public official interested only in the performance of his official duty will not be entertained. *Columbus & Greenville Ry.* v. *Miller,* 283 U.S. 96, 99-100. In *Fairchild* v. *Hughes,* 258 U.S. 126, the Court affirmed the dismissal of a suit brought by a citizen who sought to have the Nineteenth Amendment declared unconstitutional. In *Massachusetts* v. *Mellon,* 262 U.S. 447, the challenge of the federal Maternity Act was not entertained although made by the Commonwealth on behalf of all its citizens.

6. The Court will not pass upon the constitutionality of a statute at the instance of one who has availed himself of its benefits. *Great Falls Mfg. Co.* v. *Attorney General,* 124 U.S. 581; *Wall* v. *Parrot Silver & Copper Co.,* 244 U.S. 407, 411-412; *St. Louis Malleable Casting Co.* v. *Prendergast Construction Co.,* 260 U.S. 469.

7. "When the validity of an act of the Congress is drawn in question, and even if a serious doubt of constitutionality is raised, it is a cardinal principle that this Court will first ascertain whether a construction of the statute is fairly possible by which the question may be avoided." *Crowell* v. *Benson,* 285 U.S. 22, 62.

77.

Franklin D. Roosevelt: The Good Neighbor Policy

Three decades of strained relations with the Latin-American countries were reversed during the Hoover administration, largely through the work of Secretary of State Henry L. Stimson. President Roosevelt, who later named Stimson his secretary of war, resolved to continue the policy of not interfering in the internal affairs of Latin America and seeking alliances there. In an address at Chautauqua, New York, on August 14, 1936, part of which is reprinted here, the President explained his "Good Neighbor Policy."

Source: *Peace and War: United States Foreign Policy 1931-1941*, Washington, 1943, pp. 323-329.

Long before I returned to Washington as President of the United States, I had made up my mind that, pending what might be called a more opportune moment on other continents, the United States could best serve the cause of a peaceful humanity by setting an example. That was why on the 4th of March, 1933, I made the following declaration:

In the field of world policy I would dedicate this nation to the policy of the good neighbor — the neighbor who resolutely respects himself and, because he does so, respects the rights of others — the neighbor who respects his obligations and respects the sanctity of his agreements in and with a world of neighbors.

This declaration represents my purpose; but it represents more than a purpose, for it stands for a practice. To a measurable degree it has succeeded; the whole world now knows that the United States cherishes no predatory ambitions. We are strong; but less powerful nations know that they need not fear our strength. We seek no conquest: we stand for peace.

In the whole of the Western Hemisphere our good-neighbor policy has produced results that are especially heartening.

The noblest monument to peace and to neighborly economic and social friendship in all the world is not a monument in bronze or stone, but the boundary which unites the United States and Canada — 3,000 miles of friendship with no barbed wire, no gun or soldier, and no passport on the whole frontier. Mutual trust made that frontier. To extend the same sort of mutual trust throughout the Americas was our aim.

The American republics to the south of us have been ready always to cooperate with the United States on a basis of equality and mutual respect, but before we inaugurated the good-neighbor policy there was among them resentment and fear because certain administrations in Washington had slighted their national pride and their sovereign rights.

In pursuance of the good-neighbor policy and because in my younger days I had learned many lessons in the hard school of experience, I stated that the United States was opposed definitely to armed intervention.

We have negotiated a Pan American convention embodying the principle of nonintervention. We have abandoned the Platt Amendment, which gave us the right to intervene in the internal affairs of the Republic of Cuba. We have withdrawn American Marines from Haiti. We have signed a new treaty which places our relations with Panama on a mutually satisfactory basis. We have undertaken a series of trade agreements with other American countries to our mutual commercial profit. At the request of two neighboring republics, I hope to give assistance in the final settlement of the last serious boundary dispute between any of the American nations.

Throughout the Americas the spirit of the good neighbor is a practical and living fact. The twenty-one American republics are not only living together in friendship and in peace — they are united in the determination so to remain.

To give substance to this determination a conference will meet on Dec. 1, 1936, at the capital of our great southern neighbor Argentina, and it is, I know, the hope of all chiefs of state of the Americas that this will result in measures which will banish wars forever from this vast portion of the earth.

Peace, like charity, begins at home; that is why we have begun at home. But peace in the Western world is not all that we seek.

It is our hope that knowledge of the practical application of the good-neighbor policy in this hemisphere will be borne home to our neighbors across the seas.

78.

Frances Perkins: A Policy for Labor

After 1920, when women finally gained the vote, the Democratic Party, especially in New York State, pioneered in actively enrolling their support at election time. By 1932 women were a small but significant element in the New Deal coalition. President Roosevelt appointed a number of women to important jobs: Nellie Ross as director of the Mint, Ruth Bryan Owen as the first woman to achieve ministerial rank (Denmark), and Frances Perkins, who had been active in public service in New York State since 1910, as the first woman Cabinet member. Secretary of Labor Perkins was the author of numerous books, the most recent prior to the article reprinted here being People at Work *(1934). Her observation that the fundamental thing about Roosevelt was his conviction that "the people mattered" applied equally well to herself.*

Source: *Annals* of the American Academy of Political and Social Science, March 1936: "A National Labor Policy."

LABOR POLICY IN A DEMOCRACY is not a program conceived by a government. It is a program of action which the people who earn their living as wage earners and those who employ them in a profit-making enterprise must work out together in a society which develops naturally out of the work that they do and the life that they lead. The function of government is to serve as a stimulating agent to facilitate the formation of such a policy, which will be just and fair to all the people and in the line of human progress.

Hand in hand with the growth of our institutions, a labor policy is developing. It is in somewhat more than a rudimentary stage. It is, like all social institutions, a growing, living thing, subject to such

Secretary of Labor Frances Perkins visiting two of the supervisors of the Golden Gate Bridge project, San Francisco, 1935

change and revision as the economic and political consciousness of the wage-earning and employing groups, the experiences of life, and a growing sense of justness make possible. It will be realistic, flexible, practical, and based upon the habits of people and the prevailing necessities of production and distribution, rather than upon predetermined conceptions of human relationships.

Among the first items in this growing labor policy of the American government are the following:

1. That the government ought to do everything in its power to establish minimum basic standards for labor, below which competition should not be permitted to force standards of health, wages, or hours.

2. That the government ought to use its influence to bring about arrangements which will make possible peaceful settlements of controversies and relieve labor of the necessity of resorting to strikes to secure equitable conditions and the right to be heard.

3. That the ideal of government should be, through legislation and through cooperation between employers and workers, to make every job the best that the human mind can devise as to physical conditions, human relations, and wages.

4. That government should encourage such organization and development of wage earners as will give status and stability to labor as a recognized important group of citizens having a contribution to make to economic and political thought and to the cultural life of the community.

5. That government ought to arrange that labor play its part in the study and development of any economic policies for the future of the United States.

6. That the government should encourage mutuality between labor and employers in the improvement of production and in the development in both groups of a philosophy of self-government in the public interest. If labor's rights are defined by law and by government, then certain obligations will of course be expected of wage earners, and it is for the public interest that those obligations should be defined by labor itself, and that such discipline as is necessary should be self-imposed and not imposed from without. This is the basis of all professional codes of ethics in modern society.

There are many signs at the present time with the growth and the recognition of the importance and significance of the labor groups in our common civilization, that as labor gains status in the community it also imposes upon itself those rules of discipline and self-government necessary for the maintenance of that status. . . .

With the guarantee to labor of the right of free association and the provision of necessary safeguards against abuse of the right, with the establishment of the National Labor Relations Board, with the assistance of uch special industrial boards as in textiles, teel, railroad transportation, and bitumihous coal, and with the Conciliation Service of the United States Department of Labor, we should be able to look forward confidently to a fairer and more scientific handling of the problems involved in relationhips between employers and employees han we have ever had before.

This means not merely that strikes and ockouts may be fewer but that the fundamental causes of such disorders may be inelligently diagnosed and remedies quickly provided through the agency of such boards. Wage earners and employers have shown a growing disposition to avail themselves of the fair and impartial services of these government boards. They are really set up for the purpose of keeping industrial peace for the benefit of employers and workers and in the public interest. These agencies will gather authority as the years go on; and as the spirit of cooperation between employers and employees continues to grow, as they become increasingly aware that it is in their interest and in the interest of the public as well, we will find the good offices of these boards being sought more and more as a voluntary substitute for long and costly strikes and lockouts.

79.

ROBERT FROST: "Two Tramps in Mud Time"

Robert Frost has often been compared to the New England Transcendentalists of the last century, and the comparison has a certain amount of validity, although Frost himself disliked being put in critical "pigeon holes." Frost, like Emerson, Thoreau, and the others before him, seemed deeply to feel that nature confronted in solitude is a prime source of truth, that truth is ultimately personal, and that a man's main responsibility is to his own conscience. These beliefs are reflected in "Two Tramps in Mud Time," which appeared in the volume A Further Range *in 1936. The poem contains some lovely — and famous — lines about spring, but the last stanza appears to express its real point — that one's vocation and one's avocation ought to be united, in other words, that love and need should be one.*

Source: *A Further Range,* New York, 1936, pp. 16-18.

TWO TRAMPS IN MUD TIME

Out of the mud two strangers came
And caught me splitting wood in the yard.
And one of them put me off my aim
By hailing cheerily 'Hit them hard!'
I knew pretty well why he dropped behind
And let the other go on a way.
I knew pretty well what he had in mind:
He wanted to take my job for pay.

Good blocks of beech it was I split,
As large around as the chopping block;
And every piece I squarely hit
Fell splinterless as a cloven rock.
The blows that a life of self-control
Spares to strike for the common good
That day, giving a loose to my soul,
I spent on the unimportant wood.

The sun was warm but the wind was chill.
You know how it is with an April day
When the sun is out and the wind is still,
You're one month on in the middle of May.
But if you so much as dare to speak,
A cloud comes over the sunlit arch,
A wind comes off a frozen peak,
And you're two months back in the middle
of March.

A bluebird comes tenderly up to alight
And fronts the wind to unruffle a plume
His song so pitched as not to excite
A single flower as yet to bloom.
It is snowing a flake: and he half knew
Winter was only playing possum.
Except in color he isn't blue,
But he wouldn't advise a thing to blossom.

The water for which we may have to look
In summertime with a witching-wand,
In every wheelrut's now a brook,
In every print of a hoof a pond.
Be glad of water, but don't forget
The lurking frost in the earth beneath
That will steal forth after the sun is set
And show on the water its crystal teeth.

The time when most I loved my task
These two must make me love it more
By coming with what they came to ask.
You'd think I never had felt before

The weight of an ax-head poised aloft,
The grip on earth of outspread feet,
The life of muscles rocking soft
And smooth and moist in vernal heat.

Out of the woods two hulking tramps
(From sleeping God knows where last night
But not long since in the lumber camps).
They thought all chopping was theirs of
right.
Men of the woods and lumberjacks,
They judged me by their appropriate tool.
Except as a fellow handled an ax,
They had no way of knowing a fool.

Nothing on either side was said.
They knew they had but to stay their stay
And all their logic would fill my head:
As that I had no right to play
With what was another man's work for gain
My right might be love but theirs was need.
And where the two exist in twain
Theirs was the better right — agreed.

But yield who will to their separation,
My object in living is to unite
My avocation and my vocation
As my two eyes make one in sight.
Only where love and need are one,
And the work is play for mortal stakes,
Is the deed ever really done
For Heaven and the future's sakes.

80.

SELIG PERLMAN: Collective Bargaining

The New Deal saw the passage of much important legislation favoring organized labor. Laws such as the National Industrial Recovery Act of 1933 and the Wagner Act of 1935 set maximum hours and minimum wages and also strengthened the bargaining power of unions. These acts and others like them were conceived as part of the administration's overall plan to increase mass purchasing power by increasing wages and employment. Beyond that, they were intended to prevent future depressions by restoring the balance between the consuming and the producing segments of the economy. The following selection, taken from an article by the economist Selig Perlman originally titled "The Principle of Collective Bargaining," traces the history of unionism from suppression to promotion.

Source: *Annals* of the American Academy of Political and Social Science, March 1936.

COLLECTIVE BARGAINING is not just a means of raising wages and improving conditions of employment. Nor is it merely democratic government in industry. It is above all a technique whereby an inferior social class or group carries on a never slackening pressure for a bigger share in the social sovereignty as well as for more welfare, security, and liberty for its individual members. As such it is not confined to a single arena, the industrial one, where employers and labor unions meet directly, but manifests itself equally in politics, legislation, court litigation, government administration, religion, education, and propaganda. Nor is collective bargaining only a phenomenon of modern society. On the contrary, its clearest and most comprehensive manifestation was shown by the urban communities in the Middle Ages — the boroughs and the guilds in the struggle against feudal lords.

Collective bargaining as a technique of the rise of a new class is quite different from the class struggle of the Marxians. It is nominalist instead of realist. It is pragmatic and concrete instead of idealist and abstract. It is much less concerned with algebraic formulae summing up basic economic trends than with the problems of building discipline in organization and of training leadership. It derives its emotional impetus, not from the desire to displace or "abolish" the "old ruling class" but from the wish to bring one's own class abreast of the superior class; to gain equal rights as a class and equal consideration for the members of that class with the members of that other class; to acquire an exclusive jurisdiction in that sphere where the most immediate interests, both material and spiritual, are determined, and a shared jurisdiction with the older class or classes in all the other spheres. . . .

Since the union cannot prevent contact between its individual members and the employer, in the manner in which the guild prevented contact of its members and the lord, it does the next best thing and prevents *individual bargaining* by enforcing union conditions of employment, the union's rules of occupancy and tenure of the job opportunity. But wherever possible, the union tries to be the unquestioned administrator of the job opportunities, as in union print shops, where the union sits alone in judgment over the foreman who has discharged an employee, and confines its bargains with the employer to wages and hours.

ATTITUDES OF PUBLIC AUTHORITY

The employer, however, is only one of the powers with whom the union has to make terms. Public authority is the other one, and during crucial stages, even the more important of the two. Generally speaking, the attitude of the public authority toward labor's collective bargaining has passed through the stages of suppression, grudging toleration, benevolent toleration, promotion, and (lately in countries ruled by dictatorship) absorption. . . .

DEVELOPMENT OF LABOR STRATEGY

The stages in the evolution of the attitude of public authority toward labor's collective bargaining roughly accord with the stages in the development of labor strategy. The revolutionary stage coincides with the period of the unions' illegality and with the more intolerant portion of the stage of grudging toleration. Russian labor in 1904-1906 and 1917, British labor at the time of the Grand Consolidated Trades' Union and of the Chartist movement, German labor under the anti-socialist laws, and American labor in the eighties and nineties when the labor injunction made its debut — amply demonstrate that revolutionary correlation. In Russia, due to the absence in her body politic of the centers of resistance which in the countries of the Western pattern had been built up in the course of their more organic developments, labor, molded by professional revolutionaries from among the intellectuals, won a complete victory virtually by default. With that victory, collective bargaining as defined here came to an end in Russia. Elsewhere, the onrush of revolutionary labor shattered itself against the defenses of the established order.

Thereupon labor, making the best of the arrived grudging toleration by public authority, turned to a strategy of trench warfare on innumerable craft fronts, and of pounding its way inch by inch into the employer's field of prerogative. This campaign of opportunistic pressure on the many economic fronts, by means of strikes and union working rules, was supplemented by an equally opportunistic tactic on the political, legislative, and propaganda fronts. It was during this stage of many small wars, wars without formal truces, that the physiognomy of job-conscious unionism took its definite and hard shape — a hard-hitting unionism capable of great endurance but aspiring toward no millennium, only toward recognition as a legitimate partner in industrial government.

INDUSTRIAL GOVERNMENT

In fact, industrial government is labor's outstanding contribution to capitalist society. In America it began in a large way with the agreement system, erected in 1898, between the United Mine Workers and the operators in the Central Competitive Field. That agreement system became a school in which labor taught the employers the art of peaceably sharing their market opportunity instead of the former cutthroat competition. This was implemented through an elaborate wage rate structure aiming to equalize competitive costs notwithstanding geological and geographical inequalities.

The union, of course, was inspired by no philanthropy toward the employers. It merely felt that for the realization of it wn objective of job conservation and job haring, it was necessary that the operators s competitors be trained in economic good manners and sportsmanship. This industrial overnment of the mining industry disre- garded the ideology of competitive capital- sm, as well as the gospel of scientific man- gement; it advanced the economic life of he weak and it increased the costs to the onsumer. But it did so in the name of hu- manity to the producer, the job holder, and he operator alike.

In the agreement system in the men's lothing industry, established in Chicago in 911 between Hart Schaffner and Marx nd the union led by Sidney Hillman, in- dustrial government avoided conflict with fficiency, and, in time, developed a govern- ng apparatus which should be the delight of catholic-minded political scientists. In the ndustrial government under that agreement here are clearly discernible the legislative, executive, and judicial branches of govern- ment, and also the "administrative commis- ion" which combines features of all three. The "constitution," elaborated by their own ubsequent judicial interpretation, also con- ains a "bill of rights" safeguarding the em- loyer, the employee, and the union.

For instance, the employer is guaranteed gainst "stoppages" — economic "riots" as t were; the employee is protected by eco- omic "habeas corpus" proceedings against he loss of his job either through discrimi- atory discharge or from technological hange; and the union is upheld as a vigor- us bargaining agency by the grant of "par- iamentary immunity" to the "shop chair- nen" — namely, protection from discharge xcept with the preliminary consent of the mpartial "court" — and through union

preference in employment. Under this agreement system, efficiency, or progress, far from being blocked, has been encour- aged, and since 1925 perhaps somewhat un- duly so in this age of technological unem- ployment.

However, both varieties of industrial gov- ernment, in bituminous coal and in men's clothing, require, for survival, an extension over each entire industry of the standards fixed by the collective bargain. And the im- plication, as far as the attitude of public au- thority is concerned, is that collective bar- gaining has entered into the stage of pro- motion rather than that of mere toleration, however benevolent.

Dangers of Promotion

But such promotion holds its dangers, es- pecially in this country, with its labor movement unevenly developed and in many basic industries virtually lacking; for it is the rare governmental promoter of collective bargaining who will resist the temptation to try to impose his own views of what is ra- tional and good for the labor movement.

In practice, of course, it is extremely diffi- cult to draw the line between the genuine "organicism" of the labor movement, vital to its existence and vigor, and stubborn conservatism rooted in vested rights and selfishness. Especially in a time like the present, apparently a *Sturm und Drang* pe- riod in the American labor movement, union building from a blueprint, will seem to many a matter of public duty. For these the fate of Joseph II of Austria should hold a restraining lesson. Genuine reform, even in the labor movement, can come only from within.

If two New Hampshiremen aren't a match for the devil, we might as well give the country back to the Indians.
STEPHEN VINCENT BENÉT, "The Devil and Daniel Webster," 1936

81.

NORMAN THOMAS: American Socialism

Norman Thomas had a great deal of difficulty in keeping the identity of his Socialist Party clear-cut during the New Deal. He was accused by conservatives of being either a Communist or a Fascist — the terms were often interchanged — and by the Communists of belonging to the capitalist camp. It was further alleged, to Thomas' annoyance, that Roosevelt had taken over his program. Roosevelt supporters, on the other hand, were comforted by Thomas' assurance that this was not so. The following selection is taken from a book by Thomas published during the presidential campaign of 1936.

Source: *After the New Deal, What?*, New York, 1936: "The Future: Socialism?"

SOCIALISM, WE BELIEVE, is the reasonable and the only reasonable way of life and social organization in an age of interdependence and collectivism such as power-driven machinery has imposed. Socialism in this day and generation is the condition of true democracy. It is the fulfillment of the prophet's dream of brotherhood. But although socialism is the reasonable form of organization in a machine age and the desirable fulfillment of the dream of prophets, patriots, and sages, it does not follow that it is inevitable. To establish socialism requires struggle and intelligent struggle. It requires the development of new and nobler loyalties. The socialist society is not for fools or cowards. There is no foreordained assurance that man will have the wisdom to use for the social good the machinery which he had the intelligence to invent.

But half the battle for socialism will be won when men understand two things: First, that there is not room for plenty, peace, or freedom in the present disintegrating social order; and second, that socialism in itself is a thing infinitely desirable. So far we have been concerned primarily to develop the first argument; now we must turn to the second. Socialism is first of all a reasoned conviction that plenty and peace, freedom and fellowship, lie within the grasp of men. It is the assertion that our failure to conquer poverty in the midst of potential abundance is due to an acceptance of a system which is based on relative scarcity and upon the exploitation of the masses by an owning class. Socialism believes that men may be free by making power-driven machinery the slave of mankind. It believes in planned production for the use of all rather than an unplanned production for the profit of an owning class. It asserts that this type of production for use requires social ownership of land, natural resources and the principal means of production and distribution including, of course, the entire system of money, banking, and credit. In the name of social ownership of land and tools it does not propose to house men in public barracks or to take from a worker his favorite hammer, violin or typewriter, or anything else which he uses without exploiting oth ers. Socialism does intend to end absentee landlordism, but it intends to make men more, not less, secure in the occupancy and use of homes in which they live.

Because men will be more secure against the loss of their homes and their jobs there will be more real liberty. The statement that socialism will take from men civil and religious liberty is born either of malice or complete misunderstanding of the subject of socialism.

American Socialism has expressly recognized a man's right to the religion of his choice. Many socialists would go farther and quote approvingly the statement I heard a young socialist make to a woman perturbed that if she accepted socialism she would lose her religion. "Madam," said he, "one does not have to be a Christian to be a socialist, but I cannot understand how you can be a true Christian in these times and not be a socialist."

Social ownership of the great means of production and distribution is necessary for planning. It is the only basis on which we can end the dominion of profit. Even under capitalism social ownership has had an encouraging degree of success. Witness for instance such a list of publicly owned enterprises as schools, roads, parks, the post office, the Panama Canal, city water and sewer systems, power plants, and the like. They are supplemented, too, by the success of consumers' cooperatives carried on for the benefit of the consumers who are members of them and not for the private profit of any group of individuals.

It takes custom derived from a long historic development to explain how anything as utterly absurd as the legal control of private enterprises by absentee stockholders could come into existence. These stockholders know nothing about the conduct of the steel mills, electric power systems, railroads, or banks which legally they own. They are concerned only with the profit they get. Their enterprises would fail disastrously ex-

cept for the hired brains and hands employed by boards of directors to run them, not for the use of all, but for the profit of these same absentee stockholders. There was some rhyme and reason to the old individualistic capitalism where the capitalist assumed definite responsibility.

In this age, when the engineer, the technician, the manager are the key to productive enterprise, there is no reason under the sun why they should not work for society rather than for absentee owners. Logically they could do a much better job because the fact is that the interest of the absentee owners is by no means identical with the interest of the consumers, still less with the interest of the workers. So far is it from being true that the profit system puts the most advanced science and the more advanced inventions automatically to work, that, on the contrary, a great many inventions are kept off the market by the monopolists or semi-monopolists who can control them in order to protect profit. There is no reason to doubt that the engineers who have given us the modern automobile could also have added to the skill of their performance engines which would use less gasoline, but that would not suit powerful financial interests. Progress in railroad travel was held back for years by the belief, probably the mistaken belief, of directors that profits would not be increased by further improvements.

We have already accepted the estimate of experts that it would be possible to provide every American family on the average with an income equivalent to that now enjoyed by those with between $4,000 and $5,000 a year. Or, from a different angle, we have accepted the estimate of those experts who say that we could establish a minimum income for each American worker of between $2,000 and $2,500 a year without notably reducing higher incomes, except the swollen fortunes of the very rich. Economic machinery ought to be operated to make this

Norman Thomas, center rear, joins in singing at the Socialist National Convention in Cleveland, Ohio, 1936, following his nomination as a presidential candidate

great possibility a reality. It is hard to imagine any single thing which would do so much to end physical misery, mental anguish, frustration, yes, crime, as the certainty that every family worth holding together at all, every family where breadwinners are willing to work, would be guaranteed a minimum of $2,500 a year.

Above that level, at least during the transition period and the earlier stages of socialism, it would be well to reward men according to deed. Common sense and the Russian experience unite to convince us that it is better to attract men to difficult jobs, or to jobs for which well-trained workers are scarce, than to try to conscript them. One of the ways to attract men is to remunerate them according to deed. There is no such thing as perfect justice in rewarding them according to deed. Differentials in reward, particularly in the earlier stages of socialist transition, will have something to do with traditional holdovers and with the kind of pressure which different groups can exert. Nevertheless, socialism can rapidly

apply three principles to the incalculable benefit of mankind: (1) no income for any able-bodied adult without work; no long search for work in vain; (2) a minimum standard of decent living for all; (3) above the minimum an approximation to reward according to deed, far more just than that which prevails in our gamblers' world.

It will be almost the first business of a socialist society to get rid of the ugliness as well as the discomfort of the slums and shacks which now disgrace America. Even more surely, it will be the first business of socialism to see that every boy and girl born into the world shall receive food necessary for physical health, training to enable him to do the work for which he is best fitted, a chance when he comes to working age to do that work, and to do it under conditions which give him both security and leisure.

It is logically possible today to house all our people in comfort and beauty; to feed them amply; to help them through a socialized medical service to get well and stay well; to provide them economic security against the vicissitudes of life; and to substitute for the present alternation between long hours of monotonous, ill-rewarded toil and bitter unemployment a shorter working week and enriched leisure.

To establish and maintain all this Socialists do not depend upon an omnipotent and omniscient state. They regard the state as the principal instrument that must be used for the establishment of a new social order. It is the business of workers with hand and brain to gain control of government in order to accomplish this great change. Between the fascist conception of the totalitarian state as an end in itself, and the socialist conception of the state as something to be used to establish the cooperative commonwealth, there is the difference between darkness and light.

A socialist does not believe that the state is the only form of social organization which should be allowed to exist. It has no divine right. Its powers will have to be vigorously asserted and effectively used in a transition period, but as the habit of cooperation and functional self-government grows the coercive state should wither away. It should become a true commonwealth. In this connection it is encouraging that the new Soviet Constitution shows progress toward democracy and civil liberty — a decided contrast with the unchanging emphasis on dictatorship in Germany and other fascist countries. The power of the state will be necessary to effect the transfer from private to public ownership, but it should not supersede or crush consumers' cooperatives. They would admirably supplement it.

A society which is in a way to achieve a socialist revolution with a minimum of disorder and strife could well afford, as part of the price of achieving it, to offer some compensation to expropriated owners. There would be a certain equity in this as between certain classes of owners because probably certain key industries would be taken first. Such key industries as the public utilities are precisely those in which the savings of the little men are invested. For these reasons . . . socialists generally would offer compensation plus taxation, taxation that would amount to expropriation in the higher brackets. Besides income and inheritance taxes a socialist government should use what has been called a capital levy; that is a tax upon wealth in private hands. It could be paid in money, in bonds, which would be retired, thus lessening the burden of debt, or in stocks of those enterprises which the government is ready to socialize anyway. Even under capitalism such a levy is the best way to deal with the crushing burden of debt. It would be less destructive than wholesale inflation or deflation. It is a way, however, that a capitalist society finds it psychologically impossible to take.

Of course an owning class which stubbornly and blindly resists socialism and which resorts to violence against it, cannot expect compensation. On the other hand, if the day ever comes when, as it were, overnight, a smooth-running socialist society should be put into operation it would be better to cut the Gordian knot of vested right and property privilege than to try any kind of compensation. Under such a society, all except the very wealthy would be materially better off than they can ever be under any form of private ownership of the great machinery of production. And even the very wealthy might find new health to their souls!

To carry out a socialist program it is necessary that at least the key industries be taken over under a concerted plan. For example, good as publicly owned electric plants may be, it will be found unsatisfactory to try to carry on a socialized or partially socialized power industry under the capitalist economy. TVA is now doing a remarkably good job. Its success is an encouragement for the future. It is worth while as a yardstick and much more than a yardstick. But the yardstick theory, or any other theory of piecemeal socialization within the confines of capitalism, has its disadvantages in waste and confusion. Socialism is much more than the sum total of certain socialized industries. It involves a general plan impossible on the yardstick theory. It involves also a way of life to which strife between government-owned industry and its privately owned rivals offers more of disadvantage than advantage. There may be a kind of socialist emulation between publicly or cooperatively owned enterprises, but scarcely satisfactory competition between enterprises operating on a different basis and with an appeal to different ideals.

Let us assume, then, that the state has taken over the key industries; that it itself is under the control of workers with hand and brain, well organized on both the industrial and economic fronts; that its activities are supplemented by the activities of consumers cooperatives — under what plan will it control industry? It will put each socialized industry under the administrative direction of a governing authority representing the two permanent interests which always must exist in our economic life. They are the interests of man as consumer and as producer. They are not necessarily in opposition, but they are not identical. A coal miner or a textile worker has a peculiar set of interests in regard to the industry in which he invests his life. He has another set of the interests as a consumer. The interest of the workers as consumers should be dominant.

Men work to live, not live to work. It is essential for managing a world where technological advance is rapid that the primary emphasis should not be on the vested rights of workers in one particular trade, but rather on the vested rights of men to enjoy what well-managed work can create. Sidney and Beatrice Webb assert that part of the success of the Russian planned economy is due to "placing the control in the hands of representatives, not of any organizations of producers, but organizations representing the consumers." That general principle should be followed with consumers' interest dominant in the new setup. Nevertheless the unique interest of the worker in his own industry should be recognized under administration by a board on which there is representation of the general consuming interest and the particular interests of the various categories of workers employed in it. The precise form may vary in different industries. Labor unions will have a function even in a socialist society as an expression and protection of the interests of different groups of producers. They should no longer be organized consciously or subconsciously in terms of the class conflict since society or the mass of workers themselves will be the owners.

Socialized industries, each a law unto itself, cannot plan for work, leisure, security, and abundance for all unless there is over them a general economic planning council to prepare the master plan. This council is the general staff in the war against poverty. It is the expert arm of government, subject to general decisions of Congress or the electorate as to policy, but free from interference in detail. It should be composed of men and women chosen from panels suggested by engineering societies and various industrial and agricultural groups. It must make the most efficient possible use of expert skills in engineering and accounting.

It will be seen that the plan which I have outlined offers as a safeguard against bureaucratic centralization functional self-administration. It may also offer some degree of decentralization through regional machinery of government and of economic planning. That regional machinery cannot conform to present state lines or accept the dogma of states' rights because state lines have no intelligent relation to economic geography. The plan which I have suggested conserves democracy in its truest sense. It permits choices of policy and leadership to be made by those concerned in them. It recognizes that no one organization can express or carry out all a man's interests. It realizes to the full the usefulness of the expert, the engineer, and the technician, and the principle that those engaged in special tasks should have special voice in the way those tasks are carried out.

Agriculture offers somewhat greater difficulties in the earlier stages of socialization than such industries as steel, textiles, coal, or the railroads. That is partly because agriculture is in process of a delayed mechanization. The coming of the mechanical cotton picker will revolutionize hundreds of thousands of lives for better or for worse. The farmer under any kind of social order must reckon not only with new machinery and new methods but also the possibility that for his products there may be substituted the synthetic products of the chemical industry.

Mr. O. F. Wilcox, an authority on intensive agriculture, states in his book, *Reshaping Agriculture*, that it would be comparatively easy to eliminate four out of five farmers and four out of five acres under cultivation, if the best known practices of farming were adopted today. Messrs. Wayne W. Parish and Harold F. Clark, commenting on such statements as this, go on to add: "Virtually all food from wheat and corn to meat have been made in the laboratory." An engineer with more than national reputation told me recently that he doubted if cotton would be commercially grown on any important scale in America twenty years from now because cheaper ways would be found to produce cloth out of cellulose, which will supplant cotton more effectively than rayon has supplanted silk. (Incidentally, when I quoted this opinion to another high authority in the field of chemical industry he expressed great doubt of it.)

At even the most moderate estimate the contrast between what is and what might be is startling. Consider, for instance, Dr. Wilcox's statement that four-fifths of the farmers may become superfluous in contrast to the fact that under present agricultural practices we need the product of forty-one million acres more than are now in cultivation. The inevitable displacement of farm workers means that they must be absorbed in industry. There is a limit to man's need or desire for food much more rigid than the limit to his desire for other material things. It follows that socialism which will plan for a whole economy is in a far better position to handle the difficult situation than capitalism which can do nothing but subsidize scarcity in order to protect the farmers.

Socialist plans in America most assuredly do not call for the forcible elimination of a man who farms his own land. Rather he would be protected against the vicissitudes which have brought it to pass that in the fertile central valleys of California something like 35 percent of the land, I was recently told, is corporation farmed. One practical method of protection is to be found in crop insurance. A socialist government would socialize the machinery of marketing both what the farmer buys and what he sells. By taxation and otherwise it would abolish absentee landlordism. It would substitute collectives for great privately owned plantations, and train the workers in the democratic management of those collectives or cooperatives. It would enlist the farmers themselves in planning for the conservation and best use of soil. It would guide excess farm workers from the fields into other occupations. There is no inexorable limitation to employment if we set out to meet human needs rather than to preserve private profits. We can then control the rate of introduction of machinery or new technological processes according to our ability to increase production and shorten working hours.

82.

H. L. MENCKEN: American English

In the first three editions of The American Language *Mencken had argued that the American form of English was departing from its parent stem and that the differences between the two versions of the language would continue to increase. In the fourth edition, published in 1936, his thesis had changed. Since 1923, he stated in the Preface, "The pull of American has become so powerful that it has begun to drag English with it, and in consequence some of the differences once visible have tended to disappear." English writers, he declared, attributed the change to the ubiquitous American movie, but Mencken himself ascribed it — at least in part — to the fact that following World War I Americans demonstrated "an increasing inclination to throw off their old subservience to English precept and example." The following selection from the fourth edition deals with "The Hallmarks of American."*

Source: *The American Language,* 4th edition, New York, 1936, pp. 90-97.

THE CHARACTERS CHIEFLY NOTED in American English by all who have discussed it are, first, its general uniformity throughout the country; second, its impatient disregard for grammatical, syntactical, and phonological rule and precedent; and third, its large capacity (distinctly greater than that of the English of present-day England) for taking in new words and phrases from outside sources, and for manufacturing them of its own materials.

The first of these characters has struck every observer, native and foreign. In place of the discordant local dialects of all the other major countries, including England, we have a general *Volkssprache* for the whole nation, and if it is conditioned at all it is only by minor differences in pronunciation and vocabulary, and by the linguistic struggles of various groups of newcomers. No other country can show such linguistic solidarity, nor any approach to it — not even Canada, for there a large minority of the population resists speaking English altogether.

The Little Russian of the Ukraine is unintelligible to the citizen of Moscow; the Northern Italian can scarcely follow a conversation in Sicilian; the Low German from Hamburg is a foreigner in Munich; the Breton flounders in Gascony. Even in the United Kingdom there are wide divergences. "When we remember," says the *New International Encyclopedia,* "that the dialects of the counties in England have marked differences — so marked, indeed, that it may be doubted whether a Lancashire miner and a Lincolnshire farmer could understand each other — we may well be proud that our vast country has, strictly speaking, only one language."

There are some regional peculiarities in pronunciation and intonation . . . but when it comes to the words they habitually use and the way they use them all Americans, even the less tutored, follow pretty much the same line. A Boston taxi driver could go to work in Chicago or San Francisco without running any risk of misunderstanding his new fares. Once he had flattened his *a*'s a bit and picked up a few dozen localisms, he would be, to all linguistic intents and purposes, fully naturalized.

Of the intrinsic differences that separate American from English the chief have their roots in the obvious disparity between the environment and traditions of the American people since the Seventeenth Century and those of the English. The latter have lived under a relatively stable social order, and it has impressed upon their souls their characteristic respect for what is customary and of good report. Until the World War brought chaos to most of their institutions, their whole lives were regulated, perhaps more than those of any other people save the Spaniards, by a regard for precedent.

The Americans, though partly of the same blood, have felt no such restraint, and acquired no such habit of conformity. On the contrary, they have plunged to the other extreme, for the conditions of life in their country have put a high value upon the precisely opposite qualities of curiosity and daring, and so they have acquired that character of restlessness, that impatience of norms, that disdain of the dead hand, which now broadly marks them. From the first, says a literary historian, they have been "less phlegmatic, less conservative than the English. There were climatic influences, it may be; there was surely a spirit of intensity everywhere that made for short effort." Thus, in the arts, and thus in business, in politics, in daily intercourse, in habits of mind and speech.

The American is not, of course, lacking in a capacity for discipline; he has it highly developed; he submits to leadership readily, and even to tyranny. But, by a curious twist, it is not the leadership that is old and decorous that commonly fetches him, but the leadership that is new and extravagant. He will resist dictation out of the past, but he will follow a new messiah with almost Russian willingness, and into the wildest vagaries of economics, religion, morals, and speech. A new fallacy in politics spreads faster in the United States than anywhere else on earth, and so does a new fashion in hats, or a new revelation of God, or a new means of killing time, or a new shibboleth, or metaphor, or piece of slang. Thus the American, on his linguistic side, likes to make his language as he goes along, and not all the hard work of the schoolmarm can hold the business back.

A novelty loses nothing by the fact that it is a novelty; it rather gains something, and particularly if it meets the national fancy for the terse, the vivid, and, above all, the bold and imaginative. The characteristic American habit of reducing complex concepts to the starkest abbreviations was already noticeable in colonial times, and such highly typical Americanisms as *O.K., N.G.*, and *P.D.Q.*, have been traced back to the early days of the Republic. Nor are the influences that shaped these tendencies invisible today, for institution-making is yet going on, and so is language-making. In so modest an operation as that which has evolved *bunco* from *buncombe* and *bunk* from *bunco* there is evidence of a phenomenon which the philologian recognizes as belonging to the most lusty stages of speech.

But of more importance than the sheer inventions, if only because much more numerous, are the extensions of the vocabulary, both absolutely and in ready workableness, by the devices of rhetoric. The American, from the beginning, has been the most ardent of recorded rhetoricians. His politics bristles with pungent epithets; his whole history has been bedizened with tall talk; his fundamental institutions rest far more upon brilliant phrases than upon logical ideas. And in small things as in large he exercises continually an incomparable capacity for projecting hidden and often fantastic relationships into arresting parts of speech.

Such a term as *rubberneck* is almost a complete treatise on American psychology; it reveals the national habit of mind more clearly then any labored inquiry could ever reveal it. It has in it precisely the boldness and contempt for ordered forms that are so characteristically American, and it has too the grotesque humor of the country, and the delight in devastating opprobriums, and the acute feeling for the succinct and savory. The same qualities are in *rough-house, water-wagon, has-been, lame-duck, speed-cop*, and a thousand other such racy substantives, and in all the great stock of native verbs and adjectives. There is indeed, but a shadowy boundary in these new coinages between the various parts of speech.

Corral, borrowed from the Spanish, immediately becomes a verb and the father of an adjective. *Bust*, carved out of *burst*, erects itself into a noun. *Bum*, coming by way of an earlier *bummer* from the German, becomes noun, adjective, verb, and adverb. Verbs are fashioned out of substantives by the simple process of prefixing the preposition: *to engineer, to stump, to hog, to style, to author*. Others grow out of an intermediate adjective, as *to boom*. Others are made by torturing nouns with harsh affixes, as *to burglarize* and *to itemize*, or by groping for the root, as *to resurrect* and *to jell*. Yet others are changed from intransitive to transitive; a sleeping-car *sleeps* thirty passengers. So with the adjectives. They are made of substantives unchanged: *codfish, jitney*. Or by bold combinations: *down-and-out, up-state, flat-footed*. Or by shading down suffixes to a barbaric simplicity: *scary, classy, tasty*. Or by working over adverbs until they tremble on the brink between adverb and adjective: *right, sure*, and *near* are examples.

All these processes, of course, are also to be observed in the history of the English of England; at the time of its sturdiest growth they were in the most active possible being. They are, indeed, common to all tongues. "the essence of language," says Dr. Jespersen, "is activity." But if you will put the English of today beside the American of today you will see at once how much more forcibly they are in operation in the latter than in the former. The standard Southern dialect of English has been arrested in it growth by its purists and grammarians, and burdened with irrational affectations by fashionable pretension. It shows no living change since the reign of Samuel Johnson. Its tendency is to combat all that expansive gusto which made for its pliancy and resilience in the days of Shakespeare.

In place of the old loose-footedness there is set up a preciosity which, in one direction, takes the form of clumsy artificialitie in the spoken language, and in another shows itself in the even clumsier Johnsonese of so much current English writing — the Jargon denounced by Sir Arthur Quiller Couch in his Cambridge lectures. This "infirmity of speech" Quiller-Couch finds "in parliamentary debates and in the newspapers; . . . it has become the medium through which Boards of Government County Councils, Syndicates, Committees Commercial Firms, express the processes as well as the conclusions of their thought, and so voice the reason of their being." Distinct from journalese, the two yet overlap, "and have a knack of assimilating each other' vices."

American, despite the gallant efforts of the pedagogues, has so far escaped any such suffocating formalization. We, too, of course, have our occasional practitioners of the authentic English Jargon, but in the main our faults lie in precisely the opposite direction. That is to say, we incline toward a directness of statement which, at its greatest, lacks restraint and urbanity altogether, and toward a hospitality which often admits novelties for the mere sake of their novelty, and is quite uncritical of the difference between a genuine improvement in succinctness and clarity, and mere extravagant raciness.

"The tendency," says one English observer, "is . . . to consider the speech of any man, as any man himself, as good as any other." The Americans, adds a Scots professor, "are determined to hack their way through the language, as their ancestors through forests, regardless of the valuable growths that may be sacrificed in blazing the trail." But this Scot dismisses the English neologisms of the day, when ranged beside the American stock, as "dwiny, feeble stuff"; "it is to America," he admits, "that we must chiefly look in future for the replenishment and freshening of our language." I quote one more Briton, this time an Englishman steeped in the public school tradition:

> The English of the United States is not merely different from ours; it has a restless inventiveness which may well be founded in a sense of racial discomfort, a lack of full accord between the temperament of the people and the constitution of their speech. The English are uncommunicative; the Americans are not. In its coolness and quiet withdrawal, in its prevailing sobriety, our language reflects the cautious economies and leisurely assurance of the average speaker. We say so little that we do not need to enliven our vocabulary and underline our sentences, or cry "Wolf!" when we wish to be heard. The more stimulating climate of the United States has produced a more eager, a more expansive, a more decisive people. The Americans apprehend their world in sharper outlines and aspire after a more salient rendering of it.

This revolt against conventional bonds and restraints is most noticeable, of course, on the lower levels of American speech; in the regions above there still linger some vestiges of Eighteenth Century tightness. But even in those upper regions there are rebels a-plenty, and some of them are of such authority that it is impossible to dismiss them. I glance through the speeches of the late Dr. Woodrow Wilson, surely a conscientious purist and Anglomaniac if we have ever had one, and find, in a few moments, half a dozen locutions that an Englishman in like position would certainly hesitate to use, among them *we must get a move on, to hog, to gum-shoe, onery* in place of *ordinary,* and *that is going some.* I turn to the letters of that most passionate of Anglomaniacs, Walter Hines Page, and find *to eat out of my hand, to lick to a frazzle, to cut no figure, to go gunning for, nothin' doin', for keeps,* and so on. I proceed to Dr. John Dewey, probably the country's most respectable metaphysician, and find him using *dope* for *opium.* In recent years certain English magnificoes have shown signs of going the same route, but whenever they yield the corrective bastinado is laid on, and nine times out of ten they are accused, and rightly, of succumbing to American influence.

Let American confront a novel problem alongside English, and immediately its superior imaginativeness and resourcefulness become obvious. *Movie* is better than *cinema;* and the English begin to admit the fact by adopting the word; it is not only better American, it is better English. *Bill-board* is better than *boarding. Office-holder* is more honest, more picturesque, more thoroughly Anglo-Saxon than *public-servant. Stem-winder* somehow has more life in it, more fancy and vividness, than the literal *keyless-watch.* Turn to the terminology of *railroading* (itself, by the way, an Americanism): its creation fell upon the two peoples equally, but they tackled the job independently. The English, seeking a figure to denominate the wedge-shaped fender in front of a locomotive, called it a *plough;* the Americans, characteristically, gave it the far more pungent name of *cow-catcher.* So with the casting which guides the wheels from one rail to another. The English called it a *crossing-plate;* the Americans, more responsive to the suggestion in its shape, called it a *frog.*

American is full of what Bret Harte called the "saber-cuts of Saxon"; it meets Montaigne's ideal of "a succulent and nervous speech, short and compact, not as much delicated and combed out as vehement and brusque, rather arbitrary than monotonous, not pedantic but soldierly, as Suetonius called Caesar's Latin." One pictures the common materials of English dumped into a pot, exotic flavorings added, and the bubblings assiduously and expectantly skimmed. What is old and respected is already in decay the moment it comes into contact with what is new and vivid. "When we Americans are through with the English language," says Mr. Dooley, "it will look as if it had been run over by a musical comedy."

All this boldness of conceit, of course, makes for vulgarity. Unrestrained by any critical sense — and the critical sense of the pedagogues counts for little, for they cry wolf too often — it flowers in such barbaric inventions as *tasty, alright, go-getter, he-man, go-aheadativeness, tony, goof, semi-occasional,* and *to doxologize.* But vulgarity, after all, means no more than a yielding to natural impulses in the face of conventional inhibitions, and that yielding to natural impulses is at the heart of all healthy language-making.

The history of English, like the history of American and of every other living tongue, is a history of vulgarisms that, by their accurate meeting of real needs, have forced their way into sound usage, and even into the lifeless catalogues of the grammarians. The purist performs a useful office in enforcing a certain logical regularity upon the process, and in our own case the omnipresent example of the greater conservatism of the English restrains, to some extent, our native tendency to go too fast, but the process itself is as inexorable in its workings as the precession of the equinoxes, and if we yield to it more eagerly than the English, it is only a proof, perhaps, that the future of what was once the Anglo-Saxon tongue lies on this side of the water.

Standard English now has the brakes on, but American continues to leap in the dark, and the prodigality of its movement is all the indication that is needed of its intrinsic health, its capacity to meet the ever-changing needs of a restless and emotional people, inordinately mongrel, and disdainful of tradition. Language, says A. H. Sayce,

is no artificial product, contained in books and dictionaries and governed by the strict rules of impersonal grammarians. It is the living expression of the mind and spirit of a people, ever changing and shifting, whose sole standard of correctness is custom and the common usage of the community. . . . The first lesson to be learned is that there is no intrinsic right or wrong in the use of language, no fixed rules such as are the delight of the teacher of Latin prose. What is right now will be wrong hereafter; what language rejected yesterday she accepts today.

———————◆———————

Anyone who goes to a psychiatrist ought to have his head examined.

I'll give you a definite maybe.

Include me out.

In two words: im-possible.

SAM GOLDWYN, attributed

83.

Huddie Ledbetter and John Lomax: "Goodnight Irene"

For six years beginning in 1935 the Federal Arts Project provided American artists and intellectuals with funds with which to create music, art, and literature and to uncover and record hidden stores of culture throughout the land. As a result of the project, American folk songs and folk singers, among them Huddie Ledbetter, attained national fame. Ledbetter (called Leadbelly and otherwise honored as the "King of the Twelve-String Guitar") was discovered in the South by John and Alan Lomax, then on a folk-song-collecting tour. Leadbelly's theme song, which he wrote with John Lomax, became "Goodnight Irene." It was published in 1936, and the folk-singing group called the Weavers made this and other Leadbelly songs national hits in the 1950s, after Leadbelly's death.

GOODNIGHT IRENE

Irene, good night;
Irene, good night;

Good night, Irene, good night, Irene,
I'll see you in my dreams.

Last Saturday night I got married,
Me and my wife settled down,
Now me and my wife are parted,
I'm gonna take another stroll downtown.

Irene, good night; etc.

Sometimes I live in the country,
Sometimes I live in town,
Sometimes I take a great notion
To jump into the river and drown.

Irene, good night; etc.

She caused me to weep, she caused me to
mourn,
Caused me to leave my home,
But the very last words I heard her say
Was, "Please sing me one more song."

Irene, good night; etc.

Stop ramblin', stop your gamblin',
Stop stayin' out late at night;
Go home to your wife and your family;
Stay there by your fireside bright.

Irene, good night; etc.

84.

OTIS FERGUSON: Listening to Benny Goodman

In the fall of 1936 four of the world's most renowned jazzmen — Benny Goodman, Gene Krupa, Teddy Wilson, and Lionel Hampton — played together at the Cafe Rouge in New York City's Pennsylvania Hotel. Their performance inspired the following praise from Otis Ferguson, an editor of the New Republic. *Between 1933 and 1938 the craze for "hot jazz" welled to a climax. Although most of the thousands that would assemble before dawn on cold winter mornings to hear Benny Goodman's afternoon concerts were youngsters, jazz was acclaimed as good music by connoisseurs, and the love for jazz was accompanied by an unparalleled interest in classical music as well.*

Source: *New Republic,* December 30, 1936: "The Spirit of Jazz."

BENNY GOODMAN WAS BORN in what he now refers back to as the Chicago ghetto twenty-seven years ago, and about twelve years later showed up in knee pants on one of the river boats to play in a small jazz band with Bix Beiderbecke, dead now and immortal (Go away boy, Bix is reported to have said, Don't mess around with the instruments). But Benny Goodman had with him a clarinet of his own, which at that time must have been as long as he was, and he had a superior sense of music; he played with the band all right. He played around all the time in those first days, studying under good men, mastering his difficult instrument, and going to high school a little, and after that forming a band with a few boys from some sort of conservatory he attended — historic names now, Bud Freeman, Dave Tuft, Muggsy Spanier. And at the age of sixteen he went to the West Coast to join the Ben Pollack orchestra, which is as historic as the deuce. He stayed with the organization about four years, playing it out every night, working alongside such men as that force on the trombone, Mr. Jack (Big-

Gate) Teagarden, learning. When he left Pollack he worked here and there in New York, in pit and stage and radio bands, recording and later getting up a band of his own.

But that is all an interim period for most of us. The general public must have heard his music at one time or another, but there was no ballyhoo to announce where it was coming from. Then less than two years ago he started going to town for the general public, and reports came back from the Palomar in Los Angeles that you could not get within fifty yards of the stand, and afterwards you could hear over the Congress Hotel's wire in Chicago that this might have been a sedate enough ballroom before, but now Benny was in and blowing the roof off, and they were yelling from the floor.

And this winter he is to be seen in the main room at the Pennsylvania Hotel. The room, as you come in, is spacious and warm with the air of moderately well-to-do living, people and tables filling the space around the floor and around the raised walk on all four sides, waiters and captains bustling in a quiet efficiency of silver and steam and flourish. But the far side of the room is the main side, where the boys sit high and easy in their chairs and Benny Goodman stands in front, quiet or smiling into the spotlight or tilting his instrument to the rafters as they rise to the take-off. Sooner or later they will lead into one of those Fletcher Henderson arrangements of an old favorite, and the whole riding motion of the orchestra will be felt even through the thick carpets and the babble of the crowd, and those with two feet under them will move out onto the floor, because the music can be heard best when it is fulfilling its original simple purpose, coming through the ears and the good living wood underneath. As they get along into the later choruses the boys will let out a little of that flash and rhythmic power which make these separate defined instruments into something indefinable, a thumping big band with the whole room under its thumb ("Got the world in a jug"); the floor will become solid with people, even some of the bare backs and stiff shirts will jolly up noticeably and perhaps do the truck a little (dear, dear).

And then, even with the final blast of the out-chorus still echoing in the hall, everything is suddenly natural and work-a-day. The men put up their instruments, stretch, look about them, file off at random; Benny stands leafing through his music to give out the numbers for the next set, recognizing as many people as is expedient, later going off to sit at a table somewhere: How's everything, that's fine. Himself, he's on the wagon tonight; he drinks with glum heroism at a glass of plain water. "A scotch here and a soda there and where the hell are you in the morning? You know?" So now he feels better in the morning. He has a heavy voice coming from well down under the ribs and pleasant with the forthright, lively concision of popular speech.

Someone comes up, moving with vast

importance, and desires that Benny should intervene with the Selmer people. They make clarinets and it seems they've got some conspiracy of imprecise mouthpieces as against the gentleman in question: if she plays good high, then she don't play good low; likewise vice versa. Benny says come around after, he'll see; then presently out of the side of his mouth: Never *was* one of the things that would play right by itself, you have to nurse it. You know a clarinet? What's he think I can do about a damn clarinet, drive me crazy. Benny Goodman looks sadly at the scotch on the table and drinks his water.

By now a slight and quiet young man has detached himself from the gossip and joshing of the musicians hanging around in the back and drifted over to the piano — on which he has only time left to run through two numbers, if that. In a place like this, where there are too many dine-and-dancers too sure that a young man sitting at an upright piano can't be anything to hush your mouth about, Teddy Wilson is as fine an artist at starting late and quitting early as he is at his music, which is the finest. He runs through a few chords. Anyone who wants to hear it a little can move over to the piano. Some do. Just playing to amuse myself is all, Teddy says.

Well how about that Waller tune "Squeeze Me," Teddy; you used to play that pretty nice. Oh that? he says with his fine smile. I believe I forgot that one by now. He feels through the chords with unerring musical sense and listens for the turn of phrase in some backward corner of his mind — like the mind of any good jazz musician, it is a treasury and stuffed catalogue of all the songs the rest of us have thought lovely and then presently put aside for new toys. He finishes, repeats the last phrase. Hm, I *knew* I didn't have that one rightly anymore, he says, shaking his head. But the song is back for us, the song never died at all. He starts the first chords over and this time his right hand is released from concentration and free on the keyboard, and to get the pattern in music of those clear single notes without hearing the phrase as it is struck off, you would have to make some such visual image as that of a common tin plate scaled up into the sun, where there would be not only the flash and motion but the startling effect of flight, the rise and banking in curves, the hesitation and slipping off, and the plunge straight down coming suddenly. Wilson in his best mood of creation is something like that.

These nights he shows to better advantage when he comes out with the quartet. There, with something to work for, he really works and is fine in many ways. Remember that he is a Negro in a white man's world, a jazz player in a world where the thirst for music is so artificial it cannot attend with comfort anything not solemnized. And then see the quiet repose and lack of cocksureness, strut or show, the straightforward and friendly absence of assumption that comes only from a secure awareness of the dignity of a person and of his work. But even if this were the place for oversolemn pronouncements, there isn't the time. The stand is filling up again, the boys sucking on reeds, limbering up valves — doing whatever it is that musicians do with a sort of happy-go-lucky boredom. There is no more than time to say, as the first pop tune starts to go up in smoke, that memory may fade and the current musical note perish, but that fifty years around the recorded music of Mr. Teddy Wilson (now craftily surprised that the band came back so soon) should have established him where he belongs — not only great in jazz but among the best lyricists of any time or form.

Swing in, swing out, the band is up again and drawing the people out like the sun in the fable. With Krupa, Reuss (guitar) and the inspired quiet Stacey (piano) laying down a thick rhythmic base, it plays on through whatever songs are the demand of the day, making most of them sound like something. This is an organization in the line of the great jazz bands — Jean Goldkette, Fletcher Henderson, McKinney's Cotton Pickers, Ellington, Kirk et al. — a little lighter than some of these but more beautifully rehearsed and economical, and with cleaner edges. The reed section, scored as such, is more prominent than in older hot bands, giving a fuller lyric quality; but the section (five men counting Goodman) has a hard skeleton of attack and swing that supports any relative lightness of brass. The band as a whole gets its life from the rhythm men and the soloists as they take off; it is built from the ground rather than tailored — thanks to the talent, ideas, and leadership of one man.

The recent spreading of interest in good jazz to some extent made Benny Goodman's current music possible, and to some extent was made possible by Benny Goodman's music. He got good men working together, got some ace arrangements of all the good tunes, new and old, and played them wide open though bands weren't supposed to be successful that way. It wasn't so much that he made the people like it as that he gave them a chance to see what it was like when done well (too many hot bands have sounded like a barnyard until they got going around 2 A.M.). And one of the important things about his show is that he went right ahead with the same method of getting good music when it came to the old color-line bogey. He would introduce Teddy Wilson as playing with the trio, and the people would bang hands for more (they say on some nights he even had to send the rest of the band home). So hotel managers would get the point almost painlessly: and could no longer say No beforehand, on the ground that people would not stand for it. And when the trio got Lionel Hampton to play the vibraphone, the balance between black and white was even (two of each), and still no kick. Stand for it? — the people stand up from their tables just to hear it better.

They play every night — clarinet, piano, vibraphone, drums, and they make music you would not believe. No arrangements, not a false note, one finishing his solo and dropping into background support, then the other, all adding inspiration until with some number like "Stomping at the Savoy" they get going too strong to quit — four choruses, someone starts up another, six, eight, and still someone starts — no two notes the same and no one note off the chord, the more they relax in the excitement of it the more a natural genius in preselection becomes evident and the more indeed the melodic line becomes rigorously pure. This is really composition on the spot, with the spirit of jazz strongly over all of them but the iron laws of harmony and rhythm never lost sight of; and it is a collective thing, the most beautiful example of men working together to be seen in public today.

It isn't merely hell-for-leather either. Gene Krupa, a handsome madman over his drums, makes the rhythmic force and impetus of it visual, for his face and whole body are sensitive to each strong beat of the ensemble; and Hampton does somewhat the same for the line of melody, hanging solicitous over the vibraphone plates and exhorting them (Hmmm, Oh, Oh yah, Oh dear *hmmm*). But the depth of tone and feeling is mainly invisible, for they might play their number "Exactly Like You" enough to make people cry and there would be nothing of it seen except perhaps in the lines of feeling on Benny Goodman's face, the affable smile dropped as he follows the Wilson solo flight, eyes half-closed behind his glasses.

There was a special feeling among them the first morning they recorded this piece, the ghost of the blues perhaps; and when the clarinet takes up you will hear the phrases fall as clear as rain, with a sustained glow of personal essence that starts where command of the instrument (the tension of mouth, delicate fingering, etc.) leaves off. Then Hampton sings a chorus, his vibrant hoarse voice and relaxed emphasis so appropriate to the general color; and when they take up again the instruments blend so perfectly as to be indistinguishable, singing in unison with a sweet breadth of tone that goes beyond the present place and time to some obscure source of feeling and native belief. The term "swing" — no more definable in words than the term poetry — is defined at its best in this piece, where the actual beats are lost sight of in the main effect, so that the inexorable and brute lift of the time signature as carried in Krupa's great drum seems fused in the harmony and melodic line of the song. And you may say of the excitement this thing starts in the blood only that these four men are quite simple and wonderful together, that they are truly swinging.

The quartet is a beautiful thing all through, really a labor of creative love, but it cannot last forever and as the band starts again you realize that even in jazz there are several kinds of musical appreciation. For if they'll agree to put on the "Bugle Call Rag" before the end of the evening, I'll be willing to say there's nothing finer. There is some hidden lift to this old band standby, with its twenty quaint notes from the "Assembly" call dropping the barrier to a straight-out progression of simple chords — and they are off, riding it with collective assurance and fine spirit, the men in their sections, the sections balancing, the soloists dropping back with care for the total effect.

The guests are presently banked in a half-moon around the stand, unable to be still through it or move away either; and as it builds to the final solid chords, Krupa becoming a man of subtle thunder and Benny lacing in phrases, the air is full of brass and of rhythms you can almost lean on. The music seems more than audible, rising and coming forward from the stand in banks of colors and shifting masses — not only the clangor in the ears but a visual picture of the intricate fitted spans, the breathless height and spring of a steel-bridge structure.

And if you leave at the end, before the "Good-Bye" signature, you will seem to hear this great rattling march of the hobos through the taxis, lights, and people, ringing under the low sky over Manhattan as if it were a strange high thing after all (which it is) and as if it came from the American ground under these buildings, roads and motor cars (which it did). And if you leave the band and quartet and piano of the Goodman show and still are no more than slightly amused, you may be sure that in the smug absence of your attention a native true spirit of music has been and gone, leaving a message for your grandchildren to study through their patient glasses.

85.

Robert Robins: Television

Television seemed to many people to be on the verge of its great "takeoff" in 1936 (in fact, the event was delayed for fifteen years owing to the war). Important figures in the motion picture industry recognized the threat of the new medium, as is manifested by the following testimony of Robert Robins, executive secretary of the Society for the Protection of the Motion Picture Theater, before the Federal Communications Commission on June 25, 1936. At that time the motion picture industry represented an investment of $2 billion with annual expenditures for domestic and foreign advertising of $100 million and an equal amount paid in federal taxes. Robins' fear that television would destroy the movies appeared, for a decade after 1950, to be well founded, but the two mass media found a modus vivendi in the 1960s and discovered that they could both survive and prosper.

Source: VSD, July 15, 1936.

As an individual associated with the sound motion-picture industry, I wish to express my appreciation of this opportunity to bring to the attention of the Commission certain aspects of the new industry which are vitally important to both the development of television and the prevention of chaos in existing entertainment and communication fields.

Expert technical opinion holds that television services are ready for commercial exploitation. The introduction thereof threatens the capital structure of the moving-picture industry as well as its very existence. . . .

The talking motion picture is one of the major cultural factors of American life. Upward of *80 million* people go to the movies *every* week. Their habits of thought, their tastes, their standards of living are consciously and subconsciously affected by what they hear but overwhelmingly determined by what they *see*.

The economic effects of the talking motion picture have been most pronounced in the stimulation of new standards of living and have given rise to the stimulation of new industries. Overnight, the currents of style are diverted by the effect of talking motion pictures into new channels, increasing production and changing the course of industry. "Garbo-ized" hair and "Gableized" jackets alter the appearance of the nation. Talking motion pictures are universally accepted as one of the greatest social inventions of mankind.

The introduction of combined visual and aural programs into the home places the entire investment represented by the exhibition phase of the talking motion-picture industry in a very precarious position. As so eloquently expressed in the editorial of the *New York Times*, published on June 14, 1936, the eve of the present hearings, the problems facing the motion-picture industry are only now receiving adequate recognition. I quote:

> Industry has a way of ignoring the shadows cast by coming events. The railroads could not believe that the automobile and the motor trucks would deprive them of both passenger and freight; the phonograph companies dismissed radio broadcasting as of no consequence. . . . Now television looms in the offing. What will be its effect on broadcasting and on the talking motion picture?

The problem has thus been posed.

Who but those with substantial investments in the motion-picture industry can claim a greater moral and economic priority to assume the development of television? We of the motion-picture industry seek not to retard the new art but rather to promote and supplement existing arts and thereby foster the growth of new industry.

Before determining the technical details, whether relating to radio or wire channels, it is essential that the Commission take cognizance of the economic and cultural problems involved.

We propose that the most practical method of promoting this new art and consequently creating a new industry is as follows:

First, television service in its early stages must be confined to *entertainment* and *educational* purposes, such as the regular motion-picture-feature production, shorts, and newsreels, and that television must be kept *free* from advertising sponsorship.

Second, television programs must be a separate and distinct service and must be offered to the recipients on a service charge basis.

Third, rates, rules, and regulation must be determined by a competent public body.

The possible objections to this program latent in the statements made by leaders of the broadcasting industry during the progress of this hearing may best be measured by the yardstick of their own apparent success. What is that yardstick? The radio industry, according to its spokesman, represents an investment of over $1 billion. What has been the profit on this investment as judged by the fundamental doctrine of our American economic system? What earnings has this great enterprise yielded for the investment?

Out of 632 commercial broadcasting stations, how many are or have been operating at a profit? Of the 52 representative manufacturers of receiving equipment, how many have consistently paid a dividend during the course of their existence? How many of the 11 vacuum-tube manufacturers fared similarly?

The public interest, of course, also includes a fair return on capital investment.

The only true success — the scientific achievements and benefits of the art — are the result of inevitable progress, not the bounty of the business jungle. Where the rule of reason prevails, profits are very conspicuous by their presence. The two adjuncts of the broadcasting industry which have shown a consistent profit during its rise and growth are those furnishing electrical energy to activate sets and transmitters, and the telephone networks. Neither of these operates according to the rules of the jungle. . . .

Our proposed plan in no way endangers investments in the radio industry or threatens any of its social benefits. On the contrary, the plan maintains that aural broadcasting be retained as a separate and distinct service, in that portion of the spectrum best suited to its purposes; at least until such time when changes do become necessary, that a well-ordered economy guide the transition. The essential features of our plan in no way injure or render precarious the status and scope of operations of the newspaper industry or the printed word.

Past experience in the motion-picture industry demonstrates that it is uneconomic to combine advertising with a visual program. Audiences find this even *more objectionable* than an audible advertising announcement in connection with radio broadcasting.

Moreover, it is doubtful whether an advertiser, in order to obtain the real value of his advertising — because the beneficial effects of advertising are obtained by constant repetition — could afford the enormous expense entailed by providing programs acceptable for the eye. Costumes, rehearsals, talent, technicians, directors — all of the costs necessary to create one hour's entertainment as evidenced by the cost of an average motion-picture production — are estimated to run from $350,000 upward to $1

million. Without programs of this type there is no "looking-in" circulation. With no audience, there can be no service.

An eminently qualified authority on this subject, Dr. Alfred M. Goldsmith, former president of the Institute of Radio Engineers, as well as a former president of the Society of Motion Picture Engineers, stated in a press interview, I quote:

> Obstacles in the way of commercial exploitation of television are enormous. Present radio broadcasting stations are built for "blind listeners" and are not adaptable to television. Television demands, in effect, talking movie studios and all their appurtenances — stage equipment, cameramen, technicians, wardrobe sets, and properties.
>
> Like radio, television programs must be broadcast on a syndicated basis. Time schedules must be filled. News events and happenings could fill only a small part of the time schedule. If $350,000 is taken as the average production cost of a Hollywood movie lasting seventy minutes, the indicated cost of putting it on a television network would be $5,000 a minute. Hollywood's annual output of from 300 to 500 feature films would last one month in television. Could the program sponsors ever afford this?

My plan, from the labor point of view, will permit the continuance of the high wage standards and recognition of the rights of labor by the motion-picture industry, the highest known, second to none, and will create no problems of technological unemployment, but rather will increase the demand for labor's services.

This age of power also is the age of steel. Age of rust would be a better designation. If it were not for our paints and protective coatings nothing would be left of this machine civilization a hundred years hence.

WALDEMAR KAEMPFFERT

86.

Franklin D. Roosevelt: What the New Deal Has Done for Business

By 1936 the general attitude of American business toward the New Deal ranged from violent criticism to pathological hatred. Every aspect of New Deal legislation was attacked, but the main thrust focused on alleged over-regulation of the economy. Especially popular among businessmen was the accusation that Roosevelt was trying to sovietize America and destroy free enterprise. During the 1936 campaign the President answered these attacks with verve, as in the Chicago speech of October 14, reprinted below.

Source: FDR, V, pp. 480-489.

SEEM TO HAVE BEEN HERE BEFORE. Four years ago I dropped into this city from the airways — an old friend come in a new way — to accept in this hall the nomination for the presidency of the United States. I came to a Chicago fighting with its back to the wall — factories closed, markets silent, banks shaky, ships and trains empty. Today those factories sing the song of industry; markets hum with bustling movement; banks are secure; ships and trains are running full. Once again it is Chicago as Carl Sandburg saw it — "The city of the big shoulders" — the city that smiles. And with Chicago a whole nation that had not been cheerful for years is full of cheer once more.

On this trip through the nation I have talked to farmers, I have talked to miners, I have talked to industrial workers; and in all that I have seen and heard, one fact has been clear as crystal — that they are part and parcel of a rounded whole, and that none of them can succeed in his chosen occupation if those in the other occupations fail in their prosperity. I have driven home that point.

Tonight, in this center of business, I give the same message to the businessmen of America — to those who make and sell the processed goods the nation uses and to the men and women who work for them.

To them I say: Do you have a deposit in the bank? It is safer today than it has ever been in our history. It is guaranteed. Last October 1 marked the end of the first full year in fifty-five years without a single failure of a national bank in the United States. Is that not on the credit side of the government's account with you?

Are you an investor? Your stocks and bonds are up to five- and six-year high levels.

Are you a merchant? Your markets have the precious lifeblood of purchasing power. Your customers on the farms have better incomes and smaller debts. Your customers in the cities have more jobs, surer jobs, better jobs. Did not your government have something to do with that?

Are you in industry? Industrial earnings, industrial profits are the highest in four, six, or even seven years! Bankruptcies are at a new low. Your government takes some credit for that.

Are you in railroads? Freight loadings are

steadily going up. Passenger receipts are steadily going up — have in some cases doubled — because your government made the railroads cut rates and make money.

Are you a middleman in the great stream of farm products? The meat and grain that move through your yards and elevators have a steadier supply, a steadier demand, and steadier prices than you have known for years. And your government is trying to keep it that way.

Some people say that all this recovery has just happened. But in a complicated modern world recoveries from depressions do not just happen. The years from 1929 to 1933, when we waited for recovery just to happen, prove the point.

But in 1933 we did not wait. We acted. Behind the growing recovery of today is a story of deliberate government acceptance of responsibility to save business, to save the American system of private enterprise and economic democracy — a record unequaled by any modern government in history.

What had the previous administration in Washington done for four years? Nothing. Why? For a very fundamental reason. That administration was not industrially minded or agriculturally minded or business minded. It was high-finance minded — manned and controlled by a handful of men who in turn controlled, and by one financial device or another took their toll, from the greater part of all other business and industry.

Let me make one simple statement. When I refer to high finance I am not talking about all great bankers or all great corporation executives or all multimillionaires — any more than Theodore Roosevelt, in using the term "malefactors of great wealth," implied that all men of great wealth were "malefactors." I do not even imply that the majority of them are bad citizens. The opposite is true.

Just in the same way, the overwhelming majority of businessmen in this country are good citizens and the proportion of those who are not is probably about the same proportion as in the other occupations and professions of life.

When I speak of high finance as a harmful factor in recent years, I am speaking about a minority which includes the type of individual who speculates with other people's money — and you in Chicago know the kind I refer to — and also the type of individual who says that popular government cannot be trusted and, therefore, that the control of business of all kinds and, indeed, of government itself, should be vested in the hands of 100 or 200 all-wise individuals controlling the purse strings of the nation.

High finance of this type refused to permit government credit to go directly to the industrialist, to the businessman, to the home owner, to the farmer. They wanted it to trickle down from the top, through the intricate arrangements which they controlled and by which they were able to levy tribute on every business in the land. They did not want interest rates to be reduced by the use of government funds, for that would affect the rate of interest which they themselves wanted to charge. They did not want government supervision over financial markets through which they manipulated their monopolies with other people's money.

And in the face of their demands that government do nothing that they called "unsound," the government, hypnotized by its indebtedness to them, stood by and let the depression drive industry and business toward bankruptcy.

America is an economic unit. New means and methods of transportation and communications have made us economically as well as politically a single nation.

Because kidnappers and bank robbers could in high-powered cars speed across state lines, it became necessary, in order to protect our people, to invoke the power of the federal government. In the same way speculators and manipulators from across state lines, and regardless of state laws, have lured the unsuspecting and the unwary to financial destruction. In the same way across state lines, there have been built up intricate corporate structures, piling bond upon stock and stock upon bond — huge monopolies which were stifling independent business and private enterprise.

There was no power under Heaven that could protect the people against that sort of thing except a people's government at Washington. All that this administration has done, all that it proposes to do — and this it does propose to do — is to use every power and authority of the federal government to protect the commerce of America from the selfish forces which ruined it.

Always, month in and month out, during these three and a half years, your government has had but one sign on its desk — "Seek only the greater good of the greater number of Americans." And in appraising the record, remember two things. First, this administration was called upon to act after a previous administration and all the combined forces of private enterprise had failed. Second, in spite of all the demand for speed, the complexity of the problem, and all the vast sums of money involved, we have had no Teapot Dome.

We found when we came to Washington in 1933 that the business and industry of the nation were like a train which had gone off the rails into a ditch. Our first job was to get it out of the ditch and start it up the track again as far as the repair shops. Our next job was to make repairs — on the broken axles which had gotten it off the road, on the engine which had been worn down by gross misuse.

What was it that the average businessman wanted government to do for him — to do immediately in 1933?

1. Stop deflation and falling prices — and we did it.

2. Increase the purchasing power of his customers who were industrial workers in the cities — and we did it.

3. Increase the purchasing power of his customers on the farms — and we did it.

4. Decrease interest rates, power rates, and transportation rates — and we did it.

5. Protect him from the losses due to crime, bank robbers, kidnappers, blackmailers — and we did it.

How did we do it? By a sound monetary policy which raised prices. By reorganizing the banks of the nation and insuring their deposits. By bringing the businessmen of the nation together and encouraging them to pay higher wages, to shorten working hours, and to discourage that minority among their own members who were engaging in unfair competition and unethical business practices.

Through the AAA, through our cattle-buying program, through our program of drought relief and flood relief, through the Farm Credit Administration, we raised the income of the customers of business who lived on the farms. By our program to provide work for the unemployed, by our CCC camps, and other measures, greater purchasing power was given to those who lived in our cities.

Money began going round again. The dollars paid out by government were spent in the stores and shops of the nation; and spent again to the wholesaler; and spent again to the factory; and spent again to the wage earner; and then spent again in another store and shop. The wheels of business began to turn again; the train was back on the rails.

Mind you, it did not get out of the ditch itself; it was hauled out by your government.

And we hauled it along the road. PWA, WPA, both provided normal and useful employment for hundreds of thousands of workers. Hundreds of millions of dollars got into circulation when we liquidated the assets of closed banks through the Reconstruction Finance Corporation; millions more when we loaned money for home building and home financing through the Federal Housing program; hundreds of millions more in loans and grants to enable municipalities to build needed improvements; hundreds of millions more through the CCC camps.

I am not going to talk tonight about how much our program to provide work for the unemployed meant to the nation as a whole. That cannot be measured in dollars and cents. It can be measured only in terms of the preservation of the families of America. But so far as business goes, it can be measured in terms of sales made and goods moving.

The train of American business is moving ahead. But you people know what I mean when I say it is clear that if the train is to run smoothly again, the cars will have to be loaded more evenly. We have made a definite start in getting the train loaded more evenly in order that axles may not break again.

For example, we have provided a sounder and cheaper money market and a sound banking and securities system. You businessmen know how much legitimate business you lost in the old days because your customers were robbed by fake securities or impoverished by shaky banks.

By our monetary policy we have kept prices up and lightened the burden of debt. It is easier to get credit. It is easier to repay.

We have encouraged cheaper power for the small factory owner to lower his cost of production. We have given the businessman cheaper transportation rates. But, above all, we have fought to break the deadly grip which monopoly has in the past been able to fasten on the business of the nation.

Because we cherished our system of private property and free enterprise and were determined to preserve it as the foundation of our traditional American system, we recalled the warning of Thomas Jefferson that "widespread poverty and concentrated wealth cannot long endure side by side in a democracy."

Our job was to preserve the American ideal of economic as well as political democracy against the abuse of concentration of economic power that had been insidiously growing up among us in the past fifty years, particularly during the twelve years of preceding administrations. Free economic enterprise was being weeded out at an alarming pace.

During those years of false prosperity and during the more recent years of exhausting depression, one business after another, one small corporation after another, their resources depleted, had failed or had fallen into the lap of a bigger competitor.

A dangerous thing was happening. Half of the industrial corporate wealth of the country had come under the control of less than 200 huge corporations. That is not all. These huge corporations in some cases did not even try to compete with each other. They themselves were tied together by interlocking directors, interlocking bankers, interlocking lawyers.

This concentration of wealth and power has been built upon other people's money, other people's business, other people's labor. Under this concentration independent business was allowed to exist only by sufferance. It has been a menace to the social system as well as to the economic system which we call American democracy.

There is no excuse for it in the cold terms of industrial efficiency. There is no excuse for it from the point of view of the average investor. There is no excuse for it from the point of view of the independent businessman.

I believe, I have always believed, and I will always believe in private enterprise as the backbone of economic well-being in the United States.

But I know, and you know, and every independent businessman who has had to struggle against the competition of monopolies knows that this concentration of economic power in all-embracing corporations does not represent private enterprise as we Americans cherish it and propose to foster it. On the contrary, it represents private enterprise which has become a kind of private government, a power unto itself — a regimentation of other people's money and other people's lives.

Back in Kansas I spoke about bogey men and fairy tales which the real Republican leaders, many of whom are part of this concentrated power, are using to spread fear among the American people. You good people have heard about these fairy tales and bogey men too. You have heard about how antagonistic to business this administration is supposed to be. You have heard all about the dangers which the business of America is supposed to be facing if this administration continues.

The answer to that is the record of what we have done. It was this administration which saved the system of private profit and free enterprise after it had been dragged to the brink of ruin by these same leaders who now try to scare you.

Look at the advance in private business in the last three and a half years; and read there what we think about private business.

Today, for the first time in seven years the banker, the storekeeper, the small factory owner, the industrialist can all sit back and enjoy the company of their own ledgers. They are in the black. That is where we want them to be; that is where our policies aim them to be; that is where we intend them to be in the future.

Some of these people really forget how sick they were. But I know how sick they were. I have their fever charts. I know how the knees of all of our rugged individualists were trembling four years ago and how their hearts fluttered. They came to Washington in great numbers. Washington did not look like a dangerous bureaucracy to them then. Oh, no! It looked like an emergency hospital. All of the distinguished patients wanted two things — a quick hypodermic to end the pain and a course of treatment to cure the disease. They wanted them in a hurry; we gave them both. And now most of the patients seem to be doing very nicely. Some of them are even well enough to throw their crutches at the doctor.

The struggle against private monopoly is a struggle for, and not against, American business. It is a struggle to preserve individual enterprise and economic freedom.

I believe in individualism. I believe in it in the arts, the sciences, and professions. I believe in it in business. I believe in individualism in all of these things — up to the point where the individualist starts to operate at the expense of society. The overwhelming majority of American businessmen do not believe in it beyond that point. We have all suffered in the past from individualism run wild. Society has suffered and business has suffered.

Believing in the solvency of business, the solvency of farmers, and the solvency of workers, I believe also in the solvency of government. Your government is solvent. The net federal debt today is lower in proportion to the income of the nation and in proportion to the wealth of the nation than it was on March 4, 1933. In the future it will become lower still, because with the rising tide of national income and national wealth, the very causes of our emergency spending are starting to disappear. Government expenditures are coming down and government income is going up. The opportunities for private enterprise will continue to expand.

The people of America have no quarrel with business. They insist only that the power of concentrated wealth shall not be abused.

We have come through a hard struggle to preserve democracy in America. Where other nations in other parts of the world have lost that fight, we have won.

The businessmen of America and all other citizens have joined in a firm resolve to hold the fruits of that victory, to cling to the old ideals and old fundamentals upon which America has grown great.

87.

HERBERT HOOVER: The New Deal and European Collectivism

The address by ex-President Hoover, from which the following selection is taken, was delivered to the Republican National Convention in Cleveland on June 10, 1936. Although Hoover was still the dominant figure in the Party — as the wild and prolonged demonstration touched off by his appearance attested — the Republicans nominated the only Republican governor to be reelected in 1934, Alfred M. Landon of Kansas. Landon referred to himself as a "constitutional liberal," but Hoover succeeded in blunting Landon's liberal edge by injecting much of his own philosophy into the subsequent election campaign. Uncompromising opponents of the New Deal such as Hoover constantly compared the rise of Roosevelt in America to the rise of dictatorships abroad.

Source: *American Ideals Versus the New Deal*, New York, n.d., pp. 4-12.

IN THIS ROOM rests the greatest responsibility that has come to a body of Americans in three generations. In the lesser sense this is a convention of a great political party. But in the larger sense it is a convention of Americans to determine the fate of those ideals for which this nation was founded. That far transcends all partisanship.

There are elemental currents which make or break the fate of nations. There is a moral purpose in the universe. Those forces which affect the vitality and the soul of a people will control their destinies. The sum of years of public service in these currents is the overwhelming conviction of their transcendent importance over the more transitory, even though difficult, issues of national life.

I have given about four years to research into the New Deal, trying to determine what its ultimate objectives were, what sort of a system it is imposing on this country.

To some people it appears to be a strange interlude in American history in that it has no philosophy, that it is sheer opportunism, that it is a muddle of a spoils system, of emotional economics, of reckless adventure, of unctuous claims to a monopoly of human sympathy, of greed for power, of a desire for popular acclaim and an aspiration to make the front pages of the newspapers. That is the most charitable view.

To other people it appears to be a cold-blooded attempt by starry-eyed boys to infect the American people by a mixture of European ideas, flavored with our native predilection to get something for nothing.

You can choose either one you like best. But the first is the road of chaos which leads to the second. Both of these roads lead over the same grim precipice that is the crippling and possibly the destruction of the freedom of men. Which of these interpretations is accurate is even disputed by alumni of the New Deal who have graduated for conscience's sake or have graduated by request.

In central Europe the march of Socialist or Fascist dictatorships and their destruction of liberty did not set out with guns and armies. Dictators began their ascent to the seats of power through the elections providd by liberal institutions. Their weapons were promise and hate. They offered the mirage of Utopia to those in distress. They flung the poison of class hatred. They may not have maimed the bodies of men, but they maimed their souls.

The 1932 campaign was a pretty good imitation of this first stage of European tactics. You may recall the promises of the abundant life, the propaganda of hate.

Once seated in office, the first demand of these European despotisms was for power and "action." Legislatures were told they "must" delegate their authorities. Their free debate was suppressed. The powers demanded are always the same pattern. They all adopt planned economy. They regimented industry and agriculture. They put the government into business. They engaged in gigantic government expenditures. They created vast organizations of spoils henchmen and subsidized dependents. They corrupted currency and credit. They drugged the thinking of the people with propaganda at the people's expense.

If there are any items in this stage in the march of European collectivism that the New Deal has not imitated it must have been an oversight.

But at this point this parallel with Europe halts — at least for the present. The American people should thank Almighty God for the Constitution and the Supreme Court. They should be grateful to a courageous press.

You might contemplate what would have happened if Mr. Roosevelt could have appointed enough Supreme Court justices in the first year of his administration. Suppose these New Deal acts had remained upon the statute books. We would have been a regimented people. Have you any assurance that he will not have the appointments if he is reelected? . . .

So much for the evidence that the New Deal is a definite attempt to replace the American system of freedom with some sort of European planned existence. But let us assume that the explanation is simply hit-and-run opportunism, spoils system, and muddle.

We can well take a moment to explore the prospects of American ideals of liberty and self-government under that philosophy. We may take only seven short examples:

The Supreme Court has reversed some ten or twelve of the New Deal major enactments. Many of these acts were a violation of the rights of men and of self-government. Despite the sworn duty of the Executive and Congress to defend these rights, they have sought to take them into their own hands. That is an attack on the foundations of freedom.

More than this, the independence of the Congress, the Supreme Court, and the Executive are pillars at the door of liberty. For three years the word "must" has invaded the independence of Congress. And the Congress has abandoned its responsibility to check even the expenditures of money. They have turned open appropriations into personal power. These are destructions of the very safeguards of free people.

We have seen these gigantic expenditures and this torrent of waste pile up a national debt which two generations cannot repay. One time I told a Democratic Congress that "You cannot spend yourselves into prosperity." You recall that advice did not take then. It hasn't taken yet.

Billions have been spent to prime the economic pump. It did employ a horde of paid officials upon the pump handle. We have seen the frantic attempts to find new taxes on the rich. Yet three-quarters of the bill will be sent to the average man and the poor. He and his wife and his grandchildren will be giving a quarter of all their working days to pay taxes. Freedom to work for himself is changed into a slavery of work for the follies of government.

We have seen an explosive inflation of bank credits by this government borrowing.

We have seen varied steps toward currency inflation that have already enriched the speculator and deprived the poor. If this is to continue, the end result is the tears and anguish of universal bankruptcy and distress. No democracy in history has survived the final stages of inflation.

We have seen the building up of a horde of political officials. We have seen the pressures upon the helpless and destitute to trade political support for relief. Both are a pollution of the very fountains of liberty.

We have seen the most elemental violation of economic law and experience. The New Deal forgets it is solely by production of more goods and more varieties of goods and services that we advance the standard of living and security of men. If we constantly decrease costs and prices and keep up earnings, the production of plenty will be more and more widely distributed. These laws may be restitched in new phrases but they are the very shoes of human progress.

We had so triumphed in this long climb of mankind toward plenty that we had reached Mount Pisgah, where we looked over the promised land of abolished poverty. Then men began to quarrel over the division of the goods. The depression produced by war destruction temporarily checked our march toward the promised land.

Then came the little prophets of the New Deal. They announce the striking solution that the way out is to produce less and to increase prices so that people can buy less. They have kept on providing some new restriction or burden or fright down to a week ago.

At least it has enabled the New Deal to take a few hundred thousand earnest party workers to the promised land. It takes the rest of us for a ride into the wilderness of unemployment.

Can democracy stand the strain of Mother Hubbard economics for long? Will there be anything left in the economic cupboar but a bone? . . .

The New Deal may be a revolutionar design to replace the American system wit despotism. It may be the dream stuff of false liberalism. It may be the valor of muc dle. Their relationship to each other, how ever, is exactly the sistership of the witche who brewed the caldron of powerful trou ble for Macbeth. Their product is the po soning of Americanism.

The President has constantly reiterate that he will not retreat. For months, to b sure, there has been a strange quiet. Just a the last campaign was fought on promise that have been broken, so apparently th campaign is to be slipped through by eva sion.

But the American people have the righ to know now, while they still have powe to act. What is going to be done after elec tion with these measures which the Const tution forbids and the people by their vote have never authorized? What do the Nev Dealers propose to do with these unstabl currencies, unbalanced budgets, debts an taxes? Fifty words would make it clea Surely the propaganda agencies which em half a million words a day could find roor for these 50. I noticed they recently sper 300 words on how to choose a hat. It slightly more important to know the fate a nation. . . .

The Republican Party must achieve tru social betterment. But we must produc measures that will not work confusion an disappointment. We must propose a rea approach to social evils, not the prescriptio for them, by quacks, of poison in place c remedy.

We must achieve freedom in the econom ic field. We have grave problems in relatio of government to agriculture and busines Monopoly is only one of them. The Re publican Party is against the greed for pow er of the wanton boys who waste th people's savings. But it must be equally ad mant against the greed for power and exploitation in the seekers of special privilege. At one time I said: "We can no more have economic power without checks and balances than we can have political power without checks and balances. Either one leads to tyranny."

The Republican Party must be a party that accepts the challenge of each new day. The last word in human accomplishment has not been spoken. The last step in human progress has not been made. We welcome change when it will produce a fairer, more just, and satisfying civilization. But change which destroys the safeguards of free men and women are only apples of Sodom.

Great calamities have come to the whole world. These forces have reached into every calling and every cottage. They have brought tragedy and suffering to millions of firesides. I have great sympathy for those who honestly reach for short cuts to the immensity of our problems.

While design of the structure of betterment for the common man must be inspired by the human heart, it can only be achieved by the intellect. It can only be builded by using the mold of justice, by laying brick upon brick from the materials of scientific research; by the painstaking sifting of truth from the collection of fact and experience. Any other mold is distorted; any other bricks are without straw; any other foundations are sand. That great structure of human progress can be built only by free men and women.

The gravest task which confronts the party is to regenerate these freedoms.

There are principles which neither tricks of organization, nor the rigors of depression, nor the march of time, nor New Dealers, nor Socialists, nor Fascists can change. There are some principles which came into the universe along with the shooting stars of which worlds are made, and they have always been and ever will be true. Such are the laws of mathematics, the law of gravita-

United Press International

Herbert Hoover addressing an audience of 3,000 in Philadelphia in 1936. In his speech he declared that the New Deal was the first step on the road to socialism or fascism

tion, the existence of God and the ceaseless struggle of humankind to be free.

Throughout the centuries of history, man's vigil and his quest have been to be free. For this, the best and bravest of earth have fought and died. To embody human liberty in workable government, America was born. Shall we keep that faith? Must we condemn the unborn generations to fight again and to die for the right to be free?

There are some principles that cannot be compromised. Either we shall have a society based upon ordered liberty and the initiative of the individual, or we shall have a planned society that means dictation, no matter what you call it or who does it. There is no halfway ground. They cannot be mixed. Government must either release the powers of the individual for honest achievement or the very forces it creates will drive it inexorably to lay its paralyzing hand more and more heavily upon individual effort.

Less than twenty years ago we accepted those ideals as the air we breathed. We fought a great war for their protection. We took upon ourselves obligations of billions. We buried our sons in foreign soil. But in this score of years we have seen the advance of collectivism and its inevitable tyranny in more than half the civilized world. In this thundering era of world crisis distracted America stands confused and uncertain.

88.

Charles E. Coughlin: Money Changers in the Temple

Charles E. Coughlin, said Fortune in 1934, was "just about the biggest thing that ever happened to radio." Father Coughlin had turned to the new medium in 1926, and the Golden Hour of the Little Flower (broadcast directly from the altar of his Detroit Shrine of the Little Flower) reached, at its peak, upward of ten million listeners weekly. Restricting himself at first to religious subjects, Father Coughlin turned, as his audience grew, to politics, using his show as a forum for the expression of his ambivalent attitude — ranging from approval to violent attacks — toward Roosevelt and the New Deal. The formation of the Union Party in June 1936 with the backing of Coughlin's National Union for Social Justice (organized in November 1934) came as no surprise to those who had watched his rise to national prominence. The Party, backed by a coalition of Irish Catholics, supporters of the Townsend Plan, and followers of Gerald L. K. Smith (the latter included the remnants of Huey Long's Share-the-Wealthers), had high hopes in 1936, despite the history of third party failures in American politics, but it garnered less than a million votes in the November election. A portion of Father Coughlin's speech over WABC on June 19, 1936, during which he endorsed the presidential candidacy of William Lemke of North Dakota, is reprinted here.

Source: VSD, July 1, 1936, pp. 613-616.

No man in modern times received such plaudits from the poor as did Franklin Roosevelt when he promised to drive the money changers from the temple — the money changers who had clipped the coins of wages, who had manufactured spurious money and who had brought proud America to her knees.

March 4, 1933! I shall never forget the inaugural address, which seemed to reecho the very words employed by Christ Himself as He actually drove the money changers from the temple.

The thrill that was mine was yours. Through dim clouds of the Depression this man Roosevelt was, as it were, a new savior of his people!

Oh, just a little longer shall there be needless poverty! Just another year shall there be naked backs! Just another moment shall there be dark thoughts of revolution! Never again will the chains of economic poverty bite into the hearts of simple folks as they did in the past days of the Old Deal!

Such were our hopes in the springtime of 1933.

My friends, what have we witnessed as the finger of time turned the pages of the calendar? Nineteen hundred and thirty-three and the National Recovery Act which multiplied profits for the monopolists; 1934 and the AAA which raised the price of foodstuffs, by throwing back God's best gifts in His face; 1935 and the Banking Act which rewarded the exploiters of the poor, the Federal Reserve bankers and their associates, by handing over to them the temple from which they were to have been cast!

In 1936, when our disillusionment is complete, we pause to take inventory of our predicament. You citizens have shackled about your limbs a tax bill of $35 billion, most of which . . . was created by a flourish of a fountain pen. Your erstwhile savior, whose golden promises ring upon the counter of performance with the cheapness of tin, bargained with the money changers that, with 70 billion laboring hours in the ditch, or in the factory, or behind the plow, you and your children shall repay the debt which was created with a drop of ink in less than ten seconds.

Is that driving the money changers out of the temple?

Every crumb you eat, every stitch of clothing you wear, every menial purchase which you make is weighted down with an unseen tax as you work and slave for the debt merchants of America. But the $55 billion of debt bonds, held mostly by the debt merchants and the well-circumstanced of this country, have been ably safeguarded from taxation by this peerless leader who sham-battles his way along the avenue of popularity with his smile for the poor and his blindness for their plight. Is that driving the money changers from the temple?

You laborers of America who work no more than an average of 200 days a year at $5 a day are forced to contribute at least 50 days of your labor — to steal it from your wives and children, to deprive them of the conveniences and the luxuries advertised in every paper and magazine — as tribute for the benefit of the sacrosanct bondholders.

Is that driving the money changers from the temple?

You farmers of America, of whom 3,000 every week are driven over the hill to the poorhouse through the ruthless confiscation which is still protected under the guise of friendship, are forced to bear the burden of $8 billion of mortgage debt on farms at 6 percent — farms which have depreciated 50 percent during these last five years, farms which cannot be operated at a profit except temporarily through the immoral Tugwellism of destruction.

Is that driving the money changers from the temple, or is it driving Americans from their homes?

For God's command of "increase and multiply," spoken to our first parents, the satanic principle of "decrease and devastate" has been substituted.

It is not pleasant for me who coined the phrase "Roosevelt or ruin" — a phrase fashioned upon promises — to voice such passionate words. But I am constrained to admit that "Roosevelt and ruin" is the order of the day because the money changers have not been driven from the temple.

My friends, I come before you tonight not to ask you to return to the Landons, to the Hoovers, to the Old Deal exploiters who honestly defended the dishonest system of gold standardism and rugged individualism. Their sun has set never to rise again.

America has turned its back definitely upon the platitudinous platforms of "ragged individualism." Who at Cleveland dared call into question the plutocratic privilege enjoyed by the Federal Reserve bankers? Who among these moribund New Deal critics dared campaign for an annual, decent wage for the laborer and production at a profit for the farmer? Alas! These Punch and Judy Republicans, whose actions and words were dominated by the ventriloquists of Wall Street, are so blind that they do not recognize, even in this perilous hour, that their gold basis and their private coinage of money have bred more radicals than did Karl Marx or Lenin. To their system of oxcart financialism we must never return!

Review the Landon platform with its proposal to revive the gold standard, which succeeded in prostrating civilization. Hypocritically, it proposes the restoration to Congress of the right to coin and regulate money now held by the President. Pause to consider the colossal fraud that this insincere wording attempts to perpetrate upon the people of his country: "Restore to Congress the power of coining and regulating money by repealing the laws relative to such now held by the President!"

Why, every intelligent person must recognize that our objective is to restore to Congress its constitutional power to coin and regulate money, now held not by the President, not by the secretary of the treasury, but by the Federal Reserve Bank, a privately owned corporation. . . .

Alas! The temple still remains the private property of the money changers. The golden key has been handed over to them for safekeeping — the key which now is fashioned in the shape of a double cross. . . .

Neither Old Dealer nor New Dealer, it appears, has courage to assail the international bankers, the Federal Reserve bankers. In common, both the leaders of the Republicans and the Democrats uphold the old money philosophy. Today in America there is only one political party — the banker's party. In common, both old parties are determined to sham-battle their way through this November election with the hope that millions of American citizens will be driven into the no-man's-land of financial bondage.

My friends, there is a way out, a way to freedom! There is an escape from the dole standard of Roosevelt, the gold standard of Landon. No longer need you be targets in no-man's-land for the financial crossfire of the sham-battlers!

Six hours ago the birth of "the Union Party" was officially announced to the newspapers of the nation, thereby confirming information which hitherto was mine unofficially. The new candidate for President, together with his sponsors, formally requested my support, as they handed to me his platform. I have studied it carefully. I find that it is in harmony substantially with the principles of social justice.

As presented to me, this platform reads as if it were born in the hearts of a group of rebels. If you think so, you are right in thinking so, because this group rebels against the bankers' bonds, their tax-exempt bonds, their radicalism, and their financial slavery.

Who is the candidate for President of the Union Party? He is one who has left his mark for erudition in the halls of Yale University and who already has carved for himself a niche of fame in the industrial and agricultural temple of America. He is a man who has made promises in the past and has kept them. He is a battler who has entered into fights and has fought them. He is an American and not an internationalist, a liberty lover and not a slave trader, who will fight for financial freedom as did his prototype, Lincoln, who waged war for physical freedom.

I refer to Congressman William Lemke of North Dakota, who has thrown his "cap" into the presidential ring at the request of thousands of independent friends. Now that he has taken the step and has officially asked the National Union for its support, we declare him, on the strength of his platform and of his splendid record, eligible for endorsation.

He has chosen as a running mate for the vice-presidency Thomas Charles O'Brien, eminent former district attorney of Boston, counsel for the Brotherhood of Railroad Trainmen and firm exponent of social justice. For ten years before graduating from Harvard University, Mr. O'Brien labored as a baggageman.

Lemke and Yale, Agriculture and Repub-

lican! O'Brien and Harvard, Labor and Democrat!

East and West!

Protestant and Catholic, possessing one program of driving the money changers from the temple, of permitting the wealth of America to flow freely into every home!

89.

1936 *Literary Digest* Poll

The dependence on national opinion polls was a relatively new thing in 1936, but this fact did not mitigate the disastrous effects of the famous wrong guess made by the Literary Digest *in that year. A number of predictions were made regarding the outcome of the presidential election of 1936. Polls based on the modern method of statistical sampling were conducted by George Gallup and Elmo Roper; both forecast a sizeable Roosevelt victory. On the eve of the election Roosevelt computed his own chances and predicted that he would win 360 electoral votes, Landon 171. James A. Farley, Roosevelt's campaign manager, weighed all the evidence and wrote his chief on November 2: "I am still definitely of the opinion that you will carry every state but two — Maine and Vermont." Farley proved exactly right, and the* Literary Digest, *which had used the now outmoded direct mail system of polling, the results of which are reprinted here, was about as wrong as it could be, predicting that Landon would win 370 electoral votes, Roosevelt 161. Roosevelt's landslide victory helped to put the* Digest *out of business.*

Source: *Literary Digest*, October 31, 1936.

LANDON, 1,293,669; ROOSEVELT, 972,897

FINAL RETURNS IN THE *DIGEST'S* POLL OF TEN MILLION VOTERS

WELL, THE GREAT BATTLE OF THE BALLOTS in the poll of 10 million voters, scattered throughout the forty-eight states of the Union, is now finished, and in the table below we record the figures received up to the hour of going to press.

These figures are exactly as received from more than one in every five voters polled in our country — they are neither weighted, adjusted, nor interpreted.

Never before in an experience covering more than a quarter of a century in taking polls have we received so many different varieties of criticism — praise from many; condemnation from many others — and yet it has been just of the same type that has come to us every time a Poll has been taken in all these years.

A telegram from a newspaper in California asks: "Is it true that Mr. Hearst has purchased *The Literary Digest?*"A telephone message only the day before these lines were written: "Has the Republican National Committee purchased *The Literary Digest?*"And all types and varieties, including: "Have the Jews purchased *The Literary Digest?*""Is the Pope of Rome a stockholder of *The Literary Digest?*"And so it goes — all equally absurd and amusing. We could add more to this list, and yet all of these questions in recent days are but repetitions of what we have been experiencing all down the years from the very first Poll.

Problem — Now, are the figures in this Poll correct? In answer to this question we will simply refer to a telegram we sent to a young man in Massachusetts the other day in answer to his challenge to us to wager $100,000 on the accuracy of our Poll. We wired him as follows:

For nearly a quarter century, we have been taking Polls of the voters in the forty-eight States, and especially in Presidential years, and we have always merely mailed the ballots, counted and recorded those returned and let the people of the Nation draw their conclusions as to our accuracy. So far, we have been right in every Poll. Will we be right in the current Poll? That, as Mrs. Roosevelt said concerning the President's reelection, is in the "lap of the gods."

We never make any claims before election but we respectfully refer you to the opinion of one of the most quoted citizens today, the Hon. James A. Farley, Chairman of the Democratic National Committee. This is what Mr. Farley said October 14, 1932:

"Any sane person cannot escape the implication of such a gigantic sampling of popular opinion as is embraced in *The Literary Digest* straw vote. I consider this conclusive evidence as to the desire of the people of this country for a change in the National Government. *The Literary Digest* poll is an achievement of no little magnitude. It is a Poll fairly and correctly conducted."

In studying the table of the voters from all of the States printed below, please re-member that we make no claims at this time for their absolute accuracy. On a similar occasion we felt it important to say:

In a wild year like this, however, many sagacious observers will refuse to bank upon appearances, however convincing. As for *The Digest*, it draws no conclusions from the results of its vast distribution of twenty million ballots. True to its historic non-partisan policy — or "omni-partisan," as some editor described it in 1928 — we supply our readers with the facts to the best of our ability, and leave them to draw their own conclusions.

We make no claim to infallibility. We did not coin the phrase "uncanny accuracy" which has been so freely-applied to our Polls. We know only too well the limitations of every straw vote, however enormous the sample gathered, however scientific the method. It would be a miracle if every State of the forty-eight behaved on Election day exactly as forecast by the Poll.

We say now about Rhode Island and Massachusetts that our figures indicate in our own judgment too large a percentage for Mr. Landon and too small a percentage for Mr. Roosevelt, and altho in 1932 the figures in these two States indicated Mr. Hoover's carrying both, we announced:

"A study of the returns convinces us that in those States our ballots have somehow failed to come back in adequate quantity from large bodies of Democratic voters."

Our own opinion was that they would be found in the Roosevelt column, and they were. We will not do the same this year; we feel that both States will be found in the Landon column, and we are reaching this conclusion by the same process that lead to the reverse conclusion in 1932.

Pennsylvania is another State which requires special mention. Four years ago, our figures gave the State to Mr. Roosevelt, and Mr. Hoover carried it on Election day. In comparing our ballot this year with that of 1932, we find that in many cities in Pennsylvania our figures showed a much higher

rend toward Mr. Roosevelt than was justi-
ed by the election figures on Election day
n 1932. In examining the very same cities
ow we discover the reverse trend, and in
ities that in 1932 indicated an approxi-
nately 60-40 percent relationship between
Roosevelt and Hoover, we now find 60
ercent for Landon and 40 percent for Roo-
evelt.

That's the plain language of it. Many
eople wonder at these great changes in a
tate like Pennsylvania, and we confess to
onderment ourselves.

On the Pacific Coast, we find California,
Dregon, and Washington all vote for Mr.
andon in our Poll, and yet we are told
hat the Pacific Coast is "aflame" for Mr.
Roosevelt.

A State like California is always a diffi-
ult State to get an accurate opinion from
y the polling method, and we may be far
stray, yet every one should remember that
n the Gubernatorial campaign a few years
go, we took a Poll of California when it
vas believed by most of California citizens
hat Mr. Upton Sinclair would be elected
Governor, and the result of our Poll
howed that Mr. Sinclair would *not* be
lected Governor and the Poll was correct.

The State of Washington seems to be
nore favorable to Mr. Landon than either
Dregon or California. We cannot in our
'oll detect anything that would indicate a
eason for this difference.

eattle — Right here we wish to say that in
932 our Poll in Seattle gave Mr. Roose-
elt 65.43 percent of the vote, and he car-
ied that city by 61.58 percent of the vote.
n the current Poll, 1936, Seattle gives Mr.
andon 58.52 percent and Mr. Roosevelt
0.46 percent. Our readers will notice we
verestimated Mr. Roosevelt in 1932 — are
e overestimating Mr. Landon now? We
ee no reason for supposing so. And the
ree Pacific Coast States which now show
r Mr. Landon and which millions believe

will vote for Mr. Roosevelt (they may be
right) in 1924, 1928, and 1932 were correctly forecast in *The Literary Digest* Polls.

In the great Empire State, New York,
the figures for so large a State are what
might be called very close. After looking at
the figures for New York in the column at
the left, remember that in 1932 we gave
Mr. Roosevelt 46.1 percent and Mr. Hoover 43.9 percent, even closer than it is today. And yet we correctly forecast that Mr.
Roosevelt would carry the State.

And so we might go on with many
States that are very close, and some not so
close, but in which local conditions have
much to do with results, not in polls such
as our Poll but on Election day.

The Poll represents the most extensive
straw ballot in the field — the most experienced in view of its twenty-five years of
perfecting — the most unbiased in view of
its prestige — a Poll that has always previously been correct.

Even its critics admit its value as an index
of popular sentiment. As one of these critics, *The Nation*, observes:

"Because it indicates both the 1932 and
1936 vote, it offers the raw material for as
careful a prognostication as it is possible to
make at this time."

	Electoral Vote	Landon 1936 Total Vote For State	Roosevelt 1936 Total Vote For State
Ala.	11	3,060	10,082
Ariz.	3	2,337	1,975
Ark.	9	2,724	7,608
Calif.	22	89,516	77,245
Colo.	6	15,949	10,025
Conn.	8	28,809	13,413
Del.	3	2,918	2,048
Fla.	7	6,087	8,620
Ga.	12	3,948	12,915
Idaho	4	3,653	2,611
Ill.	29	123,297	79,035
Ind.	14	42,805	26,663
Iowa	11	31,871	18,614
Kans.	9	35,408	20,254

	Electoral	Landon	Roosevelt		Electoral	Landon	Rooseve
Ky.	11	13,365	16,592	Okla.	11	14,442	15,07
La.	10	3,686	7,902	Ore.	5	11,747	10,95
Maine	5	11,742	5,337	Pa.	36	119,086	81,11
Md.	8	17,463	18,341	R.I.	4	10,401	3,48
Mass.	17	87,449	25,965	S.C.	8	1,247	7,10
Mich.	19	51,478	25,686	S. Dak.	4	8,483	4,50
Minn.	11	30,762	20,733	Tenn.	11	9,883	19,82
Miss.	9	848	6,080	Texas	23	15,341	37,50
Mo.	15	50,022	38,267	Utah	4	4,067	5,31
Mont.	4	4,490	3,562	Vt.	3	7,241	2,45
Nebr.	7	18,280	11,770	Va.	11	10,223	16,78
Nev.	3	1,003	955	Wash.	8	21,370	15,30
N.H.	4	9,207	2,737	W. Va.	8	13,660	10,23
N.J.	16	58,677	27,631	Wis.	12	33,796	20,78
N.M.	3	1,625	1,662	Wyo.	3	2,526	1,53
N.Y.	47	162,260	139,277	State			
N.C.	13	6,113	16,324	Unknown		7,158	6,54
N. Dak.	4	4,250	3,666				
Ohio	26	77,896	50,778	Total	531	1,293,669	972,89

90.

"Franklin D. Roosevelt's Back Again"

Franklin D. Roosevelt was voted back into office in 1936 by the largest popular majority accorded a presidential nominee up until that time. He won 60.8 percent of the popular vote, failing to win only two states: Maine and Vermont. The following song expressed the jubilation that attended his victory and celebrates the achievements of his first term that had made him so well loved. The version presented here was adapted from a Southern mountain song by the New Lost City Ramblers in 1936.

Source: *This Singing Land*, compiled and edited by Irwin Silber,
       ® 1965 Amsco Music Publishing Co., Used by Permission.

✥ FRANKLIN D. ROOSEVELT'S BACK AGAIN

Just hand me my old Martin, for soon I will be startin'
Back to dear old Charleston, far away.
Since Roosevelt's been re-elected, we'll not be neglected,
We've got Franklin D. Roosevelt back again.

    Back again, back again,
    We've got Franklin D. Roosevelt back again,
    Since Roosevelt's been elected, moonshine liquor's been corrected,
    We've got legal wine, whiskey, beer, and gin.

I'll take a drink of brandy and let myself be handy,
Good times are coming back again.
You can laugh and tell a joke, you can dance and drink and smoke,
We've got Franklin D. Roosevelt back again.

We've got Franklin D. Roosevelt back again.
We'll have money in our jeans,
We can travel with the queen,
We've got Franklin D. Roosevelt back again.

No more breadlines we're glad to say, the donkey won election day,
No more standing in the blowing, snowing rain;
He's got things in full sway, we're all working and getting our pay,
We've got Franklin D. Roosevelt back again.

Back again, back again,
We've got Franklin D. Roosevelt back again,
Since Roosevelt's been elected, moonshine liquor's been corrected,
We've got legal wine, whiskey, beer, and gin.

91.

Stuart Chase: The Depletion of Our National Resources

An extensive campaign to save the land was ushered in by the New Deal. A Civilian Conservation Corps (CCC) was created in the spring of 1933, and, by July, 300,000 needy young men were planting trees, building dams, instituting fire-prevention procedures in the forests, and a great deal more. After the terrible dust storms of 1934, the Forest Service planted a shelterbelt of more than 200 million trees. A Soil Erosion Service aided farmers, while the Agricultural Adjustment Administration (AAA) demanded that those receiving benefits adopt soil-conserving programs. Grazing on public lands was regulated, and in 1934 a National Resources Board (NRB) was established to coordinate the effort to preserve and improve the land. The extent to which the nation's resources had been dissipated was graphically portrayed in 1936 by the economist and publicist Stuart Chase in his Rich Land, Poor Land. *A portion of the third chapter is reprinted here.*

Source: *Rich Land, Poor Land*, New York, 1936, pp. 34-47.

THE PRIMEVAL SETTING HAS BEEN EXPLORED. How does the continent look today after 300 years of occupation? Suppose we climb into a metaphorical airplane and cruise about America, first observing the whole picture, then circling to examine this area and that, finally looking into conditions underground — with the help of whatever scientific instruments may be necessary.

The basic map has changed but little: a

slit across the Isthmus of Panama, a few minor shifts in the coastline, small islands thrown up here and there or washed away, some river channels recut. But coming closer we find the cover enormously changed, as well as the denizens thereof. The old forest, the old grasslands have almost completely disappeared. Desert lands have broadened. A dust desert is forming east of the Rockies where firm grass once stood. Woodlands — and a spindly lot they are by comparison — cover only half the area the primeval forest once covered. Grazing areas are still immense but the old types of native grasses have largely gone.

On one-quarter of continental United States are new fields, bare in the winter, green with crops in the summer. Adjacent to these tilled fields are pasturelands, unknown before, of an almost equal area. On some of the old arid grasslands irrigation ditches now run, and between them is the green of crops. This is particularly noticeable around Salt Lake in Utah, in regions of the Southwest, in the Imperial and Central valleys of California. Scattered about the continent, especially along the rivers and the seacoasts, are the black clusters of cities and the smaller dots of towns and villages. Linking them run a million miles and more of highways, railroads, the tracery of power lines, and pipelines underground. . . .

Forest and native grasslands have given way to farmlands, both crop and pasture. The total farmland, including farm wood lots, approaches a billion acres, or about half the whole area. In 1630 the only parallel was the stick-furrowed fields of the Indians, which probably did not amount to a million acres all told.

Looking closer still, we see that the Indians are now clustered on a few reservations, largely in the West. On the lands over which they once hunted and grew their corn, 130 million aliens have settled, some black, some brown, but mostly white. The great herds of wild game have been replaced by domestic animals and fowl. Finally we note that in many sections the earth is pierced with holes — the shafts of mines, open-pit operations, the long drills of oil and gas and water wells.

Primeval forest, virgin soil, and the waving prairie grasses have given way to open fields, harnessed rivers spanned by steel bridges, tunneled mountains, irrigated arid lands, culm banks, oil fields, canals, drained marshes, and roaring, smoky cities. Beauty has been lost, we cry, but progress gained. Wild landscape has been replaced by cultured.

Soil

We drop 10,000 feet and look closer still. If this be progress, it is bitter tonic. The continental soil, the center of vitality, is visibly and rapidly declining. The forest cover has been stripped and burned and steadily shrinks. The natural grass cover has been torn to ribbons by steel plows and the hooves of cattle and sheep. The skin of America has been laid open. Streams have lost their measured balance, and, heavy with silt, run wild in flood to the sea at certain seasons, to fall to miserable trickles in the drier months. This land may be bristling with tall chimneys and other evidences of progress, but it has lost its old stability.

The humus is going, and when it is gone, natural life goes. Two powerful agents are destroying the soil: erosion and the loss of fertility due to mining the soil for crops. Soils which have been building steadily for 20,000 years since the last Ice Age now in a single century lose the benefits of several thousand years of accumulation. Corn yields in sections of Iowa have dropped from 50 to 25 bushels per acre within the lifetime of a man not yet old. This, remember, is the richest soil in America. In the northern humid states alone, scientists estimate that one-quarter of the original nitrogen, one-fifth of the phosphorus, one-tenth of the potassium and one-third of the sulfur have gone. The carrying capacity of pasturelands declined seriously between 1919 and 1929

The effect of erosion and mismanagement of farm land in Jackson County, Alabama, 1937; photograph by Arthur Rothstein

ccording to the National Resources Board.

The 3 billion tons of solid material washed out of the fields and pastures of America every year by water erosion contains 40 million tons of phosphorus, potassium, and nitrogen. This, of course, is in addition to losses through cropping. To load and haul away this incomprehensible bulk of rich farm soil would require a train of freight cars 475,000 miles long, enough to girdle the planet nineteen times at the Equator. Approximately 400 million tons of solid earth is dumped into the Gulf of Mexico by the Mississippi alone — the greater part of it super-soil, richer than that of the Nile. Plant food can be restored to soil that has been worn lean by cropping, but when water takes the soil itself — minerals, humus, microscopic organisms, everything — only nature can restore fertility to that land, and her rate under primeval conditions, as we have seen, is one inch in 500 years.

One hundred million acres of formerly cultivated land has been essentially ruined by water erosion — an area equal to Illinois, Ohio, North Carolina, and Maryland combined — the equivalent of 1,250,000 eighty-acre farms. In addition, this washing of sloping fields has stripped the greater part of the productive top soil from another 125 million acres now being cultivated. Erosion by wind and water is getting under way on another 100 million acres. More than 300 million acres — one-sixth of the country — is gone, going, or beginning to go. This, we note, is on land originally the most fertile.

Kansas farms are blowing through Nebraska at an accelerating rate. In the spring of 1934, the farms of the Dust Bowl — which includes western Oklahoma, western Kansas, eastern Colorado, the panhandle of Texas, and parts of Wyoming — blew clear out to the Atlantic Ocean, 2,000 miles away. On a single day 300 million tons of rich top soil was lifted from the Great Plains, never to return, and planted in places where it would spread the maximum of damage and discomfort. Authentic desert sand dunes were laid down. People began to die of dust pneumonia. More than 9 million acres of good land has been virtually destroyed by wind erosion, and serious damage is reported on nearly 80 million acres.

Taking the continent as a whole, it is reliably estimated that half of its original fertility has been dissipated by these various agents. The rate of loss tends to follow the laws of compound interest. The stricken areas grow cumulatively larger.

Soil losses due to cropping are the result of foolish marketing procedures, revolving around the one-crop system in cotton, corn, tobacco, and wheat. Losses due to erosion are the direct result of stripping the forest and grass cover from the slopes. When the tangle of roots, the sod of the native grasses, gives way to bare plowed fields with cultivated rows running up and down hill, there is nothing to hold the rain. It tears over the contours, taking the soil with it.

Forest

Not more than one-tenth of the old virgin forest remains. The Douglas firs of the Pacific Northwest are the last great stand of primeval timber. We see them coming down by high-power logging machinery, and, when they have fallen, much of the area is so devastated that trees will not grow again. The soil itself is often burned in the ensuing fires. When new vegetation starts, if at all, it is a different and poorer tree crop. These cut-over, burned-over lands are still called "forest" on the maps, but we see that almost 100 million acres is really dead land — totally unknown in the old America. This is a strange and desolate phenomenon — no farms, no productive forest, no animals, no life. In 1871, 400 square miles were burnt over in Wisconsin and 1,500 people were killed. In 1927, 158,000 forest fires were reported, and they consumed nearly 40 million acres. Meanwhile, we note that lumbermen are cutting trees of saw-timber size almost five times as fast as the stands are growing. In 1630 the reserves were 7,000 billion board feet; today the to-

tal has shrunk to 1,600 billion. In a genera tion or less, at this rate of exploitation there will be no more reserves. Wheat crop ripen every year, sometimes oftener; lumbe crops ripen every century on the average.

Grass

Some virgin timber still remains; it take patient search to find virgin grasslands. Th primeval sod has been burned, overgrazed plowed up, and destroyed. Where dry farm ing for wheat has been practised on th Great Plains, the Dust Bowl spreads Where corn has been planted on the slope in the tall grass regions, water erosio spreads. The sharp hooves of too many cat tle and the close cropping of the grass b too many sheep have torn the cover fron the open grazing lands, loosened the ancien sod, and started the gullies and dunes o both water and wind erosion. One hundre and sixty-five million acres of grazing land has been seriously depleted. As in the cas of forests, when new vegetation secures foothold, the species is inferior to the ol climax crop.

Waters

From the packed earth of the croplands the bare-burned slopes of the devastate forests, the broken sods of the grasslands rain and melting snow rush to the rivers i a fraction of the time they used to take. I some watersheds runoff which should re quire three months is carried down to th sea in a month. The rivers run red wit mud where once they were clear. Reservoir are filled, power dams rendered increasingl impotent. Lower a bucket into the Canadi an River and allow it to settle. One-quarte of the water turns out to be rich soil whic the upstream owner paid for in cash.

The baked earth of the tilled fields pre vents the rain from percolating into the ar tesian basins as it used to percolate throug the cover of forest and grass. We see th underground water table falling all over th western half of the continent. In the Dako as and Iowa the drop is serious; in the Central Valley of California, it is still more serious. Meanwhile, pumping for irrigation helps to exhaust the basins. The cool, dark reservoirs which once did so much to equalize flood and drought are sinking. The same is happening with surface reservoirs. Marshes and swamps have been drained in the hope of reclaiming good agricultural land. Sometimes the land is good and sometimes it is bad, unsuited for crops. When it is bad, fires course through the dried underbrush, as in the sterile Wisconsin and Minnesota marshes.

In the lower reaches of the rivers, the old natural side reservoirs have been blocked off by levees. Here is rich farmland, to be sure, but the rivers rise as the silt sinks, and the levees must rise higher still. In New Orleans at flood crests, the Mississippi runs high above the streets of the town. River channels are straightened and further aid the rush to the ocean. Levees break; indeed, the whole levee system nears its breaking point as a practicable engineering method for flood control.

Floods under these conditions must grow worse; droughts must grow worse. The safeguards of nature have been stripped away. In times of low water, the pollution of streams becomes an ominous menace. Each community in the watershed area dumps its untreated sewage into the drinking supply of the town below. When the river is low, sewage poisons remain unoxidized.

In uncounted streams, fish lie killed by the wastes of cities and the black refuse of mine and factory. Pollution has destroyed more fish than all the fishermen, and silt has killed more than pollution. When the sun cannot get through because of the mud, the tiny water plants die and fish lose their basic food supply. Oil wastes strangle the fish fry when they come to the surface. Sewage competes with marine life for a limited oxygen supply. Waxy sludge coats the river bottoms and kills plants there. Our

streams, according to Sears, have become watery deserts, inimical to life. Simpletons try to restock them. "To release millions of fingerlings into such an environment and expect them to live is like driving a flock of yearlings into Death Valley. . . ."

The catch of Pacific halibut and salmon fell steadily to 1930. Now, strenuous measures of conservation are reversing the trend. The Atlantic salmon has gone, unless there be a lonely school wandering the Penobscot. The Atlantic shad is greatly reduced and fishing villages are left stranded. The shellfish catch is only a fraction of what it used to be. Oysters are splendid typhoid carriers and city sewage is rank with typhoid bacilli. The extreme low-water stages of the rivers, induced by the failure of the natural reservoirs, have caused salt water to back up into the river mouths, killing rich colonies of shellfish by encouraging enemies which thrive in greater salinity. . . .

Underground

Looking below the cover of the continent we read the same story. The bowels of the earth have been cleft and robbed. Deposits painfully laid down over geological time are coming up through smoking black scars in the earth's crust to be burned, pounded, fabricated, and rusted, and eventually to vanish. Gold and silver mines have stripped away the accumulation of ages, and in placer mining have destroyed the surrounding soil as well. The sulfur fumes of copper refineries blast the vegetation of whole counties. . . . Phosphate mines destroy thousands of acres of surface soil. Coal pillars are pulled underground and farms fall in. Suffocating fires burn in abandoned mines for decades. In a single year enough petroleum and natural gas are exhausted to account for a million years of natural accumulation. A billion cubic feet of gas is daily blown into the air, "enough," says the National Resources Board, "to supply the United Kingdom twice over. It is forty times as much gas as all the Scandinavian countries use together. It is almost enough to supply every householder in the United States now consuming either natural or manufactured gas." Petroleum, copper, lead, and zinc move toward exhaustion within a generation. . . .

Landscape

Besides the material and financial loss here represented, an environment lovely to the eye has been sacrificed. The most hideous spots are the environs of mines and the slums and industrial areas of great cities. Gashed earth, culm banks, dead trees, and streams putrid with chemicals, refuse, and coal dust distinguish the mines. Cities seem to pride themselves on turning their river banks or waterfronts into majestic privies. Here cluster smoking dumps high as Bun-

ker Hill, gasworks, sewer outlets, dilapidated coal sheds, switchyards, oil refineries, slaughterhouses, glue factories, tanneries which stun the nose, and great barges laden down with garbage. Yet these waters determined the location of the city in the first place, and have often been its chief builder and nourisher. Can ingratitude go farther? European cities respect their waters and adorn their banks with parks, boulevards, and public buildings. Latin-American countries do the same. Compare the waterfront of Havana with that of Brooklyn or Hoboken.

In place of green foliage and clear water man has brought to the continent of America stinking rivers, charred forests, the incomparable filth of cities, the wretched shacks of tenant farmers along Tobacco Road.

92.

Robert M. Hutchins: American Higher Learning

Robert Maynard Hutchins served the University of Chicago for twenty-three years, first as its president (from 1929 — he assumed the post when he was only thirty years old — to 1945), and then as its chancellor (until his retirement in 1951). He early became one of the most severe critics of American higher education, aiming his criticisms especially at the chaotic fragmentation of modern knowledge, at overspecialization among both teachers and students, at the "cult" of professionalism among academics, and at what he saw as a general lowering of educational standards. In a series of lectures given in 1936 and subsequently published under the title The Higher Learning in America, *he surveyed the problems confronting higher education and offered some suggestions for improving it. Passages from the book are reprinted here.*

Source: *The Higher Learning in America*, New Haven, 1936, pp. 1-32, 70-86, 116-119.

THE MOST STRIKING FACT about the higher learning in America is the confusion that besets it. This confusion begins in the high school and continues to the loftiest levels of the university. The high school cannot

make up its mind whether it is preparing students for life or for college. Its student population is miscellaneous and variegated. The course of study is substantially uniform for all groups, whether they are prospective scientists, lawyers, clerks, or laboring men, and is apparently adjusted to the needs of only the smallest of these groups, that destined for the higher learning.

The junior college is in most places an extension of the high-school curriculum, which is there applied to an essentially similar though somewhat smaller student body. Here also the question whether the students are completing their education or are preparing to go on to the university has not been settled, and the aims of the institution are not clear.

The college of liberal arts is partly high school, partly university, partly general, partly special. Frequently it looks like a teacher-training institution. Frequently it looks like nothing at all. The degree it offers seems to certify that the student has passed an uneventful period without violating any local, state, or federal law, and that he has a fair, if temporary, recollection of what his teachers have said to him. . . . Little pretense is made that many of the things said to him are of much importance.

The university is distinguished from the college by two things: professional schools and the Ph.D. degree. At present we do not know why the university should have professional schools or what they should be like. We do not even know what the professions are. Professional education consists either of going through motions that we have inherited or of making gestures of varying degrees of wildness that we hope may be more effectual. The Ph.D. degree, because it has become a necessary part of the insignia of the college or university teacher, has lost any other meaning. But universities also do research and hope to train research men. The same degree is awarded in recognition of research. The students who are going to be teachers are put through a procedure which was designed to produce investigators. The classes, the courses, the content, and the aims of graduate work are as confused as those of the high school.

For the sake of abbreviation I have of course exaggerated the plight of the higher learning. It has, in fact, many admirable qualities, not the least of which is its friendly reception of anybody who would like to avail himself of it. But we who are devoting our lives to it should learn something from the experience of recent years. Up to the onset of the present depression it was fashionable to call for more and more education. Anything that went by the name of education was a good thing just because it went by that name. I believe that the magic of the name is gone and that we must now present a defensible program if we wish to preserve whatever we have that is of value. Our people, as the last few years have shown, will strike out blindly under economic pressure; they will destroy the best and preserve the worst unless we make the distinction between the two somewhat clearer to them.

If then the problem is to clarify the higher learning, let us examine the causes of its confusion. The first of them is very vulgar; it is the love of money. It is sad but true that when an institution determines to do something in order to get money it must lose its soul, and frequently does not get the money. Money comes to education in three ways — from students, from donors, and from legislatures. To frame a policy in order to appeal to any one of the three is fatal, and, as I have suggested, often futile as well. How much of the current confusion in universities would have been eliminated if boards of trustees had declined gifts which merely reflected the passing whims of wealthy men?

Few restricted gifts have ever been made to a university that paid the expense of receiving them. If men are supported, they are not housed or given the books and equipment they need. If buildings are given, they are not maintained. If they are maintained, they are not manned. From the financial standpoint alone the university may be worse off after the gift than it was before. And from the educational or scientific standpoint it is likely to be unbalanced and confused. Dependence on the casual interests of donors means that nobody can tell from one year to another what a university's policy is. It will become next year whatever somebody is willing to pay to make it. I do not mean, of course, that universities do not need money and that they should not try to get it. I mean only that they should have an educational policy and then try to finance it, instead of letting financial accidents determine their educational policy. . . .

Undoubtedly the love of money and that sensitivity to public demands that it creates has a good deal to do with the service-station conception of a university. According to this conception a university must make itself felt in the community; it must be constantly, currently felt. A state university must help the farmers look after their cows. An endowed university must help adults get better jobs by giving them courses in the afternoon and evening. Yet it is apparent that the kind of professors that are interested in these objects may not be the kind that are interested either in developing education or in advancing knowledge. Since a university will not be able to have two kinds of professors and at the same time remain clear as to what it is about, it must follow that extension work can only confuse the institution.

Little more can be said in justification of the attempt to teach freshmen and sophomores under the same roof and with substantially the same staff as are employed for research and graduate and professional study. Unless we exclude from the first two years all students who are not likely to be scholars and professional men or who deserve unusual opportunities for the cultivation of the mind, we must confuse an institution which should be primarily devoted to scholarship, professional education, and the training of the mind. . . .

There is only one way that I have been able to think of in which a university can entertain freshmen and sophomores and do well by them and by its university obligations at the same time. That is to take the view that the university may well try to help the system of public education by working out for it what a general education ought to be. A general education, I believe, should be given between the junior year in high school and the end of the sophomore year in college. I do not see how the public schools are ever going to command the time and intelligence to develop the organization and content appropriate to general education. I can see how a university faculty might interest itself in the problem and accelerate a solution of it.

But even with such a hope and such an attitude, the complexities of operating the first two years in a university are very serious. In the first place, few universities are so situated as to be interested or influential in the problems of public education. For those who are not so situated, the only answer is the abolition of the freshman and sophomore years. In the second place, even if a university is so situated as to develop a scheme for public education, it is doubtful whether it should do so. A university has enough trouble with the problems of the higher learning. Taking on the burden of philanthropic work, no matter how valuable, can only diminish its effectiveness in its proper field.

By one method, such philanthropy can perhaps be conducted without this sad result: the faculty dealing with general education must be independent of and even isolated from the university, close enough to it to get the advantages of its facilities and a few of its men; remote enough from it to be able to work on its problems without the interference or control of the university faculty and without interfering with or controlling that faculty. It remains to be seen whether any such organization can ever be effected and if so whether it can succeed. Nothing short of it can bring order out of the confusion produced by the conflicting aims of collegiate and university work.

The love of money means that a university must attract students. To do this it must be attractive. This is interpreted to mean that it must go to unusual lengths to house, feed, and amuse the young. Nobody knows what these things have to do with the higher learning. Everybody supposes that students think they are important. The emphasis on athletics and social life that infects all colleges and universities has done more than most things to confuse these institutions and to debase the higher learning in America. . . .

Even more important than the love of money as a cause of our confusion is our confused notion of democracy. This affects the length, the content, and the control of education. According to this notion a student may stay in public education as long as he likes, may study what he likes, and may claim any degree whose alphabetical arrangement appeals to him. According to this notion, education should be immediately responsive to public opinion; its subject matter and methods may be regulated in great detail by the community, by its representatives, or even by its more irresponsible members. . . .

Since an anti-intellectual university is a contradiction in terms, it is no wonder that the theories justifying it are very odd. There is, for instance, the great-man theory of education. Under this theory you pay no attention to what you teach, or indeed to what you investigate. You get great men for your faculty. Their mere presence on the campus inspires, stimulates, and exalts. It matters not how inarticulate their teaching or how recondite their researches; they are, as the saying goes, an education in themselves. This is a variant of the nauseating anecdote about Mark Hopkins on one end of the log and the student on the other. . . .

Another theory we have developed is the character-building theory. It may be that

we don't teach our students anything, but what of it? That isn't our purpose. Our purpose is to turn out well-tubbed young Americans who know how to behave in the American environment. Association with one another, with gentlemanly professors, in beautiful buildings will, along with regular exercise, make our students the kind of citizens our country needs. Since character is the result of choice, it is difficult to see how you can develop it unless you train the mind to make intelligent choices. Collegiate life suggests that the choices of undergraduates are determined by other considerations than thought. Undoubtedly, fine associations, fine buildings, green grass, good food, and exercise are excellent things for anybody. You will note that they are exactly what is advertised by every resort hotel. The only reason why they are also advertised by every college and university is that we have no coherent educational program to announce. . . .

The great-man theory and the character-building theory amount to a denial that there is or should be content to education. Those among us who assert that there is a content to education are almost unanimous in holding that the object of the higher learning is utility, and utility in a very restricted sense. They write articles showing that the educated get better jobs and make more money. Or they advocate changes in education that will, they think, make it more effective in preparing students to get better jobs and make more money. Here we are brought back to the love of money as a cause of our confusion. As the institution's love of money makes it sensitive to every wave of popular opinion, and as the popular opinion is that insofar as education has any object it is economic, both the needs of the universities and the sentiments of the public conspire to degrade the universities into vocational schools. To these then a distorted notion of democracy leads us to admit any and all students; for should not all our youth have equal economic opportunities?

This is the position of the higher learning in America. The universities are dependent on the people. The people love money and think that education is a way of getting it. They think too that democracy means that every child should be permitted to acquire the educational insignia that will be helpful in making money. They do not believe in the cultivation of the intellect for its own sake. And the distressing part of this is that the state of the nation determines the state of education. . . .

If there are permanent studies which every person who wishes to call himself educated should master; if those studies constitute our intellectual inheritance, then those studies should be the center of a general education. They cannot be ignored because they are difficult, or unpleasant, or because they are almost totally missing from our curriculum today. The child-centered school may be attractive to the child, and no doubt is useful as a place in which the little ones may release their inhibitions and hence behave better at home. But educators cannot permit the students to dictate the course of study unless they are prepared to confess that they are nothing but chaperons, supervising an aimless, trial-and-error process which is chiefly valuable because it keeps young people from doing something worse.

The free elective system as Mr. Eliot introduced it at Harvard and as progressive education adapted it to lower age levels amounted to a denial that there was content to education. Since there was no content to education, we might as well let students follow their own bent. They would at least be interested and pleased and would be as well educated as if they had pursued a prescribed course of study. This overlooks the fact that the aim of education is to connect man with man, to connect the present with the past, and to advance the thinking of the race. If this is the aim of education, it cannot be left to the sporadic, spontaneous interests of children or even of undergraduates. . . .

The variations that should be encouraged fall not in the realm of content but in that of method. Allowances for individual differences should be provided for by abolishing all requirements except the examinations and permitting the student to take them whenever in his opinion he is ready to do so. The cultivation of independent thought and study, now almost wholly missing from our program, may thus be somewhat advanced. And this may be done without sacrificing the content of education to the obsessions of the hour or the caprices of the young. . . .

By insisting on the permanent studies as the heart of a general education I do not mean to insist that they are the whole of it. We do not know enough to know whether certain technological work, for example, may not have a certain subsidiary value in general education for some students. Nor do I overlook the fact that since, by hypothesis, general education may be terminal for most students, it must connect them with the present and future as well as with the past. It is as important for them to know that thinking is still going on as it is for them to know what has been thought before.

The question whether certain technical work shall be allowed to be a part of general education is rather a question of method than of content, a question how to teach rather than what. Technology as such has no place in general education. If it can be justified at all, it can only be because we discover that certain principles can best be communicated through technical work. The question of present thought is largely answered by saying that it is impossible to think of a teacher who contented himself with elucidating the thought of the past without intimating that these ideas have a history running to the present day. . . .

Let us avoid all questions of administration and method. Let us assume that we have an intelligible organization of education under which there is a four-year unit, beginning at about the beginning of the junior year in high school and ending at about the end of the sophomore year in college. Let us assume that we are going to try to teach in that unit everybody who can learn from books. Let us assume further that the conclusion of their work in this unit will mark the end of formal instruction for most students. They will not go on to the university. Nevertheless, we must have a curriculum which will, in the main, do as well for those who are going on as those who are not. What shall this curriculum be?

We have excluded body building and character building. We have excluded the social graces and the tricks of trades. We have suggested that the curriculum should be composed principally of the permanent studies. We propose the permanent studies because these studies draw out the elements of our common human nature, because they connect man with man, because they connect us with the best that man has thought, because they are basic to any further study and to any understanding of the world. What are the permanent studies?

They are in the first place those books which have through the centuries attained to the dimensions of classics. Many such books, I am afraid, are in the ancient and medieval period. But even these are contemporary. A classic is a book that is contemporary in every age. That is why it is a classic. The conversations of Socrates raise questions that are as urgent today as they were when Plato wrote. In fact they are more so, because the society in which Plato lived did not need to have them raised as much as we do. We have forgotten how important they are.

Such books are then a part, and a large part, of the permanent studies. They are so, in the first place, because they are the best books we know. . . . In the second place, these books are an essential part of general education because it is impossible to understand any subject or to comprehend the contemporary world without them. . . .

You will observe that the great books of the Western world cover every department of knowledge. The *Republic* of Plato is basic to an understanding of the law; it is equally important as education for what is known as citizenship. The *Physics* of Aristotle, which deals with change and motion in nature, is fundamental to the natural sciences and medicine, and is equally important to all those who confront change and motion in nature, that is, to everybody. Four years spent partly in reading, discussing, and digesting books of such importance would, therefore, contribute equally to preparation for specialized study and to general education of a terminal variety. Certainly four years is none too long for this experience. It is an experience which will . . . serve as preparation for advanced study and as general education designed to help the student understand the world. It will also develop habits of reading and standards of taste and criticism that will enable the adult, after his formal education is over, to think and act intelligently about the thought and movements of contemporary life. It will help him to share in the intellectual activity of his time. . . .

We have then for general education a course of study consisting of the greatest books of the Western world and the arts of reading, writing, thinking, and speaking, together with mathematics, the best exemplar of the processes of human reason. If our hope has been to frame a curriculum which educes the elements of our common human nature, this program should realize our hope. If we wish to prepare the young for intelligent action, this course of study should assist us; for they will have learned what has been done in the past and what the greatest men have thought. They will have learned how to think themselves. If we wish to lay a basis for advanced study, that basis is provided. If we wish to secure true universities, we may look forward to them, because students and professors may acquire through this course of study a common stock of ideas and common methods of dealing with them. All the needs of general education in America seem to be satisfied by this curriculum.

What, then, are the objections to it? They cannot be educational objections; for this course of study appears to accomplish the aims of general education. One objection may be that the students will not like it, which is, as we have seen, irrelevant. But even if it were relevant, it is not true. Since the proposed curriculum is coherent and comprehensible, and since it is free from the triviality that now afflicts our program, students will respond to it if the teachers will give them a chance to do it. . . .

In summary, then, the university would consist of the three faculties — metaphysics, social science, and natural science. The professors would be those who were thinking about the fundamental problems in these fields. The teaching would be directed to understanding the ideas in these fields and would have no vocational aim. The student would study all three subject matters, with emphasis upon one. He would enter upon this program at the beginning of the junior year and continue in it for about three years.

Since it is desirable that the collection of historical and current data should proceed in the vicinity of the university, research institutes in the social and natural sciences may be established in connection with it, though not as part of it. Technical institutes in the same relation to the university may also be created if needed to give practical training for occupations which require a background of special knowledge and facility in special techniques. Students should in no case be admitted to technical or research institutes until they have completed their general and higher education.

We see, then, that we may get order in the higher learning by removing from it the elements which disorder it today, and these are vocationalism and unqualified empiricism. If when these elements are removed we pursue the truth for its own sake in the light of some principle of order, such a metaphysics, we shall have a rational plan for a university. We shall be able to make a university a true center of learning; we shall be able to make it the home of creative thought.

We see, too, that in such a university the dilemmas of the higher learning are resolved. The dilemma of professionalism cannot obstruct us because no distinction is made between the professional and nonprofessional disciplines. They are all studied in the three faculties and studied in the same way. Training in the techniques of the profession is left to the profession or, if necessary, to technical institutes so organized as not to confuse the university.

For somewhat similar reasons the dilemma of isolation will also cease from troubling. Disciplines will not be isolated from one another; they will be united, and by a rational principle. Professors and students will all be pursuing the truth for its own sake; they will know what truths to pursue and why. Since all students will study under all the faculties, the education they acquire will not be piecemeal or miscellaneous; it will be as unified as the university itself.

Even the dilemma of anti-intellectualism is easier to deal with. Anti-intellectualism is so much a part of the temper of the times that it will be difficult to meet this dilemma as squarely or satisfactorily as we can meet the other two. The university that I have been describing is intellectual. It is wholly and completely so. As such, it is the only kind of university worth having. I believe that it will accomplish greater political and professional results than one that is devoted to current events or vocational training.

If the country is not prepared to believe these things, it can get what it wants through the technical and research institutes I have proposed. They are so planned as to draw off the empiricism and vocationalism that have been strangling the universities and to leave them free to do their intellectual job.

If we can secure a real university in this country and a real program of general education upon which its work can rest, it may be that the character of our civilization may slowly change. It may be that we can outgrow the love of money, that we can get a saner conception of democracy, and that we can even understand the purposes of education. It may be that we can abandon our false notions of progress and utility and that we can come to prefer intelligible organization to the chaos that we mistake for liberty. It is because these things may be that education is important. Upon education our country must pin its hopes of true progress, which involves scientific and technological advance, but under the direction of reason; of true prosperity, which includes external goods but does not overlook those of the soul; and of true liberty, which can exist only in society, and in a society rationally ordered.

93.

HORACE M. KALLEN: Toward a Consumer Economy

Horace Kallen's The Decline and Rise of the Consumer, *from which the following selection is taken, was one of a number of books published between 1934 and 1936 offering "consumerism" as a permanent solution of the nation's economic problems. A system in which the consumer supplanted the producer as the prime decision-maker in the economy, consumerism was thought to combine the virtues and avoid the shortcomings of both capitalism and socialism; its main advantage, according to its advocates, was that it could counteract the practice among producers of maintaining high prices by limiting output.*

Source: *The Decline and Rise of the Consumer,* New York, 1936, pp. 415-430.

Range and Drive of the Consumer Interest

CAN THE CONSUMERS' cooperative movement incarnate its vision without doing in its own way the same violence to human nature as its rivals and competitors, without getting involved in the cruelties, the oppressions, the exploitations and injustices which characterize Communism and Fascism as fully, if not more so, as they characterize capitalism?

On the record, if the consumers' cooperative movement cannot, none has yet been born that can. The most serious disability attributed to it has been attributed by its staunchest friends and wisest interpreters. However open in principle the cooperative associations were, and however eager organized cooperators were to draw all sorts and conditions of men into cooperative society, certain sorts and conditions were automatically unable to reach to the advantages of this free association.

To obtain at all, cooperative society presupposes, Mrs. [Beatrice] Webb reasoned, a certain geographical proximity, a certain standard of living, relatively steady employment, and more or less "regular" habits. The casual laborer, moving in short, irregular intervals from job to job and home to home, living at or below the level of subsistence, is too destitute to have even the poor pennies with which the weavers of Rochdale began, too mobile to keep loyal to any organization; and there are millions upon millions of him whose life problem has thus far not been met by the method of cooperation, whether as producer or consumer.

Not only are the multitude of the industrial poor not cooperators; they are not trades unionists. Equally irregular, but for opposite reasons, are the fashionable rich, with their hunt for variety and change. They also stay beyond the reach of voluntary cooperation. Together with the multitudes of the poor, Mrs. Webb thinks, they must be compelled to cooperate, though by different methods. Like children, they must be indoctrinated and disciplined until they have grown into the social maturity needful to voluntary cooperation.

But this judgment, like the judgment of the Webbs regarding the susceptibility of transport, gas- and waterworks and other public utilities to cooperative ownership and control, is too hasty. To date the issue has been abstract and somewhat platonic. In England, neither the cooperative organization of the submerged nor the cooperative ownership and control of public utilities has become a momentous option, requiring a choice. There are still too many people *above* the subsistence level to win to the consumer movement and still too much to do in other directions to bother about deviating from the past on how to own and manage public utilities. And both are even remoter from urgency in other countries. Nowhere have they been faced and studied as practical programs requiring to be implemented and justified against alternatives. Even without a dynamic wisely directed educational establishment, cooperative membership can be at least as voluntary as citizenship is today in free countries; shareowning can be as universal as taxes and the purchase-dividend or usage-profit perhaps even more widespread than share-holding.

For though a few more than one hundred millions of the world's billion of men and women are associated together in one form or another of cooperation, the principle and method of the movement renders it in the nature of things indefinitely expansible. The more it has grown, the more it is able to grow.

Its ways and rules need to be reconciled, not so much with the casualness and destitution of the laboring multitudes as with their mobility. This reconciliation is a problem in the techniques of accountancy; a bookkeeper's problem, and the ingenuity which has solved the perplexities of the credit-enterprise structure can be relied upon to do at least as well for the expansion of cooperation. Public utilities, mines, and railroads can be owned and managed on Rochdale principles no less than fields and factories.

But more than that, the great depression of 1929-1935 has repeated the demonstration of 1844 in Rochdale that even in this new and very different age destitution is no insuperable obstacle. Thus, in 1934, twenty-five or thirty of the unemployed citizens of Grand Island, Nebraska, formed the Grand Island Self-Help Society. They assembled a capital of $24.99, and with this undertook the cooperative serving of their individual needs. A year later their capital had increased by 300 percent, they had goods on their shelves inventoried at five times the original capital, and had sold a second little group of unemployed a "washtub full of groceries" to begin their own cooperative adventure with.

Again, the most depressed section of the population of the United States is the Negro. No workers anywhere in our industrial or agricultural society could be more destitute, marginal, and mobile. In Gary, Indiana, there were 20,000 Negroes, lowest of the low, poorest of the poor. In 1932, half of them were on relief and most of them somehow not in receipt of the relief that was their due. A number fell in the way of discussing the situation, trying to figure out what they could do about it. It was a present situation — present hunger, present thirst, present need for shelter and warmth and medicine. It had to be met now, on the spot. Meeting it couldn't be postponed until after a proletarian revolution or a socialist election or a Ku Klux Klan raid (so that Mother Red Cross could practise her well-known benevolence); hunger and cold and sickness and death wouldn't wait. The one way to deal with them here and now, the discussion revealed, was the cooperative way.

Some twenty families scraped together about $24 and formed a buying club, and in less than a year the buying club grew into a store. It wasn't much of a store. Its directors were millhands and unskilled laborers, out of work; its manager and one clerk were without any experience; it was dark and poorly located and not too clean. The merchants around made fun of it. They predicted it would "go bust" before it started. But it hasn't gone bust. The membership of the now Consumers' Cooperative Trading Company of Gary, Indiana, has increased from 20 to 400. Its turnover for 1935 was more than $35,000; this is greater by one-third than the maximum sales of

the greatest long-established Negro-owned grocery store. It is today the largest Negro-owned grocery store in the United States.

Does it not seem that if either the physical or the psychic urgency is sufficient, no level of human life in the modern world is too low to be reached and lifted by the cooperative movement? But time and place must adhere. A great material urgency or a great spiritual urgency may be required to set the salvational activity in motion. Once started, however, it appears, at least as surely as any other, able to go on its own momentum. The material urgency happens: natural catastrophes, strikes, depressions may be enough to direct self-preserving action into cooperative channels. The spiritual urgency can be induced; there must be the desire to cooperate.

The desire to cooperate can be animated only through an ideal and vision of self-improvement; that is, of a consumer economy. The vision can be brought into action by education on any level of development, that of the child or that of the adult. The feel and form of cooperation may be taught . . . by any kind of organization — state, church, patriotic society, no less than the movement itself. Any may undertake to awaken men and women and children to the meaning of liberty for themselves and its attainment through the organization of liberty in the form of consumers' cooperatives.

The basic point of departure is the fact that the business of a consumer society is able, from the very moment it starts, to furnish from within itself the materials and conditions of its own success. It is one institutional structure which grows by what it feeds on and feeds on itself. For its intent can never be anything but democratic abundance. Founded on the wants of the consumer, it mounts and spreads as they multiply and diversify. This means that "the store" can grow without limit. It is not bound like the producers' organizations of the producer economy by inner and outer competition. Producer societies, no matter how democratically conceived and organized, are always restricted to their own exclusive development: They tend automatically toward monopoly; their prosperity rests on scarcity. Such a scarcity maintains itself, not by endeavoring to do better than the competitor but by destroying the competitor. It lessens jobs for workers as well as goods and quality for consumers.

This is another reason why — apart from those which have become evident in the survey of the function of the organized consumers as employer — a consumer economy is a more desirable thing for the multitude of producers purely as producers. For the multiplication and diversification of wants generates a corresponding multiplication and diversification of occupations. It means, not the shutting out of careers but the opening up of careers; an enlarged opportunity to choose occupations; and, under cooperative rule the completest possible transformation, within the limits of effectiveness, of the servilities inherent in the employer-employee relation into industrial citizenship.

Toughness, Flexibility, and Intelligence of the Cooperative Movement

COMPARED WITH THE CAPITALISM from which it is a variant, and the Socialism, the Fascism, Communism, Nazism, and other forms of state mastery which are its competitors, cooperation has grown more rapidly, more surely, more stably in any measured period than each and all of them. In a hundred years, capitalism had hardly begun to effect the modification of feudal society which the cooperative movement is obviously accomplishing in capitalist society. In fifteen or twenty years, Communism, Fascism, and Nazism have simply depressed

and impoverished the populations whose economies they rule.

Furthermore, the cooperative structure and method reveals itself to be possessed of a flexibility, a toughness which enables it to survive and to grow, without losing its integrity, in every variety of social context. It is not merely that the movement prospers alike in England and in India, in Japan and in Russia, in Ireland and in Denmark, among every variety of race, color, sect and political affiliation. It is that, short of destruction, it is able to survive, even increase, in the noxious atmosphere of Fascist Italy and amid the material and spiritual poisons of Nazi Germany.

To some degree this may be ascribed to the political "neutrality" of the movement, to its policy of avoiding "entangling alliances," to its nonpartisanship. But this "neutrality" itself, it must not be forgotten, is an expression of the very essence of democracy: it follows from the recognition of the parity of opinions, faiths, races, cultures, and other differences which call people to separate and exclusive allegiances. In effect, cooperative neutrality acknowledges the right of each of these to be. It rests upon accepting the individuality of individuals and the inviolability of the individual conscience, and presents itself to individuals and to groups as the method of combining their diversities without sacrificing them; of combining them in such a way that the prosperity of each becomes an enrichment of all and the strengthening of all becomes a reenforcement of each.

In this acknowledgment of the individuality of individuals as the prime dynamic in action resides cooperation's claim to be closer than any other movement to the passions of the human heart. By its technique of reconciling them with one another, of developing action upon a consensus born of free deliberation it allies itself with the scientific social intelligence and establishes itself as the paramount method of economic association which this intelligence has thus far been able to devise.

But the consumer movement may be called intelligent for still other reasons.

One is the immediacy of its action, the fact that the benefits it brings do not need to wait upon a change of heart in individuals or a revolution in society.

Another is that being immediate, this action does not break from the institutional course of events; it merely alters directions and changes forms. The record shows much talk of "production for use," but the prevalence in practice of the idea and feel of private property, profits, and the price system. Resting on the democratic insight of the parity of the different, requiring their equal liberty, the movement cannot wish to replace private property with state ownership. It is aware of the difficulties and dangers that come with the absenteeism intrinsic to public ownership, and its democracy rejects absenteeism. Therefore it combines the principle of individual ownership with associative use. It grows by extending the principle of private property, so that ultimately there shall be no human being so mean as not to feel that he owns, as part and parcel of his proper personal property, enough to meet well the needs of his body and to satisfy the requirements of his soul. Such an extension may bring about a change — undoubtedly it will bring about a change — in the legal form of ownership; but it will intensify and spread, rather than break with, the working psychology of possession.

Consumer cooperation also confronts "the profit motive" intelligently. If profit be the increase which is the more that comes out of the less that has been put in, if profit be the difference between the less possessed and invested and the more desired, whether as material or as psychic income, the profit motive cannot be expunged from the human heart; it can only be redirected. This the cooperative movement does. Its attitude toward profits is its attitude toward property: It may employ another word for the satisfaction of this desire for increase; it may speak of "plenty" or "abundance." But what else are these than the excess of value over investment in labor or goods, the increase which the Bible blesses and all men desire? Without profit in this sense of the word, there cannot be a consumers' economy, a life more abundant. And the general measure of the difference between cost and gain, its bookkeeping and accountancy, so to speak, gets defined in the well-known price system. This too, the consumers' economy preserves, employs, and employing, transforms.

Thus the special technique and ideology of consumers' cooperation tend little by little to effect a profound alteration of capitalist society at its roots in the habits and character of the individual. Conditioned to the attitudes and ways of consumer cooperation, a man will regard property, for example, as personal and private as ever, but its meaning will have changed. As a cooperator, he cannot be a mere absentee owner, receiving rents or dividends; he must be a functional owner, participating in direction and control. He continues to use price as his yardstick, but under cooperative conditions it is a price with consumers' gains, not pecuniary profit. The speculative production of things to sell becomes to him an activity imaginable but not experienced; he knows but the sure production of things not merely to be used, but to be used up, to be consumed. Price figures in his mind alone as the money-sign of the cost of producing, handling and distributing the goods of life under consumer control.

Moreover, because of the primacy of consumption in his psychology, the cooperator becomes more than ever aware of and sensitive to personal differences, the uncontrollable liberty of taste and sensibility, the uniqueness of the personal equation, as well as the mutual contagion and consensus of these equations. Such awareness brings new strength to the democratic principle of voluntary association, the rule of one man, one vote, upon which are based the associative form and government of consumers' cooperatives. Hence, classes, sects, castes, and the like become recessive; they cease to function in his mind as instruments for identifying individuals. He comes more and more to acknowledge individuals in their individuality, and his associative rule changes from "Live and let live" to "Live and help live." . . .

How Cooperatives, Labor Organizations, and Credit Unions Can Converge into a Consumer Economy

Now, A CONSUMERS' ECONOMY distinguishes itself from a producers' in that it does not regard work either as a right or a duty; it regards work as a means. The one right paramount upon which it seeks to rebuild the world's economy is the right to the good life. Consumers' cooperation treats production purely as an occasion or a condition or an instrument of consumption. Hence within the framework of consumers' cooperation there cannot occur between organized consumers and organized producers that exacerbated conflict about hours, wages and conditions of labor which keeps breaking into non-cooperative economies. Employers and employees being simply the same people in different roles, a consumers' economy would have neither place nor reason for the separation of labor from leisure. True, we are consumers by nature and producers by necessity; perhaps production is but a necessary evil that we would not suffer in a world which was made for us; but it does not follow that the natural conflict between our disposition and our necessities need extend beyond our individual hearts. The interval stretching from desire, through labor, to the satisfaction of desire need not be so long and so difficult as the prevailing

producers' economy has made and keeps it, even in so-called communist societies.

That leisure which gives managements and stockholders access at will to the sports, the arts, the sciences, can without conflict be extended to all employees. In a consumers' economy employing the implements and resources of modern technology, no member of the consumers' society need be under the divine curse to earn his bread by the sweat of his face for more than ten or twenty years of his life. All may enjoy the blessings of leisure from birth to their twentieth year, and from their fortieth year till they die.

Inasmuch as everyone would be a personal owner of the tools and materials of collective production, he would, as owner, exercise the rights of property as they are currently understood but without the disposition toward the creation of artificial scarcity which poisons this exercise at the source. He would be an employer, but, at the same time, he would be a worker, working, however, not for another first but for himself first. In feeling as well as in fact, he would be his own employer and his own employee. The invidious distinctions between those who live without working and those who work without living would disappear. They would be replaced by emulative distinctions of skilled effort toward the enhancement of life. The daily duration of this effort, moreover, and the number of years would, if the theoretical and technological control of nature continues to advance as it has, become automatically smaller. The dream of a four-hour day would realize itself at least as certainly as Ira Steward's dream of the eight-hour day.

The steps by which this condition might be reached can be sketched broadly, even if the details can be determined only after some of the steps have been taken.

They would start at three points and converge into the consumer economy. The first is the existing cooperative organization as a going concern. The inner subordination of all other interests — farmer, producer, credit — to the consumer interest, and the rapid and planned multiplication and confederation of consumer societies can develop with increasing precision and security.

The second is organized labor. Although the use of consumer organization as the "commissary department" of the trades-union struggle with the employer must necessarily be transitional, it can add significant speed to the transition from the producer to the consumer economy. Trades-unionists are in a position greatly to strengthen their bargaining power, to bring the immediate trades-union objectives more readily within their reach, to increase real wages and considerably to enlarge the lives of their members by devoting themselves seriously to consumer organization.

Lever's campaign of collective bargaining pressed simultaneously at the two poles of the national economy — production and consumption — would, if consistently and wisely conducted, bring about an enormous expansion of the lives and liberties of the working multitudes. For the good life is at once a function of its material conditions, its comforts, easements and luxuries; and of the leisure they make possible, the energies they set free to pursue other ends than a mere livelihood. Such dual collective bargaining would on the one hand rapidly raise the standards and conditions of employment which concern the consumer as worker; improving wages and hours and greatly widening the area of trades-union organization; on the other hand it would invincibly enrich the standards of living, which concerns the worker as consumer.

The third point is the financial surplus of the multitudes. The unexpended pennies of farmers, wage earners, white-collar workers, like the little drops of water and the little grains of sand which make the mighty ocean and the continental land, are the substantial pecuniary wealth of the nation. They constitute, as has been already noted, an accumulating surplus, pressing for investment; held by private savings banks and insurance companies and used primarily for the pecuniary advantage of the bankers, insurance men and their ilk. These pennies are a surplus of unspent wages, not unspent profits or interest or rent; their spending by the professional financier is done at the depositor's risk, not the financier's. Nor does it bring the depositor any return in the enrichment and expansion of life. If the spending were cooperative, such a return would be automatic. The application of the consumer principle and the cooperative method to the employment of this financial surplus by extending cooperative distribution and production would be a powerful engine in the modification of the competitive-producer into a cooperative-consumer economy.

Through the multiplication of cooperative banks and credit unions, and the widening of their range and powers under legal safeguards, the savings of the working multitudes could be employed to dissipate the invidious distinctions, the dependence and servility which these savings now serve to maintain. More and more employees would become their own bankers and their own employers. More and more members of the younger generation would from childhood on be enabled to grow up in purely cooperative setting and acquire the habits and outlook of the cooperative way of life.

***

Democracy is based upon the conviction that there are extraordinary possibilities in ordinary people.

HARRY EMERSON FOSDICK

94.

CARL SANDBURG: The People, Yes

The People, Yes is Sandburg's epic of America. Unique in form, it contains stories and jokes, descriptions and perorations, lyrical passages and folk sayings. Sandburg himself described it: "Being several stories and psalms nobody would want to laugh at interspersed with memoranda variations worth a second look along with sayings and yarns traveling on grief and laughter running sometimes as a fugitive air in the classic manner breaking into jig time and tap dancing nohow classical and further broken by plain and irregular sounds and echoes from the roar and whirl of street crowds, work gangs, sidewalk clamor, with interludes of midnight cool blue and inviolable stars over the phantom frames of skyscrapers." Portions of the poem — it is of book length — are reprinted here.

Source: *Complete Poems*, New York, 1950, pp. 458-460.

❧ THE PEOPLE, YES

A father sees a son nearing manhood.
What shall he tell that son?
"Life is hard; be steel; be a rock."
And this might stand him for the storms
and serve him for humdrum and monotony
and guide him amid sudden betrayals
and tighten him for slack moments.
"Life is a soft loam; be gentle; go easy."
And this too might serve him.
Brutes have been gentled where lashes failed.
The growth of a frail flower in a path up
has sometimes shattered and split a rock.
A tough will counts. So does desire.
So does a rich soft wanting.
Without rich wanting nothing arrives.
Tell him too much money has killed men
and left them dead years before burial:
the quest of lucre beyond a few easy needs
has twisted good enough men
sometimes into dry thwarted worms.
Tell him time as a stuff can be wasted.
Tell him to be a fool every so often
and to have no shame over having been a fool

yet learning something out of every folly
hoping to repeat none of the cheap follies
thus arriving at intimate understanding
of a world numbering many fools.
Tell him to be alone often and get at himself
and above all tell himself no lies about himself
whatever the white lies and protective fronts
he may use amongst other people.
Tell him solitude is creative if he is strong
and the final decisions are made in silent rooms.
Tell him to be different from other people
if it comes natural and easy being different.
Let him have lazy days seeking his deeper motives.
Let him seek deep for where he is a born natural.
    Then he may understand Shakespeare
    and the Wright brothers, Pasteur, Pavlov,
    Michael Faraday and free imaginations
bringing changes into a world resenting change.
      He will be lonely enough
      to have time for the work
      he knows as his own.

        . . . . .

      They have yarns
    Of a skyscraper so tall they had to put hinges
    On the two top stories so to let the moon go by,
    Of one corn crop in Missouri when the roots
    Went so deep and drew off so much water
    The Mississippi riverbed that year was dry,
    Of pancakes so thin they had only one side,
Of "a fog so thick we shingled the barn and six feet out on the fog,"
Of Pecos Pete straddling a cyclone in Texas and riding it to the
    west coast where "it rained out under him,"
Of the man who drove a swarm of bees across the Rocky Mountains
    and the Desert "and didn't lose a bee,"
Of a mountain railroad curve where the engineer in his cab can
    touch the caboose and spit in the conductor's eye,
Of the boy who climbed a cornstalk growing so fast he would
    have starved to death if they hadn't shot biscuits up to him,
Of the old man's whiskers: "When the wind was with him his
    whiskers arrived a day before he did,"
Of the hen laying a square egg and cackling, "Ouch!" and of
    hens laying eggs with the dates printed on them,
Of the ship captain's shadow: it froze to the deck one cold winter night,
Of mutineers on that same ship put to chipping rust with rubber hammers,
Of the sheep counter who was fast and accurate: "I just count
    their feet and divide by four,"

Of the man so tall he must climb a ladder to shave himself,
Of the runt so teeny-weeny it takes two men and a boy to see him,
Of mosquitoes: one can kill a dog, two of them a man,
Of a cyclone that sucked cookstoves out of the kitchen, up the
      chimney flue, and on to the next town,
Of the same cyclone picking up wagon-tracks in Nebraska and
      dropping them over in the Dakotas,
Of the hook-and-eye snake unlocking itself into forty pieces,
      each piece two inches long, then in nine seconds flat
      snapping itself together again,
Of the watch swallowed by the cow — when they butchered her
      a year later the watch was running and had the correct time,
Of horned snakes, hoop snakes that roll themselves where they
      want to go, and rattlesnakes carrying bells instead of rattles
      on their tails,
Of the herd of cattle in California getting lost in a giant redwood
      tree that had hollowed out,
Of the man who killed a snake by putting its tail in its mouth
      so it swallowed itself,
Of railroad trains whizzing along so fast they reach the station
      before the whistle,
Of pigs so thin the farmer had to tie knots in their tails to keep
      them from crawling through the cracks in their pens,
Of Paul Bunyan's big blue ox, Babe, measuring between the eyes
      forty-two ax-handles and a plug of Star tobacco exactly,
Of John Henry's hammer and the curve of its swing and his
      singing of it as "a rainbow round my shoulder."

               "Do tell!"
               "I want to know!"
               "You don't say so!"
               "For the land's sake!"
               "Gosh all fish-hooks!"
               "Tell me some more.
               I don't believe a word you say
               but I love to listen
               to your sweet harmonica
               to your chin-music.
               Your fish stories hang together
               when they're just a pack of lies:
               you ought to have a leather medal:
               you ought to have a statue
               carved of butter: you deserve
               a large bouquet of turnips."

               "Yessir," the traveler drawled,
               "Away out there in the petrified forest
               everything goes on the same as usual.

The petrified birds sit in their petrified nests
and hatch their petrified young from petrified eggs."

A high pressure salesman jumped off the Brooklyn Bridge and
was saved by a policeman. But it didn't take him long to sell
the idea to the policeman. So together they jumped off the bridge.

One of the oil men in heaven started a rumor of a gusher down
in hell. All the other oil men left in a hurry for hell. As he
gets to thinking about the rumor he had started he says to
himself there might be something in it after all. So he leaves for hell in a hurry.

"The number 42 will win this raffle, that's my number." And
when he won they asked him whether he guessed the number or had a system. He said he had a system, "I took up
the old family album and there on page 7 was my grand-
father and grandmother both on page 7. I said to myself this
is easy for 7 times 7 is the number that will win and 7 times 7 is 42."

Once a shipwrecked sailor caught hold of a stateroom door and
floated for hours till friendly hands from out of the darkness
threw him a rope. And he called across the night, "What
country is this?" and hearing voices answer, "New Jersey,"
he took a fresh hold on the floating stateroom door and
called back half-wearily, "I guess I'll float a little farther."

An Ohio man bundled up the tin roof of a summer kitchen and
sent it to a motor car maker with a complaint of his car not
giving service. In three weeks a new car arrived for him and
a letter: "We regret delay in shipment but your car was
received in a very bad order."
A Dakota cousin of this Ohio man sent six years of tin can
accumulations to the same works, asking them to overhaul
his car. Two weeks later came a rebuilt car, five old tin cans,
and a letter: "We are also forwarding you five parts not
necessary in our new model."
Thus fantasies heard at filling stations in the midwest. Another
relates to a Missouri mule who took aim with his heels at an
automobile rattling by. The car turned a somersault, lit next
a fence, ran right along through a cornfield till it came to a
gate, moved onto the road and went on its way as though
nothing had happened. The mule heehawed with desolation,
"What's the use?"
Another tells of a farmer and his family stalled on a railroad
crossing, how they jumped out in time to see a limited
express knock it into flinders, the farmer calling, "Well, I
always did say that car was no shucks in a real pinch."
When the Masonic Temple in Chicago was the tallest building

in the United States west of New York, two men who would
cheat the eyes out of you if you gave 'em a chance, took an
Iowa farmer to the top of the building and asked him, "How
is this for high?" They told him that for $25 they would go
down in the basement and turn the building around on its
turn-table for him while he stood on the roof and saw how
this seventh wonder of the world worked. He handed them
$25. They went. He waited. They never came back.
This is told in Chicago as a folk tale, the same as the legend of
      Mrs. O'Leary's cow kicking over the barn lamp that started
      the Chicago fire, when the Georgia visitor, Robert Toombs,
      telegraphed an Atlanta crony, "Chicago is on fire, the whole
      city burning down, God be praised!"

Nor is the prize sleeper Rip Van Winkle and his scolding wife
      forgotten, nor the headless horseman scooting through Sleepy Hollow
Nor the sunken treasure-ships in coves and harbors, the hideouts
      of gold and silver sought by Coronado, nor the Flying
      Dutchman rounding the Cape doomed to nevermore pound
      his ear nor ever again take a snooze for himself
Nor the sailor's caretaker Mother Carey seeing to it that every
      seafaring man in the afterworld has a seabird to bring him
      news of ships and women, an albatross for the admiral, a gull for the deckhand
Nor the sailor with a sweetheart in every port of the world, nor
      the ships that set out with flying colors and all the promises
      you could ask, the ships never heard of again,
Nor Jim Liverpool, the riverman who could jump across any
      river and back without touching land he was that quick on his feet,
Nor Mike Fink along the Ohio and the Mississippi, half wild
      horse and half cock-eyed alligator, the rest of him snags and
      snapping turtle. "I can out-run, out-jump, out-shoot,
      out-brag, out-drink, and out-fight, rough and tumble, no holts
      barred, any man on both sides of the river from Pittsburgh
      to New Orleans and back again to St. Louis. My trigger
      finger itches and I want to go redhot. War, famine and
      bloodshed puts flesh on my bones, and hardship's my daily bread."
Nor the man so lean he threw no shadow: six rattlesnakes struck
      at him at one time and every one missed him.

                    · · · · ·

                  The people will live on.
        The learning and blundering people will live on.
              They will be tricked and sold and again sold
          And go back to the nourishing earth for rootholds,
              The people so peculiar in renewal and comeback,
              You can't laugh off their capacity to take it.
        The mammoth rests between his cyclonic dramas.

The people so often sleepy, weary, enigmatic,
is a vast huddle with many units saying:
    "I earn my living.
    I make enough to get by
    and it takes all my time.
    If I had more time
    I could do more for myself
    and maybe for others.
    I could read and study
    and talk things over
    and find out about things.
    It takes time.
    I wish I had the time."

The people is a tragic and comic two-face:
hero and hoodlum: phantom and gorilla twist-
ing to moan with a gargoyle mouth: "They
buy me and sell me . . . it's a game . . .
sometime I'll break loose . . ."

        Once having marched
      Over the margins of animal necessity,
      Over the grim line of sheer subsistence
          Then man came
      To the deeper rituals of his bones,
      To the lights lighter than any bones,
      To the time for thinking things over,
      To the dance, the song, the story,
      Or the hours given over to dreaming,
         Once having so marched.

Between the finite limitations of the five senses
and the endless yearnings of man for the beyond
the people hold to the humdrum bidding of work and food
while reaching out when it comes their way
for lights beyond the prison of the five senses,
for keepsakes lasting beyond any hunger or death.
    This reaching is alive.
The panderers and liars have violated and smutted it.
    Yet this reaching is alive yet
    for lights and keepsakes.

        The people know the salt of the sea
        and the strength of the winds
        lashing the corners of the earth.
        The people take the earth
        as a tomb of rest and a cradle of hope.

Who else speaks for the Family of Man?
They are in tune and step
with constellations of universal law.

The people is a polychrome,
a spectrum and a prism
held in a moving monolith,
a console organ of changing themes,
a clavilux of color poems
wherein the sea offers fog
and the fog moves off in rain
and the labrador sunset shortens
to a nocturne of clear stars
serene over the shot spray
of northern lights.

The steel mill sky is alive.
The fire breaks white and zigzag
shot on a gun-metal gloaming.
Man is a long time coming.
Man will yet win.
Brother may yet line up with brother:

This old anvil laughs at many broken hammers.
There are men who can't be bought.
The fireborn are at home in fire.
The stars make no noise.
You can't hinder the wind from blowing.
Time is a great teacher.
Who can live without hope?

In the darkness with a great bundle of grief
    the people march.
In the night, and overhead a shovel of stars for
    keeps, the people march:

                    "Where to? what next?"

"California" by Dorothea Lange for the Farm Security Administration, 1936

ART AND SOCIETY

Of the government-supported public works programs that were instituted under New Deal agencies, the Federal Arts Projects of the Works Progress Administration were, collectively, probably the most interesting and, in the long run, the most significant. Thousands of unemployed artists and intellectuals were paid basic wages by the government for various creative or research projects. The Federal Theater Project sent troupes into small cities and towns unfamiliar with the stage, and produced some original works. The Writers Project devoted itself to a series of State Guides that included descriptive material, history, folklore, and photography. Artists, many of them notable in their own right, painted murals for public buildings. Musicians formed traveling orchestras. Comprehensive indexes were made for American music and composers and for American design. Despite the decadence that many claimed to see in the projects, there is no doubt that they, together with the photography done for the Farm Security Administration, were important both in spreading an awareness of culture in America and in the concerted effort they made to discover America artistically.

(Above) "Lighthouse at Two Lights" by Edward Hopper, whose stark realism dominated his painting of the American scene

Regionalism and social comment were the identifying characteristics of Thomas Hart Benton and Reginald Marsh, respectively. (Right) Benton's "Cotton Pickers, Georgia," and (below) "The Park Bench" by Marsh were both painted in the early 1930s

A growing concern with the American nvironment had been markedly present in American art for a decade or more when he Depression struck. Two strains had de- eloped, the regional approach of Benton, Wood, and Curry, and the urban school f realism of Hopper and Burchfield. While the government art projects of the WPA, devoted to "The American Scene," ffected primarily the regional school, the Depression itself prompted a rapid growth f social content in art.

Top) Grant Wood's portrayal of "Daughters of he Revolution," 1932; (right) "The Feast of Pure Reason" by Jack Levine, 1937, for WPA; bottom) "The Senate" by William Gropper, 935

Paintings done under the sponsorship of the federal government's Works Progress Administration:
(Above) John Steuart Curry's mural of John Brown done for the State Capitol, Topeka, Kan., 1940;
(below) "Western Town" by Jeune Magatow; included in an exhibit of WPA art

wo photographs from a study of the Depression for the Farm Security Administration by photographers
f the 1930s: (Above) Negro tenant farmer (rehabilitation client) in Jefferson Co., Kansas, photo-
raphed by John Vachon; (below) Mississippi plantation owner photographed by Dorothea Lange

The FSA study of the Depression covered all parts of the United States. Artist Ben Shahn was one o many who worked for the government-sponsored project. He recorded a street scene in Smithsband Kentucky (above) and one in New Orleans, Louisiana, (below)

Two photographs by Walker Evans: (Above) Negroes in front of a shop in Vicksburg, Miss.; (below) "The Gudger Family" included in James Agee's book, "Let Us Now Praise Famous Men" which told of the two men's experiences while collecting material for a magazine article in Alabama

One rather clear effect of the Depression, and a salutary one, was a renewal of the writer's involvement with society and culture in the broad sense. The temporary exile of the Twenties ended, and the human reality beneath, behind, and aside from the clap-trap of commercial, middle-class America was rediscovered. Released from the essentially private themes of an alienated generation, literature regained a balance of the personal and the social in its portrayal of American life.

(Top left) Literary critic Van Wyck Brooks; (top right) author Theodore Dreiser in 1935; (left) playwright Eugene O'Neill; (bottom left) John Dos Passos, author of "U.S.A.," published in the Thirties; (bottom right) Willa Cather, whose novels dealt with frontier life

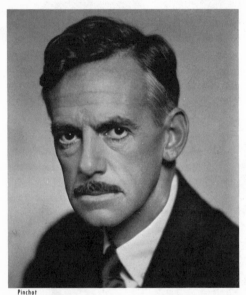

(Above) Thomas Wolfe sorting one of his manu-
cripts; (below) John Steinbeck, who wrote of the
Okie migration to California in the 1930s

(Above) James T. Farrell, whose trilogy about
"Studs Lonigan" focused on life among lower
middle-class Irish in Chicago during the 1930s;
(below) William Faulkner, author of many books
dealing with the decline of Southern culture

Four poets of the interwar years: (Above left) E. E. Cummings, an individualistic romantic who occasionally satirized the excesses of commercial "manunkind"; Robinson Jeffers, a violent chronicler of civilization in decay; (below left) Robert Frost, who developed deep metaphysical insight from spare New England images of unrivaled clarity; Ezra Pound, a major liberating force in American poetry since before World War I, was consumed by an obscure fixation on "usury" and the Jews

1937

95.

Supreme Court Reform

By the summer of 1936 the Supreme Court, acting as a conservative political force, had invalidated a number of important New Deal measures, and had in fact denied federal authority over agriculture, manufacturing, labor, and mining. Interpreting his landslide victory in November 1936 as a mandate for his program, Roosevelt decided the time had come to call the Court to a public reckoning. On February 5, 1937, the President submitted a judiciary reform bill to Congress that would have enabled him to appoint six new justices. On March 9 he addressed the nation in the speech reprinted below. The reform measure stirred up a public and congressional storm that is said to have surprised even Roosevelt, and within the year his so-called court-packing scheme was defeated. The adverse report of the Senate Judiciary Committee, issued on June 14, is reprinted here in part. Sometime during the controversy the Court itself apparently underwent a change in attitude, and its decisions became more sympathetic to New Deal legislation.

Source: 75 Congress, 1 Session, Senate Report No. 711, pp. 41-45; 1-23.

FRANKLIN D. ROOSEVELT:
Address to the People

TONIGHT, SITTING AT MY DESK in the White House, I make my first radio report to the people in my second term of office.

I am reminded of that evening in March four years ago when I made my first radio report to you. We were then in the midst of the great banking crisis. Soon after, with the authority of the Congress, we asked the nation to turn over all of its privately held gold, dollar for dollar, to the government of the United States. Today's recovery proves how right that policy was.

But when, almost two years later, it came before the Supreme Court, its constitutionality was upheld only by a 5-to-4 vote. The change of one vote would have thrown all the affairs of this great nation back into helpless chaos. In effect, four justices ruled that the right under a private contract to exact a pound of flesh was more sacred than the main objectives of the Constitution to establish an enduring nation.

In 1933 you and I knew that we must never let our economic system get completely out of joint again — that we could not afford to take the risk of another great depression. We also became convinced that the only way to avoid a repetition of those dark days was to have a government with power to prevent and to cure the abuses and the inequalities which had thrown that system out of joint. We then began a program of remedying those abuses and inequalities — to give balance and stability to our economic system; to make it bomb-proof against the causes of 1929.

Today we are only part way through that program; and recovery is speeding up to a point where the dangers of 1929 are again becoming possible, not this week or month perhaps, but within a year or two. National laws are needed to complete that program. Individual or local or state effort alone cannot protect us in 1937 any better than ten years ago.

It will take time — and plenty of time — to work out our remedies administratively even after legislation is passed. To complete our program of protection in time, therefore, we cannot delay one moment in making certain that our national government has power to carry through.

Four years ago action did not come until the eleventh hour. It was almost too late.

If we learned anything from the Depression we will not allow ourselves to run around in new circles of futile discussion and debate, always postponing the day of decision.

The American people have learned from the Depression. For in the last three national elections an overwhelming majority of them voted a mandate that the Congress and the President begin the task of providing that protection — not after long years of debate, but now.

The courts, however, have cast doubts on the ability of the elected Congress to protect us against catastrophe by meeting squarely our modern social and economic conditions. We are at a crisis in our ability to proceed with that protection. It is a quiet crisis. There are no lines of depositors outside closed banks. But to the farsighted it i[s] far-reaching in its possibilities of injury t[o] America.

I want to talk with you very simpl[y] about the need for present action in this cri sis — the need to meet the unanswere[d] challenge of one-third of a nation ill nourished, ill-clad, ill-housed.

Last Thursday I described the America[n] form of government as a three-horse tea[m] provided by the Constitution to the Ameri can people so that their field might b[e] plowed. The three horses are, of course, th[e] three branches of government — the Congress, the executive, and the courts. Two o[f] the horses are pulling in unison today; th[e] third is not. Those who have intimated tha[t] the President of the United States is trying to drive that team overlook the simple fac[t] that the President, as Chief Executive, i[s] himself one of the three horses.

It is the American people themselves wh[o] are in the driver's seat. It is the American people themselves who want the furrow plowed. It is the American people themselves who expect the third horse to pull i[n] unison with the other two.

I hope that you have reread the Constitution of the United States. Like the Bible, it ought to be read again and again. It is a[n] easy document to understand when you remember that it was called into being because the Articles of Confederation unde[r] which the original thirteen states tried t[o] operate after the Revolution showed the need of a national government with power enough to handle national problems. In its Preamble the Constitution states that it was intended to form a more perfect Union and promote the general welfare; and the powers given to the Congress to carry out those purposes can be best described by saying that they were all the powers needed to meet each and every problem which then had a national character and which could not be met by merely local action.

But the framers went further. Having in mind that in succeeding generations many other problems then undreamed of would become national problems, they gave to the Congress the ample broad powers "to levy taxes . . . and provide for the common defense and general welfare of the United States."

That, my friends, is what I honestly believe to have been the clear and underlying purpose of the patriots who wrote a federal Constitution to create a national government with national power, intended as they said, "to form a more perfect union . . . for ourselves and our posterity."

For nearly twenty years there was no conflict between the Congress and the Court. Then, in 1803, Congress passed a statute which the Court said violated an express provision of the Constitution. The Court claimed the power to declare it unconstitutional and did so declare it. But a little later the Court itself admitted that it was an extraordinary power to exercise and through Mr. Justice Washington laid down this limitation upon it: "It is but a decent respect due to the wisdom, the integrity, and the patriotism of the legislative body, by which any law is passed, to presume in favor of its validity until its violation of the Constitution is proved beyond all reasonable doubt."

But since the rise of the modern movement for social and economic progress through legislation, the Court has more and more often and more and more boldly asserted a power to veto laws passed by the Congress and state legislatures in complete disregard of this original limitation. In the last four years the sound rule of giving statutes the benefit of all reasonable doubt has been cast aside. The Court has been acting, not as a judicial body, but as a policy-making body.

When the Congress has sought to stabilize national agriculture, to improve the conditions of labor, to safeguard business against unfair competition, to protect our national resources, and in many other ways to serve our clearly national needs, the ma-

Culver Pictures, Inc.

"No Boost for the Administration Make-Up Department"; cartoon in the "New York Tribune" in 1937 in reaction to FDR's court reform plan

jority of the Court has been assuming the power to pass on the wisdom of these acts of the Congress — and to approve or disapprove the public policy written into these laws.

That is not only my accusation. It is the accusation of most distinguished justices of the present Supreme Court. I have not the time to quote to you all the language used by dissenting justices in many of these cases. But in the case holding the Railroad Retirement Act unconstitutional, for instance, Chief Justice Hughes said in a dissenting opinion that the majority opinion was "a departure from sound principles," and placed "an unwarranted limitation upon the commerce clause." And three other justices agreed with him.

In the case holding the AAA unconstitutional, Justice Stone said of the majority opinion that it was a "tortured construction of the Constitution." And two other justices agreed with him.

In the case holding the New York Minimum Wage Law unconstitutional, Justice Stone said that the majority were actually reading into the Constitution their own "personal economic predilections," and that if the legislative power is not left free to choose the methods of solving the problems of poverty, subsistence, and health of large numbers in the community, then "government is to be rendered impotent." And two other justices agreed with him.

In the face of these dissenting opinions, there is no basis for the claim made by some members of the Court that something in the Constitution has compelled them regretfully to thwart the will of the people. In the face of such dissenting opinions, it is perfectly clear that as Chief Justice Hughes has said, "We are under a Constitution, but the Constitution is what the judges say it is."

The Court, in addition to the proper use of its judicial functions, has improperly set itself up as a third House of the Congress — a superlegislature, as one of the justices has called it — reading into the Constitution words and implications which are not there and which were never intended to be there.

We have, therefore, reached the point as a nation where we must take action to save the Constitution from the Court and the Court from itself. We must find a way to take an appeal from the Supreme Court to the Constitution itself. We want a Supreme Court which will do justice under the Constitution — not over it. In our courts we want a government of laws and not of men.

I want — as all Americans want — an independent judiciary as proposed by the framers of the Constitution. That means a Supreme Court that will enforce the Constitution as written — that will refuse to amend the Constitution by the arbitrary exercise of judicial power — amendment by judicial say-so. It does not mean a judiciary so independent that it can deny the existence of facts universally recognized.

How, then, could we proceed to perform the mandate given us? It was said in last year's Democratic platform, "If these prob-

lems cannot be effectively solved within the Constitution, we shall seek such clarifying amendment as will assure the power to enact those laws, adequately to regulate commerce, protect public health and safety, and safeguard economic security." In other words, we said we would seek an amendment only if every other possible means by legislation were to fail.

When I commenced to review the situation with the problem squarely before me, I came by a process of elimination to the conclusion that short of amendments the only method which was clearly constitutional, and would at the same time carry out other much-needed reforms, was to infuse new blood into all our courts. We must have men worthy and equipped to carry out impartial justice. But at the same time we must have judges who will bring to the courts a present-day sense of the Constitution — judges who will retain in the courts the judicial functions of a court and reject the legislative powers which the courts have today assumed.

In forty-five out of the forty-eight states of the Union, judges are chosen not for life but for a period of years. In many states judges must retire at the age of seventy. Congress has provided financial security by offering life pensions at full pay for federal judges on all courts who are willing to retire at seventy. In the case of Supreme Court justices, that pension is $20,000 a year. But all federal judges, once appointed, can, if they choose, hold office for life no matter how old they may get to be.

What is my proposal? It is simply this: Whenever a judge or justice of any federal court has reached the age of seventy and does not avail himself of the opportunity to retire on a pension, a new member shall be appointed by the President then in office, with the approval, as required by the Constitution, of the Senate of the United States.

That plan has two chief purposes: By bringing into the judicial system a steady and continuing stream of new and younger blood, I hope, first, to make the administration of all federal justice speedier and therefore less costly; second, to bring to the decision of social and economic problems younger men who have had personal experience and contact with modern facts and circumstances under which average men have to live and work. This plan will save our national Constitution from hardening of the judicial arteries.

The number of judges to be appointed would depend wholly on the decision of present judges now over seventy or those who would subsequently reach the age of seventy. If, for instance, any one of the six justices of the Supreme Court now over the age of seventy should retire as provided under the plan, no additional place would be created. Consequently, although there never can be more than fifteen, there may be only fourteen, or thirteen, or twelve, and there may be only nine.

There is nothing novel or radical about this idea. It seeks to maintain the federal bench in full vigor. It has been discussed and approved by many persons of high authority ever since a similar proposal passed the House of Representatives in 1869.

Why was the age fixed at seventy? Because the laws of many states, the practice of the civil service, the regulations of the Army and Navy, and the rules of many of our universities and of almost every great private business enterprise commonly fix the retirement age at seventy years or less.

The statute would apply to all the courts in the federal system. There is general approval so far as the lower federal courts are concerned. The plan has met opposition only so far as the Supreme Court of the United States itself is concerned. If such a plan is good for the lower courts, it certainly ought to be equally good for the highest court, from which there is no appeal.

Those opposing this plan have sought to arouse prejudice and fear by crying that I am seeking to "pack" the Supreme Court

and that a baneful precedent will be established.

What do they mean by the words "packing the Court"?

Let me answer this question with a bluntness that will end all honest misunderstanding of my purposes.

If by that phrase, "packing the Court," it is charged that I wish to place on the bench spineless puppets who would disregard the law and would decide specific cases as I wished them to be decided, I make this answer: that no President fit for his office would appoint, and no Senate of honorable men fit for their office would confirm, that kind of appointees to the Supreme Court.

But if by that phrase the charge is made that I would appoint and the Senate would confirm justices worthy to sit beside present members of the Court who understand those modern conditions; that I will appoint justices who will not undertake to override the judgment of the Congress on legislative policy; that I will appoint justices who will act as justices and not as legislators — if the appointment of such justices can be called "packing the Courts" — then I say that I, and with me the vast majority of the American people, favor doing just that thing — now.

Is it a dangerous precedent for the Congress to change the number of the justices? The Congress has always had, and will have, that power. The number of justices has been changed several times before — in the administrations of John Adams and Thomas Jefferson, both signers of the Declaration of Independence, Andrew Jackson, Abraham Lincoln, and Ulysses S. Grant.

I suggest only the addition of justices to the bench in accordance with a clearly defined principle relating to a clearly defined age limit. Fundamentally, if in the future America cannot trust the Congress it elects to refrain from abuse of our constitutional usages, democracy will have failed far beyond the importance to it of any kind of precedent concerning the judiciary.

We think it so much in the public interest to maintain a vigorous judiciary that we encourage the retirement of elderly judges by offering them a life pension at full salary. Why then should we leave the fulfillment of this public policy to chance or make it dependent upon the desire or prejudice of any individual justice?

It is the clear intention of our public policy to provide for a constant flow of new and younger blood into the judiciary. Normally, every President appoints a large number of district and circuit judges and a few members of the Supreme Court. Until my first term practically every President of the United States had appointed at least one member of the Supreme Court. President Taft appointed five members and named a chief justice; President Wilson, three; President Harding, four, including a chief justice; President Coolidge, one; President Hoover, three, including a chief justice.

Such a succession of appointments should have provided a Court well balanced as to age. But chance and the disinclination of individuals to leave the Supreme Bench have now given us a Court in which five justices will be over seventy-five years of age before next June and one over seventy. Thus a sound public policy has been defeated.

I now propose that we establish by law an assurance against any such ill-balanced Court in the future. I propose that hereafter, when a judge reaches the age of seventy, a new and younger judge shall be added to the Court automatically. In this way I propose to enforce a sound public policy by law instead of leaving the composition of our federal courts, including the highest, to be determined by chance or the personal decision of individuals. If such a law as I propose is regarded as establishing a new precedent, is it not a most desirable precedent?

Like all lawyers, like all Americans, I regret the necessity of this controversy. But the welfare of the United States, and indeed of the Constitution itself, is what we all must think about first. Our difficulty with the Court today rises not from the Court as an institution but from human beings within it. But we cannot yield our constitutional destiny to the personal judgment of a few men who, being fearful of the future, would deny us the necessary means of dealing with the present.

This plan of mine is no attack on the Court; it seeks to restore the Court to its rightful and historic place in our system of constitutional government and to have it resume its high task of building anew on the Constitution "a system of living law."

I have thus explained to you the reasons that lie behind our efforts to secure results by legislation within the Constitution. I hope that thereby the difficult process of constitutional amendment may be rendered unnecessary. But let us examine that process.

There are many types of amendment proposed. Each one is radically different from the other. There is no substantial group within the Congress or outside it who are agreed on any single amendment. It would take months or years to get substantial agreement upon the type and language of an amendment. It would take months and years thereafter to get a two-thirds majority in favor of that amendment in both houses of Congress.

Then would come the long course of ratification by three-fourths of the states. No amendment which any powerful economic interests or the leaders of any powerful political party have had reason to oppose has ever been ratified within anything like a reasonable time. And thirteen states which contain only 5 percent of the voting population can block ratification even though the thirty-five states with 95 percent of the population are in favor of it.

A very large percentage of newspaper publishers, chambers of commerce, bar associations, manufacturers' associations, who are trying to give the impression that they really do want a constitutional amendment, would be the first to exclaim as soon as an amendment was proposed: "Oh, I was for an amendment all right, but this amendment that you have proposed is not the kind of an amendment that I was thinking about. I am, therefore, going to spend my time, my efforts, and my money to block that amendment, although I would be awfully glad to help get some other kind of amendment ratified."

Two groups oppose my plan on the ground that they favor a constitutional amendment. The first includes those who fundamentally object to social and economic legislation along modern lines. This is the same group who during the campaign last fall tried to block the mandate of the people. Now they are making a last stand. And the strategy of that last stand is to suggest the time-consuming process of amendment in order to kill off by delay the legislation demanded by the mandate. To them I say: I do not think you will be able long to fool the American people as to your purposes.

The other group is composed of those who honestly believe the amendment process is the best and who would be willing to support a reasonable amendment if they could agree on one. To them I say: We cannot rely on an amendment as the immediate or only answer to our present difficulties. When the time comes for action, you will find that many of those who pretend to support you will sabotage any constructive amendment which is proposed. Look at these strange bedfellows of yours. When before have you found them really at your side in your fights for progress?

And remember one thing more. Even if an amendment were passed, and even if in the years to come it were to be ratified, its meaning would depend upon the kind of justices who would be sitting on the Supreme Court bench. An amendment like the rest of the Constitution is what the justices say it is rather than what its framers or you might hope it is.

This proposal of mine will not infringe in the slightest upon the civil or religious liberties so dear to every American. My record as governor and as President proves my devotion to those liberties. You who know me can have no fear that I would tolerate the destruction by any branch of government of any part of our heritage of freedom.

The present attempt by those opposed to progress to play upon the fears of danger to personal liberty brings again to mind that crude and cruel strategy tried by the same opposition to frighten the workers of America in a pay-envelope propaganda against the social security law. The workers were not fooled by that propaganda then. The people of America will not be fooled by such propaganda now.

I am in favor of action through legislation —

First, because I believe that it can be passed at this session of the Congress.

Second, because it will provide a reinvigorated, liberal-minded judiciary necessary to furnish quicker and cheaper justice from bottom to top.

Third, because it will provide a series of federal courts willing to enforce the Constitution as written and unwilling to assert legislative powers by writing into it their own political and economic policies.

During the past half century the balance of power between the three great branches of the federal government has been tipped out of balance by the courts in direct contradiction of the high purposes of the framers of the Constitution. It is my purpose to restore that balance. You who know me will accept my solemn assurance that in a world in which democracy is under attack I seek to make American democracy succeed.

II.

Report of the Senate

THE COMMITTEE ON THE JUDICIARY, to whom was referred the bill (S. 1392) to reorganize the judicial branch of the government, after full consideration, having unanimously amended the measure, hereby report the bill adversely with the recommendation that it do not pass. . . .

The committee recommends that the measure be rejected for the following primary reasons:

1. The bill does not accomplish any one of the objectives for which it was originally offered.

2. It applies force to the judiciary and in its initial and ultimate effect would undermine the independence of the courts.

3. It violates all precedents in the history of our government and would in itself be a dangerous precedent for the future.

4. The theory of the bill is in direct violation of the spirit of the American Constitution and its employment would permit alteration of the Constitution without the people's consent or approval; it undermines the protection our constitutional system gives to minorities and is subversive of the rights of individuals.

5. It tends to centralize the federal district judiciary by the power of assigning judges from one district to another at will.

6. It tends to expand political control over the judicial department by adding to the powers of the legislative and executive departments respecting the judiciary.

This measure was sent to the Congress by the President on Feb. 5, 1937, with a message . . . setting forth the objectives sought to be attained.

It should be pointed out here that a substantial portion of the message was devoted to a discussion of the evils of conflicting decisions by inferior courts on constitutional questions and to the alleged abuse of the power of injunction by some of the federal courts. These matters, however, have no bearing on the bill before us, for it contains neither a line nor a sentence dealing with either of those problems.

Nothing in this measure attempts to control, regulate, or prohibit the power of any federal court to pass upon the constitutionality of any law — state or national.

Nothing in this measure attempts to control, regulate, or prohibit the issuance of injunctions by any court, in any case, whether or not the government is a party to it.

If it were to be conceded that there is need of reform in these respects, it must be understood that this bill does not deal with these problems.

As offered to the Congress, this bill was designed to effectuate only three objectives, described as follows in the President's message:

1. To increase the personnel of the federal courts "so that cases may be promptly decided in the first instance, and may be given adequate and prompt hearing on all appeals";

2. To "invigorate all the courts by the permanent infusion of new blood";

3. To "grant to the Supreme Court further power and responsibility in maintaining the efficiency of the entire federal judiciary."

The third of these purposes was to be accomplished by the provisions creating the office of the Proctor and dealing with the assignment of judges to courts other than those to which commissioned.

The first two objectives were to be attained by the provisions authorizing the appointment of not to exceed fifty additional judges when sitting judges of retirement age, as defined in the bill, failed to retire or resign. How totally inadequate the measure is to achieve either of the named objectives, the most cursory examination of the facts reveals. . . .

The next question is to determine to what extent "the persistent infusion of new blood" may be expected from this bill.

It will be observed that the bill before us does not and cannot compel the retirement of any judge, whether on the Supreme Court or any other court, when he becomes seventy years of age. It will be remembered that the mere attainment of three score and ten by a particular judge does not, under this bill, require the appointment of another. The man on the bench may be eighty years of age, but this bill will not authorize the President to appoint a new judge to sit beside him unless he has served as a judge for ten years. In other words, age itself is not penalized; the penalty falls only when age is attended with experience.

No one should overlook the fact that under this bill the President, whoever he may be and whether or not he believes in the constant infusion of young blood in the courts, may nominate a man sixty-nine years and eleven months of age to the Supreme Court, or to any court, and, if confirmed, such nominee, if he never had served as a judge, would continue to sit upon the bench unmolested by this law until he had attained the ripe age of seventy-nine years and eleven months.

We are told that "modern complexities call also for a constant infusion of new blood in the courts, just as it is needed in executive functions of the government and in private business." Does this bill provide for such? The answer is obviously no. As has been just demonstrated, the introduction of old and inexperienced blood into the courts is not prevented by this bill. More than that, the measure, by its own terms, makes impossible the "constant" or "persistent" infusion of new blood. It is to be observed that the word is "new," not "young."

The Supreme Court may not be expanded to more than fifteen members. No more than two additional members may be appointed to any Circuit Court of Appeals, to the Court of Claims, to the Court of Customs and Patent Appeals, or to the Customs Court, and the number of judges now serving in any district or group of districts may not be more than doubled. There is, therefore, a specific limitation of appoint-

ment regardless of age. That is to say, this bill, ostensibly designed to provide for the infusion of new blood, sets up insuperable obstacles to the "constant" or "persistent" operation of that principle.

Take the Supreme Court as an example. As constituted at the time this bill was presented to the Congress, there were six members of that tribunal over seventy years of age. If all six failed to resign or retire within thirty days after the enactment of this bill, and none of the members died, resigned, or retired before the President had made a nomination, then the Supreme Court would consist of fifteen members. These fifteen would then serve, regardless of age, at their own will, during good behavior — in other words, for life. Though as a result we had a court of fifteen members seventy years of age or over, nothing could be done about it under this bill, and there would be no way to infuse "new" blood or "young" blood except by a new law further expanding the Court, unless, indeed, Congress and the Executive should be willing to follow the course defined by the framers of the Constitution for such a contingency and submit to the people a constitutional amendment limiting the terms of justices or making mandatory their retirement at a given age.

It thus appears that the bill before us does not with certainty provide for increasing the personnel of the federal judiciary, does not remedy the law's delay, does not serve the interest of the "poorer litigant," and does not provide for the "constant" or "persistent infusion of new blood" into the judiciary. What, then, does it do?

The answer is clear. It applies force to the judiciary. It is an attempt to impose upon the courts a course of action, a line of decision which, without that force, without that imposition, the judiciary might not adopt. Can there be any doubt that this is the purpose of the bill? Increasing the personnel is not the object of this measure; infusing young blood is not the object; for if either one of these purposes had been in the minds of the proponents, the drafters would not have written the following clause to be found on page 2, lines 1 to 4, inclusive:

Provided, that no additional judge shall be appointed hereunder if the judge who is of retirement age dies, resigns, or retires prior to the nomination of such additional judge.

Let it also be borne in mind that the President's message submitting this measure contains the following sentence:

If, on the other hand, any judge eligible for retirement should feel that his Court would suffer because of an increase of its membership, he may retire or resign under already existing provisions of law if he wishes to do so.

Moreover, the attorney general in testifying before the committee (hearings, pt. 1, p. 33) said:

If the Supreme Court feels that the addition of six judges would be harmful to that Court, it can avoid that result by resigning.

Three invitations to the members of the Supreme Court over seventy years of age to get out despite all the talk about increasing personnel to expedite the disposition of cases and remedy the law's delay. One by the bill. One by the President's message. One by the attorney general.

Can reasonable men by any possibility differ about the constitutional impropriety of such a course?

Those of us who hold office in this government, however humble or exalted it may be, are creatures of the Constitution. To it we owe all the power and authority we possess. Outside of it we have none. We are bound by it in every official act.

We know that this instrument, without which we would not be able to call ourselves presidents, judges, or legislators, was carefully planned and deliberately framed to establish three coordinate branches of government, every one of them to be independent of the others. For the protection of the people, for the preservation of the rights of the individual, for the maintenance of the liberties of minorities, for maintaining the checks and balances of our dual system, the three branches of the government were so constituted that the independent expression of honest difference of opinion could never be restrained in the people's servants and no one branch could overawe or subjugate the others. That is the American system. It is immeasurably more important, immeasurably more sacred to the people of America, indeed, to the people of all the world than the immediate adoption of any legislation however beneficial.

That judges should hold office during good behavior is the prescription. It is founded upon historic experience of the utmost significance. Compensation at stated times, which compensation was not to be diminished during their tenure, was also ordained. Those comprehensible terms were the outgrowths of experience which was deep-seated. Of the fifty-five men in the Constitutional Convention, nearly one-half had actually fought in the War for Independence. Eight of the men present had signed the Declaration of Independence, in which, giving their reasons for the act, they had said of their king: "He has made judges dependent upon his will alone for their tenure of office and the amount and payment of their salaries." They sought to correct an abuse and to prevent its recurrence.

When these men wrote the Constitution of their new government, they still sought to avoid such an abuse as had led to such a bloody war as the one through which they had just passed. So they created a judicial branch of government consisting of courts not conditionally but absolutely independent in the discharge of their functions, and they intended that entire and impartial independence should prevail. Interference with this independence was prohibited, not partially but totally. Behavior other than good was the sole and only cause for interference. This judicial system is the priceless heritage of every American.

By this bill, another and wholly different cause is proposed for the intervention of executive influence, namely, age. Age and behavior have no connection; they are unrelated subjects. By this bill, judges who have reached seventy years of age may remain on the bench and have their judgment augmented if they agree with the new appointee, or vetoed if they disagree. This is far from the independence intended for the courts by the framers of the Constitution. This is an unwarranted influence accorded the appointing agency, contrary to the spirit of the Constitution. The bill sets up a plan which has as its stability the changing will or inclination of an agency not a part of the judicial system. Constitutionally, the bill can have no sanction. The effect of the bill, as stated by the attorney general to the committee, and indeed by the President in both his message and speech, is in violation of the organic law.

No amount of sophistry can cover up this fact. The effect of this bill is not to provide for an increase in the number of justices composing the Supreme Court. The effect is to provide a forced retirement or, failing in this, to take from the justices affected a free exercise of their independent judgment.

The President tells us in his address to the nation of March 9 . . .

> When the Congress has sought to stabilize national agriculture, to improve the conditions of labor, to safeguard business against unfair competition, to protect our national resources, and in many other ways to serve our clearly national needs, the majority of the Court has been assuming the power to pass on the wisdom of these acts of the Congress and to approve or disapprove the public policy written into these laws. . . .
> We have, therefore, reached the point as a nation where we must take action to save the Constitution from the Court and the Court from itself. We must find a way to take an appeal from the Supreme Court to the Constitution itself. We want a Supreme Court which will do justice under the Constitution — not over it. In our courts we want a government of laws and not of men.

These words constitute a charge that the Supreme Court has exceeded the boundaries of its jurisdiction and invaded the field reserved by the Constitution to the legislative branch of the government. At best the accusation is opinion only. It is not the conclusion of judicial process.

Here is the frank acknowledgment that neither speed nor "new blood" in the judiciary is the object of this legislation, but a change in the decisions of the Court — a subordination of the views of the judges to the views of the executive and legislative, a change to be brought about by forcing certain judges off the bench or increasing their number.

Let us, for the purpose of the argument, grant that the Court has been wrong, wrong not only in that it has rendered mistaken opinions but wrong in the far more serious sense that it has substituted its will for the congressional will in the matter of legislation. May we nevertheless safely punish the Court?

Today it may be the Court which is charged with forgetting its constitutional duties. Tomorrow it may be the Congress. The next day it may be the Executive. If we yield to temptation now to lay the lash upon the Court, we are only teaching others how to apply it to ourselves and to the people when the occasion seems to warrant. Manifestly, if we may force the hand of the Court to secure our interpretation of the Constitution, then some succeeding Congress may repeat the process to secure another and a different interpretation and one which may not sound so pleasant in our ears as that for which we now contend.

There is a remedy for usurpation or other judicial wrongdoing. If this bill be supported by the toilers of this country upon the ground that they want a Court which will sustain legislation limiting hours and providing minimum wages, they must remember that the procedure employed in the bill could be used in another administration to lengthen hours and to decrease wages. If farmers want agricultural relief and favor this bill upon the ground that it gives them a Court which will sustain legislation in their favor, they must remember that the procedure employed might some day be used to deprive them of every vestige of a farm relief.

When members of the Court usurp legislative powers or attempt to exercise political power, they lay themselves open to the charge of having lapsed from that "good behavior" which determines the period of their official life. But, if you say, the process of impeachment is difficult and uncertain, the answer is, the people made it so when they framed the Constitution. It is not for us, the servants of the people, the instruments of the Constitution, to find a more easy way to do that which our masters made difficult.

But, if the fault of the judges is not so grievous as to warrant impeachment, if their offense is merely that they have grown old, and we feel, therefore, that there should be a "constant infusion of new blood," then obviously the way to achieve that result is by constitutional amendment fixing definite terms for the members of the judiciary or making mandatory their retirement at a given age. Such a provision would indeed provide for the constant infusion of new blood, not only now but at all times in the future. The plan before us is but a temporary expedient which operates once and then never again, leaving the Court as permanently expanded to become once more a court of old men, gradually year by year falling behind the times. . . .

This bill is an invasion of judicial power such as has never before been attempted in this country. It is true that in the closing days of the administration of John Adams, a bill was passed creating sixteen new circuit judges while reducing by one the number of places on the Supreme Court. It was charged that this was a bill to use the judiciary for a political purpose by providing official positions for members of a defeated party. The repeal of that law was the first task of the Jefferson administration. Neither the original act nor the repealer was an attempt to change the course of judicial decision. And never in the history of the country has there been such an act. The present bill comes to us, therefore, wholly without precedent.

It is true that the size of the Supreme Court has been changed from time to time, but in every instance after the Adams administration, save one, the changes were made for purely administrative purposes in aid of the Court, not to control it. . . .

Shall we now, after 150 years of loyalty to the constitutional ideal of an untrammeled judiciary, duty-bound to protect the constitutional rights of the humblest citizen even against the government itself, create the vicious precedent which must necessarily undermine our system? The only argument for the increase which survives analysis is that Congress should enlarge the Court so as to make the policies of this administration effective.

We are told that a reactionary oligarchy defies the will of the majority, that this is a bill to "unpack" the Court and give effect to the desires of the majority; that is to say, a bill to increase the number of justices for the express purpose of neutralizing the views of some of the present members. In justification we are told, but without authority, by those who would rationalize this program, that Congress was given the power to determine the size of the Court so that the legislative branch would be able to impose its will upon the judiciary. This amounts to nothing more than the declaration that when the Court stands in the way of a legislative enactment, the Congress may reverse the ruling by enlarging the Court. When such a principle is adopted, our constitutional system is overthrown!

This, then, is the dangerous precedent we are asked to establish. When proponents of the bill assert, as they have done, that Congress in the past has altered the number of justices upon the Supreme Court and that this is reason enough for our doing it now, they show how important precedents are and prove that we should now refrain from any action that would seem to establish one which could be followed hereafter whenever a Congress and an executive should become dissatisfied with the decisions of the Supreme Court.

This is the first time in the history of our country that a proposal to alter the decisions of the Court by enlarging its personnel has been so boldly made. Let us meet it. Let us now set a salutary precedent that will never be violated. Let us, the Seventy-fifth Congress, in words that will never be disregarded by any succeeding Congress, declare that we would rather have an independent Court, a fearless Court, a Court that will dare to announce its honest opinions in what it believes to be the defense of the liberties of the people than a Court that, out of fear or sense of obligation to the appointing power or factional passion approves any measure we may enact. We are not the judges of the judges. We are not above the Constitution.

Even if every charge brought against the so-called reactionary members of this Court be true, it is far better that we await orderly but inevitable change of personnel than that we impatiently overwhelm them with new members. Exhibiting this restraint, thus demonstrating our faith in the American system, we shall set an example that will protect the independent American judiciary from attack as long as this government stands. . . .

The condition of the world abroad must of necessity cause us to hesitate at this time and to refuse to enact any law that would impair the independence of or destroy the people's confidence in an independent judicial branch of our government. We unhesitatingly assert that any effort looking to the impairment of an independent judiciary of necessity operates toward centralization of power in the other branches of a tripartite form of government. We declare for the continuance and perpetuation of government and rule by law, as distinguished from government and rule by men, and in this we are but reasserting the principles basic to the Constitution of the United States. The converse of this would lead to and in fact accomplish the destruction of our form of government, where the written Constitution with its history, its spirit, and its long line of judicial interpretation and construction, is looked to and relied upon by millions of our people. Reduction of the degree of the supremacy of law means an increasing enlargement of the degree of personal government. . . .

The assertion has been indiscriminately made that the Court has arrogated to itself the right to declare acts of Congress invalid. The contention will not stand against investigation or reason. Article III of the federal Constitution provides that the judicial power "shall extend to all cases in law and equity arising under this Constitution, the laws of the United States and treaties made under their authority."

The words "under this Constitution" were inserted on the floor of the Constitutional Convention in circumstances that leave no doubt of their meaning. It is true that the Convention had refused to give the Supreme Court the power to sit as a council of revision over the acts of Congress or the power to veto such acts. That action, however, was merely the refusal to give the court any legislative power. It was a decision wholly in harmony with the purpose of keeping the judiciary independent. But, while carefully refraining from giving the

Court power to share in making laws, the Convention did give it judicial power to construe the Constitution in litigated cases. . . .

The right and duty of the Court to construe the Constitution is thus made clear. The question may, however, be propounded whether in construing that instrument the Court has undertaken to "override the judgment of the Congress on legislative policy." It is not necessary for this committee to defend the Court from such a charge. An invasion of the legislative power by the judiciary would not, as has already been indicated, justify the invasion of judicial authority by the legislative power. The proper remedy against such an invasion is provided in the Constitution.

We may, however, point out that neither in this administration nor in any previous administration has the Supreme Court held unconstitutional more than a minor fraction of the laws which have been enacted. In 148 years, from 1789 to 1937, only 64 acts of Congress have been declared unconstitutional — 64 acts out of a total of approximately 58,000. . . . These 64 acts were held invalid in 76 cases, 30 of which were decided by the unanimous vote of all the justices, 9 by the agreement of all but one of the justices, 14 by the agreement of all but two, another 12 by agreement of all but three. In 11 cases only were there as many as four dissenting votes when the laws were struck down. . . .

Inconvenience and even delay in the enactment of legislation is not a heavy price to pay for our system. Constitutional democracy moves forward with certainty rather than with speed. The safety and the permanence of the progressive march of our civilization are far more important to us and to those who are to come after us than the enactment now of any particular law. The Constitution of the United States provides ample opportunity for the expression of popular will to bring about such reforms and changes as the people may deem essential to their present and future welfare. It is the people's charter of the powers granted those who govern them.

Let it be recognized that not only is the commerce clause of the Constitution and the clauses having to do with due process and general welfare involved in the consideration of this bill, but every line of the Constitution from the Preamble to the last amendment is affected. Every declarative statement in those clauses which we choose to call the Bill of Rights is involved. Guarantees of individual human liberty and the limitation of the governing powers and processes are all reviewable. . . .

Minority political groups, no less than religious and racial groups, have never failed, when forced to appeal to the Supreme Court of the United States, to find in its opinions the reassurance and protection of their constitutional rights. No finer or more durable philosophy of free government is to be found in all the writings and practices of great statesmen than may be found in the decisions of the Supreme Court when dealing with great problems of free government touching human rights. This would not have been possible without an independent judiciary. . . .

We recommend the rejection of this bill as a needless, futile, and utterly dangerous abandonment of constitutional principle.

It was presented to the Congress in a most intricate form and for reasons that obscured its real purpose.

It would not banish age from the bench nor abolish divided decisions.

It would not affect the power of any court to hold laws unconstitutional nor withdraw from any judge the authority to issue injunctions.

It would not reduce the expense of litigation nor speed the decision of cases.

It is a proposal without precedent and without justification.

It would subjugate the courts to the will of Congress and the President and thereby destroy the independence of the judiciary, the only certain shield of individual rights.

It contains the germ of a system of centralized administration of law that would enable an Executive so minded to send his judges into every judicial district in the land to sit in judgment on controversies between the government and the citizen.

It points the way to the evasion of the Constitution and establishes the method whereby the people may be deprived of their right to pass upon all amendments of the fundamental law.

It stands now before the country, acknowledged by its proponents as a plan to force judicial interpretation of the Constitution, a proposal that violates every sacred tradition of American democracy.

Under the form of the Constitution it seeks to do that which is unconstitutional.

Its ultimate operation would be to make this government one of men rather than one of law, and its practical operation would be to make the Constitution what the executive or legislative branches of the government choose to say it is — an interpretation to be changed with each change of administration.

It is a measure which should be so emphatically rejected that its parallel will never again be presented to the free representatives of the free people of America.

96.

The Future of the Great Plains

The worst drought in modern American history struck the Great Plains in 1934. Wind storms that stripped the topsoil from millions of acres turned the whole area into a vast dust bowl and destroyed crops and livestock in unprecedented amounts. The causes of the drought, which extended to 1936, went back a half century during which time cattle had first overgrazed the land, trees had been cut and not replanted, and homesteaders, responding to the demand for wheat during World War I, had exhausted the soil by extensive cultivation. In 1936 President Roosevelt established the Great Plains Committee to report "on a long term program for the efficient utilization of the resources of the Great Plains area." Its report was submitted on February 10, 1937, and is reprinted here in part.

Source: 75 Congress, 1 Session, House Document No. 144.

THE PURPOSE OF THE REPORT

IN 1934 AND AGAIN IN 1936, drought conditions in the Great Plains area of the United States became so severe that it was necessary for the federal government to take emergency steps to rescue dying cattle, relieve destitute families, and safeguard human life. The experience of the two tragic years made it evident that the drought had merely accentuated a situation which had been long developing. The agricultural economy of the Great Plains had a perilously narrow reserve. Its prosperity depended on favorable weather and markets, neither of which could be expected to be continuously present. . . .

Before going further it will be well to explain . . . what is meant by the Great Plains. Precision is more attainable in defining the western boundary, which is conveniently marked by the eastern slope of the Rocky Mountains. The eastern boundary may be indicated in one of several ways, but it is always vague. Indeed, it may be thought of as moving east or west in accordance with climatic cycles, and even with the economic and technological conditions of human occupancy. . . .

THE PRESENT SITUATION

As a productive resource, as a place to work and as a place to live, the Great Plains . . . present a disquieting picture. If there were no hope of restoration, with benefit both to the population of the area and to the nation, the present report would be only a brief final chapter in a record of failure and disaster. No such conclusions need be arrived at, yet certain facts must be faced. There are perhaps 24,000 crop farms, covering a total of 15 million acres, which should no longer be plowed. Of the range lands, probably 95 percent have declined in forage value, this decline varying from 25 to 50 percent of its original value in southwestern North Dakota to from 50 to 75 percent in southwestern Nebraska and northwestern Kansas.

These physical changes unavoidably have been accompanied by social and economic changes. There has been a marked decline in the quality of living which could be achieved by a stalwart and energetic population, which in stock and physique is not excelled in the Western world. Farmers have met the problem of holdings too small to support a family by renting additional acreage; and there has grown up a confusing, intricate, and inefficient pattern of ownerships and tenures. Tenancy has increased steadily. In eight Great Plains states (not including Oklahoma and Texas, where cotton growing outside the Plains area makes tenancy data nontypical), in 1935 more than 41 percent of all farmers were tenants. In the whole area, 35 percent of all the land in use was leased or rented in 1900; by 1935 the percentage had risen to 51. The burden of mortgages, debts, and taxes undoubtedly had rendered a much larger proportion of farmers owners only in name.

The tenant system on the Great Plains is in some respects a result rather than a cause. The situation would not be cured overnight even though it were possible to deed every acre of land in use to those who now work it. Nevertheless, tenancy has been a link in a chain of events which have led to instability of population within the region, to neglect of improvements, to low living standards, to insistence — sometimes included in the rental contract — upon a cash crop, to depletion of the soil, to destruction of the grass cover by overgrazing, and to a decline in the tangible and intangible values of community life. The nominally independent owner, harassed by his own burdens and carrying on an enterprise which is at present highly speculative, has not been able to arrest these tendencies. Depression and drought have accentuated trends long in the making. Tax delinquencies have brought about a vicious circle of higher tax rates on a diminishing tax base. The credit of the taxing units has declined as their debts have increased, and schools and other public services have suffered.

The region as a whole has not maintained its economic position; the return for energy expended has been less than for similar expenditures of energy upon the land in most other sections of the country. Despite its energy and self-reliance the population of the Great Plains has found itself in a position in which it was compelled to ask or accept outside assistance out of proportion to its numbers.

This is a matter of direct concern to the federal government and to the country as a whole. Between April 1933 and June 1936 the accumulated amounts of federal aid expended in the area ran as high in some counties as $200 per capita. Net increments to the relief population of the whole United States between 1933-34 and 1934-35 amounted to 4 percent; in New Mexico they were 19.2 percent; in South Dakota, 17.6 percent; in Oklahoma, 11.3 percent; in North Dakota, 10.9 percent. In June 1935, 20 percent of all the farmers in the spring-wheat area of the Plains were receiving relief and another 8 percent were in process of rehabilitation.

The nation can afford such relief when it is needed. It cannot afford *not* to give it when it is needed. But the integrity of community life on the Plains, the solvency of the Plains economy, and the welfare of the nation, which suffers indirectly as the population of the Plains suffers directly, demand that here, as elsewhere, a secure and stable substitute for relief be found.

The Committee has been impressed during its field trips by the certainty that in the Great Plains area it was dealing with people who desired nothing else than to earn their own living by their own efforts. It is a cruel error to regard any large portion of this population, as some uninformed commentators have done, as speculative investors whose calculations have gone wrong. Not in money alone but also in labor and endurance, they have paid for better fortune than has yet been theirs. . . .

The people of the Plains are finding their way toward an attitude of mind, deep-seated and not often brought out into the open, which will affect both their thinking and their doing. Many of the assumptions which the pioneers had found workable in other regions, under other conditions, have proved unworkable on the Plains. The Plainsman cannot assume that whatever is for his immediate good is also good for everybody — only of his long-run good is this true, and in the short run there must often be sacrifices; he cannot assume the right always to do with his own property as he likes — he may ruin another man's property if he does; he cannot assume that the individual action he can take on his own land will be sufficient, even for the conservation and best use of that land. He must realize that he cannot "conquer nature" — he must live with her on her own terms, making use of and conserving resources which can no longer be considered inexhaustible.

In this new point of view, and in this task of realizing the true and lasting values of the Great Plains, the whole nation has more than a sentimental stake. The Great Plains can be made a dependable source of a large portion of our essential food supply. Investments in their development can be rescued from uncertainty, and under proper conditions new investments can be made securely. The Plains can be transformed from a risky adventure and a recurrent liability into a stable basis of economic and social profit to their inhabitants and to the whole country.

STEPS TOWARD SOLUTION

The problem of the Great Plains offers no simple solution. Yet enough is known about conditions and their causes generally throughout the region, and in detail with respect to certain parts, to permit immediate and vigorous execution of a program of readjustment and development. Further studies of details should proceed simultaneously with the execution of the program, but the beginning of action should not be permitted to await these studies, which should in fact be a part of the program.

As the basis of a program there should be a clear analysis of the complementary parts which should be played by the various agencies which have a stake in the future of the Plains. Following is an outline of the analysis and recommendations. . . .

I. LINES OF FEDERAL ACTION

1. *Investigations and Surveys.* It is recommended that provision be made promptly for the requisite investigations and surveys to determine, insofar as it has not been done, the best uses of land, waters, and other natural resources throughout the Great Plains. These should include: the completion of topographic, hydrographic, and soil surveys; studies of climatic risks; a study of the possibilities of new irrigation projects in advantageous locations; a study of the proper size of ownership and operating units under varying conditions and in varying locations; studies in the cause and cure of erosion; and inquiries into occupational opportunities for those who can no longer make an adequate living on the land. A ten-year program should be mapped out for these additional investigations by the federal government. They are essential if the long-run development of each part of the region is to be guided intelligently.

2. *Federal Acquisition of Land in Range Areas.* It is recommended that the federal government continue the policy of purchasing scattered crop farms and other appropriate lands in areas devoted largely to grazing and most suitable for that purpose. Such purchases should be made with due caution and only after sufficient data have been accumulated to make good results probable in each case. The lands which should be acquired lie mainly in the western and more arid parts of the region. Factors to be taken into consideration should be, not only the nature of the land and its water supply but also local sentiment, the predicament of owners whose resources do not permit them to make a satisfactory living on the land they now occupy, and the possibility of rounding out the range land at the disposal of existing grazing districts or associations.

3. *Control and Use of Lands Acquired by the Federal Government in Range Areas.* In conjunction with the policy of land acquisition, it is recommended that the control of purchased lands situated within the limits of federal grazing districts be retained by a federal agency free to distribute range rights in accordance with the objectives of general rehabilitation as well as of existing priorities. Land acquired in areas where there is no public domain, or not enough to justify the organization of grazing districts under the Taylor Grazing Act, should be leased to cooperative grazing associations. In the administration of purchased lands it is essential that the federal agency cooperate with all other agencies in the formulation of rules and regulations in order to obtain best range use.

4. *Measures to Increase the Size of Farms.* It is recommended that assistance in the enlargement of undersized operating units be provided: (1) through extension of credit under suitable restrictions, and (2) experimentally through federal purchase of selected land and its subsequent lease or sale under covenants protecting its use. A minimum size of family unit for each type of land should be determined and demonstration farms should be established. This plan demands, of course, the approval and cooperation of the owner from whom the land is to be bought or leased and of the operator who is to manage it.

5. *Development of Water Resources.* The water supply of the Great Plains cannot be increased by any practicable means within human control. The best that can be done

is to regulate the varying supply at our disposal, and to adjust the land and water economy to that supply. The Soil Conservation Service has demonstrated that, generally, water can be stored by suitable farm practices in the soil itself in sufficient quantities to increase growth of grass and farm crops and to resist drought. Every effort should be made to acquaint farmers with the water-conserving measures which have been found effective. The Water Resources Committee of the National Resources Committee has pointed out that something can be done to improve the supply of water for the purposes of watering stock, but that it is not to be expected that more than 3 percent of the total area of the Great Plains can ever be irrigated. It is recommended that attention be given to the development, where natural conditions favor, of small-sized irrigation systems to water up to 1,000 acres each, to be operated in connection with storage reservoirs on tributaries or pumping plants on the major streams.

6. Resettlement. Excessive droughts in the Great Plains have resulted in the aimless and desperate migration of thousands of families in search of some means of livelihood. Many have moved to the Pacific Coast, others have settled on cheap cut-over lands, but few have improved their economic status. Many more would have been forced to leave but for public aid and relief. Until the effects of severe droughts have been sufficiently minimized by results of the long-time program, by crop insurance, or by other means, emergency measures involving some resettlement probably will be necessary.

The adoption of the recommendations of the Committee would necessarily result in a certain measure of resettlement. However, pending the completion of detailed plans for readjustments of land use, it is impossible to determine whether a further sizeable migration from the region can be avoided. Suitable opportunities should be found, if possible, within the region, but each case should receive individual consideration for its best solution.

7. Compensation to Local Governments on Account of Federal Land Acquisition. Purchase of lands by the federal government may result in shrinkage of the local tax basis. With careful consideration of each situation, provision should be made to compensate local governing bodies for the loss of tax revenues when such purchases are made. Payments made directly by the government to the counties affected might often prove inequitable, and it is suggested that payments should preferably be made directly to the states, with amounts earmarked for the counties in which acquisitions take place, but leaving to the discretion of a state administrative agency the ultimate distribution among the local units.

8. Control of Destructive Insect Pests. The control and possible eradication of insect pests which ravage periodically sections of the Great Plains should be a part of the long-range rehabilitation program. Rather than considering such destructive outbreaks as inevitable, preventive efforts through intensive research and extensive complementary experiments should be initiated on a wide front.

9. Development of Other Resources. The development of other resources, such as the vast lignite deposits which underlie the northern part of the Great Plains area, may be feasible. This would provide alternative occupation for some people. It is suggested that investigations already made by the Bureau of Mines be pursued further and that demonstration projects be established by a suitable agency to prove or disprove the economic feasibility of the use of lignite in the generation of power. Other mineral resources, where not yet fully exploited, should receive similar consideration.

II. Lines of State Action

Any action taken by the federal government should be conditioned by the extent to which the necessary complementary action is undertaken by the states. The following suggestions are made in accordance with this conviction:

1. *Legislation.* Each of the states having territory in the Great Plains area is urged to undertake a survey, as promptly as possible, with a view to necessary revision and extension of its present laws affecting land and water use and conservation. This would include laws relating to tenancy, leasing, taxing, and tax delinquency. These should be so simplified and interrelated as to avoid existing evils of lack of laws, inadequate laws, ineffective provisions for administration, and conflicts of jurisdiction.

2. *Zoning.* The principle of zoning is logically as applicable to rural territory as it is to cities and towns. It is believed that the legislatures of the several states in the Great Plains area should pass enabling laws under which their respective counties may zone land in terms of its proper use. Such legislation is deemed necessary to prevent permanent impairment of the land by unwise extension of the cultivated area during periods of supernormal rainfall or of exceptionally high prices; to give stability to land-use patterns which may be determined upon, such as a combination of stock raising and arable farming in areas which should not be given exclusively to the quick "cash crop"; to simplify and consolidate the pattern of settlement and so reduce or keep down expenses for schools, roads, and other community services; to reduce the amount of speculation in land; and generally to give permanence and greater stability to any land-improvement and land-conservation policy.

3. *Grazing Associations.* One method of improving the conditions resulting from too-small holdings and the checkerboard ownership pattern in the Great Plains is the establishment of cooperative grazing associations. The grazing association makes possible the operation of large tracts as units and in effective conjunction with adjacent dry-farming and irrigated land. It reduces destructive competition among stockmen for the use of the range and tends to eliminate overgrazing, inflation of land values, and other evils. Such associations are sanctioned under the Montana law, under the supervision of the Montana Grazing Commission, and it is suggested that this system be adapted for use in the other Great Plains States.

4. *Control of Erosion on Arable Lands.* Conservation in the Great Plains area would be greatly stimulated if each state were to adopt appropriate legislation permitting the qualified, property-tax-paying voters of a county or other division to form a soil conservation district. The Land Policy Committee, the Soil Conservation Service, and the Office of the Solicitor in the Department of Agriculture have joined in drawing up a suggestive standard law for the formation of such districts, and it is urged that the legislatures of the Great Plains states give early attention to the proposal.

5. *Tax-Delinquent Range Lands.* It is desirable that the states should avoid the resale of such lands to private individuals and should make them available for coordinated use with other public lands through cooperative grazing districts or other means.

6. *Community Organization.* The Great Plains states might well encourage local communities to make broader use of legislation permitting the consolidation of local governments and other changes in organization which would make for economy. In this way costs of roads, schools, and other public services might be reduced without loss of efficiency.

7. *Taxation.* Taxing systems in the Great

Plains states probably must continue to have their basis in the land. It is suggested, however, that prevalent modes of assessment and collection may have ceased to be suitable for the economic and social conditions that have developed; and that some revision of the taxing system which will take account of the current or average income from the land would prove to be more equitable and beneficial in the long run.

8. *Water Resources and Water Problems.* These are basic for every agency operating in the Great Plains. The states might well aid farmers in developing local water supplies for stock, etc., through tax reductions, as in Kansas; by simplifying procedures for adjudicating rights to water used; and by giving greater support to state agencies equipped to furnish engineering and other technical advice to farmers and stockmen. The example of the Montana State Water Conservation Board in facilitating small or medium-sized irrigation projects deserves imitation. In many cases highway construction can be utilized safely to assist the conservation of water. Existing state laws do not as a rule limit the amount of ground water to be pumped by any one appropriator or ensure that such water is not wasted; these defects should be remedied.

9. *Land Occupancy and Tenure.* State authorities should give attention to the forthcoming report of the Special Committee on Land Tenure appointed by the President; and should on the one hand promote ownership and permanent occupancy, and on the other hand make more equitable the position of those who continue as tenants. They should explore the possibilities of elimination of oral leases, standard forms of leases, longer duration of leases, bettering the position of tenants with respect to improvements and fixtures which they have in-

troduced, and other factors which would improve the position of tenants and encourage conservation of soil assets.

III. Local Action and Its Importance

Certain practical measures within the capacity of individuals and communities are here briefly suggested: (1) Enlargement of operating units and establishment of the family ranch or farm, or the cooperative grazing range; (2) major shifts in cropping plans to reduce the single "cash crop" and restore the more stable "balanced farm"; (3) flexible cropping plans, so that the nature of the crop each season can be adapted to the amount of moisture in the soil at planting time; (4) creation of feed and seed reserves against dry years made economical by use of the pit silo; (5) conservation of soil moisture by such means as contour plowing and listing, contour strips, terracing, leaving of stubble and crop residue in the ground, and planting of sweet clover and winter rye on sandy soils; (6) supplemental irrigation where practicable at low cost; (7) utilization of springs, wells, and other local sources of water supply where stock is to be pastured; (8) the planting wherever practicable of trees and shrubs as windbreaks on borders of fields and around houses.

All agencies — federal, state, local, and private — must cooperate in stimulating the adoption of these and other proved methods. They are a part of the intelligent adjustment to the ways of nature which must take the place of attempts to "conquer" her. But primarily the responsibility rests on the people residing in the Great Plains states. Other agencies may encourage, inform, and assist them, but the final responsibility is, and must be, their own.

97.

WOODY GUTHRIE: "So Long (It's Been Good To Know Yuh)"

Woody Guthrie is probably America's best-known balladeer, or composer of modern folk songs. The dust storms that swirled over the Great Plains from 1934 to 1936 laid waste thousands of square miles of land and forced farmers to flee westward. Guthrie, himself an "Okie," was stirred by the plight of his fellow "dust-bowl refugees" and wrote several songs about them, including "So Long (It's Been Good To Know Yuh)." "I don't know nothing about music," Guthrie once declared. "Never could read or write it. But somehow or other, when the black dust hit our country, I was among the first to blow. When it cleared off again, I woke up with a guitar in one hand and a road map in the other one."

Source: *Songs of Work and Freedom*, Edith Fowke and Joe Glazer, eds., New York, 1960.
Copyright 1950 and 1951 by Folkways Music Publishers, Inc., New York, N.Y.

ॐ SO LONG (IT'S BEEN GOOD TO KNOW YUH)

I've sung this song, but I'll sing it again,
Of the people I've met, and the places I've seen,
Of some of the troubles that bothered my mind,
And a lot of good people that I've left behind. So it's

So long, it's been good to know yuh,
So long, it's been good to know yuh,
So long, it's been good to know yuh,
What a long time since I've been home,
  And I got to be drifting along.

The sweethearts, they sat in the dark and they sparked,
They hugged and they kissed in that dusty old dark,
They sighed and they cried and they hugged and they kissed,
But instead of marriage they talked like this: Honey,

So long, etc.

I went to your family and asked them for you,
They all said take her, oh, take her, please do!
She can't cook or sew and she won't scrub your floor,
So I put on my hat and tiptoed out the door, saying:

So long, etc.

I walked down the street to the grocery store,
It was crowded with people both rich and both poor,

I asked the man how his butter was sold,
He said, one pound of butter for two pounds of gold; I said:

So long, etc.

My telephone rang and it jumped off the wall,
That was the preacher a-making a call,
He said, we're waiting to tie the knot,
You're getting married, believe it or not!

So long, etc.

The church it was jammed, the church it was packed,
The pews were crowded from the front to the back,
A thousand friends waited to kiss my new bride,
But I was so anxious I rushed her outside, told them:

So long, etc.

98.

ODETTE KEUN: TVA in Foreign Eyes

*The bill establishing the Tennessee Valley Authority was signed into law by
President Roosevelt on May 18, 1933. It implemented a program of economic and
social development for a region of about 41,000 square miles containing nearly
three million people. Specifically, TVA had three objectives: flood control of the
Tennessee River, development of navigation channels, and production and marketing
of electric power. It was the first corporation ever created by Congress and many
critics attacked it as an unconstitutional threat to the private power companies. TVA
proved highly successful and has served as a model for similar projects in other
countries. Many foreigners admired the project, among them Madame Odette Keun,
a French writer, who visited the region in 1936 and published a book about it. Her
chapter on "Social Developments" is reprinted below.*

Source: *A Foreigner Looks at the TVA*, New York, 1937, pp. 75-84.

1

THE POPULATION OF THE WATERSHED, belonging as it does to seven states, consists of different strata and follows different avocations. But perhaps one citizen in six lives in a big city. Half the inhabitants dwell on farms. The predominant classes are therefore the farmers and the small-towners, and on them the TVA has concentrated — the farmer, of the two, being its chief concern.

In great minority are the prosperous farmers on good phosphatic lands or on middling lands which they have fructified.

The typical Valley landowner lives on soil which was usually no great shakes from the start, which he bled in every conceivable way, and which now brings him in for himself and his generally large family — that stews in the same juice — from $100 to $150 a year. Then there are the tenant farmer and the sharecropper, White and Black, in varying stages of poverty and devoid, moreover, of the independence of the poor landowner. These three categories of people, their minds, their circumstances, and their future, are at the heart of all that the TVA is planning and doing.

Among the "free" farmers, the least known and the most difficult to reach are the mountaineers, and as they are numerous and constitute a poignantly human as well as an agricultural problem, I'll talk at some length about them here. The stock from which they came was, in its most remote origins, those Scotch and English Presbyterians who were planted by James I in Ulster, when he confiscated the estates of the Irish in 1607. They were called the Scotch-Irish only because they were principally of Scottish blood and had settled in Ireland, but the Irish themselves hated them bitterly as usurpers and fought them whenever they could.

As time went on, the Scotch-Irish quarrelled with the Crown, which persecuted and evicted them, and they began to emigrate to Pennsylvania. They took up land just outside the German settlements, and clashed immediately with the Indians in a series of border wars where they showed quite as much ferocity, if not more, than their enemies. They were brave, impetuous, visionary, cruel, seeing "no use in an Indian but to be a target for their bullets," and passionately devoted to the monstrous Protestant doctrines of total depravation and predestination. They were forever pushing forward to the southwest, striking at the Indians and the Whites alike, for various reasons, as they did so, until in the eighteenth century they crossed the Appalachian Mountains into utterly unknown regions.

In 1772 they established the first republic in America, based upon a written constitution, cutting loose from the seaboard and relying upon their own resources. They had nothing to do with slavery, loathed the State Church and acknowledged the authority of neither king nor aristocracy. They acknowledged no rule, indeed, save that of "outstanding merit and natural justice." They developed a savage sense of independence and individualism and all the sharply defined traits of a frontier people. They had it in them to be grim, and circumstances made them grimmer. A thorny lot.

At first they had sought out the hunting grounds and farmsteads of the plains, but when the buffalo and elk and beaver were killed off in Tennessee and in Kentucky, and the rolling savannahs were divided up in allotments and fenced and ploughed, small groups of hunters and trappers wandered into the highlands, which had remained uninhabited, and finding rich valleys and coves eminently suited for tillage, they squatted down in the mountains, put their cattle on the sumptuous grass and their axe to the splendid trees. No Negroes got there; no foreign farmers from Europe; they kept jealously and successfully to themselves.

But the population grew until the limits of subsistence were reached. The original settlers had snatched up the generous river lands, where the farmers are still comparatively well off, but those lands were very limited (the mountain slopes occupy 90 percent of the area, and 85 percent of the land has a steeper incline than one foot in five) and the rest of the people, as well as the later-comers, were forced back and back and up and up along the streams and creeks and hillsides to "scrabble" for a living. They became the real mountaineers of Tennessee and Kentucky, immured in the vast ranges, separated from all contact with the outer world, incredibly poor, superstitious, illiterate, talking a pidgin-Elizabethan, steeped in fierce religious convictions, following old-fashioned ways, wild, stubborn, proud. Civilization passed them by.

This would have been less deplorable if they had maintained their original qualities, such as they were, but nobody and nothing can stand still: you go forward or you go backward, but go you must. They went backward. Isolation, the insensate attachment of primitive folks to their place, their home and their relatives, which helped to immobilize them; lack of opportunity and therefore of ambition; no industries and no markets to which to sell their surplus products; no ready money; no roads, no schools, no hospitals; inbreeding, diseases, and a crazy diet — add to that an influx of outlaws and desperadoes who took refuge in the mountains to escape the law, and you get communities listless and shiftless through their own anemia and infected by crime from other quarters.

All these conditions were made indescribably worse by the Civil War. Most of the mountain counties were loyal to the Union and the highlanders sallied out of their fastnesses to fight on its behalf. While they were away, bandits and bushwhackers ranged through the hills, preying on those who were left defenseless and starting a network of vendettas. The South did not forgive the choice made by the mountaineers and spewed them out as traitors; and to crown all these miseries, the ungrateful Federal government imposed a prohibitive excise tax on their only real merchantable product, and drove them into the most violent outlawry through resentment of such an injustice. "Left, then," I find it said in a classic on the subject,

to their own devices, unchecked by any stronger arm, inflamed by a multitude of personal wrongs, habituated to the shedding of human blood, contemptuous of state laws that did not reach them, enraged by Federal acts that impugned, as

they thought, an inalienable right of man, it was inevitable that this fiery and vindictive race should fall speedily into warring among themselves. Old scores were now to be wiped out in a reign of terror, and the open combat of bannered war was turned into the secret ferocity of family feuds.

That's as may be. Personally, I will never admit, either for myself or for others, that we are under the inescapable necessity, except for certain physical functions, to behave like the beasts — but if we begin to discuss free will we'll never finish, so I shall just state my conviction that the mountaineers were not inexorably doomed to become as stupid, lazy, dirty, thriftless, treacherous, relentless, uglily cunning, brutal, and dishonorable as history reveals they were. I am completely unable to discern heroism and picturesqueness in their slovenly persons, their squalid houses, their primitive housekeeping, their repulsively cooked food, their mismanagement of the land — surely they could have applied themselves, during so many years, to learning a bit about *that*, their only means of keeping alive! — and the harshness, rudeness, sullenness, mutual incomprehension, and self-defensiveness which, in spite of their clannishness, seem to me the note of their family relationships.

I have been told by Army officers who were placed at the head of a depot for mountaineers when America entered the Great War and conscription was proclaimed, that out of twenty thousand highlanders assembled at that point, five thousand had to be pronounced inapt and sent back after a few weeks. They were not ill, they were not physically unfit. They were "lost." They could not adapt themselves. They mooned about; they wandered; they fell into abstractions and silences. They forgot their names. When it came to shipping them off to their homes, they did not know in what county their homes were situated, and the authorities had the devil of a job tracing their origins. For the life of me, I cannot admire a mode of existence which leads to such deterioration of the brain that human beings no longer can do anything, not only for thought and for society, but even for themselves.

However, changes are overtaking the mountaineers. The first onrush was as usual a villainous form of commercialism and exploitation — forests destroyed, mines disemboweled, lands swindled away, pitilessly enslaving factories established, traders and profiteers pouring in — against which only the shrewdest and most capable could make a stand. But if the vanguard of this odious civilization was composed of men who were playing for their own hand — much as the forefathers of the highlanders had done in their age — in their wake followed more enlightened measures and more general benefits. Roads, schools, order; county, State and Federal institutions administering a certain amount of help; and now an organization almost mystically committed to the betterment of this people. . . . For the TVA is wrapped heart and soul in the evolution of the mountaineers.

How to transform their thinking and their agricultural customs and adapt them to present conditions; how to develop their economic life, keeping them from the servitude of factories for which they are physically and mentally unsuited (and which in any case cannot absorb them any longer), and yet increase their cash income and raise their material standards to the level of those obtaining in the flourishing portions of the Valley; how to preserve their independent spirit and their culture — the TVA calls it culture: I'd call it an obsolete form of Americanism that America needs no more than Europe needs the ideology of the Corsican or the tribal pattern of the clans of the Caucasus, to speak of peoples I know — and yet teach them responsibility to society and give them a significant and useful role in the community: this is the task the TVA has undertaken.

It is especially for them and their broth-ers in the Valley that it elaborated its agri cultural program, invented its fertilizer, cre ated its Agricultural Industries Division founded its educational and training courses It is for them, plus the small-towner, that i is waging the fight for power against th Utilities. Its goal is to secure for them . more intelligent, dignified, and assured exis tence, participating in the facilities our con temporary world affords but conserving th lively characteristics of the individual: . happy balance between the Jeffersonia Dream of the self-sufficing agricultural com munity and the mechanical advantages o the Power Age. At least, I see the goal lik that, and I do not believe I have seen i awry.

The response, I must say, has been con siderable. It is true, as I have mentioned be fore, that the TVA came upon the scene a a moment when the farmer was up agains the wall; agriculture did not feed a man an his family, and despair was growing. I prices had been soaring and prospect bright, perhaps no wedge could have bee driven into rural obstinacy and traditional ism. But as it was, circumstances and th wisdom and tact of the TVA's attitud pretty soon persuaded the farmers, high landers and lowlanders alike, in spite o their caution and inveterate suspiciousness that there was a friend intensely anxious t help them, not a "passel of Yankees" com to pour scorn on their backwardness and ar rogantly tell them how to do it all. Her was real benevolence and discretion, th first manifestation, since Reconstruction, o a government's interest and care.

The mere fact . . . that in two and a hal years over twelve thousand test-demonstra tion farms have been spontaneously laid ou in a region celebrated for centuries for it ignorance and stubbornness, proves the na ture of the tie between the population o the Watershed and the TVA. And if i shows the sagacity and devotion with whic the TVA has handled that prickly proposi tion, the farmer, I concede willingly that i

so shows more alertness and gratitude on
the part of the farmer than one would have
expected to find. Indeed, the tendency
might almost become too much eagerness
for aid and guidance, though that cannot be
encouraged since it is inertia that must be
extirpated from the composition of the human animal here.

2

THE EVIL PROBLEMS of the tenant farmer and
the sharecropper, White and Black, the
TVA has not been able to touch. These are
things that can be straightened out only by
Congressional legislation. You can't urge
rotation of cover crops on a man who is
employed by a landlord, if that landlord
wants cotton on his soil; nor can you, when
you are not the Government, give half the
rural population a house and a field to start
living like freemen. Nor can you find work,
however hard you try, for all the laborers
who have been jerked out of their farm jobs
because you had to buy up the estates of
their masters for flooding purposes. All that
is not your fault, though it may be your
sorrow.

Indirectly, however, by side activities and
industries, by part-time employment in its
various projects, by free training, by diligent
searching for new places, by all sorts of ingenious efforts, the TVA does what it can
to enable the tenant and the sharecropper
who drift within its orbit to obtain a little
more security, a little more money, and perhaps even, in very fortunate cases, a little
property of their own. But that aspect of
the picture is not radiant with hope. It is
the Government alone who can get under
the skin of these very painful matters.

Another tangle concerns the people who
occupy the tracts of land the TVA is
obliged to submerge for the reservoirs of its
dams. Here human emotions are involved,
as well as concrete questions. Families had
to be removed so that engineering schemes
of national importance might be realized,
but you do not cheerfully acquiesce in the
disruption of your manner of life even
when national issues are at stake. The monetary compensation was very fair, as public
opinion recognizes, though the value of land
showed a disposition to shoot up to vertigi-
nous heights as soon as it was learned that
"government" needed it, and every owner's
estate was metamorphosed in a jiffy from
farm land into dam land, the latter costing a
hundred times more.

The TVA had to bargain, and bargain
closely, but that over, it did a lot of humane things. It explored the Valley to find
farms in the vicinity of the districts to be
flooded, at equivalent prices; it gave the
transplanted families, whenever possible, the
opportunity to choose their new homes; it
worked with Federal and county institutions to facilitate their installation in unfamiliar communities, providing them with
social contacts, arranging, as in the case of
the shifting of whole minor villages, for educational facilities in the shape of schools
and communications. Entire cemeteries had
been moved at the TVA's expense when
the time came for flooding, so that the
people should not brood upon their dead
lost irretrievably in the waters. I do not say
that the process of *transvasement* was never
accompanied by suffering and loss: in such
a gigantic enterprise every personal interest,
every personal necessity, could not always
be adequately satisfied, but what could be
done to make the lot of the perforce-
uprooted groups bearable or even to improve it, has been scrupulously tried. An interesting point is that better land or no-
better land proposed, most of the people refused to leave their hills for the plains.

3

THESE TRAITS of justice and kindness, this
ideal of a common welfare, which characterize the relations the TVA established
with the social groups existing in the Valley
come to a peak, I think, in the Labor ques-

tion, and the policies the TVA adopted in this potentially stormy field. There are more than 15,000 workers, from every rank and craft of Labor, on TVA projects in the Watershed. You can imagine what the applications were at a time when twenty million Americans were out of a job. One of the firmest rules the TVA laid down was that local labor, if it met the requirements, was to be taken on first. But it *had* to meet the requirements; patronage, favoritism, and protection were out of the question, as a good many politicians and wire-pullers immediately discovered to their great disgruntlement.

The major policies were three. The first related to the right of collective bargaining; the second to wages; the third to hours and working conditions — and these applied to colored as well as to white labor, for from the outset the TVA, quietly but persistently, hired Negroes in groups until their employment percentage tallied with the population percentage in the areas concerned: about 20 percent. The Negroes received the same wages as the Whites of the same category, the same housing and the same training. Since White labor was assured that the jobs wouldn't be pulled away from under it by the ordinary trick of using cheap colored labor, there was hardly any trouble, even when leading civic lights regretted that Negroes were being educated beyond their necessities. The TVA's answer was that neither revolt nor miscegenation was being preached, and that since the Negro was a member of the community, it was better for the community that he should be a decent citizen than an indecent one. And that was that.

I should like to see the TVA do something far broader and more decisive about the Negro, and this subject is the only one in which we do not see eye to eye; but I daresay it understands its business in the South better than I. I'm afraid that if I attempted to deal with the mixture of patho-

logical impulses and racial snobbery that i at the bottom of the attitude of the Whit toward the Black, I'd stir up a wors witch's brew.

The principle of collective bargaining which recognizes and insists on the "righ of employees to organize and bargain as body through representatives of their ow choosing, free from any and all restraint, in terference, or coercion in self-organizatio and designation of Labor's own representa tives elected fairly by majority rule," ha been observed in every detail by the TVA It made clear to its own supervisory execu tives that whatever their origins or thei previous philosophy were, the Authorit stood unshakably for the untrammeled righ of Labor to speak and act through the spe cific officials it voluntarily appointed. Dis crimination by the supervisors because o union membership or activity resulted, i the few cases where it occurred, in change in the staff.

As regards wages, the TVA believes i keeping them high. "It's not only good so cial policy but good business as well," i says. The Act provides that the Authorit in all its operations, shall pay not less tha the prevailing wage, and that due attentio shall be given to wages reached throug collective bargaining — so that when th prevailing wage is a very low one, the TVA worker has the chance to get a raise. In th event any question crops up as to what ar the prevailing rates of wages and the matte cannot be settled by conference between th duly chosen Labor spokesmen and the Au thority, it is referred to the U.S. Secretar of Labor, whose decision is final.

Schedules of rates of pay, hourly and an nual, are published and remain in force un til revision, which takes place not more of ten than once a year so that there are n sudden shattering cuts and no mysterie (By the way, the salaries of the three Direc tors are ten thousand dollars a year each. just want to remark that William Green

President of the American Federation of Labor, a proletarian not a capitalistic institution, gets twenty-five thousand a year. So do some other presidents of Unions.)

As regards hours of work, they cannot exceed eight in the twenty-four hour period; overtime work is paid for at the rate of time and one-half; during the periods of marked unemployment, hours of work are still kept consistent with a reasonable minimum income. Child labor, of course, is utterly eliminated. As regards conditions of work, the Safety Committees, the admirable Division of Hygiene (health-education program, first-aid instruction, immunization against diseases, prevention of malaria, general sanitation), the housing, catering, educational, and recreational facilities, the free training courses — I must mention some of them, they are so extraordinarily diversified and show so much mental curiosity on the part of the workers as well as so much solicitude on the part of the TVA: woodworking, general metal, automotive, electrical, ground aviation, blacksmithing, welding, plumbing, wrought-iron work, blueprint reading, even foremanship — are evidence of the determination to supply Labor with chances in the future as well as in the present. Apprenticeship, a forgotten phase everywhere in the world, has been revived. Demonstration-enterprises are run for the benefit of the employees: poultry farms, communal farm gardens, dairies, stock breeding, principles of marketing, use of farm agencies, and so forth and so on.

The TVA has further created an entirely new feature, to which no parallel can be found in any other organization — a bureau for the settlement of jurisdictional disputes, and for the maintenance of proper individual and collective relations between the supervisory personnel and the supervised workers. This section investigates complaints, makes reports to the parties concerned, and adjusts differences before they reach the stage of formal grievances. It

functions both for Whites and Blacks. (I assisted at a meeting where, among other points discussed, the Negroes, who gave me an impression of startling intelligence and moderation, objected to being invariably addressed as "son of a bitch" by certain foremen. The White head of this "Labor Relations Staff" instantly promised redress.)

There is a Workers' Council formed by the men, who debate on problems that could not be settled within the unions and groups themselves, and which thus can champion the unorganized worker: a new departure in the history of American Labor. During its three and a half years of life there has never been a strike in the TVA personnel. There has been no bluff on the part of employer or employees. The deal has been fair and square throughout on either side; the cards have been played openly and straightly; and both Capital and Labor reveal that they can be teammates, with goodwill and cooperation in a common cause, and honesty, tolerance, and patience toward problems of industrial relations.

All this seems to me exceptionally significant. When you analyze the domestic scene of a democratic country, you find that fundamentally its normal stability depends on the relations between Capital and Labor. With the exception of the Scandinavian nations where, for reasons I cannot enumerate here, admirable adjustments have been arrived at, no democratic country in Europe is a shining example of fairness; but, by and large, Capital there has been bludgeoned into a modicum of wisdom. It has been frightened into compromise. It has made concessions — and a good many concessions; sometimes, even, very difficult concessions — certainly not in a spirit of magnanimity, but of self-preservation. It has perceived that the trend of the times — queerly enough, in the fascistic lands, too — is going against it; public opinion is much more readily on the side of the workingman than of the big employer; and social legislation was, until Mr. Roosevelt appeared, incomparably more developed than in the United States.

No democratic European, whatever his party, can sympathize with the ear-splitting clamors of Tory Americans about measures most of us put through thirty-five or forty years ago, and which are now completely academic issues. They have become part and parcel of our social life and philosophy, and could no more be wrenched from them than the principle of religious freedom. In America, the fight for the social legislation we have already achieved is continuing, and the fight for political representation is only beginning. At first the foreign observer, especially if he lands in New York, which gives a thoroughly distorted and perverted view of American life (it throws the European entirely off his balance and is the chief source of the incredibly grotesque and false books we write about America; I have gone astray so dreadfully myself that I shall start my own study by earnestly petitioning the Federal Government to forbid inflexibly every European writer coming here for the first time to disembark in New York. The metropolis should only be visited on our way *home*) is tempted to think that the whole country is in violent social convulsions. That is not so at present, though it will happen in the future if the salient features of Capitalism are not modified.

Certain spots, notably the enormous industrial and shipping centers, are in violent social convulsions, and strikes have a tendency to become horrifyingly brutal, a tendency for which I blame almost exclusively the unimaginable methods the employers use to break them, aided arbitrarily, and much too often, by the authorities and official forces of the States. The methods with which the great corporations fight the strikers are caveman procedures, and I can find nothing approaching to an equivalent in any other democracy.

But broadly speaking, Labor in America is *conservative*. It is one of the most flabbergasting discoveries I have made. This conservatism is partly due to the antiquated policies of the American Federation of Labor; to its egotistic and frequently unreliable leadership; to the splitting-up of the working classes into an aristocracy of highly protected skills and crafts and a neglected and abandoned proletariat with no attention paid to the untrained laborer and to the Negro; and to such a stupefying lack of organization that out of thirty million American workers only three and a half million are unionized.

Partly, however, it is due to the temper of the American workingman himself. In general his sense of solidarity was for a very long time practically nonexistent: it is not at all effective yet. He clung with intense persistence to the traditional hope of escaping one day — soon — from the ranks of the employee into the ranks of the small entrepreneur and employer, where he would be hampered by the social legislation that would have benefited him as a simple worker. Such an ambition deprived his social outlook of all universality. He was much more ignorant and unthinking than his European colleague. He read much less. In the South, particularly, where unions were extremely rare, he was usually quite illiterate, and terrified to death of a system that could retaliate with literally murderous blows if he tried single-handedly to oppose it. Don't talk to me of the aggressiveness of the American worker, because it was a farce.

Today he is waking up. There is much less chance of passing into the higher strata; the activities of the Socialist and Communist parties are prodding him into the consciousness of the right to collective bargaining and to unionization which is his already in modern civilized countries; John L. Lewis, a gentleman who is not what could be termed a sentimentalist, is putting his class on a new footing, both industrially and politically. In two or three decades, perhaps sooner, Labor will really be a force that may tear the American domestic scene to pieces if Capitalism is obdurate. But the point I want to make is that at this stage, in spite of symptoms that reveal the possibility of an ultimate march instead of a stumbling about, Labor is still very ready to be conciliating.

After having poked a long inquiring nose into more unions, meetings, and demonstrations — pickets, too — than I can count, my unalterable conviction is that, whatever the fiery extremist groups may say or do, *the workingman* en bloc *is still no revolutionist at all*. He still has no fanatical hatred of the capitalist. He still has no feeling that the system is essentially unjust, infamous, execrable, and must be wiped off the face of the earth. He still does not hold that he is capable of taking the lead and conducting alone his country's economics. He still is prepared to sit at the foot of Capital's table and help himself to the remains of the huge dish. The one thing he insists on with growing energy and determination is that the remains should be sufficient to satisfy his reasonable necessities.

I do not say that this attitude will be his attitude eternally. I do not say that it is the intention of Labor leaders that it should be his attitude eternally. I do not say that *any* attitude can be eternal. What I wish to drive home is the fact that it is his actual attitude. His historical and mental make-up is such that he may continue in it until the community as a whole is attuned to a basic social change, if it is met with reason and equity on the part of the employer, with cooperation on the part of Capital, and with adjustments which he himself can freely formulate and practise. If these things are denied him — well, America can count on having in time a first-class bust-up.

The Labor policies of the TVA and their results prove conclusively that in a capitalistic democracy Capital need not be cannibalistic, Labor need not be revolutionary, and that the imperishable quest of man for the millennium can be pursued by evolution and adaptation instead of by blowing himself and his fellows in mud and blood to the skies. But whether autocratic Capital in this country will consent, without pressure from somebody or something more autocratic still, to take the TVA as its model, is a question on which I seem to feel a few slight doubts.

A river has no politics.
DAVID E. LILIENTHAL, when director of TVA

99.

ALOISIUS MUENCH: Rural Families and Welfare

Rural life in the Middle West during the 1930s was generally bleak. The Depression had brought falling food prices and mounting debts to farmers; the great dust storms impaired the productiveness of the soil; and young people moved off the land and into the cities in increasing numbers. In 1937 the National Catholic Rural Life Conference convened at St. Paul, Minnesota, to discuss the church's role in rural welfare. Aloisius Muench, Bishop of Fargo, North Dakota, delivered the following address in which he emphasized his church's concern for rural America, the last stronghold of the family as an economic unit.

Source: *Catholic Rural Life Objectives*, St. Paul, 1937, pp. 16-19.

The Family and Rural Welfare

THE FAMILY AS A SOCIAL INSTITUTION is stronger in rural areas than in urban centers. The farmstead is not like a shop, office, or factory to which men and women go in the morning and leave again at night, but it is also a homestead. Where farm ownership is rendered secure, the homestead is held in honor by generation after generation as it passes on from father to son. The farmstead is for all members an economic unit. Young and old, father, mother, and children have a common stake in it. The vicissitudes of the climate, the approach of the seasons for sowing and harvesting, the land, the seed, the machinery, the fowl and cattle — all evoke a daily interest around the table at mealtime or in the evening as the family gathers around the fireside. These are all important elements to hold the family together.

Once formed, the family group is less easily broken in rural areas. Divorce is less frequent among rural married people. "In large metropolitan areas, 19 percent of the homes were broken in 1930; in villages the figure was 14.7 percent, while in the country areas it was only 8.1 percent." . . . According to the fifteenth census reports, 1930, there were 100 divorced women to every 7,500 married women and 100 divorced men to every 6,400 married men in rural areas; whereas in urban districts there were 100 divorced women to 3,800 married women and 100 divorced men to every 4,700 married men. For a strictly farming population there were only 100 divorced women to 10,300 married women and 100 divorced men to every 8,000 married men. I shall not weary you with more statistics on this point. They all emphasize the fact that the marriage bond is more secure in the countryside than in urban centers.

The farm family remains also the cradle of the nation, whereas the urban family is its grave. Births have declined so rapidly in the cities that urban populations are no longer reproducing themselves. Without the migration of rural youth into the cities to make up the deficit of necessary births, cities would find their population depleted

y two-thirds within a century, assuming
hat the rate of decrease will remain what it
ow is; and as a matter of fact the trend is
o a greater and greater decline. . . .

The decline of population has serious
onsequences for education, business enter-
rise, and religion. In the cities, teachers are
inding it more and more difficult to obtain
eaching positions because of the rapid de-
line of the school population. For the last
ix years there have been 100,000 fewer ba-
ies born each year; in consequence, 2,500
ewer teachers are needed each year in the
chools. Business has not been unaware of
he shrinking of markets at home and
broad because of fewer mouths to feed and
ewer bodies to clothe and house. . . .

Religion, too, will experience the necessi-
y of making new adjustments. The Catho-
ic Church in this country is concentrated in
he cities. About 20 or 30 percent only of
Catholics are located in rural areas. This
umber is too small to make up the deficits
f births in the cities. From data thus far
vailable it is necessary to conclude that the
irth rate among urban Catholics has also
allen rapidly in the last few decades. Rural
Catholic families, however, still have many
hildren, but these families are relatively too
mall to make up for many of the 70-80
ercent of urban Catholic families that have
o children at all, or only two or three. In
rural parish of the diocese of Fargo, there
ves a Catholic mother whose descendants
umber 14 children, 117 grandchildren, and
15 great-grandchildren — 346 descendants
n all. In some rural places families are be-
inning to follow city patterns. It is esti-
nated, considering all the facts, that by
bout 1950 the population in the United
tates will be stationary.

Taken all in all, in the rural family, ideals
f virtue are sounder, religion is held in
reater honor, children obtain a better train-
ng in affairs than the youth of streets, and
he spirit of democracy is more easily
chooled where members cooperate on the
same economic basis than is the case in urban families who often live in congested
city areas, whose members are in daily contact with the materialism and sensuality of
the world and pursue each different ways of
life independent of one another and moti-
vated largely by selfish interests. Domestic
or home virtues thrive better in the rugged
atmosphere of the farm home than in the
artificial and blighting air of the city.

Private Property and Rural Welfare

THE CHURCH IS INTERESTED in rural welfare
from another point of view. It is that of
private property.

Among social institutions that touch upon
the material well-being of people, postulate
high moral qualities, and produce rich social
by-products, few, if any, are the equal of
private property. Basic to peace, order, and
progress is the security of private property.
On this account, Pope Leo XIII, almost fifty years ago, in his celebrated encyclical,
Rerum Novarum — On the Condition of
Workingmen, developed at length arguments in behalf of private property. "The
law, therefore, should favor ownership," he
wrote, "and its policy should be to induce
as many people as possible to become owners." . . .

Many excellent results will follow from
such a governmental policy. First of all,
property will be more equitably divided.
Many of the economic and social evils of
our day go back to the fact that the distribution of wealth is not more equitable.
"Wealth, therefore, which is constantly augmented by social and economic progress,
must be so distributed amongst the various
individuals and classes of society," empha-
sizes Pope Pius XI in his encyclical on the
Reconstruction of the Social Order, "that
the needs of all, of which Leo XIII spoke,
be thereby satisfied." . . .

Unfortunately, ownership in farmlands

Destitute farm families at the Farm Security Administration depot in Bakersfield, Calif., waiting for food grants; photo by Dorothea Lange

has been steadily on the decrease in this country. Recent data on the increase of tenancy in the United States is not very encouraging. Whereas in 1880, when tenancy was first measured in that year, one-fourth of all the farms in the United States were tenant-operated, fifty years later, according to the census of 1930, 42.4 percent of all farms were tenant-operated. . . . The Depression undoubtedly accelerated the increase, since financial difficulties caused many farmers to lose the farms which they once owned but now operate as tenants. . . .

It is necessary to point out that tenancy is not conducive to rural well-being whatever be the angle from which it is viewed. Since the tenant has no stake in the land, he will not utilize it to the best advantage; he will take out of it all he can, "mine the soil," as agricultural economists call it, regardless of what his method of cultivation will do to the fertility of the soil. Home, barn, granary, sheds, fences — all that is not his own will soon show the wear and tear of time; there is no ownership incentive to keep them in repair. Because the tenant must support himself and family off the farm and pay rent in some form to the owner besides, he is actually maintaining two families. In consequence his standard of living is usually lower.

From a social standpoint the tenant takes little interest in local organizations, farm bureaus, community projects, and the like. The reason is, of course, the tenant's feeling of insecurity as to his land tenure. He will form no permanent ties until he is sure of some kind of land permanence. There are reactions also on religion. "For example, in Middlewestern counties where 50 percent or more of farms are tenant operated there are only one-third as many tenants as owners listed as active church members." . . . This is but another instance of how unfavorable material conditions react unfavorably in a spiritual way. Absentee landlordism is responsible often, too, for lack of improvements, roads, schools and other community projects. These things involve the levying of taxes, to which the absentee landlord will be opposed. Unless the tenancy becomes a stepping-stone to land ownership, as for instance, in Ireland, it is ruinous to rural welfare from an economic, social, education, and religious standpoint.

A Program of Social Justice for the Farmer

WHAT PROGRAM, then, should be set forth to promote rural welfare?

First, it should be shouted from the

housetops that social justice is not merely an urban or industrial need. Its principles need to be applied also to agricultural and rural maladjustments.

Second, the experience of European countries who have suffered from tenancy evils in the past should be consulted and their legislation studied so that adequate laws shall be drawn to protect the rights of he tenants as to any property equities he may have acquired by his labor on another man's land.

Third, since fair prices to the farmers for the products he has to sell are essential for the acquisition of private property, nothing shall be left undone to safeguard the farmer's interests in this respect. This does not necessarily imply governmental action, certainly not collectivism in the guise of either Socialism or Communism. The collectivized farmer of Russia has not fared well at the hands of government officials. Wise statesmanship will provide laws and institutions that will produce of themselves public well-being and private prosperity. There is need of more organization along cooperative lines, vocational groupings, in other words, among farmers to restore the social organism that the individualism of the past century and a half destroyed.

Fourth, social justice will not remain a nebulous, intangible thing if cooperatives are established as they were in Nova Scotia under the auspices of St. Francis Xavier University. Fishermen, miners, and farmers there are cooperatively organized, and today have a better realization of social justice in a practical and concrete way than they had only some few years ago. The cooperative, whether established for purposes of production, marketing, buying, or credit facilities, seems to be the best form of organization thus far devised to protect the rights of the agriculturalist and to afford him opportunities for material development, as well as cultural and religious advancement. It is im-

perative, however, that the virus of materialism and commercialism be kept out of the life stream of the cooperatives. Their principles shall have to be carried by the ideals of social justice and social charity if they are not to go the way of modern materialistic finance capitalism.

Fifth, principles of social justice, effective tenancy legislation, sound cooperative organizations — these and other things that human ingenuity can devise for the betterment of the farmer's lot must have their focal point in the farm home. The farmstead as a homestead must be cherished as among the most priceless social institutions in the land. Upon it depends the future well-being of the nation. To allow it to fall into decay will spell decay and death for the nation.

Sixth, although the farmer produces the bread for the nation, he, too, does not live from bread alone. He himself realizes this. More than urbanites know he is interested in things of culture and religion. He hungers for them. Fortunately, great strides forward have been made in recent years with regard to social, cultural, and religious improvement of people living far from urban centers. There has been an awakening in this respect throughout the country. It is heartening to note how much has been accomplished by way of religious vacation schools, discussion clubs for adults, religious correspondence courses, motor missions, and other similar religious enterprises.

But much more needs still to be done. Those interested in the work of the National Catholic Rural Life Conference realize this. Enthusiasm for its cause must not wane; it must grow; it must be another fire that has come upon the earth to enkindle the hearts of those who have heard of neither the mission nor the message of the Conference. To you and to them I submit the outlined six-point program for consideration, discussion, and may I hope, also for action.

100.

Urban Problems

The New Deal era was the first in which attention was focused on the problems of urban development. It was obvious in the 1930s that the tendency of the population to concentrate in cities and metropolitan areas was increasing. During the 1920s more than 6 million people had exchanged a rural for an urban life, a trend only temporarily reversed during the Depression. Realizing that the nation's destiny would be profoundly affected by the cities, which now had over half of the population and even more of the wealth, the President added an Urbanism Committee to the National Resources Committee. Its report of August 9, 1937, the first to pinpoint major problems, is reprinted here in part.

Source: *Our Cities: Their Role in the National Economy*, Washington, 1937, pp. v-x.

THIS REPORT, MADE FOR THE PRESIDENT, following the request of a number of national organizations, is the first major national study of cities in the United States. The Country Life Commission reporting to President Theodore Roosevelt in 1909 explored the problems of rural living for the first time in systematic fashion, but until now there has been no similar examination of urban conditions. There have been many special studies in particular cities, but none of the place of cities in our national scheme of things.

Our nation is based upon a community of interest in the midst of diversity of occupations. The striking thing in America is not the clash of economic interests but the unity of political objectives. It is the function of the government to consider maladjustments, whether rural or urban, in the light of the national goal and to aid where possible in the solution of these problems, but not primarily as rural or urban problems, but first and foremost as American problems, as limitations on the attainment of American ideas. . . .

As America pitches back and forth between alternate depression and recurrent prosperity, it is in the nation's cities that the shadow of economic insecurity is darkest. For in the city will be found the workshop of our industrial society and the nerve center of our vast and delicate commercial mechanism. In 1935 one-fifth of all the employable persons on relief in the country were to be found in our ten largest cities. Subject to continuing unemployment, lacking the rural reserves of shelter and subsistence, the city worker is seriously handicapped in the struggle for existence.

In time of national stress the task of relief and recovery falls, not merely upon a single community or segment of the nation but upon the nation as a whole. It is the federal government that has had to assume the major burdens of providing emergency relief for the city as well as the farm, of stimulating public works in the nation's urban ceners, and even of reviving insolvent municipal finances. Of the billions of dollars devoted to public emergency relief during the period 1933 to 1936, a large percent was contributed by the federal government.

The nation's task has now become not only one of relief and recovery but of reconstruction, and this also has been recognized as in part the federal government's responsibility. Confirmed by the regulations and decisions of the highest tribunals in the land, there has been launched, along with an agricultural and fiscal plan, a nationwide program of social security and rational labor relations, principally designed to reduce the insecurities of the mass of city workers and thereby of the system of national production and consumption which rests in large part upon their welfare and their prosperity.

The nation has wisely begun to concern itself with the conservation of its human and social resources as well as the conservation of its physical resources of water, land, and minerals. These human and social resources are affected, not only by the conditions of rural life which dominated the national country life movement thirty years ago but they now include the conditions of urban life.

In looking at the urban problem, therefore, we consider it not as the concern of the city alone but as a problem of the farmer as well in that it is a problem of all the American nation. From the point of view of the highest and best use of our national resources, our urban communities are potential assets of great value, and we must consider from the point of view of the national welfare how they may be most effectively aided in their development. In the short-time run, there may be clashes of interest between urban and rural populations, competing types of production, differing demands in consumption, different hours and wages, differing standards of living, and different ways of life. But in the long run and

from the overall point of view, their interests are mutual, reciprocal, interdependent. . . .

Mechanization has produced great factories, and technology has greatly aided the output of the soil. But an indirect consequence has been the dominance of the machine over the ways of life in cities, while the machine in the country has increased the yield of farms yet diminished in many respects the value of its produce. In consequence, the man on the farm and the man in the city alike look with mingled admiration and fear at the machine which at the same time has increased their power and diminished their security.

The farm and the city have in common the problem of dealing successfully with large units of industrial organization. The farmer encounters this problem whether he buys or sells — in buying effectively what he consumes and in selling effectively what he produces for the consumption of others. Whichever way he turns, the farmer faces the industrial giants of modern America — producers and sellers of machines and merchandise, against whom he must match his wits and his economic power. The laborer in the city likewise confronts, in his struggle for wages, hours, and working conditions, and parity of purchasing power, organized units of vast strength.

The small businessman is likewise embattled. The farmer has often learned the value of associations adapted to his way of life, and the laborer and small businessman the value of associations adapted to their way of life. Through these organizations they maintain themselves against other organizations, and often glean some gains, sometimes by one group at the expense of another, without advantage to the national welfare.

Yet, viewing the whole field, it is clear that there are large numbers of farmers and large numbers of city workers whose share in our magical civilization is spelled out in terms of daily life that is drab in color and sad in tone. The crowded poverty of the one may match the lonely poverty of the other — alike cut off from the rich inheritance of the richest of modern nations.

The city has seemed at times the despair of America, but at others to be the nation's hope, the battleground of democracy. Surely, in the long run, the nation's destiny will be profoundly affected by the cities which have two-thirds of its population and its wealth. There is liberty of development in isolation and wide spaces, but there is also freedom in the many-sided life of the city where each may find his own kind. There is democracy in the scattered few, but there is also democracy in the thick crowd with its vital impulse and its insistent demand for a just participation in the gains of our civilization. There is fertility and creation in the rich soil of the broad countryside, but there is also fertility and creativeness in forms of industry, art, personality, emerging even from the city streets and reaching toward the sky. . . .

It is important to look at some of the emerging problems of urban communities and to consider such forms of guidance and support as may seem feasible and appropriate under all the circumstances.

1. The most drastic inequalities of income and wealth are found within the urban community. Relatively to their rich fellow citizens, the poor are poorer in the city than they are elsewhere despite an increasing standard of living for the city worker. Widespread poverty and cyclical unemployment and insecurity threaten purchasing power, and without continuous mass purchasing power our urban industry and mass-production economy cannot continue to function properly.

2. One of our specific economic problems is the lack of articulation among the various industries within our urban commu-

nities. Frequently the decision to locate an industry in one city or another is based upon the immediate opportunities of a particular enterprise or the desire of a community to increase the total amount of industrial activity, regardless of its effect upon the local industrial structure. Localities, by means of subsidies, tax exemption, and free sites, have indiscriminately attracted enterprises which did not mesh with the rest of the community's industries and which sooner or later helped to throw the entire industrial pattern out of gear. Under such unbalanced conditions, it is impossible to achieve a maximum employment for the available labor supply and a minimum of seasonal and cyclical fluctuations in the total payroll of the community. Instead, the results may be migrant labor, increased unemployment load, lower wages, shrunken purchasing power, loss of business, high cost of relief, untenanted property, tax arrears, and curtailed municipal services.

3. Rapid obsolescence of physical plan and plant is another problem which the American city has had to face. Villages, in all too short a period of time, have become towns, towns have become cities, and cities have turned into metropolitan centers, where brick houses replaced frame, apartment hotels succeeded residences, office buildings replaced shops and lofts, inns became grand hotels, and the early skyscrapers were converted into colossal cloud-scratchers. Some cities, on the other hand, have become deserted mill sites and dreary ghost towns. America was growing, but it was also wasting away, and traces of this deterioration are with us today in the form of many blighted neighborhoods.

4. Competing forms of transportation have left their disrupting imprint upon the national urban pattern. Located originally on natural waterways, American cities found their sister towns rising up during the canal era on new water routes. With the

coming of the railroads these canal cities met in their turn a similarly disastrous fate. Then came competing railroads, and cities again began to rival one another with excessive subsidies and cutthroat competition for rate reduction. Nor have we yet reached the end of this process. The motor truck and the passenger bus have long since entered the field of competition, and now the airplane begins to affect the national distribution of our urban centers and even the local pattern and the plan of our cities.

5. The unparalleled growth of cities has been accompanied by uncontrolled subdivision and speculative practices and by the most fantastic real estate booms, which have meant dramatic profits to a few but tragic personal losses to others and burdensome delinquent properties to the community; and this on a scale affecting the economic situation of the entire nation. The history of the recent industrial depression cannot be written without an account of the role of unsound financing and of speculation in real estate, which at times became mere gambling. We are now faced with the problem of arriving at a rational urban land policy which, while affording private owners and developers adequate opportunity for wise and profitable land uses, will curb the forms of speculation that prove calamitous to the investing and the tax-paying public.

6. Urban housing is one of the most burdensome problems the country now has to face and it calls for the nation's most serious consideration. A real property inventory of sixty-four cities made in 1934 by the Department of Commerce and the Civil Works Administration showed that more than one-sixth of 1.5 million residential dwellings were substandard, about four-fifths of the dwelling units are made of wood, about one third are over thirty years old, a large proportion are in the state of serious disrepair. Even at their most reasonable figures, rentals are so high that they exclude vast blocs of urban families from housing facilities of minimum standard.

7. Urban public health is endangered particularly in blighted areas and among low income groups. Morbidity and mortality rates in infants' diseases and tuberculosis are higher here than elsewhere, in spite of an admirable development of urban public health services. Dirt, smoke, waste, soot, grime, and the reckless pollution of water are still among the noxious enemies of city life despite valiant official attempts to regulate these evils.

8. The city with its diversity of ethnic, religious, and cultural strains is the haven par excellence of many widely varying types of personalities whose names loom large in the history of America, but in this heterogeneity the city also finds some of its weightiest problems. The various parts and participants of the urban economy are very highly specialized and the urban way of life is often socially disconnected though economically interdependent. Allegiances may become group, class, or sectional rather than community or citywide. How to prevent these strains of separation from disrupting the whole city or its civic groups or even its families, how to weave these vivid and variegated cultures into a positive civic program of intercommunication and cooperation is one of the challenging problems of the coming decades.

9. While free primary and secondary education is now widely available in urban areas, city youths in all too many cases are still barred from higher educational opportunities they might well utilize because they must all too frequently supplement the family income by going to work. Vocational education and adaptation still limp and lag behind their possibilities although much work has already been started. Adult education after so many years of enthusiasm for this form of civic enlightenment in cities is an inadequately supported service and is

still an experiment instead of an accepted responsibility of the community. Much has been accomplished through federal aid, but much more needs to be done.

10. Juvenile delinquency, organized crime, and commercial rackets are among the vexations of the city. None of our reforms in the field of criminal justice has successfully come to grips with these persistent urban problems.

11. Urban public finance is another emerging problem of vast proportions. In the recent depression, urban areas pouring millions into the national Treasury were forced to pass the hat, begging for financial support. The anomaly of the situation is the fact that the forty-eight state governments which determine the local systems of taxation are from the standpoint of total expenditures only one-half as important as all the local governments they must control. Our largest cities alone — New York, Chicago, Boston, and Detroit — have larger budgets than the states which contain them. The problem of municipal finance is becoming even more complicated with the extension of federal and state taxation to support the newer services of government, such as social security and extensive public works.

12. Another of the city's wealthiest tasks is the adjustment of the traditional scope of urban powers. In spite of its vital and growing significance as the principal instrument of public service and community control, the American city is still the legal creature of higher authorities, subject to their fiat for the most minor of powers and procedures, reaching down in one state to legislation to permit the peddling of peanuts on a municipal pier. The city is in many ways the ward of a guardian who refuses to function.

13. Our overlapping medley of independent governmental units was intended for a rural and a manorial society but never for the sprawling metropolitan regions of America and the satellite suburbs. The concrete facts of our urban and administrative life frequently defy state lines and local control. Twenty-two of our ninety-six metropolitan districts containing 26 million, or one-fifth of all our inhabitants, straddle state lines and call for a larger measure of interstate and federal cooperation in certain fields than is now found.

14. We have made striking technical advances in municipal government and for years now we have developed, contrary to opinions widely held, skill and talent and expert knowledge among our municipal career officers, but we are still faced in some cities with systematic evasions of civil service laws, irresponsible political leadership, and official tolerance of discriminatory or questionable administrative practices.

All in all there has been more widespread national neglect of our cities than of any other major segment of our national existence. Whether this is to be attributed to the absorption of our best efforts by the demands of our commercial and industrial system or by other pressing claims of national policy, it is evident that America must now set out to overcome the continual and cumulative disregard of urban policies and administration and to take into account the place of the urban community in the national economy.

In the United States there is more space where nobody is than where anybody is. This is what makes America what it is.

GERTRUDE STEIN, *The Geographical History of America*

101.

Mary Ross: Why Social Security?

The Social Security Act was passed in August 1935, and the administration of its provisions was put in the hands of a board set up as an independent government agency. As a part of its effort to explain the workings of Social Security to the public, the following pamphlet, written by Mary Ross of the Bureau of Research and Statistics, was published in 1936. A portion of the pamphlet is reprinted below.

Source: Social Security Board Publication No. 15: *Why Social Security?*, Washington, 1937, SS 1.2:So 1/2.

THE WORDS "SOCIAL SECURITY" have become popular in the last five or ten years. Actually the right and duty of a community to protect its members is as old as the records of men. Primitive tribes have rules and customs to assure the safety of all. Even pioneer American families, of course, relied on each other for help in trouble and emergencies. Barn raisings and corn huskings, which have lasted down to our times, are a survival of years when a household asked the neighbors' help in an emergency, knowing it would give its help when its turn came. . . .

Since a living was made in families, it was through families that a community made and enforced its security measures. Many of these measures remain with us today. The security of children, wives, and aged parents does not depend upon the willingness of their relatives to support them. It is written into our laws and enforced daily in our courts. It is a form of social security because we see to it as a society that relatives give this support when they can, whether they wish to or not.

As cities have grown up we have taken another series of steps for social security by banding together to pay for certain kinds of protection that no one family can provide for themselves. We have police and fire departments, for example. We make fire laws governing the kinds of buildings that people may build in safety to themselves and their neighbors. We support public-health departments. We set up traffic regulations to protect safety of life on the highways and streets.

We also have taken steps to aid helpless people who need a kind of care or an amount of protection that few families can provide for themselves. As our increasing scientific knowledge showed the need and the way, we built hospitals for the mentally sick and for people with tuberculosis. We made laws and opened clinics and special schools for crippled children.

At first, these measures to help unfortunate people dealt chiefly with those who were dangerous to others, such as mental patients and people sick with communicable diseases. More recently we realized that it is public economy as well as kindness to make sure that other disabled people get care, since often they can recover enough to earn a living for themselves. It is cheaper to cure them than to care for them for years in institutions.

About forty years ago we began to realize that security in health and life must follow people out of their homes and into the factories.

Our greatest success has come in making life safe for children. Up to about 1900 many children had gone along with their elders into the factories. In 1900 nearly a fifth of all the ten-to-sixteen-year-old children were at work. This was a larger percentage than had been found in any previous census year.

Then, state after state decided that factories were not places for children. Laws were passed to restrict child labor and to specify the conditions under which children might work, if at all. At the same time, other laws made it compulsory for children to have more chance to go to school and stay in school. In 1930 less than one-twentieth of the ten-to-sixteen-year-old children were in gainful work.

We have not yet lifted by any means all the burden of harmful labor from the shoulders of children, but most of it is gone. And in the twentieth century we have come far toward achieving what some of the colonists set themselves as a goal: the right of children to the security of an education. In 1932, President Hoover's Committee on Recent Social Trends declared that the fact that half the children of high-school age were in the high schools was "evidence of the most successful single effort which government in the United States has ever put forth."

In the past forty years many states have passed laws to promote health and safety in work for adults as well as for children — laws governing hours of work, night work, dangerous work, and the like. These are conditions which workers no longer can control for themselves as they could when they worked at home. . . .

In the past twenty years many states have taken steps to give some security to another large group of their people — the old people who never will earn again. Arizona passed the first old-age pension act in 1914. After the World War one state after another rapidly followed suit. By the end of 1930, fourteen others had put such laws on their statute books, and in the next three years ten more were added.

This wave of laws to pay regular allowances to needy old people did not come by accident or imitation. It came because of the growing percentage of old people in the population and the inability of the old to work for their living. Old age was becoming an increasingly serious problem to old people and their families and their towns and counties.

Most of the allowances given to old people under state laws have been very small. Even so, they have helped many old people to stay in their own homes and to keep their self-respect when they share the homes of others. Giving allowances has been cheaper as well as more humane than caring for old people in poorhouses.

Mothers' aid and old-age allowances are not "pensions" in the sense in which we usually use that word. Widowed mothers and old people do not get assistance just because they are widowed or have reached a certain age. They also must show that they are in need.

Regular allowances have not been given to all the needy aged and needy mothers even in states where there have been such laws. Under some of the state laws, a county chose whether or not it wished to operate under the state plan. When county and state funds ran low, even eligible applicants remained on waiting lists for months or years. Mothers' aid and old-age assistance are a modern way of giving what we used to call "charity." They are relief measures. They recognize the responsibility of counties and states to give security to people who cannot earn it for themselves and provide a more just and orderly way to meet that responsibility. . . .

Workmen's compensation acts protect workers from the costs of accidents at work. Unemployment compensation acts protect them against some of the costs of the accident of not having any job at all.

Under unemployment compensation, payrolls or wages, or both, are taxed in certain industries to pay workers in those industries a part of their wages for a time while they are unemployed through no wish or fault of their own. In some countries these payments are supplemented by governmental grants from general taxation. The tax borne by employers is a charge on industry, like other costs of doing business. When workers also are taxed, their payments are like premiums paid for fire insurance or accident insurance. The many people who run a risk pay toward meeting the loss of those on whom catastrophe falls. The lucky help pay for the unlucky. It is worth their while to do so, for they do not know when catastrophe may hit themselves.

Under the system of unemployment compensation so far established in the United States, unemployed workers still carry a large part of the loss of being without jobs. Unemployment benefits usually do not begin until a man has been out of work for several weeks. They provide only a part of the amount he would have earned. They cease after a limited period, even though he still has not found another job. Benefits paid to unemployed workers cushion the shock of losing a job, especially in short-time unemployment, which is the most usual type of unemployment in ordinary times. They make it possible for workers to keep on buying their living while they are looking for other work. In that way, these payments also benefit all those with whom these workers ordinarily deal.

Unemployment compensation is not charity or relief but a means of preventing need for relief. Through unemployment insurance, like other types of insurance, a loss which is crushing to those who incur it in any one month or year is made bearable by being distributed over large numbers of people and over a period of time. . . .

The Social Security Act of 1935 grows out of . . . many changes in American life. It consolidates our past experience in meeting insecurity. It also sets up a bulwark against some of the newer kinds of insecurity that threaten large numbers of us in this twentieth century.

Several parts of the Social Security Act deal with groups of people whose troubles we have recognized for many years. These provisions consider the people who are too young or too old to earn or are physically handicapped. The act authorizes federal grants-in-aid to enable the states to broaden and extend regular allowances for needy mothers, the needy blind, and the needy aged. It authorizes grants-in-aid for state services for child welfare, for crippled children, and for physically handicapped people who can be helped to work again. The provisions for child welfare apply especially to rural areas.

These sections of the Social Security Act draw on our national resources to help all states to do better what most or all have undertaken in some way and to some degree. They give a way to put into effect the best measures we have been able to devise for helping people who are unable to help themselves.

Other provisions of the Social Security Act recognize the risks of sickness — risks which affect all of us, young and old, rich and poor. The act authorizes federal grants-in-aid to help states to give service for the health of mothers and children and to strengthen and extend public-health services. It authorizes funds for the study of national and interstate health problems. These parts of the act promote security by preventing sickness and by giving children, especially country children, a fair start in life.

Finally, two provisions deal with insecurity in earning. They apply to groups of our people who have moved into occupations where earning often is risky. They cover a great share of the wage earners who are wholly dependent on their ability to buy a living.

Under one of these provisions, the Social Security Act sets up a framework to protect the states which wish to enact laws for unemployment compensation. Federal funds are authorized to help a state to do this by meeting the costs of administration. The Social Security Act does not say that any state must have an unemployment compensation law. It does not say what kind of law a state should have. It does say that business in a state which has unemployment compensation shall not be penalized in competition with business in states which do not.

From the beginning of 1935, when the possibility of harmony in state action became clear during the discussion of the Social Security Act in Congress, and up to April 1, 1937, forty-two states and the District of Columbia had enacted unemployment compensation laws. These laws are a beginning in making the costs of industry's fluctuations a charge upon industry rather than only on the jobless workers, who hitherto have borne the brunt of industrial change. The act thus helps states to find ways in which workers and employers can steady livelihood.

It also provides ways to build up the livelihood of wage earners in old age. The Social Security Act establishes a system of federal old-age benefits which will provide monthly payments, in 1942 and after, to many workers when they reach the age of sixty-five. The amount of a man's benefit depends on the wages he has received in his working years, after 1936, as defined in the act. Thus old-age benefits are based on wage records.

Under another provision of the act, grants are made to the states for old-age assistance. Old-age assistance is not the same as old-age benefits. In old-age assistance, federal, state, and local funds are used to help old people who lack means of their own. Regular assistance may be given to any aged person who is entitled to aid under a state plan approved by the Social Security Board. Thus, old-age assistance is helping those who now are old and in need.

Old-age benefits, on the other hand, offer future provision for large groups of people who now are working and earning. Under the plan for old-age benefits, the majority of the nation's wage earners can look forward to a definite old-age income of their own. Their old-age benefits will supplement any savings these workers have been able to make. They do not have to prove that they are needy. The benefits are theirs regardless of need.

If a worker dies before he has received his benefits, his estate receives a lump sum equal to 3½ percent of his wages counted toward benefits.

In general, the Social Security Act helps to assure some income to people who cannot earn and to steady the income of millions of wage earners during their working years and their old age. In one way and another taxation is spread over large groups of people to carry the cost of giving some security to those who are unfortunate or incapacitated at any one time. The act is a foundation on which we have begun to build security as states and as a people, against the risks which families cannot meet one by one.

The colonists and frontiersmen wanted independence. They wanted a chance for themselves and their children. They wanted a place of their own and an active share in the life of their times. There is no reason to think that our wants have changed. These are the things that most Americans ask today. What has changed is the way we take to get them. Families no longer can carve out security for themselves. Our security is the security of a people.

102.

JOEL SEIDMAN: The Sit-Down Strike

The first major sit-down strike began on December 31, 1936, when a few hundred workers seized the General Motors plants at Flint, Michigan, and remained for forty-four days, resisting all attempts to remove them and receiving food and other necessities from their allies on the outside. This new form of strike paralyzed production and prevented strikebreaking, and it was soon copied all over the country, spreading to rubber, textiles, oil refining, shipbuilding, and steel, and involving half a million workers in all. The Supreme Court declared the sit-down strike illegal in 1939, after which organized labor condemned the practice, but while it lasted it was extremely effective. The report by Joel Seidman from which the following selection is taken was published in 1937 by the League for Industrial Democracy.

Source: *New Frontiers,* January 1937: "Sit-Down."

When they tie the can to a union man,
   Sit down! Sit down!
When they give him the sack, they'll
   take him back,
   Sit down! Sit down!

Chorus
Sit down, just take a seat,
Sit down, and rest your feet,
Sit down, you've got 'em beat.
   Sit down! Sit down!

A NEW STRIKE TECHNIQUE has swept the country, arousing enthusiasm among workers and bewilderment among employers. In industry after industry, in state after state, the workers remain at their posts but refuse to work. No longer is it possible to introduce strikebreakers, for the workers are in possession. Nor are the workers readily dispersed, for they can barricade themselves in a strong defensive position. If strikebreakers or police storm the factory gate, they are clearly responsible in the eyes of the public for whatever violence may occur. The employer cannot too easily afford to alienate public opinion nor risk damage to his machinery. And so the workers remain in possession of the plant, in much more comfort and security than on the picket line. . . .

The sit-down strike should be viewed, not as an isolated occurrence but in the light of the complex social situation that gives rise to it. Those who wish to avoid it will make most progress, not by attacking the result but by removing the cause. No worker for slight cause cuts off his income, even temporarily, and it is no comfort to sleep in a factory instead of a home. If workers strike, whether by remaining in or walking out of the factory, it is because they have suffered from grievances to the limit of their endurance, and because they have learned that only by striking will their complaints be adjusted.

The rubber workers of Akron have engaged in more sit-down strikes than have any other group of workers in this country,

Culver Pictures, Inc.

"Hello, Momma, We're makin' history!"; cartoon from the "New York World Telegraph," 1937

and probably in the world. Their attitude is well expressed by Sherman H. Dalrymple, president of the United Rubber Workers of America:

> Sit-downs do not occur in plants where true collective bargaining exists. Where management does not attempt to destroy unionism by financing company unions, by the formation of vigilante groups, and by placing other obstacles in the path of legitimate union growth, there is such a spirit of cooperation between the union and management that cessations of work do not occur.
>
> Recent sit-downs in Akron have occurred because management either did not enter into fair negotiations on certain grievances or deliberately postponed decisions until resentment of the workers grew so keen that they resorted to sit-downs as a last resort.
>
> The fact that these grievances were settled satisfactorily immediately after the sit-downs definitely indicates that they could have been settled just as easily before if management had negotiated fairly with the union committee in their efforts to secure peaceful settlement of the issues involved.

It is our contention that the only way these sit-downs can be avoided in the future is through the proper application of all the rules of true collective bargaining in a spirit of fair play.

Early Uses of the Sit-down in America

IT IS IMPOSSIBLE TO DETERMINE accurately when and where the sit-down strike was first used. It seems such a logical tactic for workers to employ that there are probably many unrecorded instances, each one short in duration, going back almost as far as our modern industrial civilization. The wonder is that its use did not become widespread much earlier.

In at least two American industries it has long been common for workers to stop work without leaving their place of employment. In the anthracite coalfields the breaker boys, whose task it was to remove impurities from the coal, early formed the practice of stopping work without leaving their places when they were dissatisfied. Similarly, miners have stopped loading coal when they were not adequately supplied with timber for safety protection.

In the women's garment industry, as far back as 1910, workers have ceased operations without leaving the shop. Partly this has been done when a contract forbade strikes, the workers arguing that a mere stoppage was not a violation. These stoppages, as they were called, attracted little attention because they were usually settled within a few hours, and lacked the drama and publicity value of a picket line. Seldom, if ever, did the workers remain at their places overnight, though stoppages often continue for several days. In the Schenectady, N.Y., plant of the General Electric Company, similarly, a sit-down strike occurred as early as 1906. In 1933, 2,500 employees of the Hormel Packing Company in Austin, Minnesota, sat down for three days and won their strike against speed-up, for shorter hours and better wages. Many other instances doubtless occurred in other industries. During the Depression the unemployed in New Jersey and elsewhere took possession of legislative chambers in an effort to dramatize their plight and force more adequate relief policies.

Seamen used the sit-down strike on the Pacific Coast early in 1936. Seamen on the Panama Pacific liner *California* had signed on at the Atlantic Coast rates. In an effort to obtain the higher Pacific Coast rates, they struck for three days while the ship was at the San Pedro, California, docks. The men remained on board but refused to work. Had they struck while the ship was at sea, they would have been subject to a charge of mutiny. As it was, they narrowly escaped arrest on that charge. The line refused to reemploy the strikers when the ship reached New York, and a long strike against the International Mercantile Marine Company was the result. . . .

Rubber Workers Sit-down

IT REMAINED for the Akron rubber workers to popularize the sit-down in the United States. According to Louis Adamic it was first used by ball teams of union rubber workers who sat down on the grass or on benches and refused to play until they were provided with an umpire who was a union man. Later a dozen of them remembered this technique when they were dissatisfied with working conditions. The paralysis spread through the plant, and within an hour the dispute was settled.

The sit-down played a part in the circumstances that led up to the big Goodyear Tire and Rubber Company strike of February-March 1936. Fundamentally it was insecurity, speed-up, the threat of lower wages and longer hours, and the refusal of the company to engage in genuine collective bargaining that caused the strike. The im-

mediate cause was the laying off of 70 men in the tire division, which convinced the workers that the company planned to change from the six-hour to the eight-hour day. In protest against the layoff, 137 men engaged in a sit-down strike, whereupon they were dismissed. Mass meetings were called, and the company under pressure agreed to rehire the 137 and reconsider the suspension of the 70. Nevertheless, a strike acquired momentum and mass picketing closed down the entire plant, with 14,000 workers idle. The strike was started spontaneously and was then officially sanctioned by the union.

The rubber workers are new and enthusiastic unionists. The sit-down technique works, and so they use it as soon as an issue arises. Their officers are urging them not to stop production without first bringing their grievance to the attention of the union and the company through the regular channels. During 1936 there was scarcely a week that did not witness at least one sit-down in the rubber plants. In a single plant in less than a year no less than fifty-eight were counted, ranging in length from an hour or less to two or three days. Following one sit-down, thirty-one Goodyear strikers were charged with inciting to riot, but the charges were later dismissed. As the rubber workers become more experienced and more disciplined unionists, the sit-downs over petty issues will doubtless disappear. . . .

U.A.W.A. 1937 Model

AUTOMOBILE WORKERS took the new weapon, adapted and developed it, and with its aid brought the powerful and antiunion General Motors Corporation to terms.

A short sit-down strike had occurred in the automobile industry as early as spring, 1934, in the White plant in Cleveland. This strike was settled within several hours. The first strike in which automobile workers stayed in the plant overnight occurred in the Bendix plant in South Bend, Indiana. On Nov. 17, 1936, workers in several Bendix departments, influenced by the successful sit-downs in the Akron rubber industry, stopped work but remained at their machines. The company ordered all workers to assemble outside the plant to decide whether they wished to work. To forestall this attempted lockout, the Bendix workers determined to remain in the plant until the management came to terms. In a week victory was won.

The same day the Bendix strike ended, 900 workers in the Midland Steel plant in Detroit sat down. This strike had been planned as a stay-in, to utilize the technique used so effectively in South Bend. This strike marked the first use of the stay-in technique by automobile workers in Michigan. Again the strike ended in a smashing victory for the union. In mid-December the sit-down movement spread to the workers of the Kelsey-Hayes Wheel Company of Detroit. Two short sit-downs ended with the company's promise to negotiate; on its failure to live up to its promise the workers sat down again, this time with the determination not to resume work until they had won their demands. There was also a brief sit-down strike in the Windsor, Ontario, plant of the Kelsey Wheel Company, Ltd., a subsidiary of the Kelsey-Hayes Wheel Company. In the meantime other sit-downs were occurring in Detroit, in the plants of the Aluminum Company of America, Bohn Aluminum, and Gordon Bakery. Thus the stage was set for the big sit-down strike in Flint.

In November and December 1936, the campaign of the United Automobile Workers of America to organize the General Motors Corporation workers was nearing a climax. The auto workers enjoyed the backing of the progressive unions of the Committee for Industrial Organization. In the warfare between nonunion mass production industry and the CIO, the General Motors strike was the first major battle. Realizing that much might depend upon the outcome, both sides unstintingly threw their resources into the struggle.

In December the union requested a conference with the heads of the General Motors Corporation to engage in collective bargaining on behalf of all the corporation's employees. This request was denied, and the union was told to take up grievances with individual plant managers. At this point, in the Fisher Body plant of the corporation in Flint, Michigan, a sit-down that began inauspiciously enough was destined to have far-reaching consequences.

On December 29 the union presented a proposed contract to the plant manager in Flint requesting an answer within a week. The next morning a sit-down began in the No. 2 plant when inspectors were transferred to other jobs because they would not leave the union. Late the same day the men in No. 1 were alarmed to see dies placed on boxcars bound for Pontiac and Grand Rapids, where the union is weaker. To protect their jobs, they kept the line from starting up again and remained in possession of the plant. Slowly the tie-up spread through the vast General Motors system, as more and more plants were affected by strikes or the shortage of necessary parts. By early February almost all of the 200,000 General Motors employees were idle, and the weekly production of cars had declined to 1,500 from the mid-December peak of 53,000.

Behind the General Motors strike there was a long record of efforts by the United Automobile Workers of America to bargain collectively, with delays and evasions on the part of the corporation. Especially did the workers rebel against the speeding up of production and the spy system employed by the company. Repeated efforts of the union to win recognition and obtain a union contract came to naught, and in the meantime discrimination against union members continued.

Complaints were made to the National Labor Relations Board that General Motors had violated the law by discharging employees for union activity, using industrial spies, and dominating a company union in its St. Louis plant. Scarcely had the hearing gotten under way when the corporation sought an injunction to restrain the board from proceeding further. The injunction was denied in the Federal District Court, but a subsequent appeal and stay prevented the board from proceeding. Six months later, when the strike began, the hands of the board were still bound.

From the first the corporation officials insisted that they would not negotiate so long as the strikers held the plants. The men suspected a ruse, knowing that if they left the plants they would lose their power to prevent production. They agreed to leave, however, if the company pledged itself not to try to operate the plant or to move machinery while negotiations were in progress. The company refused.

Injunctions and Tear Gas in Flint

ON JANUARY 2 the struggle entered a new phase. Upon the company's petition, Judge Edward S. Black issued a sweeping injunction restraining the union from continuing to remain in the plant, from picketing, and from interfering in any manner with those who wished to enter the plant to work. To obey the injunction would be to concede the loss of the strike. The injunction exposed the hollowness of the company's complaint against possession of its plant, for a stay-out strike would have been crushed as surely as the sit-down had the writ been obeyed. Later, in Cleveland, the corporation was to seek an injunction against strikers who had left the plant to form a picket line. Small wonder that when the sheriff read the injunction to the Flint strikers and asked them to leave voluntarily he was laughed out of the plant.

Three days later it was discovered that the injunction judge owned stock in General Motors. The union charged that he owned 3,665 shares, worth $219,900 at the current market quotation, and the judge admitted ownership of 1,000 shares. The union thereupon petitioned the state legislature to impeach Judge Black for his violation of the statute forbidding a judge from sitting in a case in which he has an interest. The company, sensing its weak position, did not apply for the writs of body attachment which would have required the sheriff to attempt to arrest the sit-down strikers for contempt of court.

Suddenly, on January 11, the company changed its tactics. Heat in the plant was shut off, and city police mobilized in the area. Company police attempted to starve out the sit-downers, attacking carriers of food and removing the ladders by means of which food had been brought in. The sit-downers, in return, captured the gates from the company police. The city police, who had cleared nearby streets in advance, then attacked in an effort to recapture the gates. Tear-gas bombs were hurled against the sit-downers and their sympathizers outside. Strikers used the fire hoses within the plant to direct streams of water on the police and on the gas bombs.

During the battle, the sit-downers, who had until then occupied only the second floor of the plant, took possession of the entire building. For four hours the strikers fought the police, who used clubs, tear gas, and riot guns. Fourteen workers were wounded by the police gunfire, one of them seriously, and dozens were tear-gassed. Within the sound truck, union organizers took turns at the microphone, shouting encouragement to the strikers and giving direction to the battle. When the battle ended the strikers remained in victorious possession of the plants.

The county prosecuting attorney, who owned sixty-one shares of General Motors stock, jailed the wounded as they were released from the hospital, and obtained 1,200 John Doe warrants under which any strike sympathizer could be arrested. Seven of the Flint strike leaders were arrested, charged with unlawful assembly and malicious destruction of property. The union demand for the arrest of the police, company guards, and others who had been responsible for the attack was disregarded. In the meantime, National Guardsmen were mobilized and sent to Flint.

At this point, the public was relieved to learn that a truce had been arranged. General Motors agreed to enter into negotiations with the union in an effort to settle the strike, and the union, in return, agreed to evacuate all plants held by it, whether in Flint or elsewhere. One of the most important matters to be considered in the negotiations was whether the United Automobile Workers should be recognized as the sole bargaining agency for the workers. Thirty minutes before the sit-downers were to march out of the Flint plants, and after other plants had already been evacuated, the union discovered that W. S. Knudsen, executive vice-president of the corporation, had agreed to bargain collectively with the Flint Alliance, a semi-company union, semi-vigilante strikebreaking organization inspired by the company. Regarding this as a violation of the truce, the union refused to evacuate the plants, and General Motors thereupon canceled the scheduled conference. Several days later the corporation announced that 110,000 workers had signed petitions asking to be returned to work, but this number was exaggerated and the union showed that large numbers of the signatures had been obtained by intimidation.

On February 1 came the turning point in the strike. General Motors had taken the offensive, and the union had suffered defeats in Anderson, Indiana, and Saginaw, Michigan. Hearings on another application for an injunction were in progress, this time before Judge Gadola. The Flint Alliance was becoming dangerous, and there was some fear that the back-to-work movement inspired by the company might spread. Something had to be done to bolster morale. The union had again to take the offensive.

The Chevrolet plant in Flint, the scene of discrimination against union members, provided the opportunity. Of most strategic importance was plant No. 4, in which all Chevrolet motors are assembled. A hundred feet from this plant, however, was the personnel building, headquarters of company police and hired gunmen. The strategy decided upon was to make a sham attack upon plant No. 9, in the far corner of the tract. At 3:30 P.M., a sit-down started there, and the excitement brought the company police on the run. At 3:35 the union men in plant No. 6, starting to No. 9 to help, were instead directed by union leaders in the sound truck into No. 4, where a sit-down simultaneously began. The company police arrived too late, and the union was in control of the key plant, without which no production was possible. The Women's Emergency Brigade, made up of wives, mothers, and sisters of the strikers, played a heroic and important part in the battle, both at No. 9 and No. 4. They smashed windows of the plant to keep the men from being suffocated by tear gas, and with locked arms barred the police attack upon the main gate of No. 4.

On the following day, Judge Gadola issued the injunction requested by the company. Though not a stockholder, as Judge Black had been, he proved himself just as willing a servant. His injunction, similar in many ways to that issued by Judge Black a month before, was much more drastic. It ordered the union officers and the sit-downers, under penalty of $15 million, to evacuate the plants by 3 P.M. the following day, and to refrain from picketing and from interfering with the operation of the plants or the entry of strikebreakers. The sheriff was ordered to evacuate the plants within twenty-four hours. Again the strikers refused to budge, and the judge ordered them all arrested. Sheriff Wolcott, explaining that he lacked a sufficient number of deputies, refused to carry out the order unless Governor Murphy provided the aid of the National Guard.

Meanwhile, sit-downers within Fisher Body plant No. 2 and Chevrolet No. 4 were in a virtual state of siege. National Guardsmen surrounded the plants and refused to allow friends and relatives to speak to the men at the factory gates. A hunger siege at first imposed by the Guardsmen was lifted in less than a day. Reporters who tried to speak to the strikers at the gates were escorted out of the military zone at the point of bayonets. At Fisher No. 1, on the contrary, the strikers were able to receive visitors and come and go as they pleased, under no restrictions except those imposed by their own shop council.

The stumbling block to peaceful settlement of the strike remained the issue of recognition. The union, which first asked recognition as sole bargaining agent for all General Motors employees, later surrendered that claim and asked merely to be sole bargaining agent in twenty plants closed by the strike. The union proposed that, if this was agreed upon, all plants immediately resume operations, and all other points at issue be settled in conference. This the company likewise refused. Company spokesmen favored a plebiscite to determine the wishes of the men, but refused to recognize the union as sole bargaining agent in those plants where it might win a majority.

Finally, on February 11, an agreement was reached and the strike ended. Much of the credit for its settlement without further bloodshed belonged to Governor Murphy, who proved a skillful and patient mediator. Under the agreement, the United Automobile Workers was recognized as bargaining agent for its members, and the company agreed not to bargain on matters of general corporate policy with any other group from twenty struck plants without the governor's sanction. There was to be no discrimination against union men, and all court proceedings were to be dropped. Collective bargaining negotiations were to begin on February 16. The union, on its part, was to evacuate the occupied plants, refrain from recruiting on company property, and exhaust every possibility of negotiating before calling any other strike. At the same time the company announced an increase in the average wage rate of 5 cents an hour, swelling its normal annual wage bill by $25 million.

The strikers hailed the settlement as a signal victory for them. For the first time the giant General Motors Corporation had been fought to a standstill by its workers and forced to engage in collective bargaining with them. After forty-four days the sit-downers marched out of the plant, heads and spirits high, singing "Solidarity Forever." Out they came, two by two, with a large American flag at the head of the procession, to the cheers of 2,000 sympathizers assembled at the plants.

Other Sit-downs

AKRON, DETROIT, AND FLINT were not the only cities to witness the sit-down strike in the United States. Late in 1936 and early in 1937, as its popularity increased, it was employed by many other groups of workers. Automobile workers in many cities, notably Toledo, South Bend, and Kansas City, have used the sit-down technique. Glassworkers in Illinois, WPA workers in New York City and Chicago, bakers in Detroit, rubber workers in Illinois and Maryland, building service workers in New York

City, and motion-picture extras in California have used the same method. Other companies to experience sit-down tactics on the part of their workers include the Aluminum Company of America in its Detroit plant, the American Casting Company of Birmingham, the Briggs Manufacturing Company of Detroit, the United Wall Paper Company of Joliet, and the Wahl-Eversharp Pen Company of Chicago. Even a daily paper, the *Detroit News,* has experienced a sit-down strike, in this case, of its printing pressmen. A chain of retail tire shops in Chicago has also witnessed a sit-down. Submarine builders, aircraft workers, and motion-picture operators are others to use the sit-down technique. Salesgirls employed by F. W. Woolworth sat down in Detroit. There are other instances too numerous to mention.

Even hospital workers have used the sit-down strike. Early in February 1937, maintenance and service employees in a Brooklyn hospital engaged in a sit-down, demanding $15 a month for the cost of living outside. They continued to serve and feed the patients, but refused to serve doctors and nurses. Fifteen workers in the hospital laundry barricaded themselves within it to prevent its further use. After two days a compromise settlement was reached.

What are the causes of sit-down strikes? The same grievances that cause other strikes. Wages, hours, working conditions, discrimination, speed-up, layoffs, espionage — all of these have played a part. Some unusual grievances have likewise caused sit-down protests. Akron rubber workers sat down when their union president, Sherman H. Dalrymple, was beaten in Gadsden, Alabama, by thugs employed by the Goodyear Tire and Rubber Company. The Bendix employees in South Bend were aroused by favoritism to company union members and antiunion propaganda by company union leaders. Goodrich workers in Akron have

sat down to force the removal of nonunion workers. Hollywood extras sat down because casting directors were hiring society girls at low wages. Employees of the Brownhill-Kramer Hosiery Company of Philadelphia sat down to prevent removal of the machinery and moving of the business to nonunion territory. Every type of grievance has produced its quota of sit-downs. . . .

What of the Law?

UNQUESTIONABLY MOST JUDGES will hold the sit-down strike illegal under the law of trespass. The fact that the law of trespass was developed in a different social situation will be of no avail. Yet labor need not be unduly disturbed, for most weapons used by it were first held illegal. That was true both of the strike and the boycott. Indeed, strikes for certain purposes are still held illegal in many states, and the secondary boycott is also outlawed. Picketing is prohibited in many injunctions, including those issued by Judges Black and Gadola in Flint. The continued use of a logical weapon, backed by enough economic and political pressure, eventually results in its being held legal. If lobbying by labor does not force old-party legislators to declare the sit-down legal, the foundation of an independent party of labor will accomplish that end. Workers should concentrate on defeating the employer and not be too much concerned about a law that is framed largely in the interests of employers and owners.

Attacks upon the sit-down strike have already begun, and many more may be expected. Governor Hoffman of New Jersey, for example, has warned that the entire resources of the state, if necessary, would be used to eject sit-downers. In his view, workers have no more right to take possession of a factory than gangsters have to take possession of a bank. Early in 1937, legislation to outlaw the sit-down strike was being considered in Alabama and Vermont. New York City police at first refused to intervene against sit-downers. In February 1937, however, more stringent rules were put in force, under which strikers will be ejected and arrested if a formal complaint is made by the owner of a plant. In the absence of such complaint the police will not interfere so long as the strikers are orderly. Much more liberal is the attitude of Secretary of Labor Perkins, who has expressed doubt as to whether sit-downers violate any law.

Wyndham Mortimer, vice-president of the United Automobile Workers, has thus stated the case for the sit-down strike:

> Is it wrong for a worker to stay at his job? The laws of the state and nation recognize, in a hundred ways, that the worker has a definite claim upon his job; more fundamentally, it is recognized that every workman has a moral right to continue on his job unless some definite misconduct justifies his discharge. These sit-down strikers are staying at their work places; no one has a better right to be there than have these men themselves. No one else, certainly, has any right to those positions. But the sit-down strikers have performed valuable services in those factories; General Motors and the public alike have profited by those services. To call them trespassers now, and to deny their right as human beings to remain with their jobs, is logically unsound and is manifestly unjust.

The union asserts that the workers have a property right in their jobs which is superior to the company's right to the use of the property. This theory will be rejected by most judges today, but in time it may be accepted as good law. The legal concept of property rights has changed and developed with usage. In Flint the union also argued that General Motors was not entitled to an injunction on the ground that it had itself violated the laws relating to collective bargaining and therefore did not come into court with clean hands. Judge Gadola rejected this theory, though other judges have applied this general principle of equity to labor injunction cases. Gadola did not justify General Motors' actions, but merely asked whether one wrong could be righted by another wrong. This attitude is contrary to the principles of equity.

The sit-down strike has served notice on society that mere ownership does not carry with it all possible rights with reference to a factory. Those who work in it, who make it produce with their labor, and who depend upon it for their livelihood should likewise have a voice in its control. Those who invest their lives in an industry have at least as much at stake as those who merely invest their money. The sit-down strike brings these facts forcibly to public attention. It is interesting to note that, in the sit-down strike, workers are reestablishing the control over the tools of production that they lost with the Industrial Revolution. . . .

Sit-down strikes, like other types of strikes, occur when long-standing grievances of workers have brought them to the breaking point. These employers who recognize unions and deal with them fairly need have little fear of sit-downs. If all employers recognized the right of workers to organize and bargain collectively, and obtain a fair share of the fruits of industry, few strikes would occur. If, when a strike occurred, the employer made no effort to operate with strikebreakers, there would be no need for a seizure of the plant. Employers will make more progress by removing the just grievances of workers than by attacking them on the basis of property laws framed in an earlier social situation, and designed for other purposes.

The sit-down strike is here to stay. Of that workers are resolved. The law may change slowly, but change it must.

103.

Labor Racketeering

In the 1930s the word "racketeering" was used to describe the involvement of organized crime in legitimate business. With the ending of Prohibition in 1933, the underworld turned to labor unions as a field to exploit. During the intense industrial strife of the mid-Thirties, gangland hoodlums assisted labor in its struggle with management, but underworld figures later infiltrated the administrative structure of the unions to gain control of their finances. The following selection from a report published by the City Club of New York in 1937 describes the extent of their activity in labor unions.

Source: *Report on Certain Aspects of Labor Union Responsibility and Control,* New York, 1937.

RACKETEERING EXPOSED in connection with labor unions is in no sense peculiar to labor unions; it is part of a criminal pattern that has manifested itself in such diversified fields as prostitution, lottery and policy games, bail bonding, and in liquor traffic, both now and prior to repeal of the Eighteenth Amendment, as well as in legitimate forms of business activity. In each case the purpose is the unlawful extortion of tribute for the personal gain of a few individuals; in each case these individuals are found to be criminals who may be cloaked in the trappings of respectability but whose illegal activities are not confined to the labor racket.

One feature which is sometimes considered peculiar to labor racketeering is that the means employed may include practices not intrinsically illegal, namely, the threat of union sanctions, such as strikes and picketing. But the threat of lawful action is made in connection with other types of extortion. For example, the blackmailer menaces his victim with the threat of making public what may be a completely true statement of facts, or of reporting to law enforcement officers the commission by his victim of a crime. And a similar technique is found in unfair trade practices, such as trying contracts or block-booking in the motion picture industry, through which a purchaser, in order to obtain a desired article, is compelled at the same time to purchase an undesired article. In each case the means, intrinsically lawful, become unlawful only because of the element of extortion.

That the means employed by the labor racketeer may not be unlawful makes it all the more important that the problem be approached with circumspection and with appreciation of the fact that labor racketeering is but a symptom of a far larger problem. Otherwise, proper efforts tending to bring into disrepute the lawful means employed by labor racketeers for unlawful ends may also tend to discredit legitimate labor activity for legitimate ends. . . .

"Labor racketeering" consists, in essence, of the use of a labor union by racketeers to exact payments to the racketeers from the employer, from members of the union, or from both. The racketeer may himself be a union official or he may operate from without the union either through his agents or through the exercise of coercion upon intimidated union officers. The labor racketeer is often enabled to maintain his dominant position through cooperation, passive or even active, on the part of the employer, whose inertia to the existence of a racket may be partially explained by the fact that the cost of the racket is usually passed on to the consumer or to another branch of the industry, rather than borne by the employer himself. A further explanation may be found in the fact that the employer may actually profit by the racket. Thus, the employer may find it profitable to make periodic payments to a union officer in order to avoid compliance with a union rule, such as payment for overtime, or a requirement that members of the union shall not work with, or on the products of, nonunion labor. Or the employer may believe that the improvement of working conditions which may follow upon effective collective bargaining will cost him more than the labor racket.

Again, the employer may take advantage of the racket to drive a competitor out of business or to maintain prices in connection with certain types of so-called trade associations. This type of trade association, in conjunction with which labor racketeering flourishes most effectively, is usually organized and maintained in a large city and in a demoralized industry in which legitimate employer-organization is not possible or its advantages not appreciated. The initial purpose of the association, which in its more refined forms may escape the sanctions of the antitrust laws, is to obtain higher prices or to stabilize competitive conditions.

Ultimately, the visible gains to the members of the association may be so costly or the temptation to attract business by price cutting so strong that coercion becomes necessary to compel members to remain in the association or to compel competitors to join it. An effective instrument for such coercion is found in the labor racketeer, who directs threats of labor trouble against those who might otherwise be unwilling to join or maintain membership in the trade association and who may eventually obtain influence not only in the association itself but also in other branches of the trade or industry in which the association functions.

Variations in the labor racket occur under varying conditions but the fundamental technique remains the same; upon analysis, most labor rackets are found to be surprisingly similar.

The labor racketeer sometimes obtains such power that he is able to create an unnecessary type of work from which he obtains income. For example, an indictment against racketeers in a local of the Teamsters' Union charges that these racketeers through their control of trucking forced upon the dairy industry a duplication in terminal operations, resulting in a $300,000 annual increase in handling costs.

Through his dominance of the industry, the racketeer may even set up an independent business servicing the industry, patronage of which is required of employers wishing to avoid labor trouble. An outstanding example is a case in New Jersey in which a racketeer compelled contractors to patronize his construction-bonding business. Another instance is that of a racketeer in control of a motion picture operators' union who forced theater owners to purchase supplies from him.

While the membership of a union dominated by a racketeer may on the whole be better off by reason of improved conditions than in the absence of any union, the membership also suffers from labor racketeering. Exploitation of union members by the racketeer takes the form of the "sell out," most commonly in the form of agreements unduly favorable to the employer, the "kickback," through requiring union members to return part of their wages to the employer or to union officers, the exaction of excessive dues, discrimination in union privileges or in the distribution of work, waiver of union rules or contract provisions, payment of excessive salaries to union officials or diversion or embezzlement of union funds. The racketeer-controlled union may also be used as a device to combat legitimate union activity.

While the employer may in the first instance pay the cost of a racket, that cost, like the cost of any other antisocial activity, is ultimately borne by the public in the form of increased prices and industrial strife. Some employers, such as small retailers, may suffer through being unable to pass on the racket cost, but, as we have pointed out, employers may obtain benefits from the labor racket through the maintenance of the price level and the elimination of effective collective bargaining. It is an interesting commentary upon the relationship that sometimes exists between the employer and the labor racketeer that the head of an employers' association in a notoriously racket-ridden industry is reported to have asked that one of the principal convicted defendants be paroled in his custody pending an appeal. And in the recent trial of restaurant racketeers, it was brought out that substantial contributions to their defense fund were made by restaurant owners. It is true that employer groups protest the labor racket, but such protests are chiefly in the form of proposals for curbing all unions, whether corrupt or not, and, moreover, often come from groups not affected by racketeering.

The results of the labor racket may be most seriously felt by the members of the racketeer-controlled union. While the members may obtain certain apparent advantages from the existence of a union despite corrupt leadership, they are, nevertheless, exploited by the racketeer, and exploited in a manner that cannot be passed on to others. It is consequently in the primary interest of the exploited workers that labor racketeering be eliminated.

104.

WILLIAM ALLEN WHITE: The Challenge to the Middle Class

William Allen White, whose widely reprinted editorials from the Emporia (Kansas) Gazette *earned him a Pulitzer Prize in 1923, was described by his biographer Walter Johnson as "the symbol of the greatness of small-town America." Politically, White was a maverick; a staunch Republican for forty years, he nonetheless deplored the policies of Republican administrations. His support of the New Deal (except at election time) prompted Roosevelt to remark that "Bill White is with me three and a half years out of every four." In his social thinking White regarded the middle class as the guardian of American democracy, an attitude revealed in the following article published in August 1937.*

Source: *Atlantic Monthly,* August 1937.

IN NO OTHER LAND is the middle class so solidly fortified as it is in America. The constitutional prohibition against titles of nobility has done something, but not everything, and perhaps not much to strengthen the foundations of the middle-class fortification. Probably even with lords and ladies and barons and earls in this country, the rich soil, the inestimable wealth beneath the soil, the illimitable forests, the Yankee inventiveness of the race that inhabits the continent, and its isolation between the two great oceans of the globe, would have produced wealth which in modern times is the mark of social distinction, wealth so fabulous that it had to be distributed with something like equity in a middle class.

We had a new kind of human adventure on this continent. In settling the fertile land, opening the mines, and inventing methods of producing wealth from the raw materials so bountifully bestowed upon the continent, we have had two distinct advantages denied to our ancestors in Asia and in Europe. We were free from foreign wars and fears of war for a century and a half. We had the benefit of steam and its machinery in hastening the conquest of the land. Thus we developed a middle class in the United States which has seemed socially, economically, and politically impregnable. Moreover, ladders, runways, ramps, and escalators have been moving during the five generations, going up and going down from the proletariat to the plutocracy and back, but always stopping for a generation or so in the middle class. While we have had the three classes, they were not hereditary. Only a few old families survive in the plutocracy. Only a few Jukes and morons persist in the proletariat. But both plutocrat and proletariat, passing up and down, have found a salving sense of security. A middle-class complacency has been the ideal American life.

But the swift subsidence of wealth after October 1929 reacted like an earthquake shock upon the American bourgeoisie. The appearance of the unemployed not merely in millions, but in tens of millions, produced a caste with broken morale. That gave the American burghers something to think about.

For the first time in American history, labor is becoming class-conscious in a considerable area. The craft union, which grew so sturdily under the leadership of Samuel Gompers, in its philosophy was essentially not class-conscious. Its ideals were socially reactionary from the Marxian standpoint.

The appearance of the class-conscious I.W.W. just before the outbreak of the World War, and its flashes of activity during the war, were negligible in the total of labor disturbances and outbreaks in the second and third decades of the century. But the appearance of the vertical union, Mr. Lewis's CIO, is a new thing, a labor organization with a class-conscious background.

Moreover, the labor vote in the election of 1936 for the first time was cast solidly for a President and a Congress. Labor claimed naturally to have captured Washington. Not the kind of labor that hopes to rise from the craft union to a foremanship and from a foremanship to a superintendency and from a superintendency to a place in the front office. The labor solidarity that helped to win the election of 1936 for Mr. Roosevelt, the labor which contributed nearly half a million dollars to the Democratic campaign, is not bringing its hat in its hand and pulling a forelock when it enters the front office of the factory. It is not looking around to spot the chair it soon will warm. The labor that was one of the six powerful and more or less antagonistic minorities which produced the Democratic vote in 1936 was for the moment class-conscious to the core so far as leadership is concerned. It has revived the public-be-damned attitude of the elder Vanderbilt. The middle class has been able to tolerate the public-be-damned attitude from its plutocrats who were merely spoiled children. But the middle class is batting surprised and even troubled eyes when it is damned nonchalantly by the proletariat.

II

Now if other evidences were needed to convince thoughtful Americans in the middle class that they are in some jeopardy, they should be warned by the appearance in the last twenty years of a distinctly proletarian literature in their country, the first appearance of that phenomenon. Fifty years

William Allen White, editor of the Emporia, Kan., "Gazette" at Landon's headquarters in 1936

ago James L. Ford wrote a skit in which he represented Richard Watson Gilder, the editor of the *Century Magazine* in the heyday of its glossy-collared, black-tied, derby-hatted, frock-coated respectability. Mr. Gilder in Ford's sketch was standing on Fourteenth Street looking south across the literary *trocha* (a word which meant barbwire entanglement) and was pondering upon the vast treasure house of unused literary material in the slums below Fourteenth Street. To his amazement and alarm he was hailed by a denizen across the entanglement who pointed out the need in our literature of just that wealth of literary riches in the life south of the trocha. Mr. Gilder is represented by Ford as losing his poise. In the language of his literary interlocutor, "he turn up bote hands!"

Mr. Gilder has passed, and American magazines and publishers of his class have put down their hands. They have opened their doors to the proletarian writers below Fourteenth Street and all across the land. Moreover, their writers do not confine their outgivings to fiction. They have produced a distinct American proletarian philosophy, — an American proletarian dialectic, if you

will — a premise which assumes that the old American scheme of things, and particularly the middle-class scheme of things, its ideas, its economy, its philosophy, are basically false and must be not merely changed, not just converted into something better and more equitable, but utterly wiped out. If Mr. Gilder in his bowler hat, his Ascot tie and wing collar, spats, cane, and drooping moustache, could read the proletarian literature of today, he would put down his hands and turn up his toes. It would paralyze him with its violence.

This year three significant books have been written as though to order, setting forth with clarity, courage, and with more than passing tolerance for the middle-class point of view, the social, economic, and political implications of the struggle in American life which amounts, for the moment, to a challenge to the middle class. These books, by some pleasant coincidence, present three different points of view, three approaches to what must be inevitably the changing status of the American middle class. It must change, if something more devastating does not happen to it.

In *Middletown in Transition,* by Robert and Helen Lynd, we find the average Midwestern American industrial country town. Here for a hundred years the middle class has ruled. It has taken economic leadership because it has had access to capital. It has bought and owned the tools of trade. It has maintained its political rule by dividing its adversaries in the working class. This has not been consciously done. The establishment of the American two-party system has made a natural political division. Somewhat this division also cuts through the middle class. But until 1932 the political division of the middle class has represented no more class-consciousness than that of the workers. In 1932 the middle class began to shift into the Republican Party, the workers into the Democratic Party, and at the same time the Negro, who had been traditionally Republican, left the party which was proud to boast that it had struck the shackles off four million slaves.

Socially, the middle class has dominated Middletown because the middle class was the largest supporter of social institutions — the church, the college, the welfare organizations, the Chamber of Commerce, and the various community benevolences, "drives," and organized endeavors which attract community support. Since the depression, this dominance of the middle class has not seriously been shaken in the American country town — meaning by "country town" any community between five thousand and a hundred thousand where people are fairly well settled, where a considerable minority of the inhabitants has lived for two generations and an elite minority has lived for three. The older families form the bulwarks of business and politics, and man the social breastworks. The middle class in this typical country town lives on an income between two thousand and twenty thousand dollars a year. The holder of any income higher than that, whether earned or inherited, begins to put on airs of plutocracy and is of less consequence by reason of his pride.

The authors of *Middletown in Transition* have made an authentic picture of their subject. Studying the features of the portrait, we see but slight modification from the lineaments of the old American type. Its virtues are thrift, diligence, reasonable honesty, as much tolerance as the times will permit, much more knowledge than understanding, and a keen eye for the main chance — the Puritan virtues. The middle class in this community elects the sheriff, controls the police, has access to the governor, who is the head of the state militia; and in any contest with any foe, social, economic, or political, the middle class will have the tremendous advantage of the first call upon the forces of law and order. So the middle class stands for law and order as the first thing to be desired in any moment of crisis or calamity.

This typical Midwestern industrial town, which is certainly the fortress of the ruling classes, is strong enough to dominate every state between the Alleghenies and the Pacific Coast. Not more than a dozen cities in that area are large enough to produce the urban type of civilization in which the middle class is not in control of the police, in which the middle class has no idea who is sheriff and must approach the governor politely through the city boss, who might easily turn radical if votes were on the radical side. Then he might easily be convinced he might profitably betray the money side of any social, political, or economic disturbance.

III

It is urban America which has called forth *American City: A Rank-and-File History*, by Charles Rumford Walker. The American social, economic, and political scene changes quickly from the country town to the city, and a town becomes a city in America when it has attained somewhere between two and three hundred thousand population. In the city the boss rules. The boss is generally supplied with money by seekers of special privilege in the city who live in the beautiful suburbs, who control the banks, the public utilities, the industries of the place and of the region, and who form a small class-conscious group which might as well be frankly called the American plutocracy. It is not a hereditary class, but it nevertheless is a distinct group. It rules. Its money oils the political machine of the local city bosses. The political machine protects crime as far as it dares, looks after the poor in trouble, whether with the police or with the new Federal agencies that distribute work and food. This machine gives just enough to the middle class in the way of public improvements, boulevards, parks, health service, schools, traffic rules, residential zoning ordinances, pure and abundant water, reasonably low utility rates, and a plug-hat facade of respectability in the outer walls of the city hall, to keep the middle class in bounds. Speaking rather broadly, the governing classes in the American city buy the middle class with the largesse of their own taxes and fool the proletariat with benevolences — throwing in a demagogue occasionally when needed to quiet the workers' unrest.

The story of this particular American city which Mr. Walker tells is the story of the twin cities of St. Paul and Minneapolis. The time of the story is from 1933 to 1936. The social locale of the story is the working class in a series of major strikes. The point of the story is that the workers in our cities are beginning to be class-conscious. America is developing a proletariat. That word produces blood pressure in the upper and middle classes. American class-consciousness as developed in our larger cities is not necessarily, not even generally, communistic. It is not inevitably permanent. It is mildly socialistic, but not much more socialistic than either of the two Roosevelts and most of the progressive leaders of the last three decades, from La Follette and the first Roosevelt down to George Norris and Maury Maverick.

The interesting thing about the new alignment in American cities is that sometimes the city government reveals the divided loyalty of the political boss. In the past five years the boss frequently has been amenable to the workers. Always the boss has to take baksheesh from the plutocracy. Occasionally he has had to make embarrassing concessions to the proletariat in times of riot and disorder. So the poor fellow is accused of biting the hand that feeds him. But his choice is between the voters who carry the election for him, sometimes by crooked methods, and those who furnish the lubrication for his machine. In *American City* we see this conflict of interest between the political rulers of the city and those who once were its secret masters and still, in ordinary times, hold silent title to its governors. The

story Mr. Walker tells so well is not a pleasant story, but Americans should know it. It will become more and more a typical story. The rise of the city in American life injects a new x into the equation of our civilization. In that x is certainly a challenge to the middle class.

Combined with national politics and the control of city government, that x in time will produce in the equation a new living standard for labor. American labor seems to be coming into a new zone of self-respect. As a means to this self-respect, the organization of labor by industries rather than by crafts is doing something more than boosting the wages of the man at the bottom of the economic scale, the unskilled laborer. It is giving him a sense of solidarity with his fellow workers and with industry. He is stalking unabashed into the middle class. We who have been in the middle class on this continent for three hundred years will have to move over and make room. What the admission of another group will mean, no one knows. Probably not much in the way of denial to the present incumbents. There will be plenty to go around. The net of it will probably be a minimum standard of living, below which, by reason of old-age pensions, health insurance, minimum wages, the abolition of child labor, housing operated as a public utility, and various similar economic gadgets, no one who is willing and able to work will be permitted to fall. From this standard, if America remains democratic — and there is no serious sign that America is deserting permanently the democracy of the Constitution — any man will be allowed to rise and go up as far as his talents will take him, provided only that he gives genuine economic return for the rewards he takes.

IV

WHICH BRINGS US to the third book in this series, Gilbert Seldes' *Mainland*. Mr. Seldes looks squarely at all that the Lynds see in

Middletown and he does not flinch from what Mr. Walker reveals in his *American City*. But Mr. Seldes remembers and writes about something more than the industrial small town and the great urban metropolis. He adds to these the other four-ninths — the farmer, the villager, the suburbanite. These additions complete the picture of America. Three more comprehensive studies of American life could not be assembled in one season if one editor had waved his wand and published them in one volume.

Mr. Seldes sees America not as an evolutionary offshoot of Europe but as a sport in the social development of humanity. He sees us creating by the evolutionary process a new way of life — not merely higher standards of living for the masses, not merely universal education and free colleges and universities for the children of the worker as well as for those of the well-to-do. He sees us as a free people with freedom itself composing a considerable part of the actual difference in material things, with freedom and its material consequences affecting in turn the spiritual outlook of our people. He sees us as something new and strange on this planet, not merely as city dwellers in big and little towns, not as villagers or farmers, but as one people, moving incessantly up and down the economic scale with the generations, without static classes. He looks forward to an America that, for all our imperfections — they are many and obvious, and he does not blink them — shall still hold to the ancient ways. This America shall keep on living by Puritan first principles which, though modified by the exigencies of expanding civilization, were in the hearts of the men who first broke into this wilderness and later crossed the prairie and climbed the mountains and settled on the Western coast.

Mr. Seldes feels that three things are permanent in the American heart which neither the city man, the town dweller, the farmer, nor the suburbanite will ever give up: "National independence, civil freedom, and private prosperity." He feels that they are bound together, that they do not conflict, and are combined against all the powers which would attack any one of them.

V

HERE ARE THESE THREE beautiful and useful books. Each of them is a sincere piece of work, done with scholarly patience and real intelligence. Taken together, they tell the American story of today. If there be prophecy, these books are prophetic of the America of tomorrow. They make it clear that the middle class is under a genuine challenge. If what these three authors say is true, a new status of our social organization is on the horizon for the next decade. Certainly it is due before the present century closes. It is easy to say there will be changes, but no one can say what changes will come.

The thing that is happening is that Americans are trying in their own way to socialize the machines man has made and is making. The Marxians let loose a dynamic idea in the world a hundred years ago when they declared that if everyone were at work there would be enough to supply everyone with everything. But the Marxian mistake was in assuming that men would click into proper jobs. They ignored in their scheme of things the social and industrial truth — that without paying a heavy price for superintendence everyone would not go to work making anything, and there would not be enough for all. The place of organizing brains in the distributive system and the reward for those brains set the problem for America in this century.

Already the worker at the machine is in revolt at its tyranny. He will not be mechanized spiritually or socially. The whole turmoil and clamor of industry today is the worker's cry against the rigid regime of the machine. It would channel the worker's hours, rivet his spirit, and put his life on an assembly belt. He is demanding the individualism guaranteed to the middle class by our economic establishment — middle-class freedom, middle-class diversity of life, its right to culture, its access to beauty. The first thing the American industrial worker, and incidentally the American farmer, have to do is to convince their middle-class neighbors of the justice of their complaint and the fairness of their claims. When this case of the worker is established in the hearts of the middle classes, their ancient sense of right and fairness, their habit of righteousness and judgment, will make force unnecessary.

Public opinion may be depended upon to make just and even generous room for the workers. Mr. Seldes seems to feel that public opinion rises from the unexplorable spiritual forces that lie in the heart of American life. In the end they direct the course of our American civilization. These spiritual forces, which urge the glacially slow pace we keep in coming to our national verdicts and judgments in times of change and crisis, will control the decision in the struggle now pending between our plutocracy and our proletariat. Mr. Seldes clearly has faith that the righteousness that has exalted our nation for a century and a half will control the middle-class heart of America and give it power and wisdom to do full justice to the workers. As for the plutocracy, the problems it presents may easily be solved. We must not forget that our history shows this bitter irony in its commercial success: while the rich are growing richer, their brains are growing poorer.

105.

Ferdinand Lundberg: The American Plutocracy

During the Depression, at a time when more than twenty million people were depending on relief payments, the American public became more aware than ever of the continued presence of the very rich and of their undiminished high standard of living. The prestige of the very rich was never lower than during the 1930s. Besides being held responsible for the Crash itself, they were frequently charged in congressional hearings with being tax evaders and financial manipulators who preyed on the public. In 1937 Ferdinand Lundberg published an exposé that was reminiscent of the "muckraking" era, America's 60 Families. These few families, he asserted, actually formed an aristocracy that was the real government of the United States. Portions of his book are reprinted here.

Source: *America's 60 Families,* New York, 1937, pp. 3-4, 408-418.

THE UNITED STATES IS OWNED and dominated today by a hierarchy of sixty of the richest families, buttressed by no more than ninety families of lesser wealth. Outside this plutocratic circle there are perhaps three hundred and fifty other families, less defined in development and in wealth, but accounting for most of the incomes of $100,000 or more that do not accrue to members of the inner circle.

These families are the living center of the modern industrial oligarchy which dominates the United States, functioning discreetly under a *de jure* democratic form of government behind which a *de facto* government, absolutist and plutocratic in its lineaments, has gradually taken form since the Civil War. This *de facto* government is actually the government of the United States — informal, invisible, shadowy. It is the government of money in a dollar democracy.

Our concern is mainly with the sixty families, although from time to time members of the surrounding ninety-odd will enter the narrative. Under their acquisitive fingers, and in their possession, the sixty families hold the richest nation ever fashioned in the workshop of history. The whole long procession of states, nations, and empires that strained and sweated up to the threshold of the Industrial Revolution amassed much less material wealth than the United States alone possesses. The vaunted Roman Empire, for example, could be placed in the land area west of the Mississippi, with room to spare; all Europe is, indeed, only slightly larger than is the United States.

Bigness alone, however, means little; China, too, is very big. But in the economically decisive requisites of accumulated capital and equipment, technical knowledge and facilities, natural resources and manpower, the United States is unique. Yet most of its people are, paradoxically, very poor; most of them own nothing beyond a few sticks of furniture and the clothes on their backs.

The outstanding American proprietors of today tower historically over the proud aristocracy that surrounded Louis XIV, Czar Nicholas, Kaiser Wilhelm, and the Emperor Franz Joseph, and wield vastly greater power. The might of Cardinal Richelieu, Metternich, Bismarck, or Disraeli was no greater than that of private citizens, undistinguished by titles, like J. P. Morgan, Andrew W. Mellon, John D. Rockefeller, Henry Ford, and the Du Ponts. It was essentially the decision of these latter and their political deputies (so far as a single decision carried weight after the initial lines were drawn) that dictated the outcome of the World War, the greatest armed conflict in all history. Napoleon could have done no more.

The war, which raised wealthy Americans to the pinnacle of world power, obliterated huge sections of Europe's master class and set other sections adrift. In Germany and Austria-Hungary the dominant élite of wealth — landowners, bankers, and industrialists — were virtually pauperized overnight. In France and England, seriously weakened, increasingly timorous, they staggered under tax burdens, and even yet are bedeviled by grave problems upon whose tranquil solution depends their future well-being. In Russia they were simply annihilated.

Of the world's wealthy ruling classes, those of America and England alone retain the full substance, as well as the insignia and panoply, of wealth and power. Alone do they still speak confidently and act decisively for themselves, not driven to utilize bizarre intermediaries like a Hitler, a Mussolini, or a Mikado to hypnotize the multitude; they are not challenged, as in France, by powerful domestic political coalitions of the economically disfranchised. This fortunate situation is, perhaps, purely temporary; it may be undermined by the next general war. . . .

The plutocracy of the Mauve Decade was ascetic by comparison with the plutocracy of the present Black Decade. Point by point the most fantastic of the earlier extravagances, entailing the carefully studied waste of wealth produced by the people, are being duplicated or exceeded by the infinitely more monstrous extravagances of today. But in the 1890s the wholesale dissipation of wealth took place in mansions of the newly rich strung along Fifth Avenue, in plain view of journalists from the Populistic and semiradical press, or in relatively free and open Newport. Today the plutocracy is more cloistered in country estates and luxurious hostelries, and the newspapers, all owned or controlled by the millionaires, are no longer interested in holding the private life of the rich up to public scrutiny. First-class reporters are seldom sent to Newport anymore; only society editors and sports writers go there.

Where once one had merely to refer to Pulitzer's *World* to learn what the latest expensive inanity of the leisured class might be, today one has to search publications that circulate in a much more restricted area: *House and Garden, Town and Country, House Beautiful, Spur, Vogue, Vanity Fair* (recently merged with *Vogue*), *Harper's Bazaar, The New Yorker, Fortune, The Connoisseur, American Kennel Gazette, Arts and Decoration, Horse and Horseman, Yachting, Motor Boat,* etc. Sources of contemporary material are also to be found in the sycophantic "society" pages of the metropolitan newspapers, which more or less unconsciously from time to time make significant sociological revelations about the misuse and abuse of wealth. Many of the readers of these publications are, of course, merely vicarious participants in wasteful spending.

Judged by the way they squander money on vapid personal amusement and bizarre decoration, the rich are a psychopathic class, waltzing obliviously toward a hidden precipice and, apparently, dragging the nation along. Whom the gods would destroy they seemingly first make rich. Yet the personal expenditures, great though they seem to the ordinary onlooker with the needs of society in mind, are small in relation to the unprecedentedly vast incomes that accrue to the families of the plutocracy. Less than twenty-five percent of the income of multimillionaires, according to Robert R. Doane, is expended in personal channels; for try as a multimillionaire family may, it cannot spend its swollen income. To make appreciable inroads upon it there would have to be wholesale giving, and this is not *de rigueur*, as . . . in the . . . philanthropic field. . . .

To depict the extravagances of the rich families in their proper perspective let us briefly turn back to 1929 — the last highly prosperous year of record in the United States. In fateful 1929 no more than 513 Americans had a total income of $1,212,099,000, while the gross price (not profit) received by more than two million farmers for all wheat and cotton produced in 1930 was only $1,191,000,000. The 513 plutocrats could, with their 1929 income, have purchased these two basic crops, and have had enough remaining to cover the expenses of living on an extravagant scale. In 1929 no more than 14,816 Americans had taxable incomes of $100,000 upward, aggregating $4,368,152,000 — the cost of operating the national government, including the Army and Navy, for the fiscal year. This volume of revenue, going to persons sufficient in number to populate only a very small town, was thirty-eight percent of the $11,421,631,000 earned by 8,742,761 factory workers and, according to the census of manufacturers for 1929, equaled the aggregate wages of 3,339,634 factory workers. The wages of 781,830 iron and steel workers for the year aggregated only $1,239,499,000; of 737,840 food manufacturing workers, only $781,736,000; of 511,667 automobile workers, only $828,420,000. In the same year 428,128 cotton-goods workers received $322,-389,000, or $753 each, while the thirty-eight richest persons took $360,644,000, or an average of $9,490,600 each.

While the income of the rich was reduced by twenty-five to fifty percent in the ensuing depression, the incomes of ten to twenty million working-class citizens disappeared entirely for varying protracted periods. And in the "recovery period" the nation has gradually moved back to an approximation of the 1929 period, although it possesses at this writing about ten million certified paupers in contrast with approximately two million in 1929.

To obviate the need of placing a reference note after every line relative to the source of information, only occasional allusion to sources will in this chapter be made

In general, the sources are the relevant public prints since the World War.

Beard tells of a "dinner eaten on horseback" in the Gilded Age. In September 1931, Joseph E. Widener was given a "testimonial dinner" at the Biltmore Hotel, New York City, by some wealthy turfman friends. The ballroom was transformed into a replica of Belmont Park, a race track named after the Belmont family but the major owner of which is Widener; a part of the ballroom was given over to a detailed reconstruction of a corner of the park, complete to turf, a stretch of straightaway, white-painted railing, de luxe box stalls, gayly painted water buckets. As the guests sat dining in the boxes there performed before them prize mounts of the New York City Police Department, of blue-ribbon artillery and cavalry regiments, and of wealthy private owners. The palatial room resounded with the thud of hoofs, neighing of steeds, popping of champagne corks, and laughing chatter, while on the street corners outside the unemployed were selling apples.

Banquets for dogs are still given among the wealthy who make a hobby of keeping kennels, and a number of wealthy persons have established expensive canine cemeteries filled with elaborate tombstones and mausoleums. The Eleanor Speyer Hospital for dogs and cats in New York was erected by James Speyer, the banker.

As to fantastic — and expensive — parties, they are so numerous that they bewilder the inquirer. The Dorrance family (Campbell Soup) makes a regular practice of taking over the ballroom, the Clover Room, and the entire second and third floors of the Bellevue-Stratford Hotel, Philadelphia, for parties to which Wideners, Stotesburys, Dukes, Drexels, and Biddles are invited. *Fortune*, ecstatically describing one of these pretentious affairs, said, "There would be rare flowers and foliages, and hundreds of live macaws and toucans and cockatoos and parakeets and birds of paradise in cages, and showers of rose petals falling pinkly on the dancers out of an electrically activated sky." Newspapers estimated the cost per function at from $75,000 to $150,000. But these were really rather small parties.

In January, 1931, Mr. and Mrs. Henry L. Doherty arranged a coming-out party for Helen Lee Eames Doherty, daughter of Mrs. Doherty by a former marriage. This debut took place at the Mayflower Hotel, Washington, and guests were brought from New York in a special chartered train paid for by Doherty. Several floors of the hotel, in addition to the public entertaining rooms, were rented by the Dohertys for their entourage of guests, servants, and entertainers. The newspapers estimated the cost of the function at no less than $250,000. Senator Norris, citing the prevalance of unemployment, said the next day in the Senate chamber, "I don't know how they had the heart to do it."

Doherty's Cities Service Company earned distinction during the boom period by unloading huge quantities of nonvoting stock at $40 to $50 a share in a nationwide door-to-door selling campaign. The price range of this stock in 1937, after three years of rising prices, was $2.62½ to $5.37½ per share.

About the time of the quarter-million-dollar Doherty debut, Mr. and Mrs. Franklyn L. Hutton gave a party for their daughter Barbara in the Crystal Room of the Ritz-Carlton Hotel, New York. The vast interior was stage-set by Joseph Urban, famed scenic designer, to represent a moonlit garden. There were, according to the public prints, two thousand cases of champagne for one thousand guests; the aggregate cost was given at $100,000.

At the close of 1936 Mrs. Evalyn Walsh McLean, the proud possessor of the $2,000,000 Hope diamond, heiress to a mining fortune, and married into a newspaper and Cincinnati public-utilities fortune, renewed her custom of staging a lavish New Year's Eve party in Washington. The newspapers set the cost of this function, tendered to her son, John R. McLean II, at $50,000, which seems rather low in view of the details. There were 325 guests at dinner and 650 at the ball which followed. As the house on the McLean estate, Friendship, was not large enough to accommodate the guests and their equerries and footmen, Mrs. McLean ordered constructed a special wing, which was torn down after the party was over. Two orchestras played for the dancers; the cost of beverages alone was, according to the New York *Herald Tribune*, $9,000. The liquid refreshments comprised 480 quarts of champagne, 288 bottles of Scotch whiskey, 48 quarts of cocktails, 36 bottles of liqueurs, and 40 gallons of beer. The menu included several tons of tomato stuffed with crabmeat, cream-of-mushroom soup, breast of guinea hen, spinach, potatoes, ices, fruits, and coffee.

Mrs. McLean, presiding in the turmoil, wore the Hope diamond, the Star of the East (another large stone), and six diamond bracelets. She was closely guarded, as befitted a walking fortune, by fifteen private detectives and a company of Washington police, who kept vigilant eyes as well on the scintillating jewelry of the guests.

When Mrs. Marjorie Post Close Hutton married Joseph E. Davies, Washington corporation lawyer and later Ambassador to Russia, her huge apartment was bedecked "with 5,000 chrysanthemums that had been dyed blush pink at a cost of $2,000 to match the icing on the 300-pound wedding cake which the establishment's twenty-five servants, assisted by three caterers, served to fifty wedding guests." The flowers themselves cost $6,000. When the Hutton-Davies menage removed to Moscow it was reported that it ordered transported several carloads of specially prepared foods as well as furniture, ice-boxes, electric fans, and other equipment. Several hundred quarts of frozen cream were brought along, to the astonishment of Russians who pointed out that the country still had cows. During the summer of 1937 Mrs. Davies ordered two tons of frozen foods sent to Moscow for a cruise she and her husband were taking. Mrs. Davies happens to own the major interest in the General Foods Corporation, which specializes in frozen fresh products that are preserved indefinitely.

Mrs. Hutton-Davies likes to transport things long distances. She makes a practice, according to Helen Worden's *Society Circus,* of sending exotic plants from her Long Island hothouses down to her Florida estate. The plants, wrapped in cotton batting, are moved in heated railroad cars.

To celebrate her twenty-second birthday in Paris in November, 1934, the Princess Barbara Hutton Mdivani, now the Countess Haugwitz-Reventlow, gave a modest little party costing only $10,000. "We didn't think it fitting," her husband apologized, "to spend too much in these times." Among the guests, journalists discerned two princes, one duchess, three barons, thirteen counts, one earl, and one hundred lesser personages.

The plutocracy has traveled a long way since Mrs. Potter Palmer of Chicago dazzled Carlton Terrace, London, in 1909 with a puny $10,000 party and a $100,000 season. The cost of a really fashionable party is now at least $100,000 and such affairs are the rule, not the exception. It is no longer, however, the item of cost but the occasion of the cost that attracts the attention of the newspapers. At Newport throughout the summer season, in Florida during the winter, the rich families by turns entertain extravagantly with garden parties, yachting parties, costume parties, and dances, the cost of which ranges from $50,000 to $100,000 each. . . .

Whole new fields of extravagant expenditure have been opened up since the horse-and-buggy days of the 1890's. Bathrooms, swimming pools, and stamp collections take up a good deal of surplus money, while some tens of thousands of American citizens dine out of garbage cans. *Fortune* (January 1931) summarizes the bathroom fad. The Ralph Pulitzer family of New York, among the ninety second-richest clans, have their most prized bathroom embellished in a jungle motif, "walls decorated with monkeys swinging from palm trees, gaudy flamingos, and yawning crocodiles, all painted on gold canvas. . . . The tub is soft yellow, faced with black and gold marble." Continuing, "Mrs. William Stern's bath is found to be silver and green, the wall above the tub offering intimate glimpses into submarine life. . . . Just as impressive is Mrs. Seton Porter's [National Distillers' Products], with its black-and-white marble floor, jade ceiling, and mirror rising from the edge of the tub, framed in black glass." Stuart Chase, in *The New Republic*, May 25, 1927, refers to a jade-and-gold Park Avenue bathroom that cost $35,000 but he does not give the name of its owner.

The champion of champions in the bathroom sweepstakes, however, appears to be W. C. Grunow, radio manufacturer, who owns "a tub made from a single slab of Mexican onyx marble, costing $12,000 and equipped with fixtures of twenty-four carat gold plate." The gold plating, although a definite feature, has its duplicates in the fixtures of many other aristocratic bathrooms. In Mrs. Hugh Dillman's Palm Beach *palazzo*, for example, all the faucets except those in the kitchen and butler's pantry are of gold, says *Fortune*; and gold is indeed so common that much of the hardware — door hinges, knobs, metal trimming in general — in the various châteaux of the wealthy is now made of it.

The bathroom in a wealthy American's home is not, of course, synonymous with the bathroom of ordinary usage. It is usually a large vaulted chamber, with a sunken tub that may in some cases very easily be used as a swimming pool. Some of the bathrooms of the plutocracy are equipped

with gymnastic paraphernalia; all have as standard equipment such things as quartz lamps, rubbing tables, unusual lighting arrangements, and strange decorations.

Nor is the American millionaire's bathroom noteworthy for its rococo style alone. Its frequent incidence also deserves attention. Taking into consideration all the private residences and large apartments of the wealthiest families, it emerges as a fact that each family possesses at least one hundred bathrooms for the use of its own members, its guests, its servants, and its entertainers. This particular inquiry managed to isolate 723 bathrooms in the various Du Pont establishments, at which point, with much ground remaining to be covered, the quest was regretfully terminated. The Du Pont baths are plain and fancy, somber and gay, for chauffeurs and maids, for engineers and aviators, and for ladies and gentlemen.

Bathing is a frequent ceremony in upperclass life, and the member of the average wealthy family is apt to spend much time in the bath — telephoning, transacting business with secretaries and housekeepers, reading, listening to the radio or the phonograph, visiting with friends. The psychologist Freud has a theory that frequent washing of the hands marks a betrayal of a subconscious feeling of guilt. Frequent bathing, by the same token, must then mark a betrayal of an even deeper feeling of subconscious guilt.

The subject of bathing among the rich would not be complete without some mention of swimming pools. The newspaper rotogravure sections frequently regale the public with photographs of the pools of Hollywood actors, but theirs are really modest affairs. William Randolph Hearst on his San Simeon estate has an outdoor pool of Carrara marble, connected with an indoor pool for use in inclement weather. Although all the standard equipped estates have their pools, perhaps the prize of them all is to be found on the estate of the late

Henry H. Rogers at Southampton. This pool cost $250,000, and was designed in Pompeian style by Architect John Russell Pope. The interior housing arrangement is lined with colored mosaic; the lighting is indirect, and there is an outdoor counterpart. Walter Chrysler owns a "handpainted" swimming pool. The pool on the average estate is usually merely a regular part of other sports equipment. On the Long Island estate of Mrs. Dodge Sloane, for example, a separate glass building, which can be opened at will to the elements, contains an elaborate swimming pool, tennis court, and billiard and backgammon rooms. Helen Worden's *Society Circus* informs us that "the soil used for the court is tile pink, imported from France."

Upward of a thousand private pools are to be found on the estates of the wealthy.

All of the rich, to be sure, have their expensive little hobbies. The hobby of the recently deceased E. H. R. Green, son of Hetty Green, was the collecting of postage stamps. Green paid the Philatelic Agency of the United States Post Office $18,000 for a sheet of stamps merely because the illustration was printed wrong side up. Retaining the choicest specimens for himself, Green sold the balance; and the Scott Coin and Stamp Company is reported to obtain $3,300 upward from wealthy collectors for each of these stamps.

Complicated litigation is often an expensive pastime of the rich. The seven heirs of the late George Gould, for example, tied up the estate in a snarl of suits, the cost of which was estimated in 1924 by the lawyer for the estate at $2,500 an hour throughout the protracted period of the dispute.

106.

RALPH ADAMS CRAM: What Is a Free Man?

As a part of the "back to the land" movement of the Depression years, the federal government sponsored a program of subsistence homesteads that it hoped would put 25,000 families — each an economic unit — back on the farms. The program, under the auspices of the National Recovery Administration (NRA), got under way in 1934, but by mid-1935 it had attracted only 6,500 persons. At the 1937 meeting of the National Catholic Rural Life Conference, architect Ralph A. Cram, who believed in ownership of property as a prerequisite for citizenship, commented on the apparent failure of the homestead movement. Instead, he suggested ways by which society might be reconstituted without the aid of the federal government. A portion of "What Is a Free Man?" is reprinted here.

Source: *Catholic Rural Life Objectives*, St. Paul, 1937, pp. 37-41.

IN THIS COMMONWEALTH of Virginia which was Thomas Jefferson's state, I, from the Commonwealth of Massachusetts which was John Adams' state, venture to unite myself with these greatest of American statesmen in holding that he only is a free man who owns and administers his own land, craft, trade, art, or profession and is able, at necessity, to maintain himself and his family therefrom. One hundred years ago, excluding slaves, 80 percent of the male population of the United States came within this category. We were then a nation of freemen. Today less than 40 percent can be so counted. We are now, to that extent, a nation of bondmen. Here is where my paper links up with the interests — I may even call it the Crusade — of the Catholic Rural Life Conference.

I fear I can add nothing to the statement of the case I have read in one of your official documents, nor is this necessary. It is sufficient in itself, but I shall try to show one or two of the implications that seem to me to follow from the premises. Here is the statement which I am proud to make my own.

It is a distressing fact that the Jeffersonian dream of a great Western world-empire of men made free through widely distributed ownership of the means of production and the natural resources of the land is proving to be vacuous. The progressive centralization of money power is rapidly transforming the United States into a nation of propertyless people. In the industrial and distribution areas the process of disfranchisement has been under way, and with mounting intensity, for approximately a hundred years, with the result that, actually, the status of the rank and file of our so-called common people in the cities — the factory workers and the small business and tradesmen — differs but slightly from that of slavery. This is abhorrent to the American mind; it troubles the American heart. And still more important, it provides a threat to the very existence of American democratic institutions.

I would add one thing to this and enter one demurrer. It is also, we know by divine and ecclesiastical authority, inconsistent with the Catholic faith. As for its resemblance to the condition of chattel slavery, in one respect it is less advantageous to its members. The slave, at least here in the South, was assured a physical maintenance as long as he lived, and in the majority of cases, of humanitarian and Christian care in sickness and in health. The wage slave is assured of none of these things. He is a "hand," and if he has a body and soul, this is his own lookout.

It is to me self-evident that for every reason this condition of things cannot go on and this conviction is growing fast amongst thinking people. Even government is becoming conscious of it, and when government comes to realize a thing, it must indeed be obvious. In this particular quarter it is as a possible and partial solution of the unemployment problem that the land movement makes its appeal, and of course this is a matter of great value. Unfortunately, like so many other politically managed projects, this "subsistence homestead" project has been consistently mismanaged from the first. A large measure of failure has followed and consequently suspicion and discredit have followed on. If the thing could be got out of the hands of politicians, bureaucrats, and empirical theorists, and administered by private corporations financed by government grants, the results would probably be very different, but political bureaucracy and bureaucratic politicians seldom let go of what they have once had in their hands. I expect reliance must be placed on just such factors as this of the Catholic Rural Life movement.

I would note here one factor which, in addition to bureaucratic inefficiency, was responsible for the present miscarriage of the subsistence homestead project, as well as wrong in principle, and that is the reversal of values as between landholding and shop or factory work. Under government direction, subsistence from the land was made subsidiary to wage subsistence in a mill or factory. The homesteads were, as I understand it, adjuncts to a privately owned industrial plant. Mill work, on the wage system, was the primary consideration; land work just something added. If work in a mill is put first, with time off for limited agrarian pursuits, then in the end we get nowhere so far as the making of free men is concerned. The true principle is the land first with, so to speak, time off for mill work to supplement maintenance and revenue from the land.

Furthermore, this mill or factory work cannot be in some industrial plant owned and run by outside individual or corporate interests. Such industrial adjuncts as there are, and they are indispensable, must be communally owned and administered — not on a profit-making basis but on a profit-sharing basis, with the pay envelope giving place to earned dividends. Men and women acting on this basis are free, and only on this basis.

It seems to me that this factor of cooperation cannot be separated from that of individual land ownership and self-maintenance, and vice versa. What is now being done under the auspices of St. Francis Xavier University in Nova Scotia is, so far as I can judge, both a model and an inspiration. I expect it is this largely because it is not carried on under governmental or political auspices. Experience has proved that the political set-up being what it is, we must rely on civil agencies and individuals.

Edward Filene, that great Jewish merchant of Boston whose death was a great loss to the whole cooperative movement, is a shining example of what we must hope for. As you know, he gave during his lifetime $1 million to further the cooperative movement, with the beginnings at the new settlement at Greenbelt, and he has bequeathed an additional $2 million to the same cause. This is, of course, merely a residential not a self-maintenance project, but the latter is just as dependent, even more so, on cooperation for its success and for the making of truly free men. . . .

If, instead of giving or bequeathing generous sums for the founding of business schools, technological institutes, and college chairs of journalism, scenario writing, or eurythmic dancing, or still further enriching art museums which already have trouble in expending their funds except for the purchase of doubtful "old masters" or even more doubtful examples of "modernist" and "surrealist art," they would build, equip, and populate self-contained agrarian-industrial communities of human scale, they would make the most important contribution possible to the solution of most of our current social and economic problems.

The individual producer, self-sufficient, independent, and free, is indeed the answer to the problem raised by materialistic technocracy. Until we organize society in units of human scale — social, industrial, economic, and political — the social organism we have made for ourselves will continue, as in the Gadarene instance, running down a steep place into the sea. I need not remind you that this process of reestablishing the human scale of necessity carries with it the resumption of land ownership, the establishing of a cooperative mode of life, measurably in production, completely in distribution. "Free competition," i.e., internecine commercial warfare, has worked itself out to an end, and that not a pretty one.

Of course there will always be continued use of all that machinery that is truly "laborsaving," while along certain lines there will always be a certain amount of mass production under technological conditions. A blacksmith cannot make an automobile in his own smithy nor forge steel in his own backyard. Also it is to be remembered that not everyone is fitted by nature to act as a self-sufficient unit in society. Probably the major part of the 10 or 15 million unemployed of a few years ago are actually unemployable, except under strong control and definite direction. And the supply of this grade of humanity is constant.

They will of necessity find their place in the mills, factories and other industrial plants that will continue to exist though, it is to be hoped, in lesser numbers, or on corporately managed farms that may very well take on something of the character of the "collectives" as these are now conducted under the Soviets. In both cases, industrial plants and collective farms, these are only for the subnormal grades of humanity; for what we hope against hope is the normal type, the free life of independent ownership and action is the ideal that must be made real. . . .

Social and political democracy have failed because during the last hundred years what I call the High Democracy of Washington, Jefferson, and Adams has given place to the "low democracy" of Jackson, the so-called liberal philosophers and politicians of the nineteenth century, and a dispossessed proletariat. Of course, the seeds of this delusive and poisonous growth were sown long ago, in the fifteenth and sixteenth centuries. They were nurtured by the material and scientific discoveries of the eighteenth century, grew into luxuriance in the nineteenth century, and now, the abnormal growth having attained maturity, is rotting into final dissolution. As always, during the 6,000 years of man's recorded history, violent reaction follows the consummation of an epoch that has reached its term, breaking down in deserved ignominy, and we find ourselves confronted by an ever growing and widening autocracy — dictatorships, the totalitarian state, Communism, syndicalism, and all the other tyrannies that batten on the carcass of dead liberty.

I think democracy, the old and true democracy, the democracy of the Catholic monarchies of the Middle Ages, of the founders of this republic and the framers of its Constitution, is worth saving — or rather recreating. Of course, this great work cannot be accomplished without the recovery and acceptance by man of those moral sanctions *outside himself* that derive from revealed religion through a divinely established and divinely guided church. This, however, is a work of Grace; man alone seems at present unable to achieve it. Pending a new outpouring of the Holy Spirit, we can do much more in our limited human way, and one of the things we can do is to make more and more citizens of this republic, freemen, economically and industrially free; and to freemen only must be given the right to participate, through the electoral franchise, in the political determination of public affairs.

This is a hard saying, for, logically applied, it would mean that large numbers of men and women, particularly in the lower industrial and social brackets, would be disfranchised. It is also a purely academic proposition, for by no conceivable means could so drastic a revolution be accomplished. Nor would it be desirable that it should be. The ballot is a symbol, an empty symbol, if you like, but still a symbol of liberty and therefore valuable. On the other hand, it has its dangers, and one of them is that its possession deludes men into the belief that, having it, they are free men (which they are not) and that therefore they need not concern themselves with the other and more important factors of their servitude. How far they are really persuaded of the intrinsic value of the act of putting a cross before one or two names or measures determined for them by their partisan guardians and directors, is a more or less open question. In view of the fact that, except under extraordinary circumstances, not more than half the registered voters take the trouble to go to the polls, I should say that the value of the gesture was pretty well understood.

Even if this is so, the electoral franchise is held in high esteem by the majority of citizens — witness how the women fought for it — and they would properly resent any move toward taking it away from them under any pretense. Of course it was a bad blunder on the part of the Republican Party, dominated by a cabal of malignant and cynical "Reconstructionists," after Appomattox, to proclaim the electoral franchise as a "natural right" of all men (they forgot the women for the moment) instead of a privilege, a duty, and an honor, as it always had been held to be up to that unfortunate moment. Nevertheless, it happened, and became one of the major factors in the discrediting of democracy and the current breakdown of the democratic regime.

If Jefferson and Adams, Madison and Hamilton, and all the protagonists of liberty, their progenitors, time out of mind, were right in holding that the vote should be exercised only by free men, *i.e.*, possessors of *real* property (not paper certificates of indebtedness, which is what we facetiously call "securities" actually are), then the bearing of agrarianism on the political problem becomes obvious.

It seems to me that there are two considerations that follow from this. The first is that every effort must be made to change men's minds in this particular, bringing them to see that the vote is not an inalienable right of man, as such, but a high privilege, granted or withheld for cause. The second is that every movement such as this

of the Catholic Rural Life must be pushed to the limit. These are the makings of free men, and of such only, may a democracy, a republic, a monarchy, or any other polity be made.

Every man that is taken off the payroll and established on his own land, or becomes the master of his personally owned craft, trade, profession, or art — therefore his *own master* — becomes, *ipso facto*, or potentially, a free man, and as such he becomes automatically a living part of a living community.

No, I do not advocate taking the vote away from every man now on wage, but rather the making of every present wage earner an independent citizen and a free citizen by assuring him his own land or — and sometimes and — the free practice of his personally owned and conducted trade, craft, art, or profession.

107.

Franklin D. Roosevelt: Quarantine the Aggressors

The course of world events had become alarming by the late summer of 1937 when President Roosevelt began a tour of the nation designed to win support for his domestic policies. Nazi Germany was swiftly rearming; Mussolini and Hitler had formed a Fascist alliance; and in July 1937 Japan had resumed the invasion of China begun in 1931. On October 5, 1937, Roosevelt delivered the "Quarantine" Address in Chicago, which appeared to mark a reversal of the recent policy of nonintervention. The speech provoked a bitter public response. The American people, disillusioned by their experience in World War I and beset by domestic problems, were still in a predominantly isolationist mood.

Source: *Record, App.*, 75 Cong., 2 Sess., pp. 20-21.

I AM GLAD TO COME once again to Chicago and especially to have the opportunity of taking part in the dedication of this important project of civic betterment.

On my trip across the continent and back

I have been shown many evidences of the result of common sense cooperation between municipalities and the federal government, and I have been greeted by tens of thousands of Americans who have told me in every look and word that their material and spiritual well-being has made great strides forward in the past few years.

And yet, as I have seen with my own eyes, the prosperous farms, the thriving factories and the busy railroads — as I have seen the happiness and security and peace which covers our wide land, almost inevitably I have been compelled to contrast our peace with very different scenes being enacted in other parts of the world.

It is because the people of the United States under modern conditions must, for the sake of their own future, give thought to the rest of the world, that I, as the responsible executive head of the nation, have chosen this great inland city and this gala occasion to speak to you on a subject of definite national importance.

The political situation in the world, which of late has been growing progressively worse, is such as to cause grave concern and anxiety to all the peoples and nations who wish to live in peace and amity with their neighbors.

Some fifteen years ago the hopes of mankind for a continuing era of international peace were raised to great heights when more than sixty nations solemnly pledged themselves not to resort to arms in furtherance of their national aims and policies. The high aspirations expressed in the Briand-Kellogg Peace Pact and the hopes for peace thus raised have of late given way to a haunting fear of calamity. The present reign of terror and international lawlessness began a few years ago.

It began through unjustified interference in the internal affairs of other nations or the invasion of alien territory in violation of treaties and has now reached a stage where the very foundations of civilization are seriously threatened. The landmarks and traditions which have marked the progress of civilization toward a condition of law, order, and justice are being wiped away.

Without a declaration of war and without warning or justification of any kind, civilians, including women and children, are being ruthlessly murdered with bombs from the air. In times of so-called peace, ships are being attacked and sunk by submarines without cause or notice. Nations are fomenting and taking sides in civil warfare in nations that have never done them any harm. Nations claiming freedom for themselves deny it to others. Innocent peoples and nations are being cruelly sacrificed to a greed for power and supremacy which is devoid of all sense of justice and humane consideration.

To paraphrase a recent author, "perhaps we foresee a time when men, exultant in the technique of homicide, will rage so hotly over the world that every precious thing will be in danger, every book and picture and harmony, every treasure garnered through two milleniums, the small, the delicate, the defenseless — all will be lost or wrecked or utterly destroyed."

If those things come to pass in other parts of the world, let no one imagine that America will escape, that it may expect mercy, that this Western Hemisphere will not be attacked, and that it will continue tranquilly and peacefully to carry on the ethics and the arts of civilization. If those days come, "there will be no safety by arms, no help from authority, no answer in science. The storm will rage till every flower of culture is trampled and all human beings are leveled in a vast chaos."

If those days are not to come to pass — if we are to have a world in which we can breathe freely and live in amity without fear — the peace-loving nations must make a concerted effort to uphold laws and principles on which alone peace can rest secure. The peace-loving nations must make a concerted effort in opposition to those violations of treaties and those ignorings of humane instincts which today are creating a state of international anarchy and instability from which there is no escape through mere isolation or neutrality.

Those who cherish their freedom and recognize and respect the equal right of their neighbors to be free and live in peace must work together for the triumph of law and moral principles in order that peace, justice, and confidence may prevail in the world. There must be a return to a belief in the pledged word, in the value of a signed treaty. There must be recognition of the fact that national morality is as vital as private morality.

A bishop wrote me the other day:

> It seems to me that something greatly needs to be said in behalf of ordinary humanity against the present practice of carrying the horrors of war to helpless civilians, especially women and children. It may be that such a protest might be regarded by many, who claim to be realists, as futile, but may it not be that the heart of mankind is so filled with horror at the present needless suffering that that force could be mobilized in sufficient volume to lessen such cruelty in the days ahead. Even though it may take twenty years, which God forbid, for civilization to make effective its corporate protest against this barbarism, surely strong voices may hasten the day.

There is a solidarity and interdependence about the modern world, both technically and morally, which makes it impossible for any nation completely to isolate itself from economic and political upheavals in the rest of the world, especially when such upheavals appear to be spreading and not declining. There can be no stability or peace either within nations or between nations except under laws and moral standards adhered to by all. International anarchy destroys every foundation for peace. It jeopardizes either the immediate or the future security of every nation, large or small. It is, therefore, a matter of vital interest and concern to the people of the United States that the sanctity of international treaties and the

maintenance of international morality be restored.

The overwhelming majority of the peoples and nations of the world today want to live in peace. They seek the removal of barriers against trade. They want to exert themselves in industry, in agriculture, and in business that they may increase their wealth through the production of wealth-producing goods rather than striving to produce military planes and bombs and machine guns and cannon for the destruction of human lives and useful property.

In those nations of the world which seem to be piling armament on armament for purposes of aggression, and those other nations which fear acts of aggression against them and their security, a very high proportion of their national income is being spent directly for armaments. It runs from 30 to as high as 50 percent. The proportion that we in the United States spend is far less — 11 or 12 percent.

How happy we are that the circumstances of the moment permit us to put our money into bridges and boulevards, dams and reforestation, the conservation of our soil, and many other kinds of useful works rather than into huge standing armies and vast supplies of implements of war.

I am compelled and you are compelled, nevertheless, to look ahead. The peace, the freedom, and the security of 90 percent of the population of the world is being jeopardized by the remaining 10 percent who are threatening a break-down of all international order and law. Surely the 90 percent who want to live in peace under law and in accordance with moral standards that have received almost universal acceptance through the centuries can and must find some way to make their will prevail.

The situation is definitely of universal concern. The questions involved relate not merely to violations of specific provisions of particular treaties; they are questions of war and of peace, of international law, and especially of principles of humanity. It is true that they involve definite violations of agreements, and especially of the Covenant of the League of Nations, the Briand-Kellogg Pact, and the Nine Power Treaty. But they also involve problems of world economy, world security, and world humanity.

It is true that the moral consciousness of the world must recognize the importance of removing injustices and well-founded grievances; but at the same time it must be aroused to the cardinal necessity of honoring sanctity of treaties, of respecting the rights and liberties of others, and of putting an end to acts of international aggression.

It seems to be unfortunately true that the epidemic of world lawlessness is spreading. When an epidemic of physical disease starts to spread, the community approves and joins in a quarantine of the patients in order to protect the health of the community against the spread of the disease.

It is my determination to pursue a policy of peace and to adopt every practicable measure to avoid involvement in war. It ought to be inconceivable that in this modern era, and in the face of experience, any nation could be so foolish and ruthless as to run the risk of plunging the whole world into war by invading and violating, in contravention of solemn treaties, the territory of other nations that have done them no real harm and which are too weak to protect themselves adequately. Yet the peace of the world and the welfare and security of every nation is today being threatened by that very thing.

No nation which refuses to exercise forebearance and to respect the freedom and rights of others can long remain strong and retain the confidence and respect of other nations. No nation ever loses its dignity or good standing by conciliating its differences and by exercising great patience with, and consideration for, the rights of other nations.

War is a contagion, whether it be declared or undeclared. It can engulf states and peoples remote from the original scene of hostilities. We are determined to keep out of war, yet we cannot insure ourselves against the disastrous effects of war and the dangers of involvement. We are adopting such measures as will minimize our risk of involvement, but we cannot have complete protection in a world of disorder in which confidence and security have broken down.

If civilization is to survive, the principles of the Prince of Peace must be restored. Shattered trust between nations must be revived. Most important of all, the will for peace on the part of peace-loving nations must express itself to the end that nations that may be tempted to violate their agreements and the rights of others will desist from such a cause. There must be positive endeavors to preserve peace.

America hates war. America hopes for peace. Therefore, America actively engages in the search for peace.

◆

Be neutral. Be American.
WILLIAM RANDOLPH HEARST

1938

108.

Chester I. Barnard: An Incentive Economy

As one result of the large increase in the number of American corporations in the 1920s and 1930s, the so-called white-collar class — managers and executives — also increased, becoming a substantial segment of American society. It was large enough, at any rate, to be regarded as a group whose attitudes, characteristics, and desires were distinctive and merited discussion. In 1938 Chester I. Barnard, president of New Jersey Bell Telephone Company, published The Functions of the Executive *as a guide to large corporations in their personnel policies. The following selection, drawn from a chapter of the book originally called "The Economy of Incentives," is a discussion of the type of corporation employee later to be known as the organization man.*

Source: *The Functions of the Executive*, Cambridge, 1938, Ch. 11.

AN ESSENTIAL ELEMENT OF ORGANIZATIONS is the willingness of persons to contribute their individual efforts to the cooperative system. The power of cooperation, which is often spectacularly great when contrasted with that even of large numbers of individuals unorganized, is nevertheless dependent upon the willingness of individuals to cooperate and to contribute their efforts to the cooperative system. The contributions of personal efforts which constitute the energies of organizations are yielded by individuals because of incentives. The egotistical motives of self-preservation and of self-satisfaction are dominating forces; on the whole, organizations can exist only when consistent with the satisfaction of these motives, unless, alternatively, they can change these motives. The individual is always the basic strategic factor in organization. Regardless of his history or his obligations he must be induced to cooperate, or there can be no cooperation.

It needs no further introduction to suggest that the subject of incentives is fundamental in formal organizations and in conscious efforts to organize. Inadequate incentives mean dissolution, or changes of organization purpose, or failure of cooperation. Hence, in all sorts of organizations the affording of adequate incentives becomes the most definitely emphasized task in their existence. It is probably in this aspect of executive work that failure is most pronounced, though the causes may be due either to inadequate understanding or to the breakdown of the effectiveness of organization.

The net satisfactions which induce a man to contribute his efforts to an organization result from the positive advantages as against the disadvantages which are entailed. It follows that a net advantage may be increased or a negative advantage made positive either by increasing the number or the strength of the positive inducements or by reducing the number or the strength of the disadvantages. It often occurs that the positive advantages are few and meager, but the burdens involved are also negligible, so that there is a strong net advantage. Many "social" organizations are able to exist under such a state of affairs. Conversely, when the burdens involved are numerous or heavy, the offsetting positive advantages must be either numerous or powerful.

Hence, from the viewpoint of the organization requiring or seeking contributions from individuals, the problem of effective incentives may be either one of finding positive incentives or of reducing or eliminating negative incentives or burdens. For example, employment may be made attractive either by reducing the work required — say, by shortening hours or supplying tools or power, that is, by making conditions of employment less onerous — or by increasing positive inducement, such as wages.

In practice, although there are many cases where it is clear which side of the "equation" is being adjusted, on the whole, specific practices and conditions affect both sides simultaneously or it is impossible to determine which they affect. Most specific factors in so-called working conditions may be viewed either as making employment positively attractive or as making work less onerous. We shall, therefore, make no attempt to treat specific inducements as increasing advantages or as decreasing disadvantages; but this underlying aspect is to be kept in mind.

More important than this is the distinction between the objective and the subjective aspects of incentives. Certain common positive incentives, such as material goods and in some senses money, clearly have an objective existence; and this is true also of negative incentives like working hours, conditions of work. Given a man of a certain state of mind, of certain attitudes, or governed by certain motives, he can be induced to contribute to an organization by a given combination of these objective incentives, positive or negative. It often is the case, however, that the organization is unable to offer objective incentives that will serve as an inducement to that state of mind, or to those attitudes, or to one governed by those motives. The only alternative then available is to change the state of mind, or attitudes, or motives, so that the available objective incentives can become effective.

An organization can secure the efforts necessary to its existence, then, either by the objective inducements it provides or by changing states of mind. It seems to me improbable that any organization can exist as a practical matter which does not employ both methods in combination. In some organizations the emphasis is on the offering of objective incentives — this is true of most industrial organizations. In others the preponderance is on the state of mind — this is true of most patriotic and religious organizations.

We shall call the processes of offering objective incentives "the method of incentives"; and the processes of changing subjective attitudes "the method of persuasion." Using these new terms, let us repeat what we have said: In commercial organizations the professed emphasis is apparently almost wholly on the side of the method of incentives. In religious and political organizations the professed emphasis is apparently almost wholly on the side of persuasion. But in fact, especially if account be taken of the different kinds of contributions required from different individuals, both methods are used in all types of organizations. Moreover, the centrifugal forces of individualism and the competition between organizations for individual contributions result in both methods being ineffective, with few exceptions, for more than short periods or a few years.

We shall first discuss the method of incentives. It will facilitate our consideration of the subject if at the outset we distinguish two classes of incentives; first those that are specific and can be specifically offered to an individual; and second, those that are general, not personal, that cannot be specifically offered. We shall call the first class specific inducements, the second general incentives.

The specific inducements that may be offered are of several classes, for example: (a) material inducements; (b) personal, nonmaterial opportunities; (c) desirable physical conditions; (d) ideal benefactions. General incentives afforded are, for example: (e) associational attractiveness; (f) adaptation of conditions to habitual methods and attitudes; (g) the opportunity of enlarged participation; (h) the condition of communion. Each of these classes of incentives is known under various names, and the list does not purport to be complete, since our purpose now is illustrative. But to accomplish this purpose it is necessary briefly to discuss the incentives named.

(a) Material inducements are money, things, or physical conditions that are offered to the individual as inducements to accepting employment, compensation for service, reward for contribution. Under a money economy and the highly specialized production of material goods, the range and profusion of material inducements are very great. The complexity of schedules of money compensation, the difficulty of securing the monetary means of compensation, and the power of exchange which money gives in organized markets have served to exaggerate the importance of money in particular and material inducements in general as

incentives to personal contributions to organized effort. It goes without elaboration that where a large part of the time of an individual is devoted to one organization, the physiological necessities — food, shelter, clothing — require that material inducements should be present in most cases; but these requirements are so limited that they are satisfied with small quantities.

The unaided power of material incentives, when the minimum necessities are satisfied, in my opinion is exceedingly limited as to most men, depending almost entirely for its development upon persuasion. Notwithstanding the great emphasis upon material incentives in modern times and especially in current affairs, there is no doubt in my mind that, unaided by other motives, they constitute weak incentives beyond the level of the bare physiological necessities.

To many this view will not be readily acceptable. The emphasis upon material rewards has been a natural result of the success of technological developments — relative to other incentives it is the material things which have been progressively easier to produce, and therefore to offer. Hence there has been a forced cultivation of the love of material things among those above the level of subsistence. Since existing incentives seem always inadequate to the degree of cooperation and of social integration theoretically possible and ideally desirable, the success of the sciences and the arts of material production would have been partly ineffective, and in turn would have been partly impossible, without inculcating the desire of the material. The most significant result of this situation has been the expansion of population, most of which has been necessarily at the bare subsistence level, at which level material inducements are, on the whole, powerful incentives. This has perpetuated the illusion that beyond this subsistence level material incentives are also the most effective.

A concurrent result has been the creation of sentiments in individuals that they *ought* to want material things. The inculcation of "proper" ambitions in youth have greatly stressed material possessions as an evidence of good citizenship, social adequacy, etc. Hence, when underlying and governing motives have not been satisfied, there has been strong influence to rationalize the default as one of material compensation, and not to be conscious of the controlling motives or at least not to admit them.

Yet it seems to me to be a matter of common experience that material rewards are ineffective beyond the subsistence level excepting to a very limited proportion of men; that most men neither work harder for more material things, nor can be induced thereby to devote more than a fraction of their possible contribution to organized effort. It is likewise a matter of both present experience and past history that many of the most effective and powerful organizations are built up on incentives in which the materialistic elements, above bare subsistence, are either relatively lacking or absolutely absent. Military organizations have been relatively lacking in material incentives. The greater part of the work of political organizations is without material incentive. Religious organizations are characterized on the whole by material sacrifice. It seems to me to be definitely a general fact that even in purely commercial organizations material incentives are so weak as to be almost negligible except when reinforced by other incentives, and then only because of wholesale general persuasion in the form of salesmanship and advertising.

It will be noted that the reference has been to material incentives rather than to money. What has been said requires some, but not great, qualification with reference to money as an incentive — solely for the reason that money in our economy may be used as the indirect means of satisfying non-materialistic motives — philanthropic, artistic, intellectual, and religious motives for example — and because money income becomes an index of social status, personal development, etc.

(b) Inducements of a personal, nonmaterialistic character are of great importance to secure cooperative effort above the minimum material rewards essential to subsistence. The opportunities for distinction, prestige, personal power, and the attainment of dominating position are much more important than material rewards in the development of all sorts of organizations, including commercial organizations. In various ways this fact applies to many types of human beings, including those of limited ability and children. Even in strictly commercial organizations, where it is least supposed to be true, money without distinction, prestige, position, is so utterly ineffective that it is rare that greater income can be made to serve even temporarily as an inducement if accompanied by suppression of prestige. At least for short periods inferior material rewards are often accepted if assurance of distinction is present; and usually the presumption is that material rewards ought to follow or arise from or even are made necessary by the attainment of distinction and prestige. There is unlimited experience to show that among many men, and especially among women, the real value of differences of money rewards lies in the recognition or distinction assumed to be conferred thereby, or to be procured therewith — one of the reasons why differentials either in money income or in material possessions are a source of jealousy and disruption if not accompanied by other factors of distinction.

(c) Desirable physical conditions of work are often important conscious, and more often important unconscious, inducements to cooperation.

(d) Ideal benefactions as inducements to cooperation are among the most powerful and the most neglected. By ideal benefaction I mean the capacity of organizations to satisfy personal ideals usually relating to nonmaterial, future, or altruistic relations. They include pride of workmanship, sense of adequacy, altruistic service for family or others, loyalty to organization in patriotism, etc., aesthetic and religious feeling. They also include the opportunities for the satisfaction of the motives of hate and revenge, often the controlling factor in adherence to and intensity of effort in some organizations.

All of these inducements — material rewards, personal nonmaterial opportunities, desirable physical conditions, and ideal benefactions — may be and frequently are definitely offered as inducements to contribute to organizations. But there are other conditions which cannot usually be definitely offered, and which are known or recognized by their absence in particular cases. Of these I consider associational attractiveness as exceedingly, and often critically, important.

(e) By associational attractiveness I mean social compatibility. It is in many cases obvious that racial hostility, class antagonism, and national enmities absolutely prevent cooperation, in others decrease its effectiveness, and in still others make it impossible to secure cooperation except by great strengthening of other incentives. But it seems clear that the question of personal compatibility or incompatibility is much more far-reaching in limiting cooperative effort than is recognized, because an intimate knowledge of particular organizations is usually necessary to understand its precise character. When such an intimate knowledge exists, personal compatibility or incompatibility is so thoroughly sensed, and the related problems are so difficult to deal with, that only in special or critical cases is conscious attention given to them. But they can be neglected only at peril of disruption.

Men often will not work at all, and will rarely work well, under other incentives if the social situation *from their point of view* is unsatisfactory. Thus often men of inferior education cannot work well with those of superior education, and vice versa. Differences not merely of race, nation, religion, but of customs, morals, social status, education, ambition, are frequently controlling. Hence, a powerful incentive to the effort of almost all men is favorable associational conditions from their viewpoint.

Personal aversions based upon racial, national, color, and class differences often seem distinctly pernicious; but on the whole they are, in the immediate sense, I believe, based upon a sound feeling of organization necessities. For when there is incompatibility or even merely lack of compatibility, both formal communication and especially communication through informal organization become difficult and sometimes impossible.

(f) Another incentive of the general type is that of customary working conditions and conformity to habitual practices and attitudes. This is made obvious by the universal practice, in all kinds of organization, of rejecting recruits trained in different methods or possessing "foreign" attitudes. It is taken for granted that men will not or cannot do well by strange methods or under strange conditions. What is not so obvious is that men will frequently not attempt to cooperate if they recognize that such methods or conditions are to be accepted.

(g) Another indirect incentive that we may regard as of general and often of controlling importance is the opportunity for the feeling of enlarged participation in the course of events. It affects all classes of men under some conditions. It is sometimes though not necessarily, related to love of personal distinction and prestige. Its realization is the feeling of importance of result of effort because of the importance of the cooperative effort as a whole. Thus, *other things being equal*, many men prefer association with large organizations, organizations which they regard as useful, or organizations they regard as effective, as against those they consider small, useless, ineffective.

(*b*) The most intangible and subtle of incentives is that which I have called the condition of communion. It is related to social compatibility, but is essentially different. It is the feeling of personal comfort in social relations that is sometimes called solidarity, social integration, the gregarious instinct, or social security (in the original, not in its present debased economic, sense). It is the opportunity for comradeship, for mutual support in personal attitudes. The need for communion is a basis of informal organization that is essential to the operation of every formal organization. It is likewise the basis for informal organization within but hostile to formal organization.

109.

John L. Lewis: Industrial Unions

The American Federation of Labor's devotion to the principle of craft unionism prevented it from becoming an effective organizer of industrial workers during the 1930s. When its 1935 convention failed to adopt a position favorable to this hitherto ignored segment of the American working class, John L. Lewis, along with Sidney Hillman, David Dubinsky, and Thomas McMahon formed the Committee for Industrial Organization within the A.F. of L. Continuing strife in the parent body, combined with highly successful membership drives by the Committee, led the latter to break with the A.F. of L. and to form the independent Congress of Industrial Organizations (CIO) in November 1938. Lewis, president of the United Mine Workers, was named chairman of the first convention of the Congress and addressed it in that capacity.

Source: *Proceedings of the First Constitutional Convention of the Congress of Industrial Organizations*, n.p., n.d., pp. 9-12.

I PROFOUNDLY APPRECIATE the opportunity of opening this convention with greetings through President Fagan of organized labor in this great industrial section, with the greetings of His Honor, the mayor of Pittsburgh, extended in behalf of the people of this great municipality, with the greetings of the Christian churches, represented by the eminent clergymen who are present this morning, and the acclaim of our own people.

Why these greetings? Why this interest?

Why this enthusiasm? Why this acclaim? Because there has been born in America a new, modern labor movement dedicated to the proposition that all who labor are entitled to equality of opportunity, the right to organize, the right to participate in the bounties and the blessings of this country and our government, the right to aspire to an equality of position, and the right to express views, objectives, and rights on a parity with any other citizen, whatever may be his place, his condition of servitude, or the degree of world's goods which he may possess.

So that is the greeting of the Committee for Industrial Organization, assembled here and about to formalize its own internal affairs and make permanent its form of organization.

It is perhaps an interesting coincidence that fifty-seven years ago, almost to the day, the great [Samuel] Gompers founded in this city the labor movement of his generation. That labor movement served that generation in a period where the skills in American trade and industry were the skills of handicraft and not the skills of the machine age and of mass production. But time moves on and the old order changes, and, as the changes became obvious, it was more and more apparent that the labor movement and the type of organization founded in Pittsburgh fifty-seven years ago was not equal to the task of organizing or rendering service to the teeming millions who labor in American industries in this generation of our life.

Perhaps it will be illustrative to say that in fifty-four years of existence and advocation and administration of its affairs, the American Federation of Labor failed to bring to the hundreds of thousands of workers in the industries in the Pittsburgh area the blessings of collective bargaining; and during all those years the Pittsburgh industrial district was the citadel of nonunionism in America, the citadel of labor exploitation, and the recognized fortress of those financial interests and industrial interests in America who preferred to exploit and debase and degrade labor rather than recognize its existence or concede its right to fair treatment.

The old order changes, and what the American Federation of Labor could not do in fifty-four years of agitation the Committee for Industrial Organization has done in less than three years. Does that mean anything? Ask the workers in these great steel and other industrial plants within 100 miles of downtown Pittsburgh. They will tell you whether or not it means anything, and they will answer the question why they joined the CIO; they will tell you that they were not receiving the aid and succor from the American labor movement which they should have received.

The Pittsburgh area today is the most completely organized city of any city or any area in industrial America. Whether you come into Pittsburgh through the Ohio Valley, the Monongahela Valley, or the gateway of the Allegheny, you pass along miles of great industrial plants; and when you pass one of those great industrial plants in coming through any of those gateways, you pass a plant where the CIO has established collective bargaining and where the employees there are members of the CIO.

To you, Philip Murray, vice-president of the United Mine Workers of America, chairman of the Steel Workers Organizing Committee, my compliments, sir, for this superhuman task that you have accomplished in the area where you live, where the headquarters of your great organization exist. You have rendered a service, not alone to the people of Pittsburgh but to the workers in these great industries; you have rendered an outstanding and superb service to the labor movement of America, to our country, and to our flag.

In the light of that record which I have merely portrayed as indicating the events that have transpired in this area, and which may be duplicated ad infinitum in other areas, in the light of that record, why should the CIO as a movement be criticized, opposed, slandered, and vilified, denounced from the street corners by its adversaries, and constantly opposed in high places when it offers to the community, to the state, and to the nation a program of rational procedure and orderly conduct, a program of working out in a peaceful way the problems that encumber the relations of labor and industry and finance in this country?

In this steel industry to which I may aptly refer because of our presence here today, Mr. Murray and the Steel Workers organization have contracts with more than 540 corporate entities engaged in the manufacture and the fabrication of steel; and in every one of those plants, in every one of those corporations without exception, since the negotiation of those agreements, peaceful relations have obtained and mutual satisfaction prevails between management and labor — something of a record of an industry that for a lifetime, through oppressive measures, prevented the organization of its employees and denied to them the right to join the union of their choice.

But why should there be opposition and criticism of a movement that stands for orderly procedure and for a rational working out of the problems of modern industrial relationships; of an organization that is dedicated to the proposition of maintaining and supporting our democratic form of government; of an organization that is dedicated to the proposition of the right of investors to have a profit on their investment; and an organization that maintains the right to the freedom of contract relations between citizens of our republic, that is willing to lend its strength and its resources and its young men at any time to support and maintain that form of government, asking only in return that the safeguards of the Constitution and the Bill of Rights be extended to cover the most lowly, humble worker, as a right, as a privilege for an American?

These are troublous times in the world of affairs. Great and sinister forces are moving throughout the world, and he is optimistic indeed who believes that those forces will not affect Americans and will not have their impact and repercussions upon the peoples of the Western Hemisphere. Democracy is on trial in the world and in the United States. We want to preserve democracy. We cannot preserve democracy here in our own country if we encourage as a people the overwhelming tidal wave of criticism,

United Press International

John L. Lewis, chairman of the CIO, who led a strike against Republic Steel Corporation in 1937

slander, and abuse for an American institution like the CIO, that stands for the protection of the privileges of all Americans, whether they be gentiles or Jews or of any creed or religion, or any school of thought that maintains its self-respect for our institutions.

We stand appalled today at what we witness in Europe. Whose heart can fail to become anguished as he reads in the daily press of the terrible abuses and atrocities and indignities and brutalities that are now being inflicted by the German government and some of the German people on the Jews of that nation? One of the most appalling events in history, shameful indeed to our concept of the ethics of our modern civilization which we boast, harking back to the practices of the medieval ages, the torture and debasement of a great race of people who only ask the right to live.

Our Declaration of Independence says that we hold all men to be created equal. That means regardless of his creed, his color, his race, or his nationality. We foregather under that flag and we proclaim that creed, but that principle is being made a mock in the Germany of today. In Germany the labor movement was first wiped out and its leaders were harried and sent to concentration camps, and now, in progressive fury and increasing brutality, the German government is found inflicting these pogroms on the Jewish race.

I say to my fellow countrymen, and I say it to the rich and influential and wealthy gentiles of America as I say it to the rich and influential Jews of America, you cannot strike down in this country through the use of your influence, great as it may be, a powerful movement of the workers of this country under the banner of the CIO, who stand for equality of protection to any group, any minority, any religion that exists here in our country.

The United States of America is under increasing pressure in the realm of foreign affairs. The United States of America may one of these days face a great external crisis. When this mad, bloodthirsty wolf of the German government inflicts its will upon the defenseless people of Germany, of Austria, and of Czechoslovakia, and incites individuals in other countries to perpetrate the same atrocities in Europe, then it is possible that we will have to meet the German dictator as he tries to extend his domain into the realm of the Western Hemisphere.

If that day comes, who is going to sustain the United States of America? Who is going to man its industries? Who is going to send its young men to military ranks to engage in war? Labor — labor! Who is going to protect the institutions of this country, those that are meritorious? Labor! Who is going to protect the titles to property and great wealth down through the generations in America? Labor!

Who is going to do the suffering and the dying in the future but the sons and the daughters of the workers of this country?

The workers of this country will never make anything out of war; they merely work and sweat and fight and die. Someone else takes the profits. Who took the profits in the last war? Not labor. And if war comes, the United States needs the cooperation of the millions and millions of workers that are members of the CIO.

In consideration of all of these things, in consideration of the fact that we are Americans and that we believe in the principles of our government, that we are willing to fight at any time to maintain that flag, we are going to ask from those who are the beneficiaries of that service and that attitude and that policy and that loyalty, we are going to ask proper treatment ourselves — proper treatment ourselves! And I have every confidence that our government and our State Department will make emphatic representations to the German government, protesting the actions of that government in permitting these atrocities to be inflicted on the Jewish people. I say to the government of the United States if, as, and when it takes that action, the 20 million members of the CIO and their dependents will support the government and uphold its hands.

The old order changes. Neither opposition nor misrepresentation is going to destroy the existence of the CIO as a living entity, and the people in high places in America who are now using their influence, through great newspapers and publications, who have opened the sluice gates of adverse propaganda against the CIO in America, will awaken to the fact that their efforts are futile and that the day may come when they, individually, will be rushing to the CIO and begging for its protection for their special privileges and their wealth.

I express to you all my appreciation of your courteous attention while I have made these few remarks. I express with you our hope that from the deliberations of this convention may come renewed inspiration and greater confidence for the millions of workers of this country who are looking to the CIO to give them aid and assistance.

We must not forget that we have 12 million more or less unemployed people in America who have a right to work, but who have not been given work; that there are dependent upon those 12 million many more millions who are underprivileged, ill-provided for, and who are asking for a participation and are looking to this convention to devise policies, to state objectives, to lay out procedure that will cause them to have hope for the future.

I am sure that every man and woman here recognizes the great weight of responsibility upon them in their representative capacities, and that each will contribute toward the successful foundation and the final completion of this great, new, modern labor movement of the CIO.

110.

ALFRED HAYES: "Joe Hill"

Joel Emmanuel Hugglund, known to Americans as Joe Hill, emigrated from Sweden to the United States in 1901. By 1910 he was a leader of the Industrial Workers of the World on the West Coast and a popular union songwriter. In January 1914 he was arrested on a murder charge in Salt Lake City, and shortly thereafter sentenced to die. His guilt was, and continues to be, disputed. President Woodrow Wilson, the Swedish government, and organizations throughout the states tried to halt his death, but in vain. On November 18, 1915, the night before Joe Hill was shot by a five-man firing squad, a speaker at a protest meeting in Salt Lake City proclaimed that "Joe Hill will never die." The words inspired the ballad "Joe Hill," written in 1938 by Alfred Hayes and set to music by Earl Robinson.

Source: *Songs of Work and Freedom*, Edith Fowke and Joe Glazer, eds., New York, 1960.

JOE HILL

I dreamed I saw Joe Hill last night
  Alive as you and me.
Says I, "But Joe, you're ten years dead."
  "I never died," says he,
  "I never died," says he.

"In Salt Lake, Joe," says I to him,
  Him standing by my bed,
"They framed you on a murder charge."
  Says Joe, "But I ain't dead,"
  Says Joe, "But I ain't dead."

"The copper bosses killed you, Joe,
  They shot you, Joe," says I.
"Takes more than guns to kill a man,"
  Says Joe, "I didn't die,"
  Says Joe, "I didn't die."

And standing there as big as life
  And smiling with his eyes,
Joe says, "What they forgot to kill
  Went on to organize,
  Went on to organize."

"Joe Hill ain't dead," he says to me,
    "Joe Hill ain't never died.
Where working men are out on strike
    Joe Hill is at their side,
    Joe Hill is at their side."

"From San Diego up to Maine
    In every mine and mill,
Where workers strike and organize,"

Says he, "You'll find Joe Hill,"
Says he, "You'll find Joe Hill."

I dreamed I saw Joe Hill last night
    Alive as you and me.
Says I, "But Joe, you're ten years dead."
    "I never died," says he,
    "I never died," says he.

111.

Henry A. Wallace: Agricultural Policies of the New Deal

An economic recession beginning late in 1937 once again threatened the agricultural community. To help keep the farm economy stable Congress passed an Agricultural Adjustment Act in February 1938. The Act provided for production controls, soil conservation, price supports, and distribution of farm surpluses. In his 1938 report, a portion of which is reprinted here, Secretary of Agriculture Henry Wallace explained the new policies.

Source: *Report of the Secretary of Agriculture, 1938*, Washington, 1938, pp. 19-28.

There are two theories of price stabilization. One view is that it should work with factors that affect or determine prices, such as the supply of commodities, the rate of marketing, tariffs, and advertising, and let prices set themselves. Another view, in some quarters the more popular one, is that stabilization operations should fix prices outright and not bother about the ordinary price determinants. Among the most frequently proposed criteria are those of tariff equivalence, parity price, parity income, and cost of production. The tariff-equivalence criterion has considerable justification; but it assumes that industrial tariff rates, which are almost purely arbitrary, are real measures of the disparity between the positions of agriculture and industry. Therefore it is unsatisfactory.

Parity prices and parity income constitute a more justifiable norm. They give us a rough measure of the gap that must be closed if agriculture is to receive its fair share of the national income. But we cannot apply these criteria rigorously and uncritically, particularly in establishing commodity loan rates and parity or price-adjustment payments. We can calculate parity price but it may not be always a safe guide.

Over a long period the prices of agricultural products do not necessarily bear the same relations to one another and to the general price level that they did in the base period. Furthermore, parity prices for some commodities may be inconsistent with the attainment of other important goals, such as normal consumption of farm products. Indeed, such prices may even be inconsistent with the attainment of parity income for the farmers.

Parity income better expresses the idea of

equality between agriculture and industry, but it is quite difficult to measure precisely. Estimates of income from farming that goes to nonagricultural groups, of nonagricultural income earned by farmers, of the value of farm products consumed on the farm, and of other income factors can only be very rough.

In the minds of many people the plea for cost of production has a tremendous appeal. It looks synonymous with fair return. But the idea that cost alone can be used for price fixing or tariff making, either in agriculture or industry, is dubious. Almost insuperable difficulties prevent the accurate determination of costs on 6 million farms. Moreover, the enforcement of prices based on reputed costs would require a vast amount of governmental regulation, licensing, and regimentation of both farmers and middlemen.

Cost of production is a false criterion over any long period. The true guide to prices that can be maintained is the concept of economic balance. Prices of both farm and nonfarm goods should be set at levels that will encourage both maximum consumption and maximum production. The formula must keep the economic organism functioning with the least possible disturbance. We must not forget the fundamental danger in price fixing without corresponding control of supply. Almost inevitably the statistical procedure involved, as well as group pressures, will cause the price level to be fixed high enough to stimulate excessive production.

Our present many-sided agricultural program offers a better prospect. It provides a rational approach to conservation and good farming. Acreages of the major depleting and conserving crops, and desirable soil-building and conserving practices, can be distributed geographically so as to combine conservation with efficient farming and bring about balanced production. With acreages of the major crops kept within individual, county, state, and national allot-ments and goals, farmers have an assurance in years of ordinary weather of production in line with market requirements. If yields are above the average, they can take a second step under the act. They can store their crops and get a commodity loan on them from the government. If, in spite of these measures, the granary overflows, they can take a third step and vote marketing quotas on themselves and bring supplies in line with normal requirements. Conversely, the act through its ever-normal-granary feature avoids scarcity in years of drought.

Each of these steps is in the true spirit of self-government by the farmers. The first two are completely voluntary in that the individual farmer can choose whether to come into the soil conservation program or stay out, and can choose whether or not to put his corn, wheat, or cotton in storage and take a government loan. The third step, the use of marketing quotas, is an emergency step. It will not be taken unless two-thirds of the producers concerned vote for it in a referendum. . . .

For the promotion of our agricultural export trade the measure authorizes the use of funds derived from customs duties. Our reciprocal trade agreements program offers the most hope in this direction. But in periods of emergency, such as now exist with respect to wheat, it may be necessary temporarily to adopt limited export-subsidy measures in order to retain our fair share of the world market. If all nations used export-subsidy measures simultaneously as a general policy, these measures would be mutually self-defeating. They would mean international price cutting. Price wars in international trade are as disastrous as in private business. There is urgent need for an international understanding on the matter. Meantime, until the situation improves, we must take steps to keep our place in the world market and to expand the market for our farm products. Our government is doing what it can to persuade other wheat-exporting nations to join in what might be called an international ever-normal-granary plan; in a plan to stabilize the amounts of wheat offered on the world markets by each nation year after year.

One feature of the program which probably should be given greater emphasis in the future is the distribution of surpluses to low-income groups that are undernourished. This is not a sudden new idea. The department has cooperated for several years with relief agencies in distributing free supplies of food to the destitute. Some of the marketing agreements have provided for the partial disposal at low prices of surpluses in ways that do not interfere with distribution through regular channels. This feature of our program could be expanded.

Consumer demand in the low-income groups is potentially elastic for many products, and even for staples like wheat and cotton. If these groups had facilities for buying certain foods at lower retail prices, they would buy more than they do now. The plan would also increase the income of the farmers. For example, many families with low incomes buy no fresh milk and no citrus fruits. They contribute nothing to the income of the dairy farmer or citrus fruit grower. Some two-price arrangement by which low-income groups of consumers could buy surpluses at low prices while the rest of the population paid the regular market price would provide farm relief and consumer relief.

This approach to farm relief and consumer relief has recently been much discussed. There are many practical difficulties. The benefit of the lower prices should go to the consumers most in need of it, especially the needy children. It is important that the distribution should be accomplished with the cooperation of processors and distributors rather than in competition with them, in a manner that will not disrupt the existing marketing organizations; moreover, it should be done at the lowest possible cost. These are difficult problems. The department is not yet ready to undertake any ex-

tensive program of this kind, or one applied to all farm products in all parts of the country. It intends, however, to see what can be done in a small way under our present farm act.

In considering how the proposal may help farmers, we should remember that agriculture's surplus problem is not of its own making. Expansion during the World War left it with surplus capacity; our change to the creditor position reduced farm exports; our high postwar tariffs provoked retaliation and added to the export disability; new farm competition developed in Brazil, Argentina, Australia, and elsewhere; Europe struggled toward agricultural self-sufficiency; and many American industries maintained high, inflexible prices out of line with farm prices. Then came the Depression, which reduced the buying power of American consumers. These troubles of nonagricultural origin entitle agriculture to look outside itself for help in dealing with the surpluses.

If all our people could be quickly reemployed at good wages, we should not need any two-price plan; consumption would expand automatically. Indeed, the only permanent way to increase agricultural consumption is to create new buying power through increased production of nonfarm goods. But millions are unemployed; other millions get low wages; consequently, agriculture and industry stay out of balance. Agriculture produces abundantly, while industry, with frequent lay-offs, produces only what the market can absorb. Surplus farm capacity results in stocks of goods while surplus industrial capacity shows up chiefly in idle labor.

This is a painful anomaly. The consumption of industrial products potentially is almost limitless; food consumption runs up against the limitations of the human stomach. It is absurd to produce an insufficiency of desired things and simultaneously a great surplus of things already superabundant. But the anomaly persists. With Europe upset, we cannot export large surpluses on a basis that will pay for the labor and soil fertility in them. The best solution would be to work out the city problem but we do not yet know how to reanimate our urban industries. Therefore, we must resort to special means of getting crops consumed domestically. Our people will not indefinitely tolerate scarcity amid abundance, and in years of large crops both farmers and consumers will want the surpluses made available to the needy.

There are only three principal ways of dealing with farm surpluses. One is to stop producing them and to divert agricultural land and labor wholesale to other ends. Another is to store the surpluses in the hope of marketing them eventually. The third is to adjust farm production moderately through means that keep farmland and farm people employed, and to deal meantime in special ways with surpluses that accumulate unavoidably.

The third way is the only practical way; it is the way we have followed through various expedients for several years. Inevitably, in one form or another, it involves price differentials. Surpluses that remain after the ordinary market has taken what it wants bring lower prices. It is preferable to give our own people rather than foreigners the benefit of such bargain prices. Surplus disposal at home cannot entirely supplant surplus disposal abroad; prevailing conditions oblige us to offer some crops in foreign markets at low prices, with partial compensation to growers through price-adjustment payments. But we can tap new levels of demand at home as well.

Mainly the surplus problem appears in the great staple crops; but it appears also in fruits and vegetables and in livestock products, such as meat, eggs, and milk. Milk has been sold in New York City at a reduced price to low-income groups. Some similar plan might be worthwhile for some other farm products. For example, the grapefruit crop this year may be 40 million boxes or more. The maximum commercial use is only about 29 million boxes. Grapefruit of the No. 1 and No. 2 grades will fully supply the ordinary market. All of the No. 3's and culls and a part of the better grades will go to waste unless something unusual is done; but growers will have no choice if the market is too low to pay freight and handling charges. All interested groups should cooperate to get the extra grapefruit consumed. Perhaps if the farmers are willing to sell them at a sacrifice, the railroads will ship them at less than the usual rate and handlers and retailers will reduce their charges. Then the surplus grapefruit can be offered to low-income groups at low prices.

This is just one illustration of the problem. Possibly ways can be found for moving staple as well as special crops into increased consumption among low-income groups. We ought to seek out new methods of supplying these groups, partly through the reduction of distribution costs and partly through special prices. Surplus disposal at low prices to low-income groups need not mean price raising to other consuming groups. On the contrary, farm income from goods that might otherwise be wasted may allow of sales at lower prices in the ordinary market. It is a question of balance. Up to a certain point the disposal of surpluses at low prices among groups that would otherwise not be in the market makes a net addition to the farm income and lessens the urge to demand higher prices in the usual channels of trade.

An interesting variation of the ever-normal-granary idea is now in effect for dairy products. Through the Commodity Credit Corporation, funds have been advanced to a new agency, the Dairy Products Marketing Association, Inc., for the purchase of butter during the season of flush production. The plan is, if possible, to sell the butter during the season when production normally diminishes. However, in case market conditions do not permit the butter to be sold at a price that will cover all costs, the Federal Surplus Commodities Corporation will be authorized to buy it from the Dairy Products Marketing Association and distribute it to families of the needy. Through this plan, combined with the plan for stabilization of dairy-feed supplies, it should be possible to give butter prices more stability and dairy producers higher average returns than they would otherwise receive.

Other features of the present national farm program provide for marketing agreements, crop insurance, tenant-purchase operations, rehabilitation loans, submarginal-land retirement, and development of new and expanded uses for agricultural products through research. In the main our task is no longer to hunt for new ideas; the principal lines of the program are set. The task is to perfect what we have and to improve its administration. For this we shall need the full cooperation and support of all groups, and particularly of the farmers themselves.

Farmers must have an intelligent understanding of what the program means and how it works. Then they will give it their wholehearted sympathy and support. In the soil conservation and ever-normal-granary phase of the program, the job is essentially one for the farmers to do themselves. It is they who suffer most when surpluses pile up; it is they who must keep the surpluses down and at the same time use the ever-normal-granary principle as a safeguard against shortage.

There is a problem of financing. Although the Agricultural Adjustment Act of 1938 allowed for parity payments, it provided no continuing source of revenue for this purpose. Farmers cannot yet be certain that the parity principle established by Congress will be maintained. They will not be certain until some arrangement is made whereby the particular commodity concerned bears at least a part of the cost of financing its own program. Then, and only then, will a continuing source of revenue be assured. Under the early agricultural adjust-

ment programs a processing tax on the basic commodities provided necessary revenue for two and one-half years. Cooperating farmers had the assurance of the equivalent of parity prices on the domestic consumption of their products. They got part of their price from the marketplace and the rest from the government in benefit payments.

The program was self-financing and helped to balance the budget. Why should not this kind of tax be used again to finance the parity payments — at least for the export commodities, wheat and cotton — for which the new act provides? Such a tax is one important thing missing from our present farm program. It would help maintain balanced production and surplus control by assuring a continuing source of revenue to finance a portion of the program. It would help maintain parity of income by assuring a continuing source of revenue for parity payments on the commodities that do not lend themselves to price boosting through adjustment of supply.

In a democracy such as ours, economic legislation must promote certain noneconomic ends. Besides encouraging the production of wealth, it must maintain the freedom of the individual and of the community. The object cannot be exclusively material.

Man needs both bread and freedom; it is a calamity when he must barter one for the other, and the result may be the breakdown of civilization. To promote abundance, both material and spiritual, at the same time and by the same means is not easy. Increased production calls for economic and social organization, with increasing interdependence and cooperation among different economic groups. How can we achieve this and at the same time preserve freedom and democracy?

This is a complex and delicate task, which depends for its accomplishment on a blend of physical and economic science with social justice. It requires, moreover, the support of public opinion. Everything done must enlist the informed and willing cooperation of the nation as a whole; otherwise it will not be truly democratic. Efficient social cooperation without coercion is the formula, which may not be abandoned on pain of grave social disturbance.

In the Agricultural Adjustment Act of 1938 we have an important instrument for promoting the twofold objective. On the economic side the law expresses the unity of interest among different groups in agriculture and safeguards the consumer through provisions for the maintenance of a continuous and stable supply of agricultural commodities at fair prices. On the social side it applies the principle of democracy. It is a new charter of economic and political freedom for both producer and consumer. Abundance and democracy are the twin foundations. Few people doubt that, as we may infer from the majorities which the measure received in Congress, and also from the general support it obtained throughout the country. Nevertheless, both before and after the enactment of the measure, it came under a certain amount of fire.

There is still some feeling that the law may promote scarcity and not abundance, and regimentation as distinguished from democracy. A minority refuses to believe it will promote both abundance and democracy. Unless it does the nation will condemn it. There can be no true freedom without abundance and no satisfying abundance without freedom. There must be widespread understanding and approval of the principles involved; otherwise programs really democratic in conception will not have the necessary public support and will have to be dropped or modified. Moreover, the support required is urban as well as rural.

The present farm act, like its predecessor of 1933, provides in certain circumstances for the limitation of farm production. With respect to corn, wheat, cotton, tobacco, and rice it authorizes the establishment of national acreage allotments divided up among the farmers. These allotments contemplate production sufficient for the domestic and export markets, and for the provision of above-average carry-overs. Also, the measure authorizes marketing quotas for use when the granaries overflow as a means of supporting prices. The quotas regulate the movement of crops to market. Superficially, these regulations may seem opposed to the idea of abundance. Actually, they promote it by smoothing out the fluctuations of supply and price from year to year. Controlled stable production means more production in the long run than would result from uncontrolled mass swings from high to low production.

Agriculture needs crop adjustment to prevent these mass swings which lead to recurring cycles of underproduction and overproduction. Consumers need it, too, because widely fluctuating production, with its inevitable addition to the farmers' costs, means higher consumer prices in the end. . . . Consumers need protection against excessively high prices, while producers need it against excessively low prices. The groups have a common interest.

Even with the crops produced heavily for export, abundance calls for stable rather than for wildly fluctuating production. True, the domestic consumer will not go short. Our cotton and wheat crops are far above domestic wants. It would be wrong, however, for the consumer to imagine that the largest possible production of these crops means the greatest benefit to himself. With wheat or cotton production vastly in excess of the foreign and domestic demand, agricultural depression occurs and injures the urban centers. Consumers do not profit from 5-cent cotton or 30-cent wheat. Such prices reduce the retail cost of shirts or bread very little, yet they mean widespread agricultural distress, with consequent reduced agricultural buying in the cities. The fractional advantage to the consumer disappears in the associated damage to urban trade.

The ever-normal-granary features of the

AAA aim at permanent abundance. They provide, with normal yields, for supply levels of cotton, wheat, corn, tobacco, and rice at above-normal percentages sufficient to cover the usual domestic and export requirements and to build up enlarged carry-overs. In wheat and corn the carry-overs on the average will be much larger. Shifts to soil-conserving crops will improve the land and develop a production-power reserve for emergencies. Crop insurance for wheat will give farmers better protection against crop failure and consumers better protection against high prices; for the premiums will be wheat, which will add to the ever-normal-granary supply. Moreover, the community has protection against artificial shortage. Marketing quotas can be proclaimed only when supplies reach high levels, and commodity loans will be available to the farmers only when accumulating stocks threaten them with price collapse. There is no loophole for improper storage as a means of extortion. All phases of the act look toward stable, abundant production and fair prices.

Farm production that is very uneven involves high costs. No one knows the waste involved and the injury to agricultural capital and labor in the swings from high to low. And the consumer bears his share. In fact, the resulting markup in prices is loss all round; it adds nothing to the farm income and mulcts the consumer unnecessarily. Effort thrown spasmodically into production, only to be as suddenly withdrawn, is wasteful. It means excessive overhead for the occasional peak load and heavy loss periodically in the forced liquidation of flocks and herds. Uneven production wastes the soil too. In the Great Plains we purchased high production of cereals for a few years at a terrific price in soil destruction.

Stable production means more production in the end. Specialists in farm management observed long ago that the hog producer who keeps his output relatively stable from year to year and avoids the fluctua-tions of the four-year cycle earns more on the average than the man who rushes in and out of the business erratically. Relatively stable production evens out profits and losses quickly and prevents extremes. Because it is efficient and economical it is ultimately greater in volume. What applies to the individual hog producer applies also to the different branches of agriculture and indeed to the entire agricultural industry. Controlled production means abundance more of the time since it helps to obviate the alternations of glut and shortage.

Stable production in agriculture means more production in urban industry likewise. For one thing, it meshes better with the rest of the economic system. Stable production in agriculture is an important contribution to stability in the whole economy. Activity in many urban businesses, particularly in those that depend directly on agriculture for supplies, varies directly with the production of agriculture. For example, railroads, elevator companies, ginners, exporters, and other handlers of farm commodities get more out of big crops than out of small. Widely fluctuating farm production, however, obliges them to maintain a plant sufficient to carry the peak loads, and this means heavy overhead. Gain to agriculture through stability is gain to them, and gives them ultimately a larger and more profitable business.

Industries for which agriculture is primarily a market rather than a source of supplies find themselves in a different position. They depend on agriculture's buying power. Ordinarily, when farm production soars, farm income drops; whereupon sales of agricultural implements, fertilizer, farm building materials, farm furnishings, and other goods decline. This type of urban industry, equally with the type that looks to agriculture as a source of supplies, stands to benefit from a better regulation of farm production and a more even level of farm income. Gains and economies effected in agriculture through regulated production tend to be reflected throughout the industrial system, which has increased and more uniform activity. . . .

Farming and industry, including mining, comprise the base for practically the whole economic system. Each carries a superstructure of financial, technical, scientific, and legal institutions, but the taproots are fairly concentrated. Hence, increasing stability in the agricultural half of the system means increasing stability in the other, and ultimately greater production. When the historian describes this epoch, he may report that it largely bridged the gap between scarcity and abundance through the use of the ever-normal-granary in agriculture and the resulting evening out of the business cycle.

112.

JOHN COLLIER: A New Deal for the Indian

The Wheeler-Howard Indian Reorganization Act of 1934 marked a radical change in Indian policy. Under the sympathetic leadership of John Collier, commissioner of Indian Affairs, Roosevelt's New Deal policies were extended to the Indians in an effort to make them economically independent. The program included strengthening tribal governments, promoting arts and crafts, and in general respecting and encouraging the preservation of Indian culture. For the first time since the republic was founded the Indian population increased rather than decreased. A portion of Collier's 1938 report is reprinted here.

Source: *Annual Report of the Secretary of the Interior for the Fiscal Year Ended June 30, 1938,* Washington, 1938, pp. 209-211.

IN ALL OUR COLORFUL AMERICAN LIFE there is no group around which there so steadfastly persists an aura compounded of glamor, suspicion, and romance as the Indian. For generations the Indian has been, and is today, the center of an amazing series of wonderings, fears, legends, hopes.

Yet those who have worked with Indians know that they are neither the cruel, warlike, irreligious savages imagined by some, nor are they the "fortunate children of nature's bounty" described by tourists who see them for an hour at some glowing ceremonial. We find the Indians, in all the basic forces and forms of life, human beings like ourselves. The majority of them are very poor people living under severely simple conditions. We know them to be deeply religious. We know them to be possessed of all the powers, intelligence, and genius within the range of human endowment. Just as we yearn to live out our own lives in our own ways, so, too, do the Indians, in their ways.

For nearly 300 years white Americans, in our zeal to carve out a nation made to order, have dealt with the Indians on the erroneous, yet tragic, assumption that the Indians were a dying race — to be liquidated. We took away their best lands; broke treaties, promises; tossed them the most nearly worthless scraps of a continent that had once been wholly theirs. But we did not liquidate their spirit. The vital spark which kept them alive was hardy. So hardy, indeed, that we now face an astounding, heartening fact.

Actually, the Indians, on the evidence of

federal census rolls of the past eight years, are increasing at almost twice the rate of the population as a whole.

With this fact before us, our whole attitude toward the Indians has necessarily undergone a profound change. Dead is the centuries-old notion that the sooner we eliminated this doomed race, preferably humanely, the better. No longer can we, with even the most generous intentions, pour millions of dollars and vast reservoirs of energy, sympathy, and effort into any unproductive attempts at some single, artificial permanent solution of the Indian problem. No longer can we naively talk of or think of the "Indian problem." Our task is to help Indians meet the myriad of complex, interrelated, mutually dependent situations which develop among them according to the very best light we can get on those happenings — much as we deal with our own perplexities and opportunities.

We, therefore, define our Indian policy somewhat as follows: So productively to use the moneys appropriated by the Congress for Indians as to enable them, on good, adequate lands of their own, to earn decent livelihoods and lead self-respecting, organized lives in harmony with their own aims and ideals, as an integral part of American life. Under such a policy, the ideal end result will be the ultimate disappearance of any need for government aid or supervision. This will not happen tomorrow; perhaps not in our lifetime; but with the revitalization of Indian hope due to the actions and attitudes of this government during the last few years, that aim is a probability, and a real one. . . .

In looking at the Indian picture as a social whole, we will consider certain broad phases — land use and industrial enterprises, health and education, roads and rehabilitation, political organization — which touch Indian life everywhere, including the 30,000 natives of Alaska for whose health, education, and social and economic advancement the Indian Service is responsible. Lastly, this report will tell wherein the Indian Service, or the government's effort as a whole for the Indians, still falls short.

So intimately is all of Indian life tied up with the land and its utilization that to think of Indians is to think of land. The two are inseparable. Upon the land and its intelligent use depends the main future of the American Indian.

The Indian feels toward his land, not a mere ownership sense but a devotion and veneration befitting what is not only a home but a refuge. At least nine out of ten Indians remain on or near the land. When times are good, a certain number drift away to town or city to work for wages. When times become bad, home to the reservation the Indian comes, and to the comparative security which he knows is waiting for him. The Indian still has much to learn in adjusting himself to the strains of competition amid an acquisitive society; but he long ago learned how to contend with the stresses of nature. Not only does the Indian's major source of livelihood derive from the land but his social and political organizations are rooted in the soil.

A major aim, then, of the Indian Service is to help the Indians to keep and consolidate what lands they now have and to provide more and better lands upon which they may effectively carry on their lives. Just as important is the task of helping the Indian make such use of his land as will conserve the land, insure Indian self-support, and safeguard or build up the Indian's social life. . . . .

In 1887, the General Allotment Act was passed, providing that after a certain trust period, fee simple title to parcels of land should be given to individual Indians. Individual proprietorship meant loss — a paradox in view of the Indian's love for the land, yet an inevitable result, when it is understood that the Indian by tradition was not concerned with possession, did not worry about titles or recordings, but regarded the land as a fisherman might regard the sea, as a gift of nature, to be loved and feared, to be fought and revered, and to be drawn on by all as an inexhaustible source of life and strength.

The Indian let the ownership of his allotted lands slip from him. The job of taking the Indian's lands away, begun by the white man through military expeditions and treaty commissions, was completed by cash purchase — always of course, of the best lands which the Indian had left. In 1887, the Indian had remaining 130 million acres. In 1933, the Indian had left only 49 million acres, much of it waste and desert.

Since 1933, the Indian Service has made a concerted effort — an effort which is as yet but a mere beginning — to help the Indian to build back his landholdings to a point where they will provide an adequate basis for a self-sustaining economy, a self-satisfying social organization.

By the close of the fiscal year 1938, the area of the lands held in trust for the Indians by the Government had been increased to approximately 51,540,307 acres — approximately 67 percent tribally owned, and 33 percent in allotments held in trust for the benefit of individuals.

113.

Irving Berlin: "God Bless America"

Irving Berlin, one of the foremost American songwriters of the twentieth century, composed "God Bless America" in 1917 but never used the work until 1938, when Kate Smith introduced it on her radio program for an Armistice Day broadcast. The song gained an enormous and sustained popularity during World War II, and has even been suggested as a new national anthem. The proceeds from the song were turned over by Mr. Berlin to a special God Bless America Fund for distribution to the Girl Scouts and Boy Scouts of America, and the Campfire Girls.

GOD BLESS AMERICA

By Irving Berlin

While the storm clouds gather
   Far across the sea,
Let us swear allegiance
   To a land that's free;
Let us all be grateful
   For a land so fair,
As we raise our voices
   In a solemn prayer:

God bless America,
   Land that I love.
Stand beside her and guide her
   Through the night with a light from
      above.
From the mountains, to the prairies,
   To the oceans white with foam,
God bless America,
   My home sweet home.

114.

Raoul de Roussy de Sales: Love in America

Raoul de Roussy de Sales was a Frenchman who had a long and close contact with America. As a liaison officer with the American Red Cross during World War I and, from 1932 on, as a correspondent and lecturer, he wrote many witty and penetrating articles on the United States for American and French periodicals. "Love in America," a portion of which appears below, was published in May 1938.

Source: *Atlantic Monthly*, May 1938.

AMERICA APPEARS TO BE the only country in the world where love is a national problem.

Nowhere else can one find a people devoting so much time and so much study to the question of the relationship between men and women. Nowhere else is there such concern about the fact that this relationship does not always make for perfect happiness. The great majority of the Americans of both sexes seem to be in a state of chronic bewilderment in the face of a problem which they are certainly not the first to confront, but which — unlike other people — they still refuse to accept as one of those gifts of the gods which one might just as well take as it is: a mixed blessing at times, and at other times a curse or merely a nuisance.

The prevailing conception of love, in America, is similar to the idea of democracy. It is fine in theory. It is the grandest system ever evolved by man to differentiate him from his ancestors, the poor brutes who lived in caverns, or from the apes. Love is perfect, in fact, and there is nothing better. But, like democracy, it does not work, and the Americans feel that something should be done about it. President Roosevelt is intent on making democracy

work. Everybody is trying to make love work, too.

In either case the result is not very satisfactory. The probable reason is that democracy and love are products of a long and complicated series of compromises between the desires of the heart and the exactions of reason. They have a peculiar way of crumbling into ashes as soon as one tries too hard to organize them too well.

The secret of making a success out of democracy and love in their practical applications is to allow for a fairly wide margin of errors, and not to forget that human beings are absolutely unable to submit to a uniform rule for any length of time. But this does not satisfy a nation that, in spite of its devotion to pragmatism, also believes in perfection. . . .

As for the charge that the Europeans are more expert than the Americans in spoiling someone else's marital happiness, it seems to me an unfair accusation. In most cases the initiative of spoiling whatever it is that remains to be spoiled in a shaky marriage is normally taken by one of the married pair, and the wrecker of happiness does not need any special talent to finish the job.

What is quite true, however, is that the

American woman entertains the delightful illusion, that there *must* be some man on this earth who can understand her. It seems incredible to her that love, within legal bonds or outside of them, should not work out as advertised. From her earliest years she has been told that success is the ultimate aim of life. Her father and mother made an obvious success of their lives by creating her. Her husband is, or wants to be, a successful businessman. Every day 130 million people are panting and sweating to make a success of something or other. Success — the constant effort to make things work perfectly and the conviction that they can be made to — is the great national preoccupation.

And what does one do to make a success?

Well, the answer is very simple: one learns how, or one consults an expert.

That is what her husband does when he wants to invest his money or improve the efficiency of his business. That is what she did herself when she decided to "decorate" her house. In the American way of life there are no insoluble problems. You may not know the answer yourself, but nobody doubts that the answer exists — that there is some method or perhaps some trick by which all riddles can be solved and success achieved.

And so the European visitor is put to the task on the presumption that the accumulation of experience which he brings with him may qualify him as an expert in questions of sentiment.

The American woman does not want to be understood for the mere fun of it. What she actually wishes is to be helped to solve certain difficulties which, in her judgment, impede the successful development of her inner self. She seldom accepts the idea that maladjustments and misunderstandings are not only normal but bearable once you have made up your mind that, whatever may be the ultimate aim of our earthly existence, perfect happiness through love or any other form of expression is not part of the program.

ONE OF THE GREATEST moral revolutions that ever happened in America was the popularization of Freud's works.

Up to the time that occurred, as far as I am able to judge, America lived in a blissful state of puritanical repression. Love, as a sentiment, was glorified and sanctified by marriage. There was a general impression that some sort of connection existed between the sexual impulses and the vagaries of the heart, but this connection was not emphasized, and the consensus of opinion was that the less said about it the better. The way certain nations, and particularly the French, correlated the physical manifestations of love and its more spiritual aspects was considered particularly objectionable. Love, in other words — and that was not very long ago — had not changed since the contrary efforts of the puritanically minded and the romantic had finally stabilized it midway between the sublime and the parlor game.

The important point is that up to then (and ever since the first Pilgrims set foot on this continent) love had been set aside in the general scheme of American life as the one thing which could not be made to work better than it did. Each one had to cope with his own difficulties in his own way and solve them as privately as he could. It was not a national problem.

Whether or not people were happier under that system is beside the point. It probably does not matter very much whether we live and die with or without a full set of childish complexes and repressions. My own view is that most people are neither complex nor repressed enough as a rule; I wish sometimes for the coming of the anti-Freud who will complicate and obscure everything again.

But the fact is that the revelations of psychoanalysis were greeted in America as the one missing link in the general program of universal improvement.

Here was a system, at last, that explained fully why love remained so imperfect. It reduced the whole dilemma of happiness to sexual maladjustments, which in turn were only the result of the mistakes made by one's father, mother, or nurse, at an age when one could certainly not be expected to foresee the consequences. Psychoanalysis integrated human emotions into a set of mechanistic formulas. One learned with great relief that the failure to find happiness was not irreparable. Love, as a sublime communion of souls and bodies, was not a legend, nor the mere fancy of the poets. It was real, and — more important still — practically attainable. Anybody could have it, merely by removing a few obstructions which had been growing within himself since childhood like mushrooms in a dark cellar. Love could be made to work like anything else.

It is true that not many people are interested in psychoanalysis any more. As a fad or a parlor game, it is dead. Modern debutantes will not know what you are talking about if you mention the Oedipus complex or refer to the symbolic meaning of umbrellas and top hats in dreams. Traditions die young these days. But the profound effect of the Freudian revelation has lasted. From its materialistic interpretation of sexual impulses, coupled with the American longing for moral perfection, a new science has been born: the dialectics of love; and also a new urge for the American people — they want to turn out, eventually, a perfect product. They want to get out of love as much enjoyment, comfort, safety, and general sense of satisfaction, as one gets out of a well-balanced diet or a good plumbing installation.

CURIOUSLY ENOUGH, this fairly new point of view which implies that human relationships are governed by scientific laws has not destroyed the romantic ideal of love. Quite the contrary. Maladjustments, now that they are supposed to be scientifically determined, have become much more unbearable than in the horse-and-buggy age of love. Husbands and wives and lovers have no patience with their troubles. They want to be cured, and when they think they are incurable they become very intolerant. Reformers always are.

Usually, however, various attempts at readjustment are made with devastating candor. Married couples seem to spend many precious hours of the day and night discussing what is wrong with their relationship. The general idea is that — according to the teachings of most modern psychologists and pedagogues — one should face the truth fearlessly. Husbands and wives should be absolutely frank with one another, on the assumption that if love between them is real it will be made stronger and more real still if submitted, at frequent intervals, to the test of complete sincerity on both sides.

This is a fine theory, but it has seldom been practised without disastrous results. There are several reasons why this should be so. First of all, truth is an explosive, and it should be handled with care, especially in marital life. It is not necessary to lie, but there is little profit in juggling with hand grenades just to show how brave one is. Secondly, the theory of absolute sincerity presupposes that, if love cannot withstand continuous blasting, then it is not worth saving anyway. Some people want their love life to be a permanent Battle of Verdun. When the system of defense is destroyed beyond repair, then the clause of hopeless maladjustment is invoked by one side, or by both. The next thing to do is to divorce and find someone else to be recklessly frank with for a season.

Another reason why the method of adjustment through truthtelling is not always wise is that it develops fiendish traits of character which might otherwise remain dormant.

I know a woman whose eyes glitter with virtuous self-satisfaction every time she has had a "real heart-to-heart talk" with her husband, which means that she has spent several hours torturing him, or at best boring him to distraction, with a ruthless exposure of the deplorable status of their mutual relationship to date. She is usually so pleased with herself after these periodical inquests that she tells most of her friends, and also her coiffeur, about it. "Dick and I had such a wonderful time last evening. We made a real effort to find out the real truth about each other — or, at least, I certainly did. I honestly believe we have found a new basis of adjustment for ourselves. What a marvelous feeling that is — don't you think so?"

Dick, of course, if he happens to be present, looks rather nervous or glum, but that is not the point. The point is that Dick's wife feels all aglow because she has done her bit in the general campaign for the improvement of marital happiness through truth. She has been a good Girl Scout.

A man of my acquaintance, who believes in experimenting outside of wedlock, is unable to understand why his wife would rather ignore his experiments. "If I did not love her and if she did not love me," he argues, "I could accept her point of view. But why can't she see that the very fact that I want her to know everything I do is a proof that I love her? If I have to deceive her or conceal things from her, what is the use of being married to her?"

Be it said, in passing, that this unfortunate husband believes that these extramarital "experiments" are absolutely necessary to prevent him from developing a sense of inferiority, which, if allowed to grow, would destroy not only the love he has for his wife but also his general ability in his dealings with the outside world. . . .

THUS THE PROBLEM OF LOVE in America seems to be the resultant of conflicting and rather unrealistic ways of approaching it. Too many songs, too many stories, too many pictures, and too much romance on the one hand, and too much practical advice on the other. It is as if the experience of being in love could only be one of two things: a superhuman ecstasy, the way of reaching heaven on earth and in pairs; or a psychopathic condition to be treated by specialists.

Between these two extremes there is little room for compromise. That the relationship between men and women offers a wide scale of variations seldom occurs to the experts. It is not necessarily true that there is but one form of love worth bothering about, and that if you cannot get the deluxe model, with a life guarantee of perfect functioning, nothing else is worthwhile. It is not true either that you can indefinitely pursue the same quest for perfection, or that if a man and a woman have not found ideal happiness together they will certainly find it with somebody else. Life unfortunately does not begin at forty, and when you reach that age, in America or anywhere else, to go on complaining about your sentimental or physiological maladjustments becomes slightly farcical.

It is not easy, nor perhaps of any use, to draw any conclusion from all this, especially for a European who has lost the fresh point of view of the visitor because he lives here, and who is not quite sure of what it means to be a European anymore. I sometimes wonder if there is any real difference between the way men and women get along — or do not get along — together on this side of the Atlantic and on the other. There are probably no more real troubles here than anywhere else. Human nature being quite remarkably stable, why should there be? But there is no doubt that the revolt against this type of human inadequacy is very strong indeed here, especially among the women who imagine that the Europeans have found better ways of managing their heart and their senses than the Americans.

If this is at all true, I believe the reason is to be found in a more philosophical attitude on the part of the Europeans toward such matters. There are no theories about marital bliss, no recipes to teach you how to solve difficulties which, in the Old World, are accepted as part of the common inheritance.

Men and women naturally want to be happy over there, and, if possible, with the help of one another; but they learn very young that compromise is not synonymous with defeat. Even in school (I am speaking more particularly of France now) they are taught, through the literature of centuries, that love is a phenomenon susceptible of innumerable variations, but that — even under the best circumstances — it is so intertwined with the other experiences of each individual life that to be overromantic or too dogmatic about it is of little practical use. *"La vérité est dans les nuances,"* wrote Benjamin Constant, who knew a good deal about such matters.

And, speaking of the truly practical and realistic nature of love, it is a very strange thing that American literature contains no work of any note, not even essays, on love as a psychological phenomenon. I know of no good study of the process of falling in and out of love, no analytical description of jealousy, coquettishness, or the development of tediousness. No classification of the various brands of love such as La Rochefoucauld, Pascal, Stendhal, Proust, and many others have elaborated has been attempted from the American angle. The interesting combinations of such passions as ambition, jealousy, religious fervor, and so forth, with love are only dimly perceived by most people and even by the novelists, who, with very few exceptions, seem to ignore or scorn these complicated patterns. These fine studies have been left to the psychiatrists, the charlatans, or the manufacturers of naive recipes.

The reason for this neglect on the part of real thinkers and essayists may be that for a long time the standards imposed by the puritanical point of view made the whole study more or less taboo with respectable authors. And then the Freudian wave came along and carried the whole problem out of reach of the amateur observer and the artist. In other words, conditions have been such that there has been no occasion to fill this curious gap in American literature.

Of course, nothing is lost. The field remains open, and there is no reason to suppose that love in America will not cease to be a national problem, a hunting ground for the reformer, and that it will not become, as everywhere else, a personal affair very much worth the effort it takes to examine it as such. All that is necessary is for someone to forget for a while love as Hollywood — or the professor — sees it, and sit down and think about it as an eternally fascinating subject for purely human observation.

Marriage . . . is a damnably serious business, particularly around Boston.
J. P. MARQUAND, *The Late George Apley*

I like a man that takes his time.
MAE WEST

Farmer and sons walking in a dust storm in Cimarron, Okla., 1936; photo by Arthur Rothstein

THE DISPOSSESSED

Those who interpreted the Depression as a form of God's wrath were certainly reinforced when further disaster struck. Beginning in late 1933, a siege of drought and storm gripped the Plains; first the semiarid lands that had been broken during the particularly wet years just ended, then the normally viable farms of long standing dried out and literally blew away. Successive crop failures forced freehold farmers to become virtually tenants and finally drove them off the land entirely. Thus began the migration of the "Okies," a word that became the contemptuous blanket term for migrants. Whether following rumors of land and plenty or simply not knowing anything else to do, thousands upon thousands of dispossessed struck west along Route 66 in a shabby parody of the pioneers. The Promised Land failed to materialize, however; the fertile valley of California was owned in huge tracts devoted to single crops, and the only opportunity for the migrants, field work, quickly degenerated to less than slavery in the buyer's market. Hostility developed between the migrants and the people of the towns where they gathered: The "Hoovervilles" where the hopeless lived were a threat to the prevailing living standard and a source of revolution.

(Above) Dust storm in Baca Co., Colorado; (below) Sallisaw, Oklahoma, 1936; Lange photo

(Above) Kesta, Colorado, an abandoned town, 1939; (right) farmer in Pennington Co., South Dakota, 1936. This kind of marginal farming was curtailed in many areas and the people resettled under federal land reclamation programs; (below) union and nonunion workers clash outside a packing plant in Sioux Falls, South Dakota, during a strike in 1935

OPPOSITE PAGE: (Top) A migratory Mexican farm worker standing outside his home located near a pea field in Imperial Valley, Calif., 1937; (center) camp of two families along U.S. 99 in Kern Co., Calif., 1939; (bottom) living conditions of the less fortunate in Marysville, Calif., 1935. All photographs by Dorothea Lange for the FSA

(Left) Family who travelled to Tappenish in Yakima Valley, Wash., by freight train in 1939; (below) a 25-year-old itinerant on a railroad car in California, 1939; both photographs by Dorothea Lange

Library of Congress

(Left) Registering opposition to the government's migratory labor camp in Portland, Ore., 1939

European Picture Service

(Left) Police inspecting damage to the headquarters of the "Western Worker," a Communist publication in San Francisco, 1934

(Below) Demonstrators outside of City-County Building of Seattle, Wash., protesting the county's employment relief system, regarded as forced labor at slave wages

European Picture Service

(Right) Gang of pea pickers riding out to the fields in the labor contractor's truck. Generally, a percentage of the picker's take went for this transportation; (center) large scale gang labor picking carrots in the Imperial Valley, California. With gang labor the field is cleared very fast, and a saving is made on hourly pay, but the pickers, working on a piece-work basis, can earn only a few dollars a day and are quickly out of work; (below) weighing baskets of peas. The pickers are then paid by the pound, either on the spot or at the end of the day.

(All) Library of Congress

(Top) Mobile camp used by FSA to improve conditions for farm laborers; (center) a camp council meeting; (bottom) FSA distributing food to striking cotton workers in California, 1938

During the Hundred Days three major agriculture bills were passed by Congress, the most important of which was the Agricultural Adjustment Act. Though the AAA was too late to help those already driven out of the Dust Bowl, the "black blizzards" of 1934, during which dust from Oklahoma filtered into the White House itself, did serve to speed government work in both agriculture and conservation. For those already beyond the reach of the AAA, there was the Civilian Conservation Corps or direct relief.

(Top) Crew working on construction of the Grand Coulee Dam, a Columbia basin reclamation project, 1937; (bottom) CCC boys planting trees in Lolo National Forest, Montana, 1938

Numerous plans and self-help schemes appeared during the Depression; some were familiar and only gained wider popularity during the Depression, such as the idea of consumer cooperatives. Others sought panaceas: the Technocracy Movement, a chain of discussion groups, envisioned an economy without money in which technicians, controlling industry wholly on the basis of productivity and automated processes, would eliminate the need for labor. The Townsend Plan, eventually more popular than even Huey Long's "Share-the-Wealth" scheme, provided a stipend to anyone over 60 who promised to spend it in a month, the initial money coming from a national sales tax. Several Townsendites were elected to Congress

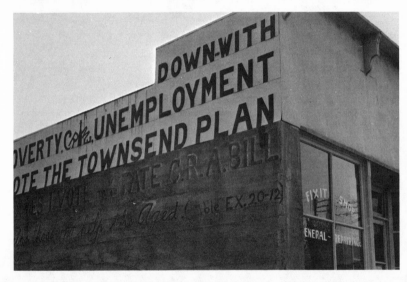

115.

A Christian Social Order

The National Catholic Welfare Conference, established by Roman Catholics after World War I, became an important instrument of social action. In 1919 the Conference adopted what became known as "The Bishop's Program of Social Reconstruction." "The ending of the Great War has brought peace," it declared, "but the only safeguard of peace is social justice. . . . Great problems face us. They cannot be put aside." During the 1930s Catholic organizations endeavored to strengthen labor unionism, to foster race relations, and to promote international peace and justice. In June 1938 the Conference adopted the following statement, prepared by the Most Reverend Edwin O'Hara, which summarized "the principles which may be regarded as basic to the development of a Christian social order in a democratic society."

Source: *Catholic Action*, Social Action Number, June 1938.

1. That industrial and financial power must not be divorced from social responsibility; those exercising such power must always have in view the good of the industry or business as a whole and also the common good.

2. That a prominent aim of industry should be to provide stable employment so as to eliminate the insecurity and the other social ills that arise from excessive changes of employment and residence.

3. That as machinery is introduced into industry workers thereby displaced should be guaranteed adequate protection.

4. That employment should be available for workers at not less than a family living income.

5. That a Christian Social Order in America will look forward to some participation by employees in profits, and management.

6. That a wide distribution of ownership of productive property should be encouraged by legislation.

7. That there should be limitations of hours of labor in keeping with human need for rest and relaxation. This is especially true in regard to the labor of women and young persons. The industrial employment of children outside of the family should be prohibited.

8. That monopoly should be controlled in the public interest.

9. That collective bargaining through freely chosen representatives be recognized as a basic right of labor.

10. That minimum wage standards be set up by law for labor unprotected by collective bargaining.

11. That the legitimacy of the profit motive in the development and conduct of business be frankly recognized; and its control in the interest of the common good should not aim at its extinction.

12. That there must be an increase of wealth produced, if there is to be an adequate increase of wealth distributed.

13. That a proper objective of monetary policy is to avoid rapid and violent fluctuations in commodity price levels.

14. That after a man has given his productive life to industry, he should be assured of security against illness and dependent old age.

15. That a balance must be maintained between industrial and agricultural population; and between the rewards for industrial and agricultural activity.

16. That a healthy agricultural system will encourage the family farm rather than the commercial farm.

17. That a Christian Social Order involves decent housing for all the people.

18. That the family, rather than the individual, is the social and economic unit: and its needs should be recognized both by industry and by the State.

19. That there are natural rights possessed by human persons and families which God has given and which the State cannot abrogate.

20. That a Christian Social Order, organized on the basis of self-governing industries, occupations and professions, according to the plan proposed by Pius XI in his Encyclical on "Reconstructing the Social Order" will establish Social Justice and promote industrial peace.

21. That a Christian Social Order can be maintained only on the basis of a full acceptance of the person and the teachings of Jesus Christ.

Beyond the enunciation of these principles, we are charged with the further responsibility of translating them into action.

116.

Report on Conditions in the South

The National Emergency Council's report on economic conditions in the South, transmitted to the President on July 25, 1938, was initially undertaken because of Roosevelt's conviction that the South presented the nation with its most serious economic problem. The highly documented report bore out his suspicion but evoked widespread criticism. Reprinted here are four of the report's fifteen sections.

Source: *Report on Economic Conditions of the South,* Prepared for the President by the National Emergency Council, n.p., n.d., Secs. 2, 5, 9, 11.

SOIL

NATURE GAVE THE SOUTH good soil. With less than a third of the nation's area, the South contains more than a third of the nation's good farming acreage. It has two-thirds of all the land in America receiving a forty-inch annual rainfall or better. It has nearly half of the land on which crops can grow for six months without danger of frost.

This heritage has been sadly exploited.

Sixty-one percent of all the nation's land badly damaged by erosion is in the Southern states. An expanse of Southern farmland as large as South Carolina has been gullied and washed away; at least 22 million acres of once fertile soil has been ruined beyond repair. Another area the size of Oklahoma and Alabama combined has been seriously damaged by erosion. In addition, the sterile sand and gravel washed off this land has covered over a fertile valley acreage equal in size to Maryland.

There are a number of reasons for this wastage:

Much of the South's land originally was so fertile that it produced crops for many years no matter how carelessly it was farmed. For generations thousands of Southern farmers plowed their furrows up and down the slopes, so that each furrow served as a ditch to hasten the runoff of silt-laden water after every rain. While many farmers have now learned the importance of terracing their land or plowing it on the contours, thousands still follow the destructive practice of the past.

Half of the South's farmers are tenants, many of whom have little interest in preserving soil they do not own.

The South's chief crops are cotton, tobacco, and corn; all of these are intertilled crops — the soil is plowed between the rows, so that it is left loose and bare of vegetation.

The topsoil washes away much more swiftly than from land planted to cover crops, such as clover, soybeans, and small grains. Moreover, cotton, tobacco, and corn leave few stalks and leaves to be plowed under in the fall; and as a result the soil constantly loses its humus and its capacity to absorb rainfall.

Even after harvest, Southern land is seldom planted to cover crops which would protect it from the winter rains. This increases erosion tenfold.

Southeastern farms are the smallest in the nation. The operating units average only seventy-one acres, and nearly one-fourth of them are smaller than twenty acres. A farmer with so little land is forced to plant every foot of it in cash crops; he cannot spare an acre for soil-restoring crops or pasture. Under the customary tenancy system, moreover, he has every incentive to plant all his land to crops which will bring in the largest possible immediate cash return. The landlord often encourages him in this destructive practice of cash-cropping.

Training in better agricultural methods, such as planting soil-restoring crops, terracing, contour plowing, and rotation, has been spreading, but such training is still unavailable to most Southern farmers. Annually the South spends considerably more money for fertilizer than for agricultural training through its land-grant colleges, experiment stations, and extension workers.

Forests are one of the best protections against erosion. Their foliage breaks the force of the rain; their roots bind the soil so that it cannot wash away; their fallen leaves form a blanket of vegetable cover which soaks up the water and checks runoff. Yet the South has cut away a large part of its forest, leaving acres of gullied, useless soil. There has been comparatively little effort at systematic reforestation. Overgrazing, too, has resulted in serious erosion throughout the Southwest.

There is a close relationship between this erosion and floods, which recently have been causing a loss to the nation estimated at about $35 million annually. Rainfall runs off uncovered land much more rapidly than it does from land planted to cover crops or forest. Recent studies indicate that a single acre of typical cornland lost approximately 127,000 more gallons of rainfall in a single year than a similar field planted to grass. Another experiment showed that land sodded in grass lost less than 1 percent of a heavy rain through immediate runoff, while nearby land planted to cotton lost 31 percent. In short, unprotected land not only is in danger of destruction; it also adds materially to the destructive power of the swollen streams into which it drains.

These factors — each one reenforcing all the others — are causing an unparalleled wastage of the South's most valuable asset, its soil. They are steadily cutting down its agricultural income and steadily adding to its cost of production as compared with other areas of the world which raise the same crops.

For example, it takes quantities of fertilizer to make worn-out, eroded land produce.

The South, with only one-fifth of the nation's income, pays three-fifths of the nation's fertilizer bill. In 1929 it bought 5½ million tons of commercial fertilizer at a cost of $161 million. And although fertilizer performs a valuable and necessary service, it does not restore the soil. For a year or two it may nourish a crop, but the land still produces meagerly and at high cost.

Moreover, Southern farmers cannot pile on fertilizer fast enough to put back the essential minerals which are washing out of their land. Each year, about 27,500,000 tons of nitrogen and phosphorus compounds are leached out of Southern soil and sent down the rivers to the sea.

The South is losing more than $300 million worth of fertile topsoil through erosion every year. This is not merely a loss of income — it is a loss of irreplaceable capital.

PRIVATE AND PUBLIC INCOME

THE WEALTH of natural resources in the South — its forests, minerals, and fertile soil — benefit the South only when they can be turned into goods and services which its people need. So far the South has enjoyed relatively little of these benefits simply because it has not had the money or credit to develop and purchase them.

Ever since the war between the states, the South has been the poorest section of the nation. The richest state in the South ranks lower in per capita income than the poorest state outside the region. In 1937 the average income in the South was $314; in the rest of the country it was $604, or nearly twice as much.

Even in "prosperous" 1929, Southern farm people received an average gross income of only $186 a year, as compared with $528 for farmers elsewhere. Out of that $186, Southern farmers had to pay all their operating expenses — tools, fertilizer, seed, taxes, and interest on debt — so that only a fraction of that sum was left for the purchase of food, clothes, and the decencies

of life. It is hardly surprising, therefore, that such ordinary items as automobiles, radios, and books are relatively rare in many Southern country areas.

For more than half of the South's farm families — the 53 percent who are tenants without land of their own — incomes are far lower. Many thousands of them are living in poverty comparable to that of the poorest peasants in Europe. A recent study of Southern cotton plantations indicated that the average tenant family received an income of only $73 per person for a year's work. Earnings of sharecroppers ranged from $38 to $87 per person, and an income of $38 annually means only a little more than 10 cents a day.

The South's industrial wages, like its farm income, are the lowest in the United States. In 1937 common labor in twenty important industries got 16 cents an hour less than laborers in other sections received for the same kind of work. Moreover, less than 10 percent of the textile workers are paid more than 52.5 cents an hour, while in the rest of the nation 25 percent rise above this level. A recent survey of the South disclosed that the average annual wage in industry was only $865, while in the remaining states it averaged $1,219.

In income from dividends and interest, the South is at a similar disadvantage. In 1937 the per capita income in the South from dividends and interest was only $17.55, as compared with $68.97 for the rest of the country.

Since the South's people live so close to the poverty line, its many local political subdivisions have had great difficulty in providing the schools and other public services necessary in any civilized community. In 1935 the assessed value of taxable property in the South averaged only $463 per person, while in the nine Northeastern states it amounted to $1,370. In other words, the Northeastern states had three times as much property per person to support their schools and other institutions.

Consequently, the South is not able to bring its schools and many other public services up to national standards, even though it tax the available wealth as heavily as any other section. In 1936 the state and local governments of the south collected only $28.88 per person, while the states and local governments of the nation as a whole collected $51.54 per person.

Although the South has 28 percent of the country's population, its federal income-tax collections in 1934 were less than 12 percent of the national total. These collections averaged only $1.28 per capita throughout the South, ranging from 24 cents in Mississippi to $3.53 in Florida.

So much of the profit from Southern industries goes to outside financiers in the form of dividends and interest that state income taxes would produce a meager yield in comparison with similar levies elsewhere. State taxation does not reach dividends which flow to corporation stockholders and management in other states; and, as a result, these people do not pay their share of the cost of Southern schools and other institutions.

Under these circumstances the South has piled its tax burden on the backs of those least able to pay in the form of sales taxes. (The poll tax keeps the poorer citizens from voting in eight Southern states; thus they have no effective means of protesting against sales taxes.) In every Southern state but one, 59 percent of the revenue is raised by sales taxes. In the Northeast, on the other hand, not a single state gets more than 44 percent of its income from this source, and most of them get far less.

The efforts of Southern communities to increase their revenues and to spread the tax burden more fairly have been impeded by the vigorous opposition of interests outside the region which control much of the South's wealth. Moreover, tax revision efforts have been hampered in some sections by the fear that their industries would move to neighboring communities which would tax them more lightly — or even grant them tax exemption for long periods.

The hope that industries would bring with them better living conditions and consequent higher tax revenues often has been defeated by the competitive tactics of the communities themselves. Many Southern towns have found that industries which are not willing to pay their fair share of the cost of public services likewise are not willing to pay fair wages, and so add little to the community's wealth.

LABOR

THE RAPIDLY GROWING POPULATION of the South is faced with the problem of finding work that will provide a decent living. Neither on the farm nor in the factory is there the certainty of a continuing livelihood, and thousands of Southerners shift each year from farm to mill or mine and back again to farm.

The insecurity of work in Southern agriculture, its changes in method and its changes in location make the labor problem of the South not simply an industrial labor problem. Neither the farm population nor the industrial workers can be treated separately, because both groups, as a whole, receive too little income to enable their members to accumulate the property that tends to keep people stable. Industrial labor in the South is to a great extent unskilled and, therefore, subject to the competition of recurring migrations from the farm — people who have lost in the gamble of one-crop share farming. On the other hand, the industrial workers, with low wages and long hours, are constantly tempted to return to the farm for another try.

As industries requiring a large proportion of skilled workers have been slow in developing, the unskilled industrial labor in the South is particularly hampered by the competition of unskilled workers from the farms who accept low wages in preference to destitution at home. Much of the South's increase in industrial activity has been brought about by the removal of cotton-goods manufacturing plants to the Southeast from higher wage areas in New England. This backbone of Southern industry ranks nationally as one of the low-wage manufacturing industries. In the South it pays even lower wages than elsewhere.

According to 1937 figures, the pay for the most skilled work in this industry is about 12 cents an hour less in the South than the pay for the same work elsewhere. The figures for the cotton-goods industry also show the large number of low-wage workers and the small number receiving high wages in the South. More than half of the workers in Southern mills earn under 37.5 cents an hour, although in the rest of the country the industry employs less than 10 percent at such low rates. In the South less than one-tenth of the workers are paid more than 52.5 cents an hour, although one-fourth of the workers in the rest of the nation's cotton-goods industry are paid above this rate.

Similar differentials between the South and other regions are found in lumber, furniture, iron and steel, coal mining, and other industries generally. The influence of the farm population's competition is shown in the unskilled occupations where these wage differentials are widest. The average differential in rates for new labor between the South and the rest of the country in twenty of the country's important industries in 1937 amounted to 16 cents an hour.

In spite of longer working hours, the total annual wages show the same discrepancy. The average yearly pay per person in industry and business in the South in 1935 was $865.41, as compared with $1,219.31 for the rest of the country.

Wage differentials are reflected in lower living standards. Differences in costs of living between the Southern cities and cities in the nation as a whole are not great enough to justify the differentials in wages that exist. In 1935 a study of costs of living

showed that a minimum emergency standard required a family income of $75.27 a month as an average for all the cities surveyed. The average of costs in Southern cities showed that $71.94 a month would furnish the minimum emergency standard. This would indicate a difference of less than 5 percent in living costs. Industrial earnings for workers are often 30 to 50 percent below national averages.

Low wages and poverty are in great measure self-perpetuating. Labor organization has made slow and difficult progress among the low-paid workers, and they have had little collective bargaining power or organized influence on social legislation. Tax resources have been low because of low incomes in the communities, and they have been inadequate to provide for the type of education modern industry requires. Malnutrition has had its influence on the efficiency of workers. Low living standards have forced other members of workers' families to seek employment to make ends meet. These additions to the labor market tend further to depress wages.

Low wages have helped industry little in the South. Not only have they curtailed the purchasing power on which local industry is dependent but they have made possible the occasional survival of inefficient concerns. The standard of wages fixed by such plants and by agriculture has lowered the levels of unskilled and semiskilled workers, even in modern and well-managed establishments. While Southern workers, when well-trained and working under modern conditions, are thoroughly efficient producers, there is not enough such employment to bring the wage levels into line with the skill of the workers.

Unemployment in the South has not resulted simply from the Depression. Both in agriculture and industry, large numbers have for years been living only half employed or a quarter employed or scarcely employed at all. In the problem of unemployment in the South, the relation between agriculture and industry becomes notably clear. Over 30 percent of the persons employed on emergency works programs are farmers and farm laborers, as compared to 15.3 percent for the country as a whole. The insecurity of Southern farmers is reflected in these figures. Seasonal wages in agriculture do not provide incomes sufficient to tide workers over the slack seasons. Part-time industrial work does not provide security the year round. As long as the agricultural worker cannot gain assurance of a continuing existence on the farm, he remains a threat to the job, the wages, and the working conditions of the industrial worker.

OWNERSHIP AND USE OF LAND

THE FARMING SOUTH depends on cotton and tobacco for two-thirds of its cash income. More than half of its farmers depend on cotton alone. They are one-crop farmers, subjected year after year to risks which would appall the average businessman. All their eggs are in one basket — a basket which can be upset, and often is, by the weather, the boll weevil, or the cotton market.

The boll weevil can be conquered, and weather hazards tend to cancel themselves out as good seasons follow bad; but the cotton market is a sheer gamble. On this gamble nearly 2 million Southern families stake their year's work and everything they own. Their only chance of making a living is tied up with the fluctuations of the world price of cotton. No other similar area in the world gambles its welfare and the destinies of so many people on a single-crop market year after year.

The gamble is not a good one. Few other crops are subject to such violent and unpredictable price variations as cotton. In 1927, cotton farmers got 20 cents a pound for their crop; in 1929 they got 16 cents; in 1931 they got 6 cents; in 1933 they got 10 cents. Only once during the last decade did the price of cotton change less than 10 percent between pickings. Three times in five years it jumped more than 40 percent — once up and twice down.

Because cotton is the cornerstone of the economy of many parts of the South, the merchants, manufacturers, businessmen, and bankers share the hazards of the farmer. The men who finance cotton farming charge high interest rates because their money is subject to far more than the normal commercial risk. As a result, the mortgage debt of Southern farm owners has been growing steadily for the last twenty years. A checkup on forty-six scattered counties in the South in 1934 showed that one-tenth of the farmland was in the hands of corporations, mostly banks and insurance companies, which had been forced to foreclose their mortgages.

This process has forced more than half of the South's farmers into the status of tenants, tilling land they do not own. Whites and Negroes have suffered alike. Of the 1,831,000 tenant families in the region, about 66 percent are white. Approximately half of the sharecroppers are white, living under economic conditions almost identical with those of Negro sharecroppers.

The pattern of Southern tenancy was set at the end of the war between the states, which left thousands of former slave owners with plenty of land but no capital or labor to work it. Hundreds of thousands of former slaves and impoverished whites were willing to work but had no land. The result was the crop-sharing system, under which the land was worked by men who paid for the privilege with a share of their harvest. It was natural under this system that landowners should prefer to have virtually all the land put in cotton or other cash crops from which they could easily get their money. Consequently, over wide areas of the South, cash-cropping, one-crop farming, and tenant farming have come to mean practically the same thing. Diversification has been difficult because the landlord and tenant usually have not been able to find a workable method of financing, producing, and sharing the return from such crops as garden truck, pigs, and dairy products.

Tenant families form the most unstable part of our population. More than a third of them move every year, and only a small percentage stay on the same place long enough to carry out a five-year crop rotation. Such frequent moves are primarily the result of the traditional tenure system, under which most renters hold the land by a mere spoken agreement, with no assurance that they will be on the same place next season. Less than 2 percent have written leases, which give them security of tenure for more than one year. Under these circumstances the tenant has no incentive to protect the soil, plant cover crops, or keep buildings in repair. On the contrary, he has every reason to mine the soil for every possible penny of immediate cash return.

The moving habit, moreover, is costly. Most renters merely swap farms every few years without gain to themselves or anybody else. The bare cost of moving has been estimated at about $57 per family, or more than $25 million annually for the tenants of the South. Children are taken out of school in midyear and usually fall behind with their studies. It is almost impossible for a family constantly on the move to take an active part in community affairs; and, as a consequence, churches and other institutions suffer. For example, in one area of North Carolina where the percentage of tenancy is low, there were 257 churches with 21,000 members. In a nearby area of high tenancy — with three and one-half times as many people — there were only 218 churches with 17,000 members.

While it is growing more cotton and tobacco than it can use or sell profitably, the South is failing to raise the things it needs. Southern farmers grow at home less than one-fifth of the things they use; four-fifths of all they eat and wear is purchased.

For example, the region has more than half of the nation's farm people, yet it raises less than one-third of the nation's pigs and cattle. Although it has more than a fourth of America's total population, it produces only one-fifth of the country's eggs, milk, and butter, one-seventh of the hay, one-eighth of the potatoes, and one-twelfth of the oats. Consequently, the South must either obtain these things from other regions and pay handling and freight charges or do without.

Too many Southern families have simply done without, and as a result they have suffered severely from malnutrition and dietary diseases. Many common vegetables are rarities in many Southern farming communities, although both soil and climate are extremely favorable to their growth. Production of foodstuffs could be increased manyfold in the South without infringing on the markets of any other region; most of the increased output could, and should, be absorbed by the very farm families producing it.

Because they have concentrated on cash crops, Southern farmers have planted relatively little of their land in alfalfa, clover, field peas, and soybeans. These and similar legumes add fertility to the soil and at the same time protect fields against washing and gullying. If widely used, they would help the farmer to protect his investment in his land and take a little of the gamble out of his business.

On the other hand, cotton, tobacco, and corn use up the natural richness of the land with great speed. Fields planted to them year after year wear out and wash away much more quickly than fields on which legumes are planted in rotation with cash crops. Yet six acres of Southern cropland out of every ten are planted one season after another in cotton, tobacco, and corn.

117.

Jonathan Daniels: Can the South Rule Itself?

Jonathan Daniels, editor from 1933 to 1942 of the Raleigh (N.C.) News and Observer, *was one of the strongest Southern supporters of the New Deal. In 1936, when the federal government was investigating the impoverished condition of the South's economy and when it regarded the South as the nation's most serious economic problem, Daniels set out on a tour to see for himself. Traveling by automobile throughout the region, he accumulated numerous impressions that were incorporated in his book,* A Southerner Discovers the South *(1938). The following selection is drawn from the book's last chapter.*

Source: *A Southerner Discovers the South*, New York, 1938: "Dixie Destination."

A TRAVELER COMES TO DESTINATIONS. Or hopes to.

I remember when I was young and Admiral Robert E. Peary and Dr. Frederick Cook were quarreling (I was a great and small partisan of Dr. Cook) that I conceived of the North Pole as such a trimmed tree trunk as the Southern Bell Telephone Company or the Carolina Power & Light Company sometimes imbedded in the sidewalk before our house. I would not have been surprised, of course, had the North Pole been a little more ornate, and a trifle more impervious to heat and cold and bug and polar bear. But it provided a definite destination for the explorer. And I think that the moment when loss of faith in Dr. Cook began to set in was when he failed to show a lantern slide of it in his illustrated lecture at the Academy of Music.

Certainly now at the end of my travels in discovery of the South I wish I had a definite destination to report — or a plan. Certainly a plan. For the South, the Philosophers at Chapel Hill tell me, will not escape without a plan or at least a planning. I agree.

All people are planners.

"I aim to plant lespedeza in that field if I ever get around to it. But it just seems natural somehow to put it in cotton."

All people are regionalists.

I discovered that when I was twelve. And I still believe that Dr. Howard W. Odum missed one of the best indices of the Southern region when he failed to determine a line on one side of which all nice children say, "No, ma'am" and "Yes, ma'am," to the teacher and on the other side of which they get laughed at for saying it by all, including teacher. Such a line, I understand, no longer exists. At any rate, when I asked my daughter about it she said, "Hunh?"

But certainly all people are planners and regionalists. The plan may not extend beyond dinner time and the region may not reach beyond the creek. Indeed, in one section of North Carolina, plan and region are combined.

"Well, I guess we'll do like the folks across the river do."

"How's that?"

"Do without."

In more ways than one that has been the regional plan of the American South, and I for one Southerner, speaking also without fear of contradiction for 25,000,000 others, am ready to find another.

This program was adopted shortly after the surrender at Appomattox and has been in force almost without interruption since. That was a grand war for the poets and the politicians, but I am beginning to wonder quite seriously whether the Civil War itself ever made any really profound difference in the life and history of the South. The war itself seems a detail almost insignificant between what went before and what came after. Mine, I suppose, was the last Southern generation reared in a combination of indignation and despair. Now, fortunately, save in a few groups devoted to a form of rebel yelling which is also a form of ancestor whooping, the Civil War as such plays little or no part in the life and thinking of the South. That means, I hope, escape from the old Do-Without Economy of the Southern States, for the chief injury inflicted upon us late Confederates by the war was the excuse which it gave us for giving up and sitting in the sun. The South was poor; the war caused it. The South was ignorant; the war made us too poor to educate. The South was slow; well, after what the damyankees did it wasn't any use to stir. The war provided a satisfying, acceptable, and even mildly exhilarating excuse for everything from Captain Seabrook's wooden leg to the quality of education dispensed at the Centennial School.

Unfortunately, like a great many simple explanations, this one did not explain. The tariff did at least as much damage in Dixie as Sherman and Grant together in making the South poor and keeping it poor. Indeed, while Grant and Sherman have gone to whatever they had coming to them, the tariff remains. The process of selling the fertility of the land along with the cotton began a long time before the Civil War and had reduced Virginia gentlemen to the unpleasant business of breeding slaves for the Deep South markets. Even now men tremble over the possible loss of cotton markets; it is a trembling like that of the old slave fearful of losing his chains. The contempt

for labor which everywhere and in all times has been an inevitable item of slavery was full grown before 1860. The hookworm was in the South but not discovered. Yellow fever, typhoid, and malaria were there but not understood. Pellagra was seen as clay eating and was considered a perverse habit of the perverted po' whites. Most of the white people were desperately poor. Most of the Negroes had instinctively developed an apparently racial shiftlessness as a shrewd labor defense under slavery long before ladies and gentlemen on the Charleston housetops applauded the firing on Fort Sumter. And Reconstruction: Mississippi had defaulted on its bonds sometime in the '40s. The Rothschilds were involved, and, if Mississippi paid her debts, the Governor said, he was fearful that they might use the money to gain control of the sepulcher of Our Blessed Savior. That would never do, so Mississippi defaulted, and there was not a Negro in the Legislature that did it.

The Civil War killed men and broke hearts and caused a tremendous amount of private suffering. But war is too spectacular. All of the major faults and flaws in Southern economy were on the way to full growth before the war began. But it served as an alibi — a magnificent alibi — for them all, and for those that came after, too. In a false present, the South had begun the adoration of a fictitious past. . . .

The South's faults were many, but the South's faults were not alone. The war and Reconstruction were important as memory of them served as a screen of emotionalism behind which moved, ever praising Lee, those unemotional gentlemen from the North who knew what they wanted and how much they would have to pay for it, which was not much. This second wave of carpetbaggers was received with honors and banquets and bands. They were the agents of the new and ever greater absentee ownership of the South. They came from the North with excellent financial connections to buy up broken-down Southern railroads and other properties, and they picked up some pretty bargains and some pretty Southerners.

The town was properly impressed when Colonel Cadwallader entertained Mr. Prentiss, the Boston banker. (It continues impressed when his name is Manaccus and he is in the garment business.) The banks of those same gentlemen who bought up Southern railroads were also deeply interested in Northern railroads. It has even been suggested that while they were ever willing to make money they were also careful not to build up Southern traffic and industry at the expense of those older developed areas of the North and East through which their older lines ran. Freight rates certainly have not been shaped to aid the industrial development of the South; instead they still sit providing inland the protection which tariffs provide on coast and frontier. Some trade tacticians feel that freight rate and tariff together made a prettier pincher than that which Grant and Sherman applied on the Confederacy.

Of course, all ownership in this modern corporate civilization assumes the pattern of absentee ownership. Stockholders, South as North, are increasingly irresponsible and uncreative as individual capitalists. But the control of capital is in the North and East, and it may be significant that the only industrial development which has taken place in the South since the industrial North overcame the country culture of the South has been in the widely dispersed manufacture of textiles and in the new big industry of the cigarette. Otherwise, the South, devoted to the culture of cotton and tobacco, the prices of which are fixed in world markets, still buys from the protected factories of the North. Its new overseers, faithful to the absentee owners, beg and plead and promise for more absentee investment and control while simultaneously they cry to hysteria in condemnation of foreign agitators among nice native labor.

There is reason for both fear and elation.

The new pincher movement upon the South has not been applied in recent years with the precision which Grant and Sherman exercised, or perhaps the body seized is a good deal less easily grasped than was the old half-dead Confederacy between Richmond and Atlanta. At any rate those capitalists, local and absentee, who are concerned for low wages in the South, and those who are concerned for sales in the South, do not seem to be acting in perfect unity. The most profoundly disturbing foreign agitators in the region are the salesmen of Chevrolets and radios, gaudy machine-stitched dresses, and other shining gadgets and gewgaws. Even the power companies, incited by TVA, are filling the towheads and the burr-heads with glittering dreams. Not only the spindle has come South, so also has the automobile. The worker and the mill have both become mobile. As whole mills may move from Massachusetts to Mississippi, so may whole philosophies.

It is not the Communists who are coming but the advertisers. The cabins of the South are wallpapered with the pages of newspapers and magazines, and so much advertising has a practically permanent appeal. There may not come to the cabin in a year enough money to meet for a month the requirements of the persuasive suggestion that it is easy to own a Packard. But if all of those who see the walls cannot read them, all of them can desire. If they lack the money, they can wish for it. They can be dissatisfied with the old Do-Without Plan of the Southern regions of the United States. They are. And those new absentees who are coming South in a movement which New England Governors call "a threat from the South" should come warned: the South has much to offer, place and people and resources and power, but it does not honestly have docility to offer. Such as it possessed is disappearing before the building of desire. And the first problem of the South today is people. It is by no means limited to the South. Indeed, it is the newly exciting question of the possibility of democracy. In contemplation of it too many people have been looking at Italy and Spain and Russia and Germany, as well as at the old democracies of England and France. It is less disturbing to consider it over water, perhaps, but the seeing is clearer in the South. Contemplate the questions:

Are the Southern people capable of serving, governing, and saving themselves?

Or must they depend for guidance in government and to decency and adequacy in living upon an oligarchy of so-called aristocrats, a committee of experts, a ring of politicians? Upon plutocrat, demagogue, or professor?

Is democracy possible in the South? (Is it possible anywhere?)

Surely, those questions are properly raised with regard to the folk of a region in which the sharp-eyed regional planners have found natural resources in superabundance, population in abundance, but a deficiency in science, skills, technology, and organization, waste in its general economy and a richness, combined with immaturity and multiple handicaps, in its culture. The trends they discovered show hesitancy and relative regression in many aspects of culture. They found the lowest incomes and the poorest fed people in America in a region which should be a garden.

Beyond those findings, I pretend to no simple, certain answers to the questions. In the first place, of course, the Southern people will not show their capability or the lack of it in a vacuum. They must work in a realm, not only patterned by their past and their prejudices but also one definitely shaped by tariffs and freight rates fixed largely at the North for the benefit of the North. It is a region governed in important degree by absentee owners and one which has been stirred deeply more frequently by reflex response to exterior criticism than by agitators, native or foreign, at work within. It is a sensitive region, more romantic than idealistic, and one which is expiating for more sins than its own, though there are enough of them.

The answers like the questions go deep into the past. Important aspects of democracy grew in the South. Much of its philosophy was shaped at Monticello by Thomas Jefferson. But Jefferson in Virginia and John Adams in Massachusetts died on the same afternoon in 1826. And sometime thereafter, perhaps at the very time it began to become solidly Democratic, the South discarded democracy. Or perhaps more fairly stated, its democracy was destroyed.

From the beginning there were Southerners, big and rich, who held to the faith that wisdom reposed only in the big and the rich and that therefore the franchise should be restricted to them. More and more democracy asserted itself against them. Requirements for voting and office were slowly but steadily scaled down. And then, after a long and passionate war, in the South the electorate was enlarged, by force from without, by thousands of Negroes and decreased by thousands of white men who had formerly borne arms as Southerners and so as Confederates and so as Rebels. The result was a condition which seemed intolerable to the most faithful Democrats. Perhaps at that time no entry of any sort by the Negroes into the rights of citizenship would have been tolerable to the South. Certainly, however, the Negroes were given no chance to be absorbed. They were hurried from slavery into a power which, in general, other men misused.

Any unemotional reader of history must recognize the similarity between the Ku Klux of the South and the Brown Shirts of Germany and the Black Shirts of Italy and the similarity of the conditions which created them. They provided a rank-and-file violence. But in the South they brought the Bourbons to power. And the native Bourbon has steadily served the large propertied classes, absentee or local, in the exploitation of the South. Almost without exception the rout of the carpetbaggers, the Negroes, and the scallywags carried the old planter class and a new promoter class to power also over the vast white mass of little farmers and storekeepers, mechanics and laborers. For them as for the Negroes, to too great an extent, democracy was in the years afterwards effectually denied.

But little men stir: And men to lead them. There was, for instance, Benjamin Ryan Tillman in South Carolina. And "Pitchfork Ben" was by no means the only name applied to him. Low Country aristocrats still snort to speak of him. After him there were others like him — and not like him. There will be more. They are Southern demagogues, some better and some worse, but all indicative of a Southern unwillingness to leave government entirely to the political gentlemen or the gentlemen of business — gentlemen who know exactly what they want and how much they will pay for it. It is only an alternative, when as in the case of such a man as Huey Long, he leaves as a political estate a power to plunder. Neither he nor his inheritors discovered that power. It always exists when the people are incapable of government or careless of government. And Southerners might be plundered by the very people who made them also for a time incapable of government. They were. And those who plundered them also saw signs of inferiority in the poverty that was left.

There are Southerners still who would more quickly deny the ability of the people of the South to manage the South than any people outside of it. They are the persisting and ineradicable Bourbons and Brigadiers who are devoted to a class before a region. That made them readier to serve as the agents of the new mastery. They still serve it and serving also themselves believe they serve the South. Their minds are still patterned in that master-slave concept which in sense of superiority applied not only to slaves but to white men lacking slaves. They apply it now to the cotton mill as well as to the plantation. Many aristocrats

in the South — and that is the name for both the Coca-Cola bottler and the member of the Society of the Cincinnati — do not believe and never have believed that the people should — if they could — govern the South. Such a faith or faithlessness leads to the unincorporated mill village and the company union. Included under it are both the kindliest paternalism and the most vicious and careless exploitation.

This lack of faith by the few great in the many small seems to me sad, but the saddest thing in the South is the fact that those at the top who do not believe in the intelligence of those at the bottom have not shown themselves capable of a leadership satisfactory to the people they assume to lead — nor, so far as I could discover, to anybody else. The market for stuffed shirts is glutted.

Finally, the people are not as disturbing as the patricians. The most encouraging thing is that the ordinary Southern whites, given fair chance and training, are showing themselves capable of performing the best types of work. This is so in the South. TVA discovered it and was surprised. Others are discovering it. And in the black and white migration to the North this generation of Southern immigrants has been able to compete with the workers already on the ground. The depression saw them shivering and jobless in every Northern city: by the thousands it sent them scurrying home again. Now they and more beside them move again. They are, of course, inadequately trained, inadequately skilled. Sometimes they are underfed. Sometimes they are sick. Sometimes they are criminal, feebleminded, perverted, insane. But they move and they will move. They march to eat. They will not be stopped. They need not be feared unless they are resisted.

But fear in the South has slandered both of them: The Southern Negro is not an incurably ignorant ape. The Southern white masses are not biologically degenerate.

Both are peoples capable of vastly more

training than they possess. Both are peoples who may hang heavy on the national advance, or help to speed and sustain it. Both are peoples who could consume and produce more wealth. And they are capable of happy, productive, peaceful life, side by side. White men and black men have shared the South's too little for a long time and, though there is more than a casual connection between hunger and lynchings, they have shared it in relative quiet, decency and peace. They would be able to build a South in terms of the South's potentiality, if together they had a chance to make and share plenty.

Increasingly the ancient and venerable Do-Without Plan is deserted. But what of a new plan for the South? The materials for its shaping have grown at the University of North Carolina in a huge, wise book, *Southern Regions of the United States.* But I believe that the new Southern plan will grow more directly from itching than from statistics. The South is awaking, scratching at new desires. A plan of course should provide the way to fulfilment, and, at the moment, the South faces the prospect of plenty with more wish than way.

"Chile, yo' eyes is bigger'n yo' belly."

But the big-eyed stage is important. Once they were sleepy. Now they stir and are wide open at last. And a regional plan is a plot from seeing to getting, from needing to wanting, to possessing. Such an ordered program in the South must include expansions of facilities for public education in a region lacking skills, for public health in a region still plagued by preventable diseases, for public welfare in a country in which the private welfare of so many is so insecure. None of these are in any sense simply Southern. The children of the South — which is the land of children in America — are more and more the adults of tomorrow in other States and so they will be the criminals or the sick or the creative or the consumers or the burdens of other States soon, very soon.

Such a plan for a new, free, fed, housed, happy South must include not merely program at home for improvement but also program in the nation for the relinquishment of advantages elsewhere over the South. Perhaps those advantages are so deeply fixed as in freight rate and tariff that to change them to give the South a chance might do vast harm elsewhere, might cause much suffering in the areas which have grown rich on advantage, like that which wrings the hearts of Northerners when they see it in the South. Perhaps the South, as New England seems now fearing, may be able to escape its single-slavery to cotton and advance to a diverse industrial and agricultural development despite the imperial advantages which New England took as its loot after the Civil War.

There was some sort of bargain then, now dimly seen. The Negroes were sold down the river again after emancipation, and the price paid was a fixed economic differentiation which left the whole South in slavery to New England instead of some of the South in slavery to other Southerners. But I mean to start no new war: the South is at last escaping from the economic occupation which succeeded the military occupation. The South is at last escaping from the more destructive Reconstruction which economically continued the South as captive. And New England is afraid: the terrible danger is that it is about to lose at last the slavery from which it profited long after Lincoln in a manner of speaking set the Negroes free. Of course everybody was free in the South, free to fight among themselves for the too little that was left when tribute was paid.

Cato the Elder was no more implacable than the Brahmans of Boston who came after the Abolitionists with considerably cooler heads. The South was not plowed up and planted with salt as Carthage was. If no more generous, Bostonians (citizens of a region and an attitude and not a town) were less wasteful. They recognized that the

South kept in its place (a place in the nation geographically similar to that of the Negro in the South) might be useful and profitable. It was. And as a Southerner at the end of discovery I ask now only that they recognize the poverty of the South as a part of the same civilization as Harvard and in a measure as the creation of the same people. Cato did not ride through Carthage on the train and blame its condition on the Carthaginians. That much only I ask of the Yankees.

A good deal more is necessary for the Southerners. Item one is escape from pretentiousness. The Southerner has deluded only himself. The boy who was brought into Savannah from Bryan County with malaria, pellagra, hookworm, and a pelvis pierced by his thighbone as a result of malnutrition nevertheless insisted in the hospital

that he was the best alligator catcher on the coast of Georgia. Perhaps he was. Maybe still one Reb can beat ten Yankees. It is irrelevant. But planning in the South must begin at the bottom where so many of its people are. There is no handle on its top by which it can be lifted. Tyranny, like that of Huey Long's, would be swifter. Government by an oligarchy of plutocrats might possibly provide a more orderly way, though it would be concerned with profits first and people only afterwards, not recognizing that there is a difference. But in the South the tyrants and the plutocrats and the poor all need teaching. One of them no more than the others. All are in the warm dark, and whether they like it or not — white man, black man, big man — they are in the dark together. None of them will ever get to day alone.

118.

JOSEPH C. GREW: Protest Against Japan's "New Order" in the Far East

When fighting broke out between Chinese and Japanese soldiers in July 1937, Japan used the incident as a pretext to launch an invasion of China. Continued Japanese advances forced the American government to reassess its policy of nonintervention in the Far East. On October 6, 1938, the government joined the League of Nations in condemning the Japanese as aggressors and protested against Japan's violation of American treaty rights. Japan replied on November 18 that the "new situation" in the Far East had nullified the traditional Open Door Policy. On December 31 the American ambassador to Japan, Joseph C. Grew, sent the following note to the Japanese government reaffirming American rights in China.

Source: PRFA, Japan: 1931-1941, Vol. I, pp. 820-826.

THE GOVERNMENT OF THE UNITED STATES has received and has given full consideration to the reply of the Japanese government of November 18 to this government's note of October 6 on the subject of American rights and interests in China.

In the light of facts and experience the government of the United States is impelled to reaffirm its previously expressed opinion that imposition of restrictions upon the movements and activities of American nationals who are engaged in philanthropic, educational, and commercial endeavors in China has placed and will, if continued, increasingly place Japanese interests in a preferred position and is, therefore, unquestionably discriminatory in its effect against legitimate American interests. Further, with reference to such matters as exchange control, compulsory currency circulation, tariff revision, and monopolistic promotion in certain areas of China, the plans and practices of the Japanese authorities imply an assumption on the part of those authorities that the Japanese government or the regimes established and maintained in China by Japanese armed forces are entitled to act in China in a capacity such as flows from rights of sovereignty and further in so acting to disregard and even to declare nonexistent or abrogated the established rights and interests of other countries, including the United States.

The government of the United States expresses its conviction that the restrictions and measures under reference not only are unjust and unwarranted but are counter to the provisions of several binding international agreements, voluntarily entered into, to which both Japan and the United States, and in some cases other countries, are parties.

In the concluding portion of its note under reference, the Japanese government states that it is firmly convinced that "in the face of the new situation fast developing in Asia, any attempt to apply to the conditions of today and tomorrow inapplicable ideas and principles of the past neither would contribute toward the establishment of a real peace in East Asia nor solve the immediate issues" and that "as long as these points are understood Japan has not the slightest inclination to oppose the participation of the United States and other powers in the great work of reconstructing East Asia along all lines of industry and trade."

The government of the United States in its note of October 6 requested, in view of the oft-reiterated assurances proffered by the government of Japan of its intention to observe the principles of equality of opportunity in its relations with China and in view of Japan's treaty obligations so to do, that the government of Japan abide by these obligations and carry out these assurances in practice. The Japanese government in its reply appears to affirm that it is its intention to make its observance of that principle conditional upon an understanding by the American government and by other governments of a "new situation" and a "new order" in the Far East as envisaged and fostered by Japanese authorities.

Treaties which bear upon the situation in the Far East have within them provisions relating to a number of subjects. In the making of those treaties, there was a process among the parties to them of give and take. Toward making possible the carrying out of some of their provisions, others among their provisions were formulated and agreed upon; toward gaining for itself the advantage of security in regard to certain matters, each of the parties committed itself to pledges of self-denial in regard to certain other matters. The various provisions agreed upon may be said to have constituted collectively an arrangement for safeguarding, for the benefit of all, the correlated principles, on the one hand, of national integrity and, on the other hand, of equality of economic opportunity.

Experience has shown that impairment of the former of these principles is followed almost invariably by disregard of the latter. Whenever any government begins to exercise political authority in areas beyond the limits of its lawful jurisdiction, there develops inevitably a situation in which the nationals of that government demand and are accorded, at the hands of their government, preferred treatment, whereupon equality of opportunity ceases to exist and discriminatory practices, productive of friction, prevail.

The admonition that enjoyment by the

nationals of the United States of nondiscriminatory treatment in China — a general and well-established right — is henceforth to be contingent upon an admission by the government of the United States of the validity of the conception of Japanese authorities of a "new situation" and a "new order" in East Asia is, in the opinion of this government, highly paradoxical.

This country's adherence to and its advocacy of the principle of equality of opportunity do not flow solely from a desire to obtain the commercial benefits which naturally result from the provisions of that principle. They flow from a firm conviction that observance of that principle leads to economic and political stability, which are conducive both to the internal well-being of nations and to mutually beneficial and peaceful relationships between and among nations; from a firm conviction that failure to observe that principle breeds international friction and ill-will, with consequences injurious to all countries, including in particular those countries which fail to observe it; and from an equally firm conviction that observance of that principle promotes the opening of trade channels, thereby making available the markets, the raw materials, and the manufactured products of the community of nations on a mutually and reciprocally beneficial basis.

The principle of equality of economic opportunity is, moreover, one to which over a long period and on many occasions the Japanese government has given definite approval. It is one to the observance of which the Japanese government has committed itself in various international agreements and understandings. It is one upon observance of which by other nations the Japanese government has of its own accord and upon its own initiative frequently insisted. It is one to which the Japanese government has repeatedly during recent months declared itself committed.

The people and the government of the United States could not assent to the establishment at the instance of and for the special purposes of any third country of a regime which would arbitrarily deprive them of the long-established rights of equal opportunity and fair treatment which are legally and justly theirs along with those of other nationals.

Fundamental principles such as the principle of equality of opportunity which have long been regarded as inherently wise and just, which have been widely adopted and adhered to, and which are general in their application are not subject to nullification by a unilateral affirmation.

With regard to the implication in the Japanese government's note that the "conditions of today and tomorrow" in the Far East call for a revision of the ideas and principles of the past, this government desires to recall to the Japanese government its position on the subject of revision of agreements. This government had occasion, in the course of a communication delivered to the Japanese government on April 29, 1934, to express its opinion that "treaties can lawfully be modified or be terminated — but only by processes prescribed or recognized or agreed upon by the parties to them."

In the same communication this government also said, "In the opinion of the American people and the American government, no nation can, without the assent of the other nations concerned, rightfully endeavor to make conclusive its will in situations where there are involved the rights, the obligations, and the legitimate interests of other sovereign states." In an official and public statement on July 16, 1937, the secretary of state of the United States declared that this government advocates "adjustment of problems in international relations by processes of peaceful negotiation and agreement."

At various times during recent decades, various powers, among which have been Japan and the United States, have had occasion to communicate and to confer with regard to situations and problems in the Far East. In the conducting of correspondence and of conferences relating to these matters, the parties involved have invariably taken into consideration past and present facts and they have not failed to perceive the possibility and the desirability of changes in the situation. In the making of treaties they have drawn up and have agreed upon provisions intended to facilitate advantageous developments and at the same time to obviate and avert the arising of friction between and among the various powers which, having interests in the region or regions under reference, were and would be concerned.

In the light of these facts, and with reference especially to the purpose and the character of the treaty provisions from time to time solemnly agreed upon for the very definite purposes indicated, the government of the United States deprecates the fact that one of the parties to these agreements has chosen to embark — as indicated both by action of its agents and by official statements of its authorities — upon a course directed toward the arbitrary creation by that power by methods of its own selection, regardless of treaty pledges and the established rights of other powers concerned, of a "new order" in the Far East. Whatever may be the changes which have taken place in the situation in the Far East and whatever may be the situation now, these matters are of no less interest and concern to the American government than have been the situations which have prevailed there in the past, and such changes as may henceforth take place there, changes which may enter into the producing of a "new situation" and a "new order," are and will be of like concern to this government.

This government is well aware that the situation has changed. This government is also well aware that many of the changes have been brought about by the action of Japan. This government does not admit, however, that there is need or warrant for any one power to take upon itself to prescribe what shall be the terms and conditions of a "new order" in areas not under its sovereignty and to constitute itself the repository of authority and the agent of destiny in regard thereto.

It is known to all the world that various of the parties to treaties concluded for the purpose of regulating contacts in the Far East and avoiding friction therein and therefrom — which treaties contained, for those purposes, various restrictive provisions — have from time to time and by processes of negotiation and agreement contributed in the light of changed situations toward the removal of restrictions and toward the bringing about of further developments which would warrant in the light of further changes in the situation, further removals of restrictions. By such methods and processes, early restrictions upon the tariff autonomy of all countries in the Far East were removed. By such methods and processes the rights of extraterritorial jurisdiction once enjoyed by Occidental countries in relations with countries in the Far East have been given up in relations with all of those countries except China; and in the years immediately preceding and including the year 1931, countries which still possessed those rights in China, including the United States, were actively engaged in negotiations — far advanced — looking toward surrender of those rights.

All discerning and impartial observers have realized that the United States and others of the "treaty powers" have not during recent decades clung tenaciously to their so-called special rights and privileges in countries of the Far East but on the contrary have steadily encouraged the development in those countries of institutions and practices in the presence of which such rights and privileges may safely and readily be given up; and all observers have seen those rights and privileges gradually being surrendered voluntarily through agreement by the powers which have possessed them. On one point only has the government of the United States, along with several other governments, insisted; namely, that new situations must have developed to a point warranting the removal of "special" safeguarding restrictions and that the removals be effected by orderly processes.

The government of the United States has at all times regarded agreements as susceptible of alteration, but it has always insisted that alterations can rightfully be made only by orderly processes of negotiation and agreement among the parties thereto. The Japanese government has upon numerous occasions expressed itself as holding similar views.

The United States has in its international relations rights and obligations which derive from international law and rights and obligations which rest upon treaty provisions. Of those which rest on treaty provisions, its rights and obligations in and with regard to China rest in part upon provisions in treaties between the United States and China and in part on provisions in treaties between the United States and several other powers, including both China and Japan. These treaties were concluded in good faith

for the purpose of safeguarding and promoting the interests not of one only but of all of their signatories. The people and the government of the United States cannot assent to the abrogation of any of this country's rights or obligations by the arbitrary action of agents or authorities of any other country.

The government of the United States has, however, always been prepared, and is now prepared, to give due and ample consideration to any proposals based on justice and reason which envisage the resolving of problems in a manner duly considerate of the rights and obligations of all parties directly concerned by processes of free negotiation and new commitment by and among all of the parties so concerned. There has been and there continues to be opportunity for the Japanese government to put forward such proposals. This government has been and it continues to be willing to discuss such proposals, if and when put forward, with representatives of the other powers, including Japan and China, whose rights and interests are involved, at whatever time and in whatever place may be commonly agreed upon.

Meanwhile, this government reserves all rights of the United States as they exist and does not give assent to any impairment of any of those rights.

The world is a fine place and worth fighting for.
ERNEST HEMINGWAY, *For Whom the Bell Tolls*

1939

119.

E. B. WHITE: The Townsend Plan

The plan known as Old Age Revolving Pensions Ltd., under the leadership of Dr. Francis E. Townsend, was one of the boldest of all those proposed during the 1930s for solving the nation's economic difficulties. A monthly pension of $200 was to be paid by the government to all unemployed people over sixty, provided they spent the money within the month. The proposal promised to alleviate the problems of the elderly and increase consumer buying at the same time. The Townsend Plan was first offered to the public in January 1934, and over the next few years gained a following of several million people who felt that New Deal legislation had passed them by. In 1939 E. B. White, columnist and humorist, wrote the following description of a meeting of Townsendites.

Source: *Harper's,* October 1939.

OVER IN THE NEXT COUNTY the Methodists have a campground, in a clump of woods near East Machias. They were in session there for about a week, and I went over on Saturday for the *pièce de résistance* — Dr. Francis E. Townsend (himself) of California. I had long wanted to see the author of America's favorite plan, and there he was, plain as day, right under the GOD IS LOVE sign.

It was a peaceful spot, though it gave one a sultry, hemmed-in feeling, as hardwood dingles often do. There was a ticket booth, where I paid my quarter; and beyond was a lane opening out into the *al fresco* temple where about six hundred people were gathered to hear the good news. They were Methodist farmers and small-town merchants and their Methodist wives and children and dogs, Townsendites from Townsend Club Number One of East Machias, pilgrims from all over the State, honest, hopeful folks, their faces grooved with the extra lines that come from leading godly, toilsome lives. The men sat stiffly in the dark-blue suits that had carried them through weddings, funerals, and Fair days. In a big circle surrounding the temple were the cottages (seventy or eighty of them), little two-storey frame shacks, set ten or a dozen feet apart, each with its front porch, its stuffy upstairs bedroom, and its smell from the kitchen. Beyond, in a nobler circle, were the backhouses, at the end of the tiny trails. The whole place, even with hymns rising through the leafy boughs, had the faintly disreputable air which pervades any woodland rendezvous where the buildings stand unoccupied for most of the year, attracting woodpeckers, sneak thieves, and lovers in season.

On the dais, behind some field flowers, sat the Doctor, patiently awaiting his time — a skinny, bespectacled little savior, with a big jaw, like the Tin Woodman. He had arrived by plane the night before at the Bangor airport a hundred miles away, and had driven over that morning for the meeting. As I sat down a voice was lifted in prayer, heads were bowed. The voice came from a loudspeaker suspended from the branch of an elm, and the speaker was talking pointedly of milk and honey. When he quit, Dr. Townsend's henchman, a baldish fellow with a businesslike manner, took the stand and introduced the man who needed no introduction, Dr. Francis E. Townsend, of California, the world's greatest humanitarian. We all rose and clapped. Children danced on the outskirts, dogs barked, and faces appeared in the windows of some of the nearest cottages. The Doctor held out his hands for silence. He stood quietly, looking round over the assemblage. And then, to the old folks with their troubled, expectant faces, he said, simply:

"I like you people very much."

It was like a handclasp, a friendly arm placed round the shoulder. Instantly his listeners warmed, and smiled, and wriggled with sudden newfound comfort.

"I have come nearly four thousand miles to see you," continued the Doctor. "You look like good Methodists, and I like that. I was raised in a Methodist family, so I know what it means."

He spoke calmly, without any platform tricks, and he sounded as though this was the first time he had ever expounded Townsendism. In words of one syllable he unfolded the plan which he had conceived, the plan which he knew would work, the plan which he promised to see enacted into law, so that all people might enjoy equally the good things of this life.

"The retirement of the elders is a matter of concern to the entire population." Grizzly heads nodded assent. Old eyes shone with new light.

"In a nation possessed of our natural resources, with great masses of gold and money at our command, it is unthinkable that conditions such as exist today should be tolerated. There is something radically wrong with any political philosophy which permits this to exist. Now, then, how did it come about?"

Dr. Townsend explained how it had come about. Flies buzzed in the clearing. The sun pierced the branches overhead, struck down on the folding music stands of the musicians, gleamed on the bare thighs of young girls in shorts, strolling with their fellows outside the pale of economics. The world, on this hot Saturday afternoon, seemed very old and sad, very much in need of something. Maybe this Plan was it. I never heard a milder-mannered economist, nor one more fully convinced of the right and wisdom of his proposal. I looked at the audience, at the faces. They were the faces of men and women reared on trouble, and now they wanted a few years of comfort on earth, and then to be received into the lap of the Lord. I think Dr. Townsend wanted this for them: I'm sure *I* did.

"Business is stymied," murmured the Doctor. "Almost half the population is in dire want. Sixty millions of people cannot buy the products of industry." The Doctor's statistics were staggering and loose-jointed, but his tone was quietly authoritative. There could be small room for doubt.

He spoke disparagingly of the New Deal, and knocked all the alphabetical schemes for employing idle men. "Do you want to be taxed for these useless and futile activities?"

His audience shook their heads.

And all the while he spoke, the plan itself was unfolding — simply, logically. A child could have understood it. Levy a two percent tax on the gross business of the country and divide the revenue among persons over sixty years of age, with the one stipulation that they spend the money ($200 a month) within a certain number of days.

"And mind you," said the Doctor, with a good-natured grin, "we don't care a rap what you spend it for!"

The old folks clapped their hands and winked at one another. They were already buying pretty things, these Methodists, were already paying off old cankerous debts.

"We want you to have new homes, new furniture, new shoes and clothes. We want you to travel and go places. You old folks have earned the right to loaf, and you're going to do it luxuriously in the near future. The effect on business, when all this money is put into circulation, will be tremendous. Just let us have two billion dollars to distribute this month, and see what happens!"

The sound of the huge sum titivated the group; two billion dollars flashed across the clearing like a comet, trailing a wispy tail of excitement, longing, hope.

"It may even be three," said the Doctor, thoughtfully, as though the possibility had just occurred to him. "America has the facilities, all we need is the sense to use them."

He said he was reminded of a story in the old McGuffey's Reader. The one about the ship flying a distress signal, and another ship came to its assistance.

"Get us water!" shouted the captain. "We are perishing of thirst."

"Dip up and drink, you fools!" answered the captain of the other ship. "You're in the mouth of the Amazon River."

"Friends," said the good Doctor, "We are in the mouth of the Amazon River of Abundance. But we haven't the sense to dip up and drink."

It was a nice story, and went well.

Suddenly the Doctor switched from words of promise to words of threat. Lightly, with bony fingers, he strummed the strings of terror. If we're going to save this democracy of ours (he said), we shall have to begin soon. You've read about strikes in the great industrial centers; in a very brief time you will read of riots. And when rioting starts, it will be an easy matter for someone to seize the armed forces of the country and put them to his own use. This has happened in Europe. It can happen here.

The glade darkened ominously. Trees trembled in all their limbs. The ground, hard-packed under the Methodist heel, swam in the vile twilight of Fascist doom. Still the little Doctor's voice droned on — calm, full of humility, devoid of theatrics. Just the simple facts, simply told.

And then the vexatious question of money to carry on with. The audience shifted, got a new grip on their seats with their behinds. The ancient ceremony of plate-passing was a familiar and holy rite that had to be gone through with. The Doctor carefully disclaimed any personal ambitions, financial or political. "I don't want a fortune," he said, confidentially. "I mean that. I don't seek wealth. For one thing, it might ruin my fine son. But it does take money to educate people to a new idea. Give us a penny a day and we'll educate the next Congress."

A joke or two, to restore amiability; another poke at Uncle Sam; another mention of the need for funds to carry on with; and the speech was over.

It had been an impressive performance.

Most speeches lack the sincerity the Doctor had given his; not many speeches are so simply made and pleasantly composed. It had been more like a conversation with an old friend. I had listened, sitting there near the musicians, with all the sympathy that within me lay, and (I trust) with an open mind. Even a middle-aged hack has his moments of wanting to see the world get along. After all, this was no time for cynicism; most of what Dr. Townsend had said, God knows, was true enough. If anybody could devise a system for distributing wealth more evenly, more power to him. One man's guess was as good as another's. Well, pretty nearly as good. I pocketed the few scribbled notes I had made and gave myself over to a mood of summer afternoon despondency and world decay.

The chairman rose and announced that the meeting would be thrown open to questions, but that the time was short, so please speak right up. It was at this point that Dr. Francis E. Townsend (of California) began quietly to come apart, like an inexpensive toy. The questions came slowly, and they were neither very numerous nor very penetrating. Nor was there any heckling spirit in the audience: people were with him, not against him. But in the face of inquiry, the Doctor's whole manner changed. He had apparently been through this sort of thing before and was as wary as a squirrel. It spoiled his afternoon to be asked anything. Details of Townsendism were irksome in the extreme — he wanted to keep the Plan simple and beautiful, like young love before sex has reared its head. And now he was going to have to answer a lot of nasty old questions.

"How much would it cost to administer?" inquired a thrifty grandmother, rising to her feet.

The Doctor frowned. "Why, er," he said. (This was the first "er" of the afternoon.) "Why, not a great deal. There's nothing about it, that is, there's no reason why it

needs to cost much." He then explained that it was just a matter of the Secretary of the Treasury making out forty-eight checks each month, one to each State. Surely that wouldn't take much of the Secretary's time. Then these big checks would be broken up by the individual State administrators, who would pay out the money to the people over sixty years of age who qualified. "We're not going to have any administrative problems to speak of, at all," said the Doctor, swallowing his spit. The little grandmother nodded and sat down.

"Can a person get the pension if they hold property?" inquired an old fellow who had suddenly remembered his home, and his field of potatoes.

"Yes, certainly," replied the Doctor, shifting from one foot to the other. "But we *do* have a stipulation; I mean, in our plan we are going to say that the money shall not go to anybody who has a gainful pursuit." An uneasy look crossed the farmer's face: very likely he was wondering whether his field of potatoes was gainful. Maybe his potato bugs would stand him in good stead at last. Things already didn't look so simple.

"How much bookkeeping would it mean for a businessman?" asked a weary capitalist.

"Bookkeeping?" repeated the Doctor vaguely. "Oh, I don't think there will be any trouble about bookkeeping. It is so simple. Every businessman just states what his gross is for the thirty-day period, and two percent of it goes to pay the old people. In the Hawaiian Islands they already have a plan much like mine in operation. It works beautifully, and I was amazed, when I was there, at how few people it took to administer it. No, there'll be no difficulty about bookkeeping."

"How will the Townsend Plan affect foreign trade?" asked an elderly thinker on Large Affairs.

Doctor Townsend gave him a queer look — not exactly hateful, but the kind of look a parent sometimes gives a child on an off day.

"Foreign trade?" he replied, somewhat weakly. "Foreign trade? Why should we concern ourselves with foreign trade?" He stopped. But then he thought maybe he had given short measure on that one, so he told a story of a corn-flakes factory, and all the corn came from some foreign country. What kind of way was that — buying corn from foreigners?

Next question: "Would a person receiving the pension be allowed to use it to pay off a mortgage?"

Answer: "Yes. Pay your debts. Let's set our government a good example!" (*Applause.*)

And now a gentleman down front — an apple-cheeked old customer with a twinkle: "Doctor, would buying a drink count as spending your money?"

"A drink?" echoed the Doctor. Then he put on a hearty manner. "Why, if anybody came to me and wanted to drink himself into an early grave with money from the fund, I'd say, 'Go to it, old boy!' " There was a crackle of laughter, but the Doctor knew he was on slippery footing. "Don't misunderstand me," he put in. "Let's not put too many restrictions on morality. The way to bring about temperance in this world is to bring up our young sons and

daughters decently, and teach them the evils of abuse. (*Applause.*) And now, friends, I must go. It has been a most happy afternoon."

The meeting broke up. Townsendites rose and started down the aisles to shake hands reverently with their chief. The chairman announced a take of eighty dollars and three cents. Life began to settle into its stride again. Pilgrims filed out of the pews and subsided in rocking chairs on the porches of the little houses. Red and white paper streamers, festooning the trees, trembled in the fitful air; and soft drinks began to flow at the booth beyond the Inner Circle. The Doctor, waylaid by a group of amateur photographers, posed in front of an American flag, and then departed in a Dodge sedan for the airport — a cloud-draped Messiah, his dream packed away in a brief case for the next performance.

On the porch of a cottage called "Nest o' Rest" three old ladies rocked and rocked and rocked. And from a score of rusty stovepipes in the woods rose the first thick coils of smoke from the kitchen fires, where America's housewives, never quite giving up, were laboriously preparing one more meal in the long, long procession. The vision of milk and honey, it comes and goes. But the odor of cooking goes on forever.

The money is always there, but the pockets change; it is not in the same pockets after a change, and that is all there is to say about money.

GERTRUDE STEIN

120.

Granville Hicks: On Leaving the Communist Party

During the 1930s many American intellectuals, disillusioned by the persisting social problems that they regarded as unalleviated by the New Deal, joined the Communist Party. One of the most prominent was Granville Hicks, an author and critic, who was fired from his position on the faculty of Rensselaer Polytechnic Institute in 1935 and became an editor of the Communist magazine New Masses. *By the end of the decade, however, there were widespread defections from the Party by those who were repelled by the Stalin purges of 1937-1938 and by the signing of the Russo-German Nonaggression Pact in August 1939. Among them was Hicks, who explained his resignation in the following communication.*

Source: *New Republic*, October 4, 1939.

I joined the Communist Party, after long hesitation, because I believed in its aims and because it seemed to offer the best way of working for those aims. As a party member, participating in its work on many levels, I became more and more convinced of its effectiveness. I am now resigning from the party because it is no longer an organization in which I can be effective.

The occasion of my resignation is the Soviet-German Pact, but that does not mean that I am prepared to condemn the pact and its consequences. I see the validity of some of the arguments put forth in its defense. Furthermore, the record of the Soviet Union compels me to suspend judgment. It is possible that history will prove the soundness and wisdom of the Soviet leaders. I am still ready to give them the benefit of the doubt. The truth is that I do not know what is happening in Europe, and until I have far more information than I have now I cannot come to any conclusion about Soviet foreign policy.

That is my immediate quarrel with the Communist Party of the United States. If the party had left any room for doubt, I could go along with it, at least for the present. But defense of the pact is now an integral part of the line and, indeed, has inevitably become the most important item of political belief. Leaders of the party have generously urged me to take all the time I wanted to make up my mind. They have sympathized with the difficulty of my decision and have not made the slightest effort to force my adherence to the party position. But they have made it clear that, if I eventually found it impossible to defend the pact, and defend it in their terms, there was nothing for me to do but resign.

In common with many of my friends, I have been much more disturbed by what has happened in the American party in the past month than by what has happened in the Soviet Union. I cannot now defend the pact, but I can conceive of history's justifying it. I can see no justification for the behavior of the party.

The party is now telling us that the pact was a necessary and wise move. If that is true, the leaders of the party should have prepared the American people for such a possibility. They tell us now that Stalin's speech last March to the Eighteenth Congress of the CPSU foreshadowed this development. This is wisdom after the event. No party leader, prior to August 21, had ever drawn such conclusions from the speech. On the contrary, when journalists predicted such a pact, they were indignantly denounced. I am not saying that advance notice should have been given to the world by the Soviets; I am saying that an analysis which ruled out the possibility of a pact was false.

Moreover, so far as one can judge from all the evidence, the leaders themselves were completely unprepared for what has happened. They were unprepared for it, and they did not understand it. If they had only said this, if they had only admitted their ignorance, the Communist Party of the United States would be intact today. But instead they insisted that the Soviet-German nonaggression pact was the greatest possible contribution to peace and democracy, and offered anything that came into their heads as proof. They rushed into print with apologetics completely devoid of clarity and logic. Only one conclusion could be drawn: if the party leaders could not defend the Soviet Union intelligently, they would defend it stupidly.

If anyone had any illusions about Moscow gold, which I may say for the sake of the record I never saw the slightest evidence of, these recent weeks should have destroyed them. Nothing could be clearer than the fact that Communists in this country had not been given the slightest inkling of what was to happen. If the leaders had frankly admitted this, if they had simply pointed to the record of the Soviet Union and asked people to wait and see, they would have strengthened the party. But they insisted on giving the impression that they were under orders from Moscow, without having the authority that a close tie with the Soviets would have given them.

The leaders of the Communist Party have tried to appear omniscient, and they have succeeded in being ridiculous. They have clutched at straws, juggled sophistries, shut their eyes to facts. Their predictions have almost uniformly been proved wrong within twenty-four hours. They have shown that they are strong in faith — which the future may or may not justify — and weak in intelligence.

One thing that particularly concerns me is the fact that as the party has retreated from one untenable position after another, it has revealed the likelihood that its domestic policy may be drastically altered. Though I have been a warm supporter of the democratic front, I have not been uncritical of the way in which the democratic-front line has been applied, and I have been willing to listen to more fundamental objections. If the American situation had greatly altered, I could conceive of adopting a different position. But I cannot accept a change that is dictated by the exigencies of Soviet foreign policy. It still seems to me essential to aid the Soviet Union, but I believe that can be done, not through stupid, unconvincing apologetics but through the building of a stanch bulwark against reaction in America.

How much strength and influence the Communist Party has lost remains to be seen, but it is my belief that the events of these past weeks have in large measure destroyed its effectiveness. I think the party did a magnificent job in building the united front. I have seen for myself that the most intelligent leaders and the hardest workers in trade unions and in every type of progressive organization were Communists. The present policy of the party is going to make such work vastly difficult, perhaps impossible. Even if the party does not abandon the policy of the democratic front, as it may, its members will be unable to build that front. When the party reverses itself overnight, and offers nothing but nonsense in explanation, who is likely to be influenced by a Communist's recommendations?

I can understand those who have been made bitter by a sense of betrayal, but I feel no impulse to denounce the Soviet Union. After all, the Soviet Union is a socialist commonwealth, and, even if it makes mistakes, its fate is of the utmost concern to every believer in socialism. I shall continue to defend its achievements, and I think my defense may be all the more effective because I am not committed to the proposition that every detail of Soviet foreign policy is necessarily and demonstrably wise and beneficent.

Furthermore, I propose to do my best to defend the Communist Party. Nothing distresses me more about leaving the party than the realization that I am leaving it at a moment when it is in extreme peril. I know as well as any party member that the pact is not the cause of the present drive against the party, and I know too that no progressive movement is safe if the party is suppressed. The whole progressive cause has suffered, and we must repair the damage as rapidly as possible. Defense of the full legal rights of the Communist Party must be an important part of the redoubled fight against reaction.

Leaving the party is as serious and difficult a step as joining it. I value my years in the party, not only for the experience and the associations but also for the opportunity they gave me of fruitful work for a cause I believed in. My problem now is how to continue that work.

121.

Harold J. Laski: Federalism and Giant Capitalism

Harold Laski of the London School of Economics was a lucid propagator of Marxism whose writings appealed to American intellectuals during the upheaval of the 1930s. He was convinced that private concentrations of capital had had their day and would be replaced by government ownership of the means of production. He attacked the federal structure in America because he felt it had come to be nothing but a bulwark of the capitalist system. Laski's opinions on federalism were summed up in an article entitled "The Obsolescence of Federalism," published May 3, 1939, and reprinted here in part.

Source: *New Republic*, May 3, 1939.

No one can travel the length and breadth of the United States without the conviction of its inexpugnable variety. East and West, South and North, its regions are real and different, and each has problems real and different, too. The temptation is profound to insist that here, if ever, is the classic place for a federal experiment. Union without unity — except in the Soviet Union and China, has variety ever so fully invited the implications of the famous definition? Geography, climate, culture, all of them seem to have joined their forces to insist that, wherever centralization is appropriate, here, at least, it has no meaning. Tradition demands its absence; history has prohibited its coming. The large unit, as in Lamennais' phrase, would result in apoplexy at the center and anemia at the extremities.

Imposed solutions from a distant Washington, blind, as it must be blind, to the subtle minutiae of local realities, cannot solve the ultimate problems that are in dispute. A creative America must be a federal

America. The wider the powers exercised from Washington, the more ineffective will be the capacity for creative administration. Regional wisdom is the clue to the American future. The power to govern must go where that regional wisdom resides. So restrained, men learn by the exercise of responsibility the art of progress. They convince themselves by experiment from below. To fasten a uniformity that is not in nature upon an America destined to variety is to destroy the prospect of an ultimate salvation.

This kind of argument is familiar in a hundred forms. I believe that, more than any other philosophic pattern, it is responsible for the malaise of American democracy. My plea here is for the recognition that the federal form of state is unsuitable to the stage of economic and social development that America has reached. I infer from this postulate two conclusions: first, that the present division of powers, however liberal be the Supreme Court in its technique of interpretation, is inadequate to the needs America confronts; and, second, that any revision of those powers is one which must place in Washington, and Washington only, the power to amend that revision as circumstances change. I infer, in a word, that the epoch of federalism is over, and that only a decentralized system can effectively confront the problems of a new time.

To continue with the old pattern, in the age of giant capitalism, is to strike into impotence that volume of governmental power which is necessary to deal with the issues giant capitalism has raised. Federalism, I suggest, is the appropriate governmental technique for an expanding capitalism, in which the price of local habit — which means, also, local delay — admits of compensation in the total outcome. But a contracting capitalism cannot afford the luxury of federalism. It is insufficiently positive in character; it does not provide for sufficient rapidity of action; it inhibits the emergence of necessary standards of uniformity; it re-

lies upon compacts and compromises which take insufficient account of the urgent category of time; it leaves the backward areas a restraint, at once parasitic and poisonous, on those which seek to move forward; not least, its psychological results, especially in an age of crisis, are depressing to a democracy that needs the drama of positive achievement to retain its faith. . . .

Giant capitalism has, in effect, concentrated the control of economic power in a small proportion of the American people. It has built a growing contrast between the distribution of that economic power and the capacity of the political democracy effectively to control the results of its exercise. It has transcended the political boundaries of the units in the American federation so as to make them largely ineffective as areas of independent government. Whether we take the conditions of labor, the level of taxation, the standards of education, public health, or the supply of amenities like housing and recreation, it has become clear that the true source of decision is no longer at the circumference, but at the center, of the state. For forty-eight separate units to seek to compete with the integrated power of giant capitalism is to invite defeat in every element of social life where approximate uniformity of condition is the test of the good life.

The poor state is parasitic on the body politic. It offers privileges to giant capitalism to obtain its taxable capacity, offers escape from the impositions of rich states in order to wrest from the wealthy some poor meed of compensation for its backwardness. It dare not risk offending the great industrial empires — cotton, coal, iron and steel, tobacco — lest it lose the benefits of their patronage. Their vested interests thus begin to define the limits within which the units of the federation may venture to move. And since the division of powers limits, in its turn, the authority of the federal government to intervene — the latter being a government of limited powers — it follows that the great industrial empires can, in fact, prevent the legislation necessary to implement the purposes of a democratic society.

The situation may, briefly, be summarized by saying that the Constitution inhibits the federal government from exercising the authority inherent in the idea of a democracy; while the risk to a state government of attack upon the conditions exacted by those industrial empires for their patronage is too great to permit the states to jeopardize what they have by issuing challenge. Whether, therefore, it be the hours of labor, the standards of health and housing, the effective organization of the trade unions, at every point the formal powers of the states are rarely commensurate with the actual authority they may venture to exercise. And it is the common citizen of the United States who pays the price of that margin between formal and effective power.

Political systems live by the results they can obtain for the great mass of their citizens. A democracy is not likely to survive on formal grounds merely; it will survive as it is able to convince its citizens that it adequately protects their powers to satisfy the expectations they deem their experience to warrant. In the present phase of American capitalist democracy, the central government largely lacks the power to implement the ends it is essential it should serve if its democratic context is to be maintained. It cannot obtain adequate standards of government in many of the major fields it seeks to enter. It is hamstrung, partly by the division of powers from which it derives its authority; partly because the Constitution has not enabled it to develop the instrumentalities essential to the purposes it must seek to fulfill.

Its effort to obtain the proper recognition of collective bargaining may be stricken into impotence by a state law against picketing. Its effort to produce proper control of public utilities may be rendered vain by local franchises granted in a period when the recognition of the need for uniformity in this field had not dawned upon the public consciousness. So, also, with conservation; with the provision of adequate educational opportunity; with the effective prohibition (a commonplace of any well ordered state) of child labor; with the coordination of relief for unemployment; with public works, especially in the utilization of the possible sources of electric power; with public-health legislation, not least in the field of maternity and child hygiene; with a proper policy of public roads — witness the breakdown of federal-state cooperation in Arkansas in 1923, in Kansas in 1926, and Maine in 1929; with a proper policy in housing. I take examples only. The central point of my argument is the simple one that in every major field of social regulation, the authority of which the federal government can dispose is utterly inadequate to the issues it is expected to solve.

I do not think this argument is invalidated by the rise of cooperation between the federal government and the states, or between groups of states. . . .

I am not arguing that the administration of government services ought to be centralized in Washington. . . . My argument is the very different one: that (a) there are certain objects of administrative control now left to the states for which they are no longer suitable units of regulation. Economic centralization makes necessary at least minimum standards of uniform performance in these objects, e.g., health, education, unemployment relief; and, in others, e.g., labor conditions, railroad rates, electric power, complete federal control without interference by the states; and (b) that the proper objects of federal supervision cannot any longer be dependent upon state consent. Where this dependency exists, state consent will be, in its turn, largely controlled by giant capitalism. That is why Delaware is merely a pseudonym of the du Ponts, and Montana little more than a symbol of the Anaconda Copper Corporation. That is why the people of the state of Washington, who ought long ago to have been permitted to have the advantage of the municipal electric-power plant of Seattle, still suffer from the division of its potential benefits through the survival of the Puget Sound Light and Power Company.

Nor would the problem be met if, instead of the states, America were divided, as writers like Professor Howard Odum suggest, into regions more correspondent with the economic realities of the situation. If America were to consist of seven or nine regions instead of forty-eight states, that would still leave unsolved the main issues if they operated upon the basis of the present division of powers, and if their consent were necessary to any fundamental change in that division. Once again, it must be emphasized that the unity which giant capitalism postulates in the economic sphere postulates a corresponding unity in the conference of political powers upon the federal government. There is no other way, up to a required minimum, in which the questions of taxation, labor relations and conditions, conservation, public utilities (in the widest sense), to take examples only, can be met.

At this point, of course, the relation of a federal system to the power of judicial review becomes fundamental. No one now believes Marshall's famous assertion that "courts are the mere instruments of the law, and can will nothing"; it has been obvious, above all since the Civil War, that the Supreme Court is the effective master of federal legislation. And it is clear, further, that this mastery is exercised in the main, not on objective tests of constitutionality (which do not exist) but upon the accident of a temporary majority's view of what it is "reasonable" for the federal government to undertake.

The Court has become a nonelective third chamber of the government which may, as in the income-tax cases, defeat for many years purposes of which its members do not happen to approve. In an epoch of rapid change, it is a grave danger to any

society that the will of a federal legislature should be subject to judicial control, and more especially when, as Marshall said, the amending process is "cumbrous and unwieldy." In a phase of liberal construction the difficulties of judicial review are obscured from the public. But the years before the controversy over the President's Court plan should be a sufficient reminder of the immense dangers lurking within it.

The view here urged, of course, looks toward a fundamental reconstruction of traditional American institutions. It is not impressed by the view, associated with the great name of Mr. Justice Brandeis, that the "curse of bigness" will descend upon any serious departure from the historic contours of federalism. The small unit of government is impotent against the big unit of giant capitalism. It may be that the very power of giant capitalism is no longer of itself compatible with the maintenance of a democratic political structure in society; there is much evidence to support this view. What, at least, is certain is this: that a government the powers of which are not commensurate with its problems will not be able to cope with them. Either, therefore, it must obtain those powers, or it must yield to a form of state more able to satisfy the demands that it encounters. That is the supreme issue before the United States today; and the more closely it is scrutinized, the more obviously does its resolution seem to be bound up with the obsolescence of the federal system.

For that system presents the spectacle of forty-nine governments seeking to deal with issues for many of which they are inappropriate as instrumentalities, whether in the area they cover or in the authority they may invoke. They are checked and balanced upon a theory of the state completely outmoded in the traditional ends upon which its postulates are based.

Giant industry requires a positive state; federalism, in its American form, is geared to vital negations which contradict the implications of positivism. Giant industry requires uniformities in the field of its major influence; American federalism is the inherent foe, both in time and space, of those necessary uniformities. Giant industry, not least, requires the opposition of a unified public will to counteract its tendency to undemocratic procedure through the abuse of power; a federal system of the American kind dissipates the unity of public opinion in those fields where it is most urgently required. And, above all, it is urgent to note that giant industry, in an age of economic contraction, is able to exploit the diversities of a federal scheme, through the delays they permit in the attainment of uniformity, to reactionary ends. Thereby, they discredit the democratic process at a time when it is least able to afford that discredit. For, thereby, the confidence of the citizen body in its power to work out democratic solutions of its problems is gravely undermined.

Men who are deprived of faith by inability to attain results they greatly desire do not long remain content with the institutions under which they live. The price of democracy is the power to satisfy living demands. American federalism, in its traditional form, cannot keep pace with the tempo of the life giant capitalism has evolved. To judge it in terms of its historic success is to misconceive the criteria by which it becomes valid for the present and the future. No political system has the privilege of immortality; and there is no moment so fitting for the consideration of its remaking as that which permits of reconstruction with the prospect of a new era of creative achievement.

122.

ROBERT A. TAFT: New Problems of Government

Robert A. Taft, eldest son of former President William H. Taft, was a U.S. senator from Ohio for fourteen years and one of the most prominent leaders of the Republican Party in this century. An opponent of the New Deal program, Taft also opposed legislation that weakened personal incentives for economic improvement or required excessive government intervention in the lives of citizens. Speaking at a meeting of the Institute of Public Affairs of the University of Virginia on July 14, 1939, Taft pointed out what he considered to be the danger of the policies of the New Deal administration. Taft, who later was nicknamed "Mr. Republican" by the American press, was serving his first term in the Senate. A portion of the July 14 speech is reprinted here.

Source: *A Republican Program*, Cleveland, 1939, pp. 21-34.

THE NEW DEAL PROGRAM has created a vast number of new problems of government. Every activity creates a new problem, and usually an interesting one. Some are well administered; some are hopelessly inefficient; all are experimental and subject to a continual change of policy. Little public attention is paid to them. Few men even in Congress have a comprehensive idea of the countless activities of government. A good many more problems have been created than solved.

But there are two great problems whose solution, in my opinion, is essential if the nation is to survive. I wish to suggest what those problems are, and how the Republicans propose to meet them.

The first and most important problem is that of unemployment. The question is how we can encourage again in the United States the tremendous volume of private enterprise which existed in the twenties. Our national income is still far below that of 1928, although there are 10 million more people today among whom it must be divided. If we could get back to the business activity of those days, we should have a $90 billion income, 40 percent larger than we have today. Any such increase would take up the greater part of the present unemployment. Unless it can be cured, we may have to admit that the whole American system of democratic government is a failure. The people may well have reason to turn to some other system under which men at least can secure work.

Whatever else has resulted from the great increase in government activity . . . it has certainly had the effect of checking private enterprise completely. This country was built up by the constant establishment of new business and the expansion of old businesses. In every city and every village throughout the country, men were constantly starting out on their own initiative to improve on the enterprises of others, or develop a new product. They put a few men to work. If successful, they expanded to employ ten or a hundred or thousands. If unsuccessful, they passed from the picture without need of government subsidy.

New methods of production were found, and small industries expanded into large industries. Men were willing to spend their time and their money in order that they might provide more completely for themselves and their family in their old age, in order that they might rise above the average standard of living and enjoy a little more luxury or a little more power. In the last six years this process has come to an end because of government regulation and the development of a tax system which penalizes hard work and success. We must and can resume the progress which returned us to prosperity after every depression, but it can only be done by a radical change in government policy.

The policy of fixing the prices of basic commodities has been frequently attempted in history, and has always failed in the end, usually resulting in lower prices for those whom it attempted to benefit. I believe that most of the laws attempting to regulate prices and wages should be repealed, although I believe in a minimum wage law to protect unorganized employees against oppression where the right of collective bargaining cannot be made effective. Laws attempting to dictate the amount of production and the method of operating agriculture and business should be repealed. Those resulting from some definite abuse should be confined to the cure of that abuse.

The SEC should confine itself to the prevention of fraud in the sale of securities. The NLRB should confine itself to seeing that the employees of each employer obtain, through collective bargaining, what they themselves really desire.

The limitation of farm production and the making of unsound loans on crops for the sole purpose of maintaining prices should come to an end.

Government competition with private industry should be confined to its present limits, and assurance given that it will not be expanded into other fields.

The government should gradually withdraw from the business of lending money and leave that function to private capital under proper regulation.

The whole tax system should be reformed to put a premium on expansion of industry and the risking of private money in the development of new and old enterprises.

The capital gains tax should be substantially modified, so that such risks as result in profit may not be subjected to high surtaxes.

Above all, the laws must be administered with a constant effort to encourage the development of private industry. There must be a real sympathy with its success, a real desire to relieve it from unnecessary harassment and discouragement. There must be a recognition of the fact that the making of profits is not a crime; that the average businessman, making a success in his own business, is an essential cog in the national machine, and ought to be encouraged, as long as it does not cost the taxpayer any money.

I am convinced that we can restore prosperity. We have come out of every past depression by the recovery of private industry. The American people are the same people they were in the twenties. They have the same ingenuity and courage and determination. Human nature is the same now as it was then. There are just as many wants unsatisfied, or more. There are just as many economic and scientific frontiers as there ever were. After all, it is fifty years since we had any physical frontiers, and most of that time we have been a prosperous nation. It can be done, but it cannot be done by government regulation of agriculture and commerce and industry.

The other new problem which must be solved is that of adjusting our expenses to our income. How can we maintain the humanitarian measures I have described within a tax system that does not completely bog down the industrial machine? If anything is certain, it is that a continuation of the present policy of reckless expenditure, without regard to taxes, can only lead to bankruptcy, repudiation, and a breakdown of our entire economic life. No government has ever continued a deficit policy without ultimate repudiation. Sooner or later the time comes when the burden of debt is so great that the people refuse to meet the expense of the interest. The temptation to pay in paper money becomes politically irresistible. Leading as it must to inflated prices, it wipes out the savings of the people and bears down most heavily on the groups with fixed income, to the benefit only of successful speculators. If we ever reach the point which Germany reached after the World War, it is doubtful if we could ever reestablish a system based on thrift and saving and investment of funds in private enterprise. The American system as we know it would not survive.

People say that the budget cannot be balanced, but of course it can be if a courageous government determines that it shall be. Expenses can be reduced; taxes can be increased. Probably a combination of both will be necessary. The people must face the fact that if we are going to give government help to the more unfortunate families, through relief, pensions, insurance, housing, and medical assistance, that help will have to be supplied by those who do not require it themselves. It cannot come from the rich, because if we confiscate all the incomes over $10,000 a year, we would only get $7 billion, and the total tax bill today is already $18 billion. It can only come from the two-thirds who are not underprivileged — from the average prudent and successful workman.

The only people who can support men and women who do not work are those who are working. Obviously the humanitarian measures must be administered as economically as possible. Pensions cannot be carelessly increased, as the Congress has just increased the old-age pension from $30 to $40, unless a majority of the people are willing to pay the taxes necessary to pay the increase. I was shocked by the fact that Wednesday a dozen senators voted a pension which would cost the people $5 billion without the slightest suggestion of any way in which the money could possibly be raised. There must be an utter repudiation of that point of view.

Furthermore, these laws should be administered so that the recipients of government assistance are not placed in a better position through that assistance than the other workmen with private jobs, who have saved their own money and have to provide the taxes. There has been too much tendency on the part of each department to look only at its own job, and try to please its wards by a liberal administration in its particular field. The man who lives in government housing should not be better off than the man who has built his own home out of his own savings. The man who gets an old-age pension should not be better off than he who has spent his life in making provision for his own old age. In short, measures to assist the lower-income groups must be administered with just as much consideration for the middle-income groups, who have to do the paying, as for the lower-income groups.

The budget can be balanced. Economy can be secured even in relief without decreasing its efficiency. If administration were returned to the localities, with full discretion to administer both work relief and direct relief in the manner best suited to local conditions, the federal government would pay less, even though it supplied two-thirds of the entire cost. There would be far more equal treatment of those on relief; more liberal treatment for direct relief clients than

today. Housing can be cheaper, and there does not need to be the large subsidy required by the present program. . . .

It is no easy task to economize. It cannot be done effectively over the opposition of the Executive, for many federal policies can be changed only by affirmative legislation, which the Executive can block. For instance, until the relief policy is completely changed, we must go on voting the appropriations required by the present WPA system. Economy cannot be secured piecemeal, for each project has its appeal, and often a very attractive appeal. Some leadership must develop a plan for balancing the budget within two years and hold Congress to it.

This is the proper function of the Executive, but if the Executive will not do it, Congress will have to create a budget committee of its own. The findings of such a committee can only be carried through with a strong leadership for economy, backed by a majority of the members in both houses of Congress. I feel confident that expenses can be reduced by several billions of dollars; that a tax system can produce the necessary income in a way that will not destroy the very income which is to provide the taxes. It can be done, but it cannot be done by neglecting the fundamental principles of common sense.

The cost of government will continue to increase, I care not what party is in power.

REED SMOOT, speech in the Senate

123.

Grace Overmyer: Report on the WPA Four Arts Project

The Works Progress Administration (WPA), established in 1935, attacked the unemployment problem by providing jobs in various public works projects. By 1939, WPA had employed over eleven million people at a cost of $6 billion. Among the most effective projects were the special programs providing work for unemployed artists. Writers prepared guidebooks, systematized archives, and performed research; painters and sculptors decorated public buildings; musicians organized symphony orchestras; and theater groups brought live drama to small towns. In 1939, the last year in which WPA received significant appropriations, Grace Overmyer issued a report on the Four Arts Project, of which a portion is reprinted here.

Source: *Government and the Arts*, New York, 1939: "Our Little Renaissance."

FROM THE STANDPOINTS both of expenditure and scope, the temporary Four Arts Projects, inaugurated by the United States in August 1935 as a measure of unemployment relief, constitute what is probably the most extensive program for artists' rehabilitation ever undertaken by a government.

Out of the original Works Progress Administration appropriation of $2 billion, the Arts Project upon their creation received an allocation of $27 million to provide suitable professional work for writers, painters, musicians, and actors whom economic conditions had deprived of their usual means of livelihood. By January 1938, the original allocation for the Arts Projects had been increased to $105 million, of which $87 million had been expended.

In a country whose previous official art activities had generally been of little public moment — often, indeed, escaping public notice altogether — the announcement late in 1935 of the government's intention to spend $27 million for the arts was received in some quarters with incredulity. By a section of the press it was praised as humane, idealistic, and farseeing; by another, denounced as unnecessary and wasteful.

The plan, however, was quickly put into operation, national and state directors were appointed, offices were established throughout the country, and, before six months had passed, approximately 40,000 men and women — of whom 75 percent were professional followers of the arts and the rest mechanical or clerical assistants — had been enrolled in the following classifications: Art Project, 5,330; Music, 15,629; Theatre, 12,477; Writers, 6,500. Of the total employed, practically two-thirds — including some of the nonprofessional assistants — had "certified as eligible for employment," which was another way of saying that these not only were without means to continue their own work but that they had in most cases reached the deadline of independent financial resources.

Were the economic assistance of a large

contingent of the country's working artists, with consequent restoration of morale and the maintenance and increasing of highly specialized skills, the only achievement of the Federal Arts Projects, their story would be worth the telling. But their total accomplishment is even greater. Begun as a human welfare movement — handicapped by temporariness, stigmatized as "relief," and dogged within by labor troubles and a thousand little human dissonances — the projects have created throughout the country the beginnings of a broad cultural awakening.

TAKING ART INTO NEW PLACES

IN VIEW of the former luxury status of art, the secret of this achievement is not far to seek. Pledged to avoid interference with "normal private employment," the workers on the Arts Projects have been obliged to take art into places where little, if any, art had ever gone before. Their efforts have of necessity been principally directed toward sections of the population unable to pay for artistic entertainment or instruction. Through the Arts Projects, free and popular-priced dramatic and musical entertainment — most of it of good, and some of excellent, quality — and free class instruction in scores of cultural branches incidental to the musical, dramatic, and graphic arts, have been brought to millions of American citizens of the economic stratum generally described as "underprivileged."

The public has been smothered in figures of the Arts Projects' accomplishments until figures have ceased to have much meaning. It is only by presenting statistics in what might be called their social context that some idea of the cultural potentialities of the work may be realized.

Of the 4 million persons who, within two years, participated in activities of the new federally sponsored Community Art Centers — combined art schools and galleries operating in eighteen states — more than half live in sections of the West, Middle West, and South in which art activities had previously been lacking; and the other half, mostly in the poorer parts of cities. Of the 25 million to 30 million persons who attended 1,700 performances by the Federal Theatre between February 1936 — the date of its first play — and the beginning of 1938, fully half were youthful products of the motion-picture era who had never before seen a performance by actors on a stage. Of the stupendous audience total of 92 million, to whom, it is estimated, the Federal Music Project, through more than 100,000 programs, brought "living music" between October 1935 and January 1938, there is reason to reckon that at least nine-tenths lacked the means to attend the high-priced performances in opera houses and concert halls with which the upper tenth of American music lovers is splendidly served.

CULTURAL REDISCOVERY OF AMERICA

IN ADDITION to their economic and social purposes, the four art groups, once established, were soon found to have other common aims. One was to devise measures which would have in them an element of permanency, that the benefits of the activities begun should not be lost after the emergency which had created the projects had passed. Another aim, which manifested itself soon after the work was sufficiently organized to have become broadly national in scope, was that of placing an emphasis on native art. Each project became a sort of road map for the cultural rediscovery of America from within. There seemed to be, on the part of project planners, a common realization that in the United States native art had been too long neglected, and foreign art too long preferred, and that the time had come at least for a national cultural stocktaking.

There seemed to be a common agreement that in return for support by the government, the projects might appropriately explore, interpret, and exhibit the artistic creations of their countrymen, particularly those of an earlier time. This is not to say that a nationalistic spirit has been fostered, that the federal actors have performed only American plays, the federal musicians played only American compositions, or the Federal Art Project painters devoted themselves exclusively to the American scene (the last, indeed, have seemed, on the whole, less inclined to adhere to native subjects than the artists of the Treasury). A thorough exploration of native art, however, involving especially a search of its history and beginnings, has been a major concern of all four groups. Except for their economic and social achievements, this general redefining of native art constitutes the greatest accomplishment of the Four Arts Projects.

THE INDIVIDUAL PROGRAMS

THE STORY of the individual programs of the Arts Projects may be told in its entirety by some vast governmental undertaking of the future, with hundreds of eager workers. Each project would make a book in itself. Each is a record, not only of benefits to working personnel and to communities served but to the advancement, within the period and place of the project's activities, of an individual art.

The statement of the individual programs which follows is necessarily incomplete. It aims, however, to record the variety and scope of those programs, of which the public, in view of the controversy that has

sometimes attended accounts of project activities, may have had a confused and partial picture.

THE ART PROJECT "PROPER"

IN WRITING of many arts and many nations, one finds oneself confronted by a linguistic paradox — or, rather, two of them. The word "art," to designate the plastic and graphic arts, is at once too broad and too narrow. Its use in this sense is comparable to that other thoroughly authorized but never entirely satisfactory custom of calling the United States *America*. Many nations, of course, come under the designation *America*, just as any and all of the fine arts are properly called *art*. But there is need for one distinctive word to limit the visual arts, no less than for one to distinguish the United States from the other Americas — as *music* unmistakably defines the art of beautiful sound, or *Canada*, our northern neighbor.

Endeavoring to be specific within the contradictions of English, one may perhaps be permitted to refer to the group which, among the Arts Projects, stands first in alphabetical order, as the *Art Project Proper*. This provides a more satisfactory label than the somewhat cumbersome one used by the project itself — *WPA Federal Art Project* — which is chiefly useful for distinguishing the painters and sculptors of this group from those working under the Treasury Department.

The personnel of the Art Project Proper includes all the numerous professional classifications (architects excepted) usually associated with art in its narrow sense — painters, sculptors, illustrators, etchers and engravers, arts and crafts workers of many types. There is even a section for photographers, whose duties largely consist in recording the activities of the various projects

Artists demonstrating for jobs in New York City in 1934, before the creation of WPA

and other public work of the government, national, state, or municipal. Several hundred art teachers are employed on the project's educational program. Unemployed architects, of whom the depression created many, have been for the most part assigned to construction projects of the WPA, where there is opportunity for utilization of their professional training.

In accordance with the rule that no private profit may be made out of work done on government time, all the works completed by the Art Project Proper are available, as indefinite loans, to tax-supported institutions, the recipient paying all but labor costs of the production. Assigned as loans instead of gifts, the works remain the property of the government. They may not be sold or given away by the institution to which they are allocated.

The art loans in the main have been enthusiastically received. It is only truthful to record, however, that there have been occasional differences of opinion between borrower and lender as to aesthetic values. Institutions and citizens in some cases have been unreceptive to the "modern" idiom, in which some, although by no means all, of the offerings of the Federal Art Project are executed. A few taxpayers have objected to the acquisition of certain murals which have a leaning toward social satire or caricature.

Despite such dissensions, ranging from mild to vehement, more than 13,000 institutions in the first three years of the project's work received loans of 186,452 artworks; and requests from hospitals, schools, and other institutions far exceeded the number that could be produced. In the total allocation there are, besides easel paintings, etchings, and lithographs, more than 1,000 murals — including mosaics and paintings in fresco, oils, and tempera — and over 1,700 sculptures. In the permanent sculptural work done for public buildings, emphasis is placed upon the creation of designs suitable to the architecture of the building. In addition to murals, sculpture, and purely decorative works, the Art Project has produced a large number of posters, maps, and diagrams. Including such items, a grand total of over a million works has been allocated by this project.

Besides the works allocated, paintings by

project artists have been purchased by the Metropolitan Museum of New York, the Phillips Memorial Gallery of Washington, and other famous galleries. Twenty-five thousand works by WPA artists are being circulated throughout the country in traveling exhibitions.

INDEX OF AMERICAN DESIGN

THE OUTSTANDING CONTRIBUTION to the history of American art of the Art Project Proper is the Index of American Design, which may be described as a work of research in the field of American decorative art of the past. The Index consists of a collection of paintings and drawings of articles in everyday use — ranging all the way from fabrics, jewelry, furniture, and cooking utensils to ships' mastheads and barn weather vanes — which are designed or decorated in patterns of distinctly American origin. Only pre-twentieth-century designs are included.

Each object pictured by the Design Index artists is thoroughly authenticated and dated, and its creator or original owner, wherever possible, identified. Libraries and museums, historical societies, and private collections are combed for material. As a result of this work, 10,000 illustrations, many of them in color, have become available as reference material for students and others making a study of American decoration. The Index operates in thirty-two states and employs more than 400 people.

INDEX OF AMERICAN COMPOSERS

FOR MANY YEARS the United States has suffered from an alleged lack of worthwhile musical creativeness. The Music Project's discovery, therefore, of nearly seventy symphonies and a dozen operas and operettas by native or resident composers comes as a gratifying surprise to those who have believed that few American composers aspired to serious creative effort.

This discovery is incidental to the compilation by the musicians' group of an Index of American Composers, which, in its aim to provide an historical record of native creative art, is similar to the Art Project's Design Index. A considerable part of the work of the Music Index staff has been devoted to identification of early compositions obtained from manuscript collections or from libraries of old music publishers. Such matters as theme sources and derivations, particularly from folk or primitive songs and tunes, are given special attention.

The Music Index, however, is not limited to pre-twentieth-century work, but is a collection of such American compositions as have historical interest or musical significance, dating from early colonial times until today. Begun in March 1936, it contained, at the end of two years, 5,500 works by about 1,500 native or resident Americans. In addition to the symphonies and operas there are disclosed 35 American concertos; and these, considering that a concerto is usually a symphony with a glorified solo part, may bring the number of orchestral works in largest form up above 100. Religious music is also generously represented, there being numerous compositions in this field, including oratorios, sacred cantatas, and liturgical works. There are also chamber music compositions, orchestral suites, band pieces, and of course many songs and instrumental solos.

The significance of the Music Index is enhanced by the fact that all the works it has collected have been given public performance by Music Project units, with the full instrumental, vocal, choral, or dramatic embellishments called for by the composer. With a total in 110 cities of 122 symphony and concert orchestras made up of players of high professional competence, 67 bands and 55 dance orchestras, as well as choral groups, opera units, and chamber ensembles, the Music Project has the requisite performing equipment for compositions of practically any kind. While the great classics supply the backbone of its best public performances, there is scarcely a program by a project orchestra which does not include at least one unfamiliar American number. A very important part of this project's service to contemporary music has been in performing little-known compositions which otherwise might have had to wait long to be heard, and in providing opportunities for concert appearances of young soloists, for whom the cost of debuts under the usual expensive and highly competitive conditions prevailing in the professional musical world would be prohibitive.

COMPOSERS' FORUM LABORATORIES

IN THE PERFORMANCE of new American works that may be described as experimental — creative efforts in unfamiliar idioms and relatively untried forms — the Composers' Forum Laboratories are fostering a purpose not served by any other agency in the country. Here the composer has not only the privilege of hearing an entire program of his own works performed with complete instrumentation but also the advantage of appraisal and suggestions from a critical and musically enlightened audience. Forum laboratories are held in New York, Boston, and Chicago, semimonthly through the music season, and at less frequent intervals in Detroit, Milwaukee, Los Angeles, and Indianapolis.

In addition to its vast performing section, this largest of the projects has maintained more than 250 music-teaching centers, in which 1,400 former private music teachers have been employed and many thousands of persons of all ages have received free class instruction, which has included the playing of practically every instrument as well as singing, musical history, theory, and composition. There is also a program for the retraining of music teachers, to which distinguished musicians and educators contribute instruction and lectures.

The Music Project has established a rigid system of audition tests, before qualified judges, for applicants for employment on the project, and only musicians who are professionally competent are accepted. Those rejected may be assigned to the recreation projects of the WPA.

THE FEDERAL THEATRE

IN ITS EFFORTS to combat the effects of mass production on public entertainment, the Theatre Project has a problem peculiarly its own. Of all the professional fields employing artists, the stage is most affected by changes described as technological and by failure of the profession to adjust itself to those changes. Even before the period of the depression, unemployment among actors had attained a degree for which the word "acute" is all too mild. A record compiled in New York in 1927-28 — at the height of the prosperity period — showed that the average of employment among 6,031 members of Equity, the actors' union, ranged from three and one-half to nine weeks a year! A well-known actor-manager has made the statement that "almost every actor is unemployed five times a year."

The Theatre Project has never, of course, been able to provide work for all the unemployed actors and stage people in the country. At the peak of its activities it had on its payroll 12,700 persons and operated 158 companies in 27 states. After the drastic cuts in project personnel in 1937 it still, with 8,500 employees, operated 99 companies in 22 states. About half of the persons employed are actors; the others, writers, designers, theatre musicians, dancers, stagehands, box-office men, ushers, maintenance workers, and the necessary secretarial and accounting forces.

In 1938 the largest Federal Theatre projects were in New York, with 4,011 persons; Los Angeles, with 1,289; Chicago, 768. More than 100 separate Federal Theatre plays were seen in New York City from February 1936 to February 1938. In the same period, community drama, under the direction of project workers, was given in New York in 390 centers located in hospitals, schools, and settlement houses. By March 1938, 1,500 of the actors employed at various times on the project had re-

turned, at least temporarily, to private jobs.

The offerings of the Federal Theatre range all the way from pure drama and the classics, through local color and sociological plays, to marionette, vaudeville, and circus performances. In the course of experiments with the theatre as a force in education and therapeutics, the project has organized hand marionette companies to work in hospitals with children having paralyzed hands. Experiments, the benefits of which are open to the entire theatrical industry, are also being carried on in theatre forms, costuming, scenery, and lighting.

124.

JOHN CROWE RANSOM: "Address to the Scholars of New England"

John Crowe Ransom, professor of English (until 1937) at Vanderbilt University, poet, and founder of the Kenyon Review, *wrote poems that were notable for their wit, irony, and delicacy. On June 23, 1939, he read the following poem, "Address to the Scholars of New England," at a Harvard University commencement ceremony.*

Source: *Poems and Essays,* New York, 1955.

ADDRESS TO THE SCHOLARS OF NEW ENGLAND

(Harvard Phi Beta Kappa Poem, June 23, 1939)

> When Sarah Pierrepont let her spirit rage
> Her love and scorn refused the bauble earth
> (Which took bloom even here, under the Bear)
> And groped for the Essence sitting in himself,
> Subtle, I think, for a girl's unseasoned rage.
>
> The late and sudden extravagance of soul
> By which they all were swollen exalted her
> At seventeen years to Edwards' canopy,
> A match pleasing to any Heaven, had not
> The twelve mortal labors harassed her soul.

Thrifty and too proud were the sea-borne fathers
Who fetched the Pure Idea in a bound box
And fastened him in a steeple, to have his court
Shabby with an unkingly establishment
And Sabbath levees for the minion fathers.

The majesty of Heaven has a great house,
And even if the Indian kingdom or the fox
Ran barking mad in a wide forest place,
They had his threshold, and you had the dream
Of property in him by a steepled house.

If once the entail shall come on raffish sons,
Knife-wit scholar and merchant sharp in thumb,
With positive steel they'll pry into the steeple,
And blinking through the cracked ribs at the void
A judgment laughter rakes the cynic sons.

But like prevailing wind New England's honor
Carried, and teased small Southern boys in school,
Whose heads the temperate birds fleeing your winter
Construed for, but the stiff heroes abashed
With their frozen fingers and unearthly honor.

Scared by the holy megrims of those Pilgrims,
I thought the unhumbled and outcast and cold
Were the rich Heirs traveling incognito,
Bred too fine for the country's sweet produce
And but affecting that dog's life of pilgrims.

There used to be debate of soul and body,
The soul storming incontinent with shrew's tongue
Against what natural brilliance body had loved,
Even the green phases though deciduous
Of earth's zodiac homage to the body.

Plato, before Plotinus gentled him,
Spoke the soul's part, and though its vice is known
We're in his shadow still, and it appears
Your founders most of all the nations held
By his scandal-mongering, and established him.

Perfect was the witch foundering in water,
The blasphemer that spraddled in the stocks,
The woman branded with her sin, the whales
Of ocean taken with a psalmer's sword,
The British tea infusing the bay's water.

But they reared heads into the always clouds
And stooped to the event of war or bread,
The secular perforces and short speech
Being labors surlily done with the left hand,
The chief strength giddying with transcendent clouds.

The tangent Heavens mocked the fathers' strength,
And how the young sons know it, and study now
To take fresh conquest of the conquered earth,
But they're too strong for that, you've seen them whip
The laggard will to deeds of lunatic strength.

To incline the powerful living unto peace
With Heaven is easier now, with Earth is hard,
Yet a rare metaphysic makes them one,
A gentle Majesty, whose myrtle and rain
Enforce the fathers' gravestones unto peace.

I saw the youngling bachelors of Harvard
Lit like torches, and scrambling to disperse
Like aimless firebrands pitiful to slake,
And if there's passion enough for half their flame,
Your wisdom has done this, sages of Harvard.

125.

ANDRÉ MAUROIS: Impressions of a Long Voyage

A frequent visitor to the United States, the distinguished French novelist, essayist, and biographer André Maurois became popular during the 1930s as a lecturer and raconteur. He traveled extensively around the country and in 1939 published a book on his experiences, Etats-Unis 39: Journal d'un voyage en Amérique. *A selection from this work is reprinted here.*

Source: TWA, pp. 554-568.

THE DAUGHTERS of the American Revolution are the women or girls whose ancestors took part a hundred and fifty years ago in the war for independence. In France we lack this type of aristocracy. The Sons of the Regicides do not hold conventions in Bourges nor the Daughters of the Victims of the Terror at Nantes. That's because our regimes followed each other so rapidly that each wiped out the loyalties of its predecessors; the conquerors of the Bastille ceased to hold reunions as soon as Bonaparte came upon the scene. In America the continuity of the regime permitted the Revolution to become hereditary and conservative.

Nevertheless, the D.A.R. this year had

troublous times. They refused to rent their concert hall in Washington to Marian Anderson, a colored singer universally admired. Mrs. Roosevelt, who belonged by right of birth to the D.A.R., with reason condemned the action and handed in her resignation. Marian Anderson sang in the open air and was acclaimed by an immense crowd. When the convention met in Washington, the ladies, somewhat penitent, tried to make peace; they voted a resolution condemning German racism. According to custom, they were invited to the White House, but the First Lady was not at home to receive them. Nevertheless, this morning, at their final meeting, they passed a vote of thanks to Mrs. Roosevelt because, their president pointed out, although Mrs. Roosevelt was absent she had ordered their sandwiches. The net effect: a large number of Negroes who have voted for the Republicans since the Civil War will vote Democratic next time.

I THINK IT WAS J. B. PRIESTLEY who last year noticed the importance of the Cinderella theme in American movies. A young girl badly dressed, badly made-up, assists in the triumph of her more fortunate sisters, not with envy, but with sorrow. Suddenly, the prince charming, a famous orchestra director, a powerful producer, an important businessman, discovers that Miss Deanna Cinderella, his typist, is the greatest singer, the greatest actress, or the greatest designer in the world, and, in a sudden reversal of roles, misery gives way to glory, just as once Scheherazade's cobbler became sultan.

Fairy tales are always true. In the Orient the cobbler could become sultan; before my very eyes Lyautey performed that miracle. In America it is literally true that magicians and fairies are ready each morning to transform a manicurist into a singer, and her bus into a limousine. Social ranks are less rigid here than elsewhere, generosity more spectacular, and success more sudden.

There are even Americans who have adopted as a vocation the search for Cinderella. Last night, for instance, friends took us to see a curious spectacle, Major Bowes' "The Amateur Hour." The scene was the broadcasting studio of a radio station. About a thousand spectators were there. Like all American programs, this was sponsored by a business firm; Major Bowes officiated for an automobile company. The salary list published by the Treasury Department informs us that he earns $450,000 a year. Any man or woman who thinks he has a singing voice, talent for acting, ability to dance or to play an instrument can write to him. If the letter seems interesting it will be answered with the offer of an audition. Among the thousands of candidates who thus come forward each week, twelve or fifteen are chosen to appear on the air before the American public.

You may thus see an unknown young man step before the microphone. "What is your name?" asks Major Bowes. — "John Hewitt." — "And what is your occupation, John?" — "I work for a building firm, Major." — "But you sing also?" — "I sing for my pleasure, but I have never taken any lessons." — "Would you like to take any?" — "There's nothing I would like better, Major . . . Music means everything to me." — "Well you sing something for us and if your voice deserves it, we will find you a teacher." John then sings, and 30,000,000 Americans listen to him, for the Amateur Hour is very popular. John has a very pleasant natural baritone voice. He has hardly finished when telephone congratulations begin to come into the basement where more than a hundred operators are ready to receive calls from all parts of the Union. Before the end of the program, Major Bowes announces that Angelo Tirani, of the B. . . Opera, offers to accept John as a pupil without charge. There, without doubt, the whole course of a life is changed.

In two minutes are laid the foundations

of future glories. Four Negro children, marvelous musicians, are so good that the Cotton Club, a famous New York night club, hires them on the spot. A little girl, gracefully charming, a new Shirley Temple, goes to Hollywood for a screen test. The public, which is kept informed of the votes registered by telephone, shares in the joy of those who triumph. Several artists are engaged by Major Bowes himself who directs a number of shows.

Without doubt, such things are also possible in Europe and we have more than once seen the destiny of a young writer transformed in a few seconds by the vote of a jury. But the *coups de théâtre* in an old country are less astonishing, and one rarely sees a whole nation take part with pleasure in their preparation. Here the fairy tale is not only possible; it is of the very essence of life. Cinderella herself becomes prima donna, is transformed into the fairy godmother, and in turn gives millions of dollars to help Cinderellas of the next generation emerge from their chrysalis. New York, Chicago, Boston, are cities full of sordid corners in which frightful miseries are hidden. But from every American city every evening rises the voice of Scheherazade, who tells stories consoling and true.

Some Americans deplore such sentimentality. "It is unhealthy," they say, "to give people this absurd confidence in the lucky accident. Better the sad realism of your French films, the shabby and hopeless lives of the residents of *Hôtel du Nord*. That is more accurate, more courageous, and more human." But those who speak in this fashion are the poets and critics of New York, already spoiled by European disillusionment. The rest of America holds to its fairy tales. . . .

WHAT TOTAL IMPRESSION does a long voyage leave? This is an immense country made up of overpopulated islands sprinkled among the prairies, the forests, and the deserts.

Among these islets of skyscrapers there is hardly any common life. The newspapers of Minneapolis are not read in Cincinnati. The great man of Tulsa is unknown in Dallas. The Negro of Georgia, the Swede of Minnesota, the Mexican of San Antonio, and the German of Chicago, Marquand's patricians, and Steinbeck's tramps are all citizens of the United States, but there is slight resemblance among them. Often in the last few months I was struck with the question of whether the unity of this country was not artificial, whether it was capable of survival.

Today, classifying, sorting out, reviewing these memories under the ocean sky, I came to an answer: This unity will come through. Despite the aspects of diversity, a common basis does exist. Let me try to enumerate the ties which strengthen American unity.

It is obviously an error to say that the interests of these regions are different, that the agricultural Middle West wants a rise in the price of wheat, that the industrial East wants wages low, that the same laws cannot satisfy both, and that they will end by separating. Diversity of production, on the contrary, renders the Union indispensable to all. The East could not get along without the Middle West, the farmer without the laborer, and economic unity prescribes political unity.

A curious unity of habits and thoughts is created by the movies, the magazines, the radio, advertising, and the newspaper chains. The daily newspaper rarely circulates beyond the limits of one state; but *Time, Life, The Saturday Evening Post, The New Yorker*, and ten others are seen everywhere; Amos and Andy are heard by more than 30,000,000 listeners; the articles of Walter Lippmann and of Dorothy Thompson are reproduced by 200 papers and read by 7,000,000 readers. Through the efforts of the Book of the Month Club the same volume is distributed in the same week from the Atlantic to the Pacific. Thus the Americans who never meet each other and who live under different skies come to have innumerable common memories and brotherly thoughts.

Little by little the American federation is transforming itself into a union, marked by the growth in importance of the role of the federal capital. In the beginning, the United States had only a small federal bureaucracy. Today the central administration is powerful and rich. Public assistance is already in large part within its province. Sooner or later that will also be true of education. Some day the railroads will be unified. One may regret that tendency, but its power cannot be denied.

Finally, most of the citizens of the United States are united by a common faith; they believe in their institutions and in the virtues of liberty. They believe in the possibility of a better future for a free people. They even hope that an understanding of free peoples everywhere will some day prevent most wars. In a word, they are optimists.

Or, more accurately, they were. The extent and persistence of unemployment, the length of the crisis, the stalemate in economic experimentation, have struck deeply at this American faith. The young men and women in the universities, the workers in the factories, the farmers on the marginal lands begin to ask if the system is likely to live long. Foreign propaganda, communist and totalitarian alike, stirs up their resentment. Roosevelt appeases discontent somewhat by distributing acquired wealth; but when the day comes when the reserves are exhausted, it will not be easy to govern America.

Basically, the problem lies not in a choice between two opposing solutions, communism or fascism, Roosevelt or laissez-faire, but in a levy on each theory for the elements of validity it contains. Hegel's formula — thesis, antithesis, synthesis — is always true. A directed economy does not function well; total liberalism is unhappily no longer possible. Absolute laissez-faire presumed that the passions and desires of individuals, their hopes and their fears, would assure the equilibrium of the market by millions of compensations. That was once true. But in a world where propaganda and information spread in a few seconds throughout the planet, happy indifference no longer serves as counterfoil to error, ignorance is no longer the marvelous buffer that deadens the follies of the reasoning reason. The machine has lost its regulator. And, of course, how can one speak of classical liberalism in a period of cartels, of trusts, of monopolies? But to reinforce by a state economy the existing rigidity of the mechanism would be to act like a man with high blood pressure who takes adrenalin to raise it.

What must be done? I believe we must act the cautious doctor, try what we have, let that alone which works, try what remedies are at hand, increase the doses of medicines which seem to succeed, change the method if it seems to fail, and, above all, keep up the patient's morale. It seems to me that the weakest point in the recent American experiences was that they were almost all directed against someone. One class was ranged against another. No government can thus construct an enduring system. A government has the right to be firm; it has the right to be severe and to demand a respect for the laws; but it has not the right to hate. We will not emerge from our present difficulties by class war, but by love and by a mutual effort of intelligence and understanding.

Nothing will kill the movies except education.
WILL ROGERS

126.

CULBERT L. OLSON: Migratory Labor and Civil Liberties

Some of the worst poverty in the nation existed among the migrant farm workers of California. These people, who followed the harvest season from section to section, were recruited from the poorest segments of society and received the lowest possible pay for their work. Attempts to organize the workers met with little success, partly because the workers never remained in one place very long but also because employers were not above resorting to violence. In 1939 a subcommittee of the Senate Committee on Education and Labor, under its chairman, Robert M. La Follette, Jr., of Wisconsin, visited California to investigate violations of the workers' civil liberties. In December Governor Culbert Olson of California gave testimony to the committee, from which the following selection is taken.

Source: *Violations of Free Speech and Rights of Labor, Hearings Before a Subcommittee of the Committee on Education and Labor, U.S. Senate,* 76 Congress, 2 Session, Washington, 1940, Pt. 47, pp. 17244-17254.

AT THE OUTSET, gentlemen, I should like to say that of all the grave and serious problems which the present administration has inherited from prior administrations, none is, perhaps, more acute than that of migratory farm labor in this state. . . .

A migratory worker is likely to be regarded as a stranger or "alien" in the many communities in which he is forced to work during the course of a single year. Many migratory workers are not, of course, residents of the counties in which they are employed during those periods when, for example, labor disputes may occur. Thus they lack not only the security necessary to give bargaining strength but the means of political retaliation for unfair or illegal treatment. If they are residents of any one county in California, they are seldom residents of those counties in which the denial of civil liberties is likely to occur. Strangers, in any community, particularly in rural communi-

ties, are regarded with a certain amount of provincial suspicion and potential ill will.

Migratory workers, particularly with the large degree of turnover that is common in agricultural employment in this state, seldom have an opportunity to make themselves generally known in any one community. One year they may work in a given number of counties, and the next year they may follow an entirely different route. It is impossible to state, with any degree of accuracy, how many migratory workers are actually residents of California; nor can it be estimated what percentage have been able to comply with statutory requirements in order to vote. But it is safe to say that a very large percentage of migratory workers in California during any given period are not voters.

As long as this state of affairs continues to exist, unequal treatment at the hands of certain local law-enforcement agencies in the state is likely to occur. In the last analysis, it is largely because migratory workers are a socially disadvantaged class in California that their civil liberties have been frequently violated. For the most part, they lack the means, individually and collectively, to defend themselves against illegal practices of the type that will be revealed during the course of your investigation.

Another factor which has encouraged undue interference with the right of agricultural labor to bargain collectively in this state is the physical difficulties involved in organization. It is inherently difficult, for example, for a nondescript army of migratory workers to organize themselves into trade unions.

On many occasions, over a period of forty years, agricultural workers have attempted to organize for purposes of collective bargaining in California. But the physical difficulties involved have been almost as influential in discouraging organization as the undue influence of employer groups. I can but mention merely a few of these difficulties: the lack of understanding among different racial groups; the low earnings resulting in inability to support or maintain an organization once effected; the difficulty of maintaining an organizational structure during the period of seasonal unemployment; and the constant influx of new workers unfamiliar with local conditions. Your own investigations have clearly indicated that workers must organize for self-protection. As long as workers are not organized in California agriculture, they are likely to be subjected to discriminatory treatment of one kind or another, and, as long as the bulk of agricultural workers are migratory workers, difficulties of the type I have mentioned will hinder organization.

It is quite impossible to understand the difficulties of protecting the civil liberties of agricultural workers in California apart from an understanding of the psychological tensions which make for bitterness in labor disputes in this field. Because of the nature of our agriculture, crops in this state represent an enormous investment in money, time, and effort on the part of employers. Many of these crops are, moreover, perishable in character. Certain areas of the state emphasize off-season production in which the element of timing in reaching a particular Eastern market is of the greatest importance to the grower.

It is quite natural, under these circumstances, that growers should regard, with great bitterness, any stoppage of work during the harvest season. Crops in this state must be harvested quickly or an entire year's investment may be lost. A great amount of the rancor and bitterness which many farm groups in this state feel toward organized labor can be traced to this constant fear of possible interruption of work during the harvest season.

Under the other hand, the miserable living and working conditions of migratory labor, the appalling low earnings available for this type of labor at present make workers desperate. The bitterness which these conditions create among workers is just as intense as the bitterness felt by growers during a labor dispute. Fear is the element that has created the appalling bitterness, which in the past has too frequently resulted in riots, bloodshed, and murder — a fear of the loss of crops on the part of growers — fear of starvation on the part of workers. As long as this psychological tension exists — and it exists in California today — the problem of maintaining civil liberties is inherently difficult.

It is not only the growers and workers who are under the type of economic pressure that I have mentioned, for many of the townspeople in the rural areas also become involved in the same complex of forces. Many areas in the state are directly dependent upon agriculture. It is understandable, therefore, that in these areas the entire community should feel that it is directly involved in the outcome of a particular labor dispute.

The townspeople themselves become active partisans, usually on the side of the grower interests, and the entire community is divided into hostile camps. Many townspeople in the rural areas have slight sympathy for migratory labor. During the peak labor periods, their hospitals are overcrowded, their schools are overrun with new pupils, and their various social agencies are burdened with the problems incident to this annual influx of nonresident workers. Having slight direct contact with the workers themselves, it is natural that they should regard them as outsiders or strangers. We have had several instances in the past, in California, where vigilante groups have been recruited in the towns. This circumstance does not make the problem of protecting civil liberties any easier in California.

One unfortunate phase of this entire problem of maintaining and protecting civil liberties in the agricultural areas is that until quite recently the workers involved had not developed competent leadership out of their own rank and file.

Sensing the desperate plight of the workers and realizing that they lacked elements of leadership, organizers have entered the rural areas, unfamiliar with local conditions, and have attempted in their zeal to right in a single season the accumulated wrongs and injustices of fifty years. These ultramilitants, not even understanding the temperament of the people among whom they were working, have too often indulged in fiery oratory and have too frequently urged the adoption of methods which would be indefensible in metropolitan areas, but which, when applied in rural areas, constitute grave provocation. These hair-trigger situations which arise in the fields in California make strenuous demands upon the self-restraint and the good sense of every group involved. There is no place in such situations for firebrands, either among employers or employees.

Agricultural labor in California should develop, out of its own ranks, an intelligent, competent, and, above all, a tactful and statesmanlike leadership — a leadership capable of full realization of the acute psychological tensions and economic pressures involved; a leadership that will, in the fullest and deepest sense, really represent the aims and aspirations of farm labor. This leadership must recognize that, if their cause is to be successful, they must win and maintain the confidence of the people of this state. In order that a well-informed and responsible leadership may be developed, there is a great need for workers' education in this field. The presence of irresponsible elements, who assume the functions of leadership and who have no deep roots or ties in the rural communities, only complicates the problem of safeguarding civil liberties in California.

The introduction of modern methods of dealing with industrial relations in the field of farm labor is not going to come about overnight. It is, in fact, an objective that it will take time to achieve in this state under the most favorable circumstances. The swiftness and ease with which it is achieved will largely depend upon the extent to which each group can understand the point of view of the other.

What I deplore in this entire situation is the lack of mutual understanding. The use of violence is in direct relation to the lack of such understanding. Violence, in fact, is proof perfect of utter misunderstanding. This administration will not tolerate further violence in California agriculture from either side or from any elements. I take advantage of this occasion to serve notice to employers and to employees, and in particular to local law-enforcement agencies in the rural counties, that we intend to maintain not only civil liberties but the public peace in this state. We are prepared to go to any lengths, even to the point of calling out the National Guard and invoking martial law, to see to it that order is maintained and that the laws are equally and impartially enforced.

I intend, moreover, to follow up such incidents as the disturbance in Madera this fall and to see to it, in this and in all other similar incidents, that the law is not enforced with an unequal hand. The sense of justice and of fair treatment of the people of this state has been exhausted and public sentiment will not tolerate a recurrence of the Salinas situation of 1936 or the Stockton cannery strike of 1937, or of Madera in 1939.

Moreover, there are certain practical considerations which make the problem of protecting the rights of agricultural workers difficult in this state. Most disputes occur, of course, during the harvest or peak labor periods, and the harvest seasons are seldom of more than a few weeks' duration. Consequently, disturbances arise quickly and are usually over in a short time. An explosion will occur, and before the state executive can ascertain whether or not the local law-enforcement agencies are performing their duties equally and impartially, the strike will be over. We have discovered, therefore, that the best way to protect the civil liberties of agricultural workers is to attempt to prevent strikes from occurring — to intervene before the breach occurs.

The possibility of such effective intervention for the purpose of preventing strikes in California agriculture is limited at the present time by reason of the stand that has been consistently taken by organized farm groups in California to the effect that they are opposed to the application of the principles of collective bargaining for agricultural labor. Again and again these same groups, as you will doubtless learn during the course of your investigation, have not only actively opposed the formation of trade unions but have publicly stated that under no circumstances would they bargain collectively with the duly designated representatives of their employees. Encouraged by the fact that there is no legal compulsion at the present time to force recognition or collective bargaining, these same groups have carried the fight further and have unduly interfered with every attempt that has been made to bring into play the principles of collective bargaining which have long been recognized nationally as the best approach to the problem of employer-employee relations in industry. . . .

As you have doubtless discovered in the course of your investigations elsewhere, intimidation of workers can take as many forms as the ingenuity of employers can devise. There is a kind of intimidation which exists in the agricultural field of California today which is exceedingly difficult to correct by executive action. Where, for example, the bulk of migratory workers reside during the course of their seasonal employment in private labor camps located upon the premises of their employers, there is an element of coercion employed in the circumstances of their housing.

In the first place, they are under the direct surveillance of foremen, labor contractors, and bosses; they cannot help but be aware of the fact that they can be summarily evicted; they have scant opportunity under these circumstances to hold meetings or to discuss the problems arising in connection with their employment. If they are evicted, as almost invariably happens during a labor dispute, they must by force of necessity provide some type of improvised community camp, and, in general, they never have the means to lay out or establish a decent camp, with the result that, the moment they are evicted, local health officers are brought into action and they are hounded from place to place in their efforts to find temporary shelter. The hardship which this works is bad enough insofar as grown men are concerned. It is, of course, far more deplorable insofar as women and children are concerned.

And the matter of the lack of independent residence has a direct bearing on the problem of the organization of agricultural workers for mutual aid and protection and upon the problem of protecting their civil liberties. Coupled with this situation is the circumstance that again, by force of necessity, many agricultural workers make their purchases at company stores, usually in the form of credit allowed by the employer and paid for in the form of scrip, counters, or orders upon the store itself. This circumstance has particular significance in those instances, quite common, where workers congregate in a given area in advance of the season or where the seasonal operation is for some reason delayed.

Under these circumstances they are forced to seek credit, which is extended by the owner or by the contractor, so that the workers find themselves indebted to a particular employer or contractor before working operations have commenced, and under these circumstances — and faced with the necessity of seeking additional credit in order to survive, they are inevitably coerced, and in many instances work at wage rates and under conditions that they would not voluntarily accept. Also, when the foremen of a given ranch are deputized and there are many instances where this situation exists, and where, in connection with their being deputized they carry guns, this fact cannot escape the attention of employees. All of these circumstances have to be taken into consideration in considering the problem of civil liberties. . . .

With respect to the undue interference with the right to collective bargaining, I call your attention to the strike at Marysville, Calif., which also occurred during the present administration. I understand that you intend to go into this incident fully, so I shall not comment upon the matter other than to indicate that my efforts at concilia-

tion and mediation were opposed from the outset by the employer involved, and that its opposition was encouraged and supported by the Associated Farmers.

By way of summation it can be said that the problem of protection of civil liberties of agricultural labor in California is made extremely difficult by reason of —

First, the economic pressures involved.

Second, the pattern of the employment of minority racial groups and the fact that many such groups are still employed.

Third, the very nature of migratory labor itself.

Fourth, the reluctance of individual employers of large numbers of agricultural laborers, encouraged by such employer groups as the Associated Farmers, to recognize the marked trend throughout the nation in the direction of using accepted principles of collective bargaining as a means of avoiding labor strife, as long as it obtains, will make for strife in California agriculture, and will thereby make the problem of protection of civil liberties a difficult one in this state.

Lastly, the physical difficulties are themselves formidable, namely, the extent of the area in which employment takes place and the very large number of workers involved and the shortness of the period of their employment.

We feel, therefore, that the emphasis in the protection of civil liberties should be placed upon measures designed to prevent the occurrence of labor disputes and to decasualize agricultural labor employment in California.

As long as an army of workers of this magnitude remains, so to speak, outside the general social, economic, and political life of the state in the local communities in which they reside or find employment, the problem of protecting their civil liberties will be very great.

127.

JOHN STEINBECK: Okies

The dust storms of the middle 1930s forced thousands of agricultural workers to abandon the Great Plains for the greener fields of the West Coast. The most vivid portrayal of the plight of these migrant workers was John Steinbeck's The Grapes of Wrath, the Pulitzer Prize novel in 1939. It depicted the life of a migrant family driven from the dust bowl of Oklahoma to California and the problems they faced working under an almost feudal system of agriculture. Provoking bitter anger among Western landowners, the novel succeeded in arousing widespread sympathy for the migrant worker and established Steinbeck as the foremost American novelist of the Great Depression. Passages from the novel are reprinted here.

Source: *The Grapes of Wrath*, New York, 1939, Chs. 14, 17, 19, 21.

THE WESTERN LAND, nervous under the beginning change. The Western States, nervous as horses before a thunder storm. The great owners, nervous, sensing a change, knowing nothing of the nature of the change. The great owners, striking at the immediate thing, the widening government, the growing labor unity; striking at new taxes, at plans; not knowing these things are results, not causes. Results, not causes; results, not causes. The causes lie deep and simple — the causes are a hunger in a stomach, multiplied a million times; a hunger in a single soul, hunger for joy and some security, multiplied a million times; muscles and mind aching to grow, to work, to create, multiplied a million times. The last clear definite function of man — muscles aching to work, minds aching to create beyond the single need — this is man. To build a wall, to build a house, a dam, and in the wall and house and dam to put something of Manself, and to Manself take back something of the wall, the house, the dam; to take hard muscles from the lifting, to take the clear lines and form from conceiving. For man, unlike any other thing organic or inorganic in the universe, grows beyond his work, walks up the stairs of his concepts, emerges ahead of his accomplishments. This you may say of man — when theories change and crash, when schools, philosophies, when narrow dark alleys of thought, national, religious, economic, grow and disintegrate, man reaches, stumbles forward, painfully, mistakenly sometimes. Having stepped forward, he may slip back, but only half a step, never the full step back. This you may say and know it and know it. This you may know when the bombs plummet out of the black planes on the market place, when prisoners are stuck like pigs, when the crushed bodies drain filthily in the dust. You may know it in this way. If the step were not being taken, if the stumbling-forward ache were not alive, the bombs would not fall, the throats would not be cut. Fear the time when the bombs stop falling while the bombers live — for every bomb is proof that the spirit has not died. And fear the time when the strikes stop while the great owners live — for every little beaten strike is proof that the step is being taken. And this you can know — fear the time when Manself will not suffer and die for a concept, for this one quality is the foundation of Manself, and this one quality is man, distinctive in the universe.

The Western States nervous under the beginning change. Texas and Oklahoma, Kansas and Arkansas, New Mexico, Arizona, California. A single family moved from the land. Pa borrowed money from the bank, and now the bank wants the land. The land company — that's the bank when it has land — wants tractors, not families on the land. Is a tractor bad? Is the power that turns the long furrows wrong? If this tractor were ours it would be good — not mine, but ours. If our tractor turned the long furrows of our land, it would be good. Not my land, but ours. We could love that tractor then as we have loved this land when it was ours. But this tractor does two things — it turns the land and turns us off the land. There is little difference between this tractor and a tank. The people are driven, intimidated, hurt by both. We must think about this.

One man, one family driven from the land; this rusty car creaking along the highway to the west. I lost my land, a single tractor took my land. I am alone and I am bewildered. And in the night one family camps in a ditch and another family pulls in and the tents come out. The two men squat on their hams and the women and children listen. Here is the node, you who hate change and fear revolution. Keep these two squatting men apart; make them hate, fear, suspect each other. Here is the anlage of the thing you fear. This is the zygote. For here "I lost my land" is changed; a cell is split and from its splitting grows the thing you hate — "We lost our land." The danger is here, for two men are not as lonely and perplexed as one. And from this first "we" there grows a still more dangerous thing: "I have a little food" plus "I have none." If from this problem the sum is "We have a little food," the thing is on its way, the movement has direction. Only a little multiplication now, and this land, this tractor are ours. The two men squatting in

a ditch, the little fire, the side-meat stewing in a single pot, the silent, stone-eyed women; behind, the children listening with their souls to words their minds do not understand. The night draws down. The baby has a cold. Here, take this blanket. It's wool. It was my mother's blanket — take it for the baby. This is the thing to bomb. This is the beginning — from "I" to "we."

If you who own the things people must have could understand this, you might preserve yourself. If you could separate causes from results, if you could know that Paine, Marx, Jefferson, Lenin, were results, not causes, you might survive. But that you cannot know. For the quality of owning freezes you forever into "I," and cuts you off forever from the "we."

The Western States are nervous under the beginning change. Need is the stimulus to concept, concept to action. A half-million people moving over the country; a million more, restive to move; ten million more feeling the first nervousness.

And tractors turning the multiple furrows in the vacant land.

THE CARS OF THE MIGRANT PEOPLE crawled out of the side roads onto the great cross-country highway, and they took the migrant way to the West. In the daylight they scuttled like bugs to the westward; and as the dark caught them, they clustered like bugs near to shelter and to water. And because they were lonely and perplexed, because they had all come from a place of sadness and worry and defeat, and because they were all going to a new mysterious place, they huddled together; they talked together; they shared their lives, their food, and the things they hoped for in the new country. Thus it might be that one family camped near a spring, and another camped for the spring and for company, and a third because two families had pioneered the place and found it good. And when the sun went down, perhaps twenty families and twenty cars were there.

In the evening a strange thing happened: the twenty families became one family, the children were the children of all. The loss of home became one loss, and the golden time in the West was one dream. And it might be that a sick child threw despair into the hearts of twenty families, of a hundred people; that a birth there in a tent kept a hundred people quiet and awestruck through the night and filled a hundred people with the birth-joy in the morning. A family which the night before had been lost and fearful might search its goods to find a present for a new baby. In the evening, sitting about the fires, the twenty were one. They grew to be units of the camps, units of the evenings and the nights. A guitar unwrapped from a blanket and tuned — and the songs, which were all of the people, were sung in the nights. Men sang the words, and women hummed the tunes.

Every night a world created, complete with furniture — friends made and enemies established; a world complete with braggarts and with cowards, with quiet men, with humble men, with kindly men. Every night relationships that make a world, established; and every morning the world torn down like a circus.

At first the families were timid in the building and tumbling worlds, but gradually the technique of building worlds became their technique. Then leaders emerged, then laws were made, then codes came into being. And as the worlds moved westward they were more complete and better furnished, for their builders were more experienced in building them.

The families learned what rights must be observed — the right of privacy in the tent; the right to keep the past black hidden in the heart; the right to talk and to listen; the right to refuse help or to accept, to offer help or to decline it; the right of son to court and daughter to be courted; the right of the hungry to be fed; the rights of the pregnant and the sick to transcend all other rights.

And the families learned, although no one told them, what rights are monstrous and must be destroyed: the right to intrude upon privacy, the right to be noisy while the camp slept, the right of seduction or rape, the right of adultery and theft and murder. These rights were crushed, because the little worlds could not exist for even a night with such rights alive.

And as the worlds moved westward, rules became laws, although no one told the families. It is unlawful to foul near the camp; it is unlawful in any way to foul the drinking water; it is unlawful to eat good rich food near one who is hungry, unless he is asked to share.

And with the laws, the punishments — and there were only two — a quick and murderous fight or ostracism; and ostracism was the worst. For if one broke the laws his name and face went with him, and he had no place in any world, no matter where created.

In the worlds, social conduct became fixed and rigid, so that a man must say "Good morning" when asked for it, so that a man might have a willing girl if he stayed with her, if he fathered her children and protected them. But a man might not have one girl one night and another the next, for this would endanger the worlds.

The families moved westward, and the technique of building the worlds improved so that the people could be safe in their worlds; and the form was so fixed that a family acting in the rules knew it was safe in the rules.

There grew up government in the worlds, with leaders, with elders. A man who was wise found that his wisdom was needed in every camp; a man who was a fool could not change his folly with his world. And a kind of insurance developed in these nights. A man with food fed a hungry man, and thus insured himself against hunger. And when a baby died a pile of silver coins grew at the door flap, for a baby must be well buried, since it has had nothing else of life.

An old man may be left in a potter's field, but not a baby.

A certain physical pattern is needed for the building of a world — water, a river bank, a stream, a spring, or even a faucet unguarded. And there is needed enough flat land to pitch the tents, a little brush or wood to build the fires. If there is a garbage dump not too far off, all the better; for there can be found equipment — stove tops, a curved fender to shelter the fire, and cans to cook in and to eat from.

And the worlds were built in the evening. The people, moving in from the highways, made them with their tents and their hearts and their brains.

In the morning the tents came down, the canvas was folded, the tent poles tied along the running board, the beds put in place on the cars, the pots in their places. And as the families moved westward, the technique of building up a home in the evening and tearing it down with the morning light became fixed; so that the folded tent was packed in one place, the cooking pots counted in their box. And as the cars moved westward, each member of the family grew into his proper place, grew into his duties; so that each member, old and young, had his place in the car; so that in the weary, hot evenings, when the cars pulled into the camping places, each member had his duty and went to it without instruction: children to gather wood, to carry water; men to pitch tents and bring down the beds; women to cook the supper and to watch while the family fed. And this was done without command. The families, which had been units of which the boundaries were a house at night, a farm by day, changed their boundaries. In the long hot light, they were silent in the cars moving slowly westward; but at night they integrated with any group they found.

Thus they changed their social life — changed as in the whole universe only man can change. They were not farm men any more, but migrant men. And the thought, the planning, the long staring silence that had gone out to the fields, went now to the roads, to the distance, to the West. That man whose mind had been bound with acres lived with narrow concrete miles. And his thought and his worry were not any more with rainfall, with wind and dust, with the thrust of the crops. Eyes watched the tires, ears listened to the clattering motors, and minds struggled with oil, with gasoline, with the thinning rubber between air and road. Then a broken gear was tragedy. Then water in the evening was the yearning, and food over the fire. Then health to go on was the need and strength to go on, and spirit to go on. The wills thrust westward ahead of them, and fears that had once apprehended drought or flood now lingered with anything that might stop the westward crawling. . . .

Once California belonged to Mexico and its land to Mexicans; and a horde of tattered feverish Americans poured in. And such was their hunger for land that they took the land — stole Sutter's land, Guerrero's land, took the grants and broke them up and growled and quarreled over them, those frantic hungry men; and they guarded with guns the land they had stolen. They put up houses and barns, they turned the earth and planted crops. And these things were possession, and possession was ownership.

The Mexicans were weak and fled. They could not resist, because they wanted nothing in the world as frantically as the Americans wanted land.

Then, with time, the squatters were no longer squatters, but owners; and their children grew up and had children on the land. And the hunger was gone from them, the feral hunger, the gnawing, tearing hunger for land, for water and earth and the good sky over it, for the green thrusting grass, for the swelling roots. They had these things so completely that they did not know about them any more. They had no more the stomach-tearing lust for a rich acre and a shining blade to plow it, for seed and a windmill beating its wings in the air. They arose in the dark no more to hear the sleepy birds' first chittering, and the morning wind around the house while they waited for the first light to go out to the dear acres. These things were lost, and crops were reckoned in dollars, and land was valued by principal plus interest, and crops were bought and sold before they were planted. Then crop failure, drought, and flood were no longer little deaths within life, but simple losses of money. And all their love was thinned with money, and all their fierceness dribbled away in interest until they were no longer farmers at all, but little shopkeepers of crops, little manufacturers who must sell before they can make. Then those farmers who were not good shopkeepers lost their land to good shopkeepers. No matter how clever, how loving a man might be with earth and growing things, he could not survive if he were not also a good shopkeeper. And as time went on, the business men had the farms, and the farms grew larger, but there were fewer of them.

Now farming became industry, and the owners followed Rome, although they did not know it. They imported slaves, although they did not call them slaves: Chinese, Japanese, Mexicans, Filipinos. They live on rice and beans, the business men said. They don't need much. They wouldn't know what to do with good wages. Why, look how they live. Why, look what they eat. And if they get funny — deport them.

And all the time the farms grew larger and the owners fewer. And there were pitifully few farmers on the land any more. And the imported serfs were beaten and frightened and starved until some went home again, and some grew fierce and were killed or driven from the country. And the farms grew larger and the owners fewer.

And the crops changed. Fruit trees took the place of grain fields, and vegetables to feed the world spread out on the bottoms: lettuce, cauliflower, artichokes, potatoes — stoop crops. A man may stand to use a scythe, a plow, a pitchfork; but he must crawl like a bug between the rows of lettuce, he must bend his back and pull his long bag between the cotton rows, he must go on his knees like a penitent across a cauliflower patch.

And it came about that owners no longer worked on their farms. They farmed on paper; and they forgot the land, the smell, the feel of it, and remembered only that they owned it, remembered only what they gained and lost by it. And some of the farms grew so large that one man could not even conceive of them any more, so large that it took batteries of bookkeepers to keep track of interest and gain and loss; chemists to test the soil, to replenish; straw bosses to see that the stooping men were moving along the rows as swiftly as the material of their bodies could stand. Then such a farmer really became a storekeeper, and kept a store. He paid the men, and sold them food, and took the money back. And after a while he did not pay the men at all, and saved bookkeeping. These farms gave food on credit. A man might work and feed himself and when the work was done, might find that he owed money to the company. And the owners not only did not work the farms any more, many of them had never seen the farms they owned.

And then the dispossessed were drawn west — from Kansas, Oklahoma, Texas, New Mexico; from Nevada and Arkansas families, tribes, dusted out, tractored out. Carloads, caravans, homeless and hungry; twenty thousand and fifty thousand and a hundred thousand and two hundred thousand. They streamed over the mountains, hungry and restless — restless as ants, scurrying to find work to do — to lift, to push, to pull, to pick, to cut — anything, any burden to bear, for food. The kids are hungry. We got no place to live. Like ants scurrying for work, for food, and most of all for land.

We ain't foreign. Seven generations back Americans, and beyond that Irish, Scotch, English, German. One of our folks in the Revolution, an' they was lots of our folks in the Civil War — both sides. Americans.

They were hungry, and they were fierce. And they had hoped to find a home, and they found only hatred. Okies — the owners hated them because the owners knew they were soft and the Okies strong, that they were fed and the Okies hungry; and perhaps the owners had heard from their grandfathers how easy it is to steal land from a soft man if you are fierce and hungry and armed. The owners hated them. And in the towns, the storekeepers hated them because they had no money to spend. There is no shorter path to a storekeeper's contempt, and all his admirations are exactly opposite. The town men, little bankers, hated Okies because there was nothing to gain from them. They had nothing. And the laboring people hated Okies because a hungry man must work, and if he must work, if he has to work, the wage payer automatically gives him less for his work; and then no one can get more.

And the dispossessed, the migrants, flowed into California, two hundred and fifty thousand, and three hundred thousand. Behind them new tractors were going on the land and the tenants were being forced off. And new waves were on the way, new waves of the dispossessed and the homeless, hardened, intent, and dangerous.

And while the Californians wanted many things, accumulation, social success, amusement, luxury, and a curious banking security, the new barbarians wanted only two things — land and food; and to them the two were one. And whereas the wants of the Californians were nebulous and undefined, the wants of the Okies were beside the roads, lying there to be seen and coveted: the good fields with water to be dug for, the good green fields, earth to crumble experimentally in the hand, grass to smell, oaten stalks to chew until the sharp sweetness was in the throat. A man might look at a fallow field and know, and see in his mind that his own bending back and his own straining arms would bring the cabbages into the light, and the golden eating corn, the turnips and carrots.

And a homeless hungry man, driving the roads with his wife beside him and his thin children in the back seat, could look at the fallow fields which might produce food but not profit, and that man could know how a fallow field is a sin and the unused land a crime against the thin children. And such a man drove along the roads and knew temptation at every field, and knew the lust to take these fields and make them grow strength for his children and a little comfort for his wife. The temptation was before him always. The fields goaded him, and the company ditches with good water flowing were a goad to him.

And in the south he saw the golden oranges hanging on the trees, the little golden oranges on the dark green trees; and guards with shotguns patrolling the lines so a man might not pick an orange for a thin child, oranges to be dumped if the price was low.

He drove his old car into a town. He scoured the farms for work. Where can we sleep the night?

Well, there's Hooverville on the edge of the river. There's a whole raft of Okies there.

He drove his old car to Hooverville. He never asked again, for there was a Hooverville on the edge of every town.

The rag town lay close to water; and the houses were tents, and weed-thatched enclosures, paper houses, a great junk pile. The man drove his family in and became a citizen of Hooverville — always they were called Hooverville. The man put up his own tent as near to water as he could get; or if he had no tent, he went to the city dump and brought back cartons and built a house of corrugated paper. And when the rains came the house melted and washed away. He settled in Hooverville and he scoured the countryside for work, and the little money he had went for gasoline to look for work. In the evening the men gathered and talked together. Squatting on their hams they talked of the land they had seen.

There's thirty thousan' acres, out west of here. Layin' there. Jesus, what I could do with that, with five acres of that! Why, hell, I'd have ever'thing to eat.

Notice one thing? They ain't no vegetables nor chickens nor pigs at the farms. They raise one thing — cotton, say, or peaches, or lettuce. 'Nother place'll be all chickens. They buy the stuff they could raise in the dooryard.

Jesus, what I could do with a couple pigs!

Well, it ain't yourn, an' it ain't gonna be yourn.

What we gonna do? The kids can't grow up this way.

In the camps the word would come whispering. There's work at Shafter. And the cars would be loaded in the night, the highways crowded — a gold rush for work. At Shafter the people would pile up, five times too many to do the work. A gold rush for work. They stole away in the night, frantic for work. And along the roads lay the temptations, the fields that could bear food.

That's owned. That ain't our'n.

Well, maybe we could get a little piece of her. Maybe — a little piece. Right down there — a patch. Jimson weed now. Christ, I could git enough potatoes off'n that little patch to feed my whole family!

It ain't our'n. It got to have Jimson weeds.

Now and then a man tried; crept on the land and cleared a piece, trying like a thief to steal a little richness from the earth. Secret gardens hidden in the weeds. A package of carrot seeds and a few turnips. Planted potato skins, crept out in the evening secretly to hoe in the stolen earth.

Leave the weeds around the edge — then nobody can see what we're a-doin'. Leave some weeds, big tall ones, in the middle.

Secret gardening in the evenings, and water carried in a rusty can.

And then one day a deputy sheriff: Well, what you think you're doin'?

I ain't doin' no harm.

I had my eye on you. This ain't your land. You're trespassing.

The land ain't plowed, an' I ain't hurtin' it none.

You goddamned squatters. Pretty soon you'd think you owned it. You'd be sore as hell. Think you owned it. Get off now.

And the little green carrot tops were kicked off and the turnip greens trampled. And then the Jimson weed moved back in. But the cop was right. A crop raised — why, that makes ownership. Land hoed and the carrots eaten — a man might fight for land he's taken food from. Get him off quick! He'll think he owns it. He might even die fighting for the little plot among the Jimson weeds.

Did ya see his face when we kicked them turnips out? Why, he'd kill a fella soon's he'd look at him. We got to keep these here people down or they'll take the country. They'll take the country.

Outlanders, foreigners.

Sure, they talk the same language, but they ain't the same. Look how they live. Think any of us folks'd live like that? Hell, no!

In the evening, squatting and talking. And an excited man: Whyn't twenty of us take a piece of lan'? We got guns. Take it an' say, "Put us off if you can." Whyn't we do that?

They'd jus' shoot us like rats.

Well, which'd you ruther be, dead or here? Under groun' or in a house all made of gunny sacks? Which'd you ruther for your kids, dead now or dead in two years with what they call malnutrition? Know what we et all week? Biled nettles an' fried dough! Know where we got the flour for the dough? Swep' the floor of a boxcar.

Talking in the camps, and the deputies,

fat-assed men with guns slung on fat hips, swaggering through the camps: Give 'em somepin to think about. Got to keep 'em in line or Christ only knows what they'll do! Why, Jesus, they're as dangerous as niggers in the South! If they ever get together there ain't nothin' that'll stop 'em.

Quote: In Lawrenceville a deputy sheriff evicted a squatter, and the squatter resisted, making it necessary for the officer to use force. The eleven-year-old son of the squatter shot and killed the deputy with a .22 rifle. . . .

THE MOVING, QUESTING people were migrants now. Those families who had lived on a little piece of land, who had lived and died on forty acres, had eaten or starved on the produce of forty acres, had now the whole West to rove in. And they scampered about, looking for work; and the highways were streams of people, and the ditch banks were lines of people. Behind them more were coming. The great highways streamed with moving people. There in the Middle- and Southwest had lived a simple agrarian folk who had not changed with industry, who had not farmed with machines or known the power and danger of machines in private hands. They had not grown up in the paradoxes of industry. Their senses were still sharp to the ridiculousness of the industrial life.

And then suddenly the machines pushed them out and they swarmed on the highways. The movement changed them; the highways, the camps along the road, the fear of hunger and the hunger itself, changed them. The children without dinner changed them, the endless moving changed them. They were migrants. And the hostility changed them, welded them, united them — hostility that made the little towns group and arm as though to repel an invader, squads with pick handles, clerks and storekeepers with shotguns, guarding the world against their own people.

In the West there was panic when the migrants multiplied on the highways. Men of property were terrified for their property. Men who had never been hungry saw the eyes of the hungry. Men who had never wanted anything very much saw the flare of want in the eyes of the migrants. And the men of the towns and of the soft suburban country gathered to defend themselves; and they reassured themselves that they were good and the invaders bad, as a man must do before he fights. They said, These goddamned Okies are dirty and ignorant. They're degenerate, sexual maniacs. Those goddamned Okies are thieves. They'll steal anything. They've got no sense of property rights.

And the latter was true, for how can a man without property know the ache of ownership? And the defending people said, They bring disease, they're filthy. We can't have them in the schools. They're strangers. How'd you like to have your sister go out with one of 'em?

The local people whipped themselves into a mold of cruelty. Then they formed units, squads, and armed them — armed them with clubs, with gas, with guns. We own the country. We can't let these Okies get out of hand. And the men who were armed did not own the land, but they thought they did. And the clerks who drilled at night owned nothing, and the little storekeepers possessed only a drawerful of debts. But even a debt is something, even a job is something. The clerk thought, I get fifteen dollars a week. S'pose a goddamn Okie would work for twelve? And the little storekeeper thought, How could I compete with a debtless man?

And the migrants streamed in on the highways and their hunger was in their eyes, and their need was in their eyes. They had no argument, no system, nothing but their numbers and their needs. When there was work for a man, ten men fought for it — fought with a low wage. If that fella'll work for thirty cents, I'll work for twenty-five.

If he'll take twenty-five, I'll do it for twenty.

No, me, I'm hungry. I'll work for fifteen. I'll work for food. The kids. You ought to see them. Little boils, like, comin' out, an' they can't run aroun'. Give 'em some windfall fruit, an' they bloated up. Me, I'll work for a little piece of meat.

And this was good, for wages went down and prices stayed up. The great owners were glad and they sent out more handbills to bring more people in. And wages went down and prices stayed up. And pretty soon now we'll have serfs again.

And now the great owners and the companies invented a new method. A great owner bought a cannery. And when the peaches and the pears were ripe he cut the price of fruit below the cost of raising it. And as cannery owner he paid himself a low price for the fruit and kept the price of canned goods up and took his profit. And the little farmers who owned no canneries lost their farms, and they were taken by the great owners, the banks, and the companies who also owned the canneries. As time went on, there were fewer farms. The little farmers moved into town for a while and exhausted their credit, exhausted their friends, their relatives. And then they too went on the highways. And the roads were crowded with men ravenous for work, murderous for work.

And the companies, the banks worked at their own doom and they did not know it. The fields were fruitful, and starving men moved on the roads. The granaries were full and the children of the poor grew up rachitic, and the pustules of pellagra swelled on their sides. The great companies did not know that the line between hunger and anger is a thin line. And money that might have gone to wages went for gas, for guns, for agents and spies, for blacklists, for drilling. On the highways the people moved like ants and searched for work, for food. And the anger began to ferment.

Oklahoma migrant stalled on the California desert in 1937; photo by Dorothea Lange
Library of Congress

128.

Albert Einstein: Letter to President Roosevelt

By 1939 a number of nuclear physicists in Western Europe and the United States knew of the theoretical possibility of uranium fission. Many of these scientists were refugees from the Nazi-dominated parts of Europe. As war grew imminent, they became apprehensive that the Germans would secure a quick victory by producing an atomic bomb. In March 1939 Enrico Fermi, a refugee from Mussolini's Italy, met with officials of the Navy Department to impress upon them the importance of atomic energy in war but without much success. As a last desperate effort to convince the government of the urgency of carrying on nuclear research, the Hungarian-born physicist Leo Szilard persuaded Albert Einstein, who was held in the highest regard by government officials, to write the following letter to President Roosevelt. Dated August 2, the letter was not delivered until October 11. Within a month the President established a research committee and by the autumn of 1940 the government had awarded sizeable contracts. On December 2, 1942, the first self-sustained chain reaction was achieved by Fermi's group at Chicago.

Source: *The Atomic Age,* Morton Grodzins and Eugene Rabinowitch, eds., New York, 1963, pp. 11-12.

Some recent work by E. Fermi and L. Szilard, which has been communicated to me in manuscript, leads me to expect that the element uranium may be turned into a new and important source of energy in the immediate future. Certain aspects of the situation which has arisen seem to call for watchfulness and, if necessary, quick action on the part of the administration. I believe, therefore, that it is my duty to bring to your attention the following facts and recommendations.

In the course of the last four months it has been made probable — through the work of Joliot in France as well as Fermi and Szilard in America — that it may become possible to set up a nuclear chain reaction in a large mass of uranium, by which vast amounts of power and large quantities of new radium-like elements would be generated. Now it appears almost certain that this could be achieved in the immediate future.

This new phenomenon would also lead to the construction of bombs, and it is conceivable — though much less certain — that extremely powerful bombs of a new type may thus be constructed. A single bomb of this type, carried by boat and exploded in a port, might very well destroy the whole port together with some of the surrounding territory. However, such bombs might very well prove to be too heavy for transportation by air.

The United States has only very poor ores of uranium in moderate quantities. There is some good ore in Canada and the former Czechoslovakia, while the most important source of uranium is Belgian Congo.

In view of this situation you may think it desirable to have some permanent contact maintained between the administration and the group of physicists working on chain reactions in America. One possible way of achieving this might be for you to entrust with this task a person who has your confidence and who could perhaps serve in an unofficial capacity. His task might comprise the following:

(*a*) To approach government departments, keep them informed of the further development, and put forward recommendations for government action, giving particular attention to the problem of securing a supply of uranium ore for the United States.

(*b*) To speed up the experimental work, which is at present being carried on within the limits of the budgets of university laboratories, by providing funds, if such funds be required, through his contacts with private persons who are willing to make contributions for this cause, and perhaps also by obtaining the cooperation of industrial laboratories which have the necessary equipment.

I understand that Germany has actually stopped the sale of uranium from the Czechoslovakian mines which she has taken over. That she should have taken such early action might perhaps be understood on the ground that the son of the German undersecretary of state, Von Weizsacker, is attached to the Kaiser-Wilhelm-Institut in Berlin, where some of the American work on uranium is now being repeated.

Index of Authors

*The numbers in brackets
indicate selection numbers
in this volume*

ADAMIC, LOUIS (March 23, 1899-Sept. 4, 1951), author. Born Yugoslavia; became U.S. citizen (1918); wrote *Dynamite* (1931), *The Native's Return* (1934), *From Many Lands* (1940), *The Eagle and the Roots* (1952). **[62]**

ALLEN, FREDERICK LEWIS (July 5, 1890-Feb. 13, 1954), editor and author. An editor (1914-16) of the *Atlantic Monthly*, (1916-17) of the *Century*, and (1923-53) of *Harper's* magazine; wrote *Only Yesterday* (1931), *Since Yesterday* (1940), *The Big Change* (1952). **[7, 26]**

AMERINGER, OSCAR (fl. 1932), journalist. Editor of the *American Miner* and of the (Oklahoma) *American Guardian*. **[28]**

ANDERSON, SHERWOOD (Sept. 13, 1876-March 8, 1941), author. Wrote poetry, novels, and short stories (*Winesburg, Ohio*, 1919; *The Triumph of the Egg*, 1921; *Horses and Men*, 1923; *Death in the Woods*, 1933). **[8]**

BARNARD, CHESTER I. (Nov. 7, 1886-June 7, 1961), businessman. President of New Jersey Bell Telephone Company; national president of the USO during World War II; president (1948-52) of the Rockefeller Foundation. **[108]**

BARRETT, E. BOYD (fl. 1929), journalist. **[5]**

BEARD, CHARLES A. (Nov. 27, 1874-Sept. 1, 1948), historian and educator. Professor of politics (1907-17) at Columbia University; a founder of the New School for Social Research, N.Y.C.; wrote *American Government and Politics* (1910), *An Economic Interpretation of the Constitution* (1913), *The Rise of American Civilization* (1927), *A Basic History of the United States* (1944). **[20]** See also Author Index, Vols. 13, 14.

BERLE, ADOLF A. (Jan. 29, 1895-   ), lawyer and diplomat. Consultant (1918-19) to the Paris Peace Commission; assistant secretary of state (1938-44) under F. D. Roosevelt; ambassador to Brazil (1945-46); professor (1927-   ) at Columbia University Law School. **[32]** See also Author Index, Vols. 16, 17.

BERLIN, IRVING (May 11, 1888-   ), composer. Born Russia; wrote scores for musical comedies (*Music Box Revue*, 1921; *Annie Get Your Gun*, 1946) and motion pictures, including the songs "Alexander's Ragtime Band," "Always," "All Alone," "Remember," "White Christmas," and "God Bless America." **[113]**

BORAH, WILLIAM E. (June 29, 1865-Jan. 19, 1940), lawyer and public official. U.S. senator from Idaho (from 1907); chairman (1924-33) of the Senate Foreign Relations Committee; sponsored Constitutional amendments for a national income tax and direct election of senators. [6] See also Author Index, Vol. 14.

BORSODI, RALPH (fl. 1920-1933), social reformer. Wrote *National Advertising vs. Prosperity*, *The Distribution Age* (1927), *Flight from the City*. [50]

BRANDEIS, LOUIS D. (Nov. 13, 1856-Oct. 5, 1941), jurist. Special counsel for the people in minimum wage and work hour law cases in Illinois, Ohio, California, and Oregon (1907-14); associate justice (1916-39) of the U.S. Supreme Court. [33, 76] See also Author Index, Vol. 13.

CHASE, STUART (March 8, 1888-   ), economist and author. Investigator (1917-22) for U.S. Federal Trade Commission; associated (1922-39) with Labor Bureau, Inc. and (1940-41) with the Tennessee Valley Authority; wrote *A New Deal* (1932), *Rich Land, Poor Land* (1936), *The Proper Study of Mankind* (1948). [91]

CLARK, BENNETT CHAMP (Jan. 8, 1890-July 13, 1954), lawyer and public official. U.S. senator from Missouri (1933-45); associate justice (from 1945) of the U.S. Court of Appeals in the District of Columbia. [74]

COFFMAN, LOTUS D. (Jan. 7, 1875-Sept. 22, 1938), educator. Dean (1915-20) of the college of education and president (from 1920) of the University of Minnesota; wrote or edited many books and articles on teacher-training. [22]

COLLIER, JOHN (May 4, 1884-   ), sociologist. A founder and secretary (1910-14) of the Board of Review of Motion Pictures; director (1915-19) of the National Training School for Community Workers; secretary (1923-33) of the American Indian Defense Association; editor (1926-33) of *American Indian Life*; commissioner of Indian Affairs (1933-45); director of the National Indian Institute; president of the Institute of Ethnic Affairs. [112]

CONVERSE, FLORENCE (April 30, 1871-   ), author. Contributor to *The Churchman*

and the *Atlantic Monthly*; wrote novels, poems, and two histories of Wellesley College. [29]

COUGHLIN, CHARLES E. (fl. 1936), clergyman. Founder (1938) of the Christian Front; published *Social Justice*. [88]

COWLEY, MALCOLM (Aug. 24, 1898-   ), author. Literary editor (1929-44) of the *New Republic*; edited collections of Faulkner, Hawthorne, and Whitman; translated from the French works by Paul Valéry and André Gide; wrote *Exile's Return* (1934), *The Dry Season* (1941), *The Literary Situation* (1954). [34]

CRAM, RALPH ADAMS (Dec. 16, 1863-Sept. 22, 1942), architect. Professor of architecture (1914-21) at Massachusetts Institute of Technology; supervising architect (1907-29) for Princeton University; consulting architect for Bryn Mawr and Wellesley colleges; planned Rice Institute and buildings for Williams College, Phillips Exeter Academy, and the U.S. Military Academy; designed St. Thomas Church, N.Y.C. [106]

CRANE, HART (July 21, 1899-April 27, 1932), poet. Wrote *White Buildings* (1926), *The Bridge* (1930), *Collected Poems* (1933). [15]

CUMMINGS, E. E. (Oct. 14, 1894-Sept. 3, 1962), poet and artist. Wrote prose works (*The Enormous Room*, 1922; and *Eimi*, 1933), plays, and poetry characterized by typographical nonconformity and stylistic originality (*XLI Poems*, 1925; *Is 5*, 1926; *&*, 1926; *Collected Poems*, 1938; *One Times One*, 1944; *95 Poems*, 1958). [17] See also Author Index, Vols. 14, 16.

DANIELS, JONATHAN W. (April 26, 1902-   ), journalist and author. Editor (1933-42, 1948-   ) of the *Raleigh* (N.C.) *News and Observer*; administrative assistant (1943-45) and press secretary (1945) to F. D. Roosevelt; U.S. representative to the United Nations; wrote *A Southerner Discovers the South* (1938), a biography of Harry S. Truman (1950), and *The Time Between the Wars* (1966). [117]

DAVIS, CHESTER C. (Nov. 17, 1887-   ), agricultural and financial administrator. Editor and manager (1917-21) of the

Montana Farmer; administrator (1933-36) of the U.S. Agricultural Adjustment Administration; president (1941-51) of the St. Louis Federal Reserve Bank; associate director (1951-54) of the Ford Foundation. **[49]**

DENNIS, LAWRENCE (fl. 1935), banker, journalist, and author. **[70]**

EINSTEIN, ALBERT (March 14, 1879-April 18, 1955), theoretical physicist. Born Germany; professor at the universities of Zürich, Prague, and Berlin; director of the Kaiser Wilhelm Physical Institute; to U.S. (1933); member (1933-45) of the Institute for Advanced Study, Princeton; published accounts of his special (1905) and general (1916) theories of relativity; received Nobel Prize for Physics (1921). **[128]** See also Author Index, Vol. 16.

FEARING, KENNETH (July 28, 1902-June 26, 1961), journalist and author. Reporter for Chicago City News Bureau; wrote poetry (*Angel Arms,* 1929; *Dead Reckoning,* 1938; *Afternoon of a Pawnbroker,* 1943) and novels (*The Hospital,* 1939; *The Loneliest Girl in the World,* 1951). **[72]**

FERGUSON, OTIS (fl. 1936), an editor of the *New Republic.* **[84]**

FITZGERALD, F. SCOTT (Sept. 24, 1896-Dec. 21, 1940), author. Wrote short stories (*Flappers and Philosophers,* 1920; *Tales of the Jazz Age,* 1922; *All the Sad Young Men,* 1926) and novels (*This Side of Paradise,* 1920; *The Great Gatsby,* 1925; *Tender is The Night,* 1934). **[25]**

FORD, HENRY (July 30, 1863-April 7, 1947), automobile manufacturer. Organizer, president (1903-18, 1943-45), and sole owner after its first few years, of Ford Motor Co., during his tenure the world's largest auto manufacturer; sailed for Europe aboard the Ford "Peace Ship" (1915-16) in a futile attempt to end World War I. **[40]** See also Author Index, Vol. 14.

FROST, ROBERT (March 26, 1874-Jan. 29, 1963), poet. Professor of English (1916-20, 1924, 1926-38, 1949-63) at Amherst; professor of poetry (1939-43) at Harvard and (1943-49) at Dartmouth; among his books of poetry are *A Boy's Will* (1913),

North of Boston (1914), *Mountain Interval* (1916), *New Hampshire* (1923), *West-running Brook* (1928), *A Further Range* (1936), *A Witness Tree* (1942), and *In the Clearing* (1962). **[79]** See also Author Index, Vols. 13, 14, 16.

GARLAND, JIM (fl. 1932), miner and songwriter. **[31]**

GREW, JOSEPH C. (May 27, 1880-May 25, 1965), diplomat. Secretary of U.S. embassies at Vienna (1911-12) and Berlin (1912-16); secretary-general of U.S. commission at Paris Peace Conference (1918-19); minister to Denmark (1920) and Switzerland (1921); ambassador to Turkey (1927-31) and Japan (1931-41); undersecretary of state (1924-27) under Coolidge and (1944-45) under F. D. Roosevelt. **[118]**

GUTHRIE, WOODY (July 14, 1912-Oct. 3, 1967), Oklahoma balladeer. Composed folk songs, including "So Long (It's Been Good to Know Yuh)," "Tom Joad," and "Union Maid." **[97]** See also Author Index, Vols. 16, 17.

HAND, LEARNED (Jan. 27, 1872-Aug. 18, 1961), jurist. Judge (1909-24) of U.S. District Court, N.Y.; judge (1924-39) and chief judge (1939-51) of the U.S. Court of Appeals for the Second Circuit. **[51]**

HAYES, ALFRED (fl. 1938), songwriter. **[110]**

HICKS, GRANVILLE (Sept. 9, 1901-   ), novelist and literary critic. Editor (1934-39) of *New Masses* magazine; literary editor (1951-58) of *New Leader* magazine; contributing editor (1958-) for *Saturday Review;* wrote *The Great Tradition — An Interpretation of American Literature* (1933); edited *The Living Novel* (1957). **[120]**

HOOVER, HERBERT CLARK (Aug. 10, 1874-Oct. 20, 1964), mining engineer, relief administrator, and statesman. Thirty-first President of the United States (1929-33); chairman of American relief commissions (1914-15) in London and (1915-19) in Belgium; U.S. food administrator (1917-19); director (1921) of relief in Eastern Europe; secretary of commerce (1921-28) under Harding and Coolidge; organized

U.S. relief operations in Europe after World War II; chairman (1947, 1953) of federal Commissions on Organization of the Executive Branch. **[18, 39, 87]** See also Author Index, Vols. 14, 17.

HOPKINS, HARRY L. (Aug. 17, 1890-Jan. 29, 1946) relief administrator and public official. Administrator (1933-35) of Federal Emergency Relief Administration and (1935-38) of the WPA; secretary of commerce (1938-40) under F. D. Roosevelt; presidential envoy (1941) to Russia and Great Britain; head of lend-lease program (1941); special assistant to Roosevelt (1942-45). **[57]**

HUGHES, CHARLES EVANS (April 11, 1862-Aug. 27, 1948), jurist and statesman. Governor of New York (1907-10); associate justice (1910-16) of the U.S. Supreme Court; candidate (1916) for President of the United States; secretary of state (1921-25) under Harding and Coolidge; member (1926-30) of The Hague Tribunal; judge (1928-30) on the Permanent Court of International Justice; chief justice (1930-41) of the U.S. Supreme Court. **[66]**

HUTCHINS, ROBERT M. (Jan. 17, 1899-   ), educator. Dean (1927-29) of Yale Law School; president (1929-45) and chancellor (1945-51) of the University of Chicago; president (1954-) of the Fund for the Republic and president of the center for the Study of Democratic Institutions; wrote *The Higher Learning in America* (1936) *Some Observations on American Education* (1956). **[92]** See also Author Index, Vol. 16.

JAMES, EDWIN L. (June 25, 1890-Dec. 3, 1951), journalist. Reporter (1910-14) for newspapers in Baltimore, Pittsburgh, and Albany; associated (from 1915) with the *New York Times* (1918-30) in Europe, (1931-32) as assistant managing editor, and (from 1932) as managing editor. **[12]**

JEFFERS, ROBINSON (Jan. 10, 1887-Jan. 20, 1962), poet. Wrote *Tamar and Other Poems* (1924), *Cawdor* (1928), *Thurso's Landing* (1932), and *Be Angry at the Sun* (1941); adapted Euripides' *Medea* for American production (1946). **[75]** See also Author Index, Vol. 14.

JOHNSON, HUGH S. (Aug. 5, 1882-April 15, 1942), lawyer and soldier. Devised plan (1917) for the Selective Service System and supervised (1917-18) its operations; administrator (1933-34) of the National Recovery Administration and (1935) of the Works Progress Administration in New York City; columnist (from 1934) for Scripps-Howard newspapers. **[65]**

KALLEN, HORACE M. (Aug. 11, 1882-   ), educator. Professor of philosophy (1918-) and dean of the graduate faculty of political and social science (1944-46) at the New School for Social Research, N.Y.C.; wrote *Why Religion* (1927), *A Free Society* (1934), *Modernity and Liberty* (1947). **[93]**

KEUN, ODETTE (1890-   ), French author. **[98]**

KEYNES, JOHN MAYNARD (June 5, 1883-April 21, 1946), English economist. Staff member (1915-19) of British Treasury and its principal representative at Paris Peace Conference (1919); editor (from 1912) of the *Economic Journal*; vice-president of the World Bank and Monetary Fund; wrote *The Economic Consequences of the Peace* (1919), *The General Theory of Employment, Interest and Money* (1936). **[59]**

LA FOLLETTE, ROBERT M., JR. (Feb. 6, 1895-Feb. 24, 1953), public official. U.S. senator from Wisconsin (1925-47) and chairman of the Senate Civil Liberties Committee; Washington business consultant (from 1947). **[21]**

LASKI, HAROLD J. (June 30, 1893-March 24, 1950), British political scientist. Taught (1914-16) at McGill University, Canada, and (1916-20) at Harvard; professor of political science (from 1926) at the London School of Economics; wrote *The Problem of Sovereignty* (1917), *Communism* (1927), *Liberty in the Modern State* (1930), *The American Presidency* (1940), *Reflections on the Revolution of Our Time* (1943). **[121]**

LEDBETTER, HUDDIE (fl. 1936-1951), folk singer. Known as "Leadbelly, King of the Twelve-String Guitar." **[83]** See also Author Index, Vol. 17.

LEWIS, JOHN L. (Feb. 12, 1880-   ), coal miner and labor leader. Vice-president (1917-20) and president (1920-60) of the United Mine Workers' Union; organizer (1911-17) for the American Federation of Labor; organized (1935) the Committee (later Congress) of Industrial Organizations, which withdrew from the AF of L in 1936; president (1935-40) of the CIO. [109]

LEWIS, SINCLAIR (Feb. 7, 1885-Jan. 10, 1951), novelist and playwright. Worked (1908-16) as a journalist and editor; wrote *Main Street* (1920), *Babbitt* (1922), *Arrowsmith* (1925), *Elmer Gantry* (1927), *Dodsworth* (1929), *Cass Timberlane* (1945); first American to receive the Nobel Prize for Literature (1930). [14] See also Author Index, Vol. 14.

LIPPMANN, WALTER (Sept. 23, 1889-   ), editor and author. Assisted in preparation of the Fourteen Points and the League of Nations plan for the Paris Peace Conference (1918-19); a co-founder (1914) and editor of the *New Republic*; syndicated political columnist (1931-67) for the *New York Herald Tribune*; wrote *Public Opinion* (1927), *A Preface to Morals* (1929), *The Good Society* (1937), *U.S. Foreign Policy: Shield of the Republic* (1943), *Essays in the Public Philosophy* (1955). [56] See also Author Index, Vols. 13, 14, 16, 17, 18.

LOMAX, JOHN A. (Sept. 23, 1867-Jan. 26, 1948), folklorist. President (1912-13) of the American Folklore Society; edited several collections of folk songs, including *Cowboy Songs and Other Frontier Ballads* (1910), *Plantation Songs of the Negro* (1916), and *American Ballads and Folk Songs* (with Alan Lomax, 1934). [83]

LONG, HUEY (Aug. 30, 1893-Sept. 10, 1935), lawyer and politician. Noted demagogue and head of a powerful political machine; governor of Louisiana (1928-31); U.S. senator (from 1931); employed dictatorial techniques to advance his "Share-the-Wealth" plan; assassinated during a speaking appearance at Baton Rouge, La. [69]

LOVETT, ROBERT MORSS (Dec. 25, 1870-Feb. 8, 1956), educator and author.

Teacher (1893-1909) and professor (from 1909) of English at the University of Chicago; wrote novels (*Gresham*, 1904; *A Winged Victory*, 1907), plays (*Cowards*, 1914), *Preface to Fiction* (1930), and several anthologies. [54]

LUNDBERG, FERDINAND (fl. 1937), author. Wrote *Imperial Hearst* (1936), *America's 60 Families* (1937). [105]

LYND, HELEN MERRELL (1897-   ), sociologist. Wife of Robert S. Lynd and with him co-author of *Middletown — A Study in Contemporary American Culture* (1929) and *Middletown in Transition* (1937); wrote *England in the 1880's* (1945). [2]

LYND, ROBERT S. (Sept. 26, 1892-   ), sociologist. Professor of sociology (1931-60) at Columbia; husband of Helen Merrell Lynd and with her co-author of *Middletown — A Study in Contemporary American Culture* (1929) and *Middletown in Transition* (1937); wrote *Knowledge for What?* (1939). [2]

MACLEISH, ARCHIBALD (May 7, 1892-   ), poet, teacher, and public official. Librarian of Congress (1939-44); assistant secretary of state (1944-45) under F. D. Roosevelt; professor (1949-62) at Harvard University; wrote poetry (*Tower of Ivory*, 1917; *New Found Land*, 1930; *Conquistador*, 1932; *Actfive and Other Poems*, 1948), essays, and verse plays (*The Hamlet of A. MacLeish*, 1928; *J.B.*, 1957). [13] See also Author Index, Vols. 16, 18.

MAUROIS, ANDRÉ (July 26, 1885-Oct. 9, 1967), French author. Born Émile Herzog; wrote novels, essays, critical studies (*Proust: Portrait of a Genius*, 1949), biographies (*Lélia: the Life of George Sand*, 1952; *The Three Dumas*, 1957), and histories (*A History of England*, 1958; *From the New Freedom to the New Frontier*, 1963). [125]

MEANS, GARDINER C. (June 8, 1896-   ), economist and author. Associated (1927-33) with Columbia Law School in economic research; economic adviser (1933-35) to secretary of agriculture; member (1933-35) consumers' advisory board of NRA; director of industrial section (1935-39) National Resources Commission; economic adviser (1939-40) National Resources Planning Board; fiscal analyst (1940-41) Bureau of the Budget; associated (1943-54) with CED; economic consultant (1957-59) Fund for the Republic; wrote *The Structure of American Economy* (1939). [32, 64]

MENCKEN, H. L. (Sept. 12, 1880-Jan. 29, 1956), editor and satirist. Editor and writer (from 1899) for four Baltimore newspapers; literary critic (1908-23) and co-editor with G. J. Nathan (1914-23) of *Smart Set;* co-founder with Nathan and editor (1924-33) of the *American Mercury;* wrote *Prejudices* (in series, 1919-27), *In Defense of Women* (1917), *The American Language* (1919 ff.), and an autobiography (3 vols., 1940-43). [82] See also Author Index, Vol. 14.

MUENCH, ALOISIUS (Feb. 18, 1889-Feb. 15, 1962), Roman Catholic prelate. President of the National Catholic Rural Life Conference; elevated to cardinal (1959). [99]

MÜLLER-FREIENFELS, RICHARD (1882-), German psychologist and philosopher. Professor of aesthetics and psychology at the Berlin Academy of Music; wrote *The Mysteries of the Soul* (1929), *The Psychology of Art,* and *Philosophy of Individualism.* [1]

NIEBUHR, H. RICHARD (Sept. 3, 1894-July 5, 1962), clergyman. Brother of Reinhold Niebuhr; professor of Christian ethics (from 1938) at Yale Divinity School; wrote *The Kingdom of God in America* (1937), *Christ and Culture* (1951), *Social Sources of Denominationalism* (1954). [73]

NUGENT, WILLIAM HENRY (fl. 1929), journalist and sportswriter. [4]

OLSON, CULBERT L. (fl. 1939-1943), public official. Governor of California (1939-43). [126]

OVERMYER, GRACE (fl. 1939), author. [123]

PEFFER, NATHANIEL (June 30, 1890-April 12, 1964), educator and authority on Far Eastern affairs. Professor of international relations (from 1938) at Columbia University; wrote a number of books on international affairs. [46]

PERKINS, FRANCES (April 10, 1882-May 14, 1965), social worker and public official.

Executive director (1917-19) of New York Council of Organization for War Service; member (1919-21, 1929-33) of New York Industrial Commission and (1923-33) of New York Industrial Board; secretary of labor under F. D. Roosevelt; member (1945-53) of Civil Service Commission; wrote *The Roosevelt I Knew* (1946). [78]

PERLMAN, SELIG (Dec. 9, 1888-Aug. 14, 1959), economist. Born Poland; became U.S. citizen (1913); professor of economics (from 1909) at the University of Wisconsin; wrote *A Theory of the Labor Movement* (1928). [80]

RANSOM, JOHN CROWE (April 30, 1888-), poet and literary critic. Teacher (1914-27) and professor (1927-37) of English at Vanderbilt University; professor of poetry (1937-58) at Kenyon College and editor (1939-59) of the *Kenyon Review;* wrote *Chills and Fever* (1924), *Selected Poems* (1945, rev. 1964). [124]

REECE, FLORENCE (fl. 1931), songwriter. Wife of Sam Reece, a union leader in the Kentucky coal fields; wrote "Which Side Are You On?" during the 1931 Harlan County miners' strike. [24]

RICHBERG, DONALD R. (July 10, 1881-Nov. 27, 1960), lawyer. General counsel (1933-35) for the National Recovery Administration; executive director (1934-35) of the National Emergency Council; wrote *Tents of the Mighty* (1930) and *Government and Business Tomorrow* (1943). [42]

ROBINS, ROBERT (fl. 1936), motion picture industry executive. [85]

ROOSEVELT, FRANKLIN D. (Jan. 30, 1882-April 12, 1945), lawyer and statesman. Thirty-second President of the United States (1933-45) and the only President to be elected to a third (and a fourth) term; assistant secretary of the Navy (1913-20) under Wilson; governor of New York (1929-33); initiated national administrative and legislative reforms known as the "New Deal"; chief architect of the United Nations. [36, 38, 43, 45, 47, 58, 67, 68, 77, 86, 95, 107] See also Author Index, Vol. 16.

Ross, Mary (fl. 1937), editor and author. Associate editor (c. 1935) of *Survey Graphic* magazine; staff member (c. 1936) of the Bureau of Research and Statistics, Social Security Board. **[101]**

Rourke, Constance M. (Nov. 14, 1885-March 23, 1941), author. Instructor in English (1910-15) at Vassar College; wrote *Trumpets of Jubilee* (1927), *American Humor* (1931), *The Roots of American Culture* (1942). **[27]**

Roussy de Sales, Raoul de (March 5, 1896-Dec. 3, 1942), French journalist. Liason officer for the American Red Cross during World War I; assistant director for the Rockefeller Foundation in France; American correspondent (1932-c.1940) for French newspapers. **[114]**

Sandburg, Carl (Jan. 6, 1878-July 22, 1967), poet and author. Poetry collections include *Cornhuskers* (1918), *Smoke and Steel* (1920), *The People, Yes* (1936), and *Complete Poems* (1950); edited collections of folk songs (*The American Songbag*, 1927); wrote histories (*Abraham Lincoln — The Prairie Years*, 1926; *Abraham Lincoln — The War Years*, 1939). **[94]** See also Author Index, Vols. 13, 14.

Seidman, Joel (fl. 1937), labor leader. Member of the League for Industrial Democracy. **[102]**

Sherwood, Robert E. (April 4, 1896-Nov. 14, 1955), author. An editor (1920-28) of *Life* magazine; wrote plays (*The Petrified Forest*, 1935; *Idiot's Delight*, 1936; *Abe Lincoln in Illinois*, 1939; *There Shall Be No Night*, 1941) and motion picture stories (*The Best Years of Our Lives*, 1946). **[3]**

Slichter, Sumner H. (Jan. 8, 1892-Sept. 27, 1959), economist. Instructor of economics (1919-20) at Princeton; professor (1920-30) at Cornell; professor of business economics (from 1930) at Harvard Business School; member of the American Academy of Political and Social Science; wrote many books on industry-labor relations and economics. **[42]**

Soule, George Henry (June 11, 1887-   ), editor and author. Director (1922-   ) of the National Bureau for Economic Research; editor (1924-47) of the *New Republic;* wrote *The Useful Art of Economics* (1929), *The Future of Liberty* (1936), *Prosperity Decade: From War to Depression, 1917-1929* (1947), *The New Science of Economics* (1964). **[35]**

Steinbeck, John (Feb. 27, 1902-Dec. 20, 1968), writer. War correspondent (1942-45); received Nobel Prize for Literature (1962); wrote *Tortilla Flat* (1935), *In Dubious Battle* (1936), *Of Mice and Men* (1937), *The Grapes of Wrath* (1939), *Cannery Row* (1945), *East of Eden* (1952), *The Winter of Our Discontent* (1961). **[127]**

Stimson, Henry L. (Sept. 21, 1867-Oct. 20, 1950), lawyer and public official. Secretary of war (1911-13) under Taft; special representative to Nicaragua (1927); governor of the Philippine Islands (1927-29); secretary of state under Hoover; chairman (1932) of U.S. delegation to the Disarmament Conference; secretary of war (1940-45) under F. D. Roosevelt. **[16]** See also Author Index, Vol. 13.

Sutherland, George (March 25, 1862-July 18, 1942), jurist and public official. U.S. representative from Utah (1901-03); U.S. senator (1905-17); U.S. counsel (1921) at The Hague; associate justice (1922-38) of the U.S. Supreme Court. **[33]** See also Author Index, Vol. 14.

Taft, Robert A. (Sept. 8, 1889-July 31, 1953), lawyer and political leader. Son of William Howard Taft; Ohio legislator (1921-26, 1931-32); U.S. senator (from 1939) and Republican majority leader in the Senate (1953); co-sponsor of the Taft-Hartley Labor-Management Relations Act (1947). **[122]** See also Author Index, Vol. 16.

Thomas, Norman (Nov. 20, 1884-Dec. 19, 1968), Socialist politician. Ordained in Presbyterian ministry (1911) but resigned (1931); founder and editor (1918-21) of *The World Tomorrow* and editor (1921-22) of *The Nation;* six times (1928-48) Socialist Party candidate for President of the United States; wrote *America's Way Out — A Program for Democracy* (1930), *The Test of Freedom* (1954), *Socialism Re-examined* (1963). **[81]** See also Author Index, Vol. 14.

TOLLER, ERNST (Dec. 1, 1893-May 22, 1939), German author and political agitator. Leader of social revolutionary movements in Germany following World War I, for which he was imprisoned (1919-24); banished (1933) from Germany by Nazis, and fled to New York; wrote poetry, plays, and an autobiography. [10]

WALLACE, HENRY A. (Oct. 7, 1888-Nov. 18, 1965), agriculturist and public official. Vice-President of the United States (1941-45) under F. D. Roosevelt; on staff (1910-29) of *Wallace's Farmer*; editor (1929-33) of *Wallace's Farmer and Iowa Homestead*; secretary of agriculture (1933-40) under F. D. Roosevelt; head (1941) of Economic Defense Board; secretary of commerce (1945-46) under Roosevelt and Truman; editor (1946-47) of the *New Republic*. [48, 61, 71, 111] See also Author Index, Vol. 16.

WHITE, E. B. (July 11, 1899-   ), humorist and essayist. A contributing editor to the *New Yorker* and principal author of its "Talk of the Town" column; author of "One Man's Meat" column in *Harper's* magazine; wrote *Is Sex Necessary?* (with James Thurber, 1929), *One Man's Meat* (1942, 1944), *The Wild Flag* (1946), *The Second Tree From the Corner* (1953). [53, 119] See also Author Index, Vol. 16.

WHITE, WILLIAM ALLEN (Feb. 10, 1868-Jan. 29, 1944), journalist and author. Known as "the Sage of Emporia" for his work as owner and editor (from 1895) of the *Emporia* (Kan.) *Gazette*; wrote *The Real Issue and Other Stories* (1896), *A Puritan in Babylon* (1938), *The Changing West* (1939), *Autobiography* (1946). [104] See also Author Index, Vols. 12, 13, 14.

WOOLSEY, JOHN M. (Jan. 3, 1877-May 4, 1945), jurist. A founder (1901) of the *Columbia Law Review*; member (1928-42) of advisory committee on international law at Harvard Law School; judge (1929-43) of U.S. District Court for the Southern District of New York. [52]